D0444325

Walking in
Britain

David Else
Sandra Bardwell
Gareth McCormack
Helen Fairbairn
Peter Cruttenden
David Wenk
Christopher Somerville

LONELY PLANET PUBLICATIONS
Melbourne • Oakland • London • Paris

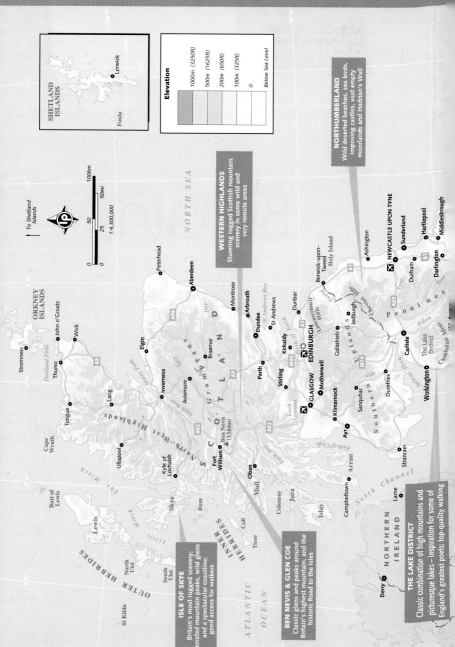

SHETLAND ISLANDS

Lerwick

Foula

Elevation

1000m (3250ft)
500m (1625ft)
200m (650ft)
100m (325ft)
0

Below Sea Level

To Shetland Islands

0 50 100km
0 25 50mi

1:4,300,000

NORTH SEA

NORTHUMBERLAND
Wild deserted beaches, sea birds, imposing castles, vast empty moorlands and Hadrian's Wall

WESTERN HIGHLANDS
Stunning rugged Scottish mountain scenery in some wild and very remote areas

ORKNEY ISLANDS

Stromness
Thurso
John o'Groats
Wick
Tongue
Pentland Firth
Lairg
Cape Wrath
Ullapool
The Minch
Butt of Lewis
Lewis
OUTER HEBRIDES
North Uist
South Uist
St Kilda
Kyle of Lochalsh
Skye
Rum
Coll
Tiree
Mull
Colonsay
Jura
Islay
INNER HEBRIDES
Campbeltown
North Channel
Larne
NORTHERN IRELAND
Derry

Peterhead
Aberdeen
Dee
Elgin
Inverness
Aviemore
Loch Ness
Grampians
Braemar
North-West Highlands
Fort William
Ben Nevis (1344m)
Oban
Arran
Ayr
Kilmarnock
Sanquhar
Dumfries
Southern Uplands
Stranraer
Firth of Clyde

Montrose
Arbroath
Dundee
St Andrews Bay
St Andrews
Firth of Forth
Perth
Stirling
SCOTLAND
GLASGOW
Motherwell
EDINBURGH
Galashiels
Lammermuir Hills
Jedburgh
Berwick-upon-Tweed
Holy Island
Ashington
NEWCASTLE UPON TYNE
Tyne
Sunderland
Durham
Hartlepool
Middlesbrough
Darlington
Tees
Pennines
Cheviot Hills
Carlisle
Eden
The Lake District
Workington
Kirkcaldy
Dunbar
Lochmaben
Southern Uplands

BEN NEVIS & GLEN COE
Classic glens and peaks around Britain's highest mountain, and the historic Road to the Isles

ISLE OF SKYE
Britain's most rugged scenery; serrated mountain peaks, wild glens and a spectacular coastline; good access for walkers

THE LAKE DISTRICT
Classic combination of high mountains and picturesque lakes – inspiration for some of England's greatest poets; top-quality walking

ATLANTIC OCEAN

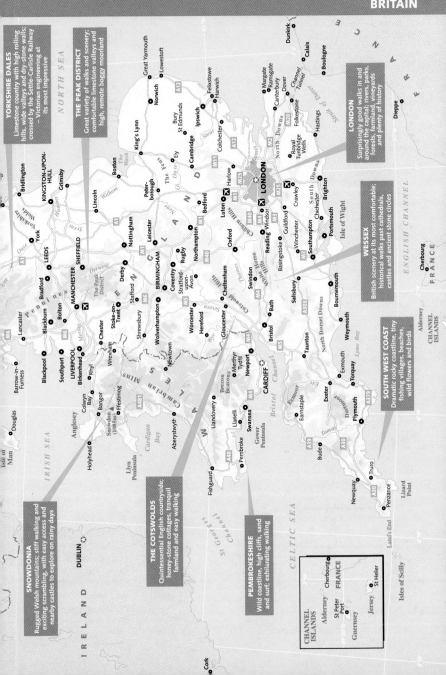

BRITAIN

YORKSHIRE DALES
Limestone country with high rolling hills, wide valleys and dry-stone walls; crossed by the Settle-Carlisle Railway – Victorian engineering at its most impressive

THE PEAK DISTRICT
Great variety of walks and scenery: comfortable limestone valleys and high, remote boggy moorland

LONDON
Surprisingly good walks in and around the capital: rivers, parks, forests, farmland, vineyards and plenty of history

WESSEX
British scenery at its most comfortable: historical walks past cathedrals, castles and ancient stone circles

SOUTH WEST COAST
Dramatic rocky coastline, tiny fishing villages, beaches, wild flowers and birds

SNOWDONIA
Rugged Welsh mountains; stiff walking and exciting scrambling, with easy access and nearby castles to explore on rainy days

THE COTSWOLDS
Quintessential English countryside: honey-stone cottages, tranquil farmland and easy walking

PEMBROKESHIRE
Wild coastline, high cliffs, sand and surf; exhilarating walking

Walking in Britain
2nd edition – August 2001
First published – May 1997

Published by
Lonely Planet Publications Pty Ltd ABN 36 005 607 983
90 Maribyrnong St, Footscray, Victoria 3011, Australia

Lonely Planet Offices
Australia Locked Bag 1, Footscray, Victoria 3011
USA 150 Linden St, Oakland, CA 94607
UK 10a Spring Place, London NW5 3BH
France 1 rue du Dahomey, 75011 Paris

Photographs
Many of the images in this guide are available for licensing from
Lonely Planet Images.
email: lpi@lonelyplanet.com.au

Main front cover photograph
View across the Mamores from Ben Nevis (Gareth McCormack)

Small front cover photograph
Looking across to Glencoe from Ben Nevis (Gareth McCormack)

Southern England photograph p101
South West Coast Path (Andrew Marshall & Leanne Walker)

Northern England photograph p229
Hadrian's Wall (Andrew Marshall & Leanne Walker)

Wales photograph p375
Walkers heading for Crib Goch, Snowdonia NP (Eoin Clarke)

Wales photograph p376
Sunrise on Mt Snowdon range (Grant Dixon)

Scotland photograph p447
Descending to Glencoe (Gareth McCormack)

ISBN 1 86450 280 0

text & maps © Lonely Planet 2001
photos © photographers as indicated 2001

Printed by Craft Print International, Singapore

Contents

1

The Walks	Duration	Standard	Season
LONDON REGION			
The Jubilee Walkway	6 hours	easy	all year
The Centenary Walk	1 or 2 days	easy	all year
The Thames Path (East)	6 days	easy	all year
The North Downs Way (West)	2 days	easy	all year
The North Downs Way (East)	2 days	easy	all year
WESSEX			
The Clarendon Way	9–11 hours	easy	all year
The Kennet & Avon Canal	1 or 2 days	easy	all year
The Ridgeway (West)	3 days	easy	all year
The Thames Path (West)	6 days	easy	all year
THE ISLE OF WIGHT			
The Tennyson Trail	5–6½ hours	easy	all year
DARTMOOR			
A South Dartmoor Traverse	7–8 hours	medium	all year
A North Dartmoor Circuit	5–6 hours	medium	all year
NORFOLK			
A Broads Walk	6–8 hours	easy	all year
The Norfolk Coast Path	3 days	easy	all year
THE COTSWOLDS			
The Cotswold Way	7 days	easy-medium	all year
Bourton & the Slaughters	6 hours	easy	all year
SOUTHERN ENGLAND LONG-DISTANCE PATHS			
The South Downs Way	8 days	easy-medium	all year
The South West Coast Path (Cornwall Section)	14 days	medium-hard	Mar–Oct
THE PEAK DISTRICT			
The Edale Skyline	6 hours	medium	Mar–Oct
The Limestone Way	2 days	easy-medium	all year
THE YORKSHIRE DALES			
The Dales Way	6 days	medium	Mar–Oct
The Three Peaks	9–12 hours	hard	Mar–Oct
Wharfedale & Littondale	5–6 hours	easy-medium	any
THE LAKE DISTRICT			
The Cumbria Way	5 days	medium	Mar–Oct
The Fairfield Horseshoe	5–7 hours	medium	Mar–Oct
Helvellyn & Striding Edge	5–6 hours	medium-hard	Mar–Oct
Fairfield & Dovedale	5–7 hours	medium-hard	Mar–Oct
A High Street Circuit	6–8 hours	medium	Mar–Oct
A Scafell Pike Circuit	5–6½ hours	medium-hard	Mar–Oct
THE NORTH YORK MOORS			
The Cleveland Way	9 days	medium	all year
Falling Foss & Fylingdales	5–7 hours	easy-medium	all year
The Farndale Skyline	6½–8 hours	easy-medium	all year

The Walks *continued*	Duration	Standard	Season
NORTHUMBERLAND			
A Hadrian's Wall Walk	3 days	easy-medium	Mar–Oct
A Northumberland Coast Walk	5–6½ hours	easy	all year
NORTHERN ENGLAND LONG-DISTANCE PATHS			
The Coast to Coast Walk	12 days	medium	Mar–Oct
The Pennine Way	16 days	medium-hard	Mar–Oct
THE BRECON BEACONS			
A Brecon Beacons Ridge Walk	6½–8 hours	medium	Mar–Oct
PEMBROKESHIRE			
The Pembrokeshire Coast Path	15 days	medium-hard	Mar–Oct
A Preseli Hills Circuit	6–8 hours	medium	all year
SNOWDONIA			
The Snowdon Horseshoe	5–7 hours	hard	Mar–Oct
A Snowdon Traverse	5–7 hours	medium-hard	Mar–Oct
Tryfan & the Glyders	5–7 hours	hard	Mar–Oct
The Carneddau	4–6 hours	medium	Mar–Oct
A Beddgelert Valley Walk	3–4 hours	easy	all year
WALES LONG-DISTANCE PATHS			
The Glyndŵr's Way	9 days	medium	Mar–Oct
The Offa's Dyke Path	12 days	hard	Mar–Oct
THE CENTRAL HIGHLANDS & ISLANDS			
The Ptarmigan Route *	4½–5 hours	medium	May–Sept
A Goatfell Circuit	6–7½ hours	medium-hard	May–Sept
Cock of Arran	3½–4 hours	easy-medium	May–Sept
BEN NEVIS & GLEN COE			
A Glen Coe & Glen Etive Circuit	5 hours	medium	May–Oct
Buachaille Etive Mòr	5–6 hours	medium-hard	June–Oct
Ben Nevis	6–8 hours	medium-hard	June–Oct
The Road to the Isles	6–9 hours	medium-hard	May–Oct
THE CAIRNGORMS			
A Cairn Gorm High Circuit	4–5 hours	medium-hard	May–Sept
Chalamain Gap & the Lairig Ghru	6–6½ hours	medium-hard	May–Sept
THE WESTERN HIGHLANDS			
The Five Sisters of Kintail	6¾–8 hours	hard	May–Sept
Beinn Alligin *	6–8 hours	medium-hard	June–Oct
An Teallach *	7½–9 hours	hard	June–Oct
THE ISLE OF SKYE			
Coast & Cuillin (Elgol to Sligachan)	8–9 hours	medium	April–Oct
Bruach na Frithe	6–8 hours	medium-hard	June–Oct
SCOTLAND LONG-DISTANCE PATHS			
The Southern Upland Way	9 days	medium-hard	April–Oct
The West Highland Way	7 days	medium	April–Oct

* no public transport

The Maps

Scotland p448

ATLANTIC OCEAN

Outer Hebrides

Isle of Skye

SCOTLAND

EDINBURGH

Northern England p230

NORTHERN IRELAND

BELFAST

IRELAND

Irish Sea

DUBLIN

Wales p376

ENGLAND

NORTH SEA

NETHERLANDS

Channel

WALES

CARDIFF

LONDON

BELGIUM

Isle of Wight

English Channel

FRANCE

Southern England p102

0	200	400km
0	100	200mi

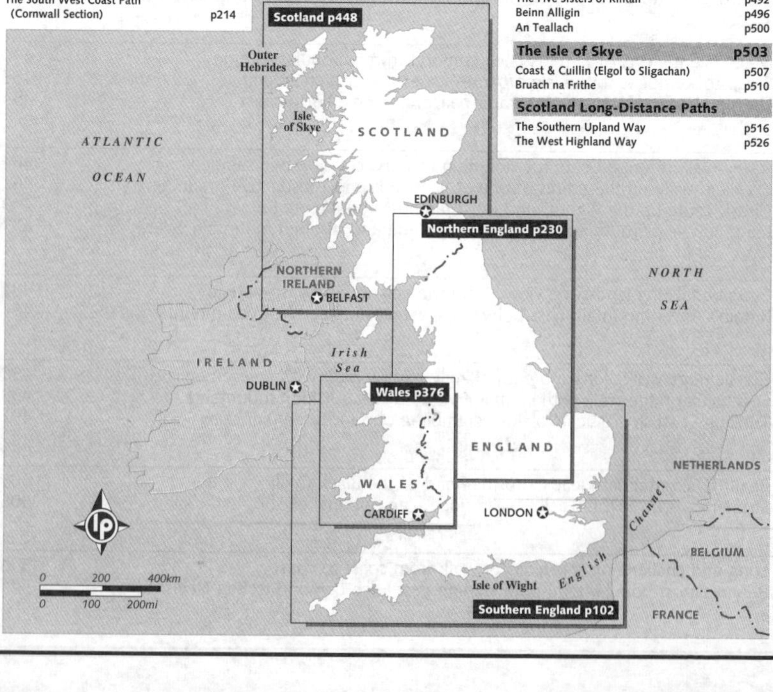

The Authors

David Else

David Else was born in London and over the following decades slowly trekked northwards via Wiltshire, South Wales and Derbyshire to his present base on the edge of the Peak District in Northern England. Originally introduced to the great outdoors as a cyclist, David's own walking in Britain started during university years when any chance to head for the hills was always taken in preference to visiting the library. His first long-distance path was the Pennine Way, done on a bicycle in the days before mountain bikes were invented, and when passing ramblers found such illegal escapades amusing. Now much more respectable, although still rarely seen in libraries, David is a full-time writer, dividing his time between Britain and Africa. His other books for Lonely Planet include *Trekking in East Africa*, *Southern Africa*, *West Africa* and *Malawi*. He has also contributed to *Tanzania*, *East Africa* and *Africa on a shoestring*.

Sandra Bardwell

After graduating with a thesis on the history of national parks in Victoria, Sandra worked as an archivist and then historian for the National Parks Service. She has been a dedicated walker since joining a bushwalking club in the early 1960s, and became well known through a newspaper column and as the author of several guidebooks. In 1989 Sandra and her husband Hal retired to the Highlands of Scotland where they live in a village near Loch Ness. She has walked for Lonely Planet in Italy, Ireland, France and Australia, and has now renewed her enthusiasm for Scotland's hills and glens.

Gareth McCormack

After finishing a degree in law in 1995 Gareth travelled, walked and climbed his way across Asia, Australia and New Zealand for 18 months. This trip inspired a radical career turnaround and he is now a writer and photographer based in Ireland. He is a regular contributor to the magazine *Walking World Ireland* and co-authored Lonely Planet's *Walking in Ireland*, *Walking in France* and *Walking in Australia*. Every year he tries to spend several months photographing wild and beautiful parts of the world.

Helen Fairbairn

A year spent teaching English on the French Caribbean island of Guadeloupe convinced Helen of the benefits of life in the sun, and she regularly escapes the dark winters of Ireland to rekindle her relationship with things more exotic. A mountain lover and a dedicated kayaker, the wild areas of the world seem to hold a particular attraction for her.

Peter Cruttenden

Born in Western Australia and raised for a time in England, Pete gained his love of the outdoors by tramping through many of Australia's national parks as a teenager. Extended walks in Nepal and Tasmania's Cradle Mountain National Park formalised the addiction and he dreams of tackling other sections of the Himalayan range and exploring the Andes. Pete recently left Lonely Planet's Melbourne office after a four-year stint, during which time he co-wrote *Read This First: Asia & India* and contributed to the first three editions of *Out to Eat – Melbourne*.

David Wenk

A creature of the outdoors at heart, David has spent much of the past three years holed up in Lonely Planet's London office, offering cartographic skills and technical know-how to the book production team. He frequently promises himself he'll get out more. Growing up without a television on a remote farmstead in upstate New York, David is well versed in the manufacture of goat's cheese and maple syrup, and was once a stellar musician. Long an admirer of landscape fair, David finds rambling the British countryside a perfect panacea to London life. Thankfully, modesty precludes him from regaling the office staff with tales of aerial derring-do from his brief yet colourful career as a pilot.

Christopher Somerville

Christopher endured walking expeditions as a child, abhorred them in his teens and then grew to love them again. These days he is one of Britain's best-known travel journalists and writers, with over 20 books to his name. His features on walking and exploring all corners of Britain, Ireland and Europe appear regularly in the *Sunday Times*, *Daily Telegraph* and other newspapers, and on BBC Radio.

FROM THE AUTHORS

David Else A big thank you goes to my wife, Corinne, who assisted with initial research and joined me on a great selection of British footpaths, from the South Downs to the far north of Scotland, from West Wales to East Anglia, testing buses, ferries, cafes, B&Bs, pubs and hostels en route. Thanks also to various friends who joined us; without their company, humour and sandwiches we'd have never made it.

Special thanks go to various specialists who gave me their thoughts and the benefit of their experience, including Roly Smith (Chairman, Outdoor Writers Guild), Jill Leheup (for wildlife information) and Jim Walker (National Trails Marketing Consultant).

Thanks also to the co-authors of this book: Sandra Bardwell, Helen Fairbairn, Gareth McCormack, David Wenk, Pete Cruttenden and Christopher Somerville. My name goes down as coordinating author but I really couldn't have done it without them.

A big thank you also to the staff at the national park offices, walking and hostel organisations, conservation bodies and, especially, Tourist Information Centres for their professional knowledge and always helpful service. And finally thanks to all the National Trail officers, other countryside officials, guides and footpath association members who so willingly gave their time and expertise: David Hiscock, David McGlade, Jos Joslin, Huw Rees, Jim Saunders, Mark Townsend, Rab Jones, Jo Ronald, Malcolm Hodgson, Karl Gerhardsen, Steve Westwood, Anne Glover, Jill Hobbs, Eric Wallis, Ros Love.

Sandra Bardwell Thanks are due to Jim Strachan, Speyside Way Ranger, and Alasdair Macleod, Great Glen Way Ranger, for freely giving of their time; to Calum Macfarlane, Scottish Natural Heritage, for information and advice; the Warden at Kendoon Youth Hostel for a helping hand; and to Martin Rodgers for his infinite patience behind a photocopier. David Else's inspirational diligence and good humour were greatly appreciated, while sharing an enthusiasm for Scotland's hills with Gareth and Helen made the project even more enjoyable. Hal's companionship and support are deeply appreciated.

Gareth McCormack First of all thanks to Helen for taking on the walks that my poor knee couldn't face – and making the sandwiches a disproportionate number of times. Such is the existence of an LP walking guide author. Thanks also to the Clancys for company in Glen Coe and to Sandra Bardwell for correspondence and advice.

Helen Fairbairn First of all huge thanks are due to Gareth, who was like a light shining into all the murky corners of LP house style. I'm sure it would have been much harder on my own! Thanks also to Nick and Sandra for very positive support. Cheers to Kate and Cian for coming over from Ireland and entertaining us for the weekend – we'll get you up Aonach Eagach next time! Huge appreciation also to my sister, Mags, whose very comfortable flat in Edinburgh offered a much-needed recovery haven.

Peter Cruttenden Firstly, a huge vote of thanks must go to Glyndŵr's Way project officer, Rab Jones, who gave me heaps of time and assistance, as well as the privilege of walking the new trail long before it opened to the public. Thanks, too, to Joyce Connolly, who saved me when things went pear-shaped; to Matt Fletcher, Claire and Bando for fun and frivolity in Bath; to Matt and Joyce again for their companionship on the trail; to David Else for his advice and guidance; to the staffers in Lonely Planet's London and Paris offices for their friendly faces and useful equipment; to Rebecca Cole for her unswerving support and last-minute assistance; and to all the inn-keepers in southern England and mid-Wales for their grand establishments and outstanding beer. Finally, thanks to Darren and Micki Nash for their generosity, hospitality and absurdly steep staircase. Here's cheers to a friendship rekindled.

This Book

The 1st edition was compiled by David Else with the assistance of a team of contributors. For this edition, the team of intrepid walkers was once again led by David Else as coordinating author, with material used from Lonely Planet's *Cycling Britain* and *Britain*. David was responsible for updating the lion's share of the book. Sandra Bardwell researched the Central Highlands & Islands, Cairngorms and Other Walks in Scotland chapters, and contributed to the Western Highlands and Scotland Long-Distance Paths chapters. Gareth McCormack and Helen Fairbairn updated the Ben Nevis & Glen Coe and Isle of Skye chapters, and contributed to the Scotland Long-Distance Paths chapter. Peter Cruttenden took on the Wales Long-Distance Paths chapter and the Cotswold Way. Christopher Somerville researched the Thames Path and David Wenk tamed the Cleveland Way.

From the Publisher

Walking in Britain was guided along the way by Emily Coles (coordinating editor), Helen Rowley (coordinating designer) and Andrew Smith (coordinating cartographer). Editorial assistance was provided by Jennifer Garrett, Janet Brunckhorst, Peter Cruttenden, Andrew Bain and Anne Mulvaney. Chris Klep, Eoin Dunlevy and Jacqui Saunders all helped with the mapping, and Mark Germanchis provide timely layout advice. To illustrate the book, Matt King commissioned the talents of Jane Smith, Kate Nolan, Kelli Hamblet, Hugh d'Andrade and Martin Harris, while cartoons were drawn by Clint Curé and the cover was designed by Jamieson Gross. Photographic assistance was provided by Lonely Planet Images staff Annie Horner, Brett Pascoe and Gerard Walker.

Thanks

Thanks to all the readers who wrote in with comments about *Walking in Britain*. Their voices live on in this edition:

Eliane Dosker & Maarten Adelmeijer, Tracy Stewart, Nicky Robinson, Ann Garner, Harry Bitten, Reg Tripp, Michelle Hawkins, Sam Trafford, Michael Turner, Chris Ashford, Julia Merrifield, Richard & Esther Hollis, Ann Garner, Chris Hollis, Conrad & Janet Yanis, John & Barbara Else, Jeff Kingston, Roger Slade, Bryn Thomas, Pat Yale, Charlotte Hindle, Rob Beckley, Miles Roddis, Rod Grant, Angela Kalisch, Robin Saxby, Alf Alderson, Chris & John Harvey, W Barrett, M & J Beed, Pauline Beiliwik, Wendy & Gerry Broad, Phillip Crampton, Eliane Dosker, Judson Ford, Cyril Frances, CJ Francis, Richard K Greave, Zach Rohaizad Roj Haron, CM Hill, Maureen Holberry, Elizabeth Howard, Edgar Locke, Chris Lofty, Michael Mee, Jenny Mitcham, Stephen Mitchell, Matt Moore, Lance Pierce, Ian Plenderleith, Elizabeth Poole, Antje Strauch, BL Underwood, Patricia Ward, Guido Witmond, Michael Woods and some chap called Tony Wheeler.

Foreword

ABOUT LONELY PLANET GUIDEBOOKS

The story begins with a classic travel adventure: Tony and Maureen Wheeler's 1972 journey across Europe and Asia to Australia. Useful information about the overland trail did not exist at that time, so Tony and Maureen published the first Lonely Planet guidebook to meet a growing need.

From a kitchen table, then from a tiny office in Melbourne (Australia), Lonely Planet has become the largest independent travel publisher in the world, an international company with offices in Melbourne, Oakland (USA), London (UK) and Paris (France).

Today Lonely Planet guidebooks cover the globe. There is an ever-growing list of books and there's information in a variety of forms and media. Some things haven't changed. The main aim is still to help make it possible for adventurous travellers to get out there – to explore and better understand the world.

At Lonely Planet we believe travellers can make a positive contribution to the countries they visit – if they respect their host communities and spend their money wisely. Since 1986 a percentage of the income from each book has been donated to aid projects and human rights campaigns.

Updates Lonely Planet thoroughly updates each guidebook as often as possible. This usually means there are around two years between editions, although for more unusual or more stable destinations the gap can be longer. Check the imprint page (following the colour map at the beginning of the book) for publication dates.

Between editions up-to-date information is available in two free newsletters – the paper *Planet Talk* and email *Comet* (to subscribe, contact any Lonely Planet office) – and on our Web site at www.lonelyplanet.com. The *Upgrades* section of the Web site covers a number of important and volatile destinations and is regularly updated by Lonely Planet authors. *Scoop* covers news and current affairs relevant to travellers. And, lastly, the *Thorn Tree* bulletin board and *Postcards* section of the site carry unverified, but fascinating, reports from travellers.

Correspondence The process of creating new editions begins with the letters, postcards and emails received from travellers. This correspondence often includes suggestions, criticisms and comments about the current editions. Interesting excerpts are immediately passed on via newsletters and the Web site, and everything goes to our authors to be verified when they're researching on the road. We're keen to get more feedback from organisations or individuals who represent communities visited by travellers.

Lonely Planet gathers information for everyone who's curious about the planet – and especially for those who explore it first-hand. Through guidebooks, phrasebooks, activity guides, maps, literature, newsletters, image library, TV series and Web site we act as an information exchange for a worldwide community of travellers.

Research Authors aim to gather sufficient practical information to enable travellers to make informed choices and to make the mechanics of a journey run smoothly. They also research historical and cultural background to help enrich the travel experience and allow travellers to understand and respond appropriately to cultural and environmental issues.

Authors don't stay in every hotel because that would mean spending a couple of months in each medium-sized city and, no, they don't eat at every restaurant because that would mean stretching belts beyond capacity. They do visit hotels and restaurants to check standards and prices, but feedback based on readers' direct experiences can be very helpful.

Many of our authors work undercover, others aren't so secretive. None of them accept freebies in exchange for positive write-ups. And none of our guidebooks contain any advertising.

Production Authors submit their raw manuscripts and maps to offices in Australia, USA, UK or France. Editors and cartographers – all experienced travellers themselves – then begin the process of assembling the pieces. When the book finally hits the shops, some things are already out of date, we start getting feedback from readers and the process begins again …

WARNING & REQUEST

Things change – prices go up, schedules change, good places go bad and bad places go bankrupt – nothing stays the same. So, if you find things better or worse, recently opened or long since closed, please tell us and help make the next edition even more accurate and useful. We genuinely value all the feedback we receive. A well travelled team reads and acknowledges every letter, postcard and email and ensures that every morsel of information finds its way to the appropriate authors, editors and cartographers for verification.

Everyone who writes to us will find their name in the next edition of the appropriate guidebook. They will also receive the latest issue of *Planet Talk*, our quarterly printed newsletter, or *Comet*, our monthly email newsletter. Subscriptions to both newsletters are free. The very best contributions will be rewarded with a free guidebook.

Excerpts from your correspondence may appear in new editions of Lonely Planet guidebooks, the Lonely Planet Web site, *Planet Talk* or *Comet*, so please let us know if you *don't* want your letter published or your name acknowledged.

Send all correspondence to the Lonely Planet office closest to you:

Australia: Locked Bag 1, Footscray, Victoria 3011
USA: 150 Linden St, Oakland, CA 94607
UK: 10A Spring Place, London NW5 3BH
France: 1 rue du Dahomey, 75011 Paris

Or email us at: talk2us@lonelyplanet.com.au

For news, views and updates see our Web site: www.lonelyplanet.com

WALKING YOU THROUGH THIS GUIDEBOOK

Walking is an individual pursuit and we expect that people will use our guidebooks in individual ways. Whether you carry it in your backpack or read it as you walk along (not recommended near cliffs), a Lonely Planet walking guide can point your wandering spirit in the right direction. Never forget, however, that the finest discoveries are those you make yourself.

What We've Packed All Lonely Planet guidebooks follow roughly the same path, including the walking guides. The Facts about the Country chapter provides background information relevant to walkers, ranging from history to weather, as well as a detailed look at the plants and animals you're likely to encounter on the track. Facts for the Walker deals with the walking practicalities – the planning, red tape and resources. We also include a special Health & Safety chapter to help combat or treat those on-track nasties. The Getting There & Away and Getting Around chapters will assist in making your travel plans.

The walking chapters are divided into regions, encompassing the walks in those areas. We start each walk with background, planning and how to get to/from the walk information. Each walk is detailed and highlights en route are included in the text. We also suggest where to rest your weary feet and fill your empty stomach. You will have earned it.

Maps Maps are a key element of any Lonely Planet guidebook, particularly walking guides. The maps are printed in two colours, making route-finding a snap, and show everything from town locations to the peaks around you. We strive for compatability between word and image, so what you read in the text will invariably feature on the map. A legend is printed on the back page.

Navigating the Guidebook The traditional 'map and compass' for a Lonely Planet guidebook are the contents and index lists but, in addition, the walking guides offer a comprehensive table of walks, providing thumbnail information about every described walk, as well as a table of maps.

Although inclusion in a guidebook usually implies a recommendation we cannot list all the good places. Exclusion does not necessarily imply criticism. There are a number of reasons why we might exclude a place – sometimes it is simply inappropriate to encourage an influx of travellers.

Preface

Visitors to Britain may expect to see Buckingham Palace or Big Ben, but few will make the trip for that reason alone. The 'other' Britain many people come for is the countryside – Wordsworth's idyllic Lake District, the bleak but beautiful moors of *Wuthering Heights*, Jane Austen's manicured meadows, or Braveheart's wild and forbidding country. Not surprisingly, by far the best way to discover it all is on foot. Britain is a nation of walkers – nearly eight in 10 of us enjoy a regular ramble – with good reason.

Whether you are spending a week exploring the breath-taking wilderness of the Cairngorms or just stopping off for a stroll around Stonehenge, you are in for a treat. The British countryside is extraordinary in its geographic diversity. It is also guardian to many relics from our past and is undoubtedly an intrinsic part of our national heritage. It is easy to see why it has enthused and inspired artists and poets for centuries.

Fortunately, the tracks and byways once tramped by our ancestors are now protected throughout England and Wales as an extensive and much-loved network of public rights of way. Scotland too has a long tradition of people being able to walk with reasonable freedom over open country. You are also welcome to wander through our public forests, and some benevolent landowners, including the National Trust, voluntarily open their sumptuous grounds for you to explore.

Access to the countryside will soon be further enhanced with the implementation of a freedom to roam over millions of acres in England and Wales and, hopefully, an extension in public access provisions in Scotland. Once in place, access to these vast areas of wild, uncultivated countryside and their heart-stoppingly beautiful landscapes will provide infinite pleasure to walkers from home and abroad.

However, rural Britain is not a theme park. It remains, as it has for centuries, home and workplace for many people, and this must be respected. However much you enjoy your visit, the phrase 'take nothing but photographs and leave nothing but goodwill' serves well.

Britain is crammed with the remnants of thousands of years of human occupation including mystical stone circles, Roman roads, Bronze Age settlements, ancient battlefields and many more. It is difficult to travel anywhere without encountering, whether you realise it or not, some evidence from the past, so researching an area before walking there will enrich your experience no end. This book provides an excellent opportunity for you to do just that.

Wherever you intend to go, let me extend a warm welcome on behalf of the Ramblers' Association. Those visiting from abroad will never want to go back; those of you from the UK will wonder why you waited so long to try it.

Have a fantastic time!

**Nick Barrett, Chief Executive
Ramblers' Association**

Nick Barrett is Chief Executive of the 130,000-member Ramblers' Association. Formed in 1935, the association promotes walking as a recreation, and campaigns to protect Britain's footpaths and the natural beauty of the countryside. It has successfully lobbied for the creation of Britain's national parks and, more recently, for the introduction of a statutory freedom to roam over open country. The Ramblers' Association also provides an extensive information service. Many of Britain's national walking trails were originally proposed and surveyed by association members, and much of the rights of way network has been maintained by the association's volunteers.

Introduction

One of the best ways to experience the varied landscape of Britain, and an ideal way to meet the people, is to go walking. Walkers can enjoy the extensive footpath network and the traditional 'right to roam' in many areas, which lets you walk over hills and mountains, beside rivers and lakes, through valleys and across moors. Other attractions include traditional villages and small country towns, where two British institutions – the pub and the B&B – make walking so pleasurable. The traveller can also experience historic sites, good public transport, excellent maps and – for many visitors – few language problems. Some people rave about hardy expeditions through the untamed wilderness of North-West Scotland, while others love the accessibility and human scale of Southern England's gentle fields and farmland. There really is something for everyone.

Walking in Britain is for visitors from overseas and locals looking for a single book that covers the whole country. We describe a selection of routes, ranging from easy to hard and from a few hours to a few weeks, with something suitable for all types of walker. The options for walking in Britain are almost limitless, so providing a complete list is impossible, but what we have included is enough to keep you busy for a long time!

The day walks are samples of what each area has to offer. Most are circular, so you start and finish in the same place, and we often use the same starting point for various routes, so you can be based in one place and go in different directions each day. Several linear day walks can be extended into two days – ideal for a weekend or if you simply want to keep going! We also outline shorter alternatives, good if you only want to walk for a morning or afternoon. Likewise, the long-distance paths don't have to be followed in their entirety – you can do just a couple of days if you prefer. Some day walks and long-distance paths in this book deliberately overlap, giving you even more scope for several walks in the same area.

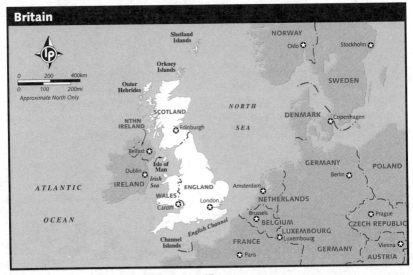

Britain

17

Many different types of accommodation are available in Britain; where you stay may depend on how much money you want to spend or how much time you have. On the long routes you may want to carry all your gear and camp, or you may prefer to travel light, staying in hostels, B&Bs or hotels. Many walkers visit several areas, so we also include details on local transport: how to get to the start of a route, how to get away at the end and how to 'escape' halfway. The book covers many other subjects regarding walking in Britain, including visitors centres, local guidebooks and maps, guided walks and so on. This book has just about everything you need.

We have concentrated on the national parks and other more popular areas simply because these are where the walking is best! Some of the routes are long-time classics, others are personal favourites based on our own local knowledge. We have also described a few out-of-the-way routes and provided brief outlines of many more places, which you can enjoy exploring. Have fun and let us know how you get on so your information can be used for the next edition.

Facts about Britain

Before you read this book some essential definitions are required. The state of Great Britain (shortened to 'Britain') is made up of three countries – England, Wales and Scotland. The United Kingdom (UK) consists of Great Britain, Northern Ireland and some semiautonomous islands such as the Isle of Man and the Channel Isles. The island of Ireland consists of Northern Ireland and the Republic of Ireland. The latter, also called Eire, is a completely separate country. The British Isles is a geographical term for the whole group of islands that make up the UK and the Republic of Ireland.

It is quite usual to hear 'England' and 'Britain' used interchangeably, but you should if possible avoid this, especially in Wales or Scotland, where it may well cause offence. (Calling a Scot 'English' is like calling a Canadian 'American' or a New Zealander 'Australian'.) Visitors can plead ignorance and get away with an occasional mix-up, but some of the worst offenders are the English themselves, many of whom seem to think that Wales and Scotland *are* parts of England. This naturally angers the Scots and Welsh, fuelling nationalist sentiments. This is usually completely misunderstood by the English, who simply think their neighbours carry ancient and unreasonable grudges.

HISTORY

A major aspect of walking in Britain is passing historical sites and features. In a single day you could follow a Roman road, pass a Bronze Age burial mound and visit a 13th-century cathedral. Within a few miles you could walk through prehistoric stone circles and beneath the arches of a Victorian railway viaduct. You might see battle sites, grand castles, humble workers' cottages or ancient Celtic crosses. Of course you'll also see stretches of open countryside and wilderness, but very few of these have completely escaped the effects of human activity.

Britain's history, spanning several millennia, is complex and can be quite difficult to grasp. This very brief historical outline will help you put things in order and perspective. It is followed by a more detailed section on the history of walking in Britain.

4000 BC – Neolithic (Stone Age) people arrive in Britain from mainland Europe
3000 – construction of ceremonial complexes such as Stonehenge and Avebury
800 – arrival of the Celts from central Europe; beginning of the Bronze Age
500 – Celts divided into two main tribes: Britons in the south, Picts in the north; start of the Iron Age
AD 43 – Roman invasion of Britain
122 – Emperor Hadrian decrees a wall across northern Britain to keep out the Picts, having failed to conquer them
313 – Romans bring Christianity to Britain after its acceptance by Emperor Constantine in Rome
410 – end of Roman power in Britain
5th & 6th centuries – migration of Angles and Saxons from northern Europe to Britain; Celts absorbed or forced to move to the extreme northern and western parts of the British Isles; Scotti people reach south-western Scotland from northern Ireland
635 – St Aidan founds monastery on Lindisfarne, which becomes a major centre of Christianity
7th & 8th centuries – three powerful Anglo-Saxon kingdoms emerge – Northumbria, Mercia and Wessex
8th century – King Offa of Mercia orders a dyke (defensive ditch) to mark the border between his Anglo-Saxon kingdom and Celtic Wales
9th century – Norse and Danish invaders conquer parts of northern and eastern Britain, and many settle; in southern Britain, Wessex remains Anglo-Saxon under King Alfred the Great
843 – Pict culture disappears after a Scot, Kenneth MacAlpin, is crowned king of the north (the territory later becomes known as Scotland)
9th & 10th centuries – repeated attacks on the Welsh by Anglo-Saxon tribes
10th century – Edward the Elder gains control of northern 'Danelaw' territories and southern Wessex, uniting England for the first time
1066 – Norman Conquest of Britain led by William the Conqueror
1085 – Doomsday Book is produced; a census of England's people, land and potential
1215 – signing of the Magna Carta by King John, ending the absolute authority of the monarchy

1272–1307 – Edward I establishes his authority over Wales and moves the Scots' coronation stone to England

1314 – England defeated by Robert the Bruce, King of Scotland, at the Battle of Bannockburn

1337 – start of the Hundred Years' War between England and France

1349 – Black Death in England kills more than 1.5 million people, one-third of the population

1381 – Richard II suppresses the Peasants' Revolt

1400–06 – Owain Glyndŵr leads a Welsh rebellion against England but is defeated by the army of Henry IV

1445–85 – 'War of the Roses' between the Houses of York and Lancaster; Edward IV of York is victorious and Henry VI of Lancaster dies in the Tower of London

1483 – twelve-year-old Edward V and his brother murdered in the Tower of London, possibly by Richard III

1485 – Henry Tudor becomes King Henry VII

1536 – start of the Dissolution of the Monasteries by Henry VIII, famous for his six wives; Church of England established

1558 – Elizabeth I becomes queen; enter William Shakespeare, Walter Raleigh and Francis Drake

1560 – Scottish parliament creates Protestant church independent of Rome and the monarchy

1567 – Mary Queen of Scots is imprisoned

1603 – James VI of Scotland also becomes James I of England

1605 – Guy Fawkes' Gunpowder Plot to blow up the Houses of Parliament fails

1625 – Charles I becomes king

1644 – start of the Civil War between Royalists and Parliamentarians

1649 – Charles I executed; establishment of the Commonwealth, ruled by Oliver Cromwell

1660 – restoration of the monarchy by parliament and the crowning of Charles II as king

1688 – William of Orange defeats James II at the Battle of the Boyne to take the crown of England

1707 – the Act of Union joins Scotland and England under a single parliament

1714 – Queen Anne, the last of the Stuart monarchs, dies; the Hanoverian kings reign

1715 – first Jacobite Rebellion attempts to restore the Stuart monarchs to the throne

1745 – second Jacobite Rebellion led by Charles Stuart ('Bonnie Prince Charlie')

1746 – Bonnie Prince Charlie flees Britain after defeat at the Battle of Culloden

1750s – start of the Industrial Revolution

1837–1901 – reign of Queen Victoria

1840s–1860s – 'The Clearances' of people from the land in the Highlands of Scotland

1914–18 – WWI

1919–21 – Anglo-Irish War results in independence for the Republic of Ireland; six counties in the north became Northern Ireland and remain part of the United Kingdom

1936 – King Edward VIII abdicates the throne to marry Mrs Simpson, a US divorcee; George VI is made king

1939–45 – WWII

1952 – George VI dies

1953 – Elizabeth II is crowned

1999 – devolution in Britain; Scottish Parliament and Assembly of Wales established

History of Walking

Prehistory Many routes enjoyed by present-day walkers were first trodden by prehistoric humans, for whom walking was obviously the only means of getting around. A good example of this is the Ridgeway, dubbed the oldest road in Europe because of its continuous use for at least 5000 years. It is now a national trail through Southern England, passing Bronze Age burial mounds, Iron Age hillforts and modern power stations – truly a walk through history. Its chronicler, JRL Anderson, said there was something humbling in tripping over a stone that may have stubbed a human toe 10,000 years ago.

It used to be accepted knowledge that prehistoric people kept to the ridges and hilltops because valleys were marshy or heavily forested, but archaeological research in places like the Somerset Levels has discovered a well-developed network of lowland tracks, such as the so-called 'Sweetway', which crossed even the most inhospitable swamps.

The earliest tracks linked settlements or hunting grounds, but archaeological evidence suggests that commerce also existed in prehistoric times. The discovery in Southern England of beautifully polished axeheads manufactured in North Wales or the Lake District shows that trade routes were well established across the country.

Alfred Watkins, in his book *The Old Straight Track*, claimed prehistoric sites were linked by an unseen system of tracks called 'ley lines'. This is open to dispute and dismissed by serious archaeologists. Even so, there are still many 'ley hunters' walking in Britain.

Romans & Anglo-Saxons Some prehistoric routes, such as the Icknield Way and Watling Street, were later followed by ruler-straight roads constructed by Roman legions during their 400-year occupation of most of Britain from the 1st century AD. In turn many Roman roads have been followed by today's main roads; for example, the A5 from London to North Wales follows much of Watling Street, while the Fosse Way is largely followed by modern roads from Exeter, through the Cotswolds and across the Midlands to Lincoln. Many Roman roads have also been followed by modern footpaths, such as the Pennine Way, Dales Way and Peddars Way (all described in this book).

After the Romans abandoned their British province, the Anglo-Saxon people (originally from northern Germany and around the Baltic), who became the foundation stock of modern England, largely ignored the Roman roads and set up villages away from the Imperial network. It was these settlers who created most of the villages that are such a typical feature of the modern British landscape. The footpaths that linked the villages developed into the current British rights-of-way network, which is now almost exclusively used for leisure purposes, and jealously guarded by local people and organisations such as the Ramblers' Association. (The concept of rights of way is discussed in more detail under Place Names & Terminology in the Facts for the Walker chapter.)

Middle Ages During the Middle Ages (AD 500 to the 15th century) important trade routes were widened into 'drove roads' for the easier transportation of livestock and goods, sometimes over vast distances. Some routes from Scotland into England were several hundred miles long. 'The Galloway Track' in Yorkshire is just one reminder of these times. (Many drove roads later became rights of way enjoyed today by walkers.)

Other important trade routes crossed the high country in the north of England, where trains of up to 50 packhorses were the big trucks of their day. The single-file causeways (locally called 'causeys'), built to cross boggy sections, were often paved, or 'pitched', with large stone slabs. These causeways still make excellent walking routes and modern restoration work on routes such as the Pennine Way has reverted to using the same historical construction paving techniques.

Another reason for walking during this period was spiritual. There was an established network of pilgrim routes leading to important religious sites such as Canterbury, Walsingham and Winchester. Geoffrey Chaucer's *The Canterbury Tales* describes the various types of people (including the well-to-do who were mainly horse riders) who made the journey to the shrine of St Thomas à Becket at Canterbury. Much of this route is followed by today's North Downs Way National Trail.

The 18th Century Drove roads remained important until the 17th century or later. Throughout Northern England and Scotland other early highways were military roads, built mainly in the 18th century by English armies attempting to control 'rebellious' Scots. Many of these routes exist today, either followed by modern highways or as rough tracks, used by walkers, winding through the glens. Also in Scotland, many of today's tracks and paths follow 'coffin roads', used by locals to carry their dead to burial grounds.

In the latter part of the 18th century a very important shift occurred in attitudes towards walking. Until this time most people walked out of necessity – whether it be for work, trade or pilgrimage – and the hills and mountains were not regarded as places of enjoyment. But a group of writers and poets, who became known as 'the Romantics', glorified nature as a source of inspiration rather than a source of horror. The leaders of this new movement were often walkers, realising that the best way to appreciate the wonders of the natural world was on foot.

One of the greatest exponents of the joys of walking and nature was the poet William Wordsworth. From his homes in the Lake District, Wordsworth would walk in the surrounding hills and valleys with his sister

Dorothy, taking the notes that later became such classic works as *The Prelude*.

As his reputation grew, Wordsworth gathered a nucleus of like-minded writers around him. One was opium addict Thomas de Quincey, who estimated that Wordsworth's legs (which were 'certainly not ornamental') must have walked at least 175,000mi during his lifetime. It was, said de Quincey:

'...a mode of exertion which, to him, stood in the stead of alcohol and all other stimulants whatsoever to the animal spirits; to which, indeed, he was indebted for a life of unclouded happiness, and we for much of what is most excellent in his writings.'

Another Romantic writer who settled in the Lake District was Samuel Taylor Coleridge, who became a close friend of the Wordsworths. Coleridge is credited with one of the earliest recorded rock climbs in the district with his ascent of Broad Stand on Scafell Pike during a 100mi walk in 1802.

Encouraged by the Romantic poets, or perhaps merely to escape the horrors of wheeled transport, 'pedestrian touring' became popular. In 1801 a 78-year-old Birmingham businessman, William Hutton, walked from his home along Hadrian's Wall and back again – a round trip of 600mi. His entertaining account is a classic in walking literature, as is George Borrow's *Wild Wales*, published in 1862, in which this eccentric linguist colourfully recounted his adventurous 239mi walking tour, including an ascent of Snowdon.

The Industrial Revolution Most of the best-known early walkers came from the upper or middle classes – among them intellectuals such as Charles Dickens. But by the earliest years of the Industrial Revolution, members of the lower classes – the factory workers – were also walking in the countryside for enjoyment.

As early as 1777 there was a flourishing botanical society at Eccles in Lancashire and its millworker members thought nothing of 'rambling' 30mi or 40mi on a Sunday afternoon searching for interesting specimens on the moors. They were not alone.

According to the British Association for the Advancement of Science, the Manchester district was 'the scene of one of the most remarkable manifestations of popular science which has ever been recorded'.

But the Enclosure Acts of the early 19th century resulted in the wholesale appropriation of large areas of moor and mountain in England, Wales and Scotland, which formerly had been 'common land' – open to all. Many ramblers were forcibly excluded from walking where they wished by stick-wielding gamekeepers charged with protecting grouse that their masters would later shoot. Many long-established rights of way were extinguished during this period.

One interesting by-product of the Highland Clearances in Scotland was the establishment of stalkers' tracks. As shooting for sport (stalking) became an increasingly popular pastime of the idle rich, tenants lucky enough not to be thrown off their land were put to work building paths for their masters to follow on foot or pony. Masterpieces of construction, many are still in use today – very useful for walkers in mountain areas.

Early Walking Organisations In a response to the landowners' moves an Association for the Protection of Ancient Footpaths in the Vicinity of York was founded in 1824, followed two years later by the Manchester Association for the Preservation of Ancient Footpaths, later to become the Peak District & Northern Footpath Preservation Society. (Waymarks of this still-active organisation are often seen where paths meet public roads.) The Manchester association, in the words of one of its founders:

'...spread among the country gentlemen a wholesome terror of transgressing against the right of the poor to enjoy their own without anyone to make them afraid.'

Despite these bold words, access to the high moors of the Pennines and Peak District was still strictly limited, and in 1877 the Hayfield and Kinder Scout Ancient Footpath Association reported that the public, 'imagining that what was once their own is now their own, have not infrequently come into unpleasant collision with gamekeepers'.

Thomas Arthur Leonard, a Congregational minister from Colne, Lancashire, founded the Co-operative Holidays Association (CHA) in 1897. Its aim was to provide working-class people with walking holidays for the price of a week's wages. Leonard later formed the more austere Holiday Fellowship because he felt that, despite its origins, the CHA was becoming 'too middle-class in spirit and conservative in...ideas'.

By this time rambling clubs were springing up all over the country. Among the earliest was the Sunday Tramps, formed among London intellectuals in 1879 by the mountaineer Leslie Stephen. Soon to follow were the Manchester YMCA Rambling Club and the Forest Ramblers Club, based in Epping Forest, formed in 1884. Clubs were also formed around Glasgow and Edinburgh.

One of the most active of these early clubs was the Sheffield Clarion Ramblers, founded in 1900 by GHB Ward and named after the *Sheffield Clarion*, a socialist newspaper. Ward personified the self-taught nature of these early northern ramblers; his annual Clarion Handbooks are filled with home-spun axioms such as 'A rambler made is a man improved' and 'The man who never was lost never went very far'. Ward, like most of the ramblers' leaders of the time, was a life-long campaigner for access to the forbidden moorlands of the Peak District.

The 1920s & 1930s After WWI, soldiers returning from the trenches to 'a land fit for heroes' were still faced with 'Keep Out' signs when they went for a walk on the moors. Ramblers from the northern cities of England campaigned for access to the Pennine moors, while their Scottish counterparts campaigned for access to (among others) the hills of Perthshire. In response, landowners erected 'Trespassers will be Prosecuted' signs but these were known as 'wooden liars' by ramblers because trespass was not a criminal offence. The situation was made worse by the strong-arm tactics of some gamekeepers, and there were many unpleasant incidents.

Meanwhile rambling clubs had formed themselves into regional federations based on the major cities, and in 1931 the National Council of Ramblers' Federations was set up. In 1935 this became the Ramblers' Association (RA) – still at the forefront of campaigns for walkers' rights in England and Wales today.

From the very start the ramblers had three main issues on their agenda: the creation of national parks, the protection of rights of way, and access to mountains and moorland. Things came to a head in the early 1930s when a series of well-attended open-air rallies was held in the Peak District. Deliberate trespasses were organised, culminating in 'The Battle of Kinder Scout' – a major landmark in the history of British walking (see the boxed text on page 24).

Postwar Years & Late 20th Century
Although some access victories were achieved in the 1930s, the creation of national parks had to wait until after WWII. The postwar Labour government was committed to national parks, based on the visionary 1945 report of architect, planner and rambler John Dower, which in turn was based on the principles of protected wilderness areas established in the USA in the late 19th and early 20th centuries. In 1949 parliament passed the National Parks & Access to the Countryside Act, which led to the creation of parks in England and Wales.

The first park was created in 1951 in the Peak District, scene of the great access battles of the 1930s, and access agreements were negotiated with landowners so that today over 80 sq mi of once-forbidden moorlands are open, allowing walkers their cherished freedom to roam, subject to a common-sense set of by-laws.

The 1949 Act also set up the National Parks Commission (later the Countryside Commission, now the Countryside Agency), which was charged not only with the creation of national parks and other protected areas but also with the creation of long-distance paths (LDPs). The first and best known of these was the Pennine Way, a 270mi route from the Peak District to the

Scottish border, which was established in 1965. Through the following decades many more LDPs were established by the Countryside Commission, county councils, local rambling groups and other organisations. In the 1990s LDPs managed by the Countryside Agency were renamed national trails.

The 1949 National Parks & Access to the Countryside Act was modified by the Environment Act of 1995, which made all national parks free-standing local authorities, divorced from their respective county councils. This Act also amended national park purposes to include conserving and enhancing the natural beauty, wildlife and cultural heritage of parks, and promoting opportunities for the understanding and enjoyment of their special qualities to the public.

The Battle of Kinder Scout

In the spring of 1932 some members of the communist-based British Workers' Sports Federation (BWSF) were forced off the Peak District high moorland of Bleaklow by abusive gamekeepers. They resolved to come back in force, and a 'mass trespass' over Kinder Scout was organised and advertised locally. Kinder Scout, at 636m, was the highest point of the Peak District, visible from the streets of Manchester yet uncrossed by any public path.

On 24 April 1932, a bright Sunday morning, about 400 ramblers set off from the small town of Hayfield towards the summit of Kinder, determined to exercise what they saw as their 'right to roam'. They soon outpaced their police escort and made their way up a right of way in a small valley called William Clough, before deliberately setting off cross-country. They were met by a small force of gamekeepers. Some scuffles occurred and a gamekeeper fell with an injured ankle.

Five of the mass trespass ringleaders were arrested and eventually tried in Derby where they received a total of 17 months' imprisonment. Ironically, it was the severity of the sentences that united the rambling establishment, which until then had been opposed to the direct action of the BWSF.

Despite some successes, however, walkers still had not gained the right to roam freely on all mountains and moorland. In the postwar years, and then particularly through the 1980s and 1990s, the Ramblers' Association (by now one of Britain's foremost pressure groups with over 100,000 members) and several other bodies continued vigorously campaigning for that 'right to roam' – a right enjoyed by walkers in most other European countries.

Changes for a New Millennium In late 2000 the campaigning work finally paid off when the Countryside & Rights of Way Act was passed by Parliament. The Countryside Agency called it 'the most significant step taken for people to enjoy the countryside since national parks were established 50 years ago'. Among its many provisions, this new law finally allows walkers to walk where they want – within sensible limits and subject to restrictions for management and conservation interests – on designated and mapped uncultivated mountains and moorland, as well as on other open areas (such as downland and common land) in England and Wales. Most of the land still remains privately owned and bodies known as access forums will decide on disputes. (Scotland has its own legal system and separate access laws; these are covered in the boxed text 'Access in Scotland & the Concordat' on p451.)

The new law also allows landowners to voluntarily open up other areas such as woodland or meadows, which wouldn't normally be included in the principle of the 'right to roam' across open, uncultivated land. Additionally, the new law requires local councils to properly maintain all the rights of way in their area. There are also many provisions for improved protection of wildlife and conservation areas called Sites of Special Scientific Interest (SSSIs).

In practice, the situation for walkers on the ground won't immediately change much but, from 2001 to 2010, the improvements in access, both to open land and on rights of way, will become increasingly apparent and should add to the enjoyment of walkers.

Other major changes due include the establishment of two new national parks in England – the South Downs in Sussex and the New Forest in Hampshire – and two new national parks in Scotland. The English parks should be legally created by 2003 and are due to be 'on-stream' by 2005, but the Scottish parks may be fully operational earlier than this. See the boxed text 'National Parks for Scotland' on p478.

GEOGRAPHY

The geography of Britain is extremely varied, so it's easier to outline the main features by focusing on each country.

England

Covering just over 50,000 sq mi, England can be divided into four main geographical areas. Northern England is dominated by the Pennines, a series of mountains, hills and valleys stretching for 250mi in a central ridge from Derbyshire to the border with Scotland. The Pennine Way National Trail winds through this range. To the west are the scenic Cumbrian Mountains of the Lake District, especially popular with walkers, containing England's highest point, Scafell Pike, measuring 978m.

The central part of England is known as the Midlands, mainly flat, heavily populated and an industrial heartland since the 19th century.

The South-West Peninsula, also known as the West Country, has a rugged coastline, good beaches and a mild climate, making it a favourite holiday destination. The South West Coast Path, Britain's longest national trail, and the wild, grass-covered moors of Dartmoor and Exmoor are popular areas with walkers.

The rest of the country is usually lumped together as the South-East, a region of rolling farmland and several densely populated towns and cities, including London, the capital of both England and Britain. To the south are hills of chalk known as downs, including the North Downs (followed by another national trail), stretching from London to Dover, where the chalk is exposed as the famous white cliffs.

Wales

Covering just over 8000 sq mi, Wales is surrounded by sea on three sides. Its border to the east with England still runs roughly along Offa's Dyke, a giant earthwork constructed in the 8th century. Wales has two major mountain national parks: Snowdonia in the north and Brecon Beacons in the south. At 1095m, Snowdon is the highest peak in Wales. The population is concentrated in the south-east, along the coast between Cardiff (the capital) and Swansea, and in the Valleys (a former mining centre) that run north from here.

Scotland

Scotland covers about 30,000 sq mi, two-thirds of which is mountain and moorland and therefore very popular with walkers. The Central Lowlands run from Edinburgh (the capital and financial centre) in the east to Glasgow (the industrial centre) in the west, and include the industrial belt and the majority of the population. A coastal plain runs all the way up the east coast. Between the Central Lowlands and the border with England are the Southern Uplands – an area of rolling hills and deep valleys. To the north of the Central Lowlands are the Highlands, a vast, sparsely populated area where most of the major mountain ranges are found. Ben Nevis, at 1322m the highest mountain in Scotland and Britain, is near the town of Fort William. The most spectacular (and most remote) mountains are those in the far north-west.

Scotland has 790 islands, 130 of them inhabited. The Western Isles comprise the Inner Hebrides and the Outer Hebrides. Two other island groups are Orkney and Shetland, the northernmost part of the British Isles.

CLIMATE

In keeping with its geography, the weather of Britain varies widely from place to place and from day to day, so visitors will soon sympathise with the locals' conversational obsession with the weather. The following section provides an overview. For more details, see When to Walk in the Facts for the Walker chapter.

The winter months (November, December, January and February) are generally

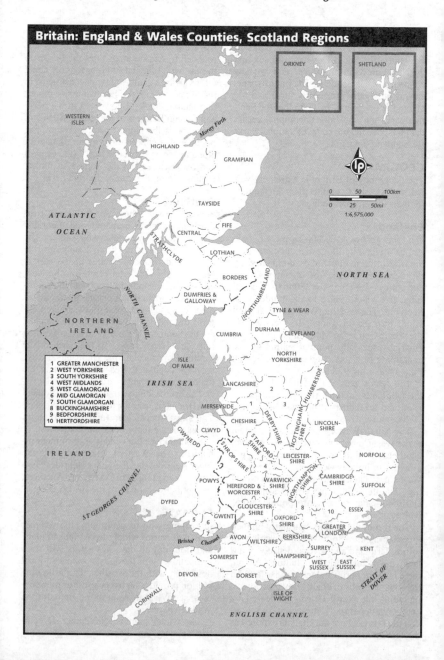

least pleasant for walking. It's cold and the days are short, although the hills are less crowded. Snow and ice intermittently cover many highland areas from about December, making walking on hills and mountains potentially dangerous without experience, although nothing can be more exhilarating than a walk in clear sunlight across a snow-covered mountain. Generally, the farther east you go the drier it gets and the farther north you go the colder it gets (although temperature is also greatly influenced by altitude).

Through the rest of the year (March to October) the weather can be good for walking – often dry and cool, and sometimes even warm. In summer temperatures can be hot and you'll need sunscreen to avoid getting burnt, even if it's windy and overcast.

England

Climatologists classify England's climate as 'temperate maritime', for which read 'mild and damp'. In winter light winds that blow off warm seas stop inland temperatures falling very far below 0°C and keep summer temperatures from rising much above 30°C. The average high in Southern England, from June to August, is 21°C and the average low is 12°C. It tends to be colder in the north of England but not as cold as in Scotland. Rainfall is greatest in hilly areas, such as the Lake District and Pennines, but you can expect some cloudy weather and rain anywhere in Britain at any time.

Wales

Temperatures are about on a par with England's but Wales gets a bit more rain. That said, the closeness of the mountains to the coast means you encounter very different climatic conditions within a relatively short distance. In practice this means if it's raining, it will be fine somewhere nearby. It also means you can get sun, then rain, then sun again within a couple of hours.

Scotland

'Varied' may be a vague description but it perfectly describes Scotland's climate. One good thing about the weather is that it does change quickly – a rainy day is often followed

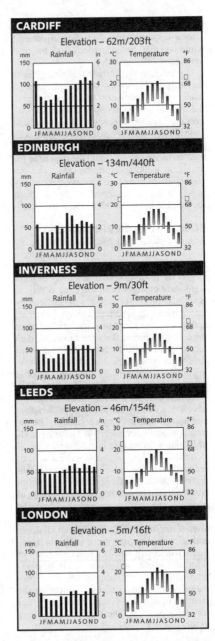

by a sunny one. In the mountains there are also wide variations over short distances; while one glen broods under cloud, the next may enjoy full sunshine.

Considering the latitude (Edinburgh is as far north as Moscow), you might expect a colder climate but warm Atlantic winds give the west coast a relatively mild climate, with average summer highs of 19°C. May and June are generally the driest months (as with the rest of Britain, rainfall generally decreases as you go east) and the best time for mountain walking. Note, however, that the Highlands can have extreme weather at any time; in the Cairngorms snow has been recorded in *every* month of the year.

ECOLOGY & ENVIRONMENT

Britain is small and has been inhabited by people for thousands of years, so it's hardly surprising that the countryside today is largely the result of human activity. The most significant changes occurred after WWII, as Britain's push for food self-sufficiency meant farming practices changed dramatically, which in turn had a dramatic effect on the country's native flora and fauna. Modern farming methods included linking small fields into vast prairie-like areas by removing the thick hedgerows – a valuable wildlife habitat – that once separated them. Since 1946 tens of thousands of miles of hedgerow have been destroyed, along with the plant and animal species they contained. The destruction continues; since 1984 a further 23% of Britain's hedgerows have disappeared.

Britain's wildlife habitats have also been reduced over the last 50 years through numerous other practices, including the increased use of pesticides, blanket planting of conifers, massive house- and road-building schemes, and the construction of out-of-town shopping centres. But it's not all doom and gloom. Despite these overwhelming odds Britain still boasts a great diversity of flora and fauna, and some of the best examples of natural habitats are now protected, to varying degrees, thanks to the creation of national parks and other similar conservation areas. These are discussed later in this chapter.

Britain's coast has also been subjected to more than its fair share of abuse from human activity. Damage to dunes by holiday-makers has led to erosion and the consequent loss of plant life and nesting sites. More worrying still is the issue of sea pollution. The massive spillage from an oil tanker near Milford Haven on the Pembrokeshire coast in 1996 caused devastation and brought the issue into sharp focus. But memories seem short and oil tankers continue to be a threat to Britain's coast. At the same time, sewage and industrial waste (some of it toxic and even radioactive) continue to be dumped at sea.

Equally serious is the persistent over-fishing of the seas around Britain. As commercial offshore fishing methods become increasingly efficient, fish stocks are reduced and fish are unable to reproduce at sustainable rates. This leads to a decline in vital food supplies for birds and sea mammals, while quotas introduced to control the over-fishing also have devastating effects for the people whose livelihoods depend on this trade. In many parts of Britain trawlers are mothballed while fishermen flounder on the dole and wait for stocks to recover.

Perhaps the most controversial environmental issue in Britain today concerns fox hunting. Groups of red-coated horse riders, complete with horns and hounds, are a classic image of the British (and especially English) countryside, but anti-hunting sentiment runs strong, particularly in urban areas, and many people see hunting as a cruel activity. However, hunting is a primarily rural phenomenon, largely (although not exclusively) tied up with social class, and pro-hunters argue that about 20,000 foxes are killed by hunts every year, compared to the 40,000 killed by vehicles or 100,000 that are trapped or shot, and that hunting provides much-needed employment in country areas. In January 2001 MPs overwhelmingly voted to ban fox hunting but the House of Lords delayed the bill's progress through Parliament. Major pro-hunt and countryside demonstrations are planned for 2001. Hunting has been increasingly

continued on page 40

Fauna & Flora of Britain

The wide variety of plants and animals in Britain reflects the surprisingly diverse range of natural habitats found in these small islands, although Britain's isolation since the last ice age has left its diversity more limited than other countries of northwest Europe. The diversity of habitats is partly due to Britain's range of climatic influences, from cold Arctic winds to the warm southern waters of the Gulf Stream.

Farming is the dominant land use throughout Britain, responsible for the manicured pattern of the countryside and the hills bereft of trees. Most of Britain's indigenous fauna are woodland creatures that have more or less adapted to the mix of habitats. Some, like kestrels and red foxes, are ubiquitous while others, like the Dartford warbler and dormouse, have clearly defined habitats and very restricted ranges.

This section is not intended to be a comprehensive guide. Rather, it gives an overview of the sort of things that you might see while walking. Note, however, that many British plants and animals are small and sometimes hidden away. You often need patience and perseverance to get the most out of studying the wildlife here. Don't be discouraged, though; there is such a variety of species that your efforts will be rewarded, and if you appreciate the wealth of life above and below, your walking will undoubtedly be enhanced.

NICOLA WELLS

Manicured patterns of farmland, Scotland

GRASSLAND & FARMLAND

Probably the best examples of grassland are found on the chalk downs in Southern England (notably on the South Downs) and in the limestone areas farther north, such as the Peak District and Yorkshire Dales.

Most traditional grassland has disappeared from Britain in the last 50 years, principally because it has been ploughed up and replaced with ryegrass, or because it has been fertilised, leading to the overgrowth of a few vigorous species. However, some grasslands and meadows are now protected, and are home to a great profusion of wild flowers, each month bringing a fresh array.

Cowslips (*Primula veris*) and **primroses** (*P. vulgaris*) both have yellow flowers in April and May, and have similar cabbage-like leaves. They are easy to distinguish as cowslips have a cluster of flowers on one stalk, while primroses have one stalk for each flower. Later in the year **meadow buttercups**

DAVID TIPLING

Cowslip

Title page: Puffin with sand eels.
Photograph by Nicholas Reuss.

Common spotted orchid

Blue tit

Badger in the wild

(*Ranunculus acris*) produce golden yellow flowers, while **knapweed** (*Centaurea scabiosa*) flowers look like tiny purple pineapples; both these plants can cover a whole meadow in colour. Orchids also thrive in this environment. **Common spotted** (*Dactylorhiza fuchsii*) and **early purple orchids** (*Orchis mascula*) have large pinkish flowerheads, while the **bee orchid** (*Ophrys apifera*) is surprisingly easy to overlook despite its bee-like flowers.

With the flowers come insects. If the meadows have trees nearby, a variety of birds can be sighted, including **blue tits** (*Parus caeruleus*), **great tits** (*P. major*), **blackcaps** (*Sylvia atricapilla*) and the occasional **green woodpecker** (*Picus viridis*), seen stabbing at the anthills. You may also hear the warbling song of a **skylark** (*Alauda arvensis*) as it flutters high over more open farmland.

Slow worms (*Anguis fragilis*) live in a variety of dampish habitats. While they look like snakes and are often attacked by scared people, they are actually legless lizards and, like almost all British wildlife, are completely harmless.

With the belated realisation that farm hedgerows support a great deal of wildlife, farmers are now encouraged by bodies such as English Nature to maintain their hedgerows and 'set aside' the perimeters of fields to grow wild. These areas serve as havens for many birds such as **robins** (*Erithacus rubecula*); one of Britain's smallest birds, **wrens** (*Troglodytes troglodytes*); and **yellowhammers** (*Emberiza citrinella*). Hedges also provide cover for flocks of **finches**, preyed upon by **sparrowhawks** (*Accipiter nisus*), which come from nowhere at tremendous speed.

The most common hedgerow tree is **hawthorn** (*Crataegus monogyna*) with its white spring blossom providing early nectar for hungry insects and its red berries eaten by many creatures, including flocks of **fieldfares** (*Turdus pilaris*) and **redwings** (*Turdus iliacus*) visiting Britain in early winter. **Elder** (*Sambucus nigra*) is another berry-bearing shrub that feeds birds and small mammals in the autumn. **Blackberries** (*Rubus fruticosus*) are also abundant in the hedgerows and a welcome snack for walkers in the countryside.

If you notice an area where a lot of earth has been dug up, try sitting quietly nearby at dusk. You may be lucky enough to see a **badger** (*Meles meles*) trundle past. On warm evenings **pipistrelle bats** (*Pipistrellus pipistrellus*) patrol the hedges, catching tiny midges.

Hedgerows and (ironically) road or motorway verges frequently support large populations of small mammals, attracting **kestrels** *(Falco tinnunculus)*. **Barn owls** *(Tyto alba)* are a fantastic sight as they fly silently along hedgerows, looking and listening for the faint rustle of a vole or shrew. They are often called ghost bird or screech owl for very good reason.

Weasels *(Mustela nivalis)* and **stoats** *(M. erminea)* are sometimes seen bounding between hedgerows on quiet country lanes. Both are ferocious hunters and look similar, except that the stoat has a black tip to its tail. In rural Wales or Scotland you may see a **buzzard** *(Buteo buteo)*, Britain's most common large raptor, perched by the roadside.

Another common bird is the **pheasant** *(Phasianus colchicus)*. Their nervous habit of leaving cover just at the last moment makes them ideal for shooting, and they were originally introduced from Russia for this purpose. Pheasants, now considered naturalised, are commonly seen in a variety of habitats, including farmland, woodland and moorland.

Rabbits *(Oryctolagus cuniculus)* are extremely common in Britain, having recovered from the myxomatosis epidemic of the 1950s. **Brown hares** *(Lepus capensis)*, with longer legs and ears, choose to stay in the open where they can see predators, so are often visible. Territorial battles between males in early spring give rise to the expression 'mad as a March hare'.

Barn owl

Pheasant cock

WOODLAND

Several thousand years ago Britain was almost entirely covered with woodland. Then Neolithic farmers began clearing small areas of trees, and the process of deforestation never really stopped until well into our own time. Large areas of native woodland survived until about the mid-16th century when demand for timber for shipbuilding, charcoal and firewood denuded the country's forests. Further large-scale deforestation during the Industrial Revolution reduced tree cover to a mere 2% or 3%.

As long ago as 1919 the Forestry Commission, a government agency, was established to halt this decline with a plan to plant five million acres (two million hectares) of trees, mainly in Northern England, Scotland and Wales, by 2000. Substantial grants for landowners ensured that this target was achieved by the early 1980s. Today Britain has about 8% tree cover,

Gnarled English oak

Wood anemones

still one of the lowest figures for any country in Europe (Italy has 22%, France 27%). What's more, most of these trees are closely spaced conifers, which severely restrict smaller bushes and undergrowth, and in turn result in greatly reduced insect and bird populations. Before a pine forest becomes too dense you may see birds such as **goldcrests** *(Regulus regulus)*, **coal tits** *(Parus ater)* and **siskins** *(Carduelis spinus)* but most of these will eventually depart, leaving eerily silent woodlands.

The environmental problems caused by conifers have been recognised for a few decades, but only in more recent times has there been a switch to establishing new 'broad-leaved' woodlands. Mainly deciduous trees are planted, such as **oak** *(Quercus* spp*)*, **ash** *(Fraxinus excelsior)*, **hazel** *(Corylus avellana)* and **rowan** *(Sorbus aucuparia)*, which support an enormous biodiversity. The New Forest and the Forest of Dean are examples of this type of habitat. Surprisingly, the most wooded county in Britain is Surrey, despite its proximity to London. The soil is too poor for agriculture and so the trees remain.

In spring, before the canopy is fully developed, enough sunlight reaches the ground to encourage a carpet of woodland flowers such as **wood anemones** *(Anemone nemorosa)* and **bluebells** *(Endymion nonscriptus)*. These trees and plants encourage numerous insects, which in turn attract birds. Common summer visitors are **willow warblers** *(Phylloscopus trochilus)* and **chiffchaffs** *(P. collybita)*. These inconspicuous small olive-brown birds are distinguished by their song: Willow warblers sing a descending cadence of notes, while the chiffchaff makes a noise like its name.

Also in woodland, your eye may be caught by a **tree creeper** *(Certhia familiaris)*, a small brown bird with a white chest, scuttling up trees in search of insects. By contrast, the greyish-blue **nuthatch** *(Sitta europaea)* can climb both up and down the bark.

Listen carefully and you may hear a **greater spotted woodpecker** *(Dendrocopus major)* drumming on dead trees to announce its presence, or spot this black-and-white bird flying off with a deeply undulating style.

Seed eaters are common year-round. These include **woodpigeons** *(Columba palumbus)*, who call 'my toe hurts Teddy', and **jays** *(Garrulus glandarius)*. The latter are large buff-brown birds that show vivid blue and white patches on their wings. They have a harsh voice and bury acorns during autumn to feed themselves through the winter.

Willow warbler

NICHOLAS REUSS

RICHARD MILLS

Spring is a good time to rise early and catch the 'dawn chorus' of birds singing to mark their territories and attract mates. On a night excursion, you may spot the plump, red-brown shape of a **tawny owl** *(Strix aluco)*, which often breeds close to human habitation.

Hedgehogs *(Erinaceus europaeus)* search leaf litter for insects and earthworms and will roll into a spiny ball at the first sign of danger. Sadly this is no protection against the motor car, and they are more likely to be seen as a roadside casualty than alive in the wild.

Other woodland mammals include **fallow deer** *(Cervus dama)*, smaller than red deer (see Moorland later) and distinguished by white spots. They are the most common woodland deer of England and Wales. **Roe deer** *(Capreolus capreolus)* are even smaller and prefer open woodland. In the absence of large predators all deer do considerable damage to young trees, and are culled in most areas. **Red foxes** *(Vulpes vulpes)* are very widespread. Originally a nocturnal woodland animal, foxes have adapted well to a scavenging life in country towns and even on the edges of cities. **Grey squirrels** *(Sciurus carolinesis)* have also proved very adaptable. Introduced from North America, they have almost entirely replaced smaller native **red squirrels** *(S. vulgaris;* see the boxed text below).

RICHARD MILLS

Hedgehog

The Red Squirrel

The red squirrel used to be commonplace in woodland, but is now one of Britain's most endangered species. Populations have declined significantly over the past 50 years to about 150,000, following the importation of the larger grey squirrel from America. The problem isn't that grey squirrels attack their red cousins. The problem is food. Greys are able to eat hazelnuts and acorns when they are still very green, but reds can only eat these nuts when they are ripe. But the greys get there first, and there's not much left for the reds. Once grey squirrels have arrived in an area the reds are usually gone within about 15 years.

RICHARD MILLS

Paradoxically, the enlightened policy of planting broad-leaved woodland rather than coniferous provides a further threat to the reds, as they are more adept than greys at getting the seeds out of pine cones. However, even this advantage is threatened, because the indomitable greys are learning the technique.

Red squirrels are now mainly confined to Scotland, Ireland and to isolated populations in the Lake District, Norfolk and the Isle of Wight. Initiatives by environmental groups such as the WWF are now underway to try to halt its further decline.

Pine marten

In the Scottish highlands there are a few areas where the native Caledonian forest (mostly Scots pine – *Pinus sylvestris*) grows naturally, allowing light to reach the understorey of **juniper** *(Juniperus communis)* and **holly** *(Ilex aquifolium)*. Resident native birds include the spectacular **crossbill** *(Loxia curvirostra)*. If there is water nearby you have a chance of spotting an **osprey** *(Pandion haliaetus)*. Some are now satellite tagged and their migration to West African coasts in the winter can be followed on a fascinating Web site (**W** www.rutlandwater@u-net.co.uk/ospreys). **Wildcats** *(Felis sylvestris)* live in dense woodland in the Highlands of Scotland, but are under threat and rarely seen. By contrast, **pine martens** *(Martes martes)* are again being seen in some forested regions, especially in Scotland. Now fully protected, they have a beautiful brown coat with a conspicuous yellow throat patch.

HEATHLAND

Areas of land called 'heath' are generally low with poor soils, typified by **gorse** *(Ulex europaeus)* and **heather** (family Ericaceae) plants. The season for heather to flower is autumn, when the moors are covered in purple. Other characteristic plants are **broom** *(Cytisus scoparius)* and, increasingly in some areas, **bracken** *(Pteridium* spp). **Bilberry** *(Vaccinium myrtillus)* bushes, recognised by the tiny blue-black fruit they produce in the summer, may be interspersed with the heather, particularly on higher ground.

Heathland used to be widespread in southern Britain, but most has now disappeared as agriculture, roads and property development take their toll. Pockets remain, most notably in the New Forest and parts of Surrey.

Heathland birds include **meadow pipits** *(Anthus pratensis)*, small brown birds that have a habit of flying up from the path ahead so you never quite get a good look. **Stonechats** *(Saxicola torquata)* are a common sight, often perched on a gorse bush, calling a metallic 'chak chak', like the sound of two stones banged together. After dark you may hear the distinctive churring song of **nightjars** *(Caprimulgus europaeus)*.

Britain's only venomous snake, the **adder** *(Vipera berus)*, is found throughout the mainland in dry, open country and is easily recognised by the dark zigzag stripe down its back. This snake grows to about 70cm and, although poisonous, its bite is rarely fatal.

Heather and gorse growing on a hillside

Common stonechat

MOORLAND

This is essentially heathland on higher ground, and supports a similar collection of plant life. Classic moorlands include Dartmoor, the northern Peak District, the North York Moors, the North Pennines and the uplands of Scotland, which not coincidentally are also some of the best parts of Britain for walking.

As you stride across these moors you will almost inevitably scatter **red grouse** *(Lagopus lagopus)*, another nervous game bird. The elegant **curlew** *(Numenius arquata)* breeds in upland areas and lives on the coast. **Golden plovers** *(Pluvialis apricaria)* are beautifully camouflaged but are noticed by their mournful cries. **Wheatears** *(Oenanthe oenanthe)* are another moorland bird; the males are a handsome grey with black patches and a white rump. **Merlins** *(Falco columbarius)* are dark fast-flying falcons that hunt smaller birds. White-rumped **hen harriers** *(Circus cyaneus)* can also sometimes be seen hunting low over the moors. **Short-eared owls** *(Asio flammeus)* glide or hover on long rounded wings in daylight hours. These three birds of prey are all also seen in coastal marshes and estuaries.

Many of the high moors are covered extensively with peat, but these areas have declined dramatically in the last few decades due to the commercial use of peat for gardens and the establishment of large pine plantations. Originally a woodland mammal, **red deer** *(Cervus elaphus)* herds survive on Exmoor and Dartmoor, in the Lake District and in larger numbers in Scotland. Males grow a pair of large antlers between April and July, which are shed again in February. Their long-term future as a species is threatened by interbreeding with the introduced **sika deer** *(Cervus nippon)*.

MOUNTAINS

There are mountains (as opposed to hills) in Snowdonia (Wales) and the Lake District (England), but the vast majority of Britain's high mountains are in Scotland, particularly in the west and north-west. Unique to these areas are many hardy alpine plants such as **purple saxifrage** *(Saxifraga oppositifolia)*, **mossy saxifrage** *(S. hypnoides)*, **rock speedwell** *(Veronica fruticans)* and **mountain avens** *(Dryas octopetala)* – best looked for on rocky ledges or under stones, where sheep can't get to them. One of the best places to see this type of vegetation is at Cwm Idwal in

Red grouse

Red deer

Mountain avens

Yellow iris

NICHOLAS REUSS

Kingfisher

DAVID TIPLING

Snowdonia, where the ledges known as the Hanging Gardens have been a botanists' paradise for years.

In central Wales there has been a successful project to reintroduce **red kites** *(Milvus milvus)*; these fork-tailed mountain birds are a spectacular sight. On the high peaks in Scotland you may see the grouse's northern cousin, the **ptarmigan** *(Lagopus mutus)*, dappled brown in the summer but white in the winter. **Snow buntings** *(Plectrophenax nivalis)* are scarce breeders on Scottish mountain tops but a regular winter visitor along the shores of the east coast where they form large flocks. **Golden eagles** *(Aquila chrysaetos)*, Britain's largest birds of prey, glide and soar along ridges and in thermals. Principally found in the mountains of Scotland, a few heavily protected pairs also breed in the Lake District.

FRESHWATER AREAS

Streams and rivers in lowland areas are abundant with life in the summer. On the banks, **meadowsweet** *(Filipendula ulmaris)* produces masses of fragrant creamy flowers, while hairy **willowherb** *(Epilobium hirsutum)* has more discreet pinkish flowers with white star-shaped stamens. **Yellow irises** *(Iris pseudacorus)* grow tall with slender, blade-like leaves and have their roots in water. Mayflies emerge from aquatic larvae en masse and provide a feast for birds and fish. The iridescent **kingfisher** *(Alcedo atthis)* is most often seen as a flash of bright blue disappearing down the river, disturbed from its fishing perch. **Little grebes** *(Tachybaptus ruficollis)* are fun to watch as they pop up from underwater foraging, while **grey herons** *(Ardea cinerea)* silently stalk at the water's edge, and **moorhens** *(Gallinula chloropus)* noisily boss each other around. Moorheans are black birds with red bills; they are often confused with **coots** *(Fulica atra)*, which have black feathers but white bills.

Also found in lowland freshwater areas, **grass snakes** *(Natrix natrix)* are Britain's longest snakes. Completely harmless, they are greyish green and have a pale ring on the neck.

By contrast to lowland watery areas, upland streams are often fast running and crystal clear. The abundance of insects both in and above the water encourages the presence of birds. The thrush-like **dipper** *(Cinclus cinclus)* has a white bib and searches underwater crevices for fly larvae, while **grey wagtails**

(Motacilla cinerea), more yellow than grey, twist and turn in the air to catch adult flies.

Pairs of **great crested grebes** *(Podiceps cristatus)* put on a fancy bonding display in summer, with long-neck rubbing and lots of splashing. **Mallards** *(Anas platyrhynchos)* are widespread; the male is instantly recognisable with a striking glossy, dark green head, while the female is better camouflaged. **Tufted ducks** *(Aythya fuligula)* are dainty divers, usually seen in breeding pairs or in larger groups in winter. **Teals** *(Anas crecca)* are small ducks with lovely chestnut heads and dark green eye stripes. **Pintails** *(A. acuta)* have long tails, while **shovelers** *(A. clypeata)* have spatulate bills.

Marshes and reedbeds, such as those found in the Norfolk Broads, are an ornithological paradise. Nesting birds, such as **reed buntings** *(Emberiza schoeniclus)*, **redshanks** *(Tringo totanus)* and, very rarely, **bitterns** *(Botaurus stellaris)*, may be seen. Look for **marsh harriers** *(Circus aeruginosus)* gliding low overhead.

Closer inspection reveals a number of springtime flowers. **Marsh orchids** *(Dactylorhiza* spp) have purple flower spikes, **bogbean** *(Menyanthes trifoliata)* have hairy star-like white flowers, and **marsh marigolds** *(Caltha palustris)* form spectacular clusters of glossy yellow flowers.

Water voles *(Arvicola terrestris)* were once the most common aquatic mammal in Britain. This endearing rodent has been all but wiped out by the **American mink** *(Mustela vison)*. Originally introduced to stock fur farms, some escaped and have become widespread, much to the detriment of many smaller native mammals. Now protected, **otters** *(Lutra lutra)* are beginning to make a comeback after suffering from the effects of polluted water, habitat destruction and from persecution by anglers. They are mainly nocturnal and inhabit the banks of rivers and lakes. In Scotland they frequently live on the coast.

COASTAL AREAS

The dramatic cliffs and beaches round the coast of Britain, particularly in Cornwall, Pembrokeshire and North-West Scotland, are a marvellous sight, especially during early summer when they are home to thousands of breeding sea birds. **Guillemots** *(Uria aalge)*, **razorbills** *(Alca torda)* and **kittiwakes** *(Rissa tridactyla)*, among others, all fight for space on impossibly crowded rock ledges. Other birds, such as

DAVID TIPLING

Tufted duck

NICHOLAS REUSS

Razorbill

NICHOLAS REUSS

Sea holly

jackdaws (Corvus monedula), also make use of holes in the cliffs for nesting. **Puffins** (Fratercula arctica) have distinctive rainbow beaks and can be seen burrowing to make their nests. **Gannets** (Morus bassabus) are one of the largest sea birds and make dramatic dives for fish, often from a great height.

Estuaries and mudflats are feeding grounds for numerous migrant wading birds. Handsome **black-and-white oystercatchers** (Haematopus ostralegus) with long red bills are a familiar sight. Flocks of small **ringed plovers** (Charadrius hiatus) may skitter along the sand, then rise in a compact bunch. **Lapwings** (Vanellus vanellus) have a distinctive crest and look black and white from a distance. They have a jerky flight and a strange squeaky 'pee wit' call. All the wading birds feed on molluscs and crustaceans, but each species has a slightly different bill that allows them to feed from a different level in the mud. Ducks, such as teal (see Freshwater Areas earlier) and **wigeon** (Anas penelope), with its golden crown, and several species of geese are also found here. Plants, such as **glasswort** (Salicornia europaea) and **sea lavender** (Limonium vulgare), also flourish on muddy saltmarshes.

Even dunes and beaches, which may appear inhospitable, support a range of plant life, including the tough **marram grass** (Ammophila arenaria) that holds the sand together. Other specialised plants that thrive on the dunes include marsh orchids (see Freshwater Areas earlier) and creeping willow. These in turn bring in a variety of butterflies and grasshoppers. Even shingle beaches can support plants such as **sea holly** (Eryngium maritimum) and **sea milkwort** (Glaux maritima). Some birds, including oystercatchers and **black-headed gulls** (Larus ridibundus), choose to nest on the dunes, so you should take great care if walking in quiet sandy areas (although you're unlikely to see nesting birds on busy beaches).

Two species of seal frequent British coasts. The larger **grey seal** (Halichoerus grypus) is more often seen than the **common seal** (Phoca vitulina). When walking the Pembrokeshire Coast Path it's worth staying an extra day at St David's to go sea-mammal watching or kayaking along the coast. **Common dolphins** (Delphinus delphis) and **harbour porpoises** (Phocoena phocoena) sometimes compete with nearby canoeists to perform aquabatic feats.

NICHOLAS REUSS

Atlantic grey seal

continued from page 28

combined with many other urban-versus-rural issues that remain high on the political agenda, and the situation is still fluid and volatile. Visitors are well advised only to listen to any conversations about hunting, especially in country pubs.

Conservation Groups

There are many groups in Britain involved in environmental conservation. International campaigning organisations, such as the World Wide Fund for Nature (WWF), Greenpeace and Friends of the Earth, include British issues in their portfolios. Several other local organisations concentrate on British issues, and many of these own land that you may cross or pass by when walking, or historic sites near the route that you may want to visit. These include:

The National Trust (☎ 020-8315 1111, e en quiries@ntrust.org.uk, W www.nationaltrust.org .uk) 36 Queen Anne's Gate, London SW1H 9AS. This is a conservation charity (not a government agency) and major landowner with estates, wilderness areas, parks and woods all over England and Wales, plus about 600mi of coastline, which receive some 40 million visitors every year. The trust also owns many formal gardens and historic buildings. You do not normally need to pay to enter open land owned by the trust, but for special gardens and buildings an entrance fee is usually payable. You can become an annual member of the National Trust for £30 (there are discounts for families and under 25s) and then get free entry to sites run by the National Trust and the National Trust for Scotland. Similar organisations overseas may have reciprocal arrangements with the National Trust, allowing members free entry.

The National Trust for Scotland (☎ 0131-234 9300, e information@nts.org.uk, W www.nts .org.uk) 5 Charlotte Square, Edinburgh EH2 4DU. The Scottish organisation is also a major landowner, with similar objectives and responsibilities to its namesake in England and Wales, although concerned more with protection of landscapes. Membership gets you free or reduced rates at their properties, where an entrance fee is charged. The annual fee is £27 (discounts for families and under 25s). Reciprocal arrangements exist with The National Trust (England and Wales) and other similar bodies overseas.

Royal Society for the Protection of Birds (☎ 01767-680551, W www.rspb.org.uk) The Lodge, Sandy, Bedfordshire SG19 2BR. The RSPB runs more than 100 bird reserves. For £20 per year members get free entry to these reserves and a quarterly magazine.

Scottish Natural Heritage (☎ 0131-447 4784, fax 446 2277, W www.snh.org.uk) 12 Hope Terrace, Edinburgh EH9 2AS. Set up in 1992, SNH is the government body responsible for caring for Scotland's natural heritage. It's strongly decentralised and has 11 area offices – the best points of contact locally. SNH advises the government on natural heritage issues, owns and manages reserves, operates many grant schemes to promote nature conservation, supports Countryside Ranger services and produces a wide range of publications.

Wildlife Trusts (☎ 01636-677711, W www .wildlifetrust.org.uk) The Kiln, Waterside, Mather Road, Newark NG24 1WT. This organisation consists of numerous local groups actively involved in the care of nature reserves, along with conservation and education projects.

The Woodland Trust (☎ 01476-581111, W www .woodland-trust.org.uk) Autumn Park, Dysart Rd, Grantham NG31 6LL. This body buys and conserves woods and forests all over Britain and allows walkers free access to many of them.

NATIONAL PARKS & OTHER PROTECTED AREAS
National Parks

William Wordsworth, famous poet and walker, suggested in 1810 that the Lake District should be 'a sort of national property, in which every man has a right and interest who has an eye to perceive and a heart to enjoy'. But it took more than a century before the Lake District became a national park and it was very different from the 'sort of national property' Wordsworth envisaged.

Today there are 11 national parks in England and Wales – Brecon Beacons, Dartmoor, Exmoor, Lake District, Norfolk and Suffolk Broads, Northumberland, North York Moors, Peak District, Pembrokeshire Coast, Snowdonia and Yorkshire Dales. Two more parks, the New Forest and the South Downs, will be created by 2003. The situation in Scotland is different. No national parks existed until 2000, when two new parks were proposed. See the boxed text 'National Parks for Scotland' on p478.

'National park' is the highest designation for landscape protection in Britain but this title can cause some confusion. Firstly, parks are not owned by the nation. All the land is private, belonging to farmers, individual landowners, companies and conservation organisations. Just to increase the confusion, large sections of several national parks are owned by the National Trust but, despite the similar name, this private charity has no direct link with the national park administrative authorities. Secondly, these are not 'parks' of wilderness, as in many other countries. In the national parks of Britain are roads, railways, villages and towns. About 250,000 people live and work inside national park boundaries, some of them in industries that do great damage to their supposedly protected landscapes.

But don't despair! National parks also contain vast tracts of wild and open mountain and moorland, rolling downs and river valleys, and other areas of quiet countryside, all ideal for walking. These are still among the most scenic areas of Britain but being aware of their actual status will lessen the surprise for some visitors.

National parks are administered by national park authorities (NPAs) – freestanding bodies, independent of county council control – which perform a difficult tightrope act: balancing land conservation with both the needs of the local people who live and work in them, and the huge number of recreational visitors. NPAs represent a typically British compromise and, in cases of conflict, they often find themselves in a no-win situation.

The current total number of visits to British national parks is over 100 million every year. Some conservationists believe parks are counterproductive; they claim that making an area a national park creates an increase in visitors, which puts unsustainable pressure on the land and local resources. It seems there is never an easy solution.

Areas of Outstanding Natural Beauty

The second tier of protection in England and Wales covers Areas of Outstanding Natural Beauty (AONBs). There are about 40 such areas – including the Cotswold Hills and the North Pennines – all of which have excellent walking. Local county councils within AONBs have a responsibility for the landscape. Although they don't have the teeth of a national park authority, their powers are strengthened under the Countryside & Rights of Way Act 2000 (see the History of Walking earlier in this chapter).

National Scenic Areas

In Scotland, National Scenic Areas (NSAs) have been set aside where local authorities must have special concern for the landscape. Examples of these areas are Ben Nevis and Glen Coe, the Cairngorms, North Arran and Kintail. Again, all these areas are ideal for walking and are described in this book.

National Nature Reserves

These were established under the 1949 National Parks Act and are administered by English Nature, Scottish Natural Heritage (SNH) or the Countryside Council for Wales. Nature conservation is an important focus of National Nature Reserves (NNRs), but agriculture, forestry and recreation may also be involved. All NNRs are privately owned – sometimes by conservation organisations. In Scotland, SNH owns some NNRs, itself, including Beinn Eighe, Britain's first NNR. There's much variety among Scotland's 70 NNRs. Most are accessible and the more popular have a ranger service.

Other Designated Areas

As well as national parks, AONBs and NNRs, there are many other types of protected areas in Britain and an even greater number of connected abbreviations. Conspiracy theorists claim that the sheer number of governmental organisations charged with environmental protection is a deliberate move to prevent any one body becoming too powerful. Whether this is true or not, there are two important points to remember: Like national parks, most designated areas consist of privately owned land; and these special designations do not normally affect rights of way – where they exist, you can use them without worry.

National Parks & Other Protected Areas

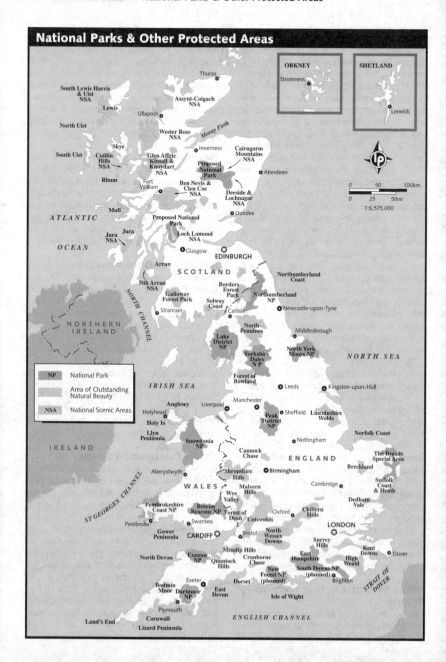

One protected area popular with walkers is a Heritage Coast. As the name suggests, these are particularly scenic or environmentally important areas of coastline. Sites of Special Scientific Interest (SSSIs) protect the most important areas of wildlife habitat and geological formation in Britain. Environmentally Sensitive Areas (ESAs) and Countryside Stewardship Schemes (CSSs) are intended to protect farmland and make it more accessible to the public, although critics, such as the Ramblers' Association, claim such schemes are ineffective and under-utilised.

POPULATION & PEOPLE

Britain has a population of over 56 million, or about 600 inhabitants per sq mi – one of the most crowded islands on the planet. To these figures you can factor in an annual influx of nearly 20 million tourists. (On a busy summer's day, most of these seem to be on the summit of Scafell Pike.)

England's population is 48 million, with most people living in and around London and in the Midlands and northern sprawls of Birmingham, Manchester, Liverpool, Leeds, Sheffield and Newcastle. Wales has a population of around three million, mostly based in the south around Cardiff, Swansea, Newport and the industrial Valleys area. Scotland has a population of just over five million people; the largest cities are Glasgow, Edinburgh, Aberdeen and Dundee. The northern Highlands region of Scotland, containing much of Britain's finest walking country, is the most sparsely populated administrative area in Britain, with an average of 20 people per sq mi – that's 30 times less than the national average.

SOCIETY & CONDUCT

It's difficult to generalise about a homogenous British culture – mainly because there isn't one! Even the words 'Britain' and 'British' in this context were invented comparatively recently. British 'culture' (if it exists) contains characteristics of at least three countries (England, Wales and Scotland), as well as Ireland and various offshore islands. The country has also been greatly influenced by immigrants from all over the world.

The British Love of Animals

The British, and especially the English, are widely believed to love their animals – mainly pets – more than their children. The Royal Society for the Prevention of Cruelty to Animals (note the regal status) was established before the National Society for the Prevention of Cruelty to Children – and still rakes in more donations. As an outsider you'll notice that although striking up conversation with a stranger is very unusual, many British people are quite happy talking to another person's dog.

This special affection for dogs means these particular pets can get away with anything. On city streets pet dogs on leads obstruct pedestrians and crap all over the parks and pavements. In rural areas pet dogs chase sheep, disturb wildlife and – you've guessed it – crap on the footpaths. Of course, it isn't the dogs' fault, it's the owners', but these anti-social habits are all tolerated to an incredible degree by most Brits.

Dog owners are convinced that 'Keep Dogs on Lead' signs don't apply to *their* dogs and often let them run around, and think it especially cute when they approach other people. If, while out walking, you're terrified by the unwanted attentions of a giant muddy hound, be prepared for the usual response from the owner – 'Don't worry, he's only being friendly'.

CLINT CURÉ

A major factor that runs through British culture and society, even in these egalitarian days, is class. Brits are often defined as working class, middle class or upper class. Although the days of peasants docking their caps to the lord of the manor may be gone, some Brits still judge others according to their place of birth, school, club, accent, family name and family wealth (and how long they've had it), rather than according to their skills and personality.

Many visitors arrive with strong preconceptions about British characteristics, the most common being that the British are reserved, inhibited and stiflingly polite. But it's important not to confuse British tradition with English tradition. While these characteristics may apply in some parts of England (notably the south and south-east) and to people from the middle and upper classes, in general they simply don't. Visit a pub, a nightclub, a football match or a seaside resort, or go walking in the hills and parks, and other characteristics like uninhibited, tolerant, exhibitionist, passionate, aggressive, sentimental, hospitable and friendly might spring to mind.

Having said that, you should be aware many people are wary of strangers in the street or on public transport. If you're obviously a tourist battling with directions, there's no problem – locals are happy to help. But try starting a general conversation at the bus stop and people will stare at you as if you're mad.

Dos & Don'ts

Britain is a reasonably tolerant place, so it's not easy to cause offence without meaning to. However, a few tips will be useful.

Probably the greatest insult you can give the Welsh or Scottish is to refer to them as English, or tell them how much you like being 'here in England', when you mean 'here in Wales' or 'here in Scotland'.

As in many parts of the world, differences of politics and religion exist in many parts of Britain, and many British people hold strong opinions. These normally lie beneath the surface but not that far below. As a visitor you should resist from being too opinionated about British politics and religion, especially in pubs or other public places. The same goes for football.

LANGUAGE

The English language is perhaps Britain's most significant contribution to the modern world. In the 'home country', though, the language continues to evolve and there are many English words which would not be recognised or understood in other English-speaking countries. On top of this are regional accents and dialects, which can sometimes be impenetrable for foreigners and often difficult for people from other parts of England too!

But English is not Britain's only language. In parts of Wales the Welsh language is spoken (see the boxed text 'Welsh Language' on p388). This is Celtic in origin, completely different from English, and difficult for foreigners (including those from England) to pronounce. It's spoken as a mother tongue by many, so don't be surprised or insulted (as some English folk are) when Welsh people use their own language in places such as pubs and shops.

In Scotland, English is the universal language and the first language for everyone. Gaelic, another language of Celtic origin, is spoken as a second language, mainly in the North-West and Western Isles. Gaelic has made a comeback from near extinction, encouraged by government agencies, and Gaelic education is flourishing from nurseries to universities, a renaissance mirrored in music, literature and broadcasting. A different language, Lowland Scots, or Lallans, with multiple European origins including English and Norse, is also spoken quite widely in the southern part of Scotland.

See the Glossary at the back of this book for explanations of some peculiarly English, Welsh and Scottish terms, including those relevant to walking.

Facts for the Walker

The information in this chapter is aimed at walkers visiting Britain (although some of it will also be useful to British walkers too). For more information about the country, a general guidebook is recommended – several Lonely Planet titles are listed under Books later in this chapter.

HIGHLIGHTS

Simple highlights are difficult to pick out because so much depends on your own interests and experience, but the following categories should help you choose between the many possible options.

Coastal Scenery

The rollercoaster cliffs of Cornwall and Pembrokeshire are hard to beat. This is the place for birds, seals, wild flowers, secluded beaches, traditional fishing villages and fantastic views. For a wilder edge go for Scotland's west coast and islands.

High Mountains

Snowdonia and the Lake District provide wonderful high-level walking, although the terrain and weather are not to be taken lightly. Most serious and most rewarding are the wild, rugged and remote mountains of Scotland.

Long-Distance Paths

The Coast to Coast Walk has it all. Transecting Northern England, it takes you through a wonderful variety of landscapes, from coast to high mountain, to wild dale and tranquil farmland. It can be busy, but don't let that stop you. For a longer view of the sea, tackle the scenic and surprisingly strenuous Pembrokeshire Coast Path or the South West Coast Path.

Typical English Countryside

For country cottages and classic English farmland you can't beat the Cotswolds. The Yorkshire Dales also supply postcard scenery, with a slightly harder edge.

Weekend Walks

There are many to choose from, but consider the Norfolk Coast Path, a Brecon Beacons Ridge Walk, the Limestone Way in the Peak District, or the Coniston to Keswick section of the Cumbria Way in the Lake District.

Wilderness Areas

Without a doubt, North-West Scotland is Britain's finest wilderness area. It is not easy to get to, has unpredictable weather and you need sound navigation skills, but it's unrivalled in beauty. Easier to reach are Rannoch Moor in central Scotland or Glyndŵr's Way through Mid-Wales.

River Walks

The Thames Path is a long-distance riverside classic, with a lot of variation as it meanders from countryside to city centre. The Dales Way follows the beautiful River Wharfe through the Yorkshire Dales for up to a week. (See also the boxed text 'Waterway Walks' on p49.)

Bird Walks

The Northumberland coast is a must for keen birdwatchers, with a side trip to the nearby Farne Islands, home to thousands of sea birds. The Norfolk coast also has several excellent bird reserves.

Ancient Sites

Dartmoor has a wealth of standing stones, burial mounds and Bronze Age settlements. Or you can walk the Ridgeway in Wessex from England's time-worn stone circle at Averbury, past Neolithic long barrows and mysterious figures carved in chalk hillsides.

Multiactivity Areas

If you want to mix walking with other activities, coastal Pembrokeshire is great for sea kayaking and sea-cliff climbing. Inland, the hills of the Peak District offer some of the best mountain biking and rock climbing in Britain.

SUGGESTED ITINERARIES

The possibilities for wonderful walking in Britain are almost endless, and it would take a lifetime to cover them all. So don't try. But it's worth noting that distances between walking areas are not vast and transport is reasonable, so you can, if you want, reach several different areas in a reasonably short time.

One Week

If you have only a week, consider heading for just one of the classic walking areas, such as the Lake District, Snowdonia, the Yorkshire Dales or the Peak District. There is more than enough to keep a walker happy for seven days in any of these places. If you yearn for the wilds of Scotland, the area around Ben Nevis and Glen Coe is accessible and relatively compact.

Two Weeks

In two weeks you could visit several different areas, perhaps in the same part of the country. A tour of Southern England could encompass walking from Winchester to Salisbury on the Clarendon Way, continuing to Bath and the Cotswolds for a few days, then heading down to the high moorland of Dartmoor and possibly spending some time on the South West Coast Path. The Cotswolds also link in neatly with Wales.

Walking Festivals

During the summer months, many towns and country areas organise walking festivals featuring a few days of guided walks, often coinciding with an annual carnival or other event. The aim is usually to encourage more people into the pastime of walking, or for established walkers to meet other like-minded people. Dates change from year to year and are hard to pin down, but regular festivals are mentioned in the relevant walk chapters. A major week-long event with literally hundreds of walks all over the country is organised every August by the Ramblers' Association (w www.ramblers.co.uk).

Farther north, you could combine the Yorkshire Dales with the Lake District, possibly also tying in a visit to southern Scotland – the island of Arran is accessible and a perfect introduction. In the far north-west of Scotland, a visit to the Isle of Skye, the Torridons and the mountains around Ullapool is perfectly possible in a fortnight.

Alternatively, go for the satisfaction of completing one of Britain's long-distance footpaths (LDPs), many of which take around two weeks, such as the Coast to Coast Walk, Cleveland Way or the Cornwall section of the South West Coast Path. Alternatively, do a shorter LDP, such as the Dales Way, Cotswold Way, Cumbria Way or South Downs Way National Trail (which all take about a week), and combine this with day walks in the same or neighbouring area.

A Month or More

If you are in Britain for a month, you could do an LDP and visit several completely contrasting areas, eg, by combining the West Highland Way in Scotland with mountains farther north, or with a visit to Northumberland or the Peak District. If you do a route like the Coast to Coast Walk, which passes through several areas (in this case the Lake District, Yorkshire Dales and North York Moors), you could take time out from the route and do some day walks from a single base. In Southern England you could combine the coast of Cornwall with the rolling hills of Dartmoor, the chalk hills of Wessex and the flatlands of Norfolk. In Wales you could walk across Snowdonia and round the coast of Pembrokeshire – another wonderful combination of coastline and mountains.

If you are visiting Britain for longer than a month, you may be working, in which case there are many great options for weekend walking close to the main centres. London itself has many good walks, and even places that seem far away, such as the Peak District and the Brecon Beacons, are actually very easily reached. If you are here for more than a month and *not* working, the possibilities become endless. Try to get to several contrasting areas and don't forget to build in some rest days!

Our objective was to walk through the fields and villages of Britain. Wandering through pastureland and across cropped paddocks (an experience not readily available to most Australians) has left us with a real feel for the English countryside. There was not one moment which could be described as boring.

Phillip Crampton

WHEN TO WALK

The best seasons for walking in Britain are spring, summer and autumn. This means March to October/November. July and August are school holidays and the busiest months, especially around coasts and national parks. In winter some accommodation closes, restaurants have shorter hours and public transport options are reduced. See Climate in the Facts about Britain chapter for a discussion of regional climates.

Generally speaking, the farther north you go, the longer winter lasts and the shorter the walking season is. While lower and coastal areas of Scotland may enjoy seasons similar to those in England and Wales, in the high mountains of Scotland the best time for walking is from May to September. (If you're camping, June to August can be unpleasant because of the midges – see the boxed text.)

During the Scottish winter, snow and ice make most mountain walking routes impassable without an ice axe, crampons and specialist knowledge. 'Technical' winter walks of this nature are beyond the scope of this book.

Away from the high mountains, you can walk the rest of Britain at any time of the year. Even in winter the weather is never bad enough to make conditions technical. In fact, a beautiful crisp midwinter's day is always preferable to one of the damp, misty days that can easily occur in high summer.

The time of year also affects hours of daylight. In summer in Northern England it is light from around 5am to 9pm, while in winter it is light between 8am and 5pm. In Southern England the differences are less pronounced, but in Scotland during summer it gets dark for only a few hours around midnight and your days are luxuriously long. Conversely, during winter in southern

Scotland or Northern England you only have about seven or eight hours of daylight to play with – down to just five or six in northern Scotland.

WHAT KIND OF WALK?

Many visiting walkers ask, 'What is walking in Britain actually like?' and 'What are my options?'. The answer to the first question is: There is no easy answer, as landscapes, weather, path conditions, access

Midges

Between June and August in rural Britain (especially in Northern England and most notoriously in western Scotland), millions of tiny flying insets called midges take to the evening air. Their bite is not painful or dangerous, but it is very annoying. Ways to counter the attack include midge repellents, anti-midge hats with bee-keeper-style netting, or simply staying indoors for the evening hours – easy if you're in a hotel, harder if you're camping (unless there's a pub nearby!). Hardy Highland walkers love to tell stories about being forced to swelter in a tent for hours to escape being eaten alive. Others tell of finding it hard to breathe as thousands of the pesky insects crawl up their noses. The end result is that for many walkers May and September – between the snow and the midges – are the best two months to be in Scotland.

CLINT CURÉ

rules, distances and a host of other factors vary greatly between different routes and areas. But with such a range, Britain has something for every kind of walker, and that answers the second question: You can do anything from gentle half-day rambles through farmland to multi-day routes across wild mountains, plus, of course, anything in between. There are also numerous companies offering guided walking holidays, for walkers who would like more support (for a list of specialist tour companies, see Guided Walks later in this chapter).

Generally speaking, the lower and more cultivated the landscape, the easier the walking, with clear paths and signposts. In mountain and moorland areas, if the route is popular there will be a path (although sometimes this is faint), but not many signposts. If the route is rarely trodden, there may be no visible path at all and absolutely no signposts, so you'll need a detailed map and compass for navigation.

Walking is one of the most popular pastimes in Britain, and every weekend millions of people take to the countryside for a stroll or day-long march that nearly always ends somewhere that sells tea or beer. Thus, an infrastructure for walkers exists and makes everything easy. Most towns and villages in walking areas have shops or a Tourist Information Centre (TIC) selling maps, walk leaflets and local guidebooks.

There are two aspects of walking in Britain that make this country unlike many others in the world. The first is the principle of 'rights of way', allowing walkers to cross privately owned land on paths or tracks open to the public. Nearly all land in Britain is privately owned, from tiny cultivated areas to vast tracts of open wilderness, but the right of way cannot be overruled by the actual owner. If there is a right of way, you can walk through fields, woods and even farmhouse yards as long as you keep to the correct route and do no damage.

The second unique aspect of walking in Britain is the vast network of rights of way, totalling about 140,000mi (225,000km). You can sometimes walk for just a few miles and encounter many forks and junctions with paths all leading in different directions. In some areas this network of paths has existed for thousands of years, so the concept of a single, recently created trail leading for miles through the wilderness simply doesn't exist here. Even national trails and other long routes are, in fact, just one way of linking many shorter paths.

In Scotland the situation regarding access and rights of way is different from that in England and Wales. More details are given in the boxed text 'Access in Scotland & the Concordat' on p451 in the Central Highlands & Islands chapter.

Day Walks
In this book the day walks have been chosen as the best examples in each area. Some walks are classics, while others are more obscure. Most day walks are circular so you can start and finish in the same place. Others are linear, but you can still get back to base by using public transport. Some longer day walks can be walked at a slower pace over two days.

Long-Distance Paths
In Britain, long-distance paths (LDPs) are usually considered to be more than about 40mi (65km), taking at least two days to complete. The longest are several hundred miles long and take many weeks. Some long routes are national trails administered by the Countryside Agency, with better signposting and maintenance.

LDPs without national trail status are sometimes termed 'recreational routes' and are administered by local councils, often with assistance from local rambling groups. Some LDPs have no official status at all, having been invented by a solitary guidebook writer, yet may be walked by thousands of people every year.

Some walkers 'do' an LDP in one go, taking one or two weeks, but many complete shorter sections, maybe covering the whole trail over a series of weekends. LDPs are also a catalyst for a whole range of circular walks, taking in a section of the main route, then branching off and looping back to the starting point by other paths.

CLOTHING & EQUIPMENT

You may come to Britain to combine walking with 'normal' travel. Most clothing and equipment is suitable for both, but anything you don't have can easily be bought in markets, shops and outdoor gear stores as you need it. For a full list of walking gear, see the Equipment Check List later in this section.

Clothing

The basics for general travel include two pairs of trousers, shorts or a skirt, a few T-shirts or shirts, underwear, socks, a warm sweater or sweatshirt, shoes, sandals or thongs, and a weatherproof coat. For walking, you'll need to add more gear. The advice here is weighted towards more serious walking on hills or mountains. You can compromise for lowland walks.

It is best to use several layers of clothing, to add or peel off to maintain your comfort. Starting next to the skin, cotton is OK, but much better in hot or cold weather are vests and T-shirts made from a synthetic material that 'wicks' sweat away.

For the middle layer, synthetic 'fleece' (which comes in many different types) is ideal, and two thin layers much better than a single thick one. For conditions that are windy but not wet, use a lightweight windshirt made from a thin breathable fabric. You can also buy fleece or pile tops with waterproof and/or windproof membranes or covers, but these reduce the flexibility of your layering system.

Legwear should have some 'give' to allow freedom of movement. Tracksuit-style trousers specially designed for outdoor activities are very popular, as are lightweight windproof trousers made from synthetic microfibre, often called 'trekking trousers' when a lot of pockets are added. Denim jeans are heavy and slow-drying, so save them for the pub in the evening.

For the outside layer, a good set of waterproofs – jacket and trousers – is advisable for lowland walks and absolutely essential for upland areas. Fabrics that 'breathe' improve your comfort level. The jacket should have a storm flap over the main zip, drawcords at waist and lower hem, and a hood – ideally with a stiffened peak to keep rain off your face and cutaway sides to ensure peripheral vision. Waterproof trousers should have zips so they can be pulled on over boots.

Other essentials are a warm hat and gloves. And, not forgetting Britain's varied weather, you should also have a wide-brimmed or peaked hat for sun protection in the summer.

Footwear

Even if the rest of your gear is not top flight, you should never compromise on footwear – the key to an enjoyable walk. Walking shoes or trainers (running shoes) are fine for short or lowland walks, but for upland or mountain routes, boots made of fabric or

---

Waterway Walks

Britain has an extensive network of canals and navigable waterways built in the early days of industry, mostly used today for leisure purposes. When canals were built, boats were pulled along by horses. Today these towpaths are good for walkers – especially those who don't like hills!

Some waterway towpaths have been turned into long-distance routes, including the Kennet & Avon Canal and the Thames Path, covered in the Wessex and London Region chapters of this book.

Other waterways with good walking possibilities include the Llangollen Canal in Wales, which is partly followed by the Offa's Dyke Path (also described in this book); the Caledonian Canal in Scotland; the Oxford Canal, which winds through the heart of central England; and the big daddy of them all, the Grand Union Canal linking London and Birmingham (which, incidentally, has its own waterway network and more miles of canal than Venice).

If you want to know more about Britain's waterways, several books on canal walks are available. A marvellous series of full-colour map guides, including the *Kennet & Avon Canal*, *The Thames Path*, *The Grand Union*, *The Oxford Canal* and *The Llangollen Canal*, is published by GeoProjects.

leather are highly recommended. Remember that some paths in Britain can be very rough.

Don't spend loads of money on boots, then skimp on socks. Get good ones. Synthetic or synthetic-and-wool loop-stitch socks provide the best cushioning. Flat seams avoid causing discomfort. Using one or two pairs of socks comes down to personal preference,

although thin liner socks are often useful for fine-tuning the fit.

Gaiters are very useful when walking in Britain, where conditions underfoot can be wet, rough, boggy or all three. They don't need to be of the extreme 'yeti' type, which are fixed to your boot with a rubber seal. They just need to keep the infamous British mud from seeping over the top of your boot.

Equipment

Backpack Your No 1 essential item is a backpack – called a rucksack in Britain. If you're walking and carrying all your stuff, you'll need a large backpack. Many visitors travel with a large bag, but leave it wherever they stay (or use a baggage service – see the boxed text 'Baggage Services') and walk with only a small day-pack for lunch, camera, waterproofs etc.

Tent For walking in Britain a tent is not essential, although you may choose to camp for flexibility or economy. You won't need anything too high-tech, as you are unlikely to be camping in hurricane conditions (although conditions can get pretty blowy in autumn, and torrential rain is always a possibility at any time of year), but it should be light enough to carry easily.

Sleeping Bag For summer lowland conditions your sleeping bag can be fairly light, but for upland camping in spring or autumn you'll need something rated 'three-season'.

Stoves & Fuel For cooking, open fires are generally not allowed, but the stove you use comes down to personal preference. Stoves using methylated spirits (ethyl alcohol) are very popular, safe and low maintenance. Fuel can be easily bought in supermarkets, hardware shops and outdoor gear shops.

Some stoves run on petrol (gasoline), and the unleaded variety can be bought from any filling station. Super-refined petrol for stoves (called Coleman fuel, Shellite or white gas) and gas cartridges of various sizes can be bought from outdoor gear stores. Kerosene is called paraffin in Britain, and is also available from hardware shops and some outdoor

---

Baggage Services

On many long-distance paths in Britain, you can use a baggage service to carry your bags from one overnight stop to the next while you walk with just the things you need that day. Going without a heavy pack means you can cover greater distances if required, or simply enjoy your walking more. Some companies require you to book the whole route itinerary in advance, while others can be hired for just one or two stages (eg, if you suddenly get tired or strain an ankle), as long as you phone the evening before to let them know. The usual charge is about £5 per bag per stage, but some companies charge a bit extra for a door-to-door service, while others charge less and leave your bag at an agreed point (eg, a central hotel or pub) close to where you're actually staying. Some deliver door-to-door *and* charge competitive rates, so it is worth phoning around to see what's on offer. Individual companies are listed in the relevant walk description sections.

Two main players are Sherpa Van Project and Brigantes Baggage Couriers. Part of a larger walking holiday company, Sherpa Van Project (☎ 020-8569 4101, e info@sherpavan.com, w www.sherpavan.com) covers a very wide selection of routes in Scotland, Wales and Northern and Southern England. It also offers a Trail Planner for self-guided tours and an accommodation booking service. Brigantes Baggage Couriers (☎ 01729-830463, e mike@pikedaw.freeserve.co.uk, w www.pikedaw.freeserve.co.uk/walks) specialises in the Pennine Way, Dales Way and other routes in Northern England. Along with a baggage service, it also offers walking holidays and accommodation booking.

gear shops, although not many stoves use this fuel these days, so it is harder to find. Note also that in Scotland, towns with outdoor gear shops, or any shops selling fuel for stoves, are few and far between, so stock up whenever you can.

Buying & Hiring Locally

In popular walking areas, most towns (and even small villages) have outdoor gear shops where you can buy clothing, boots, socks, tents, sleeping bags, maps, guidebooks and anything else you may need for walking. Hiring equipment is much harder – very few shops offer this service (none at all in Scotland), and what they do hire may be limited to backpacks and possibly waterproofs. It is better to have all your own gear.

MAPS & NAVIGATION

In theory Britain has now moved to metric weights and measures although nonmetric (imperial) equivalents are still used in many situations, including mapping. Some maps have a scale of one inch to 1mi (which is 1:63,360 in case you wondered), while most

---

Equipment Check List

This list is a general guide to the things you might take on a walk. Your list will vary depending on the kind of walking you want to do, whether you're camping or planning on staying in hostels or B&Bs, and on the terrain, weather conditions and time of year.

Equipment
☐ backpack and waterproof liner
☐ camera and spare film
☐ emergency food (high-energy)
☐ map, compass and guidebook
☐ medical kit*, toiletries and insect repellent
☐ pocket knife
☐ repair kit
☐ sleeping sheet
☐ sunglasses and sunscreen
☐ survival bag or space blanket
☐ torch (flashlight) with spare batteries and bulb (globe)
☐ towel, soap and toilet paper
☐ water containers
☐ water purification tablets/solution or filter
☐ whistle (for emergencies)

Clothing
☐ gaiters
☐ training shoes or sandals
☐ shorts and trousers
☐ socks and underwear
☐ sunhat
☐ sweater, fleece or windproof jacket
☐ thermal underwear
☐ T-shirt and long-sleeved shirt with collar
☐ walking boots and spare laces
☐ warm hat, scarf and gloves
☐ waterproof jacket with hood
☐ waterproof overpants

Camping
☐ cooking, eating and drinking utensils
☐ dishwashing items
☐ matches, lighter and candle
☐ sleeping bag
☐ sleeping mat
☐ spare cord
☐ stove and fuel
☐ tent (check pegs, poles and guy ropes)
☐ toilet trowel

Optional Items
☐ altimeter and/or barometer
☐ backpack cover (waterproof)
☐ binoculars
☐ day-pack
☐ emergency distress beacon
☐ GPS receiver
☐ lightweight groundsheet
☐ mobile phone
☐ notebook and pencil
☐ swimming costume
☐ walking poles or stick

* see the Medical Kit Check List in Health & Safety

road atlases are published with scales of one inch to 3mi or 4mi (and don't even quote a ratio figure). Even metric maps with scales of 1:50,000 or 1:25,000 (the most popular for walking) are still called 'one-inch' or '2½-inch' by die-hard ramblers.

Small-Scale Maps

To get from place to place you'll need a small-scale map of the whole of Britain. The best introductory map of the country is published by the British Tourist Authority (BTA) and is widely available for a small fee from BTA offices around the world (contact details are listed under Tourist Offices later in this chapter). If you're combining driving with walking you will need a road atlas showing smaller roads (to reach the start of a walk). The Ordnance Survey's *Motoring Atlas of Great Britain* is good, but the *Big Road Atlas – Britain*, produced by the Automobile Association (AA), is even better, as national trails are marked on it. Both are at scales of one inch to 4mi and cost about £7 to £9.

Large-Scale Maps

Britain is covered by an excellent series of maps published by Ordnance Survey (OS), once part of the military and now a government agency. Most useful for walkers are the Landranger series, covering the whole

Trig Points

Trig (short for trigometric) points, also called survey cairns, are concrete, stone or brick pillars, about 1m tall, used for the making of Ordnance Survey maps. These pillars are marked on maps, and a real life-saver if you're walking in the mist and need a bit of navigational confirmation. As the OS does not use trig points any more (since most maps are made by aerial surveys and other means), some trig points have been removed. However, in popular walking areas local rambling groups and other interested parties have 'adopted' trig points, promising to keep them in good repair for the benefit of other walkers.

country at a scale of 1:50,000 (£5.25); the Outdoor Leisure series, covering areas such as national parks at 1:25,000 (£6.50); and the Explorer series, covering other areas at 1:25,000 (£5.50). Some parts of the country are still covered by the Pathfinder series at 1:25,000, but these are gradually being phased out. No bad thing, say walkers, as some of the Pathfinders covering Scotland are now seriously out of date.

Recently published OS 1:25,000 maps have amazingly accurate detail and are ideal for walkers, especially in lowland areas. However, the sheer degree of detail can be confusing in mountain areas and many walkers prefer 1:50,000 or 1:40,000 maps instead.

Despite their popularity, OS maps have a number of quirks. One of these is that boundaries (national, county, parliamentary constituency) are marked more clearly than paths – particularly on 1:25,000 maps. In fact the boundaries *look* like paths, and many inexperienced walkers get lost trying to follow a row of dots on the map that turns out to be a border. OS maps also mark rights of way even when no visible path exists on the ground. Conversely a path may exist that *isn't* shown on the map because it isn't legal. Note also that words that aren't proper nouns have capital initial letters (eg, Sheepfold, Sinkholes), making it hard to distinguish between features and actual place names. And finally, note that OS uses different symbols on 1:25,000 and 1:50,000 maps (eg, footpaths are green dashes on the former and red dashes on the latter). But don't be put off by these gripes. OS maps are still among the best in the world. Once you're used to the idiosyncrasies you'll never need to be lost.

The new kid on the block is a company called Harvey, with maps that are becoming increasingly popular with walkers simply because they are specifically designed for them. For example, if a path exists on the ground, it's shown on a Harvey map; if it doesn't exist, it isn't shown. 'Invisible' boundaries are also not shown, so although you may not know when you've passed from Yorkshire to Cumbria, it also means you won't follow the frontier. Another great advantage is that Harvey maps are based on logical walking areas, whereas two OS maps sometimes meet in the middle of a mountain. Harvey maps are also printed on waterproof paper, and most are available in two types: Walker's Maps at a scale of 1:40,000 (£5.75) and Superwalker Maps at 1:25,000 (most around £7.45).

Another main player is Footprint Maps, specialising in map guides to major walking areas of England, Wales and Scotland, such as the Lake District, Snowdonia and Loch Lomond. Each features several suggested walking routes plus a handy series of strip maps for national trails, including the Pennine Way, the Cleveland Way and the West Highland Way (most priced £3.50 or less).

Also worth looking out for if you're walking the Thames Path, the Kennet & Avon Canal or in the Norfolk Broads are the excellent maps of Britain's inland waterways produced by GeoProjects, a specialist mapping company. Although aimed primarily at boaters, these maps are very good for walkers too.

Full details of recommended maps for walks described in this book are listed under Planning in the introduction to each walk. For information on this book's custom-drawn walking maps, see Maps in This Book under Walks in This Book later in this chapter.

Buying Maps

To buy maps of Britain, large bookshops and outdoor gear shops will usually keep a good stock of OS and Harvey maps, covering most parts of Britain. Smaller shops and TICs will stock maps of the local area.

If you're in London, before setting off to visit other parts of Britain you can buy maps at Stanfords (☎ 020-7836 1321, e customer .services@stanfords.co.uk), 12–14 Long Acre, London WC2E 9LP, or purchase direct from the company's Web site (W www .stanfords.co.uk). You can order OS maps on-line direct from OS (W www.o-s.co.uk). Other map specialists include Latitude Map Mail Order (☎ 01707-663090, fax 663029), 34 The Broadway, Darkes Lane, Potters Bar, Herts EN6 2HW, and the UK-based on-line specialist Maps Worldwide (W www.ma psworldwide.com), which stocks OS and Harvey maps, as well as a good range of walking guidebooks and accommodation handbooks.

GPS

Originally developed by the US Department of Defense, the Global Positioning System (GPS) is a network of satellites that beam encoded signals back to earth. GPS receivers can decode these signals to give users an extremely accurate reading of their location (to within 30m). It should be understood, however, that a GPS receiver is not a substitute for a detailed map and compass. It is expensive, vulnerable to breakdowns and will only work properly in the open. Directly below high cliffs, near large bodies of water or in dense tree-cover, the signals from a crucial satellite may provide inaccurate readings. Check out the Web site W www.trimble.com/gps/howgps/gpsf ram2.htm if you want to learn more about GPS receivers.

WALKS IN THIS BOOK

The Walks Table near the start of this book gives a rundown of all the routes we describe, with their distances, standards, seasons and a summary of the walk. Where walking seasons are given as 'all year', these are usually *best* done during dryer, warmer periods, ie, spring, summer and autumn.

Route Descriptions

In the introduction to each walk, the Direction, Distance & Duration section discusses the practical features of the route: the recommended direction, variations in distance and duration, waymarking and any other special conditions readers should be aware of. Possible shorter or longer alternatives to the described walk are also outlined here.

Day walks are usually circular, and we give details of where to stay before and afterwards. The route is broken into natural stages, eg, from the base to the mountain summit, then from the summit to a village, and from the village back to a base.

Long-distance path descriptions are divided into daily stages, each ending at a place with accommodation. Suggestions are given

Navigation in Britain

Some footpaths and trails in Britain are not well signposted, particularly in highland areas, so it is absolutely essential that you can read a map and navigate with a compass. All survey maps have the 'national grid' marked on them. This is a series of vertical (north-south) and horizontal (west-east) lines, which are a vital part of the map-reading process, allowing you to pinpoint exact positions and find your direction in relation to north. Grid references in Britain are usually a six-figure number, sometimes preceded by two letters for further clarification. If you are not familiar with grid references, the system is explained on all Ordnance Survey (OS) and Harvey maps.

Remember that grid north (ie, north on the map) and magnetic north (ie, north on the compass) are not the same, and not fixed; you need to take account of magnetic variation. In 2000 magnetic north was about 3.5 degrees west of grid north, and expected to decrease by about one degree over the following five years. This means that when you are transferring a compass bearing between map and 'field', or vice versa, you need to add or subtract 3.5 degrees respectively.

If coming from Australia, you may find your compass doesn't work properly. This isn't a joke. It won't point backwards, but the needle will dip down and stick to the base-plate rather than swinging freely in a horizontal position. This is because the attraction of magnetic north varies slightly in different parts of the world, so compasses have to be calibrated accordingly. There are five main types: northern, northern tropical, equatorial, southern tropical and southern. You need the northern type for Britain, and if you're coming from another region, you'll have to buy one when you arrive. You can get very cheap compasses for a few pounds, but these may not be reliable. The cheapest good-quality types start from about £10, but for serious mountain walks larger models are recommended, with a dial showing each degree and a hand-size plate.

for different stages so you can adjust the daily mileage to suit your own ability.

Throughout the descriptions we have used general compass bearings (eg, 'head northwest' or 'keep south of east as you leave the river'). Precise compass bearings have been used rarely, and only where necessary.

Level of Difficulty

The walks in this book are divided into five categories: easy, easy-medium, medium, medium-hard and hard.

Easy Routes use good, clear paths on mostly flat or rolling ground, and are suitable for people with children aged 10 and above. They can be followed without needing a compass (you may need a map, though).

Medium Routes cross higher ground and require exertion. Paths may be rough and distances are longer. You will definitely need a map and need to know how to use a compass. The route may involve steep ascents where you may have to use your hands for balance.

Hard Routes are just that – hard. They are tough in terms of landscape, length and duration. Competence using a map and compass is essential, and on steep ascents you may have to use your hands in places to pull yourself up. Note, however, routes that require technical rock climbing or mountaineering are avoided in this book.

Times & Distances

The times given in this book reckon on most walkers covering about 2.5mph (4km/h) with an extra hour for every 300m to 500m of ascent. This gives *walking* times that allow for a few short stops (map reading, photos etc), but not for long stops. It also assumes good weather.

So if conditions are kind and you don't stop much, you'll find the timings given about right. If you prefer to linger longer or there's a chance of bad weather (always a possibility in mountains), then you should add extra time – about 10% for straightforward walks and up to 50% for serious mountain routes. If you are carrying a heavy load, then your speed will drop even more.

Walking times that factor in breaks for lunch and sightseeing etc, are estimated under Direction, Distance & Duration in the introduction to each walk.

Britain uses both metric and imperial systems of measurement. We have reflected this by using both also. When converting from one to the other we have usually rounded up or down to the nearest half-mile or 0.5km. This may give rise to small inconsistencies between measurements, but nothing significant.

Maps in This Book

The maps in this book are intended to show the general routes of the walks we describe. They are primarily to help locate the route within the surrounding area and are not detailed enough in themselves for route finding or navigation. You will still need a properly surveyed map at an adequate scale, showing important relief features (recommended in the Planning section for each walk).

A continuous 'highlight' line of brown stipple shows the entire route covered by the text. Alternative routes are shown with a dashed brown stipple line. Start and finish points are marked with boxes, and campsites, lookout points and other symbols are also indicated. Map symbols are interpreted in the Map Legend at the back of this book.

Most chapters have a regional map showing the gateway towns or cities, principal transport routes and the borders of the walk areas mapped in greater detail.

Altitude Measurements

Britain uses both metric and imperial systems, but for altitudes metres are used more often, with significant heights also given in feet. The maps discussed under Maps & Navigation earlier are usually very accurate on heights of mountains, although rounding up or down can create minor inconsistencies between measurements in feet and metres.

Place Names & Terminology

We've used local British terminology for features in walk descriptions and on maps.

Roads & Lanes Visitors from overseas will find the following definitions useful:

road – any sealed highway, usually wide enough for two vehicles
main road or **A-road** – road linking larger towns, with a number (A45, A569 etc)
B-road – local road, smaller than an A-road, with a number (B345, B6578 etc)
dual carriageway – main road where the traffic is divided by a central reservation
motorway – major dual carriageway, linking cities (equivalent to interstate highways in the USA and Australia)
street – road in a town or city, usually with houses and a proper name
lane – local country road, smaller than a B-road, sometimes called a C-road, usually only wide enough for one car, or two at a squeeze
dirt road – road that is not sealed but can still be easily used by motor vehicles
track – road that is not sealed, and not easily used by vehicles (eg, used mainly by farm tractors), sometimes called a 'green lane'

You may see the term 'metalled road' – a road that has been surfaced, usually with tar (bitumen), but sometimes with cobbles or stones. Tar is also called 'Tarmac' in Britain, leading to the clumsy term 'tarmacked road'.

Rights of Way In England and Wales a right of way allows you to cross private land. There are three main types of right of way:

footpath – for walkers only
bridleway – for walkers, horse riders and cyclists
byway open to all traffic – for walkers, riders and any kind of vehicle (abbreviated to BOAT or byway)

A further category is 'permissive path', where a landowner has volunteered an access route, but there is no right of way. Another is 'road used as public path', old roads that fell out of use long ago and never had sealed surfaces. These are being reclassified as either bridleways or byways. It is very important to note that not all dirt roads, tracks and paths are necessarily rights of way.

Rights of way do exist in Scotland but they are not always shown on maps. There is, however, a Scottish Rights of Way &

Access Society (☎ 0131-558 1222, e srws @scotways.demon.co.uk, W www.scotways .demon.co.uk), which does much to publicise routes that have (or deserve) legal status. These include old drove roads, military roads mostly built in the 18th century for English troops based in Scotland, and coffin roads to churches. The society's guide *Scottish Hill Tracks*, available direct from the society or from James Thin's booksellers in Scotland, is invaluable. Scottish rights of way are further discussed in the boxed text 'Access in Scotland & the Concordat' on p451.

Signposts & Waymarks Most rights of way in England, Wales and Scotland are signposted where they meet roads or other rights of way. Coloured arrows are usually used: yellow for footpaths, blue for bridleways, red for byways. The sign may simply say 'Public Footpath', or give more detail, such as the name of the next village, usually with the distance.

Waymarks are small arrows, circles or dots of paint that indicate you are still on the right of way, usually fixed to gateposts, stiles etc. The same colour code is normally used. Areas with a lot of footpaths have a lot of yellow waymarks, so don't assume they all lead the way you want to go. Waymarking is better in some areas than in others, according to the diligence of the

---

Never Mind the Bealachs – Learn Local Geography

In different parts of Britain geographical features have various names, according to local dialect. For example, a stream is a *beck* in the Lake District or a *burn* in Scotland; a valley can be a *cwm* in Wales, a *glen* or *strath* in Scotland, or a *coombe* in Southern England; a pass or low point between hills is a *bwlch* in Wales, a *haus* in the Lake District or a *bealach* in Scotland and, just to keep you on your toes, the French word *col* is also often used. For more local words see the Glossary at the back of this book.

---

local authority; sometimes they're missing. That's why you need a map.

Some walks – especially LDPs – may also have waymarks specific to that route. For example, all national trails in England and Wales are marked with an acorn symbol, while national trails in Scotland are marked with a thistle in a hexagon. Other routes have their own 'trademarks': a ram's head for the Limestone Way, a bishop's hat for the Clarendon Way, a Celtic cross for St Cuthbert's Way and so on.

Note that the spellings of place names on signposts may be slightly different from those on maps, or even those in this guidebook, particularly in Scotland and Wales.

Climbing & Scrambling The term 'climbing' has generally been avoided in this book to avoid confusion with rock climbing or technical mountaineering (which none of the routes described involve).

For walkers in Britain 'scrambling' has quite a specific meaning. Scrambling comes somewhere between walking and climbing, where you need your hands as well as your feet to follow a steep, rocky section of path, which may be a 'step' just a few metres high or a ridge several hundred metres long! Quite often a scramble is not too technically difficult but is made more exciting by height or exposure, ie, sheer drops on both sides! Some scrambles, however, can be very demanding, and there is a definite overlap between hard scrambling and easy rock climbing. If you like excitement and are already competent on exposed rock, you can buy dedicated scrambling guides in bookshops, outdoor gear shops and TICs in mountain areas where scrambling is possible (particularly, Snowdonia, the Lake District and many parts of Scotland).

Don't let any of this worry you. If you like to keep your hands firmly in your pockets, nearly all of the sections of scrambling on routes in this book can be avoided.

GUIDED WALKS

In national parks and some other areas, guided walks (varying from a few hours to a day) are usually available, led by a ranger or local expert with a small fee (£1 to £3) usually payable. More details are given in the individual chapters.

If you want a more extended guided walk, several companies run walking tours in Britain. These are either based at one or two centres with day walks in various directions, or are linear tours, going by foot from place to place while baggage is carried in a van. Some companies arrange tours led by experienced guides, which leave on certain dates for a set duration. Others arrange 'self-guided' tours where all accommodation and baggage transfer is prebooked, with map and instructions provided so you can go at your own pace. Of course, with self-guided holidays you can go when you like, and usually do not join a group.

We have listed a small selection of walking companies below. For more details contact the companies directly. Only national and regional companies are listed here. Smaller outfits covering specific areas are detailed in the walk chapters. Several of the organisations listed here are well used to catering for foreign visitors and have agents and representatives in Australia, New Zealand, the USA and many other countries around the world.

The Ramblers' Association (see Useful Organisations for contact details) produces a good list of walking tour operators (including smaller outfits), and the *Green Britain* leaflet produced by the British Tourism Association (BTA) carries advertisements. Other publications carrying advertisements are mentioned under Magazines later in this chapter.

Contours Walking Holidays (☎ 01768-867539, ⒺA info@contours.co.uk, Ⓦ www.contours .co.uk) Smithy House, Stainton, Cumbria CA11 0ES. This company offers a wide range of tours in Scotland, England and Wales, led by experienced guides, along many famous LDPs, such as the West Highland Way, Cumbria Way and Pembrokeshire Coast Path, plus single-base holidays in popular and more unusual areas of Britain. Self-guided tours (where all routes and accommodation are arranged, but you go at your own pace) are also available.

Discovery Travel (☎ 01904-766564, Ⓔ discoverytravel@compuserve.com) 12 Towthorpe Rd, Haxby, York YO32 3ND. A Northern England walk specialist, organising guided and self-guided tours on several LDPs, with accommodation, maps, route descriptions and door-to-door baggage transfer.

Country Guide Holidays (☎ 0113-257 5996) 72 Thornhill St, Leeds LS28 5PD. A small and friendly company specialising in Northern England (Yorkshire Dales and Moors, Peak District and Northumberland), with weekend (from £105) and full week options (£310) on circular walks and LDPs such as the Dales Way.

Countrywide (☎ 01942-241432, Ⓔ reservations @countrywide-walking.org) Miry Lane, Wigan, Lancashire WN3 4AG. This long-standing company offers a very wide range of walking holidays all over Britain, of various lengths and standards, using experienced leaders and providing accommodation in country guesthouses. Three night breaks at a single base start at about £120, while seven nights on the Cotswold Way costs £449.

C-N-Do Scotland (☎ 01786-445703, Ⓔ info@cn doscotland.com) Unit 32, STEP, Stirling FK7 7RP. This company specialises in Scotland with a varied program of tours from St Cuthbert's Way in the Scottish Borders to the Kintail Ridges in the Highlands and the remote island of Rum in the Outer Hebrides. Leaders are experienced and fully qualified, and accommodation can be in guesthouses, B&Bs or youth hostels.

Classic Walking (☎ 020-8905 9556, Ⓔ info @hfholidays.co.uk) Imperial House, Edgware Rd, London NW9 5AL. Part of the well-respected HF Holidays group, this company organises guided holidays on many LDPs in Britain, plus an extensive program of single-base holidays in various parts of the country.

Instep Walking Holidays (☎ 01903-766475, Ⓔ walking@instephols.co.uk) 35 Cokeham Rd, Lancing, West Sussex BN15 0AE. This company offers a range of self-guided walking tours on LDPs in England and Wales. Routes include Offa's Dyke Path, the South Downs Way and South West Coast Path, plus more unusual canal walks. Prices vary according to the length of the route and the number in your group, but start at £370 per person for two people on a six-day trip.

North-West Frontiers (☎ 01854-612628, Ⓔ nwf @compuserve.com) 18A Braes, Ullapool IV26 2SZ. This experienced outfit specialises in western and North-West Scotland, including the Isle of Skye and the Outer Hebrides.

Sherpa (☎ 020-8577 27171, Ⓔ sales@sherpa-walking-holidays.co.uk, Ⓦ www.sherpa-walking-holidays.co.uk) 131A Heston Rd, Hounslow TW5 0RD. This company organises walking holidays right round the world, and in its own backyard as self-guided treks on the Cumbria Way, Dales Way, West Highland Way and several other long routes. In Britain all tours are self-guided, using Sherpa's Trail Planner service – you decide when you want to leave and how far to walk each day, where you want to stay and at what kind of budget, then Sherpa books all the B&Bs and hotels for you. Several people have recommended this service – it saves you a lot of ringing around. Also tied in is the Sherpa Van – for more details, see the boxed text 'Baggage Services' on p50.

SYHA Breakaway Holidays (☎ 01786-891400, ⓔ syha@syha.org.uk, ⓦ www.syha.org.uk) 7 Glebe Crescent, Stirling FK8 2JA. The SYHA runs youth hostels all over Scotland, and offers a wide range of walking holidays, using hostels as a base, or going from hostel to hostel on LDPs. Holidays include gentle walking and some very exciting mountain trips – ideal if you want to experience the highlands, but don't have the necessary expertise. As a price sample, eight days on the West Highland Way cost £360, five days in Torridon cost £220. Navigation, winter skills and mountaineering courses are also available.

Walkabout Scotland (☎ 0131-661 7168, ⓦ www.walkaboutscotland.com) 2 Rossie Place, Edinburgh. This company offers a range of day trips from Edinburgh to surrounding mountains, including Ben Lomond, The Cobbler and Buachaille Etive Mór, all for £40 per person with transport, guide and lunch.

YHA Holidays (☎ 0870-241 2314, fax 01629-581062, ⓔ reservations@yha.org.uk, ⓦ www.yha.org.uk) PO Box 67, Matlock, Derbyshire DE4 3YX. The YHA runs hostels all over Britain (see Useful Organisations and Accommodation later in this chapter for details) and organises walking holidays using the hostels with qualified leaders and full-board accommodation. A weekend (two nights) of easy walking in the Peak District costs about £85. Six days of serious, hostel-to-hostel walking in North Wales or six days on the Cumbria Way cost £299.

RESPONSIBLE WALKING

Some general principles for responsible walking in Britain are contained in the Country Code, promoted by national parks and other similar bodies. If you're planning to camp 'wild', you should adhere to the Backpack Camping Code; this is based on principles developed by Dartmoor National Park, but is applicable anywhere (see the boxed text 'Respecting the Environment').

A particularly important aspect of responsible walking in Britain concerns rights of way. The legal aspects of rights of way are discussed under Place Names & Terminology earlier. In England and Wales, these rights of way are as much a part of the 'Queen's Highway' as a main road, and walkers have the same right to use them unhindered by obstructions. However, it is also your responsibility to keep to the right of way and not wander across other parts of the private land through which it passes.

If a right of way is obstructed, walkers are permitted to remove enough of the obstruction to pass. Sometimes a right of way may

---

Respecting the Environment

Country Code
- Guard against all risk of fire
- Fasten all gates
- Keep dogs under control
- Keep to paths across farmland
- Avoid damaging fences, hedges and walls
- Leave no litter – take it home
- Safeguard water supplies
- Protect wildlife, wild plants and trees
- Go carefully on country roads
- Respect the life of the countryside

Backpack Camping Code
Remember that all land in Britain is privately owned, but camping may be tolerated on open mountain and moorland.

- Don't camp in fields enclosed by walls without permission
- Don't camp within sight of roads, houses or popular recreational areas
- Don't stay on a site for more than one night (occasionally two is tolerated)
- Keep groups small and avoid pitching where another tent has recently been
- Bury excrement away from campsites
- Don't light fires and handle stoves carefully
- Avoid fouling water sources with soap or waste
- Take all litter out – don't bury rubbish
- Leave the site as you found it

go straight across a field that has been sown with crops and the path has been completely covered. In such cases walkers can go legally (but carefully) through crops, but discretion is advised as no farmer will appreciate damage to property and it is more responsible to walk round the edge of the cropfield.

There are some places where walkers can move beyond the rights of way through areas of unenclosed and uncultivated moorland or mountain, although these are still privately owned, eg, by the National Trust, which is dedicated to unrestricted access. In Scotland, which has a different legal system, there are fewer rights of way, but generally speaking there is greater access to open country (for more details, see the boxed text 'Access in Scotland & the Concordat' on p451). Nearly all the routes described in the Scotland chapters cross land with no access restrictions. You should, however, be prepared to avoid areas where you might disrupt deer stalking and grouse shooting (which take place mainly between early August and late October) and lambing (from mid-April to late May). This is particularly important if you explore areas not covered in this book.

Note that access may be restricted to certain areas (eg, because of fire danger in dry summers). At these times, notices are usually put up to inform walkers, and it is your responsibility to adhere to them.

Considering the size of Britain, and its complex rights of way system, in practice there are surprisingly few rules and regulations. Mostly it comes down to common sense. If there's no stile and you have to climb over a wall to cross a field, the chances are you shouldn't be there.

WOMEN WALKERS
Walking is enjoyed by everyone in Britain – old and young, male and female – walking singly or in small groups. From a personal safety angle, women are very unlikely to get mugged or accosted in the countryside, so walking alone in most rural areas is not a risk (although in wild and remote mountains, it is always wise to go in pairs in case of accident).

Some LDPs pass through towns or down-at-heel suburbs, or through parks and woods on the edge of cities, and here unfortunately there may be a danger of attack or assault. Women, especially lone women, are often seen as easy victims by attackers, so some common-sense precautions need to be taken.

WALKING WITH CHILDREN
Many parts of Britain are ideal for walking with children under the age of 10. But many other parts are not – being too high, too steep or requiring too much effort to reach. Several of the routes in this book are suitable for kids aged 11 to 15 – mostly the day walks graded 'easy', but as much depends

Do Walkers Shit in the Woods?

Yes – quite often. So it is something that has to be discussed and not coyly skirted around.

Ideally, when out walking you should use toilets where provided, but sometimes that's just not possible, so if you have to 'go' in the great outdoors, please do it responsibly. Defecate at least 100m away from water, paths and campsites; dig a hole and bury your excrement if possible – it will break down in the soil. The hole should be deep enough (around 15cm) to prevent animals from being attracted by the smell and digging it up – which can spread disease. Do *not* simply cover excrement with a stone. If you really can't bury it, it is better out in the sun, where it breaks down more quickly.

Bury toilet paper (biodegradable paper is good for this), or ideally carry it out in a bag and dispose of it properly when you get to a toilet. Tampons and sanitary pads should always be carried out. A sealable plastic bag inside a paper or canvas bag keeps things safe and out of sight.

After all this malarkey, don't forget to wash your hands! But, please, *not* in a river or stream. Collect some water in a cup and wash you hands away from the water. Packs of moist tissues are useful – but carry out used tissues too.

on attitude and enthusiasm as on fitness or ability. Long-distance walks are another matter; some young people don't have the stamina for multi-day routes, but for those over 16 many of the national trails are feasible, although in some cases the daily distances may need to be trimmed. Lonely Planet's *Travel with Children* contains plenty of useful information. Some guidebooks written specifically for families are listed under Books later in this chapter.

USEFUL ORGANISATIONS

Britain has a huge number of organisations that administer or promote walking, outdoor activities and other countryside matters. Some are useful to join as they provide services such as handbooks and discounts for members. Others you might want to contact for information. Conservation bodies are listed under Ecology & Environment in the Facts about Britain chapter earlier.

Backpackers' Club (☎ 01395-265159, e wjbeed @genie.co.uk) 49 Lyndhurst Rd, Exmouth, Devon EX8 3DS. While these days 'backpacking' means budget travel, this organisation promotes backpacking in its original sense: lightweight and self-contained camping in rural or wilderness areas, travelling by foot. It provides information and a directory of camping areas for members.

British Mountaineering Council (BMC; ☎ 0161-445 4747, e office@thebmc.co.uk, w www .thebmc.co.uk) 177 Burton Rd, Manchester M20 2BB. The BMC has a bias towards rock climbing and mountaineering, but also represents hill walkers. A wide range of leaflets and booklets is available on safety, access and other aspects, also available through the BMC's Web site.

Camping & Caravanning Club (CCC; ☎ 024-694995) Greenfields House, Westwood Way, Coventry CV4 8JH. The CCC is Britain's leading club for users of caravans, campervans and 'big tents', but it also caters for lightweight campers. It owns several campsites around the country, with excellent facilities like hot showers, laundrettes and shops, where members get cheap rates, and it lists or certifies several hundred more. The club handbook (free to members) contains a huge list of campsites.

English Heritage (membership ☎ 01793-414910, e members@English-heritage.org.uk, w www .english-heritage.org.uk) PO Box 570, Swindon SN2 2YR. This government agency has responsibility for conserving historic monuments, including castles, stately homes, stone circles and major sites like Hadrian's Wall. Admission to some is free, but others charge between £1 and £4. The walks in this book pass many English Heritage sites, so joining is worth considering if you are a history fan. The companion organisations are Historic Scotland (☎ 0131-688 8800, w www.historic-scotland.gov.uk) and Welsh Historic Monuments (☎ 029-2050 0200), also called Cadw. You can become a member or 'friend' of any of these bodies for an annual fee and get free entry into the properties they administer. For tourists, passes for three days, a week or two weeks are also available.

Long-Distance Walkers Association (w www .ldwa.org.uk) This club is for those who like long day walks – more than 20mi (32km) – or multi-day walks in rural or mountainous areas. It also promotes challenge walking (covering set distances within a set time). Contact details change annually – see the Web site for details.

Mountaineering Council of Scotland (☎ 01738-638227, w www.mountaineering-scotland .org.uk) The Old Granary, West Mill St, Perth PH1 5QP. The council represents mountaineers, climbers and hill walkers in Scotland. It can help members with information, particularly on issues of access and freedom to roam. It produces a useful book called *Heading for the Scottish Hills* (although this hasn't been updated since 1966) and can recommend qualified mountain guides if you're not competent to go alone. Its vast Web site covers topical issues.

Ramblers' Association (☎ 020-7339 8500, e ram blers@london.ramblers.org.uk, w www.ramblers .org.uk) Camelford House, 87–90 Albert Embankment, London SE1 7TW. This is Britain's largest and most active national walking organisation. It produces a great range of booklets and leaflets (cheap or free) covering aspects of walking in Britain ideal for visitors from abroad. Also exceedingly useful is the annual *The Rambler's Yearbook & Accommodation Guide* (see the Books section later in this chapter), free to members or £5 to nonmembers. The Ramblers' Association has offices in Scotland and Wales and 400 local groups around the country, which you can hook up with if you're spending a while in one place. The association also organises regular national walking festivals, with hundreds of free guided walks. The Ramblers' Web site has events, campaigns, advice, contact details and a list of publications for sale on-line.

Scottish Youth Hostels Association (SYHA; ☎ 01786-891400, e syha@syha.org.uk, w www .syha.org.uk) 7 Glebe Crescent, Stirling FK8 2JA.

The SYHA runs a network of hostels, many in walking areas. Reciprocal agreements with other countries (including England and Wales) apply. The colourful *Scottish Youth Hostels* handbook lists details of every SYHA hostel and is invaluable.

Youth Hostels Association (YHA; general inquiries ☎ 0870-870 8808; Walking Holidays, group reservations and LDP bookings ☎ 241 2314; fax 01629-581062; e reservations@yha .org.uk; customer services e customerservices @yha.org.uk; w www.yha.org.uk) PO Box 67, Matlock, Derbyshire DE4 3YX. The YHA owns and runs a network of hostels in England and Wales, offering cheap but comfortable accommodation to walkers, cyclists and travellers. For more information on the hostels themselves, see Accommodation later in this chapter. To use YHA hostels, citizens of England and Wales must be YHA members. Visitors from abroad must be a member of their own national hostel organisation or a member of Hostelling International (HI), which can be joined in Britain. You can join at any hostel or through the address above; membership costs adults £12. This also covers you for SYHA hostels in Scotland and HI hostels worldwide. YHA members get discounts on outdoor gear and the invaluable *YHA Accommodation Guide*, listing every YHA hostel in England and Wales, with details of facilities, prices, opening days and times, local transport and so on. If you're already a member of another hostelling organisation, you can buy the guide for £3. The YHA also produces a good range of leaflets (free) and booklets (a small charge) describing hostel-to-hostel walks in various parts of the country. Yet another useful YHA service is the Booking Bureau, which allows you to book a string of hostels in one go along several LDPs including the Coast to Coast Walk, Pennine Way and Cumbria Way.

TOURIST OFFICES
Local Tourist Offices
There are Tourist Information Centres (TICs) all over Britain. Every city and large town has at least one, and even small places in tourist areas have TICs open from April until the end of October, or a Village Information Point – a noticeboard or leaflet dispenser, usually in the village shop. TICs give advice on accommodation, often with a Book-A-Bed-Ahead (BABA) service, and have plenty of information about their region, including walking routes.

Some TICs are run by regional and local tourist boards. Others are national park authority initiatives and have additional information on wildlife and conservation matters.

Most TICs open from 9am to 5pm Monday to Friday, although in popular tourist areas they may also open weekends and stay open later in the evening. Larger TICs stay open all year, but from October to March smaller TICs are often closed. Some TICs have 24-hour computer databases that can be accessed even when the office is closed. Others put posters in the window with basic information about accommodation etc.

Relevant TICs are listed in the walk chapters of this book.

Tourist Offices Abroad
The British Tourist Authority (BTA) represents the main tourism bodies of England, Scotland and Wales overseas, with more than 40 offices around the world (some are listed below).

The BTA produces an extensive collection of information, quite a lot of it free, including accommodation lists and a very good leaflet called *Green Britain*, which covers walking and other outdoor activities, listing routes, contacts, maps and walking tour companies. Some places may also stock the older but more specific *Britain for Walkers* leaflet. The BTA can also advise on public transport passes; see the Getting Around chapter. A very useful BTA booklet called *Scenic Britain by Bus* is full of tips and route suggestions.

You can also get information on the following Web sites: w www.bta.org.uk and w www.visitbritain.com. The Britain visitor atlas at w www.visitmap.com is also useful. Walkers can go straight to w www.visitbri tain.com/walking, or for specifics on Scotland and Wales try w www.visitscotland .com and w www.visitwales.com.

Australia (☎ 02-9377 4400, fax 9377 4499, e visitbritainaus@bta.org.uk) Level 16, The Gateway, 1 Macquarie Place, Circular Quay, NSW 2000
Canada (☎ 888-847 4885, fax 905-405 1835) 5915 Airport Rd, Suite 120, Mississauga, Ontario L4V 1T1

France (☎ 01 44 51 56 20, fax 01 44 51 56 21)
Maison de la Grande Bretagne, 19 rue des
Mathurins, 75009 Paris
Germany (☎ 069-971123, fax 9711 2444,
ⓔ gb-info@bta.org.uk) Westendstrasse 16–22,
60325 Frankfurt
Ireland (☎ 01-670 8000, fax 670 8244)
18–19 College Green, Dublin 2
Japan (☎ 03-5562 2546, fax 5562 2551)
Akasaka Twin Tower 1F 2-17-22, Akasaka
Minatu-ku, Tokyo
Netherlands (☎ 020-689 0002, fax 689 0003,
ⓔ britinfo.nl@bta.org.uk) Stadhouderskade 2,
1054 ES, Amsterdam
New Zealand (☎ 09-303 1446, fax 377 6965,
ⓔ bta.nz@bta.org.uk) 17th Floor, NZI House,
151 Queen St, Auckland 1
South Africa (☎ 11-325 0343, 325 0344,
ⓔ johannesburg@bta.org.uk) Lancaster Gate,
Hyde Park Lane, Hyde Park 2496
USA (☎ 212-986 2200, 800-462 2748,
ⓔ travelinfo@bta.org.uk) Suite 701, 551 Fifth
Ave, New York, NY 10176

VISAS & DOCUMENTS
Passports
All foreign citizens entering Britain need a
passport, valid for the whole period of stay
and at least six months after. You do not need
your passport to travel between England,
Scotland and Wales.

Visas
Citizens of Australia, Canada, New
Zealand, South Africa or the USA do not
need a visa for Britain. Tourists from these
countries are given 'leave to enter'; you can
stay for up to six months but are prohibited
from working. European Union (EU) citizens do not need a visa to enter Britain.
Visitors from most other countries need a
visa; however, requirements can change
and you should check with your nearest
British embassy before travelling.

Travel Insurance
Visitors from overseas should take out a
travel insurance policy to cover theft, loss
and medical expenses. There's a wide variety available so read the fine print to make
sure your policy suits your needs. Some
specifically exclude 'dangerous activities',
which can include walking.

Some policies pay doctors or hospitals
direct. Others require you to pay on the spot
and claim later. Check that ambulances or
an emergency flight home are included in
your policy.

Citizens from EU countries may be eli-
gible for free medical treatment in Britain if
required (see Predeparture Planning in the
Health & Safety chapter for more details).

Driving Licence
Overseas visitors intending to buy or hire a
car can use their own driving licence for 12
months. An International Driving Permit
(IDP), available from your national driving
association, helps officials make sense of
your local licence. If you're a member of a
national driving association, ask about reciprocal services (touring maps, information,
breakdown help, technical advice etc).

Student & Youth Cards
For young travellers, the International Student Identity Card (ISIC) gets you discounts
on some public transport and to museums
and sights. If you're under 26 but not a student, you can get a Federation of International Youth Travel Organisations (FIYTO)
card, which gives much the same discounts.
Student travel agencies can advise on these.

EMBASSIES & CONSULATES
British Embassies & Consulates Abroad
British embassies abroad include the fol-
lowing:
Australia (☎ 02-6270 6666, fax 6270 6653,
ⓦ www.uk.emb.gov.au) Commonwealth Ave,
ACT 2600
Canada (☎ 613-237 1530, fax 232 2533,
ⓦ www.britain-in-canada.org) 80 Elgin St,
Ottawa, Ontario KIP 5K7
France (☎ 01 44 51 31 00, fax 01 44 51 31 28,
ⓦ www.amb-grandebretagne.fr) 35 rue du
Faubourg Saint Honoré, 75008 Paris
Germany (☎ 030-201 840, fax 201 84159,
ⓦ www.britischebotschaft.de) Unter den
Linden 32–34, 10117 Berlin
Ireland (☎ 01-205 3822, fax 205 3890,
ⓦ www.britishembassy.ie) 29 Merrion Rd,
Ballsbridge, Dublin 4
Japan (☎ 03-3265 5511) 1 Ichiban-cho,
Chiyoda-ku, Tokyo

Netherlands (☎ 070-427 0427, fax 427 0345,
W www.britain.nl) Lange Voorhout 10,
2514 ED, The Hague
New Zealand (☎ 04-472 6049, fax 471 1974,
W www.brithighcomm.org.nz) 44 Hill St,
Wellington 1
South Africa (☎ 21-461 7220) 91 Parliament St,
Cape Town 8001
USA (☎ 202-588 6500, fax 588 7850,
W www.britainusa.com) 3100 Massachusetts
Ave NW, Washington DC 20008

Embassies & Consulates in Britain

All embassies are based in London, although
some countries also have representation in
Edinburgh and Cardiff. Countries include:

Australia (☎ 020-7379 4334, fax 7240 5333)
Australia House, Strand, London WC2
Canada (☎ 020-7258 6600, fax 7258 6333)
1 Grosvenor Square, London W1
France (☎ 020-7838 2050, fax 7838 2046)
58 Knightsbridge, London SW1
Germany (☎ 020-7824 1300, fax 7824 1435)
23 Belgrave Square, London SW1
Ireland (☎ 020-7235 2171, fax 7245 6961)
17 Grosvenor Place, London SW1
Japan (☎ 020-7465 6500) 101 Piccadilly,
London W1
Netherlands (☎ 020-7590 3200, fax 7590 3458)
38 Hyde Park Gate, London SW7
New Zealand (☎ 020-7930 8422, fax 7839
4580) New Zealand House, 80 Haymarket,
London SW1
South Africa (☎ 020-7930 4488) Trafalgar
Square, London WC2
USA (☎ 020-7499 9000, fax 7495 5012)
24 Grosvenor Square, London W1

CUSTOMS

When you enter Britain at an airport or sea-
port, there are strict allowances for the quantity of goods you may import duty-free.
These are: 200 cigarettes or 250g of tobacco,
2L of still wine plus 1L of spirits or another
2L of wine, 60cc of perfume, 250cc of eau de
toilette, and all other goods to the value of
£145. Along with the usual red and green
customs channels, there is a blue channel if
no duty is payable because you bought your
goods in another EU country where duties
have already been paid. The rules allow importation of any amount, within reason, *for
individual consumption*. It is illegal to resell.

MONEY
Currency

Britain's currency is the pound (£), sometimes called the 'sterling pound', divided
into 100 pence (p). Notes (paper money)
come in £5, £10, £20 and £50 denominations. (The £50 notes can be difficult to
change – avoid them if possible.) The word
'pence' is rarely used; like its abbreviated
written counterpart, it is pronounced 'pee'.

Scotland has its own central bank and its
major banks issue their own notes and coins,
including a £1 note, although the values are
the same as in the rest of Britain. Scottish
notes and coins are legal tender anywhere in
Britain, although shopkeepers in Southern
England and Wales may be reluctant to accept them. 'English' money will be accepted
anywhere in Scotland.

Exchange Rates

This is what your own currency is worth in
pounds and pence.

country	unit		pound
Australia	A$1	=	£0.35
Canada	C$1	=	£0.45
EU	€1	=	£0.60
France	10FF	=	£0.95
Germany	DM1	=	£0.30
Ireland	IR£1	=	£0.80
Japan	¥100	=	£0.60
New Zealand	NZ$1	=	£0.30
South Africa	R10	=	£0.85
USA	US$1	=	£0.70

Exchanging Money

Cash Nothing beats cash for convenience,
but of course it is a risky way to carry *all* your
money. To get cash as soon as you arrive, all
major airports have 24-hour exchange bureaus. These will exchange your foreign cash
or travellers cheques into pounds cash. To
save queuing (especially if you've had a long
flight), exchange some money into pounds in
your home country, so you are covered at
least for the first week or so.

Travellers Cheques In Britain, travellers
cheques are rarely used for everyday trans-
actions (as they are in the USA) except at

Watch Out for the Euro

By 2002 most countries in the European Union (of which Britain is a member) will have a single currency called the euro. Until then, francs, marks and so on will remain in place or share equal status with the euro. In the UK things are different. The pound will continue to be the unit of currency as the British government has decided not to adopt the euro for the time being. You're likely to see some of the acrimonious debate on the issue in the press during your visit.

major hotels, so you need to exchange them for cash. Do this at a bank or exchange bureau, but be careful as some (not all) bureaus seem to offer good exchange rates, but frequently levy outrageous commissions.

Some TICs and post offices in tourist areas also offer this service, but remember banks and post offices may only open from Monday to Friday and Saturday morning (see the Business Hours section later). Rates and commissions vary slightly, so it may be worth shopping around.

Credit & Debit Cards Cards are very useful. You can use them to get cash, either dealing with a clerk in a bank or through an automatic teller machine (ATM), usually called a 'cash machine' or 'cashpoint' in Britain. Before leaving home, ask your bank or card company which machines in Britain will accept your card.

Cards are widely accepted at large hotels, guesthouses and YHA hostels, and at restaurants and larger pubs. Some pubs and shops offer 'cash-back' on debit cards – they charge the card with a higher amount and you get the change in cash – which can save going to banks at all. You can also use cards for long-distance train and coach travel, or for buying petrol or other goods worth more than about £10.

On the Walk

When walking in Britain you should note that small establishments in rural areas, such as shops, pubs and B&Bs, always prefer cash. Many walking areas are away from towns, so you have to plan carefully. Wherever you go, carry enough cash for a week to 10 days, especially if you hit the only town with a bank on Sunday.

Security

Carrying cash or cards while walking is not a risk in the countryside or wilderness. However, a few routes pass through large towns (and sometimes not the most salubrious parts) or through parks and woodland on the edge of cities, where a slight danger may exist and some common-sense precautions need to be taken.

Costs

A daily budget is hard to pin down. At the bottom end, you could get away with a total of £10 to £15 per day, and £20 per day is entirely feasible. Move up a few comfort notches and you'll be on £30 to £50 per day. Stay in smart hotels, eat in fancy restaurants, take a few taxis, and a top-end daily budget could be £75 to £100.

More than anything, your type of accommodation determines how much you'll spend (see Accommodation later in this chapter for

Tipping

In Britain, waiters in restaurants normally expect a tip of around 10% of the bill, but you should pay this only if you're satisfied with the service. It is not automatic. Some restaurants automatically include a 'service charge' of 10% to 15% onto the bill, but this should be clearly advertised. If the service was satisfactory you must pay, or explain the reasons for your dissatisfaction to the manager. You do not add a further tip.

If you eat in a pub, the tipping situation is fluid. If you order and pay for your food at the bar, tips are not expected. If you order at the table and the food (and the bill) is brought to your table, restaurant-style, then a tip may be appropriate – if the food and service has been good of course!

price details). Transport is the other big expense, but its cost is harder to quantify as it depends not on how long you stay, but on how far you go and how many different areas you visit. The Coach & Train Fares tables in the Getting Around chapter provide some indication of public transport prices. Petrol costs between 80p and £1, although it varies around the country.

For food, in towns or cities you can get by on £5 per day by purchasing basics from supermarkets. When walking, camping or hostelling you may be self-catering anyway, so £5 to £10 per day will see you through nicely. If you have meals at hostels or cheap restaurants, £10 per day will also be your baseline. A bar meal in a pub will be about £5, while a mid-range restaurant main course will set you back £7 to £10. Beer may not be classed as an essential by some, but just for the record, a pint will cost you £2.50 to £3 in London and £1.50 to £2.25 around the country.

Taxes & Refunds

In Britain most prices include Value-Added Tax (VAT), which is currently 17.5%. This is levied on virtually all goods except books and food from shops. Restaurants must by law charge VAT in their menu prices. Overseas visitors can claim back the VAT on major purchases that are not consumed in Britain, although shops where you buy goods have to be part of the refund scheme – and not all of them are. Participating shops should carry a 'Tax-Free Shopping' sign in their window.

POST & COMMUNICATIONS
Post

If you don't have a permanent address, mail can be sent to poste restante in the town or city where you are staying. American Express Travel offices will also hold cardholders' mail free of charge.

Within Britain, first-class mail (27p per letter) is quicker and more expensive than 2nd-class mail (19p). For letters weighing up to 10g, air-mail to EU countries costs 27p, to non-EU European countries 36p, and to the Americas and Australasia 45p.

Telephone & Fax

Most public telephone booths in Britain take coins, pre-paid phonecards or credit cards.

There are several different call charges: local calls (where no area code is required) are cheapest, local area calls (up to a radius of about 20mi) are more expensive, and national calls (anywhere else in the UK) are more again. The cheapest rates for domestic and international calls apply at weekends and between 6pm and 8am on weekdays. Service calls (eg, weather information lines) are charged at a higher rate than normal phone calls – from 50p to £1 per minute.

Area codes are listed with each phone number throughout the book. Other codes worth knowing about are:

service	code
Britain (UK) country code	
(to phone Britain)	☎ 44
call is free to caller	☎ 0800
call is free to caller	☎ 0808
call is free to caller	☎ 0500
emergency (fire, police	
or ambulance)	☎ 999
international direct-dial code	
(to phone from Britain)	☎ 00
international directory assistance	☎ 153
international operator	☎ 155
local & national operator	☎ 100
local call Rates apply	☎ 0845
national call rates apply	☎ 0870
national directory assistance	☎ 192
premium rates apply	☎ 090

Beware of other codes that may indicate you're calling a mobile phone (ie, codes not starting with 01 or 02, if not included in the list here). This is usually considerably more expensive than calling a conventional phone.

If you need to send or receive a fax, many TICs, newsagents and other shops offer a public service.

Mobile Phones Britain uses GSM 900/1800, which is compatible with the rest of Europe and Australia but not with North America or Japan (although some North

Americans have GSM 1900/900 phones that do work here). If you have a GSM phone, check with your service provider about compatibility with Britain and beware of calls being routed internationally.

Mobile phones (cell phones) can be useful when walking, either as a safety aid – although only in dire emergencies (not for sprained ankles or when simply lost) – or for phoning ahead to check B&Bs if you haven't booked. Be aware, however, that your mobile may not work on every walk we cover.

Phonecards There's a wide range of local and international phonecards. For local calls within Britain you're usually better off with a local card, available from newsagents and other shops in denominations of £1 to £10.

Lonely Planet's eKno Communication Card is aimed specifically at independent travellers and provides budget international calls, a range of messaging services, free email and travel information. You can join on-line at ⓦ www.ekno.lonelyplanet.com or by phone from Britain by dialling ☎ 0800-376 1704. Once you have joined, to use eKno from Britain dial ☎ 0800-169 8646 (or ☎ 0800-376 2366 from a payphone).

Email
All cities, most towns and even some villages have cybercafes or public Internet bureaus. Hotels, hostels and larger B&Bs may also offer this service. Other places to try are libraries and TICs – even if the latter don't offer this service, they'll know where to send you. Free web-based email is available through eKno (ⓦ www.ekno.lonely planet.com), mentioned under Phonecards.

INTERNET RESOURCES
Britain is second only to the USA in its number of Web sites and there are plenty to interest walkers and travellers. Towns, tourist boards, national parks, LDPs, attractions, B&Bs, hotels and transportation companies all have Web sites. You will find many listed throughout this book. Web sites relevant to walking routes or for local organisations are listed in the Information and Planning sections of the walk chapters. Other Web sites

are listed under Useful Organisations, Tourist Offices and Accommodation in this chapter, and under the public transport headings in the Getting Around chapter.

Note that some of the most popular walking routes have several competing sites: an official one authorised by the national park or national trail, and several commercial sites (some masquerading as 'official'); the latter type varies considerably – some are very useful, others are not always reliable.

The Internet is also a rich resource for travellers in general. You can research your trip, hunt down bargain air fares, book hotels, check on weather conditions or chat with locals or other travellers and walkers about the best places to visit (or avoid!).

There's no better place to start your Web explorations than the Lonely Planet Web site (ⓦ www.lonelyplanet.com), featuring the Thorn Tree bulletin board, where you can ask questions before you go or dispense advice when you get back, and the subWWWay, which links you to the most useful travel resources elsewhere on the Internet.

BOOKS
This book cannot cover every aspect of walking in Britain – a great number of other books are available. This section will guide you between the shelves. Detailed guidebooks to specific routes and areas are listed in the relevant sections. Many guidebooks are produced by small publishers (some are listed here), which may not be easy to locate outside their local areas.

Lonely Planet
For general travel around the country, Lonely Planet's *Britain* guide is an excellent companion to this book. For more detail there are separate guides to England, Scotland and Wales, as well as city guides to London and Edinburgh. Those who want to get to grips with local forms of English should get hold of Lonely Planet's *British Phrasebook*.

For keen walkers interested in exploring more of the wild areas of Scotland and discovering timeless Ireland, check out Lonely Planet's *Walking in Scotland* and *Walking in Ireland*.

Walking Guidebooks

A walking guidebook is to carry with you (books about walking that you probably wouldn't carry are listed under Walking Handbooks following), and it seems that every bit of footpath in Britain has been covered at least once. Some guidebooks describe one route, others describe many. They range from bland step-by-step instruction manuals to lovingly crafted works of art combining eloquent route descriptions with carefully researched background information. In fact, there are so many guidebooks that the choice can be daunting, and this is one of the reasons we produced *Walking in Britain*.

Route Guidebooks These books describe a single route in great detail, often step by step. Some cover the route only, others include extra details on accommodation, history or wildlife. For example, the official national trail guides published by Aurum include detailed descriptions and incorporate relevant sections from OS 1:25,000 maps.

Area Guidebooks These books cover large areas such as a district or national park. Some are all-encompassing, eg, the classic *The Pictorial Guides to the Lakeland Fells* by Alfred Wainwright. For north of the border, *Exploring the Far North West of Scotland* by Richard Gilbert is a particularly well-regarded book.

Pathfinder Guides published by Jarrold are excellent area guidebooks; each describes about 25 walks of varying lengths and standards, from a few hours to a day in duration, clearly shown on an extract from the relevant OS map.

If you're travelling with children, look out for the Family Walks series published by Scarthin Books; there are about 50 titles covering the country, each with a good selection of 'high interest, low mileage' walks.

Other area guidebooks have a specific theme, with titles like *Mostly Downhill in the Yorkshire Dales* or the more challenging *Hard Walks in the Pennines*.

Another popular theme is the Pub Walks series (one set published by Countryside Books and another by Sigma). All included routes have at least one pub, with details on the food, beer, atmosphere, facilities and so on. If you're looking for a challenge to earn your pint, get *The Pubhiker's Guide* by Mick Payne, which promises 'real walks and real ale'!

If you have other tastes and interests, chances are they'll be catered for. Published series include Teashop Walks, Wildlife Walks, History Walks, River Walks, Canal Walks, Literary Walks and thousands of other titles, some bordering on the bizarre: How about *Circular Walks to Peak District Aircraft Wrecks*?

Local Guidebooks These cover fairly small areas, such as the countryside around a single town, with a number of walks (usually circular) in that area. They are often available only from local newsagents, gift shops and TICs for a modest price. Some are listed in specific route descriptions in this book.

National Guidebooks These cover entire countries, usually with a specific angle. Most useful for keen and hardy walkers is *200 Challenging Walks in Britain & Ireland* by Richard Gilbert, combining brief route outlines and descriptions with maps and photos, covering some of the finest routes and walking areas in the British Isles. The routes are drawn from three best-selling large-format books, *Classic Walks*, *Wild Walks* and *Big Walks* – which are ideal for inspiration before your trip.

Another classic is *The Munros* by Donald Bennet. This Scottish Mountaineering Club (SMC) Hillwalkers' Guide is published by Cordee and the Scottish Mountaineering Trust. A 'Munro' is a mountain in Scotland higher than 914m, the metric equivalent of 3000ft – the magical height at which mountains take on an extra significance for walkers. (See the boxed text 'Munros & Munro Bagging' on p452.) This book – the Munro-baggers' bible – lovingly describes all of them (around 277, although the actual figure is always hotly debated) with maps, photos and route descriptions. It makes a good souvenir, even if you don't bag the set, and is a worthy purchase as some proceeds from the sale go to mountain conservation in Scotland. In the same series are *The Corbetts and Other Scottish Hills* (Corbetts are Scottish mountains over 2500ft) and several district guides – these are mentioned in more detail in the relevant Scotland chapters.

Also highly recommended is *Scottish Hill Tracks* by Donald Bennet (does this guy ever get home?) & Cliff Stone, published by the Scottish Rights of Way Society. It covers more than 300 routes around and through the mountains, all over Scotland, following historical rights of way, coffin roads and drove roads.

Walking Handbooks

Walking handbooks are designed to inspire or inform (or both) before you head off on your walk. For this reason they are almost as valuable as practical guidebooks, but not a substitute for them.

The High Mountains of Britain & Ireland by Irvine Butterfield. This is a truly beautiful book, covering every mountain over 914m (3000ft). This naturally includes all the Munros in Scotland (see National Guidebooks earlier for an explanation of Munros), plus 'honorary Munros' in other parts of the British Isles. Each chapter covers a group of mountains, with maps, photos, outlines of routes, overall descriptions and excellent colour photos. For peak baggers this is all you need, but unfortunately it is too big to carry on a walk. To overcome this, *The High Mountains Companion* contains the condensed text, with all the photos and other frills left out – slim enough to fit in a pocket.

The High Peaks of England & Wales by Paul Hannon. This book covers in detail all the mountains south of the Scottish border over 2500ft (the equivalent to Scotland's 'Corbetts'), mainly in the Lake District and Snowdonia, but with a few unexpected giants elsewhere too. Just for completeness, the 3000ft summits are also included, and the whole book is illustrated with full-colour maps and photos.

Land's End to John O'Groats and *Coastwalk* by Andrew McCloy. These books are for those who want really long walks. The first describes three routes from one end of Britain to the other (for many walkers the 'End-to-End' is a great goal), with all you need for initial planning. The second book describes a route round the entire coastline of England and Wales. Both books

also suggest shorter sections, ranging from a few days to a few weeks.

The Long Distance Walkers Handbook published by the Long Distance Walkers Association and A&C Black. This book lists and briefly describes about 550 long-distance walks in Britain; indispensable for mile eaters in search of inspiration.

The Mountains of England & Wales by John & Ann Nuttall. This is another useful almanac, divided into one volume per country, providing a definitive list of all mountains over 600m (2000ft), with descriptions of fine circular day walks that take them all in; ideal for peak baggers south of the Scottish border.

Munro's Tables by DA Bearhop. This book lists all Munros in Scotland (over 3000ft) plus the latest lists of Corbetts (over 2500ft), Donalds (over 2000ft), and even Grahams (who knows!).

The Munroist's Companion by Robin N Campbell. This book has more than you could really want to know on the subject: articles on Munro himself, a definition and classification of Munros, technical advice on peak bagging and short articles by Munro aficionados.

The Relative Hills of Britain by Alan Dawson. This is the list to end all lists. Forget Munros: These are the Marilyns, the name for any hill or mountain which is *relatively* high, ie, 150m (about 500ft) above its surroundings, whatever its actual altitude. Anyone who thought British walkers were obsessive will have their suspicions unequivocally confirmed by this book, although the bland statistics are balanced by some interesting facts and tongue-in-cheek observations on the art and lore of peak bagging.

Safety on Mountains by Andy MacNae et al. An inexpensive and potentially vital handbook covering all the skills and equipment you need when venturing into the British mountains, especially in winter. This book is backed by the British Mountaineering Council and the Mountain Leader Training Board.

Accommodation & Food Guides

There are many general guidebooks to places to stay and eat in Britain, with useful information to complement detailed route guidebooks. We list a few here, concentrating on those of particular interest to walkers.

Bed & Breakfast Guest Accommodation published by the English Tourism Council. This large (800 pages) book lists all B&Bs, inns, guesthouses and other small establishments in England that have been registered and graded by this official body. There are similar books for Wales and Scotland. These are available in TICs in Britain and from BTA offices overseas. Town and county tourist boards also produce leaflets and booklets listing local registered and graded accommodation, also available from TICs (free of charge). See the Accommodation section for more details.

Highland Hostels Not all independent hostels in Scotland are included in the *Independent Hostel Guide Scotland* (listed later). This supplementary list is available from Highland Hostels, Aite Cruinnchidh, 1 Achluachrach, By Roy Bridge, Inverness-shire PH31 4AW, or at **w** www.highland-hostels.co.uk.

The Independent Hostel Guide published by the Backpacker's Press (☎/fax 01629-580427, **e** davedalley@aol.com) 2 Rockview Cottages, Matlock Bath, Derbyshire DE4 3PG. The guide covers 250 independent hostels in Britain (ie, not part of national hostel organisations, such as the YHA), from basic bunkhouses in rural areas to lively backpackers lodges in cities, and is ideal for outdoor enthusiasts and budget travellers. It is available in some TICs and outdoor shops, by mail order from the publisher (£5 plus postage) or through Wilderness Press (fax 510-558 1696, **e** Jones@WildernessPress.com), 1200 5th St, Berkly CA 94710-1306, USA.

Independent Hostel Guide Scotland produced by and available from Independent Backpackers Hostels Scotland (☎/fax 01478-640254, **e** skyehostel@lineone.net, **w** www.hostel-scotland.co.uk), Croft Bunkhouse & Bothies, Portnalong, Isle of Skye IV47 8SL. This is a fold-out leaflet with full details of about 90 independent hostels throughout Scotland. Comes with a Highlands and islands travel map. Available from TICs or by post for 52p within Britain or two international reply coupons from overseas.

The Rambler's Yearbook & Accommodation Guide published by the Ramblers' Association. The Ramblers' very handy yearbook is free to members or can be bought by mail order for £5 (see Useful Organisations earlier for contact details). It contains a good summary of walkers' rights, a list of 50 popular LDPs with details of maps, guidebooks, and a large list of B&Bs and guesthouses that welcome walkers.

Room at the Inn by Jill Adam. Many pubs and inns offer accommodation, and can be ideal places to stay. This book lists pubs that offer a combination of good food, memorable beer and good accommodation.

Stilwell's Bed & Breakfast published by Stilwell. This book, arranged by county, briefly lists and describes several thousand B&Bs (including farms, inns and small hotels) across Britain in a very accessible way. The associated Web site (**w** www.stilwell.co.uk) is also very useful.

Stilwell's National Trail Companion published by Stilwell. This is an adaptation of *Stilwell's Bed & Breakfast*, listing every B&B and every pub providing accommodation and food on or near all Britain's national trails and about 30 other LDPs. They are listed in order, as you walk along the route, which makes planning overnight stops very easy. If you're doing several long routes and nothing else, this book is absolutely ideal.

Travel

The First Fifty by Murial Gray. A perfect book if you like mountains but can't stand the intensity of male-dominated peak bagging, by a hip TV personality who also happens to like hill walking, and likes even more to de-bunk the fastidious nature of some other writers on Scotland.

Hamish's Mountain Walk by Hamish Brown. A very readable account of a historic first and extraordinarily long continuous round of the Munros, by an extremely well-known Scottish mountain writer. There's also *Hamish's Groat's End Walk* (across Britain from John O'Groats to Lands End), and *Climbing the Corbetts*, among others.

Notes from a Small Island by Bill Bryson. This is not specifically a walking book, although the author does travel by foot in places, but it is a highly entertaining, deeply perceptive study of Britain and a continuous best seller.

Plowright follows Wainright by Alan Plowright. The author takes up walking to keep fit and discovers the works of the near-legendary guidebook writer Alfred Wainwright. Inspired, Plowright then follows Wainwright along the Pennine Way and across the Coast-to-Coast, paying tribute to his mentor and describing evocative landscapes and eccentric fellow walkers encountered along the way.

Walking in Britain by John Hillaby. This book is a collection of writings about various parts of the country by local experts, designed to enthral and inspire rather than simply inform. This book was published in 1988 and is already a bit dated. His other books include *Journey Through Britain*, published even earlier but capturing the spirit of the age, and possibly destined to become a walking classic.

Natural History

The Complete Guide to British Wildlife by Arlott, Fitter & Fitter is a handy field guide, well suited to visitors with a general interest.

It is nicely illustrated and covers everything from obscure fungi to tall trees in a neat and accessible format.

If your interest in wildlife is more casual, go for the very portable and reasonably priced series of Gem Guides, published by Collins. This includes *Birds*, *Insects*, *Trees*, *Fish*, *Wild Flowers* and many more. If you need more detail, the slightly larger Wild Guides series (also Collins), with accessible information and colour photos, includes *Birds*, *Trees*, *Mushrooms & Toadstools*, *Butterflies & Moths* and *Flowers*. A similar series of Pocket Guides (published by Mitchell Beazley) includes *Butterflies*, *Trees* and *Wildflowers*, combining in-depth coverage with a handy format – ideal for walkers. Collins publishes separate guides for Scottish wild flowers and birds.

Buying Books

Most towns have bookshops, and in walking areas even small village stores will stock a selection of maps and guidebooks on the surrounding area. TICs also sell local maps and guidebooks. If you want to buy books before you arrive in a walking area, some national park authorities and national trail offices offer a mail-order book service (see the relevant sections in the walk chapters for details).

Books on Birds

Walking and birdwatching go particularly well together. One of the best field guides for keen amateurs is the award-winning *Pocket Guide to Birds of Britain & Europe* by Heinzel, Fitter & Parslow. Similarly handy, and highly rated by birdwatchers, especially for beginners, is the *Birdwatcher's Pocket Guide* by Peter Hayman (published by Mitchell Beazley), designed for speedy reference with clear illustrations and notes on distinctive features. If you want to choose destinations according to what you may see, *Top Birding Spots* by David Tipling is recommended, with colour maps and photos, covering 400 birdwatching sites in Britain and Ireland.

If you're staying in London, some of the shops listed under Supplies & Equipment in the London Region chapter also sell walking guidebooks. Another source is The Travel Bookshop (☎ 020-7229 5620), on Blenheim Crescent, W11; this has a good stock of walking guides to Britain, and is also reputed to have been the inspiration for the bookshop in the film *Notting Hill*. Other large central bookshops in London, which also stock guidebooks, include three in the Waterstone's chain (on Charing Cross Rd, Gower St and Piccadilly – the latter is the largest bookshop in Britain).

Alternatively, try on-line booksellers such as Maps Worldwide, with contact details under Buying Maps earlier. Also good are Amazon.com (www.amazon.com) and its UK subsidiary (www.amazon.co.uk). Both carry a good range of British guidebooks, including relatively small and obscure titles, and annual booklets such as national trail accommodation guides.

MAGAZINES

Walking magazines can be a great source of information for visitors to Britain. Most contain news of walking events, equipment, clothing reviews etc. They also have features on day walks or weekend routes around the country, which can be a great source of inspiration. Also useful are the advertisement sections, full of information on walking holiday companies, guides, accommodation etc. *TGO* (The Great Outdoors) has been around for years, combining a traditional pedigree and a modern look with excellent news coverage and route suggestions. *Trailwalker* and *Country Walking* also offer plenty of route suggestions, lively and informative articles and very good sections of advice for people new to walking.

WEATHER INFORMATION

The most potentially dangerous aspect of walking in Britain is the changeability of the weather, especially in highland or coastal areas, where low cloud, fog, rain and snow can mean trouble for unprepared walkers. Sometimes the problem is minor – you get lost in the mist for half an hour – but sometimes it is more serious as temperatures drop below freezing.

Before you go walking always check the weather. In national parks and tourist areas, weather bulletins are posted at TICs, hostels, outdoor gear shops and cafes frequented by walkers.

There are also several telephone information services. For WeatherCheck telephone ☎ 0900-133 3111 and, on the prompt, add a number for the area of the country you're interested in, then listen to the tape. The service includes special hill walkers' information for Scotland, North Wales and the Lake District.

Another to try is WeatherCall: First dial ☎ 0891-5004, then add two digits for the area you want, eg, 15 for North Wales or 19 for the Lake District. At any time you can jump to a menu which gives you the two digits to dial for all parts of Britain. Part of this service is Mountaincall, which supplies specialist information for walkers to the three main mountain areas of Britain: First dial ☎ 0891-5004, then 41 for the Western Highlands of Scotland, 42 for the Eastern Highlands or 49 for Snowdonia.

Similar services are advertised in walking magazines and at TICs. Calls to these numbers cost 60p per minute.

On-line weather forecast sites include Met Office Weather (W www.met-office.gov.uk) and the BBC Weather Service (W www.bbc .co.uk/weather).

TIME

Britain is home to Greenwich Mean Time (GMT), now more commonly called Universal Time Coordinated (UTC). To give you a rough idea, Britain is on the same time (plus or minus one hour) as much of Western Europe, while Eastern Europe is a couple of hours ahead. Sydney is 10 hours ahead of GMT, while San Francisco is eight hours and New York five hours behind GMT. Britain uses daylight saving (called 'British Summer Time' or BST) so that the whole country is one hour ahead of GMT from late March to late October. Most public transport timetables use the 24-hour clock, but in everyday conversation it is very rarely used; instead people refer to 9am or 9pm etc.

ELECTRICITY

The standard voltage throughout Britain is 240V AC, 50Hz. Plugs have three square pins and adapters are widely available.

WEIGHTS & MEASURES

Britain is in a period of awkward transition when it comes to weights and measures, as it has been for the last 25 years and probably will be for another 20. Most British people still think and talk in 'imperial' units – pounds (lb) and ounces (oz) – even though since January 2000 goods in shops have to be sold in kilograms. And nobody knows their weight in pounds (like Americans do) or in kilograms (like the rest of the world); Brits weigh themselves in 'stones', which is a unit of 14 pounds. When it comes to volume, things are even worse. Most liquids are sold in litres or half-litres, except milk and beer, which come in pints. Petrol stations sell petrol priced in pence per litre, but measure car performance in miles per gallon. Great, isn't it?

For length, most British people still use the old units of inches, feet and yards, but on maps the heights of mountains are now given in metres only. So walkers, more than any other section of the population, have become familiar with the 'new' metre measure, although some still prefer to convert back to feet (multiplying, roughly, by three).

Despite this drift towards metres, very few British people are familiar with kilometres. All distances on road signs are in miles, and it is more usual to see distances on footpath signs given in miles too, although a few kilometre equivalents do creep in occasionally. One annoying result of this intransigence is that on signposts 'mile' is often abbreviated to 'm', which to everyone in the world except the sign-makers means 'metre'.

In this book we have reflected this rather wacky and typically British system of mixed measurements. In the route descriptions, daily distances along footpaths are mostly given in miles (with kilometre equivalents), while mountain heights are given in metres (with some feet equivalents). That's the way things are in Britain, and who are we to swim against the tide? For conversion tables, see the back of this book.

BUSINESS HOURS

Business hours for offices, shops and post offices are traditionally Monday to Friday from 9am to 5pm. All shops and large post offices are also open on Saturday from 9am to 5pm, while supermarkets and neighbourhood shops keep longer hours and also open on Sunday. Small shops may close for lunch from 12.30pm or 1 to 2pm. In country towns, there may be an early closing day for shops – usually Tuesday, Wednesday or Thursday – which means they shut all afternoon on that day, although in tourist areas shops stay open every day during 'the season' (April to September or October). Beware particularly of cafes that claim to stay open all year, but turn out to be closed when you troll up on a wet and blustery day.

PUBLIC HOLIDAYS

Public holidays (called 'bank holidays' in Britain) are:

New Year's Day 1 January
Bank Holiday 2 January (Scotland)
Good Friday the Friday before Easter Sunday
Easter Monday the Monday after Easter
  Sunday (not in Scotland)
May Day Bank Holiday first Monday in May
Spring Bank Holiday last Monday in May
Summer Bank Holiday first Monday in August
  (Scotland), last Monday in August (outside
  Scotland)
Christmas Day 25 December
Boxing Day 26 December

Most banks and businesses are closed on public holidays. Museums and other attractions generally stay open for most public holidays except Christmas Day and Boxing Day. In tourist areas, shops will also stay open on public holidays, but post offices may close. In Scotland, however, 'bank holidays' still have that meaning: the banks are closed but most other things stay open. Scottish towns normally have a spring and autumn holiday, but dates vary from year to year and town to town.

ACCOMMODATION

The accommodation you use while walking in Britain is as varied as the routes you follow, and the range of choices (from basic bunkhouses to smart hotels) is all part of the attraction.

As Australians in Britain we like to walk through villages, stopping overnight in old inns when possible. We are keen bushwalkers at home, but in Britain do not wish to duplicate our Australian walks. A pint in a pub at the end of a day's walking through English fields and meadows is most enjoyable.

Phillip Crampton

Camping

Many cities and towns, especially near popular walking areas, have campsites, although these are usually some distance from the centre, which can be awkward if you want to go in for shopping or something to eat. Facilities are usually good, with rates of about £3 to £5 per person.

Once you get into the countryside there are many options for camping, although a tent is not essential for any of the walks described in this book. Campsites range from a field where the cows have been, with a tap and a basic toilet (charging £1 to £2.50 per person per night), to smarter affairs with hot showers, a shop, bar, children's playground etc (for around £5). Some campsites cater for big tents or caravans on long stays and are not set up for passing walkers.

If you plan to explore an area by doing several day walks from a single base, camping is a good-value option. National parks and other walking areas have many campsites, although they can be busy in summer. Most LDPs are also fairly well served, and if you ask nicely farmers may permit your tent in their field on a one-off basis. Remember all land is private in Britain, so if you camp without permission you could be moved on rather aggressively. If you can't find anyone to ask, be very discreet. Use your common sense too: don't camp in crop fields, for example.

Before you arrive in Britain, forget the backwoods bushwalk type of camping of Australasia and North America where you can pitch a tent anywhere. It just doesn't work like that here except in parts of Scotland and remote areas of England and Wales (ie, more than half a day's walk from an official site or any other form of accommodation) where 'wild camping' may be tolerated by landowners. If you camp wild, be meticulous. Leaving a mess spoils things for the next walkers, possibly endangers wildlife and makes landowners less likely to allow camping in the future.

A final note: Always carry a stove. Open fires are not normally allowed on official sites or for wild camps. They can be dangerous and quite often there isn't enough wood anyway.

Shelters & Bothies

Very simple shelters exist in some remote parts of England and Wales but are most common in Scotland, where they are called bothies. They are not locked or guarded, and those in Scotland are maintained on a voluntary basis by the Mountain Bothies Association (MBA). You're expected to stay one or two nights only, groups of more than three are discouraged and you need cooking equipment, sleeping bag and mat. There's no charge. In the last few years some bothies in popular areas have been overused to the point of destruction. Consequently, the MBA prefers the location of others to remain fairly secret. Some walks in this book pass near bothies but unless essential they are not listed. Where bothies are already marked on maps they can hardly be considered secret, so are listed if relevant. Whatever, if you find a bothy and use it, that's fine. But leave it as you found it (or better).

Camping Barns

A camping barn is usually a converted farm building providing shelter for walkers, with wooden sleeping platforms and a cooking area, often in one room, and basic toilets outside. You need everything you'd need for camping except a tent. Although most camping barns are privately owned (usually by a farmer), some are organised collectively and run by a national park or by the

YHA (see Hostels following). They cost around £2 to £4 per night.

Bunkhouses

The next grade up from camping barns are bunkhouses. They usually have stoves for heating and cooking and may supply utensils. Sleeping platforms may have mattresses but you'll still need a sleeping bag. Other facilities may include showers and a drying room. Most charge around £5 to £7.50 per night. Some top-end bunkhouses are like hostels and charge similar rates, ie, around £10.

Hostels

There are two types of hostel in Britain: those run by the YHA or SYHA (see Useful Organisations earlier in this chapter) and those run by independent hostels.

YHA and SHYA hostels have male and female dormitories, showers, a drying room, lounge and an equipped kitchen for self-catering. Most provide meals as well. Many YHA hostels also have double rooms, or rooms with four bunks, often with their own bathroom. The days of big dorms and queues for the shower are passing (although with improved facilities and standards come increased prices).

There are several large YHA hostels in cities and big towns, usually with a busy cosmopolitan atmosphere, charging around £10 to £12 per night, or up to £22 in London.

In country areas, YHA hostels are graded as follows:

small – ranging from fairly basic to quite comfortable, usually in remote areas, ideal for walkers, usually closed from 10am to 5pm, charging around £7 to £8

medium or **diverse** – with more facilities, easy to reach, often in popular country areas, about £10

large – busy and with many facilities, often catering for school and youth groups, activities arranged, about £11

Charges listed here (varying slightly between hostels) are for members. It costs £12 to join. If you're not a member you can join at the first hostel you use or pay a premium of about £2 per hostel. Obviously if you're using more than a handful of hostels it's cheaper to join. Under-18s pay £6 to join and about 75% of the adult overnight rates. Meals (which are optional) cost about £3 for breakfasts and packed lunches, and from £4 for evening meals – often large and very good value.

The deal at SYHA hostels in Scotland is similar: It costs £6 to join (£2.50 for under 18s). Hostels are graded according to 'stars' (between one and three) awarded by the Scottish Tourist Board. Prices reflect the standard of the hostel but are also determined by its position. A simple hostel in a remote area will cost about £6 to £7, one with more facilities might be £9 to £11, while very popular city locations (such as Edinburgh) charge £13 to £16. Under-18s pay about 85% of the adult rates.

Making Reservations

When booking a room at a hostel, hotel or B&B, check where it is in relation to your walking route. In country areas, postal addresses include the nearest town but this may be 20mi away! (Some accommodation guides include map references.)

Some remote B&B owners will pick you up by car – but check if there's a charge. Remember also that there may be no pub serving food nearby. Some B&Bs provide evening meals, if booked in advance, or a lift to the pub.

Most hostels have self-catering facilities, so being in a remote area is no problem if you've got adequate supplies. Most YHA hostels also provide meals.

When booking larger B&Bs and YHA hostels by phone, you can pay up front by credit card. Independent hostels and small B&Bs often accept phone bookings but do not require a deposit. If you book ahead and your plans change, please phone and let your accommodation know. Owners lose money by holding beds for people who never turn up while turning away others who arrive on spec.

And finally, note that many B&Bs and hotels raise their rates in busy times (usually summer), so be prepared for prices that are slightly different from those indicated in this book.

Independent hostel facilities and prices vary considerably: In rural areas, some are simple bunkhouses (charging around £5), some are good bunkhouses (around £9) and some are almost up to B&B standard, charging £10 or more. In cities, independent hostels can cost £15 for a dorm bed and £20 or more for a private room.

Independent hostels in cities are often called backpackers hostels, aimed at young budget travellers from around the world. These are usually very lively with a range of rooms (doubles or dorms), a bar, cafe, Internet service, laundry facilities and so on. Prices range from £10 to £20. (Some independent hostels in London have been described as 'backpacker ghettos', noisy, very crowded and with few facilities, so you may want to choose carefully.)

Reservations are usually possible at hostels; at larger places you can pay in advance by credit card. At YHA hostels, opening times and days can vary; always check these before turning up.

B&Bs & Guesthouses

The B&B (bed and breakfast) is a great British institution. Basically, you get a room in somebody's house. Small B&Bs may only have one guest room so you'll really feel like part of the family, while larger B&Bs may have up to 10 rooms and more facilities.

B&Bs in country areas often offer a special welcome for walkers. You might stay in a village house, an isolated cottage or a farmhouse surrounded by fields. Breakfasts are traditionally enormous – just right to set you up for a day in the hills (see the boxed text 'British Breakfasts' on p76 for a rundown on the menu). In country areas, many B&Bs also offer evening meals (from around £10) and packed lunches (from around £3), although these must be ordered at least a day in advance. In these enlightened days nearly all places will do a vegetarian breakfast, although this may be of the 'extra-egg-no-bacon' type. The only downside of B&Bs for keen walkers is that breakfasts are invariably served between 8am and 9am, which can be awkward if you want to make an early start.

Bookings are preferred at B&Bs, and recommended (or essential) at popular periods. But if you're on a flexible itinerary you can turn up and take a chance; places with spare rooms hang a 'Vacancies' sign outside. If you phone to reserve and the place is full, ask if the owner can recommend another place nearby. Most B&Bs cooperate with each other in this way.

B&B prices are usually quoted per person (as in this book, unless otherwise stated) but may be based on two people sharing a twin room. Lone walkers have to pay between 20% and 50% extra, and some B&Bs simply won't take singles. When you're looking for a B&B note that small places are often listed under the name of the owner, eg, Mrs Jones, or the address, eg, 6 Green St.

Price differences are usually reflected in the facilities: At the bottom end (£12.50 to £14 per person) you get a simple bedroom and share the bathroom with other guests. Smarter B&Bs charge about £15 to £20 and have extras like a TV or coffee-making facilities, and a private bathroom (either down the hall or en suite). Bathrooms are just that – they contain a bath. Showers are less usual.

Note the use of the term 'B&B': You can stay *at* a B&B but some hotels and inns *do* B&B. Note also that in towns and cities some B&Bs are set up for long-term residents – sometimes for homeless people on welfare. Even if they had room they would not normally take in passing walkers.

'Guesthouse' can be just another name for a B&B, although sometimes they tend towards a small hotel. Prices range from £15 to £30 per person per night, depending on the quality of the food and accommodation.

The useful Stillwell Web site (W www .stilwell.co.uk) covers B&B and guesthouse accommodation in Britain specifically for walkers, arranged by area and LDP. Another useful portal is W www.muddybootswelc ome.com, which links to various Spotlight Guide sites covering accommodation and other aspects of LDPs.

One last tip: If you're doing an LDP, try to avoid starting on a weekend as that's when most people start, and demand for accommodation swells at following overnight

spots along the route. Several B&Bs on routes like the Coast to Coast Path are quite quiet most of the week and then have to turn people away on the busy one or two nights when most walkers come through.

Inns & Pubs

As well as selling drinks and meals (see Food following), pubs and inns sometimes offer B&B, particularly in country areas. These can be good fun since they place you at the centre of the community. Rates are normally

> ### Totting up the Stars & Diamonds
>
> Most accommodation in Britain is registered with a local tourist board. Throughout Britain hotels are graded and awarded stars (from one star to five stars) according to their standards. B&Bs in Scotland and Wales are also awarded stars, while in England they are awarded diamonds.
>
> Often, the number of stars is based on facilities and standards rather than character, atmosphere or the attitude of the staff. Many two-star places are owner-managed, where guests get a personal welcome, while some five-star places can feel a bit impersonal. Awarding diamonds to smaller places attempts to rectify this – small places without many facilities but with friendly, top-quality service can still get a high diamond rating.
>
> In Scotland (and at least partly in Wales) hostels and budget accommodations are also graded using stars. Hostels in England are not graded but stars or diamonds (or maybe some other symbol – a walking boot?) may be introduced in the near future.
>
> It's also worth noting that establishments have to pay to be graded and listed in tourist publicity. This is expensive so many rural B&Bs don't register, even though they are absolutely fine. Thus accommodation lists provided by TICs are not complete. Although the places they list usually meet the set standards, if you use these lists as your only source you might miss out on a real gem.

about £15 to £25 per person. The difference between an inn and a pub is technical and not worth worrying about but just to confuse things some pubs are called hotels.

Hotels

The term hotel can be used to describe a wide range of accommodation, from simple local pubs with a few rooms to grand country houses. The term also describes medium-sized places varying widely in quality and atmosphere, which can charge from about £30/40 to more than £100/150 for a single/double. Some hotels are excellent value. Some overcharge. More details are given in the route descriptions throughout this book.

FOOD

The nature of walking in Britain means you're never more than a day's walk (two at the most) from a shop, cafe, pub or restaurant selling food. The range of meals available varies considerably, but vegetarians will be pleased to know that their choice has increased markedly in the last five years or so, with many (although not all) pubs and restaurants making a real effort to provide a choice of interesting non-meat dishes (not just omelette and quiche!).

Where to Eat

Whether out on the hills or back at base at the end of the day, walkers often have a good choice of places to eat.

Cafes In many walking areas, your route may pass a cafe (or café). In Britain, the accent is often omitted, and a British cafe (pronounced caffy, or shortened to caff) is nothing like its stylish continental European namesake. Most are simple places serving cheap, filling food at reasonable prices (£2 to £4). Cafes are always open for lunch, some until 6 or 7pm, and some also early in the morning for breakfast. Around Britain are a number of classic cafes popular with walkers and climbers and often as famous as the mountain routes nearby.

Teashops Slightly more upmarket than cafes are teashops, which serve snacks and light meals as well as tea and coffee, usually at slightly higher prices. Most have a menu in the window, so you can check the choice before entering.

Pubs Most pubs – especially those in country areas frequented by tourists – serve snacks or bar meals, and make ideal places to eat at lunchtime or in the evening after your walk. Some cheap pub food doesn't vary much from cafe fare, but many pubs offer a good, interesting menu and reasonable prices (around £5 to £7). Some pubs are closer to restaurants, with very good food and higher prices (around £10 to £12). Many pubs actually do both, with cheaper food served in the bar, and a pricier, more formal restaurant. Gourmets should consult *Good Pub Food* by Susan Nowak, listed under Books earlier in this chapter.

When walking in the British countryside you'll come across pubs that call themselves a 'Free House'. This, unfortunately, doesn't mean there's no charge for the beer. It means the pub is privately owned, not part of a chain or belonging to a large brewery.

British Breakfasts

If you stay in B&Bs or visit cafes you will encounter a phenomenon called the 'Full English Breakfast' in England, and the 'Full Breakfast' everywhere else. This consists of bacon, sausage, egg, tomatoes, mushrooms, baked beans and fried bread. In B&Bs it's proceeded by cereals, served with tea or coffee and followed by toast and marmalade. In Scotland you may get oatcakes instead of fried bread. In northern Britain (if you're really lucky) you may get black pudding – a mixture of meat and fat.

If you don't feel like eating half a farmyard it's quite OK to ask for just the egg and tomatoes. Some B&Bs offer other alternatives, such as kippers (smoked fish) or a 'continental breakfast' – which completely omits the cooked stuff and may even add something exotic like croissants.

These free houses are often worth seeking out as they tend to offer personal management, and good beer and food, whereas some chain pubs (like chain hotels) can be a bit impersonal. Pubs owned by (or 'tied' to) small local breweries are often of a similarly high quality.

For more information on British pubs, see Drinks later.

Restaurants More expensive than pubs or teashops, but usually with a wider choice, are restaurants, where prices for a main course usually start at about £5 or £6, and can rise to £10 or £15 at places that make an effort with interesting and good-quality menus. At the top of this category are the real high-class establishments, where excellent food, service and surroundings are reflected in the higher prices.

Buying Food

If you're camping or self-catering, you can buy supplies as you go. When walking, you're rarely more than a day or two from a village shop selling bread, milk, tinned or dried groceries, and fresh fruit and vegetables (although there may be little choice in the latter). Relevant shops for re-supplying on long walks are listed in the route descriptions. If your route passes a town of any size, you can also enjoy takeaways: fish and chips, baked potatoes and burgers.

DRINKS
Alcholic Drinks

The most popular alcoholic drink in Britain is beer (see the boxed text 'British Beer'), but wines and spirits are also widely available. Beer is usually served in pints, but you can ask for a 'half' (a half pint). You

---

British Beer

What the British call beer is technically 'ale' – usually brown in colour and more often called 'bitter'. What most people from the New World know as beer (usually yellow) is called 'lager' in Britain. There are some British lagers, but imported brands (including Foster's and Budweiser) have infiltrated in a big way, so foreigners can be reassured by familiar names. However, when in Britain you should definitely try some good British beer.

If you've been raised on the 'amber nectar', a traditional British bitter may come as a shock – a warm, flat and expensive shock. Part of this is to do with the way it is often served (hand pumped, not pressurised) and the climate (beer here doesn't need to be chilled). Most important, though, is its integral flavour; it doesn't need to be cold or fizzed up. (Drink a warm flat lager and you'll see it has very little actual flavour.)

And flavour is the key. Once you've got used to British beer, you can start experimenting with some of the hundreds of different regional types, all with varying textures, tastes and strengths. When these beers are served in a natural way – usually by hand pump – they are called 'real ales', and the difference between these and mass-produced lagers is the same as between fine wines and industrial plonk, or between gourmet food and a burger.

The other key feature is that these beers are 'live', and change their taste slightly while in the barrel, although they only have a shelf life of a few weeks and must be looked after properly (which is why many pubs don't serve real ale). Beware also of pubs that claim to serve real ales, but give the barrels as much care as they do the cigarette machine. There's nothing worse than a *bad* pint of real ale.

An organisation called the Campaign for Real Ale (CAMRA) promotes the sensible drinking and understanding of traditional British beer, and recommends pubs that serve good beer. Look for their endorsement sticker on pub windows, or get a copy of the very useful *Good Beer Guide* published by CAMRA (£12), which lists pubs by county and location. You can obtain more information from the Web site (**w** www.camra.org.uk).

When walking or travelling in Britain, it is well worth seeking out pubs that serve good real ale. If a pub owner looks after the beer properly, chances are everything else is well looked after too.

can also buy beer, home-produced or imported, in bottles.

The pub (along with B&Bs) is another great British institution. One of the great pleasures of walking in Britain is stopping at a pub for lunch. A pint or two is also very welcome after a good long walk on the hills. Many walkers plan a route around a midday beer, or go to a certain mountain because the nearby pub is good. There's even a range of 'pub-walk' guidebooks.

Most pubs in Britain are open from 11am to 11pm. Others open only at lunchtimes (from 11am to 3pm) and evenings (from 7 to 11pm). The bell for last orders rings at 10.45pm. On Sunday they close at 10.30pm. (These laws are likely to be relaxed over the next few years.)

You can sometimes buy takeaway drinks from a pub, but it is more usual to go to a shop or 'off-licence', where it is cheaper.

Nonalcholohic Drinks

The British are great tea drinkers, and in cafes used to walkers the tea comes in large mugs. Only in a few cafes can you get something exotic like Earl Grey or lapsang souchong, and coffee is frequently the instant type. At teashops you often have a better choice of teas (including herbal), served in cups and saucers, and the coffee may be filter or of better quality. In cafes, teashops and pubs you can get fruit juices and all the usual international brands of fizzy drink. Many pubs also serve tea and coffee at lunchtimes.

On the Walk

Even when you're walking you'll often pass a pub, cafe or shop where you can buy drinks. Even so, if you're walking for more than a few hours it is worth carrying some water. And if you're going all day without a cafe stop, then carrying water is definitely recommended – and essential in hot weather.

In high remote areas, hardy walkers drink straight from streams (some say the peaty taste in Scotland is the next best thing to whisky!), but you never know if there's a dead sheep upstream, and if you haven't got a strong constitution this isn't recommended. However, if you don't want to lug too much water with you, it is easy enough to carry some water purifying equipment. For more advice on filters and purification, see Water in the Heath & Safety chapter. Note also that in some parts of Britain, such as on high mountains and in chalk areas above the spring line, ground water can be hard to find.

One final note about pubs – some welcome walkers straight off the path; others are less keen to have mud and other countryside matters deposited on their carpets. Some pubs have a specific walkers bar with a stone floor and 'Muddy Boots Welcome' signs. Alternatively, where no such sign exists, it is perfectly acceptable to take your boots off and pad around in your socks (look for the other walkers' boots piled up on the porch), although this isn't always advisable if your morning has been a bit sweaty or you've been up to your knees in bogs!

Health & Safety

Compared to many other countries around the world, Britain has no major health hazards but there are a few things to be aware of. Keeping healthy while walking and travelling depends on your predeparture preparations, your daily health care and how you handle any medical problem that does develop. While the potential problems can seem quite frightening, in reality very few walkers in Britain experience any trouble. The sections that follow aren't intended to alarm but they are worth a skim before you go.

PREDEPARTURE PLANNING
Medical Cover

Citizens of European Union countries are covered for emergency medical care upon presentation of an E111 form, which you must get before you travel; ask at your doctor or local health service. Although the form entitles you to free treatment in government clinics and hospitals, you will have to pay for medicines and dental treatment. Once home, you may be able to recover some costs from your national health service.

Visitors from other countries will need adequate health insurance. See Travel Insurance under Documents in the Facts for the Walker chapter for details.

Immunisations

No immunisations are required for Britain but before any trip it's important to make sure you are up to date with routine vaccinations such as diphtheria, polio and, most importantly, tetanus.

First Aid

It's a good idea at any time to know the appropriate responses in the event of a major accident or illness, and it's especially important if you are intending to walk in a remote area. Consider learning basic first aid on a recognised course before you go, or including a first-aid manual with your medical kit (and reading it). Although detailed first-aid instruction is outside the scope of

this guidebook, some basic points are listed under Traumatic Injuries later in this chapter. Prevention of accidents and illness is just as important – read the Safety on the Walk section for more advice. You should also be aware of how to summon help should a major accident or illness befall you or someone with you – read the Rescue & Evacuation section.

Other Preparations

If you are concerned about your health, have a full checkup before you go. It's far better to have problems treated at home than to find out about them halfway up a mountain. It's also sensible to have a dental checkup since toothache on the trail far from help can be a miserable experience. If you wear glasses, take a spare pair and your prescription.

If you need a particular medicine, take enough with you. Take part of the packaging showing the generic name, rather than the brand, as this will make getting replacements easier. It's also a good idea to have a legible prescription or letter from your doctor to prove that you legally use the medication to avoid any problems at customs.

STAYING HEALTHY
Hygiene

To reduce the chances of contracting an illness, you should wash your hands frequently, particularly before handling or eating food. There are a number of antibacterial preparations, available at outdoor gear shops, which can be a wise investment.

Take particular care to dispose carefully of all toilet waste when you are on a walk. See the boxed text 'Do Walkers Shit in the Woods?' under Responsible Walking on p59 in the Facts for the Walker chapter.

Nutrition

A good diet is just as important (or more so) on the trail as when you're at home. Make sure your diet is well balanced, with protein, fruit, grains and carbohydrates.

Medical Kit Check List

Following is a list of items you should consider including in your medical kit – consult your pharmacist for the names of brands available in your country. Most items will be readily available in Britain:

First-Aid Supplies
☐ adhesive tape
☐ butterfly closure strips
☐ crepe bandage
☐ elasticised support bandage – for knees, ankles etc
☐ gauze swabs
☐ nonadhesive dressings
☐ scissors
☐ sterile alcohol wipes
☐ sticking plasters (Band-Aids)
☐ thermometer (note that mercury thermometers are prohibited by airlines)
☐ triangular bandage and safety pins
☐ tweezers

Medications
☐ antidiarrhoea and antinausea drugs
☐ antibiotics – consider including these if you're travelling well off the beaten track; see your doctor as they must be prescribed and carry the prescription with you
☐ antifungal cream or powder – for fungal skin infections and thrush
☐ antihistamines – for allergies, eg, hay fever; to ease the itch from insect bites or stings; and to prevent motion sickness
☐ antiseptic, eg, povidone-iodine – for cuts and grazes
☐ calamine lotion, sting relief spray or aloe vera – to ease irritation from sunburn and insect bites or stings
☐ cold and flu tablets, throat lozenges and nasal decongestant
☐ painkillers, eg, aspirin or paracetamol, or acetaminophen in the USA – for pain and fever
☐ rehydration mixture – to prevent dehydration, eg, due to severe diarrhoea; important when travelling with children

Odds & Ends
☐ eye drops
☐ insect repellent
☐ sunscreen and lip balm
☐ water purification tablets or iodine

Water

Many diseases are carried in water in the form of bacteria, protozoa, viruses, worms and insect eggs etc. When walking in Britain it's wise not to drink from streams and rivers, although many people do.

Water Purification The simplest way of purifying water is to use a chemical agent, such as chlorine and iodine, in tablet or liquid form, available from outdoor gear shops and pharmacies. Follow the recommended dosages and allow the water to stand for the correct length of time. Chlorine tablets will kill many pathogens, but not some parasites like *Giardia* and amoebic cysts. Iodine is more effective, but remember that too much iodine (regular use for several weeks) can be harmful.

Your other option is a water filter. There are two main kinds. Total filters take out all parasites, bacteria and viruses, and make water safe to drink, but they are expensive and relatively heavy – although good models weigh less than a litre of water. Simple filters (which can be a nylon mesh bag) are lighter and take out dirt and larger foreign bodies from the water so chemical solutions can work more effectively. It's very important when buying a filter to read the specifications, so you know exactly what it removes from the water and what it doesn't.

Common Ailments

Blisters This problem can be avoided. Make sure your walking boots or shoes are well worn in. At the very least, wear them on short walks before tackling longer outings, and make sure your boots fit comfortably with enough room to move your toes. Boots that are too big or small will cause blisters.

Similarly for socks – be sure they fit properly. Wear socks specifically made for walkers, with no seams rubbing. Wet and muddy socks can also cause blisters, so even on a day walk carry a spare pair. Keep your toenails clipped but not too short.

If you do feel a blister coming on, treat it sooner rather then later. Apply a sticking plaster, or preferably a special blister plaster, which acts as a second skin.

Fatigue A simple fact – walking injuries often happen towards the end of the day. While tiredness can simply be a nuisance on an easy walk, it can be life-threatening on exposed ridges or in bad weather. Never attempt a walk that is beyond your capabilities. If you feel below par, have a day off or take a bus. To reduce the risk, don't push yourself too hard – take rests every hour or two and build in a good lunch break. Towards the end of the day, turn down the pace and increase your concentration. You should also eat properly throughout the day to replace energy used. Things like nuts, dried fruit and chocolate are all good, high-energy food.

Knee Pain Many walkers feel the judder on long steep descents. When dropping steeply, to reduce the strain on the knee joint (you can't eliminate it) try taking shorter steps which leave your legs slightly bent and ensure that your heel hits the ground first and you roll your foot forward naturally, as you would when walking on level ground.

Some walkers find that tubular bandages help, while others use hi-tech, strap-on supports. Walking poles are very effective in taking some of the weight off the knees.

MEDICAL PROBLEMS & TREATMENT
Environmental Hazards

Walkers are at more risk than most groups from environmental hazards such as sun and snow. The risk, however, can be significantly reduced by applying common sense.

Sun Protection against the sun should always be taken seriously, particularly in the rarefied air and deceptive coolness of the mountains.

Warning

Self-diagnosis and treatment can be risky, so you should always seek medical help. An embassy, consulate or five-star hotel can usually recommend a local doctor or clinic. Note that we have used generic rather than brand names for drugs throughout this section – check with a pharmacist for locally available brands.

Slap on the sunscreen and a barrier cream for your nose and lips, wear a broad-brimmed hat whenever the sun appears and protect your eyes with good-quality sunglasses, particularly when walking near water or snow.

Dehydration Dehydration is a potentially dangerous and generally preventable condition. Sweating and inadequate fluid intake are the most common causes in walkers, but other important causes include diarrhoea and vomiting – see Diarrhoea later. The first symptoms are weakness, thirst and passing small amounts of very concentrated urine. This may progress to drowsiness, dizziness or fainting, and finally coma.

It's easy to forget how much fluid you are losing via perspiration while you are walking, particularly if a strong breeze is drying your skin quickly. You should always maintain a good fluid intake – a minimum of 3L a day is recommended.

Cold Too much cold can be just as dangerous as too much heat. This is particularly relevant when walking in winter – especially in Scotland or other mountainous areas.

Hypothermia If the body loses heat faster than it can produce it hypothermia occurs. It is surprisingly easy to get dangerously cold due to a combination of wind, wet clothing, fatigue and hunger, even if the air temperature is above freezing. Adequate clothing, food and drink (and a 'space blanket' or 'bivvy bag' for emergencies) are essential.

Symptoms of hypothermia are exhaustion, numb skin (particularly toes and fingers), shivering, blue or grey pallor, slurred speech, irrational or violent behaviour, lethargy, stumbling, dizzy spells, muscle cramps and violent bursts of energy. Irrationality may take the form of sufferers claiming they are warm and trying to take off their clothes.

To treat mild hypothermia, first get the sufferer out of the wind and/or rain, remove their clothing if it's wet and replace it with dry, warm clothing. Give them hot liquids – not alcohol – and some high-energy, easily digestible food. Do not rub victims; instead, allow them to slowly warm themselves. The recognition and treatment of mild hypothermia is the only way to prevent severe hypothermia, which is a critical condition.

Infectious Diseases

Diarrhoea Simple things like a change of water, food or climate can cause mild diarrhoea, but a few rushed toilet trips with no other symptoms is not indicative of a major problem. More serious diarrhoea is caused by infectious agents transmitted by faecal contamination of food or water, or from one person's hand to another. Paying particular attention to personal hygiene, drinking clean water and taking care of what you eat are important measures to take to avoid this.

Dehydration is the main danger. Under all circumstances *fluid replacement* (at least equal to the volume lost) is essential. Clean water is best but weak black tea with a little sugar, or soft drinks allowed to go flat and diluted 50% with clean water are all good. With severe diarrhoea a rehydrating solution is preferable to replace minerals and salts lost. If you have small amounts of concentrated urine, you need to drink more. Keep drinking small amounts often.

Gut-paralysing drugs such as diphenoxylate or loperamide can be used to bring relief from symptoms, although they do not actually cure the problem. Only use these drugs if you do not have access to toilets, eg, if you *must* travel. These drugs are not recommended if you have a high fever or are severely dehydrated.

In certain situations antibiotics may be required. In Britain you are never more than a day from a doctor, so seek medical advice rather than self-administering.

Fungal Infections Sweating liberally, probably washing less than usual, and going longer without a change of clothes can mean long-distance walkers risk picking up fungal infections. While an unpleasant irritant, this presents no danger. To avoid this wear loose, comfortable clothes, wash when you can and dry yourself thoroughly. Try to expose the infected area to air or sunlight as much as possible and apply an antifungal cream or powder like tolnaftate.

Traumatic Injuries

Sprains Ankle and knee sprains are common injuries for walkers, particularly when crossing rugged terrain. To help prevent ankle sprains in these circumstances, you should wear boots with adequate ankle support. If you suffer a serious sprain, immobilise the joint with a firm bandage, and relieve pain and swelling by keeping the joint elevated for 24 hours and, where possible, by using ice or a cold compress. Take simple painkillers to ease the discomfort. If the sprain is mild, you may be able to continue your walk after a couple of days. For more severe sprains, seek medical attention, as you may need an X-ray to rule out the possibility of a broken bone.

Major Accident Falling or having something fall on you, resulting in head injuries or fractures (broken bones), is always possible when walking, especially if you are crossing steep slopes or unstable terrain. Following is some basic advice on what to do if a person suffers a major fall:

- make sure you and other people with you are not in danger
- assess the injured person's condition
- stabilise any injuries
- seek medical attention as soon as possible – see the Rescue & Evacuation section later

If the person is unconscious, immediately check they are breathing – clear their airway if it is blocked – and have a pulse by feeling the side of the neck rather than the wrist. If they are not breathing but have a pulse, you should start mouth-to-mouth resuscitation immediately. Move the sufferer as little as possible in case their neck or back is broken, and keep them warm; insulate them from the ground if possible.

Check for wounds and broken bones. Control any bleeding by applying firm pressure to the wound. Bleeding from the nose or ear may indicate a fractured skull. Don't give the person anything by mouth, especially if they are unconscious.

Indications of a fracture are pain, swelling and discolouration, loss of function or deformity of a limb. Don't try to straighten a

Everyday Health

Normal body temperature is up to 37°C (98.6°F); more than 2°C (4°F) higher indicates a high fever. The normal adult pulse rate is 60 to 100 beats per minute (children 80 to 100, babies 100 to 140). As a general rule the pulse increases about 20 beats per minute for each 1°C (2°F) rise in fever.

Respiration (breathing) rate is also an indicator of illness. Count the number of breaths per minute: between 12 and 20 is normal for adults and older children (up to 30 for younger children, 40 for babies). People with a high fever or serious respiratory illness breathe more quickly than normal. More than 40 shallow breaths a minute may indicate pneumonia.

displaced broken bone. Nondisplaced broken bones can be splinted. Fractures associated with open wounds (compound fractures) require more urgent treatment as there is a risk of infection. Dislocations, where the bone has come out of the joint, are very painful and should be treated as soon as possible.

Broken ribs are painful but usually heal by themselves and do not need splinting. If breathing difficulties occur, or the person coughs up blood, medical attention should be sought urgently, as it may indicate a punctured lung.

Internal injuries are more difficult to detect and, if suspected, medical attention should sought urgently. Watch for shock, which is a specific medical condition associated with a failure to maintain circulating blood volume. Signs include a rapid pulse and cold, clammy extremities. A person in shock requires urgent medical attention.

Some general points to bear in mind are:

* Simple fractures take weeks to heal, so don't need fixing straight away but should be immobilised to protect from further jury. Compound fractures need much more urgent treatment.
* If you splint a broken bone, check regularly that the splint is not cutting off the circulation to the hand or foot.
* Most cases of brief unconsciousness are not associated with any serious internal injury to the brain but any person who has been knocked

unconscious should be watched for deterioration. The sufferer should get a medical checkup within a few days and if there is any sign of deterioration, medical attention should be sought straight away.

Cuts & Scratches

Even small cuts and grazes should be washed well and treated with an antiseptic. Dry wounds heal more quickly, so where possible avoid bandages and sticking plasters, which can keep wounds wet. Infection in a wound is indicated by the skin margins becoming red, painful and swollen. More serious infection can cause swelling of the whole limb and of the lymph glands. In this case seek medical attention.

Burns

Immerse the burnt area in cold water as soon as possible, then cover it with a clean, dry sterile dressing. Keep this in place with plasters for a day or so in the case of a small, mild burn, but longer for more extensive injuries. Medical help should be sought for severe and extensive burns.

Bites & Stings

There are very few biting and stinging things to worry about when walking in Britain. Midges are an annoyance (see the boxed text 'Midges' under When to Walk on p47 in the Facts for the Walker chapter) but not actually a health risk.

Bees & Wasps Bee and wasp stings are usually painful rather than dangerous. However, in people who are allergic to them severe breathing difficulties may occur and urgent medical care is required. Calamine lotion or sting relief spray will ease discomfort and ice packs will reduce the pain and swelling.

Ticks If you're walking through dry, grassy areas where animals graze there is a chance small biting insects called ticks may attach themselves to you. They can cling for hours or even days and can cause skin infections, so you should check all over your body if you have been walking through potentially tick-infested areas.

If found, press down around the tick's head with tweezers, grab the head and gently pull upwards. Avoid pulling the rear of the body as this may squeeze the tick's gut contents into you, increasing the risk of infection. Smearing chemicals on the tick will not make it let go and is not recommended.

Women's Health

Antibiotic use, synthetic underwear, sweating and contraceptive pills can lead to fungal vaginal infections, especially when walking or travelling in hot conditions. Fungal infections are characterised by a rash, itch and discharge and are usually treated by nystatin, miconazole or clotrimazole pessaries or vaginal cream. Maintaining good personal hygiene and wearing loose-fitting clothes and cotton underwear may help prevent these infections.

SAFETY ON THE WALK

By taking a few simple precautions, you'll reduce significantly the odds of getting into trouble while walking in Britain. See the boxed text 'Walk Safety – Basic Rules' for a list of simple precautions to take. For information on the clothes and equipment you should take with you when walking, consult Clothing & Equipment in the Facts for the Walker chapter.

Dangers

You're very unlikely to be mugged in the British countryside, although some long routes (eg, the Thames Path) do pass through towns and cities where the usual precautions for urban areas should be taken. Generally, though, walking in Britain is an easy and enjoyable way to see the country and, with correct planning, it is remarkably free of danger. However, the more remote high routes we describe in this book are not suitable for novices. If you are new to walking it is better to start on some of the easier lowland walks described in this book or consider improving your skills by joining a course before heading for lofty summits.

Other dangers to watch out for when walking through farmland are the temporary electric fences. These are designed to control cattle but they are often placed near (or across) footpaths. They are often no more than a thin strand of wire and can be difficult to see, but they pack a punch, so beware. It's actually illegal for farmers to put electric fences (or any barrier) across a right of way.

In farmland too, watch out for untethered guard dogs and dangerous bulls. The Ramblers' Association advises you treat both with caution. If confronted, back away slowly and report the situation to police if you consider it dangerous to the point of being unlawful.

Some walks described in this book cross areas of land that are used by the army for training. When manoeuvres are under way live ammunition may be used, so walkers are not allowed to enter. Red warning flags are raised around the area at these times. There are usually noticeboards too, which list the days and times that the area is closed to the public. When the red flags are not flying you can cross the land, but you should still keep to paths and beware of unidentifiable metal objects lying in the grass. If you do find anything suspicious, don't touch it. Make a note of the position and report it to the police after your walk.

Crossing Rivers

While walking in mountain areas you may have to ford a river or stream swollen with floodwater or snowmelt. Trying to cross a

fast, deep river is risky and potentially fatal. The first rule is: Don't cross it. Wait for a while to see if the water goes down or go upstream to check for a safer crossing place. If this doesn't work, and you really *have* to get across, there are many ways to go about this. Some tips and methods are described below:

• Look for the widest part of the river, where the river will flow more slowly.
• Loosen your backpack straps, so if you slip, you can shrug it off and not be pulled under.
• A common river-crossing practice for a group of people is to face upstream and cross 'crab-wise'. One person should stand behind the other, holding the person in front at the waist – it's much harder for the water to knock you over this way.
• If you're fording alone, plant a stick or your walking poles upstream to give you greater stability and help you lean against the current. Walk side-on to the direction of flow so that your body presents less of an obstacle to the rushing water.

Lightning

If a storm brews, avoid exposed areas. Lightning has a penchant for crests, lone trees, small depressions, gullies, caves and cabin entrances, as well as wet ground. If you are caught out in the open, try to curl up as tightly as possible with your feet together and keep a layer of insulation between you and the ground. Place metal objects, such as metal-frame backpacks and walking poles, away from you.

Rescue & Evacuation

If someone in your group is injured and can't move, leave a member of the party with them while another one or more goes for help. If there are only two of you, leave the injured person with as much warm clothing, food and water as it's sensible to spare, plus the whistle and torch. Take careful written note of the location (including a map reference) and mark the position with something conspicuous – an orange bivvy bag or perhaps a large stone cross on the ground.

If you need to call for help, use these internationally recognised emergency signals. Give six short signals, using a whistle, a yell or the flash of a light, at 10-second intervals, followed by a minute of rest. Repeat the sequence until you get a response. The response is three signals at 20-second intervals, followed by a minute's pause.

If possible you should get to a telephone. Public phones in country areas are marked on maps, but in *real* emergency situations the owners of remote farms or houses will let you use theirs. Dial ☎ 999 (the national emergency number – free of charge) and ask for the headquarters of the police in the area where you are (eg, North Wales, the Lake District). The police will coordinate with the appropriate mountain rescue service, and possibly with army or air force helicopters. Be ready to give information on where an accident occurred (including that all-important map reference), how many people are injured and the injuries sustained. If ringing from a mobile phone, don't forget to leave your own number for further contact.

Remember that most mountain rescue teams in Britain are staffed by volunteers. These teams get some commercial sponsorship but are funded by donations from the public. You'll notice collection boxes in pubs and cafes in mountain areas, and even if you've come down safely you may want to make a small donation of a pound or two.

Mobile Phones

If you're using a mobile phone (cell phone), they are, of course, very useful in emergency situations but remember that they may not get a signal in remote areas, especially if you're in a valley. It's very important to use the mobile *only* in genuine emergencies. There are too many stories of people using their mobile phone to call the mountain rescue team because they are simply lost or have forgotten their sandwiches.

A Final Word

Much of the above may sound pretty daunting. That's good. With a bit of luck it will make you respect the mountains and have a safe time while you're exploring them. Most of the advice comes down to common sense, so with some of that and some preparation or training if required, you should be fine.

Getting There & Away

AIR
Airports & Airlines

London's Heathrow and Gatwick are the main airports for intercontinental flights. A few flights from North America and Asia also go to Manchester, and some flights to/from North America go to Glasgow.

Flights from Europe arrive at Heathrow and Gatwick, as well as London's other airports (Stanstead, Luton and London City) and other airports throughout Britain, such as Manchester, Birmingham, Edinburgh and Glasgow.

Most major airlines (and a lot of the more obscure ones too) have services between Britain and most parts of the world. For flights to/from other European countries, also look out for the new breed of discount, no-frills airlines, such as Buzz (☎ 0870-240 7070, W www.buzzaway.com), Go (☎ 0845-605 4321, W www.go-fly.com), easyJet (☎ 0870-600 0000, W www.easyjet.com) and Ryanair (☎ 0870-156 9569, W www.ryanair.com). Note, however, that it's possible these airlines may not continue such bargain basement prices into the unforeseen future. Bear in mind also that some of the European airports Ryanair flies to are secondary fields far from the cities they claim to serve. Always check where they really fly to and what transport links are available. These discount airlines are not usually on travel agents' computerised reservations systems or travel Web sites such as W www.travelocity.com and W www.expedia.com. To check their fares you'll have to call their reservation numbers or visit their Web sites (which often have extra discounts for tickets bought on the Internet).

Buying Tickets

When you're looking for air fares, go to a travel agent rather than directly to the airline (unless it's one of the low-cost carriers). From time to time, airlines do have promotional fares and special offers, but generally they only sell fares at the official listed price. For an idea of what travel agents offer (and how to contact them) check the adverts in travel magazines or weekend newspapers.

The other option is to book on the Internet; many airlines (full-service and no-frills) offer some excellent fares to Web surfers. However, online super-fast fare generators are no substitute for a travel agent who knows all about special deals, has strategies for avoiding stopovers and can offer advice on everything from airline vegetarian food to travel insurance.

The days when some travel agents would routinely fleece travellers by running off with their money are, happily, almost over. Paying by credit card sometimes offers protection, as most card issuers provide refunds if you can prove you didn't get what you paid for. Similar protection can be obtained by buying a ticket from a bonded agent, such as one covered by the Air Transport Operators License (ATOL) scheme in the UK. Agents who only accept cash should hand over the tickets straight away and not tell you to 'come back tomorrow'.

Warning

The information in this chapter is particularly vulnerable to change: prices for international travel are volatile, routes are introduced and cancelled, schedules change, special deals come and go, and rules and visa requirements are amended. Airlines and governments seem to take a perverse pleasure in making price structures and regulations as complicated as possible. You should make sure you understand how a fare (and ticket you may buy) works, and get opinions, quotes and advice from as many airlines and travel agents as possible before you part with your hard-earned cash. The details given in this chapter should be regarded as pointers only and are not a substitute for your own careful and up-to-date research.

After you've made a booking or paid your deposit, call the airline and confirm that the booking was made. It's generally not advisable to send money (even cheques) through the post unless the agent is very well established – some travellers have reported being ripped off by fly-by-night mail-order ticket agents.

You may decide to pay more than the rock-bottom fare by opting for the safety of a better known travel agent. Firms such as STA Travel, which has offices worldwide, Council Travel in the USA and Travel CUTS in Canada are not going to disappear overnight and they do offer good prices to most destinations.

After purchasing your ticket, if you want to change your route (most tickets don't allow this) or dates, you can contact the airline or the nearest branch of your travel agent. Airlines only issue refunds to the purchaser of a ticket – usually the travel agent who bought the ticket on your behalf. Many travellers change their routes halfway through their trips, so think carefully before you buy a ticket that is not easily changed or refunded.

Travellers with Special Needs

Most international airlines can cater to people with special needs – travellers with disabilities, people with young children and even children travelling alone. Travellers with special dietary requirements (vegetarian, kosher, etc) can request appropriate meals. If you have any special needs let the airline know as soon as possible so they can make arrangements. Remind them when you reconfirm your booking and again when you check in at the airport.

Airlines usually allow babies up to two years of age to fly for 10% of the adult fare, although a few may allow them free of charge. Reputable international airlines usually provide nappies (diapers), tissues, talcum and all the other paraphernalia needed to keep babies clean, dry and half-happy. For children aged between two and 12, the fare on international flights is usually 50% of the regular fare or 67% of a discounted fare.

Departure Tax

All domestic flights and those to destinations within the European Union (EU) from Britain carry a £10 departure tax. For flights to cities outside the EU you pay £20. This is usually built into the price of your ticket.

Ireland

On air routes between Britain and Ireland, competition means you can usually get a discount ticket for as little as £50.

Continental Europe

For flights between Britain and continental Europe there is not much variation in fares between London and the main European cities, but there can be a big range of prices to any one destination. Fares can vary according to season, time and the special offers available. Expect to pay the equivalent of about £50 to £200 (both one way and return) on major airlines or a bit less on low-cost carriers. Travel agents generally have a number of deals on offer, so shop around.

The USA & Canada

There's a lot of competition on flights between the USA and Britain. Fares on major airlines flying between London and the US east coast start at US$300 in winter (December to February), US$400 in spring (March to May) and autumn (September to November), and US$600 in summer (June to August). From the west coast fares are about US$100 higher. Air fares to/from Canada tend to be about 10% higher than those sold in the USA.

Australia & New Zealand

There are a lot of competing airlines and a wide variety of air fares for flights between Europe and Australasia. Expect to pay anywhere from A$1800 in the low season to A$3000 in the high season for return tickets. Round-the-world (RTW) tickets are often real bargains and can sometimes work out cheaper than a return flight, especially from New Zealand.

Africa

Nairobi (Kenya) and Johannesburg are probably the best places in East and South

Africa to buy tickets. Some major airlines have offices in Nairobi, which is a good place to determine the standard fare before you make the rounds of the travel agencies. Getting several quotes is a sensible idea as prices are always changing. As a rough guide, return tickets from Johannesburg start at US$1500.

LAND
Border Crossings
Britain is an island and the border is the coast! (The UK's only land border is between Northern Ireland and the Republic of Ireland.) Upon entering Britain you'll find the usual array of immigration officers, passport controls and customs posts. There are also borders between England, Scotland and Wales but no customs or immigration to deal with.

Bus
You can travel between Britain and continental Europe by long-distance bus (called a coach in Britain). The coach either drives onto the train and gets carried through the Channel Tunnel or it uses a ferry (included in the ticket price). Eurolines (☎ 0870-514 3219, Ⓦ www.eurolines.com), a division of National Express, has an enormous network of European destinations, with a main office in London and agents all over Europe. Nearly all services arrive in London's Victoria Station, from where you can get onward services to all parts of England, Scotland and Wales (see the Getting Around chapter for details).

Long-distance buses are slower and less comfortable than trains, but they are cheaper, especially if you qualify for the discount available to people under 25 or over 60.

Some sample one-way/return adult fares and journey times are: Amsterdam £32/45 (nine hours), Barcelona £79/111 (22 to 24 hours), Berlin £39/65 (22½ hours), Brussels £32/45 (seven hours) and Dublin £24/44 (11 hours).

At peak times in summer (when you should add between 5% and 10% to the above fares), you should make reservations a few days in advance. Also note that on

trips from places such as Barcelona, you'll pay the same price and save about 20 hours and lots of sanity by getting a special fare with a discount airline.

Train
Eurostar (in the UK ☎ 0990-186186, in France ☎ 08 36 35 35 39, Ⓦ www.eurostar .com) is a high-speed passenger train that runs through the Channel Tunnel between London and Paris or Brussels, with stops in Lille and Calais in France and Ashford in England. The trains run around 16 times a day and the journey takes about three hours to/from Paris (less to/from Brussels).

You can buy tickets from travel agencies, major train stations or by phoning Eurostar directly. The Eurostar Web site often has special deals. The second-class one-way fare from Paris or Brussels is an eye-opening £110. While the price is similar to the airlines, there are numerous special and discount fares. It's not uncommon for there to be a £79 return fare. There are also discount fares for children and those aged 12 to 25 or more than 60.

Slower but much cheaper train services run from London to various European destinations, with a ferry ride in between. (Trains go to a port where you catch a ferry, then board another train on the other side.)

Car & Motorcycle
Thanks to the Channel Tunnel you can now 'drive' between Britain and Europe. In fact what you actually do is drive to a terminal, drive onto a shuttle train, effectively a rolling road, which carries you through the Tunnel, then drive off the other end. These shuttle trains run 24 hours a day, departing up to four times an hour in each direction from 6am to 10pm, and every hour between 10pm and 6am. Eurotunnel terminals are clearly signposted and connected to motorway networks. British and French customs and immigration formalities are carried out before you drive on to Eurotunnel. Travel time from motorway to motorway, including loading and unloading, is one hour; the shuttle itself takes 35 minutes. A one-way trip during high season for a car and its

passengers costs from £130, and for a motorcycle the cost is around £72. You can make an advance reservation (☎ 0870-535 3535, **W** www.eurotunnel.com) or pay by cash or credit card at a check-in booth.

If you're coming from Europe by car, there are motorways from all the main ferry ports and the Channel Tunnel that converge on the M25 motorway around London. You can use this (often clogged) artery to skirt the city and drive on to other destinations.

SEA

There's a bewildering array of ships sailing between Britain and continental Europe, which you can use with a car or as a foot passenger. Eurotunnel and low-fare airlines mean ferry fares are often quite competitive – although structures are very complex and vary according to time of day or year, length of stay and the size of car (if you're driving). Return tickets may well be much cheaper than two one-way fares; vehicle tickets seem costly but may also cover driver and passengers.

Most ferries from continental Europe serve the ports on the southern coast of Britain, and

several serve ports such as Hull and Newcastle in northern England – very handy if this is where you're heading for walking.

You will definitely have to plan ahead to find the best deals. Because of the wide array of fares, the listings below are limited to high-season return fares for a single foot passenger and one car plus driver (unless otherwise stated).

Ireland

There's a great variety of ferry services from Ireland to Britain using modern car ferries. From south to north, ferry possibilities include the following:

Cork to Swansea Swansea Cork Ferries has a 10-hour crossing that costs £68/378 (for up to five people and one car). It operates several times each week mid-March to early November.

Rosslare to Fishguard & Pembroke To/from Pembroke, Irish Ferries has two daily crossings that take just under four hours. The fares are £20/179. To/from Fishguard, Stena Line has two daily regular ferries that take 3½ hours and cost £40/179. The frequent catamaran service takes under two hours and costs £50/209.

Ferry Companies Serving Britain

Europe to Britain

Brittany Ferries	☎ 0870-901 2400	**W** www.brittany-ferries.co.uk
DFDS Seaways	☎ 0870-533 3000	**W** www.dfdsseaways.co.uk
Fjord Line	☎ 0191-296 1313	**W** www.fjordline.no
Hoverspeed	☎ 0870-240 8070	**W** www.hoverspeed.co.uk
P&O European Ferries	☎ 0870-242 4999	**W** www.poef.com
P&O North Sea Ferries	☎ 01482-377177	**W** www.ponsf.com
P&O Scottish Ferries	☎ 01224-572615	**W** www.poscottishferries.co.uk
P&O Stena Line	☎ 0870-600 0600	**W** www.posl.com
Smyril Line	☎ 01224-572615 (UK agent)	**W** www.smyril-line.fo
Stena Line	☎ 0870-570 7070	**W** www.stenaline.com

Ireland to Britain

Irish Ferries	☎ 0870-517 1717	**W** www.irishferries.ie
P&O Irish Sea	☎ 0870-242 4777	**W** www.poirishsea.com
Sea Containers Ferries	☎ 0870-552 3523	**W** www.steam-packet.com
Stena Line (see above)		
Swansea Cork Ferries	☎ 01792-456116	**W** www.swansea-cork.ie

Dublin & Dun Laoghaire to Holyhead Irish Ferries has two daily slow ferries to/from Dublin that take a little over three hours and cost £40/189. Fast ferries travel four times daily, take two hours and cost £50/239. Stena Line has several slow ferries a day to/from Dublin that take 3¾ hours and cost £184 (foot passengers not accepted). Stena fast ferries go to/from Dun Laoghaire in less than two hours and cost £50/229.

Dublin to Liverpool Sea Containers Ferries has daily catamaran services, which take 3¾ hours and cost £50/249.

Belfast to Stranraer Stena Line has several daily slow ferries, costing £40/189 for the three-hour trip. The frequent fast ferry service, taking only 1¾ hours, costs slightly more.

Belfast to Troon Sea Containers Ferries has several daily catamarans, charging £50/249 for the 2½-hour trip.

Larne to Cairnryan P&O Irish Sea has at least two daily slow ferries, which take 2¼ hours and cost £42/238. Frequent fast ferries cost £50/290 and take one hour.

France

The shortest ferry link is between Dover or Folkestone and Calais or Boulogne. P&O Stena Line ferries take one hour and 15 minutes and cost £48/321. Hoverspeed's Seacats (large catamarans) take 45 minutes from Dover to Calais (£48/330) and 55 minutes from Folkestone to Boulogne (£48/298).

Hoverspeed catamarans between Dieppe and Newhaven are £56/360.

P&O European Ferries run between Portsmouth and Cherbourg or Le Havre, and take five to six hours (seven to eight hours at night). Fares for both are £60/190.

Spain

From Plymouth, Brittany Ferries operates at least one ferry a week to Santander, on Spain's north coast. The journey time is 24 hours; fares cost £154/460.

P&O European Ferries operates a service twice a week between Bilbao and Portsmouth (35 hours). Fares cost £100/440.

Scandinavia

Until you see the ferry possibilities, it's easy to forget how close Scandinavia and Britain are. This is why Nordic kings once ruled parts of northern Britain, and why the

Vikings found British villages so convenient for pillaging.

One of the most interesting boat possibilities is between Bergen (Norway) and Shetland, from where you can reach mainland Scotland. Smyril Line operates a weekly ship from late May to early September. The trip costs £40 for each foot passenger travelling one way, accommodation is in a berth, and it takes about 13 hours.

Norway's Fjord Line operates ferries all year between Newcastle in northern England and Stavanger or Bergen in Norway. They sail three times a week in summer and twice-weekly at other times. The journey takes 20 hours or 27 hours, respectively. The fare for foot passengers is about £200.

DFDS Seaways has two to three ferries a week between Harwich and Esbjerg (Denmark), a 20-hour trip. Fares are £168/276 and include a berth in an economy cabin.

The Rest of Continental Europe

Hoverspeed operates Seacat catamarans between Dover and Oostende (Belgium) at least three times a day (£28/215, two hours).

DFDS Seaways has three ferries a week between Harwich and Hamburg, Germany (£168/276, 20 hours). The fare includes a berth in an economy cabin. Stena Line has two fast ferries a day between Harwich and Hoek van Holland, near Rotterdam in the Netherlands (£44/260, four hours).

P&O North Sea Ferries sail daily between Hull and Rotterdam (13 hours) or Zeebrugge in Belgium (13½ hours). Fares on both routes cost £81/136.

DFDS Seaways has daily services between Newcastle and IJmuiden, near Amsterdam in the Netherlands (£118/256, 15 hours). The fare includes a berth in an economy cabin.

WALKING HOLIDAYS

Most of the British walking holiday companies listed under Guided Walks in the Facts for the Walker chapter cater for visitors from overseas, who use Web sites for information and book by email. If you prefer to arrange a trip through a company based in your own country, the following outfits may serve as a good start point:

Continental Europe

Active Tours (☎ 8374-589 9525, fax 5899 530, e info@activetours.de, w www.activetours.de) Alpenrosenweg 20 D-87463 Dietmannsried, Germany. Adventure trips worldwide, including a range of walking holidays in Britain.

The USA

As well as the companies listed below, have a look at the following Web sites, which list a large number of companies offering a range of activites: w www.adventureseek.com, w www.away.com and w www.journeyquest.com. The prices of walking tours arranged in the USA vary enormously according to the length of the trip and the type of accommodation provided, but as a very rough guide you can expect to pay around US$1000 for a week.

Backroads (☎ 510-527 1555, fax 510-527 1444, w www.backroads.com) 801 Cedar St, Berkeley, California 94710-1800. Walking tour company offering a six-day trip to the Cotswolds.

Country Walkers (☎ 800-464 9255, 888-742 0770, e info@countrywalkers.com, w www.countrywalkers.com) PO Box 180, Waterbury VT 05676. A worldwide company with tours in Cornwall, the Cotswolds and the Lake District.

Cross Country International Walking Tours (☎ 1800-828 8768, fax 914-677 6077, e xcintl@aol.com, w www.walkingvacations.com) PO Box 1170, Millbrook, NY 12545. A good range of walking holidays all over Britain, including the Lake District, Cornwall, the Cotswolds, Yorkshire and a Scottish castles walk.

English Lakeland Rambler (☎ 800-724 8801, 212-505 1020, e britwalks@aol.com, w www.ramblers.com) 18 Stuyvesant Oval, New York NY 10009. A good range of tours in the Lake District, plus (despite the name) Scotland and the Cotswolds.

Great Outdoors Recreation Pages (GORP; ☎ 1877-440 4677, fax 303-444 3999, e info@gorptravel.com, w www.gorp.com) PO Box 1486, Boulder, Colorado 80306. A major travel holiday company offering numerous walking trips of varying duration to destinations in England and Scotland.

Walking the World (☎ 800-340 9255, 970-498 0500, e walkingtheworld@aol.com, w www.walkingtheworld.com) PO Box 1186, Fort Collins CO 80522. A specialist in holidays for over-50s with walks in many countries, including England and Wales.

Wilderness Travel (☎ 800-368 2794, fax 510 558 2489, e info@wildernesstravel.com, w www.wildernesstravel.com) 1102 Ninth St, Berkeley, California 94710-1211. A major adventure tour operator with a small selection of walks in the Lake District and Scotland.

Australia

Adventure World (☎ 02-9956 7766, fax 9956 7707, e sydney@adventure.world.com.au, w www.adventureworld.com.au) 73 Walker St, North Sydney, NSW 2060. An adventure travel specialist with a small range of walking tours, including some in Britain.

Ecotrek: Bogong Jack Adventure (☎ 08-8383 7198, fax 7377) PO Box 4, Kangarilla SA 5157. Adventure trips around the world, including a range of walking holidays to the Lake District, Yorkshire Dales and on the Coast to Coast path.

Getting Around

This chapter outlines your options for getting to – or between – the various walking areas. Specific details on getting to the start of (and away from) walks are given in the individual chapters. It's worth emphasising that just about every walk in this book can be reached by public transport, although in a few areas it's by a once-weekly bus or something equally rare, and you'll need determination and some skilful deciphering of timetables to get where you want to go. Mostly, though, the walks of Britain can easily be reached by bus or train (and sometimes boat), which is particularly useful for visitors and for anyone else who just wants to leave the car at home. In some national parks public transport is positively promoted and you can reach even quite obscure areas with remarkable ease.

Generally speaking your options for getting around Britain are: long-distance buses, nearly always the cheapest option for long journeys; trains, quicker but more expensive; and planes, even more expensive and rarely necessary. For local travel (eg, reaching the start of a walk from the nearest town), bus travel is normally your only option, although you may also use a taxi.

Public transport in Britain is mostly of a high standard, but through the 1980s and much of the 1990s government policies favoured road transport, allocating billions of pounds each year to the construction of new roads. There has been only the slightest shift in policy in the years since the late 1990s. The result is reduced, although slowly improving, public rail and bus services, particularly in country areas.

For walkers, using public transport has advantages. You can take a bus or train to the starting point, do a linear walk for as many hours or days as you like, then return by bus or train from the other end, with no worries about parking or returning to a car.

One thing to remember when asking locals for public transport information is that those with cars are often unaware that their own town or village is quite well served, and will blissfully tell you there is 'one bus a week' when there are actually three or four per day. Always contact Tourist Information Centres (TICs) or travel information phone lines for details.

You can get good brochures and leaflets public transport options from your nearest British Tourist Authority (BTA) office – see

National Transport Information

All public transport in Britain is privately (as opposed to state) owned. The railway system was reorganised recently and is now a fairly complicated setup, with 27 separate companies running services. Obtaining accurate bus and coach information can be equally confusing, with many small bus companies operating locally. Your best option is to contact one of the following telephone numbers or Web sites for transport and travel information across Britain.

Bus
National Express
   ☎ 0870-580 8080
   w www.gobycoach.com

Train
Railtrack
   w www.railtrack.co.uk
National Rail Enquiry Service
   ☎ 0845-748 4950
   w www.nationalrail.co.uk
The Trainline
   w www.thetrainline.com

General
UK Public Transport Information
   ☎ 0870-608 2608
   w www.pti.org.uk
Countrygoer
   w www.countrygoer.org
Train, Bus and Coach Hotline
   ☎ 0906-891 0910

Tourist Offices in the Facts for the Walker chapter. Especially useful is *Scenic Britain by Bus* – full of tips and route suggestions.

AIR
Domestic Air Services
Most cities in Britain are linked to London by air, but unless you're travelling very long distances (eg, from the south of England to the north of Scotland), planes are only marginally quicker than trains once you include the time it takes to get to/from airports.

The main operators of domestic flights are British Airways, British Midland, KLM uk, easyJet, Go and Ryanair. Their prices vary enormously according to when you fly and when you buy the ticket, but travel agents can guide you through the maze (although some of the bargain airlines deal directly with the public by phone or on-line – see the Getting There & Away chapter for contact details). For example, a return ticket from London to Edinburgh on British Airways costs from around £120 on special to around £270 full fare. British Midland generally has cheaper flights, especially on weekdays, although they may also have more restrictions. Easy-Jet flights between London and Edinburgh

---

Domestic Airline Reservations

British Airways
  ☎ 0845-773 3377
  w www.british-airways.com
British Midland
  ☎ 0870-607 0555
  w www.britishmidland.com
easyJet
  ☎ 0870-600 0000
  w www.easyjet.com
Go
  ☎ 0845-605 4321
  w www.go-fly.com
KLM uk
  ☎ 0870-507 4074
  w www.klmuk.com
Ryanair
  ☎ 0870-156 9569
  w www.ryanair.com

---

start at £29 but you have to be quick to get them; you'll more likely pay £59 to £79.

BUS
Long-Distance Buses
Public road transport in Britain is nearly all privately owned. National Express (☎ 0870-580 8080, w www.gobycoach.com) runs the largest national network of long-distance buses (called 'coaches' in Britain), which serve all of England and Wales. Scotland's long-distance coaches are run by Scottish Citylink (☎ 0870-550 5050, w www.citylink.co.uk), which is part of the National Express group and ties in with National Express services in Northern England.

Most useful for walkers from overseas who want to fly in and head straight for the hills are the National Express services direct from Heathrow and Gatwick airports to all parts of Britain, bypassing central London. These are more expensive but, weighed against the extra cost and hassle of going into London and out again (possibly staying overnight), are good value. If you arrive in the late evening and the coach to your walking destination doesn't leave until the next morning, it may be worth staying in a hotel near the airport.

Details of local bus services are under Local Transport at the end of this chapter.

Bus Passes
National Express and Scottish Citylink share several passes. The Discount Coach Card costs £9 per year and offers 30% off fares for full-time students and those aged 16 to 25, or 60 plus. International Student Identity Cards (ISIC) or passports are accepted as proof of age. The National Express Travel Pass allows unlimited coach travel within a specified period. It's available to all overseas visitors but it must be bought outside Britain, usually from a Eurolines agent. The cost ranges from five days for £65/50 (adults/under 26) to 30 days for £185/145. The Tourist Trail Pass allows unlimited travel on all services and can be bought abroad or at National Express agents in Britain, including at Heathrow and Gatwick airports; adults pay £49 for a three-day pass,

£79 for any five days of travel in a 10-day period, and £179 for 15 days in 30. You can get another 20% to 30% off this with the Discount Coach Card.

Several smaller local companies have passes allowing unlimited travel for a day or a week in certain areas (such as the popular Lake District). These can be bought in

Coach/Bus Fares from London

The sample fares below are for unrestricted one-way and return travel from London on the National Express coach (bus) system. Within each category, the first fare is available to anyone and the second fare requires one of the National Express discount cards (see Bus Passes earlier).

If you can avoid travelling on Friday, you can save a few pounds off these fares. National Express has advance purchase fares on some routes that also save a few pounds, so it's worth checking if your trip qualifies for such a fare. In markets close to London there are day return fares that cost just a bit more than the regular one-way fare.

On some of the routes below you will have to change buses one or more times.

road mileage from London	destination	best time (hours)	one way (£)	return (£)
51	Brighton	1¾	7.50/6	12.50/10
54	Cambridge	2	8/6.50	12.50/10
56	Canterbury	2	8/6.50	12.50/10
57	Oxford*	1¾	7	7.50
71	Dover	2½	9.50/7.50	15/12
83	Salisbury	2¾	12/9.50	18/14
92	Stratford	2¾	11/10	16/13
106	Bath	3	11.50/9.50	22/17
110	Birmingham	2½	10/9	15/12
115	Bristol	2¼	11/11	18/18
131	Lincoln	4¾	19.25/13.75	28.25/20.75
150	Shrewsbury	4½	12.50/10.50	18/15
155	Cardiff	3¼	14/11.50	24/19.50
172	Exeter	3¾	16.50/13.50	30/24
184	Manchester	4	15/13	25/19.50
188	York	4	18/15	28/23
193	Liverpool	4½	15/13	25/19.50
211	Aberystwyth	7¼	19.25/13.75	28.25/20.75
215	Scarborough	5¾	22/18	34/26
255	Durham	4¾	20/16	32/25
299	Carlisle	5½	22/18	33/27
375	Edinburgh	8	22/18	33/27
397	Glasgow	7	22/18	33/27
434	Dundee	8¼	26/21	41/33
450	Perth	8¼	26/21	41/33
503	Aberdeen	10½	28/22	46/37
536	Inverness	12	30/24	47/38

* Operated by Oxford Tube (☎ 01865-772250). Fares are for an unrestricted one-way and a one-day return ticket; an open return is £9.50.

advance or on the first bus. Sometimes an all-day ticket is cheaper than a ticket for a single long ride. Some passes cover rail and bus travel as well (see Rail Passes later in this chapter). Local Tourist Information Centres (TICs) or bus information phone lines can give more details.

Postbus

Many rural places are served by postbuses – vans collecting or delivering mail that also carry passengers. They are ideal for walkers heading for remote locations and great for tours through the most remote and beautiful areas of Britain, even if you stay in the van! For information and timetables contact the Postbus Helpline (☎ 01246-546329) or customer services (☎ 0845-774 0740).

Backpacker Buses

Bus tours aimed at young and groovy budget travellers can be a useful way of getting around, as most offer a hop-on, hop-off facility. This allows you to travel between cities and other popular areas, get off where you like, stay for a few days, then pick up the next tour that comes through. Stray Travel Network (☎ 020-7373 7737, e enquiries @straytravel.com, W www.straytravel.com) covers a regular circuit between London, Bath, Wales, the Lake District, Edinburgh, York, Oxford and back to London. Ticket options include three days of travel over a two-month period for £79, or six days in a four-month period for £129. The similar Radical Travel Network (☎ 0131-557 9393, W www.radicaltravel.com) operates Border Raiders tours covering the highlights of England, Scotland and Wales, and Haggis tours in Scotland.

TRAIN

Despite the cutbacks of the last two decades, Britain has an impressive rail service, including a number of lines through sparsely populated country, which are very handy for walkers travelling to remote areas. A combination of travel by rail and foot is one of the best ways to see Britain.

The former state-owned British Rail was privatised in the 1990s and now about 25 different companies run train services. The main routes are served by express trains. Local railways are served by slower 'stopping trains'. A separate company, Railtrack, owns and maintains the tracks and stations.

For very long journeys you can use an overnight sleeper train. The most useful and one of the most scenic is the service between London and Scotland.

The secrets for successful train travel are to get a discount pass if you're using the train a lot, buy your ticket as far in advance as possible, ask for the cheapest ticket available (always give the clerk time to check – they find the system cumbersome too) and ask what restrictions it may have. If you figure out and fully exploit the system you can save a lot of money travelling by train. You'll also gain a lasting insight into an insane bureaucracy.

Information & Tickets

You can get information or buy tickets at any train station. Alternatively, for timetables you can check the Railtrack Web site (W www.railtrack.co.uk) or the UK Public Transport Information service (☎ 0870-608 2608, W www.pti.org.uk). For tickets, contact a commercial site such as Trainline (W www.thetrainline.co.uk). Or you can phone the National Rail Enquiry Service (☎ 0845-748 4950); a helpful human voice will tell you all the times you want, then give you the phone number of the train operator for purchasing a ticket.

There are two classes of train travel: First-class seats cost 30% to 50% more than standard (2nd) class and, except on very crowded trains, are not worth the extra money. Unless otherwise stated, the prices quoted in this book are for 2nd-class adult, one-way tickets. Return tickets are sometimes double the one-way price but often only a few pounds more.

There are many different types of tickets for any journey, and with almost as many discount passes and railcards available (see the next sections), the permutations seem endless. On top of this, the various train companies all have their own complex discount schemes and special offers, not unlike airlines. These come and go throughout the year so you have to shop around if you want to be sure you are getting the best fares. And just like the airlines, the cheapest fares have certain restrictions, such as limited

London to Scotland by Rail

Did you know you could get on a train in London in the evening, have a meal and a good night's sleep, even breakfast in bed, and then get off next morning in the stunning mountains of Scotland? Late every evening (except Saturday) the *Caledonian Sleepers* leave London's Euston Station bound for Glasgow or Edinburgh (arriving around 7am), and then on to Fort William or Inverness (arriving at noon).

The route to Inverness eventually leads to Kyle of Lochalsh – gateway to the Isle of Skye. Between Glasgow and Fort William the train runs on the West Highland Railway, surely the most beautiful yet underrated train journey in the country. As you go north the magic continues; beyond Fort William the train runs on to Mallaig, from where it's a short ferry ride to the Isle of Skye. There's also a branch line to Oban, gateway port to the Outer Hebrides.

On both lines you can leave the train at an intermediate station and head straight for the hills. For example, from Aviemore you can reach the Cairngorms, and from the West Highland Railway stations you can aim for nearby peaks as you step off the platform.

With returns from Scotland leaving in the evening and arriving back in London around 8am the next day, it makes short walking breaks for mountain-starved southerners exceedingly possible, and is ideal for visitors if you've only got a few days to spare.

ScotRail (☎ 0845-755 0033, W www.scotrail.co.uk) currently charges £89 return for an Apex ticket (see Information & Tickets for an explanation of Apex) between London and Glasgow/Edinburgh, and £109 return for an Apex ticket between London and Fort William/Inverness. You can make inquiries and reservations on the Web site.

seating or minimum-stay. Many special fares are nonrefundable, so if you miss your train, you're stuck.

Some special fare tickets, such as Apex (advance purchase excursions), must be bought in advance. If you want your tickets sent by post, you must purchase them at least five working days before travel. Otherwise, you can collect them at a station. Children under five travel free while those aged between five and 15 pay half price for most tickets, and full fare for Apex and Super-Apex. See the boxed text 'Rail Fares from London' for ticket prices.

The following are the main classifications of fares:

Single – valid for a one-way journey at any time on the day specified; expensive but you can usually get on and off at several stops along the way

Day Return – valid for a return journey at any time on the day specified; relatively expensive

Cheap Day Return – valid for a return journey on the day specified, but there are time restrictions such as not being allowed to travel on a train that leaves before 9.30am

Open Return – for outward travel on a stated day and return on any day within a month

Apex – a cheap return fare; you must book at least seven days in advance, but seats are limited

SuperApex – a very cheap return fare for journeys on certain lines; you must book at least 14 days in advance; again, seats are limited

Train Passes

Passes are for multiple journeys within a given period. The following are just some of those available. A good travel agent or main train station will give you more details.

BritRail Passes There are two main types of BritRail pass. They are popular with visitors but are *not available in Britain* and must be bought in your country of origin. BritRail Classic passes are for consecutive days of travel. Prices for adult standard class are US$265 for eight days, US$400 for 15 days, US$505 for 22 days and US$600 for 30 days. (Anyone who gets their money's worth out of the last pass should qualify for some sort of award for heroism.) Youth passes for those aged between 15 and 25 cost US$215/280/355/420. BritRail Flexipass is usually a better option for travellers as you don't have to get on a train every day and ride for hours to get value for money. They are good for a certain number of days within a 60-day period. Prices for adults standard class are US$235 for four days, US$340 for eight days and US$515 for 15 days. Youth passes attract a 25% discount.

Rail Fares from London

The following are sample 2nd-class (standard) fares in effect between London and selected destinations at the time of writing. One-way ticket prices are for unrestricted tickets that allow for stopovers along the journey. Day Return fares are the cheapest return tickets that have no advance purchase requirement; however, you have to do all your travelling on the same day. These are only shown for destinations under two hours from London. One night or more return tickets are the cheapest tickets that allow for one or more nights away. These often have advance purchase requirements and other restrictions. Where there is more than one route between London and a destination, the faster route is shown, although the slower one is likely to be cheaper.

For ease of comparison, the destinations are shown in the same order as the bus fares from London, even though there are great variations in the rail mileage versus the road mileage (see the boxed text 'Coach/Bus Fares from London' earlier). Also, note that the journey times are the best possible and may involve one or more connections.

rail mileage from London	destination	best time (hours)	one way (£)	day return (£)	one night or more return (£)
51	Brighton	¾	13.70	14.60	18.80
56	Cambridge	1	14.50	14.60	18.80
62	Canterbury	1½	15.90	15.40	17.10
64	Oxford	¾	15.10	14.80	18.90
77	Dover	1¼	19.80	18.30	20.60
84	Salisbury	1¼	22.50	21.90	26.70
121	Stratford	1¾	20	19.50	22.50
107	Bath	1½	34	31	25.50
110	Birmingham	1½	43.50	27	15
118	Bristol	1½	36	32	18.50
137	Lincoln	1¾	37	39	21
156	Shrewsbury	2½	55	-	18
151	Cardiff	2	43.50	-	23
174	Exeter	2	39	-	28
184	Manchester	2½	85	-	20
188	York	2	58	-	23
194	Liverpool	2½	79	-	20
237	Aberystwyth	5¼	71	-	29
230	Scarborough	2¾	60	-	29
254	Durham	2¾	74	-	23
299	Carlisle	3½	91	-	27
393	Edinburgh	4	86	-	30
402	Glasgow	5	91	-	53
452	Dundee	5¾	89	-	50
450	Perth	6	89	-	50
524	Aberdeen	6½	90	-	66
568	Inverness	8¼	91	-	50

Freedom of Scotland Travelpass – This comprehensive and very good value pass covers all rail services in Scotland, plus those north of Berwick and Carlisle in England, and includes free or discounted rides on ferries, postbuses and some bus routes. A pass for four days' travel in eight days costs £79, eight in 15 costss £109 and 12 in 15 costs £119. These passes can be bought in Britain.

Freedom of Wales Rover FlexiPass – These provide unlimited travel on all Welsh trains and many bus services as well. The passes are valid for eight days' travel within a 15-day period and cost £92. A Regional Rover for just north and central Wales is cheaper.

Railcards

Railcards get you discounts on tickets, up to 33% on most fares (except certain heavily discounted tickets). They include the Young Persons Railcard if you're aged between 16 and 25 or studying full time, Senior Railcard for over 60s, Disabled Persons Railcard and a Family Railcard. The cards all cost between £14 and £20, are valid for one year and most are available from major train stations.

CAR & MOTORCYCLE

If you've come to Britain to combine walking with some general motorised touring, a vehicle helps you reach remote places and is better for travelling quickly, independently and flexibly. For a short visit you can hire a car (it's very difficult to hire a motorcycle); for a longer visit you might consider buying a car and selling it again when you leave.

If you decide to hire, you might be better off making arrangements in your home country. In Britain, a small car with four seats (carrying two in reasonable comfort, three at a pinch and four if you leave the luggage behind) can be hired from about £30 per day or about £120 per week (with unlimited mileage). A larger car is about £180 per week. Check local tourist news sheets, *Yellow Pages* phone directories and London-based free publications such as *TNT*. Big-name firms charge more than small local companies, but rates are competitive and always changing, so it's worth ringing around. If you want a car with automatic transmission you must specify this in advance.

Petrol costs between about 80p and £1 per litre (usually more expensive in remote areas) and diesel is a few pence cheaper. This is expensive by American or Australian standards, but distances aren't great.

Road Rules

For details on British road rules, get hold of a booklet called *The Highway Code*, which is often available in TICs and post offices. For an outline of the different types of road in Britain, see Place Names & Terminology in the Facts for the Walker chapter.

Briefly, vehicles drive on the left-hand side of the road; front seat belts are compulsory and if belts are fitted in the back they must be worn; the speed limit is 30mph (48kph) in built-up areas, 60mph (96kph) on single carriageways and 70mph (112kph) on dual or triple carriageways; you give way to your right at roundabouts (traffic already on the roundabout has the right of way); and motorcyclists must wear helmets.

Parking

If you park your car at the start of a walk, you have to get back to it eventually. This is not usually difficult on the day walks covered in this book, as most are circular, but it can be more trouble on long-distance walks as these are usually linear. Many B&Bs at the start of long routes offer long-term parking; you can leave your car at the B&B while walking and return by public transport (and stay another night). Several baggage-carrying companies also offer long-term parking or will transport you back to pick up your car. Details for individual walks are given in the long route descriptions in the walk chapters.

If you're leaving your car for the day while you're walking, just *finding* a place to park can be difficult in more popular areas. Car parks in national parks usually cost from £2 to £4 per day, although some are free. In some places secure parking is hard to guarantee, so ask local walkers about the situation if you're in doubt. Most importantly, never park your car on the side of narrow country lanes or across gateways to fields where they might block tractors and

Road Distances (Mi)

	London	Aberystwyth	Bath	Birmingham	Cambridge	Cardiff	Dover	Edinburgh	Glasgow	Holyhead	Inverness	Manchester	Oxford	Penzance	Stranraer	Thurso	Windermere	York
London	---																	
Aberystwyth	480	---																
Bath	236	142	---															
Birmingham	128	119	97	---														
Cambridge	150	213	174	101	---													
Cardiff	241	115	56	107	213	---												
Dover	274	310	200	203	121	233	---											
Edinburgh	195	335	384	293	337	393	457	---										
Glasgow	208	331	384	291	349	393	490	45	---									
Holyhead	192	106	245	155	246	209	351	327	321	---								
Inverness	360	493	544	453	500	558	648	159	171	486	---							
Manchester	197	133	181	88	153	188	283	218	335	125	378	---						
Oxford	56	156	66	63	80	109	148	362	355	212	518	154	---					
Penzance	312	313	213	278	368	232	365	56	563	409	722	358	265	---				
Stranraer	414	346	398	304	361	406	503	133	88	334	267	226	371	576	---			
Thurso	652	626	655	590	630	685	740	290	298	585	130	300	650	858	368	---		
Windermere	259	443	251	150	248	250	350	148	145	182	310	81	220	415	163	423	---	
York	209	480	236	128	150	241	274	195	208	192	360	71	185	405	228	482	112	---

other agricultural vehicles. You may come back to find you car has been towed away, none too carefully, by an angry farmer.

BICYCLE

Many visitors to Britain travel around by bike. Distances between places of interest are relatively short, and the country's network of minor roads and lanes makes for excellent touring. A combination of cycling and walking is a great way to discover some of Britain's quieter areas, especially as bikes are allowed to ride on byways and bridleways but *not* footpaths – see Place Names & Terminology in the Facts for the Walker chapter.

You can bring your own bike or rent locally; many national parks and other walking areas described in this book have hire centres. Of the long-distance paths described in this book, the South Downs Way can be covered by bike as well as on foot, and the western half of the Ridgeway National Trail is open to cyclists.

The BTA publishes a useful, free leaflet called *Green Britain* with some suggested cycling routes, lists of cycle holiday companies and other helpful information. Many regional TICs have information on local cycling routes and places where you can hire bikes. Of course your best source of information is Lonely Planet's *Cycling Britain*.

If you're touring by bike for more than a few weeks it might be worth joining the Cyclists' Touring Club (☎ 01483-417217, e cycling@ctc.org.uk, W www.ctc.org.uk), 69 Meadrow, Godalming, Surrey GU7 3HS. Members can get comprehensive information about cycling in Britain (and elsewhere in Europe), suggested route sheets (on and off-road), lists of local cycling contacts and clubs, details of recommended accommodation and organised cycling holidays, a cycle hire directory, and a mail-order service for maps and books for cyclists. Some cycling organisations outside Britain have reciprocal membership arrangements.

HITCHING

Hitching is never entirely safe in any country and we don't recommend it. Travellers who decide to hitch should understand that they are taking a small but potentially serious risk. However, getting around Britain by hitching is reasonably easy, except in built-up areas where you'll need to use public transport. It's against the law to hitch on motorways; you have to use approach roads, nearby roundabouts or petrol stations. In country areas, where public transport and any kind of traffic is thin on the ground, the old hitchers' rule comes into play – the fewer the cars, the better your chances.

If you're just hitching locally (ie, from a hostel to the start of a walk or back to camp at the end of the day), your chances of getting a lift are good, especially if you look like a walker. It will probably be other walkers that stop to help you out. In some remote parts of Scotland, hitching is so much a part of getting around that local drivers may stop and offer lifts without you even asking.

BOAT

The major ferry destination in the south of Britain is the Isle of Wight, with services from Southampton and Lymington. These are covered in the Isle of Wight chapter.

In the Highlands and islands of Scotland, ferries are essential. Caledonian MacBrayne (CalMac, ☎ 0870-565 0000, Ⓦ www.calmac .co.uk) is Scotland's major ferry operator with services to most inhabited islands, including Arran and Skye (both covered in this book). If you plan to spend some time here, CalMac's Island Hopscotch travel passes are usually a good deal.

LOCAL TRANSPORT
Bus & Train

Once at your destination, each city, town or county has several small, private bus companies that operate locally. Because many country services are designed for people going to school or work there may be few midday services and even fewer at weekends. This isn't a major problem but you do have to bear it in mind when planning

walks. In towns, buses only pick up at designated bus stops. In rural areas some buses may stop anywhere it's safe, as long as you make it clear you want to get on or off. This system is called 'hail and ride'.

In many areas there may be more than one bus company serving on the same route, each with its own timetable, which can make planning complicated. It's always best to check details with a TIC or with a local transport information phone line – numbers are given throughout this book. In many cases, local information lines are being phased out in favour of the UK Public Transport Information inquiry line (☎ 0870-608 2608), which will automatically connect you to an operator in the area you're phoning from (who can also help with other areas), although it will be a year or two before this fully takes over from every local phone service. You can also check the associated Web site, (Ⓦ www.pti .org.uk), which is very comprehensive on some areas, although patchy on others.

As well as buses, several national parks are crossed by railway lines and well served by stopping trains, which can often be a very quick and comfortable way to get into the countryside. A very useful Web site for walkers is Countrygoer (Ⓦ www.country go er.org), which covers in great detail all public transport options (bus and train) for reaching national parks, also with background on the parks themselves, suggested routes combining walks and public transport, plus useful links to other related sites.

Taxi

In London and some other big cities, taxi fares are expensive, but in smaller cities and towns they are usually quite reasonable – about £1 to £1.50 per mile. Thus a taxi is definitely worth considering to get to an out-of-the-way hostel or the beginning of a walk, or if the next bus isn't due for several hours, especially if there are three or four people to share the fare. Local taxis are listed in the relevant sections. Alternatively you can dial National Cabline (☎ 0800-123 444), which automatically puts you though to your nearest taxi firm.

Southern England

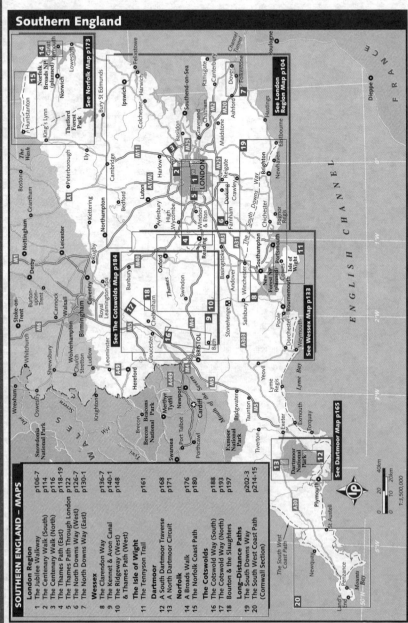

Southern England

London Region

London is the capital of England, the capital of Britain and one of the largest cities in Europe. If you've come to Britain for sightseeing, London has some of the most famous sights in the world (Tower Bridge, Big Ben, Trafalgar Square and all), and there are more attractions in the surrounding counties of Essex, Hertfordshire, Berkshire, Surrey and Kent, known collectively as the Home Counties.

If you've come to Britain specifically for walking, you'll probably want to head for Cornwall or the Lake District as soon as possible but, perhaps surprisingly, there are many opportunities for walking in and around London too. We're not talking wilderness here but exploring a city on foot can be one of the best ways to see it. Walking also provides an excuse to explore areas that many visitors never reach.

INFORMATION
Maps
Lonely Planet produces a very handy *London City Map*, which includes several maps of different scales, from the whole of Greater London down to detail of the inner centre. A street directory such as the trusty *London A-Z* is always useful. Ringbound editions are about £6.

For maps covering individual walks, see Planning in the introduction to each walk.

Books
There's a plethora of books about London and the surrounding Home Counties. This chapter describes walk-specific information only, so it's essential you get a general guidebook to London, which lists places to stay and eat and helps you get around, as well as providing more information on places of interest.

Of course we highly recommend Lonely Planet's own *London* guide. More portable is Lonely Planet's *London Condensed*, which includes several descriptions of short walking tours.

For a slightly different angle, *Discovering Off-beat Walks In London* by John Wittish & Ron Phillips (published by Shire Publications) is a fascinating and affordable pocket guide. The same publisher has *Discovering Country Walks in North London* by Merry Lundow and *Discovering Walks in Surrey* by Angela Haine & Susan Owen, both rather quaint and homespun in feel, but cheap and handy with many good suggestions for walks outside the city.

Information Sources
By far your best source of walking information in and around the capital is the Web site of the very active London Walking Forum ([W] www.londonwalking.com). The Ramblers' Association, Britain's largest and most active national walking organisation, is a useful contact for information on walking in London and the rest of Britain (for contact details, see Useful Organisations in the Facts for the Walker chapter).

Guided Walks
Time Out magazine provides a weekly listing of guided walks in its Around Town section. The London Tourist Board has a special guided tours and walks information line (☎ 09064-123431), and the London Walking Forum Web site ([W] www.londonwalking.com) lists several guided walk operators.

LONDON
London's main Tourist Information Centre (TIC) is in Victoria train station and is open daily. There are a lot of free leaflets to pick up, including on walks and walking, but if you've got specific inquiries the queues can be very long at peak holiday times.

There are also major TICs at Waterloo International Terminal, Liverpool Street train station, and Heathrow Airport Terminal 3 (arrivals). There are smaller TICs at the other Heathrow terminals, at Gatwick, Stansted, Luton and London City airports, Paddington train station and Victoria Coach Station.

For advance inquiries by mail or fax, contact the London Tourist Board (fax 020-7932 0222), Glen House, Stag Place, London SW1E 5LT; or make use of the Visitorcall system: Dial ☎ 09064-123 and then add 400 for information on events, 403 for exhibitions, 422 for rock concerts and 435 for accommodation advice. Calls are charged at 60p per minute and can only be dialled within the UK.

General tourism Web sites (with links to London sites) are listed in the Facts for the Walker chapter. Or go straight to the London tourism site W www.londontown.com.

Time Out magazine, published weekly, is a staggeringly detailed listing of London entertainment, attractions, art and much besides. There are many free listing magazines; *TNT* is the best known (call ☎ 020-7373 3377 for the nearest distribution point).

Supplies & Equipment

The YHA Adventure Shop (☎ 020-7836 8541), 14 Southampton St WC2, is an excellent place to stock up on a wide range of camping and walking gear. Among other

continued on page 112

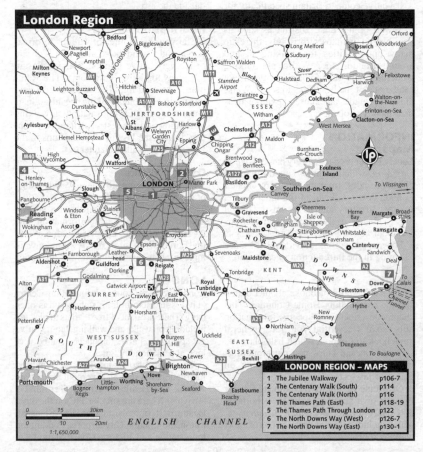

London Region

	LONDON REGION – MAPS	
1	The Jubilee Walkway	p106-7
2	The Centenary Walk (South)	p114
3	The Centenary Walk (North)	p116
4	The Thames Path (East)	p118-19
5	The Thames Path Through London	p122
6	The North Downs Way (West)	p126-7
7	The North Downs Way (East)	p130-1

The Jubilee Walkway

Distance	12mi (19.5km)
Duration	6 hours
Standard	easy
Start/Finish	Leicester Square

Summary A fascinating walk through the streets of ancient and modern London, taking in many popular sights along both sides of the River Thames

The Jubilee Walkway is a route through London, created in 1977 (as the Silver Jubilee Walkway) to celebrate the 25th anniversary of Queen Elizabeth II's accession to the throne. It passes some of the finest sights in the city (and we've taken the liberty of suggesting a few additional loops), including Buckingham Palace, Big Ben, St Paul's Cathedral, Tower Bridge and the Tower of London. It also goes along the south bank of the River Thames, which gives excellent views of the great buildings on the northern side.

Direction, Distance & Duration

The route is circular, running both north of the River Thames and along its south bank. The official start and finish is Leicester Square. You can of course start anywhere and go in either direction, but we describe it clockwise. The route is signed with silver metal discs marked with a crown and set into the footpaths and pavements; many are scuffed by the passing of countless feet but have survived the past 25 years pretty well.

The total distance is 12mi, which will take about six hours of walking, but at least double this time if you stop to look at the sights and probably double it again if you go into just some of the famous buildings and other sights along the way. It's best to allow two days, or even four!

Below: Buckingham Palace

ELLIOT DANIEL

The Jubilee Walkway

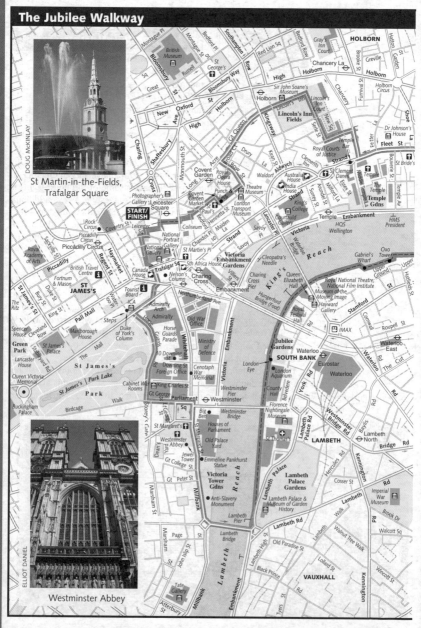

St Martin-in-the-Fields, Trafalgar Square

DOUG McKINLAY

Westminster Abbey

ELLIOT DANIEL

The Jubilee Walkway

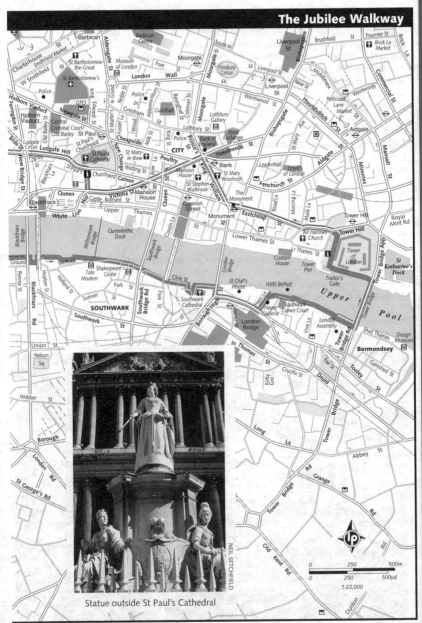

Statue outside St Paul's Cathedral

NEIL SETCHFIELD

1:22,000

PLANNING

This brief route outline can't do justice to the many fascinating sights passed along the route. You'll definitely need a good street map and a guidebook to give you more details on places of interest. See Information earlier for some suggestions. Numerous information boards along the route explain features passed and interpret the scenes from bridges and other view points. A specific leaflet on the Jubilee Walkway is planned, so ask at a TIC about this.

THE WALK
Leicester Square to Lambeth Bridge

Leicester Square was once a quiet public garden – now it's most famous for its cinemas and movie premiers, when the stars arrive to pose for pictures and make hand prints in the pavement.

From here, the official route heads south, past the National Gallery and **Trafalgar Square**, dominated by Nelson's Column, along the Mall and then left down Horse Guards Rd. You may prefer to go along Whitehall instead and past the entrance to **Downing St**, where the prime minister lives at No 10.

Determined sightseers could branch off westwards to visit **Piccadilly Circus**, with its famous statue of Eros, and even continue through Green Park or St James's Park to **Buckingham Palace** (London home of the Queen), before heading back east again.

Whichever way you go, your next major feature is the **Houses of Parliament**, dominated at the north end by St Stephen's Tower, commonly called **Big Ben** (actually the name of the bell inside). The route

Below: The National Gallery and Trafalgar Square

LEE FOSTER

goes south past **Westminster Abbey** (the coronation place of monarchs since at least the 11th century, and final resting place of Chaucer, Darwin and many other famous names). You get your first sight of the River Thames just before **Lambeth Bridge** – which you cross to the south bank.

Lambeth Bridge to Tower Bridge

For the next few miles the route stays off the roads and follows walkways next to the river. After passing **Lambeth Palace** (London residence of the Archbishop of Canterbury), there are excellent views of the Houses of Parliament and the nearby Westminster Bridge. Go past the **London Eye**, a giant wheel giving spectacular views over the city, and under Waterloo Bridge. From here the south bank becomes the **South Bank**, an area of theatres, studios, museums, galleries and concert halls, with a lively surrounding atmosphere despite the ugly concrete 1960s architecture.

Next pass the **Tate Modern**, a former power station now a world-class art gallery, and the silver thread of the **Millennium Bridge** spanning the river. There's a fine view of St Paul's Cathedral through a gap in the north bank riverside buildings. Walk past the **Shakespeare's Globe**, a recreation of the Bard's original theatre, and go under Southwark Bridge and the rail bridge to Cannon Street Station, rattling with trains and home to flocks of pigeons (don't look up).

Right: South Bank statue beside the National Theatre

JULIET COOMBE

Now you're in **Southwark** (pronounced suth-ark) once a separate town outside London, famous for its taverns, brothels and theatres, which flourished beyond the control of the city's law makers. From here, the route moves inland slightly away from the river and down Clink St (site of a former prison), past **Southwark Cathedral** and under **London Bridge**, almost without noticing. Go up the steps and out to the middle of the bridge for great views up and down the river.

A confusing set of paths leads you back to the riverside. Be sure to visit **Hayes Galleria**, a converted warehouse and dock (one of many that used to line the south bank), now with shops and cafes centred round a large and fantastical metal sculpture.

As you pass the site of the new London Assembly (back by popular demand after being abolished in the 1980s, with a high-profile Mayor of London), your view over the river is dominated by **Tower Bridge** – one of London's most famous landmarks. Before crossing to the north bank, with luck you may see the roadway swing open to let a ship through.

Tower Bridge to Leicester Square

On the north bank of the River Thames, the official route loops through **St Katharine's Dock**, now a fancy marina with waterside pubs, shops and cafes, but it's more interesting to walk west along the embankment between the river and the **Tower of London**. Built originally by William the Conqueror shortly after the Battle of Hastings in 1066, the tower has been added to by many subsequent monarchs; it is now home to the Crown Jewels and ceremonial guards called Beefeaters.

Below: Tower Bridge

NEIL SETCHFIELD

The path leaves the river and enter the **City of London** (usually just called the City), a separate entity, governed by a corporation more than 900 years old. Today this is London's banking and financial centre. If you thought the City was old, next stop **All Hallows by the Tower**, a church dating from 675.

Turn back to more recent times as you pass **the Monument**, which commemorates the 1666 Great Fire of London, and wander up King William St to the **Mansion House**, since around 1750 the residence of the Lord Mayor of London. (Just to keep you on your toes, this is not the Mayor of London based at the London Assembly back by Tower Bridge.) Nearby are two potent symbols of the country's financial prowess: the **Bank of England** and the **Stock Exchange**.

From Mammon to God and the next highlight: **St Paul's Cathedral**, designed by Sir Christopher Wren, one of London's greatest architects, and built between 1675 and 1710. From here, the route takes you over Ludgate Circus (once an execution site), down Fleet St (once London's newspaper centre), past the Royal Courts of Justice (where TV crews wait for the latest celebrity trial to end) and through Lincoln's Inn Fields (London's legal centre), touching **Drury Lane** (and skirting a cluster of famous theatres) and continuing down Bow St (where the 'Bow Street Runners' in the 1750s became the forerunner of London's police force).

Round the corner and back to the present: **Covent Garden**, the epitome of trendy modern London, with shops, cafes and a lively street atmosphere. (Even this place has its roots in history, though; it was a fruit and flower market for centuries, and the name comes from a convent that stood here for centuries before that.) Time to sit down, have a coffee, watch a busker or buy an 'I love London' hat. It's a short stroll back to Leicester Square and the end of the walk.

Below: Twinings Building decoration, Fleet Street

ELLIOT DANIEL

continued from page 104

outlets, there's a branch (☎ 020-7938 2948) at 174 Kensington High St W8.

The national Camping & Outdoor Centre chain has two branches in London, one in the City (☎ 020-7329 8757), 41 Ludgate Hill EC4, and another in Pimlico (☎ 020-7834 6007), 27 Buckingham Palace Rd SW1. Taunton Leisure (☎ 020-7924 3838), 557–561 Battersea Park Rd SW11, also has a good reputation.

Places to Stay & Eat
Accommodation in London is expensive and in demand. The peak tourist months (between June and August) are the busiest; definitely book ahead if you plan to visit during these times.

London is the UK's undisputed culinary capital, and the growth in the number of restaurants and cafes – some 8500 at the last count – has made the city much more international. The best way to stay abreast of the choice is to read the latest newspaper reviews and *Time Out* magazine. Among the regularly updated local food guides, Lonely Planet's *Out to Eat – London* is, of course, to be recommended.

JULIET COOMBE

Lunch is calling – keep an eye out for bakery signs as you walk around London

Getting There & Away
See the Getting There & Away and Getting Around chapters for advice about getting to/from London. For travel information in and around the capital, phone London Travel Information (☎ 0207-222 1234).

The Centenary Walk

Distance	15mi (24km)
Duration	6–7 hours
Standard	easy
Start	Manor Park
Finish	Epping
Gateways	London, Harlow

Summary A mix of urban parks and ancient forest, with walking mostly on flat or undulating tracks, which can be muddy after rain. An optional extension to Chipping Ongar stretches the route to 23mi (37km).

The Centenary Walk offers good walking surprisingly close to the centre of London – the starting point is a mere 5mi from St Paul's Cathedral. It runs through Epping Forest, on the northern edge of the city – a remnant of the royal forest that covered much of the county of Essex in the 12th century. In following years, as kings lost interest in hunting, the forest diminished until by the 1850s little remained. The possible loss of a much-used recreation area (allied to early stirrings of the environmental movement) caused the City of London to act. In 1878 legislation was introduced that made the City of London 'conservator' of the forest with a charter to keep it public and preserve its natural aspect. Since then the forest has remained popular, particularly among walkers who make good use of the network of paths and bridleways. It was to celebrate the 100th anniversary of the Epping Forest Act that the Centenary Walk was devised in 1978.

The forest has a continuous biological history dating from the last ice age, but for more than 1000 years it has been greatly influenced by human activity, managed for firewood, timber and grazing purposes, and as a hunting ground for the monarch. Beech, oak and hornbeam are common forest trees, many of which have been pollarded – 'beheaded' around 3m above ground level to produce a cluster of branches that are later relopped for firewood. Pollarding mostly ceased in the last century but left a remarkable legacy of weirdly contorted trees seen along the route.

On the southern part of the route the forest is undeniably embedded in urban development, but its setting becomes much more rural to the north. Some parts of the route are heavily used on summer Sundays, so if you prefer a solitary walk choose another day.

The Centenary Walk ends at Epping town. Beyond here a long-distance path called the Essex Way extends for 81mi on waymarked paths through farmed countryside and sizeable woodlands to the North Sea port of Harwich. We have described a possible extension to the Centenary Way along the Essex Way to the ancient market town of Chipping Ongar (see Alternatives following).

Direction, Distance & Duration
This linear walk can be done in either direction, but south to north is much more pleasing as you head out of town into the countryside. From Manor Park to Epping is 15mi (24km), requiring about six to seven hours of walking. With stops for lunch and places of interest, you should allow seven to eight hours.

Alternatives You can reduce the length of the walk and cut out the more built-up sections by starting at the suburbs of Leytonstone or Chingford, reducing the distance to Epping to 12mi or 7mi, respectively.

If you want to lengthen the walk, you can carry on from Epping to Chipping Ongar, described under Optional Extension at the end of the walk description. This is 8mi (13km) long and needs three to four hours of walking (with stops allow four to five hours). The total from Manor Park to Chipping Ongar is 23mi (37km), taking about nine to 11 hours. This is quite a feasible option for strong walkers, as the route is not difficult, although it would best be done on a long summer's day.

Another option is to start at Chingford and go all the way to Chipping Ongar – a comfortable day's walk of 15mi (six to 7½ hours of walking), avoiding the more urban part of the route. A final alternative for the whole way from Manor Park to Chipping Ongar is to spread the walk over two days, overnighting along the way.

PLANNING
Maps
The southern part of the Centenary Way is on Ordnance Survey (OS) Landranger 1:50,000 map No 177 *(East London)*, and the northern section is on No 167 *(Luton & Hertford)*, which also covers the Essex Way section to Chipping Ongar. The OS Explorer 1:25,000 map No 174 *(Epping Forest & Lee Valley)* covers the whole forest but not the southern part of this route. An inexpensive *Epping Forest* pictorial map, which marks the route of the Centenary Walk, is available from the Epping Forest Information Centre (see Information Sources following).

Books
Most useful are *The Centenary Walk* booklet, published by Epping Forest Conservators, and *The Essex Way* booklet, published by Essex County Council. For more options *Short Walks in Epping Forest* by Fred Matthews describes 24 routes. For background, try *Epping Forest Through the Ages* by Georgina Green or the *Official Guide to Epping Forest*, describing its history and management. All are available at the Epping Forest Information Centre and can be posted on request.

Information Sources
The Epping Forest Information Centre (☎ 020-8508 0028) at High Beach, south of Epping (and on the Way), has a wide range of information, a bookshop and a permanent display. The centre runs an extensive program of guided walks on forest topics.

PLACES TO STAY & EAT
If you're staying in central London it is easy to do the walk then return to your accommodation from Epping or Chipping Ongar by

public transport. If you decide to stay overnight on the route, the charming *Epping Forest YHA Hostel* (☎ 020-8508 5161), at High Beach, charges £9.80. In Epping, B&Bs include *Brooklands* (☎ 01992-575424), charging £40/50 for en suite singles/doubles; and *Thatched House* (☎ 01992-578353), at Bell Common, charging £29/59. For B&B in Chipping Ongar, *The King's Inn* (☎ 01277-365183) is recommended.

You can obtain a comprehensive *Accommodation List* from the Epping Forest Information Centre at High Beach.

For food, there are many pubs along the way that serve meals and bar snacks. More details are given in the route description. Epping and Chipping Ongar also have a choice of restaurants.

GETTING TO/FROM THE WALK
Bus & Train Both train and tube (London's underground railway) services start early in the morning and end late in the evening, with several an hour, although with a reduced service on Sunday. Manor Park is reached from Liverpool Street train station (from where trains also go to Chingford). Use the tube (Central Line) to reach Leytonstone and Epping (the terminus).

From Chipping Ongar regular buses go several times a day back to Epping, leaving from the point where the Essex Way meets the main road near Budworth Hall. From Epping you can join the tube network and get back to central London.

THE WALK
Manor Park to Chingford
8mi (13km), 3–3½ hours
From Manor Park train station turn left along a street called Forest Drive, which soon brings you to a large grassy open space called Wanstead Flats. Head diagonally across the grass aiming towards twin high-rise buildings in the distance.

After a mile, you cross a road and continue towards the left edge of some houses on the far side of another road, which you also cross. Go along a track with grassland on your left, then fork right through woodland, and then left and right round a brick

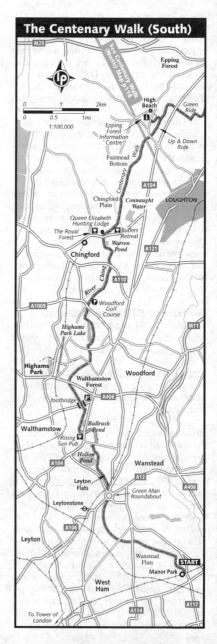

The Centenary Walk (South)

wall to reach a busy main road and the Green Man Roundabout – named after a nearby pub. (The walk could be joined here from nearby Leytonstone tube station.)

Cross over the roads feeding the roundabout (or use the pedestrian tunnel), and on the other side is Leyton Flats – another largely grassland area. Head across this, through a belt of trees, past Hollow Pond and straight ahead through woodland to a road that you cross. Go past a pond and some attractive houses on your right to enter a road called College Place. At its end, veer left through the forest, crossing a road to reach the **Rising Sun Pub**, then re-entering the woodland with Bullrush Pond on your right. Turn right and go along a white posted track (for horses) until a narrow path on your left leads up a grassy bank to cross a footbridge over a road. From here there are panoramic views over the city and suburbs of London.

To continue, fork left, following posts through a subway under the North Circular Rd, into the woods of **Walthamstow Forest** and past an area where in 1992 the Epping Forest Conservators repollarded trees as an experiment. For perhaps 1000 years much of the forest would have looked like this.

Cross a road and continue with a high-rise building on the left. Keep left as you go downhill and then oxver a road and along the right-hand side (east) of **Highams Park Lake**. At its end go uphill through trees to pick up a grassy track leading onto and over a road to Woodford Golf Course. Continue on the track, later with a fairway on the right, then go uphill and through trees along a wide grassy strip.

The route skirts round the eastern edge of the suburb of Chingford, crossing a road to reach Whitehall Plain. It then continues alongside the little River Ching, turning left over a bridge. Go uphill to the left of Warren Pond to meet and cross a road opposite the distinctive **Queen Elizabeth Hunting Lodge**, on the north side of Chingford (see the boxed text for some history). Just to the left of the Hunting Lodge is **The Royal Forest**, a reasonable pub which serves lunches at the bar. To the right is **Butlers Retreat**, which also provides refreshments.

Chingford to Epping
7mi (11km), 3–3½ hours
If you skipped the southern, more urban part of the Centenary Way, the route can be joined here from nearby Chingford train station.

From Queen Elizabeth Hunting Lodge go towards the fountain behind Butlers Retreat and turn right (with a pond on the right) and down a wide grassy track to the right of Chingford Plain. Cross a ditch and turn left along a wide gravel-surfaced track through woods. Go over a junction of tracks and continue uphill, round an overgrown pond on the right, and on through forest for 1.5mi, to eventually reach a large grassy area called Fairmead Bottom. Go left uphill as the track winds through beechwoods, crosses a small road and becomes Up and Down Ride.

Take a left fork after about 800m and then left again down a hard track to reach Epping Forest Information Centre at **High Beach** (so called because the soil here is quite sandy), where Queen Victoria dedicated the forest to the people in 1882. Years later the dedication is not forgotten and this area is busy at weekends. Nearby, **The King's Oak** pub serves lunches, while the green **tea hut** serves drinks and cakes.

From High Beach retrace your steps to the main route and go left at the fork. Cross the main road to a car park and continue ahead

Queen Elizabeth Hunting Lodge & Butlers Retreat

The Queen Elizabeth Hunting Lodge, despite its name, dates from Henry VIII's time (mid-16th century). It's open to visitors on afternoons from Wednesday to Sunday. Tradition says that Henry waited here to hear the cannon signalling that Anne Boleyn had been beheaded at the Tower of London. And then went hunting! Nearby, Butlers Retreat was one of many 'retreats' established in the late 19th and early 20th century. These were opened to provide alcohol-free alternatives to pubs, seen as being a major cause of drunkenness for the working people who escaped on Sunday from the factories and docks of London's East End.

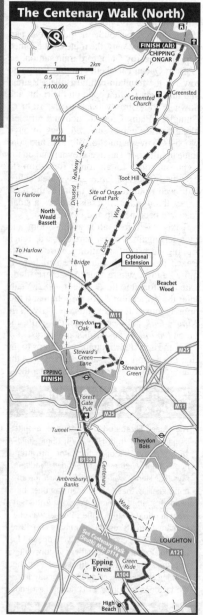

The Centenary Walk (North)

0 1 2km
0 0.5 1mi
1:100,000

FINISH (Alt)
CHIPPING
ONGAR

Greensted
Church — Greensted

A414

Toot Hill

To Harlow

North
Weald
Bassett

Site of Ongar
Great Park

To Harlow

Disused Railway Line

Essex Way

Bridge

Optional
Extension

Beachet
Wood

M11

Theydon
Oak

Steward's
Green
Lane

Steward's
Green

M25

M11

EPPING
FINISH

Forest
Gate
Pub

M25

Tunnel

Theydon
Bois

B1393

Ambresbury
Banks

Centenary Walk

See Centenary Walk
(South) Map p114

LOUGHTON

A121

Epping
Forest

Green
Ride

A104

High
Beach

on a surfaced track, which after 500m joins another main track, where you turn left. This is **Green Ride**, cut through the forest in 1880 so Queen Victoria could go on a commemorative carriage-ride after her dedication. For the next 2.5mi follow Green Ride through woodland and across two roads.

After the second road and 200m beyond another track on the left, it is worth a short detour slanting left into the woodland to the impressive **Ambresbury Banks** earthworks – an Iron Age defensive structure dating from around 500 BC. According to local legend, a British uprising led by Queen Boudicca was put down here by the Romans in AD 60.

Eventually the track arrives at a grassy area with a cricket pitch to the left. In the 1970s this part of the forest was threatened with the construction of the M25 motorway and major environmental battles were fought to prevent it being severed. These were successful and today the motorway is in a tunnel a couple of metres below you.

Go past the cricket pavilion to a gravel track and turn right onto a footpath with a pond on the left. Follow this over a road (the nearby *Forest Gate* pub does excellent lunches) and continue over Bell Common – a narrow strip of scrub, grass and trees between a main road to the left and houses to the right.

At the end of the common follow Hemnall St (past a little house where Lucien, son of Camille Pissarro the French Impressionist painter, lived for many years) to Station Rd, then turn right to reach Epping train station – the end of the Centenary Way.

Optional Extension: Chipping Ongar
8mi (13km), 3–4 hours
This stage, along the first part of the Essex Way, can be added on to your walk along the Centenary Way.

From Epping train station take the footbridge over the railway line and then a path (past an apartment block called Bower Court), which soon leads across fields to meet **Steward's Green Lane** (in medieval times part of the main road between London and East Anglia). The lane takes you, after about half a mile, to the *Theydon Oak* pub. A little beyond the pub turn left on a gradually rising path, the attractions of which are not entirely spoilt by the M11 motorway over to the right, as you pass through 2mi of interesting ancient woodland. You also cross the motorway (fortunately a bridge is provided).

Look out for the ditch and banks marking the boundary of the site of **Ongar Great Park**, the first recorded deer park in England, mentioned in early 11th-century documents. Most of the way to Toot Hill – the name means lookout post – the path runs through this ancient park. The *Green Man* pub (like its namesake near the start of the route, it is named after the ancient, legendary spirit of the woods) in Toot Hill village is OK for a drink and snack, but full meals can be pricey.

Just past the end of the village a path on the right leads across fields alongside a hedge. Turn left by Widows Farm and continue across a lane by a wood, then through fields to **Greensted Church**, a remarkable survivor from the 10th century or earlier, possibly the oldest wooden church in the world.

Behind the church a fine descending path known as the Avenue – a double row of stately elm trees failed to survive Dutch Elm Disease in the 1970s but replanting has been done – leads directly to the heart of Chipping Ongar. This small town has a range of interesting features, including an 11th-century **church** and **castle**, and some attractive old houses, and makes a suitably scenic finish to your walk through history.

The Thames Path (East)

Distance	90mi (145km)
Duration	6 days
Standard	easy
Start	Pangbourne
Finish	Thames Barrier
Gateways	Reading, London

Summary A six-day walk along a popular national trail that follows the winding River Thames past historic towns to the heart of the capital.

The Thames Path National Trail divides very neatly into two sections near the town of Reading, about 40mi west of central London.

The more rural western section is described fully (along with general information about the whole route) in the Wessex chapter, later in this book.

In this chapter we describe the eastern section of the Thames Path, which winds through famous and historical towns, such as Henley-on-Thames and Windsor, before becoming a major artery through the heart of the capital itself.

Direction, Distance & Duration

The route is described west to east, starting from Pangbourne, near Reading, and ending at the Thames Barrier. The total distance for this eastern section is 90mi (145km), split over six days.

day	from	to	mi/km
1	Pangbourne	Henley-on-Thames	15/24
2	Henley-on-Thames	Maidenhead	15/24
3	Maidenhead	Staines	14/22.5
4	Staines	Kingston upon Thames	15/24
5	Kingston upon Thames	Battersea	15/24
6	Battersea	Thames Barrier	16/25.5

Alternatives The days are numbered from Pangbourne but you may prefer to skip Reading and begin at Henley-on-Thames, which is easy to reach by train from London. Other alternatives are discussed under Planning in the introduction to the Thames Path in the Wessex chapter.

PLANNING

Details on books and accommodation, along with contact details for the Thames Path National Trail Office, are given in the general Planning section for the Thames Path in the Wessex chapter.

Maps

OS Landranger 1:50,000 maps covering the eastern section of the Thames Path are No 175 *(Reading & Windsor)*, No 176 *(West London)* and No 177 *(East London)*.

Of the OS Explorer 1:25,000 series, you will need No 159 *(Reading, Wokingham & Pangbourne)*, No 160 *(Windsor, Weybridge & Bracknell)*, No 161 *(London South, Croydon & Esher)*, No 171 *(Chiltern Hills West, Henley-on-Thames & Wallingford)*, No 172 *(Chiltern Hills East, High Wycombe & Maidenhead)* and No 173 *(London North, Harrow & Enfield)*.

Information Sources

TICs along this part of the walk include Reading (☎ 0118-956 6226), Henley-on-Thames (☎ 01491-578034), Marlow (☎ 01628-483597), Windsor (☎ 01753-852010) and Kingston upon Thames (☎ 020-8547 5592). London is covered under Information in the introduction to this chapter.

GETTING TO/FROM THE WALK

Bus & Train Reading is linked to London and other parts of the country by National Express coach and local bus, but by far the easiest way to reach Reading is by train. Deep in the commuter belt, the town has very regular services to/from London, Bristol, Oxford and other cities in west and central England. Pangbourne, on the Oxford line, also has a train station, with regular trains to/from Reading and London.

At the end of the route, it's a short half-mile walk southwards through down-at-heel streets from the Thames Barrier to the nearest bus route, where you can get a bus to Greenwich and from there join the tube network. Alternatively, it's a 15-minute walk west to Charlton train station, from where trains run to Charing Cross train station in central London.

Car Reading is just off the M4 motorway, and Pangbourne is north-west of Reading on the A329.

The walk ends at the Thames Barrier in Eastmoor St, off the A206, about 1mi west of Woolwich or 1mi east of the junction

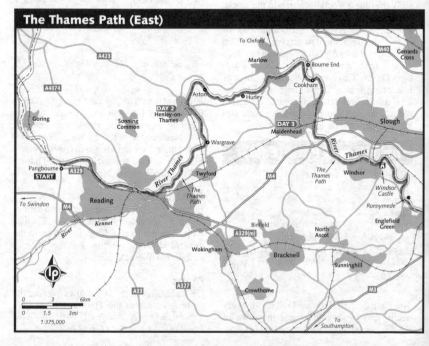

The Thames Path (East)

with the A102(M) motorway. Leaving a car in the car park is not advisable for more than a few hours.

Riverbus On the last section of the route, a riverbus (☎ 020-7930 3373) runs between the Thames Barrier and Westminster five times a day from Easter to October. Boat services (☎ 020-8305 0300) also run between Greenwich and the Thames Barrier four times a day in the autumn, more frequently in summer and sketchily from November to December.

THE WALK
Day 1: Pangbourne to Henley-on-Thames
15mi (24km), 6 hours
The first part of today's walk has a countryside feel. Beyond Reading, you can feel the influence of London; a high proportion of residents along the Thames are commuters and an air of affluence prevails.

From Pangbourne it's a short distance to Mapledurham Lock, where the path leaves the River Thames and takes you through a housing estate. This is well signposted and leads to a short section along the main A329. Just before Beethoven's Hotel (formerly the Roebuck), look out carefully for the path back down to the river. From here a fairly urban section leads you into Reading (pronounced reding).

Reading is a dull city but it does have some historical sites – chiefly the fascinating **archaeological finds** housed in Reading's Museum and Art Gallery in the town centre – and accommodation options. Signs of industry line the river as you pass the important junction with the Kennet & Avon Canal. (A day walk along the Kennet & Avon from Bath to Bradford-on-Avon is described in the Wessex chapter). Despite these attractions, you'll probably want to push on to Henley-on-Thames (often just referred to as Henley).

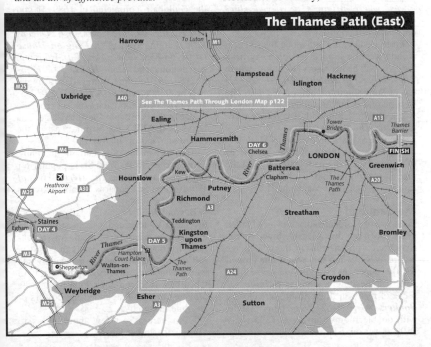

The Thames Path (East)

Henley-on-Thames

Best known for its internationally renowned **rowing regatta** in the first week of July (when accommodation is very hard to find), Henley is an old town with plenty of charm and character.

There's B&B at *Vine Cottage (☎ 01491-573545, 53 Northfield End)* with rooms from £19; or *Mervyn House (☎ 01491-575331)*, for £30. *The Red Lion (☎ 01491-572161)*, an upmarket hotel by Henley Bridge, has double rooms at £152.50.

There are plenty of restaurants in town. *The Villa Marina (☎ 01491-575262)* serves Italian meals, while pubs such as the *Anchor* and the *Row Barge* are friendly and serve good food.

Day 2: Henley-on-Thames to Maidenhead

15mi (24km), 6 hours

This section of the walk passes through well-kept countryside and prosperous towns, where Britain's privileged elites once enjoyed their entertainment (and scandals) and still do today.

From Henley, it's 3mi along the river (in regatta week, a short diversion away from the river will be necessary) to **Aston**, where *The Flower Pot Hotel (☎ 01491-574721)* has en suite singles/doubles at £39/49. The historic and beautiful village of **Hurley** is worth a short detour and, if you time it for lunch, try *The Rising Sun*.

From here it's a mile or so to Marlow – a busy town with plenty of shops and places to stay and eat. The path leads on, past the marina at Bourne End, over the river and through Cookham to Maidenhead.

Maidenhead

The town of Maidenhead has an air of faded glory, like a run-down seaside town. By the river there's still a sense of the golden age before WWI, when this was a playground for the upper and middle classes. While some of the hotels, such as *Skindle's* – scene of many an illicit affair – are closed, *Boulters (☎ 01628-621291)* retains its style, with double rooms starting at £135 (only £100 at weekends).

By Maidenhead Bridge, comfortable B&B is available from £29 at *Bridge Cottage Guest House (☎ 01628-626805)* or the nearby *Ray Corner Guest House (☎ 01628-632784)*, which charges from £40.

Day 3: Maidenhead to Staines

14mi (22.5km), 5½ hours

Today the river weaves under roads and railways as the influence of London becomes increasingly apparent, but there are still some green and quiet sections to enjoy.

From Maidenhead there are a few miles of riverside walking with a surprisingly rural feel. Added to this is a sense of grandeur as the meadows open out onto a stunning view of **Windsor Castle** high above the river, one of Britain's greatest surviving medieval strongholds and the residence of royalty since 850. It is well worth a visit but very busy at weekends and holiday periods.

Surrounding the castle is the town of **Windsor**, with fine old cobbled streets and the **Guildhall**, completed in 1689. If you want to overnight here, central B&Bs are *Mrs Hughes (☎ 01753-866036, 62 Queens Rd)*, charging from £30; *Langton House (☎ 01753-858299, 46 Alma Rd)*, from £60 per double; and *Alma House (☎ 01753-862983, 56 Alma Rd)*, from £40 for a single.

If heading for the *YHA Hostel (☎ 01753-861710)*, as you approach Windsor cross the bridge at the A332 into Clewer village. The hostel is in Mill Lane, a mile west of the centre of Windsor. It costs £10.85.

There are plenty of restaurants and pubs. *Francescoes*, in Peascod St, is popular for pizza and pasta, while *The Merry Wives of Windsor*, on St Leonards St, also provides good food.

Beyond Windsor, the towpath was closed by Queen Victoria and walkers still have to divert along a busy main road. Any republican feelings this engenders can be given full vent at **Runnymede** – a meadow site where democratic history was made in 1215 when barons forced King John to sign the *Magna Carta* and so ended the powers of absolute monarchy.

From here it's a few more miles to Staines, the end of the day.

Staines

Once an important river crossing, Staines is now a lacklustre commuter town that serves primarily as a convenient stopping point rather than a place to explore.

Accommodation options include **Penton Guest House** (☎ 01784-458787, 39 Penton Rd) with B&B from £25; and **Rose Villa** (☎ 01784-458855, 146 Commercial Rd) with B&B from £25.

A short walk from the river before reaching Staines is the quiet village of **Englefield Green**, where you can find B&B at **Bulkeley House** (☎ 01784-431287), on Middle Hill, charging £60 for a twin.

Day 4: Staines to Kingston upon Thames

15mi (24km), 6 hours

Today you encounter greater variety in the housing along the river. Flats, bungalows and even houseboats line the path, creating a sense of tidy suburbia. But it's not totally built up, and there are long stretches of meadows and fields.

From Staines it's a straightforward 8mi to Shepperton Lock, where a company called Nauticalia runs a ferry across the river every quarter-hour from 10am to 6pm, with longer hours in the summer and on weekdays. This allows you to choose either the north bank or the slightly shorter south bank path to Walton Bridge.

Your next highlight is England's grandest Tudor structure, **Hampton Court Palace**, presented to King Henry VIII by his then lord chancellor, Cardinal Wolsey. It is a beautiful building with superb grounds and a famous 300-year-old maze. The path runs alongside the grounds.

Kingston upon Thames

On the fringe of Greater London, Kingston upon Thames is a distinct town in its own right – and a very desirable place for well-heeled suburbanites. For accommodation, one good bet is **16 Chivenor Grove** (☎ 020-8547 0074), Royal Park Gate, offering decent B&B for £40. In the town itself you could try **281 Richmond Rd** (☎ 020-8546 7389) with B&B from £15.

Day 5: Kingston upon Thames to Battersea

15mi (24km), 6 hours

On this penultimate day, the countryside along the Thames retains a semirural air. Along the river are sections of parkland, open common and ornamental gardens.

From Kingston the Thames Path runs along the east bank and then, from Teddington Lock, simultaneously along both banks of the river. Choose what's best for you – there are several sites of interest along the river – although as far as Kew the east bank is definitely preferable. From Putney the buildings finally drag themselves up to dominate both sides of the river, and from now on you are well and truly in the city. You can, of course, cross and recross on the many bridges that link the two banks. These are shown on the Thames Path Through London map.

Battersea

Once you reach Battersea, the rest of London is easily accessible by bus or on foot. North of the river is Chelsea, Sloane Square or, a little farther on, Earls Court. To the south is Clapham. All have plenty of accommodation options. Refer to one of the general London guidebooks listed under Information in the introduction to this chapter. Once you've found a place, you're better off staying for two nights and returning by public transport when you've finished the walk the next day.

Day 6: Battersea to the Thames Barrier

16mi (25.5km), 6½ hours

This day's walk takes you through the heart of London – past buildings, bridges and historical sites that feature prominently on the standard tourist route. You'll also pass curious nooks and crannies, which you might not have otherwise visited.

From Battersea the Thames Path runs along both sides of the river, so you'll have to choose the side that seems most interesting. If you can't decide, we'd recommend the south bank to Tower Bridge, as this passes several interesting sites and the views

LONDON REGION

The Thames Path Through London

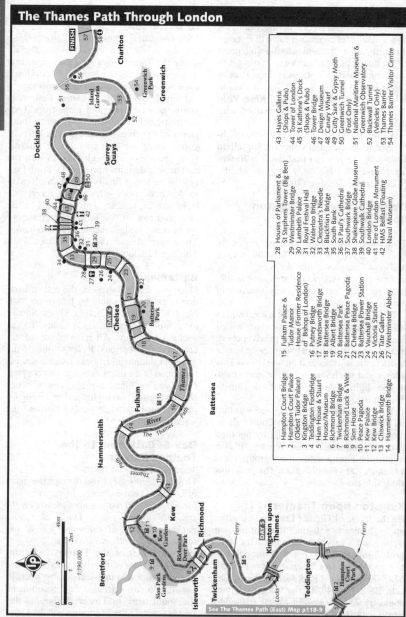

See The Thames Path (East) Map p118-9

1   Hampton Court Bridge
2   Hampton Court Palace & Tudor Palace (Oldest Tudor Palace)
3   Kingston Bridge
4   Teddington Footbridge
5   Ham House & Stuart House/Museum
6   Richmond Bridge
7   Twickenham Bridge
8   Richmond Lock & Weir
9   Sion House
10 Peace Pagoda
11 Kew Palace
12 Kew Bridge
13 Chiswick Bridge
14 Hammersmith Bridge

15 Fulham Palace & Tudor Manor House (Former Residence of Bishop of London)
16 Putney Bridge
17 Wandsworth Bridge
18 Battersea Bridge
19 Albert Bridge
20 Battersea Park
21 Battersea Peace Pagoda
22 Chelsea Bridge
23 Battersea Power Station
24 Vauxhall Bridge
25 Victoria Station
26 Tate Gallery
27 Westminster Abbey

28 Houses of Parliament & St Stephens Tower (Big Ben)
29 Westminster Bridge
30 Lambeth Palace
31 Royal Festival Hall
32 Waterloo Bridge
33 Cleopatra's Needle
34 Blackfriars Bridge
35 South Bank
36 St Paul's Cathedral
37 Southwark Bridge
38 Shakespeare Globe Museum
39 Southwark Cathedral
40 London Bridge
41 Fire of London Monument
42 HMS Belfast (Floating Naval Museum)

43 Hayes Galleria (Shops & Pubs)
44 Tower of London
45 St Kathrine's Dock (Shops & Pubs)
46 Tower Bridge
47 Design Museum
48 Canary Wharf
49 Cutty Sark & Gypsy Moth
50 Greenwich Tunnel (Foot Only)
51 National Maritime Museum & Greenwich Observatory
52 Blackwall Tunnel (Vehicles Only)
53 Thames Barrier
54 Thames Barrier Visitor Centre

across to the north bank are often superb. For more details of the section between Lambeth Bridge and Tower Bridge, see the Jubilee Walkway earlier in this chapter. Some walkers finish at **Tower Bridge**; this famous landmark makes a fitting end to the trip.

Beyond Tower Bridge, the final sections of the Thames Path weave through the detritus of the old London docks and industry, although this can be interesting in itself and many places are being regenerated. Some sections of the route follow pleasant riverside embankments past yacht marinas and renovated warehouses; other sections follow dirty streets or dodge through forlorn parks, tower blocks, waste-ground and other unattractive areas where you can't even see the river. You have to take the rough with the smooth.

You can still choose either the north bank or the south bank. The former passes more places of interest but involves more road walking, although there are plans to open up more riverside frontage in the future. The latter keeps closer to the river. Whichever way you go, you can't miss the glass-clad, pyramid-peaked tower that marks the flagship business development of **Canary Wharf** in a regenerated London Docklands. Its futuristic architecture symbolises the brash aspirations of the plutocratic 1980s.

At Greenwich the two routes rejoin and there's plenty to see: the **Cutty Sark** sailing ship, the **National Maritime Museum** and, of course, the Prime Meridian marked out at the **Old Royal Observatory**, which gave its name to Greenwich Mean Time. There are also a couple of nice pubs for lunch.

Beyond Greenwich, the last few miles take in some parkland, old wharves, busy roads, scrap-metal yards and forgotten back streets. In other words, the real London that tourists rarely see. At present you have to cut across the neck of the Greenwich peninsula before reaching the **Millennium Dome**, but soon, it's hoped, a path will be opened next to the river all the way round the peninsula. Be prepared for changes – including, possibly, the disappearance of the Dome itself if a sensible plan can't be agreed for it. Negotiations for its future use were ongoing at the time of writing.

Nearing journey's end you can see ahead the great silver shells of the **Thames Barrier** (the gates are raised in high-water conditions to prevent the capital from flooding). The barrier's visitors centre tells the story of the Thames through history, of the building of the barrier and of recent attempts to clean the river up. Pass under the control tower – look out for the bas-relief murals – to finish at the *Barrier Cafeteria*, with a terrace overlooking the river. Time for a cake and cup of tea to celebrate!

The North Downs Way

The North Downs is an elongated area of hills and chalk ridges running through south-eastern England between Farnham, south of London, and Dover, on the coast of the English Channel. The North Downs Way National Trail follows this natural line, passing through two Areas of Outstanding Natural Beauty with panoramic views, leafy woods, grassy downland, nature reserves, farmland, orchards and vineyards, and ending with chalk cliffs of Dover, the famous white cliffs of Dover.

The modern walkers' route keeps close, for many miles, to the Pilgrims Way. This is a Victorian interpretation of the ancient route taken by Christians from Canterbury to Winchester for the festival of St Swithen, and more recently from Winchester to Canterbury in celebration of St Thomas à Becket. Other historical features include Neolithic long barrows (burial mounds), medieval castles, 1970s motorways and the entrance to the Channel Tunnel.

On a map the route appears trapped in outer London's cobweb of roads. In reality, however, it bypasses most towns and you usually feel deep in the English countryside, not infrequently with the path very pleasantly to yourself.

Towards the end of the walk, at Boughton Lees, the path splits: The southern stretch takes walkers along the cliffs to Dover, while the northern loop goes via Canterbury.

Here we describe the two best sections of the route as separate walks: the far western end from Farnham to Dorking, and the far eastern end from Ashford to Dover. Both sections take two days to cover and make ideal weekend excursions from London.

Direction, Distance & Duration

The North Downs Way National Trail is traditionally followed west to east and the two sections we describe follow that pattern. The route has a total length of 157mi (251km), walkable in 12 days.

As a national trail the route is waymarked with acorn symbols and specific signs, but there are a few places where the waymarks fizzle out, so you'll definitely need a map.

PLANNING
Maps

For the western section of the walk that we describe, you need OS Landranger 1:50,000 maps No 186 *(Aldershot & Guildford)* and No 187 *(Dorking & Reigate)*. For the eastern section, you need No 179 *(Canterbury & East Kent)*.

Books

The *North Downs Way National Trail Guide* by Neil Curtis & Jim Walker has a detailed route description, background information and sections from OS maps that cover the route. The pocket-sized *North Downs Way – A Practical Handbook* costs just £2.95 and lists hotels, pubs, cafes, shops and places of interest; unfortunately, however, the information is presented in a very confusing manner. These and several other books and maps are available from local TICs or by mail order from Kent County Council (☎ 01622-221526). For more background, *Discovering the North Downs Way*, produced by Shire Publications, is full of fascinating historical anecdotes.

Information Sources

TICs on the North Downs Way include Farnham (☎ 01252-715109), Guildford (☎ 01483-444333), Ashford (☎ 01233-629165), Folkestone (☎ 01303-258594) and Dover (☎ 01304-205108).

Surrey County Council and Kent County Council have dedicated walking information lines, which include information on the North Downs Way: for Surrey, ☎ 0845-600 9009, e walkssurrey@surreycc.gov.uk; for Kent, try ☎ 01622-221529 or e walkkent @kent.gov.uk.

Specific details on the route are available from the North Downs Way National Trail Office (☎ 01622-221525, e northdownsway @kent.gov.uk). Also useful is the Web site at w www.nationaltrails.co.uk, which covers the North Downs Way and three other paths in Southern England.

PLACES TO STAY & EAT

The route is well served with B&Bs and hotels, although most are a mile or so off the path. We provide some suggestions in the route description. For a wider choice use *The Rambler's Yearbook & Accommodation Guide* and *Stillwell's National Trail Companion* (details are given under Books in the Facts for the Walker chapter), or the *North Downs Way – A Practical Handbook*, mentioned under Books earlier. For walkers on a budget there are only two YHA hostels. Camping possibilities are similarly limited, except near the coast where holiday sites cater for caravans and family campers.

At the end of each day there are pubs, restaurants or cafes, but noon options can be sparse, especially on the eastern end of the route, so it's best to take a packed lunch.

GETTING TO/FROM THE WALKS

Bus Farnham, Dorking, Ashford (near Wye), Folkestone and Dover can all be reached by National Express coach from London and by local bus from other towns, but are more easily reached by train.

Train Farnham, Guildford and Dorking are all London commuter towns with very regular train services to/from London Waterloo or London Victoria train stations (around four times per hour during the week and at least hourly at weekends). There is also an east-west train service between Farnham, Guildford and Dorking, which makes getting back to the start very easy.

Folkestone and Dover are busy ports, so have frequent and fast rail links to London (Charing Cross). The main line to Folkestone goes through Ashford (the station is called Ashford International), from where Wye can be reached. Alternatively, Wye can be accessed from London on trains to Margate.

Car Farnham is just off the A3, which runs between London and Portsmouth. Dorking is on the A24 between London and Worthing.

For the eastern section, Wye is north of Ashford, which is just off the M20 motorway between London and Folkestone, while Dover is reached via the M2 from London and A2 from Canterbury, or via the A20 from Folkestone.

The North Downs Way (West)

Distance	24mi (38.5km)
Duration	2 days
Standard	easy
Start	Farnham
Finish	Dorking
Gateways	Farnham, Dorking

Summary The western section of a popular national trail within easy reach of London. This is an excellent weekend excursion.

Direction, Duration & Distance

Listed here are the walking times for this two-day section. You should add an hour or two to each day for stops along the way, and possibly even for wine tasting.

day	from	to	mi/km
1	Farnham	Guildford	11/17.5
2	Guildford	Dorking	13/21

THE WALK
Farnham

Farnham is an old market town with some attractive Tudor buildings and red-brick Georgian houses and facades, as well as a famous **castle** with a Norman keep. The TIC (☎ 01252-715109) is at the council offices on South St.

Walker-friendly B&Bs include *Sleepy Hollow* (☎ 01252-721930, 1 Broomleaf Corner), off Waverley Lane (B3001), just up the hill from the start of the walk, where B&B costs £20/35 per single/double; and *Sandiway* (☎ 01252-710721, e john@shortheath.freeserve.co.uk, 24 Shortheath Rd), in the southern section of town, with just two rooms from £22/40. Also good is *High Wray* (☎ 01252-715589, 73 Lodge Hill Rd), about a mile south of the centre towards Tilford, charging from £20. If you book ahead, the people here will send you a 'safe way to walk from Farnham' leaflet and recommend a handy short cut onto the North Downs Way, which avoids the busy centre of town.

Top-end options include *The Bush Hotel* (☎ 0870-400 8225), on the Borough – a charming, old-fashioned place dating from the 17th century. Double rooms cost £145 from Sunday to Thursday, but only £45 for B&B on Friday and Saturday.

Many of Farnham's pubs serve good-value food. In the centre are *The Lamb*, on Abbey St, and *The Waverley Arms*, near the station. *The Shepherd & Flock*, on Moor Park Lane about 1.5mi east of the centre, has also been recommended.

Day 1: Farnham to Guildford
11mi (17.5km), 5–6 hours

Today's walk is a fairly gentle introduction to the national trail. For most of the way you pass through woodland and open fields. Be prepared to clamber over some stiles!

The day starts near the train station, meanders a bit around the suburbs, crosses the River Wey and then aims decidedly east. To your north is the distinctive long hill called **Hog's Back**. For these first 6mi, paths are fairly easy and level, except for a steep up-hill section before the village of Puttenham. *The Good Intent* is a friendly cosy pub on the main street, ideally placed for lunch, with giant 'doorstep' sandwiches for £2.50 and bar meals for around £4.

A mile or so past Puttenham the trail passes under the very busy A3, which links London and Portsmouth. Nearby is *Compton Tea Room*, not quite as busy as the A3, which serves food until 5.30pm.

The last 3mi are almost straight uphill, passing through the Losely Estate, then dropping steeply back towards the River Wey, from where a path leads northwards into Guildford centre.

Guildford

As the capital of Surrey, Guildford (pronounced gillford) has some fine old buildings, cobbled streets and a ruined **castle** with a 12th-century keep. The TIC (☎ 01483-444333) is on Tunsgate, an old street in the town centre. For somewhere to stay, the large and very central *'Y' Centre (☎ 01483-532555)*, formerly the YMCA, is on Bridge St, close to the bus station and charging £29.

B&B options include **Weybrook House** (☎ *01483-302394, 113 Stoke Rd*), charging from around £20; **Quiet Ways** (☎ *01483-232347, 29 Liddington Hall Drive*), 2mi north-west of the centre, with just two en suite rooms, charging £25/38 for a single/double; and the small and friendly **Crawford House Hotel** (☎ *01483-579299*, e *cliffbotfield@btclick.com, 73 Farnham Rd*), west of the centre, charging from £28 for singles and £42 to £47 for doubles.

Guildford has many places to eat, especially around the castle. Among the pubs, **The King's Head**, on King's Rd, serves good beer and food, while the **Old Ship Inn**, south of the centre on Portsmouth Rd, is livelier.

Shalford

In the village of Shalford, south of Guildford and about a mile south of the route, **The Laurels** (☎ *01483-565753*), with a big garden, good breakfasts and lots of cats, is recommended. B&B costs £22. Nearby, **The Seahorse** is a large pub with excellent ambience, great service and good evening meals from £6 to £9.

Day 2: Guildford to Dorking

13mi (21km), 6–7 hours

Today the route reaches the Downs proper. The route climbs higher than yesterday's and can get crowded, which is not surprising as there are some great views.

From Guildford centre, retrace your steps southwards beside the River Wey to meet the route and cross the bridge to aim east once again. Cross the A281 north of Shalford and follow the road (Pilgrims Way) until it bears left (keep a look out for the white cottage on the right). Cross the road and follow a track used by local horse riders past a small car park and on up through the Chantries. You eventually reach St Martha's Hill, with a tiny 12th-century **church** on top, and some lovely views over the rolling patchwork hills.

Drop down the hill on a sandy track, passing the junction where a route called the Downs Link heads off south to join the South Downs Way (described later in this book). At the bottom of the hill go left along a road for a short stretch, then up again to **Newlands Corner**. The site has a large car park, visitors centre, toilets and a takeaway **snack bar**, catering for people who come to admire the nearby views and (at weekends) large groups of motorcyclists. It's quite a busy place, so you may wish to use the facilities and hurry on.

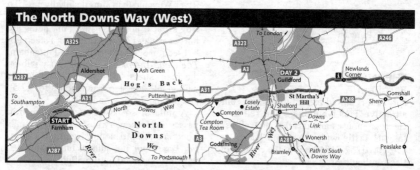

The North Downs Way (West)

Beyond Newlands Corner the route levels out, and becomes easy walking through some beautiful sections of shaded and enclosed woodland, with huge arches of branches and dappled sunlight on the path. There are occasional glimpses through the trees over the North Downs and across the flatlands, called the Weald, to the South Downs beyond.

At Ranmore Common you reach **St Barnabas Church**, built in 1859 and known as the Church on the North Downs Way. About a mile north, the *YHA Hostel (☎ 01306-877964)*, at Tanner's Hatch, costs £8 (self-catering only); this place was once famously basic but a recent renovation makes it more comfortable without losing any of the 're-mote' atmosphere.

On the route a gravel track descends through **Denbies Wine Estate** (see the boxed tex), which has a *cafe-restaurant* ideally placed to revive flagging walkers. From here it's a mile or so to Westhumble, which has a train station on the line to London. Dorking is just over a mile south via the A24.

If you've still got a couple of hours to spare before going to Dorking, it's worth continuing east along the path, up steeply and then along the escarpment edge of **Box Hill** for some of the best views in the area. Bibliophiles should look out for the *Literary Walk at the Foot of Box Hill* leaflet available in local TICs, describing the links of several authors (including John Keats, Daniel Defoe and Jane Austen) with the area. (Keen Austen fans will recall the key scene in *Emma* between the heroine and the enigmatic Mr Knightley, which took place here.)

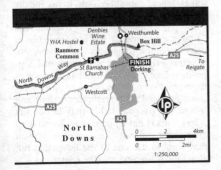

Denbies Wine – Not Quite Champagne?

A visit to Denbies Wine Estate (☎ 01306-742 0020, w www.denbiesvineyard.co.uk), the largest vineyard in England, is highly recommended. Along with a stylish cafe-restaurant under a glass-domed roof and a well-stocked shop, there are daily tours of the wine cellars, a ride on an indoor 'people mover' and the opportunity for wine tasting.

Frustratingly for the company, although the chalk hills of the North Downs are geologically identical to those in the Champagne region of France, and even though Denbies uses the same grapes as its French competitors, it can't call its sparkling wine champagne because of copyright law. It's called 'brut cuvée' instead and tastes just as good – and it's English!

Dorking

The quaint old market town of Dorking has a fine **church** with one of the tallest spires in the country, cute cobblestone courtyards and a good range of places to stay and eat.

Walker-friendly B&Bs include *Fairdene Guesthouse (☎ 01306-888337)*, on Moores Rd, with single/double B&B for £27/45. On Rose Hill, very near the centre, are a couple of good places: *The Waltons (☎ 01306-883127, e thewaltons@rosehill5.demon .co.uk, No 5)*, charging from £20 for singles and £35 to £40 for doubles; and *The Gardners (☎ 01306-887209, e gardner8rh@aol .com, No 8)* with B&B from £20 to £25.

Another option is the smart *Chart House (☎ 01306-882040, e jillattfield@online .rednet.co.uk)*, on the leafy south-west edge of town, charging from £35/40 for B&B.

At the top of the range, *The White Horse Hotel (☎ 0870-400 8282)*, on the High St, charges from £135 per double midweek and £70 at weekends.

Pubs in the centre that do food and good beer include *The Kings Arms*, on West St, and the *Surrey Yeoman*, on the High St. Also good for food is *The Pilgrim (☎ 01306-889951)*, on Station Rd, which has straightforward B&B for £25/40.

The North Downs Way (East)

Distance	22mi (35.5km)
Duration	2 days
Standard	easy
Start	Wye
Finish	Dover
Gateways	Ashford, Dover

Summary The eastern section of the North Downs Way, following part of the Pilgrims Way and ending with a final stretch along the white cliffs of Dover, is an excellent two-day jaunt.

Direction, Duration & Distance

Listed here are the walking times for the eastern section of the North Downs Way. Factor in some extra time for lunch stops etc.

day	from	to	mi/km
1	Wye	Folkestone	16/25.5
2	Folkestone	Dover	6/10

THE WALK
Wye

The pretty town of Wye has a good choice of places to stay and eat. Walker-friendly B&Bs include *Selsfield (☎ 01233-812133, 46 Oxenturn Rd)*, just east of town, a comfortable place charging £25/40 for singles/doubles; and *Riverside (☎ 01233-813098)*, on Bridge St, just west of the centre, charging £30/40.

Riverside is next door to *The Tickled Trout* pub, which serves good food; or you can go a little farther to *The New Flying Horse Inn (☎ 01233-812297)*, on Upper Bridge St, where B&B costs about £40/50 per double. Another pub option is *The Kings Head Hotel (☎ 01233-812418)*, on Church St, with B&B for around £40 per double and bar meals for about £5.

Day 1: Wye to Folkestone
16mi (25.5km), 7–8 hours

Today's walk is long and quite hard but rewards your efforts with wonderful views all around. The route crosses high rolling downland and open farmland, with just a few short woodland sections for a change of scenery.

The North Downs Way goes through Wye, so you can easily pick it up by the church or off the road leading north out of town. The route itself aims eastwards and climbs steeply up onto Wye Down. At the top of the hill there's a fork that's quite easy to miss. You have to keep looking behind for the waymark on your right, indicating a right (east) turn. It's not visible when coming from the west.

The route goes through **Wye Nature Reserve**, then follows lanes and tracks down to the straggling village of Stowting, where *The Tiger Inn* is a good place for lunch. There's a steep push out of Stowting up Cobb's Hill to Farthing Common.

The route then meanders over the downs above Postling and crosses several other paths. With missing waymarks at vital points it can be easy to lose your way. Keep a close eye on the map and keep to high ground across a large field that dips down in the middle (avoid walking too far to the right). Cross a lane and enjoy a steep climb up Tolsford Hill, marked by radio masts just north of the summit.

From here make sure you keep aiming east (the Saxon Shore Way diverges south). From this point the North Downs Way shares the Saxon Shore Way route all the way to Dover. Follow signs for both, descending through woods to skirt just east of Etchinghill. From here the path ascends sharply and loops through fields along the top of the edge of the downs. There are great views over Folkestone and – it has to be said – the M20 motorway and the Channel Tunnel Terminal, where cars drive onto trains for the underground ride to France.

Keep heading east, crossing over the A20 (a busy extension of the motorway) as it goes through a tunnel, to reach the A260, which is a slightly less busy main road. Opposite is East Crete Rd, which is the route of the North Downs Way, but to go into Folkestone you need to turn right (south) here and follow the pavement that runs beside the A260. This is not a pleasant walk and hard after today's already long mileage, so you may want to use one of the buses that run along the main road into the centre.

GRAHAM BELL

GRANT DIXON

NICHOLAS REUSS

NICHOLAS REUSS

NICHOLAS REUSS

NICHOLAS REUSS

DAVID TIPLING

Clockwise from Top Left: Guillemots gather onshore during the breeding season; Scots pine cones and heather; puffins lined up and facing into the wind; great spotted woodpecker; a thick carpet of bluebells in a beech forest; berries on a hawthorn bush

VERONICA GARBUTT

Stepping back in time on the Thames Path at Runnymede, birthplace of the *Magna Carta*

CHARLOTTE HINDLE

East-west meridian, Greenwich

VERONICA GARBUTT

The July Henley Royal Regatta, traditional since 1829

DAVID ELSE

The Avebury stone circle stands as a vivid reminder of the ancient origins of the Ridgeway trail

Folkestone

There's lots of accommodation here, but this seaside resort gets very busy in summer so book ahead. For assistance contact the TIC (☎ 01303-258594) on Harbour St. Highly recommended is *The Park Inn Hotel* (☎ *01303-252000, 2 Radnor Park Rd*), opposite the train station. This is a quiet and friendly pub, rather shabby on the outside but renovated and soundproofed inside, with en suite singles/doubles for £20/30. It serves good bar food and very reasonable meals in the attached restaurant. Another walker-friendly option is *Sunny Lodge Guesthouse* (☎ *01303-251498,* e *linda.dowsett@btclick .com, 85 Cheriton Rd*), west of the centre, charging from £35 for doubles. There are many more B&Bs along the same road.

Folkestone has a fair selection of eating options. Good pubs doing food include *The Lifeboat*, on North St, a small quiet place; and *Wetherspoons*, a large chain pub stylishly converted from a former church.

Capel-le-Ferne

If you want to avoid the bright lights of Folkestone, 2mi farther on in the small town of Capel-le-Ferne you can get B&B for £18 at *Xaipe* (☎ *01303-257956, 18 Alexandra Rd*), a small bungalow just off the route (and in case you wondered, it's Greek for something like happiness).

Day 2: Folkestone to Dover

6mi (10km), 3–4 hours

The final stretch of the route is a short, sharp and very dramatic coastal walk, where the path sticks close to the edge of the cliffs – a heady experience for vertigo sufferers.

From Folkestone regain the path just before Capel-le-Ferne and the **Battle of Britain Memorial**, a simple statue set in a propeller design, which commemorates pilots from Britain, Australia, New Zealand, Canada and many other countries killed during this period of WWII.

The route then rollercoasts across the top of the white cliffs of Dover through tufty grasslands and wild gorse bushes. This is where the North Downs meet the English Channel. Formed by the relentless erosion

of the sea, the cliffs have been a symbol of homecoming for sailors for many centuries and are still an icon of Englishness today – protected as a Heritage Coast. This is also a popular walking and strolling area, although the path is quite overgrown, which can sometimes obscure waymarks. There isn't much space between the busy A20 on your left and the edge of the cliffs on your right (between the devil and the deep blue sea?), but there's still room for several paths and it's important to check carefully you're on the right one. If you want the views, avoid taking a right turn onto the Warren & Fossil Trail (just past the *Cliff Top Café*) as this leads down to shore level.

As you get near Dover, the route is not clear, so take care. By a big white house there's a fork; ignore the mud track on the right and take the gravel path that forks left towards the gate with the 'No Motorcycling' sign on it. This soon turns into an unattractive but fairly flat concrete path, still passing through long grass and gorse bushes.

When the harbour first comes in to view, there is a very steep descent as you walk along the spine of the cliff through meadows colourful with seasonal flowers. With the busy main road still on your left, you face one more steep uphill, then another descent as the salt air really hits you and the beaches come into view. The route into the centre of Dover is very well signposted as you use a pedestrian tunnel to walk under the A20, then continue though, up and behind a housing estate.

The final mile or so leads you up again through an area called Western Heights – you'll see why! When we passed the battlements of **Drop Redoubt** (a historic fort), the North Downs waymark was broken; if you're in doubt, continue walking round the top of the hill and start descending as the sea appears ahead of you. You'll reach Cow Gate, an entrance to the Western Heights and the end of the route. From here it's a short walk downhill into Dover town centre or out to the newly developed De Bradelei Wharf shopping complex on the seafront, a picturesque place to rest aching feet and have a nice patriotic cuppa!

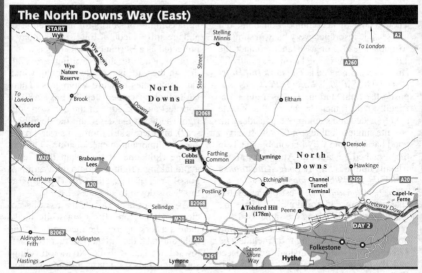

The North Downs Way (East)

Dover

Dover is a very busy passenger port, best known for its white cliffs – which you've just walked over – and **medieval castle**. The TIC (☎ 01304-205108) on Townwall St, near the seafront, can guide you through the huge choice of places to stay.

Budget options include the large and busy *YHA Hostel* (☎ 01304-201314, 306 London Rd), charging £10.85. Walker-friendly B&Bs include *Bleriots* (☎ 01304-211394, 47 Park Ave), charging from £18; and *Amanda Guesthouse* (☎ 01304-201711), on Harold St, at £36 per double. *St Martin's Guesthouse* (☎ 01304-205938, 17 Castle Hill Rd), at £45 per double (with reductions in the low season), is also recommended.

Good places to eat include the *The Red Lion*, at Charlton Green near the YHA Hostel. *Blakes*, in Castle St, is a bar-restaurant, which has also been recommended.

Other Walks

The Jubilee Walkway, described earlier in this chapter, takes in many great sights of London, but this, of course, is only a taster

and the city offers many more opportunities for exploring on foot. Several of the guidebooks mentioned under Information in the introduction to this chapter contain suggestions for city street routes.

PARK WALKS

To get away from the streets, you could consider a long walk through London's glorious parks. You could start in St James's Park and go east to west through Hyde Park and Kensington Gardens. Or try a south to north route, tying in all or any of Battersea Park, Ranlagh Gardens, Hyde Park, Regent's Park and Hampstead Heath, using buses or tubes to skip the street sections in between. To the south-west are the larger open areas of Richmond Park and Wimbledon Common. On a clear day, and armed with a picnic, a walk like this is guaranteed to banish urban blues.

Another park option is the **Green Chain**, a well-signposted and highly recommended 40mi network of walks in south-east London connecting many parks, commons, woods and other open spaces. Essentially the Chain stretches from the outer suburbs of Thamesmead and Erith, on the banks of the River Thames, through Plumstead, Eltham

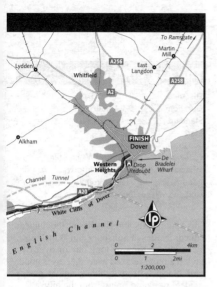

and Beckenham to Crystal Palace. A major branch goes through Charlton, linking this line to the Thames Barrier. Access is very easy as the whole route is well served by public transport, and you can do short or long stretches. A free leaflet on the route is available from local TICs and a set of 10 weather-proof route cards (£3.50) is available from The Green Chain Project (☎ 020-8921 5028), PO Box 22119, London SE18 6WY. You can also check the Web site at Ⓦ www.greenchain.com.

On the other side of London, the **Lea Valley Walk** is a 50mi linear route from Limehouse, in the East End, along the valley of the River Lee, winding a green way between the suburbs and towns of Tottenham, Enfield, Waltham Abbey, Hertford and Harpenden to reach Luton, north of the capital. Of course, you don't have to do the whole route; it's very well served by public transport all along the walk. The route goes through country parks and nature reserves, beside lakes and reservoirs, over golf courses and beside canals. The southern sections of the walk are undoubtedly urban but it becomes surprisingly rural as you go north. You can get leaflets, route maps and more

details from the Lee Valley Park Information Centre (☎ 01992-702200, Ⓦ www.leevalle ypark.org.uk), Abbey Gardens, Waltham Abbey, Essex EN3 1XQ.

THE RING & THE LOOP
The Green Chain walk mentioned earlier is part of a complete circuit of London called the **Capital Ring** – a mix of city streets, parks, gardens and other open suburban spaces. This 72mi route is divided into 15 stages. At the time of writing, only part of the route had been completed, but there's still enough to keep you busy for several days! The rest of the route was due to open by mid-2001.

For a long-distance option try the **London Loop**, a 150mi outer circuit taking full advantage of the many green spaces that line the capital's fringe – many with a surprisingly rural feel. The route also passes several villages with attractive pubs for lunch. This is an ideal way to sample the countryside and yet still be in reach of the city centre.

Of course, you don't have to do the Ring or the Loop in one go. In fact they're designed to be done in short sections, tied in with a circular route, or using bus and train to get back to your start. Some excellent leaflets on these routes are available; each has a map of every section, describes points of interest along the way and details how the start and end can be reached by public transport. The leaflets are available from libraries and local TICs, and more information on the ring and the loop is available from London Walking (Ⓦ www.londonw alking.com). A dedicated London Loop guidebook is due to be published by Aurum Press in 2001.

LONG-DISTANCE PATHS
As well as the Thames Path and the North Downs Way, some other long walks described elsewhere in this book are within fairly easy reach of London. These include the Clarendon Way (in the Wessex chapter) and the South Downs Way (in the Southern England Long-Distance Paths chapter). For more ideas, see the Other Walks in Southern England chapter.

Wessex

In the 9th century Wessex was one of several British kingdoms, ruled most famously by the much admired King Alfred the Great (849–899) from his capital at Winchester. At its greatest extent Wessex included much of western, southern and south-central England. The word is a derivation of 'West Saxons', hence also Essex and Sussex (although no Nossex). Much later, the Wessex name was resurrected and immortalised when the author Thomas Hardy (1840–1928) based many of his pastoral novels in this part of Britain, including the much-read *Tess of the d'Urbervilles* and *Far from the Madding Crowd*.

Today Wessex no longer officially exists, but the name is used as a convenient catch-all for the area, which includes the counties of Dorset, Hampshire, Somerset, Wiltshire and Berkshire, and much of the fertile Thames Valley.

As in Thomas Hardy's day, this is still a largely rural region – and there are many opportunities for walking. Most routes are straightforward, often spectacular without being overbearing, and can be walked at any time of the year. They are also within easy travelling distance of the popular tourist centres of London, Salisbury, Winchester and Bath.

In this chapter we describe two short walks – the Clarendon Way and the Kennet & Avon Canal – plus sections of some long-distance paths (LDPs) – the time-worn Ridgeway and Thames Path National Trails. There are also some suggestions for other walks in the region.

GETTING THERE & AWAY

For specific information on public transport services in the Wessex area, see Getting to/from the Walk under individual walks. Alternatively, the Getting Around chapter lists several public transport inquiry lines that provide details of both national and local bus and train services: See the boxed text 'National Transport Information' on p92.

The Clarendon Way

Distance	27mi (43.5km)
Duration	9–11 hours
Standard	easy
Start	Salisbury
Finish	Winchester
Gateways	Salisbury, Winchester

Summary A long but straightforward walk on good paths and tracks, through woods, farmland and villages, and over rolling hills.

This route starts and finishes at the ancient cathedral cities of Salisbury and Winchester. It can be done in one long day or over two days at a more relaxed pace. Access is good, particularly to/from London, and it makes an ideal weekend break from the city.

The route derives its name from the medieval Clarendon Palace, now ruined, which is passed on the walk a few miles east of Salisbury. The route has several more historical features, including the remains of a Roman road, several Bronze Age tumuli (ancient burial mounds) and a Civil War battle site.

It's also a walk through Britain today; a classic Southern English landscape of fields, woods, farms and quiet rivers, plus cosy pubs, manor houses, neat thatched cottages and narrow country lanes frequented by very smart cars.

Direction, Distance & Duration

The walk can be made in either direction, although west to east may be more comfortable weather-wise. The 27mi requires nine to 11 hours' walking time, so you're looking at 10 to 12 hours overall. This can be a push in one day, particularly if you make any sightseeing pauses, so you may prefer to stretch it over two. There are no camping or hostel options along the route, forcing those on a tight budget to do the walk in one go. Waymarking is reasonable – the symbol is a bishop's mitre (ceremonial hat) – but a map is definitely required.

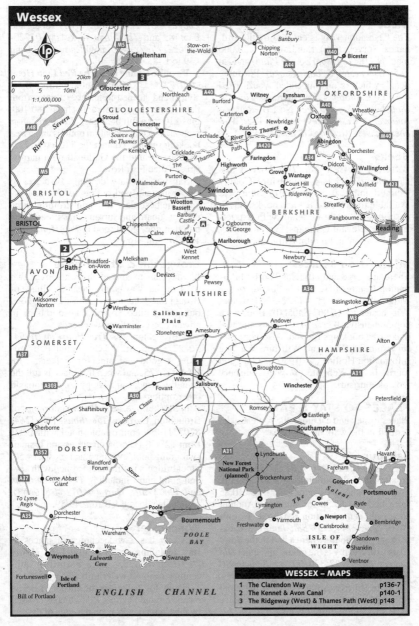

Wessex

1:1,000,000

WESSEX – MAPS	
1 The Clarendon Way	p136-7
2 The Kennet & Avon Canal	p140-1
3 The Ridgeway (West) & Thames Path (West)	p148

WESSEX

PLANNING
Maps
The Clarendon Way is covered by the Ordnance Survey (OS) Landranger 1:50,000 maps No 184 *(Salisbury & the Plain)* and No 185 *(Winchester & Basingstoke)*. For more detail, which is recommended, you'll need the OS Explorer 1:25,000 maps No 130 *(Salisbury & Stonehenge)*, No 131 *(Romsey, Andover & Test Valley)* and No 132 *(Winchester, New Alresford & East Meon)*.

Books
Walks in Wessex: The Test Way & the Clarendon Way is a Hampshire County Council publication by Barry Shurlock, available from local TICs and bookshops. It describes the route in detail, with extracts from the relevant OS maps, and covers accommodation and food possibilities.

Information Sources
There are large and efficient Tourist Information Centres (TICs) at both ends of the walk – Salisbury (☎ 01722-334956) and Winchester (☎ 01962-840500). Both have comprehensive *Where to Stay* lists and will make free bookings for you. Also very useful is the Salisbury and Wiltshire Walking Information Hotline (☎ 01980-623255) and tourist board Web site (W www.salisbury .gov.uk/tourism).

PLACES TO STAY & EAT
Places to stay and eat along the route are described in the walk description.

Salisbury
The busy *YHA Hostel (☎ 01722-327572)* is an attractive old building on Millford Hill, just east of the city centre, charging £10.85 for a bed and £5.50 for camping. Another cheap and central option is *Matt & Tiggy's (☎ 01722-327443, 51 Salt Lane)*, a backpackers guesthouse where a bed in the dorm costs £10. Nearby is the quaint and quiet *Old Bakery (☎ 01722-320100, 35 Bedwin St)* with B&B from £18/38 for singles/doubles.

Castle Rd (the A345, between the inner ring road and Old Sarum) has a wide choice of B&Bs, including *Leena's (☎ 01722-*

335419, No 50), from £25/46; *Victoria Lodge (☎ 01722-320586, No 61)*, for around £35/48; and *Hayburn Wyke (☎ 01722-412627, No 72)* with doubles ranging from £39 to £48.

If you're feeling rich, *The Red Lion Hotel (☎ 01722-323334)*, on central Milford St, is stylish and steeped in history (it dates from the 13th century), with rooms from £80/100, plus £10 for a full breakfast. For more information on accommodation options and a free booking service, contact the TIC (☎ 01722-334956), behind the Guildhall on a narrow street called Fish Row.

Salisbury has a wide range of places to eat, from fast-food outlets to fine restaurants; the best place to begin strolling is the market square and surrounding streets. One pub that does good food is *The Haunch of Venison*, on Minster St.

Broughton & Stockbridge
If you plan to spread the walk over two days, the halfway point is near the village of Broughton. Accommodation there is good but quite limited, so you'll need to book in advance, especially at weekends.

In Broughton, *Yew Tree House (☎ 01794-301227)*, opposite the Greyhound pub, provides a good welcome for walkers, with B&B for £25, and when this place is full the friendly owners are happy to recommend other options.

In Stockbridge, a small town north-east of Broughton, *Carbery Guesthouse (☎ 01264-810771)* is a comfortable hotel with B&B from £28/50 (£35/54 en suite) and a small swimming pool; evening meals cost £14.50. Stockbridge's main street is lined with several good pubs, including *The Three Cups* and *The White Hart (☎ 01264-810663)*, which also does B&B for £49/59.

Winchester
This city has a wide choice of places to stay, including a very central *YHA Hostel (☎ 01962-853723)*, in a beautiful 18th-century restored water mill, charging £9.

Handy for walkers is the cluster of B&Bs on and around St Cross Rd (which is crossed by the Clarenden Way on the edge of the city centre) within half a mile to a mile of the cathedral. These include *67 St Cross Rd* (☎ *01962-863002)*, charging from £20; *Florum House* (☎ *01962-840427,* [e] *florum .house@barclays.net, No 47)*, a small hotel with 10 rooms, charging £46/61 for en suite singles/doubles and offering discounts for two nights; *5 Ranelagh Rd* (☎ *01962-869555,* [e] *thefarrells@easicom.com)*, a very walker-friendly place, charging from £22 (or £50 for an en suite double); and *85 Christchurch Rd* (☎ *01962-868661)*, near the junction of Stanmore Rd and St Cross Rd, from £23. *Mrs Wright* (☎ *028-9385 5067, 56 Cross Rd)* has also been recommended. For more accommodation options and a free booking service, contact the TIC (☎ 01962-840500), in the Guildhall on Broadway (the main street), near the cathedral.

For food in Winchester you have a wide choice. Worthy of comment are *Pizza Express* in a renovated 18th-century building on Bridge St, near the statue of King Alfred, – light years away from the usual plastic and polished steel – and *The Eclipse Inn*, near the cathedral, serving homely food in quaint surroundings. There are several other good old pubs nearby and most do food in the evenings.

GETTING TO/FROM THE WALK

Bus Salisbury and Winchester are linked by regular National Express coaches to London and other parts of the country. Local bus services run between Winchester and Salisbury roughly every two hours (less frequently on Sunday); all go via Stockbridge, some via Broughton and some via King's Somborne. If you want to cut the first few miles from the walk described, buses from Salisbury and Andover stop at Pitton and Middle Winterslow.

Train Salisbury and Winchester are on the outer edges of the capital's commuter belt, so there are frequent trains to/from London, as well as the Midlands and the southern coast of England.

Car Salisbury is on the A30, easily reached from London. Winchester lies just off the

M3 between London and Portsmouth. Salisbury and Winchester are linked by the A30 and the B3049 (via Stockbridge).

THE WALK
Salisbury to King's Somborne
14mi (22.5km), 4½–5½hours

The route starts at Salisbury Cathedral (see the boxed text) and heads out of town along Milford St. Begin by following signs for the YHA hostel ('Youth Hostel') – there are none for the Clarendon Way. Go under the inner ring road, up Millford Hill, down a suburban path called Millford Hollow and along Millford Hill Rd, which crosses the Bourne River. Surprisingly quickly, you're out in the country.

Keep heading east along a lane called Queen Manor Rd, and look out for the first noticeable waymarks on the right, onto a path across a field and up King Manor Hill. Looking back, the path points straight towards the cathedral, still towering above any other building in Salisbury.

From the top of the hill, continue through woodland and pass the remains of **Clarendon Palace** where, in 1164, Henry II hosted an early skirmish in the long power

---

Salisbury & the Cathedral

Salisbury is famous for its cathedral, but this bustling town (officially a city) is not just a tourist trap. Markets have been held twice weekly for over 600 years and the jumble of stalls still draws large crowds. The town's architecture, including some very beautiful half-timbered buildings, is a blend of every style since the Middle Ages.

Salisbury Cathedral is one of the most beautiful in Britain. The architecture is uniformly Early English, a style characterised by pointed arches, flying buttresses and a rather austere feel. The architectural uniformity is due to its rapid construction – between 1220 and 1266 – a remarkably short time for such a mammoth project.

The cathedral is open daily; to enter, a donation of £3 is requested.

struggle between crown and church. The 'turbulent priest' Thomas à Becket was present and was killed six years later at the king's behest. An overgrown stretch of a wall is all you can see today, but the historical buildings conservation agency, English Heritage, was busy tidying it up in mid-2000, so the site may be open to visitors when you pass.

At a fork just after the palace, keep straight on the main track for 100m, then branch left onto a narrow footpath through pleasant woodland all the way to the pretty little village of Pitton. From the crossroads, head south-east briefly (nearby, the village *shop* sells drinks, food and ice creams), pass *The Silver Plough* pub and turn immediately left (north) into a lane lined with houses. The lane turns into a path over the hill to reach a road by the very attractive flint **church** of West Winterslow.

Cross the road and go down a track with the church on your right. Go through a gate and cross the small field to a stile, and then a larger field to another stile where you pick up a path leading north-eastwards to Middle Winterslow. The waymarks seem to have disappeared here and the path may be obscured by grass or crops, so this short section is potentially confusing. Keep a close eye on your map.

The path eventually leads you out of the fields, through a children's play area on the edge of the cricket pitch and then along another path to meet a road in the centre of Middle Winterslow village. Go straight on down a lane and another path for 500m or so. On the edge of the village the route hooks up with a former Roman road (originally between Old Sarum, near Salisbury, and the port of Clausentum, near Southampton). The map reading is easier – you pretty much go straight ahead for several miles – and now you've crossed from Wiltshire to Hampshire, the signposting is much better.

Follow the route of the Roman road along a track to the north of a small village (effectively an eastward extension of Middle Winterslow) called the Common and then eastwards in a straight line for about 2mi. At Buckholt Farm, the Clarendon Way leaves the Roman road and goes over a hilly area before descending into the sleepy village of Broughton.

If it's time for a rest, Broughton's pair of pubs, *The Greyhound* and *The Tally Ho*,

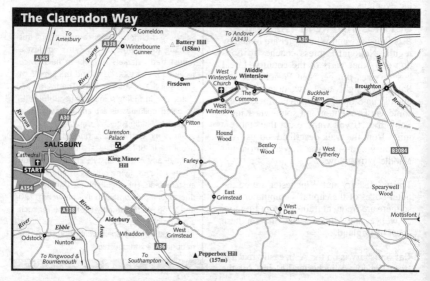

The Clarendon Way

await the weary and thirsty walker. Nearby, **St Mary's Church** has a fine dovecote in its churchyard, demonstrating that intensive animal rearing is not a new invention. Battery pigeons were raised in this circular structure in medieval times, with 3½ tons of young pigeons slaughtered each year.

The route leads along Rectory Lane out of Broughton, over Wallop Brook and behind some large houses, then across fields (many full of pigs) to Houghton. A narrow lane leads to two footbridges across the crystal clear waters of the **River Test**, where a rash of 'private' signs indicates a premier trout stream. If there's one thing the English value highly it's their fishing rights. Rumour has it that even Prince Charles had to join a waiting list for membership of the local angling club.

Just after the river, the route crosses an old railway track, which is part of the Test Way, an LDP through Hampshire. If you want to call it a day, turn left to reach Stockbridge; otherwise go up the steep hill, then follow the lane down to King's Somborne – yet another pretty little village, although straddling the busy A3057 road it's not as peaceful as others. There's a *pub* to slake

any walking thirst or hunger. The village *shop* (closed on Sunday), with a bench by the stream, is an alternative spot for refreshment and rest.

King's Somborne to Winchester
13mi (21km), 4½–5½ hours

Leave King's Somborne on the lane heading north-east towards Ashley, then on the edge of the village take a path on the right. This leads uphill through fields and woods to briefly join the Roman road again, before it zigzags around more fields and takes you up to the summit of **Beacon Hill**. This splendid view point is topped by a curious, pyramid-like monument marking the burial place of a horse which, in 1733, tumbled into a local quarry during a hunt. Apparently, neither the horse its nor rider was injured, and the grateful owner changed his mount's name to Beware Chalkpit, which went on to win several races.

If it's a weekend you're likely to meet a crowd of people for the next few miles as the route crosses **Farley Mount Country Park**, with a rather confusing tangle of walking paths and bridleways. The Clarendon waymarks disappear at some junctions,

WESSEX

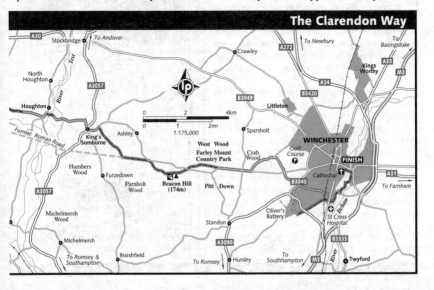

The Clarendon Way

but if in doubt follow the bridleway (marked by red poles with horseshoe symbols) through the woods. The Clarendon Way once again meets the Roman road, which is now also a modern road, then branches off to loop north and then south past farms and a golf course.

The country lane becomes a suburban street as you enter the outskirts of Winchester. At a junction with the busy B3040, go straight onto Stanmore Rd. The official route turns at the first right and follows Oliver's Battery Rd to **Oliver's Battery**, the site where Cromwell forced the city to surrender during the Civil War. However, this section through the suburbs is fiddly and the latter section, down a narrow sunken track at the back of a housing estate, is far from salubrious. It's much better to continue

downhill on Stanmore Rd and under the railway bridge to meet another main road (the B3355). Turn right here, then left just before a pub called *The Bell*, where you rejoin the Clarendon Way. Nearby is **St Cross' Hospital**, a charitable home founded in 1137 for '13 poor impotent men so reduced in strength as rarely or never able to raise themselves without the assistance of one another'.

From here the Way leads across beautiful water meadows beside the River Itchen, then through a series of narrow streets and arches round ancient Winchester College. Once again it's worth diverting from the official Clarendon waymarks, following instead the signs to Winchester Cathedral, where you can finish the walk at the grand cathedral door.

Winchester & the Cathedral

If one place lies at the centre of English history and embodies the romantic vision of an English heartland, it is Winchester – a beautiful city surrounded by water meadows and rolling chalk downland. Despite this, it seems to have escaped tourist inundation – certainly compared with theme parks like Bath.

Alfred the Great and many successors made Winchester their capital, and William the Conqueror came here to claim the crown of England. The Domesday Book was also written here, but much of the present-day city dates from the 18th century, by which time the town had settled down as a prosperous market centre.

Winchester Cathedral was built between 1079 and 1093, shortly after the Norman Conquest of 1066. In the 13th century the cathedral was extended in the Early English style, and from the mid-14th century the Norman nave was completely rebuilt in a late Gothic style called 'perpendicular', characterised by large windows, fan vaults and an emphasis on vertical lines. The cathedral's internal detail outshines the comparatively mundane exterior, and makes an interesting contrast with Salisbury Cathedral, where the exterior is wonderful and the interior less inspiring.

The cathedral is open daily from 7.15am to 6.30pm and a £2 donation is requested.

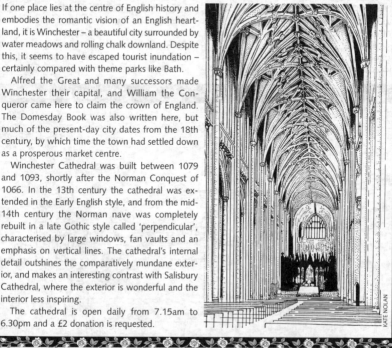

KATE NOLAN

The Kennet & Avon Canal

Distance	10mi (16km)
Duration	4–5 hours
Standard	easy
Start	Bath
Finish	Bradford-on-Avon
Gateways	Bath, Devizes, Salisbury

Summary A flat and relatively short waterway walk through delightful countryside with a good taste of Britain's early industrial heritage. An optional extension doubles the distance and offers contrasting scenery, as well as more canal-side attractions.

The Kennet & Avon Canal was built between 1794 and 1810 to join London and Bristol, two of the most important ports in the country, by linking the Rivers Avon and Kennet. The project was completed before the days of mechanisation, so most construction was done by workmen called navigators ('navvies') using little more than picks and wheelbarrows. When completed, goods were carried along the canal in barges called narrowboats, towed by horses.

In the late 19th and early 20th centuries, canals had to compete with railways and then road transport for the movement of freight. By the 1960s much of the Kennet & Avon was in an unusable state. However, since the early 1980s dedicated enthusiasts have rebuilt the canal, providing a new lease of life and several new uses never foreseen by the navvies. People in pleasure cruisers, rowing boats and canoes enjoy the waterway, along with anglers, while walkers and cyclists (and the occasional horse) can follow the towpath. There is usually plenty of room for all considerate users.

One of the most interesting sections of the canal is from Bath to Bradford-on-Avon, as the route involves a fascinating series of bridges, tunnels and impressive aqueducts. Other attractions include the canal boats, canal-side pubs and good bird life.

Direction, Distance & Duration

This linear walk can be done in either direction. We describe the route from Bath to Bradford-on-Avon, assuming you'll return to Bath by train. Or you could overnight in Bradford-on-Avon.

From Bath to Bradford-on-Avon it's a flat 10mi (16km) stretch, which takes about four to five hours of walking. Add some extra time for lunch and admiring the aqueducts, and you will probably need about six hours.

Alternatives If you don't want to go all the way to Bradford-on-Avon, you can walk as far as Avoncliff (8.5mi from Bath), from where you can catch a train back to Bath.

If you've got more time, you can continue along the canal from Bradford-on-Avon to Devizes. This provides a change of scenery – from enclosed river valley to open farmland – and includes the 'flight' of 16 closely stepped locks at Caen Hill, one of the most spectacular features on Britain's entire inland waterway system. The distance from Bradford-on-Avon to Devizes is 11.5mi (18.5km), requiring another five to six hours of walking. This optional extension (slightly longer than the main walk itself!) is described at the end of the walk description.

If you do the extension, it brings the total distance from Bath to Devizes up to 21.5mi (34.5km), which most people will need nine to 11 hours to cover. However, because the route is flat and easy underfoot, strong walkers could do it in around seven to eight hours – not too demanding on a long summer's day.

Alternatively, you might like to spread the whole route over two days, overnighting at Bradford-on-Avon (and possibly at Devizes too) before returning to Bath.

PLANNING
Maps & Books

The OS Landranger 1:50,000 maps No 172 *(Bristol & Bath)* and No 173 *(Swindon & Devizes)* cover the route described here. For more detail on the whole canal and a bargeful of very useful information, the *Kennet & Avon Canal Map & Guide*, published by GeoProjects, is highly recommended.

The Kennet & Avon Walk by Ray Quinlan covers the whole canal, plus river walks at either end, from the mouth of the Avon, near Bristol, to Westminster in central London.

Information Sources

TICs are located at Bath (☎ 01225-477101), Bradford-on-Avon (☎ 01225-865797) and Devizes (☎ 01380-729408). Also useful are British Waterways (☎ 01380-722859, W www .britishwaterways.co.uk) and the Kennet & Avon Canal Trust (☎ 01380-721279, W www .katrust.demon.co.uk), which has done much of the canal's restoration work.

PLACES TO STAY & EAT

The main towns on this walk along the Kennet & Avon Canal are very well served by places to stay and eat. Additionally, near the canal are several good country pubs, ideally placed for lunch or refreshment; a selection is described in the walk description.

Bath

At the start of the route, Bath has accommodation and facilities for all tastes and budgets, as befits a major tourist destination. These are listed under the Cotswold Way in the Cotswolds chapter.

Bradford-on-Avon

Bradford-on-Avon has several places to stay. Nearest the canal, just over the bridge from the Canal Tavern, is *The Barge Inn* (*☎ 01225-863403*), charging from £25/35 per single/double and does good bar food. Nearby, *The Old Cottage* (*☎ 01225-868414*, *e bedandbreakfast@theoldcottage .fsbusiness.co.uk*), now swallowed up in a new housing estate called Spencers Orchard, is a very walker-friendly B&B with rooms for £25/38 (or £55 en suite).

On the main street leading from the canal to the Town Bridge (which crosses the River Avon) are several pubs and teashops, including *The Riverside Inn* (*☎ 01225-863526*), not surprisingly overlooking the river. It has simple en suite rooms from £35/47 and provides meals every evening except Sunday.

On the other side of the Town Bridge, *The Swan Hotel* (*☎ 01225-868686*) charges from £50/70; eating options include bar food or a meal in the restaurant. Up from here in price and position is the beautifully converted *Bradford Old Windmill* (*☎ 01225-866842*), charging £79 to £99 for double rooms; it's not cheap but the views, atmosphere and friendly welcome are worth it.

Back on the canal path, just 1mi outside town on the way towards Devizes, *The*

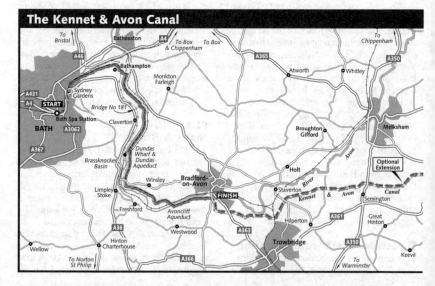

The Kennet & Avon Canal

WESSEX

Locks (☎ *01225-863358, 265 Trowbridge Rd*) has B&B for £20. *The Beehive* pub, next door, does very good evening meals and is busy with diners at weekends.

For more information on other B&Bs in the Bradford-on-Avon area, contact the TIC (☎ 01225-865797), on Silver St near the Town Bridge.

Devizes

The old market town of Devizes is not as touristy as Bath or Bradford-on-Avon, and so has a smaller, but perfectly good, choice of places to stay.

Near Foxhangers Wharf, before you reach Devizes, *Foxhangers Farm* (☎ *01380-828254)* does B&B from £38 a double, plus *camping* for £6 per tent. In town, B&Bs include *Greenfields* (☎ *01380-729315)*, near the top of the Caen Hill Locks, charging £25/45; and *Eastfield House* (☎ *01380-721562),* on the canal beyond The Wharf, charging from £36 to £40 per double.

Around the central marketplace are several atmospheric old coaching inns, including *The Bear Hotel* (☎ *01380-722444)* with B&B from £59/86, and *The Black Swan* (☎ *01380-723259)* with B&B from £50/70.

All pubs also do food, and the town has several other cafes and restaurants.

For more information, contact the TIC (☎ 01380-729408).

GETTING TO/FROM THE WALK

Bus Bath is regularly linked to all parts of the country by National Express coach. At the end of the route, buses go regularly from Bradford-on-Avon back to Bath, but it's far easier to use the train (see the next section). For onward travel, there's a bus about six times daily from Bath via Bradford-on-Avon all the way to Salisbury.

From Devizes there are buses back to Bath. Alternatively, you can get the Trans-Wilts Express bus which runs about 10 times daily (less frequently on Sunday) from Devizes via Avebury to Swindon, on the main railway line between London and Bath. There's also a bus to Salisbury. For more details, phone the Wiltshire Bus Enquiry Line (☎ 08457-090899).

Train Bath is served by mainline trains with regular connections to/from London, Swindon and Bristol. There are about 20 trains per day each way between Bath and Bradford-on-Avon (only 10 on Sunday).

Car Bath is on the A4 east of Bristol and south of the M4 motorway. Bradford-on-Avon is on the A363 between Bath and Trowbridge. Devizes is south of the A4 on the junction of the A361 and A342.

THE WALK
Bath to Bradford-on-Avon

10mi (16km), 4–5 hours

With your back to the Bath Spa station entrance, go right and follow the footpath sign under the railway arch to cross a footbridge over the River Avon. Turn left, then after 50m turn left again to reach the start of the canal near the lock gates separating it from the river. That's the tricky navigational bit over! You keep to the towpath now for the rest of the walk.

There can be few quieter, or more attractive, ways of leaving Bath. The path passes grand **Cleveland House**, straddling the canal, and then **Sydney Gardens**, once a very fashionable quarter where two more bridges were built to hide the narrowboats from sensitive aristocrats.

You soon reach Bathampton (2.5mi from the start) where *The George Inn* serves drinks and food, but if it's too early for a stop, continue along the path, now heading south. After Bridge No 181 (they are numbered from Reading) there are woods on the right, while a beautiful stretch of countryside unfolds to your left.

About 5mi from Bath, you cross to the other bank. This is Dundas Wharf, where boats often tie up or divert down a small section of the Somerset Coal Canal, which meets the Kennet & Avon here. About 500m away, at **Brassknocker Basin**, is the very pleasant *Angelfish Café* (open daily for teas, snacks and lunches) and another wharf with toilets and a small exhibition about the canal's history.

The main canal towpath, and our route, crosses the River Avon on the remarkably ornate **Dundas Aqueduct**, named after the first chairman of the canal company but designed by engineer John Rennie.

Farther on, just past Bridge 175 above Limpley Stoke, you may find a *tea garden* open – look for the sign hidden in the hedge. Another few miles brings you to **Avoncliff Aqueduct** – longer, higher and even more splendid than Dundas. This takes you back across the river, and you have to loop down under a tunnel to reach the towpath on the other side of the canal. Nearby, *The Mad Hatter* tearoom and restaurant is open until 5pm daily in summer (except Monday) and on weekends during winter. The busy *Cross Guns* pub offers sandwiches from £2 and bar meals for around £5 to £7.

The last 1.5mi takes you into Bradford-on-Avon. Look out for the famous **Tithe Barn** on your left – this is well worth a visit (see the boxed text 'Bradford-on-Avon'). Nearby are several craft shops and a cafe.

The end of this walk is marked by a bridge over the canal. Next to the bridge is *The Canal Tavern*, which does a fair range of bar meals, and the *Lock Inn Cottage* with its canal-side gardens, cosy interior and vast

Bradford-on-Avon

The old country town of Bradford-on-Avon holds plenty of interest, so it's worth having a look around. The Town Bridge dates from 1610 and is noted for its 'lockup' (small prison) built into the central pier – probably so inmates could be jeered at by passing citizens.

Some magnificent mill buildings remain alongside the river, dating from the 17th and 18th centuries when Bradford-on-Avon reached its peak as a weaving centre and West Country wool was highly prized across Britain and Europe.

Also crossing the river is the medieval Packhorse Bridge, over which produce was carried to the immense Tithe Barn – built in 1341 and still standing today despite 100 tons of stone tiles on the roof.

Up on the hill overlooking the town is the tiny Saxon church of St Laurence. It was founded in the 7th or 8th century, but put to secular use and eventually forgotten when a new church was constructed. It was rediscovered around 1856 and has been returned to its original condition.

array of drinks, snacks and meals, including the famous Boatman's Breakfast (£4). You can also rent bicycles and canoes, which may provide an alternative way of covering the route.

Before leaving the canal, cross the road to see the lock, basin and dry dock on the other side. From The Canal Tavern it's less than half a mile to the centre of Bradford-on-Avon. If you have time to spare before going back to Bath, between the train station and the Town Bridge is *Mr Salvat's Coffee Room* in a delightful old building which was last 'modernised' in the 17th century. It now serves a tempting range of hot drinks, cakes and lunches.

Optional Extension: Devizes
11.5mi (18km), 5–6 hours

This stage starts at the bridge by The Canal Tavern. The first few miles out of Bradford-on-Avon take you through fancy marinas complete with fashionable waterfront apartments, then past some less appealing industrial premises, before reaching the comparative tranquillity of the open country beyond Hilperton. Midweek this stretch of path should be quiet, increasing your chances of seeing bird life at close quarters.

A good place to stop for a drink or lunch is the *Somerset Arms* at Semington (5mi from Bradford-on-Avon and just 400m off the route), with good beer, big sandwiches for £3 and bar meals for £5 to £7. Just beyond is a set of locks, then an open stretch to Seend Cleve where the old *Barge Inn* (now modernised) also serves good food.

Three miles beyond Semington, near Sells Green, turn off the canal at bridge No 149 to reach *The Three Magpies*, which has a reasonable daytime menu and camping facilities. Beyond here, locks become more frequent as the canal starts to work uphill towards Devizes.

Devizes

Devizes is an old town where traders have come to set up stalls in the market square every Thursday for the past few centuries. More than once in the recent past locals have dressed up in 18th-century gear to be extras in films based on Thomas Hardy books. With old stone and half-timbered buildings surrounding the square, hardly anything else needs to be changed.

In the square you'll find the TIC, a choice of teashops and restaurants, plus plenty of pubs providing food, and this is also where buses arrive and leave. Look out for the market cross, which tells the story of Ruth Pierce who, in 1753, asked God to strike her dead if she lied about the price of corn – and was immediately hit by a thunderbolt.

There's also the Old Town Hall, dating from 1750, the Elizabethan houses of St John's Alley, and the Devizes Museum, which also has displays on Stonehenge and the Avebury stone circle (see the boxed text 'Avebury Stone Circle' in this chapter) – useful if you're heading that way next.

Bank-side activity also increases as you pass **Foxhanger Wharf** and cross to the other side of the canal; anglers like the wider and deeper waters here, with some very large specimens being caught.

Beyond Foxhangers you pass under a small road bridge and reach the bottom of **Caen Hill Flight** – a chain of 16 closely stepped locks, which are just part of the 35 needed to give this artificial waterway a spectacular height gain of 90m in slightly more than 6mi. With luck, as you walk up the hill you'll see narrowboats negotiating the long haul up or down. *Lock Cottage Tearoom* provides sustenance halfway along.

At the top of the flight, go under a main road bridge and, at the next bridge, go up the ramp to the road. Turn right over the canal, then right along the towpath for a short distance before crossing back over the canal again on Bridge 140 to reach **Devizes Wharf Centre** – a fitting place to end your walk. The centre has a canal exhibition, shop, theatre and the *Wharfside Restaurant*. Devizes town centre is just a few streets away.

The Ridgeway (West)

Distance	44mi (71km)
Duration	3 days
Standard	easy
Start	Overton Hill, near Avebury
Finish	Goring
Gateways	Devizes, Swindon, Reading
Summary	A popular and straightforward national trail through high, rolling chalk hills and farmland, with great views and a rich historical background.

The Ridgeway is dubbed 'Britain's oldest road' and archaeological evidence confirms that this ancient route has been used for at least 5000 years. It follows a line of high chalk hills, avoiding forested plains and valleys, thus making travel easier for early Stone Age walkers. It is one of many ancient routes that linked south-west England with the east coast.

Although the original Ridgeway crossed the country, the modern Ridgeway National

Trail follows only part of this ancient route and is divided into two very distinct sections. The western section, described here, crosses the North Wessex Downs (an Area of Outstanding Natural Beauty – AONB) over open country with few roads and villages, providing excellent views when the skies are clear and a bleak grandeur when the storm clouds brew. Historical reminders abound as the route passes Stone Age burial mounds and Iron Age forts, and the massive stone circle at Avebury.

Beyond the Thames Valley, which neatly cuts the route in two, the eastern section of the Ridgeway winds through the very different landscape of the Chiltern Hills – also an AONB, but more densely populated with numerous villages and small towns, along with notably more woodland. This part of the route is described briefly in the Other Walks in Southern England chapter.

The Ridgeway National Trail is an ideal summer route, when mild gradients and dry paths make the walking effortless and enjoyable. In winter the paths can be muddy and the bare chalk slippery, but it's not too difficult if you take care, making it a good year-round walk.

Direction, Distance & Duration

The Ridgeway is a linear route and, as a national trail, well waymarked with acorn symbols and signs. We recommend going west to east, to keep the wind mostly behind you. The official start to the trail is Overton Hill, which is nothing more than an uninspiring car park near West Kennet on the main A4 road west of Marlborough. A more interesting option is to start at the fascinating Avebury Stone Circle – an appropriate introduction to this walk through ancient British history – and join the Ridgeway from here, missing the first few miles of the official route.

The total distance for the whole route is 85mi (136km) with the western section covering 44mi (70.5km), although you will need to add a few extra miles to get to/from your accommodation. Most people do this section in three days, and the most convenient places to begin and end each day are:

day	from	to	mi/km
1	Avebury	Ogbourne St George	9/14.5
2	Ogbourne St George	Court Hill	21/34
3	Court Hill	Goring	14/22.5

Hours given in the description are walking times only – remember to add extra for lunch, sightseeing, rests etc.

Alternatives Day 1 on this route is short but allows for visiting Avebury Stone Circle before setting out. The middle day is long, although not too arduous, and easily possible for fit walkers. However, you can space the walk differently by continuing beyond Ogbourne St George to the villages of Bishopstone or Ashbury; both have B&B options. This makes Days 1 and 2 about 15mi each.

As with all LDPs, you can do just a small section of the Ridgeway or a circular route taking in a stretch of the main trail.

An interesting long-distance alternative would be to do the western section of the Ridgeway (as described here) and then, at Goring, switch to the Thames Path and continue for another six days to London, as described in the London Region chapter. For an even longer option, see Other Walks in Southern England.

PLANNING
Maps

The western section of the Ridgeway is on OS Landranger 1:50,000 maps No 173 (*Swindon & Devizes*) and No 174 (*Newbury & Wantage*); these maps are fine, as the going is straightforward. Very useful is *The Ridgeway* strip map published by Harvey. The strips are wide enough to show villages off the route where you might divert for accommodation and, like all Harvey maps, are waterproof and hardwearing. The Footprint *Ridgeway* strip map is lighter and cheaper, although not as detailed.

Books

The official national trail guide is *The Ridgeway* by Neil Curtis, which contains a good detailed description, background information and extracts from OS 1:25,000 maps, although these are only useful if you don't detour more than a few miles off the route.

Absolutely invaluable is *The Ridgeway National Trail Companion*, published by the National Trails Office (see Information Sources later in this section), which covers accommodation, services and facilities along and near the trail. Organised in a logical fashion, it also lists recommended maps and books, provides background historical and wildlife information, and even tells you where to water your horse! Get it from local TICs (£4) or by post inside Britain (add 75p) from the National Trails Office.

The same office also produces a very handy *Ridgeway Bus & Train Guide* (free of charge), which details all public transport to, from and across the route, and the *Ridgeway Routes Pack*, which describes a good selection of circular walks that include sections of the main national trail.

Information Sources

For general accommodation and transport inquiries, TICs near the route include Avebury (☎ 01672-539425), Marlborough (☎ 01672-513989) and Wantage (☎ 01235-760176). Ridgeway National Trails Office (☎ 01865-810224, fax 810207, ℮ email@rway-tpath.demon.co.uk) should be your first contact for route information. Also very useful is the Web site at ⓦ www.nationaltrails.gov.uk, which covers the Ridgeway and three other national trails in Southern England.

PLACES TO STAY & EAT

The western section of the Ridgeway passes *through* only one village – all others are a mile or two off the route, and there aren't that many with places to stay and eat, so careful planning is required (as are advance reservations in summer). Some B&Bs do a pick-up, drop-off service. Camping is also possible, and there are two YHA hostels. We provide some suggestions in the route description. For a wider choice, use *The Ridgeway National Trail Companion* (mentioned under Books in the Planning section for this walk) or *The Rambler's Yearbook &*

Accommodation Guide or *Stillwell's National Trail Companion* (for details, see Books in the Facts for the Walker chapter).

Along the trail there are no handy cafes and pubs for midday stops, so it's best to carry lunch supplies. Most villages mentioned as overnight halts have small food shops. It's also important to carry enough water (especially in summer) as the route is above the spring line and there are few opportunities for refills.

GETTING TO/FROM THE WALK

A free booklet called *Ridgeway Bus & Train Timetable* with comprehensive details of all public transport serving the Ridgeway is available from the Ridgeway National Trail Office (for contact details, see Information Sources under Planning earlier) and from local TICs.

Bus Swindon can be reached from most parts of the country by National Express coach. You then take the Trans-Wilts Express bus, which runs about 10 times daily (less on Sunday) between Swindon and Devizes via Avebury. There are also buses to Avebury from Salisbury. On Sunday, from late April to late October, the Ridgeway Explorer bus runs between Swindon and Reading via many points along the national trail.

Train No trains go to Avebury but many go to Swindon and Salisbury, from where you can catch a bus. You can also get a train to Pewsey (which is on a main line between London and south-western England), from where Avebury is a scenic 6mi walk.

Goring, at the end of this section of the route, is on a main line between London and Reading, Oxford and Stratford-on-Avon, with frequent trains in both directions.

Car Avebury is 2mi north of the main A4, about 10mi south of Swindon, and is easily reached from most parts of the country on the M4 motorway.

At the end of the western part of the route, Goring is on the A329, off the A4074 between Reading and Oxford, also easily reached from the M4.

THE WALK
Avebury

The village of Avebury is surrounded by a gigantic **stone circle**, larger than Stonehenge, plus several other historic sites and an excellent **museum** (see the boxed text 'Avebury Stone Circle' for details). It also has a TIC (☎ 01672-539425).

Places to stay in Avebury include *Manor Farm* (☎ *01672-539294*), on the High St, charging £40/55 for singles/doubles. Another option is *The Red Lion* (☎ *01672-539266*), picture-postcard twee on the outside but a regular pub on the inside and favoured by local motorcyclists at weekends. B&B costs £40/60, there's a good range of beer, and meals (including steak and Stonehenge pie) cost around £4.

B&Bs just outside the village, in the 'suburb' of Avebury Trusoe, are *6 Beckhampton Rd* (☎ *01672-539588*), charging £36 per double; and *Manor Farm* (☎ *01672-539243*) with a double room for £45. Near the official start of the route, at West Overton, *Cairncot* (☎ *01672-861617*) does B&B from £20.

Aspiring druids can stock up on charms and all sorts of Celtic goodies at the Henge Shop, while walkers may enjoy the takeaway sandwiches at the village *shop*. There is also a *tearoom* in the village. Avebury

Antiques (☎ 01672-539436) is also worth a visit. The exceedingly friendly lady here is happy to advise visitors on local sights and places to stay, and can provide information on transport to nearby Cherhill, which has several more B&B options. These include *Poacher's Croft* (☎ *01249-812587*), on the A4 about 3mi from Avebury, with just one room sleeping up to four people. The cost is around £20, with a reduction if four people stay in the room. Another option in Cherhill is the *Cricketers Rest* (☎ *01249-812388*).

Day 1: Avebury to Ogbourne St George

9mi (14.5km), 4–5 hours

This first day's walk is through classic Wiltshire downs scenery, with rolling hills of grass and wheat, and occasional clumps of trees on the horizon. The whole area is dotted with mysterious mounds and ancient standing stones.

From The Red Lion pub head east along a narrow lane, which soon becomes a rough track, leading uphill through fields to meet the Ridgeway 1.5mi from the village. Turn left here and keep going for three days!

About 5mi from Avebury the route goes through **Barbury Castle** (an Iron Age hillfort); there are toilets nearby and a small *cafe* at the warden's bungalow (often closed in bad weather). There's also a water tap.

Beyond Barbury the route approaches the northern edge of the downs and the views get better – across to the giant town of Swindon and the more scenic Vale of White Horse. Follow Smeathe's Ridge across open farmland and descend to the village of Ogbourne St George.

Ogbourne St George

The Ridgeway skirts the village but you'll probably go in to take advantage of the friendly *Parklands Hotel* (☎ *01672-841555*, e *enquiries@parklandshoteluk.co.uk*), which serves lunches, sandwiches, snacks and evening meals (main courses around £10), and has single/double non-smoking rooms for £45/60. It also provides packed lunches and the friendly owner can arrange taxis to carry luggage to your next

---

Hikers, Bikers & 4WDs

Most of the western section of the Ridgeway consists of rights of way defined as 'Byway' or 'Road Used as Public Path' (RUPP). This means walkers share the route with cyclists, horse riders and occasional 4WDs 'leisure vehicles', which doesn't cause too much of a problem, although hooves and tyres can churn up the ground in wet weather, making walking tricky. On several parts of the trail, separate footpaths run parallel to the main track giving walkers a chance to avoid vehicles and the ruts they make in bad weather. A Code of Respect for all users has been introduced and this is clearly posted at places where the Ridgeway crosses conventional roads.

Avebury Stone Circle

The stone circle at Avebury dates from around 2600–2100 BC, between the first and second phase of construction at Stonehenge. With a diameter of about 350m, it's one of the largest in Britain. The site originally comprised an outer circle of 98 standing stones, many weighing up to 20 tons, although not worked to shape like at Stonehenge.

The circles remained largely intact through the Roman period, when the site may have already been a tourist attraction. A Saxon settlement grew up inside the circle from around AD 600. In medieval times, when the power of the church was strong and fear of paganism stronger, many of the stones were deliberately buried. In the early 18th century, when the village began to expand, stones were broken up for building material. Fortunately, local resident William Stukely (1687–1765) extensively surveyed the site. Modern archaeological site surveys commenced in the early 20th century. In 1934, under the supervision of Alexander Keiller, buried stones were located and resurrected, and markers were placed where stones had disappeared. The wealthy Keiller actually bought Avebury in order to restore 'the outstanding archaeological disgrace of Britain'.

The modern roads into Avebury neatly dissect the circle into four sectors. To see everything, start from the High St and walk round the circle in an anticlockwise direction. In the south-west sector there are 12 standing stones, including the Barber Surgeon Stone where the skeleton of a man was found buried. The south-east sector starts with the huge Portal Stones – the entry into the circle from an ancient road called West Kennet Ave. The north-west sector has the most complete collection of standing stones, including the massive 65-ton Swindon Stone – one of the few never to have been toppled.

The Alexander Keiller Museum is a good place to start your exploration; it helps explain the purpose, construction and subsequent decay of the Avebury Circle, and houses a collection of finds from the sites.

overnight stop. Nearby, *The Inn with the Well* (☎ 01672-841445), formerly The Old Crown Inn, has double rooms for £40 with £50, including breakfast, and a good choice of bar food. On the edge of the village, *Foxlynch Farm* (☎ 01672-841307) offers B&B in a comfortable self-contained 'bunkroom' for £15, and camping for £4.

Day 2: Ogbourne St George to Court Hill
21mi (34km), 8–10 hours
This is a long day, but the route is straightforward and not too tiring. With an early start you should have no problems.

From Ogbourne St George rejoin the Ridgeway with a stiff uphill climb. The path continues up to Liddington Hill, the trail summit at 277m. Nearby is **Liddington Castle**, another Iron Age fort, which is reached by a permissive footpath, offering a fine panorama, spoilt only by the scar of the M4 motorway. You descend a chalky track and walk along a busy road for about 200m, before turning right onto a lane that crosses the M4 and leads to the hamlet of Fox Hill. Here you will find *The Shepherds Rest* (the only pub to be found on the whole western section of the trail), which offers fresh coffee, a wide range of beers and good meals in the £9 to £12 range.

About 200m from here the Ridgeway rejoins the rough track, the surface switching over the next few miles between grass, shale, tar, gravel and bare chalk – which is slippery when wet. You pass over high ground with more wonderful sweeping views to the north. (If the weather is hot, remember to carry enough water for this stretch.)

About 1.5mi off the path, the village of Bishopstone has B&Bs, including the secluded and idyllic *Cheney Thatch* (☎ 01793-790508), charging from £20 (also with a marquee budget option); *Prebendal Farm* (☎ 01793-790485, ℮ prebendal@aol.com), charging £25; and *The True Heart Inn* (☎ 01793-790080), which charges around £20 for B&B, offers good food and allows camping on its grounds.

A mile or two farther on, in **Ashbury**, the very friendly people at *The Village Stores*

(☎ *01793 710262*) offer B&B for around £25, and also run a taxi and luggage transfer service. The shop is open every day and sells groceries, packed lunches, toiletries, books and maps. Nearby, *The Rose & Crown Hotel* (☎ *01793-710222*) does B&B for £40/60 per single/double and offers a good choice of bar food from £5, and meals from £8 to £10 in the smarter restaurant.

The next feature on the Ridgeway is **Wayland's Smithy**, where legend tells of horses being left overnight and reshod by morning, although in reality it's an unusual 'chamber barrow' burial site. Beyond here is another fine fort, **Uffington Castle**, from where you get views across the Vale of White Horse, with the chalky outline of the aforesaid animal cut in the turf just below.

Another fine rolling section of open downland follows, with the path ahead often visible for miles. As you continue, do stop occasionally and look back – the views are stunning that way too.

Court Hill & Letcombe Regis

Where the trail crosses the A338, turn left (north) and follow the road for 500m, turning left again to reach Court Hill. Here is the Ridgeway Information Centre, which contains an interesting exhibition, and *Ridgeway YHA Hostel* (☎ *01235-760253*), where beds cost £9 and camping £4.50.

The nearest B&Bs are at Letcombe Regis, about 1.5mi north-west. The thatched *Quince Cottage* (☎ *01235-763652*) charges from £20; *The Old Vicarage* (☎ *01235-765827*) is comfortable and ivy-clad, and charges £23; the quiet *Gwastad* (☎ *01235-766240*) charges £20; and the friendly *Regis Bed & Breakfast* (☎ *01235-762860*, e *millie_rastall@hot mail.com*) has singles/doubles from £23/40 and an en suite double for £45, plus three-course dinners for £9. You can get evening meals at *The Greyhound* pub.

If these B&Bs are full, the nearby town of Wantage (famous for being the birthplace of King Alfred) has a wider choice.

The Ridgeway (West) & Thames Path (West)

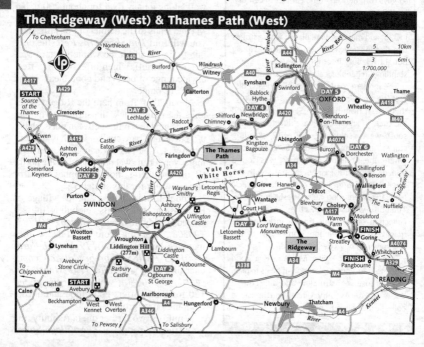

Day 3: Court Hill to Goring
14mi (22.5km), 5–6 hours
This day is one of transition, with your final miles on high, open downland before a descent to the wooded Thames Valley.

Retrace your steps to the Ridgeway and continue along the northern edge of the downs, now also following the route of an ancient defensive dyke called **Grim's Ditch**. About 2mi from Court Hill – as the route follows a wide, grassy track – look to the right for the **Lord Wantage Monument**. The noble lord commemorated here was a philanthropic landowner and commander of a battle in the 19th-century Crimean War – it's said he planted clumps of trees on his estate in the same formation as troops on a battlefield!

As you continue along the trail, you'll see signs of the racehorse activity for which the area is famous, as well as the cooling towers of Didcot power station and the former Atomic Energy Research Establishment at Harwell, but none of this affects the calmness of the surrounding downland.

About 6.5mi from Court Hill, the Ridgeway goes under the busy A34 by way of a pedestrian tunnel (with some murals added for your enjoyment). A mile beyond here, the track is paved with concrete and there is a broad grass verge. Look for the sharp left turn off the paved section and keep your eye open for signs as the route weaves round fields, with several paths leading off to the left and right.

After Warren Farm you are faced with 3mi of almost continuous descent through an area called Streatley Warren, where rabbits were farmed in medieval times. Initially the track is stony but, on reaching another Warren Farm, it turns into a lane running past a few houses. After the remoteness of the last few hours, the first signs of civilisation may be a shock, but you'll soon be passing more houses and then a golf course, before reaching a road junction with the busy A417. Turn right to reach the next junction with the even busier A329 and then go straight into the village of Streatley, where a left turn at the traffic lights will lead across a very scenic stretch of the River Thames into the small town of Goring.

If you decide to overnight in Streatley, before crossing the river to Goring go straight at the traffic lights to reach the *YHA Hostel* (☎ 01491-872278), which charges £10.85. Nearby, *The Bull* pub serves meals.

Goring
In Goring, just over the bridge, *Riverside Tearooms* does cakes and meals until 6pm. The High St has banks and shops (including one open daily to 10pm). Also on the High St, *The Miller of Mansfield Hotel* (☎ 01491-872829) charges £42/55 for singles/doubles (about £10 extra en suite) and provides good food in the restaurant. Nearby, on the corner of Manor Rd and Station Rd, the traditional cottage-like *John Barleycorn Inn* (☎ 01491-872509) has beer, meals for around £6 to £9 and B&B for £27/42. Just up Station Rd is another recommended pub, *The Catharine Wheel* (☎ 01491-872379), with food most evenings (not on Sunday) from £20. Across the railway line and near the station on the edge of town, *The Queens Arms* (☎ 01491-872825) is a straightforward pub with no-frills B&B for £25. Along Wallingford Rd, *14 Mountfield* (☎ 01491-872029) offers walker-friendly B&B from £23. In the Arcade, running between High St and Station Rd, there's a *cafe* open until 5pm daily. If you don't want pub food, try the nearby *Chef King Chinese Restaurant*.

The Thames Path

The River Thames marks the northern limits of the legendary land of Wessex and is followed from its source by the Thames Path National Trail – an LDP that takes 12 to 14 days of walking. This trail is divided very neatly at the town of Reading, providing two sections that can each be traversed in a week. Reading is also a transition point, where the Thames changes from a rural river to a major waterway with urban overtones.

Here we describe the western section of the route and also include most of the introductory information. The eastern section is described in the London Region chapter.

The Thames is a lowland river and the source is a mere 107m above sea level. Geological barriers are few so the river has an easy time of it, ambling towards the sea, losing height slowly with no tumbling falls or rapids to ripple its surface. The walking is correspondingly straightforward. The Thames Path takes the walker through a rich vein of English countryside, history and culture, past unspoilt pastures and market towns, across broad flood plains and slicing through large settlements, including the heart of 'the Big Smoke' – London.

While the scenery around the river can be beautiful if unspectacular, the history is fascinating. Some of the most historically significant towns and villages of Southern England grew up on the Thames and are often worth a brief diversion.

Within the early miles the immature river has been diverted to provide water for millponds, and later for locks, weirs and cuts (canals), all customising the Thames for human use. Having said that, you'll also see evidence of occasional rebellion where the river has escaped its artificial boundaries and flooded the surrounding lands. Regular commemorative stones mark high floods, particularly in 1897 and 1947 when enormous devastation was caused. There were also major floods in the autumn of 2000, when the owners of many riverside houses found their ground floors under water.

Direction, Distance & Duration

This book covers a 12-day walk that takes you from the source to the Thames Barrier (a series of massive flood-prevention gates raised in high-water conditions to prevent London from being flooded). It can be walked in either direction, but going downstream is more satisfying, following the remote and rural stream as it develops into a magnificent river. The Thames Barrier is a fitting end to the walk, whereas arriving at the source, an indistinct depression in a field, can be a bit of an anticlimax.

The Thames Path is between 170mi and 180mi; our route measures 173mi. You will see some references to distances nearer 200mi, but this includes the trail in London

where it runs along both sides of the river simultaneously. Many walkers stop (or start) the route at Kew or Richmond, on the outer limits of London. This misses a large section of the walk through the capital that, although built up and urban, provides views and experiences not found on the standard walking trails.

Waymarking is mostly good, although vital signs do occasionally come loose and route finding can be tricky when the trail detours away from the river. The route continues to be improved and, as it does, the signing will improve too.

Alternatives The first two days could be combined, but it makes for a long and tiring first day over rough paths. In the more populous sections, downstream of Oxford, there are more accommodation options and plenty of scope to extend or shorten the days.

The meanders on the river provide many opportunities for short cuts. Some can be a few hundred metres, others can skip miles, although to leave the river too often defeats the whole purpose of the route. If you do decide to cut across a loop, make sure you keep to public rights of way – most of the land you walk through is private and often intensively farmed.

A more pleasing way to save miles is to take one of the many boat cruises along the river, from places such as Oxford, Henley-on-Thames and Windsor.

PLANNING
Maps

Even though you're following a river, a map is essential to put the trail in a wider context and to help guide you through the diversions or away from the trail to your accommodation. The whole route is covered by the OS Landranger 1:50,000 maps, listed under Maps in the Planning section for the western and eastern sections of the trail. Even more useful are OS Explorer 1:25,000 maps, also listed.

Carrying all these maps would be expensive and heavy. Instead, a very useful single map showing the whole route is *Thames, the River & Path*, published by GeoProjects and available in local TICs or shops catering for the leisure boat market. It is not quite detailed enough to be relied upon totally for walking, but used in conjunction with the maps in *The Thames Path National Trail Guide* (see Books) it will be fine. It also includes a wealth of background information and many useful phone numbers.

Books

The Thames Path National Trail Guide by David Sharp is the most comprehensive guide available, with the route described from the source to the Thames Barrier; it also features the relevant sections of OS maps. *The Thames Path* by Leigh Hatts, revised in 2000, describes the route going upstream from the Thames Barrier to the source.

Most useful is *The Thames Path National Trail Companion*, a compendium of practical information, including details of camping, B&B and hotel accommodation along the river. This is available from local TICs or direct by post (£4.95 plus 90p postage in Britain) from the Thames Path National Trail Office (listed in the following Information Sources entry), which can also supply you with useful leaflets on public transport to points along the trail.

A classic of English literature is *Three Men in a Boat* by Jerome K Jerome, a whimsical tale of a trip up the Thames, which is worth putting in your backpack for evening reading.

Information Sources

For route specifics, your first contact should be the Thames Path National Trail Office (☎ 01865-810224, fax 810207, ✉ email @rway-tpath.demon.co.uk), or the associated Web site (W www.nationaltrails.gov .uk), which covers the Thames Path and three other national trails in Southern England. TICs along the route are listed under Information Sources in the Planning section for each walk.

Guided Walks

The Thames Path National Trail Office publishes a guided walks program – some combining boat trips and walks. Various commercial organisations offer guided walks in Oxford, Windsor and London; TICs have details.

PLACES TO STAY & EAT

The Thames, having being a major trading route, retains a legacy of inns, hotels, guesthouses and B&Bs. These are less common in the early sections (the un-navigable part of the river), but once you pass Lechlade the options increase. There are YHA hostels at Oxford, Streatley and Windsor. If you want

---

History of the Thames Path

The Thames Path National Trail was officially opened in 1996 (the final route is still being established in some places), although the idea of a route along the river was first mooted as early as the 1920s. Only in the mid-1980s did serious efforts to develop the trail begin. This process, promoted by the Ramblers' Association and sponsored by the Countryside Commission (now the Countryside Agency), has involved the cooperation of 23 local authorities, as well as the National Rivers Authority (now the Environment Agency) and the Port of London Authority.

The trail downstream from Lechlade is loosely based on the towpath that used to run beside the navigable river. In the 17th century towpath construction was hindered by some powerful riverside landowners who obstructed the efforts of the Thames commissioners to develop the river as a business route. Thus the towpath frequently jumps over the river to avoid the land of uncooperative landowners. Once ferries operated at these points, but these are now redundant and instead walkers have to divert away from the river. Some of these diversions cut through scenic areas, but others are not so pleasing. Several new lengths of trail closer to the river have been opened to avoid the worst of these.

Remember, as you're walking, that the final route of the Thames Path is still evolving and you should be prepared for further improvements as the last few gaps in the riverside route are filled.

WESSEX

to camp there are plenty of sites; a list is available at TICs along the route. Some farmers may allow camping on their land, but you must always ask permission. Even in the early rural stages a village or town is never far away, so getting supplies should not be any problem.

The Thames Path (West)

Distance	83mi (133.5km)
Duration	6 days
Standard	easy
Start	Thames Head
Finish	Pangbourne
Gateways	Kemble, Cirencester, Reading

Summary A straightforward walk through beautiful English countryside and fascinating historical sites.

Direction, Distance & Duration

Hours given for each day's distance are walking times only. You will need to add extra for lunch, sightseeing etc. The most convenient stages are listed in the table, while alternatives to the suggested route are discussed under Planning in the introduction to the Thames Path earlier.

day	from	to	mi/km
1	Thames Head	Cricklade	10/16
2	Cricklade	Lechlade	11/17.5
3	Lechlade	Newbridge	16/25.5
4	Newbridge	Oxford	14/22.5
5	Oxford	Dorchester	16/25.5
6	Dorchester	Pangbourne	16/25.5

PLANNING
Maps

OS Landranger 1:50,000 maps covering the western half of the Thames Path are No 163 (*Cheltenham & Cirencester*), No 164 (*Oxford*), No 175 (*Reading & Windsor*), No 176 (*West London*) and No 177 (*East London*).

Of the OS Explorer 1:25,000 series, you will need No 159 (*Reading, Wokingham & Pangbourne*), No 160 (*Windsor, Weybridge & Bracknell*), No 161 (*London South, Croydon & Esher*), No 168 (*Stroud, Tetbury &*

Malmesbury), No 169 (*Cirencester & Swindon, Fairford & Cricklade*), No 170 (*Abingdon, Wantage & Vale of White Horse*), No 171 (*Chiltern Hills West, Henley-on-Thames & Wallingford*), No 172 (*Chiltern Hills East, High Wycombe & Maidenhead*), No 173 (*London North, Harrow & Enfield*) and No 180 (*Oxford*).

Information Sources

For advice on accommodation and transport, TICs along this section of the Thames Path can be found at Cirencester (☎ 01285-654180), Oxford (☎ 01865-726871), Abingdon (☎ 01235-522711) and Wallingford (☎ 01491-826972).

PLACES TO STAY & EAT

A general discussion of accommodation and supplies along the route is given under Places to Stay & Eat in the introduction to the Thames Path earlier. Kemble and Cirencester, described in detail here, are two possible overnight options near the start of the walk.

Kemble

B&Bs in the village of Kemble include *The Willows* (☎ *01285-770667*), conveniently near the train station, charging from £26; and the decent *Smerrill Barns* (☎ *01285-770907*), 1mi north of Kemble, charging £45. *The Thames Head Inn* (☎ *01285-770259*) is near the source with B&B from £35 and camping at £5 a night.

Cirencester

Cirencester is a larger and more interesting place to stay than Kemble. At the junction of three Roman roads, including the Fosse Way, it was the second-largest city in Roman Britain. Today the town has a fascinating **museum** plus several fine historical buildings, many dating from medieval times when Cirencester was a wealthy wool-trade centre. The **church** of St John the Baptist is particularly magnificent. The TIC (☎ 01285-654180) is in Corn Hall in the Market Place.

Near the centre of Cirencester, the 18th-century *Golden Cross Inn* (☎ *01285-652137*) provides B&B from £20. Closer to the start of the walk, the *Royal Agricultural College* (☎ *01285-889924*) provides comfortable rooms from £24.50 to £58. At the top end, *The Jarvis Fleece Hotel* (☎ *01285-658507*) is central and provides good rooms from £79 for a single, with special offers at weekends.

GETTING TO/FROM THE WALK

Bus Hourly buses run between Cirencester and Chippenham (on the main London to Bristol railway line) via Kemble, and another bus runs approximately hourly between Kemble and Cirencester. Further details are available from Gloucester Public Transport Information (☎ 01452-425543).

At the end of this walk, the most convenient way to leave Pangbourne is by train (see the next section). Reading is linked to London and other parts of the country by National Express coach and local bus.

Train There are regular train services to Kemble from London and from Birmingham via Cheltenham.

At the end of this section, Pangbourne is on the Oxford line and has regular trains to/from Reading and London. Like Pangbourne, Reading is deep in the commuter belt with very regular train services to/from London, as well as Bristol, Oxford and other cities in west and central England.

Car The start of the trail is Thames Head, 2mi north of the village of Kemble, which is on the A429 between Cirencester and Chippenham. Customers of the Thames Head Inn (on the A443, about 1mi southeast of the junction with the A429) can leave cars here for a few hours, but there's no long-term parking.

At the end of this section of the Thames Path, Pangbourne is north-west of Reading on the A329, while Reading is just off the M4 motorway.

THE WALK (see map p148)

The village of Kemble is a walkable 2mi south of the start, and the town of Cirencester is 5mi north-east. From Kemble, leave the village on the minor road heading north-west

to Tarlton until it meets the A433. Turn right to reach the *Thames Head Inn*, then carry on along the A433 towards the railway bridge. After about 50m, just before the bridge, there are gates on your left. Go through the abandoned goods yard, parallel to the railway line, to reach a stile which takes you across the tracks (beware of trains). On the other side, follow the path to a gate, then go diagonally across the meadow to a copse of trees where you will find the official source of the Thames marked by an engraved stone. Don't expect a gushing fountain here! Most of the year this 'source' is dry, although the surrounding field can be boggy from underground water. But this is the official source, so this is where our walk begins.

Day 1: Thames Head to Cricklade
10mi (16km), 4 hours
This is a day of anticipation as the minor dip in a field develops into a real river, which flows past cultivated fields, fallow meadows and picturesque villages.

From the river's source follow the trail southwards, over the main roads to the east of Kemble and then through the edge of the village of Ewen (from the Saxon word *aewylme*, meaning 'river source'). By this time you should indeed be beside the infant Thames (also called the Isis as far as Abingdon), which you follow to Neigh Bridge and the lakes of the Cotswold Water Park – once gravel pits, these now provide leisure amenities for the area.

The old and pretty village of **Ashton Keynes** has a couple of *pubs* and makes a suitable lunch stop. There may be some confusion after you leave Ashton Keynes, taking the path signposted to Waterhay. The route crosses a road on the south-eastern side of the village into a sports field. The fields beyond this have been replaced by gravel pits. The path continues on a narrow causeway between two flooded gravel pits not shown on the latest OS maps. (Note that after heavy rain and/or a south-westerly gale this section can become flooded. In this case, do not enter the sports field from Ashton Keynes but continue along Rixon Gate Rd to a sharp left bend, where you turn right along a

WESSEX

marked bridlepath.) After about half a mile the new causeway path joins an unmade track. Turn left here and then right at the first footpath, which is signposted 'Cricklade 3 miles' and marked as the Thames Path. You are now back on the official route.

About a mile before Cricklade, just as you reach North Meadow, there is a bridge over the river. The official route is planned to cross the river and lead you down the south bank into Cricklade. At the time of writing, however, this was not yet signposted and it was easier, more straightforward and more picturesque to take the path through the Meadow by the north bank.

Cricklade

The sleepy old Roman town of Cricklade has churches and buildings with fine examples of architecture from Norman times to the present. Accommodation is available in two old coaching inns which are both in the main street – *The White Hart Hotel* (☎ 01793-750206), charging from £35; and *The Bear Inn* (☎ 01793-750005), from £20.

Day 2: Cricklade to Lechlade
11mi (17.5km), 4½ hours
The river is now well established, but not yet navigable. Accordingly there is no continuous riverside path and two sections of today's walk are by road, although improvements are planned.

From Cricklade, the trail follows the river for about 1.5mi to Water Eaton Footbridge, after which the route can be confusing. Continue along the south bank of the river on a newly opened section of path for less than a mile. Just inside a plantation the path turns right to reach a track; turn right along this to the road at Water Eaton Cottages, where you turn left for the final distance into Castle Eaton. At the time of writing, negotiations were under way, but still inconclusive, for extending the path along the bank of the river all the way into Castle Eaton.

Castle Eaton is the largest settlement you will pass today. In the village, *The Red Lion* has a garden overlooking the river and serves filling pub food.

After Castle Eaton, the route follows a lane, some paths, a rather unpleasant road and (with relief) a final stretch of river into Lechlade.

Lechlade

This is a quintessential Cotswold town, which owes its wealth to trade on the Thames, although it's slightly back from the river. The church spire is visible from afar. At St Johns Lock look out for the reclining figure of **Old Father Thames**, a concrete statue with a colourful history. Originally placed at the river source, it was relocated in 1974 because of problems with vandals.

There is a wide choice of accommodation. B&Bs include the *Apple Tree Guesthouse* (☎ 01367-252592) with double rooms at £36; and *Cambrai Lodge* (☎ 01367-253173), in Oak St, offering B&B at £25. In

North Meadow Nature Reserve

North Meadow, outside Cricklade, is the most remarkable site for wild flowers along the entire length of the Thames Path. This vast, open field, more than 100 acres in area, is in a floral time warp, a throwback to the more ecologically friendly farming practices of pre-mechanised agriculture. North Meadow was never enclosed; instead, it has been grazed each year between August and February since as long as anyone can remember. Wild flowers grow in richly 'dunged' soil and they are given time to set seed before the meadow is cut for hay.

As a result, North Meadow is a wonderful, richly coloured carpet of wild flowers each spring and early summer – orchids, yellow rattle, saxifrages and scores of others. Most importantly, it is by far the most abundant site in Britain for snake's head fritillary, a very rare and beautiful flower with a spotted, drooping head that varies from purple to white. At other places you would jump for joy if you were sharp-eyed enough to spot one fritillary specimen. In North Meadow, in April and early May you would have to walk with your eyes closed *not* to see them.

the market square the **Red Lion** (☎ *01367-252373*) provides B&B from £20.

Day 3: Lechlade to Newbridge
16mi (25.5km), 6½ hours
The remote and rural feel of the Thames is retained, although the river is now a substantial waterway, crossed by historic bridges and locks.

From Lechlade it's 5mi of lovely riverside walking to **Radcot** – the scene of Civil War clashes and the site of the oldest existing bridge on the Thames. In Radcot, *The Swan* (☎ *01367-810220*) does adequate B&B from £25.50. Along the way you'll also see reminders of a later conflict: pillboxes (small fortified emplacements) built in WWII as a defence against invasion.

Another 3mi and you reach Tadpole Bridge where *The Trout Inn* provides a welcome drink and a wide-ranging menu. B&B is planned for 2001. Beyond here riverside paths lead past Chimney Nature Reserve to Shifford Lock, from where you continue for 2mi into Newbridge.

Newbridge
This river crossing has a pub on each side, but only the one on the north bank, *The Rose Revived* (☎ *01865-300221*), has accommodation, charging £57.50 a double for B&B. There are more options in the village of Kingston Bagpuize, about 2mi south, or you could push on to Bablock Hythe.

Day 4: Newbridge to Oxford
14mi (22.5km), 5½ hours
Today's walk is another scenic section, but as you get near Oxford the river banks get perceptibly busier.

From Newbridge, it's 3.5mi to **Bablock Hythe**, where the *Ferryman Inn* (☎ *01865-880028*) provides functional rooms, charging £50 a double for B&B. Beyond here you leave the river for 2.5mi. As an alternative, ask the landlord of the Ferryman Inn about his irregular ferry service – in more or less continuous operation for the last 1000 years – across the river. This will allow you to follow the path that runs along the east bank and rejoin the official trail at Pinkhill Lock.

It's another mile to **Swinford Bridge**, one of the last two remaining toll bridges over the river. The *Talbot Inn* on the north bank makes a good lunch stop.

For the next few miles the trail is better defined and the distant hum of traffic comes as quite a shock after four days of quiet. More leisure craft are moving on the river and, before you realise it, the Thames has brought you into the heart of Oxford.

Oxford
Much of the fascinating history and architecture in Oxford is based around the university, but the city is also a regional trade centre. In medieval times, wool from the Cotswolds often passed through Oxford and, in this century, heavy industry (notably car manufacturing) was established here. Being a working city, rather than just a university town, means that Oxford isn't as quaint as Cambridge but, boasting 650 buildings officially designated with historical or architectural merit (most within easy reach of the centre), this is a city worth discovering.

The TIC (☎ 01865-726871) is on Gloucester Green. *The Oxford Town Trail* leaflet can be obtained here and tours start from here daily. Accommodation is plentiful. Some central possibilities include *Oxford Backpackers* (☎ *01865-721761, 9A Hythe Bridge St*), charging from £11; and the *YHA Hostel* (☎ *01865-762997*), which costs from £10.85. Another cheap option during holiday periods is college-owned accommodation such as the *Rachel Trickett Building* (☎ *01865-274907*), at St Hugh's College, with rooms from £25. For B&B try *The Falcon Hotel* (☎ *01865-511122*), on Abingdon Rd, charging £35/68 for singles/doubles; or the smarter *River Hotel* (☎ *01865-243475*), on Botley Rd, with doubles from £70 to £81.

Day 5: Oxford to Dorchester
16mi (25.5km), 6½ hours
This stage could be described as the heart of the walk, with a fascinating mix of riverside views and historical buildings, especially ecclesiastical remains. The river is active and you'll likely see punts, rowing eights and hired cruisers out and about.

From Oxford the trail runs along the west bank, past Iffley Lock and Sandford Lock. About 4mi out of Oxford, the **Kings Arms** makes a pleasant refreshment spot. Alternatively, continue for another 4mi to Abingdon – an attractive and well-established market town with a fine range of former **monastic buildings** near the river, and a very handsome 17th-century **County Hall** in the marketplace. Abingdon has plenty of lunch opportunities and is a possible overnight stop. A good B&B is **Helensbourne** (*☎ 01235-530200*), in East Saint Helens St, from £30. The TIC (*☎ 01235-522711*) is at 25 Bridge St.

If you're only stopping for lunch, don't linger too long – it's still another long 8mi to Dorchester.

Dorchester & Around

Sometimes called Dorchester-on-Thames, to distinguish it from its namesake in Dorset, this was a Roman garrison town and a Saxon bishopric. It still has a historical atmosphere, sustained in part by the large number of antique shops. For B&B try the **George Hotel** (*☎ 01865-340404*) at £62.50, or the **White Hart** (*☎ 01865-341082*) at £65 – both in the High St. Cheaper alternatives are available in adjacent villages. **Dinckley Court** (*☎ 01865-407763*), in Burcot, has rooms with a river view from £35/50 for a single/double. You could also try **North Farm** (*☎ 01865-858406*), in Shillingford, with singles/doubles from £28/46.

Day 6: Dorchester to Pangbourne

16mi (26km), 6½ hours

Today the Thames wanders through the serene Chiltern Hills and the trail occasionally strays onto higher ground away from the river.

From Dorchester, the trail goes through the pleasant towns of Benson and Wallingford (which both have accommodation options). Wallingford TIC (*☎ 01491-826972*) is in the Town Hall. At the village of **Moulsford**, if you are feeling culinary and fiscally flush you could stay at *The Beetle & Wedge Riverside Hotel* (*☎ 01491-51381*),

characterised in *The History of Mr Polly* by HG Wells and now famed for its good food. Rooms start from £95.

Next comes Goring, another lunch or overnight possibility. For details see Day 3 of the Ridgeway walk (which crosses the river and the Thames Path here) earlier in this chapter. From Goring it's a few easy miles to Pangbourne.

Pangbourne & Whitchurch

On opposite sides of the Thames, the towns of Pangbourne and Whitchurch are connected by a toll bridge. In Whitchurch, *The Rectory* (*☎ 0118-984 3219*), on the High St, has twin rooms for £50. In Pangbourne, *The George Hotel* (*☎ 0118-984 2237*) – once home to Kenneth Grahame, author of *Wind in the Willows* – has singles/doubles from £60/£65. *The Copper Inn* (*☎ 0118-984 2244*), on Church Rd, does B&B for £45; and the homely *Weir View House* (*☎ 0118-984 2120, 9 Shooters Hill*) charges from £28. *The Swan*, opposite, serves good pub food. The town itself has a number of places where you can eat and perhaps celebrate reaching the halfway point of the walk.

If you're continuing downstream, the rest of the Thames Path route is described in the London Region chapter.

Other Walks

THE WILTSHIRE DOWNS

The Wiltshire Downs is an area of chalky grassland and sparsely wooded hills, forming a broad west-east band between the towns of Devizes, Marlborough, Swindon, Wantage and Newbury. Also known as the North Wessex Downs, this area is combined with the Chiltern Hills, north of the Thames Valley, to form an important AONB.

The Wiltshire Downs area is traversed by the Ridgeway National Trail – described earlier in this chapter. From Avebury (near the start of the Ridgeway), several day walks are possible, taking in sections of the Ridgeway. Another good target is the mysterious Neolithic earth pyramid of **Silbury Hill** and the nearby West Kennet Long Barrow – an ancient burial mound. Alternatively, to the west of Avebury is **Cherhill Down** (pronounced cherril), which is high and easily accessible, and topped by a monument and giant white horse carved in the chalk (see the 'Wessex Chalk Figures' boxed text on p158). Places to stay in Cherhill and Avebury are listed in the Ridgeway section.

South of Avebury is the small town of Pewsey, which makes a good base for exploring the quiet rural **Vale of Pewsey**, between the Wiltshire Downs and Salisbury Plain. Pewsey is on a main line between London and the West Country, so access is easy. It is also the base for a unique public transport system called 'the wriggly bus', which serves outlying villages. Within walking distance of Pewsey are two more white horse figures carved on the hillsides, several tumuli and other prehistoric remains. The **Kennet & Avon Canal**, which is described as far as Devizes earlier in this chapter, runs through the Vale of Pewsey to Hungerford, Newbury and eventually to Reading where it meets the River Thames (as described in The Thames Path section of this chapter).

To the west of Salisbury Plain, the **West Wiltshire Downs** is an area of grassy hills and escarpments near the town of Westbury, south-east of Bath. Together with the quiet farmland and heath of Cranborne Chase, this forms another important AONB. Nearby is another famous white horse figure carved on the hillside.

An excellent series of walks along the **Wiltshire's White Horse Trail** wind around the West Wiltshire and North Wessex Downs, joining up eight white horses and many other historical sites, passing through tranquil farmland, meadows, hills and quiet villages. The whole 90mi route is waymarked and can be done neatly in one week, but it's also designed so you can follow shorter sections for a just day or two, either on a circular walk or returning to the start by public transport. Good bases are Devizes (described in the Kennet & Avon Canal walk), Avebury (in the Ridgeway walk), Marlborough, Westbury or Pewsey. A helpful series of route cards is available from local TICs, or by mail order by phoning the very useful Wiltshire

Walking & Cycling Hotline (☎ 01980-623255). You can also check the Web site at Ⓦ www.wiltshiretourism.co.uk.

SALISBURY PLAIN

Salisbury Plain is a wide, empty area of rolling grassland surrounded on the north by a steep escarpment and on the south by the valleys of the Rivers Wylie and Test. To explore Salisbury Plain you could base yourself in the city of Salisbury itself (covered in the Clarendon Way earlier in this chapter), which is easy to reach and has a good range of places to stay and eat, as well as several sites of interest. The TIC sells local walking guides and can provide leaflets and advice about walking in and around Salisbury and on Salisbury Plain. Note that much of the area is an army firing range that's closed to the public at certain times, so most options for walkers keep pretty much to the edge of the plain rather than crossing it. You'll have to choose your routes carefully.

While you're in the area, ask about the **Sarcen Way**, a 26mi route across the rarely visited heart of the plain, linking the stone circles of Stonehenge and Avebury. Unfortunately some parts of this route are only open on certain days of the year but, if you coincide with these, it is well worth doing.

If all this sounds too much, the quiet villages and classic English farmland of the **Hampshire Avon Valley**, north of Salisbury towards Amesbury and Stonehenge, offer a comforting contrast to the wide open plains.

Another way to explore Salisbury Plain might be from Warminster, a large town about 20mi north-west of Salisbury, on the edge of the plain and only a few miles south of Westbury (described under the Wiltshire Downs earlier). From Warminster a 20mi circular walk called the **Imber Perimeter Path** loops round the army area via the villages of Bratton, West Lavington, Tilshead and Chittern. (The village of Imber itself is in the heart of the range. The people were moved out in 1943 and since then the village has remained closed to the public, except for a few days each year.) If you don't want to do the whole circuit, a short out-and-back walk on the hills above Warminster takes

WESSEX

Wessex Chalk Figures

Much of the rolling downland and farming country of Wessex covers a large area of chalk. The vegetation is only a thin green cloak of grass covering the white ground, and gives rise to the practice of cutting pictures into hillsides. The technique is simple – mark out your picture and cut away the green grass and topsoil to reveal the white chalk below. The picture needs periodic maintenance, but not much. Some of the chalk figures may date back to Bronze Age times, although the histories of the oldest figures are uncertain.

Wessex has many chalk figures and Wiltshire has more than any other county. Most are horses, and include those at Cherhill and Uffington (near the Ridgeway – which lends its name to the nearby Vale of White Horse), plus several more near Pewsey and Westbury. There's another good one at Osmington near Weymouth.

The tradition has continued into the 20th century. During WWI soldiers based at Fovant, west of Salisbury, cut a series of army badges into a nearby hillside, and a New Zealand regiment left a gigantic kiwi on a hillside at Bulford, a few miles east of Stonehenge.

Although Wiltshire goes for sheer quantity, in other parts of Wessex the locals go for sheer style. Probably the most impressive chalk figure is Dorset's 180ft-tall Cerne Giant (on a hillside near the village of Cerne Abbas in Dorset), with his even more notable 30ft penis.

JANE SMITH

Uffington's White Horse

you to the white horse chalk figure (see the boxed text) and Iron Age fort above Westbury. Another nearby attraction is Cradle Hill, where many UFO sightings have been claimed by enthusiasts.

LONG-DISTANCE PATHS
The South West Coast Path

A highlight of the southern part of Wessex is the English Channel coast of Dorset and South Devon, parts of which are billed as the English Riviera on account of their mild climate (although don't expect Cannes). This stretches from Poole to Exmouth via Weymouth and Lyme Regis, and for walkers this is the route followed by the Dorset section of the South West Coast Path (see the Southern England Long-Distance Paths chapter).

The Wessex Ridgeway

Another good option through the heart of the region is the Wessex Ridgeway (not to be confused with the Ridgeway National Trail). This excellent 140mi route starts at Marlborough in Wiltshire and heads south, taking in several of Wessex's special highlights, including Avebury Stone Circle, the northern and western edge of Salisbury Plain, a section of the picturesque Wylie Valley (running parallel to the Imber Perimeter Path, mentioned earlier), Cranborne Chase and the huge chalk giant of Cerne Abbas, then runs through the heart of Thomas Hardy country to finish on the South Devon coast at Lyme Regis – famous for its fossils. A handy guidebook is *The Wessex Ridgeway* by Alan Proctor.

The Isle of Wight

The Isle of Wight, 23mi (37km) long by 13mi (21km) wide, lies only a few miles off the Hampshire coast. Its name is thought to come from *wiht*, an ancient word meaning 'lifted' – from the sea. During their occupation of Britain, the Romans named the island Vectis and built several villas here; perhaps the mild climate and sea views were reminders of their Mediterranean home.

Today the pleasant weather still attracts visitors and holiday-makers, particularly to the busier eastern side of the island. The weather is also good for walking, and on the quieter western side of the island there's at least a week's worth of walking on a marvellous network of footpaths through fields and villages, over the downs (rolling hills) and along the coast.

The local authorities have put a lot of work into maintaining and signposting their paths, and the island also has a very good bus service for getting to the start or from the end of walks. If you're new to walking in Britain, or you're not looking for high peaks and wilderness, the Isle of Wight is an excellent place to start. As our sample walk we describe a popular route through the heart of the western side of the island, and at the end of the chapter we outline several other options.

INFORMATION
Maps & Books

Ordnance Survey (OS) Landranger 1:50,000 map No 196 *(The Solent & Isle of Wight)* and OS Outdoor Leisure 1:25,000 map No 29 *(Isle of Wight)* both cover the whole island. The 1:25,000 scale provides better detail.

Tourist Information Centres (TICs) stock a very handy little booklet called *Coastal Path & Inland Trails on the Isle of Wight*, produced by the Isle of Wight Council Rights of Way Department, which covers the Tennyson Trail and many others, with maps and route descriptions. For more ideas see *A Walker's Guide to the Isle of Wight* by Martin Collins & Norman Birch.

Information Sources

TICs include Cowes, Newport, Ryde and Yarmouth. They can provide leaflets, books, maps etc, but for phone inquiries there's a single number: ☎ 01983-813818. For accommodation bookings, phone ☎ 01983-813813. It's also worth checking out the Web sites at W www.islandbreaks.co.uk and W www.isle-of-wight-tourism.gov.uk.

Guided Walks

Walking tours (short or long, guided or self-guided) are run by Step by Step Holidays, a good flexible company based at the Hambledon Hotel (☎ 01983-862403, e hambledon @netguides.co.uk) in Shanklin, on the east side of the island.

For walkers with a social bent, the Isle of Wight walking festival is held every May and includes more than 100 guided walks and other events.

GETTING THERE & AROUND

The Getting Around chapter lists several public transport inquiry lines that provide details of both national and local bus and train services: See the boxed text 'National Transport Information' on p92.

Bus On the mainland there are regular National Express coaches to Southampton and Portsmouth, although fewer to Lymington. On the Isle of Wight there are regular buses between West Cowes and Newport, and between Alum Bay and Newport (via Yarmouth). Timetables are posted at the Newport bus station and at the Alum Bay terminus, or you can phone the Timetable Hotline (☎ 01983-827005). If you're staying for a few days, various money-saving passes are available.

Train Southampton and Portsmouth have frequent train services to/from London and can easily be reached from other parts of the country. Trains on the Isle of Wight cover only the east side of the island.

Ferry Red Funnel ferries (☎ 023-8033 4010, W www.redfunnel.co.uk) ply the route between Southampton and West Cowes (from where you can easily reach Newport) every half-hour for much of the day. Wightlink ferries (☎ 0870-582 7744, W www.wightlink .co.uk) travel hourly between Lymington and Yarmouth (near Freshwater) for £8.90. If you're coming from London or the South-East, the handiest Wightlink ferries run from Portsmouth to Fishbourne (£8.90 return) and Ryde (£10.90 to £12.10 return), from where you can easily reach Newport.

Car Both ferry services carry vehicles but prices depend on the size of car and the time of year. As a sample, the return fare for a car (and one driver) is £75 in the high season between Lymingon and Yarmouth, or Portsmouth and Fishbourne. At mainland ports there are big car parks where you can leave your car for a couple of days and go on the ferry as a foot passenger.

The Tennyson Trail

Distance	14mi (22.5km)
Duration	5–6½ hours
Standard	easy
Start	Carisbrooke
Finish	Alum Bay
Gateways	Newport, Southampton
Summary	Enjoyable walking on clear paths through woods and farmland, and across rolling coastal downs with views of the sea.

The Tennyson Trail is named after the 19th-century poet, Alfred Lord Tennyson, who lived on the Isle of Wight. As a lover of the outdoors he'd probably have approved of this route, which runs along a chalk ridge through the quieter western side of the island and finishes on high sea cliffs where fine views and a spectacular lighthouse are the major attractions.

Direction, Distance & Duration
This linear route runs for 13mi from Carisbrooke (near Newport in the centre of the island) via Freshwater Bay to the Needles at the extreme western end of the island. From here it's another mile to Alum Bay where the route ends and you can find transport back to the start. This takes five to 6½ hours of walking, so with stops you should allow about seven to eight hours. Before walking you should buy picnic material; the only place for refreshments is at Freshwater Bay – two-thirds of the way through the walk.

For this walk you could base yourself in Newport and return there by bus at the end. However, Freshwater (near the end of the walk, just north of Freshwater Bay) is a more pleasant place to stay, so you may choose instead to catch an early bus to Newport then walk back.

PLACES TO STAY & EAT
Freshwater & Totland
These overgrown villages combine to form one town with banks, shops and a good choice of places to stay.

Heathfield Farm Campsite (☎ 01983-756756), on the north side of Freshwater, is mainly for caravans, but genuine walkers are charged £6.50 per tent. *Totland Bay YHA Hostel* (☎ 01983-752165) charges £10.85 and is very handy for the end of this walk.

B&Bs in Freshwater include the *Traidcraft Shop & Tearoom* (☎ 01983-752451, 119 School Green Rd), charging £15. Attached to an interesting fair-trade and wholefood store, the service includes a vegetarian breakfast. *The Royal Standard Hotel* (☎ 01983-753227) is an imposing and characterful hotel-pub on School Green Rd, with B&B from £21 and good meals in the hotel restaurant.

In Totland, B&Bs include *Sandford Lodge* (☎ 01983-753478, 61 The Avenue), a peaceful, well-kept place and *Sandy Lane Guesthouse* (☎ 01983-752240), on Colwell Common Rd, a large comfortable family house. Both charge from £20.

For a meal or drink in a fine location, the *Waterfront Restaurant* down on the beach overlooking Totland Bay has snacks from £2, light meals for £5 and main courses from £5 to £10. *The Red Lion* (☎ 01983-754925), on Church Place in Freshwater, is an old (and slightly snooty) ivy-covered pub very highly

The seafood always comes fresh at the lively fishing village of Wells-next-the-Sea, Norfolk

Standing on the edge of Britain at the Bedruthan Steps, Cornwall, South West Coast Path

The twin towers of the abandoned Crowns Mine, near Pendeen Watch, South West Coast Path

The Cotswold Way begins in the heart of fashionable Bath, a stone's throw from a cappuccino

regarded for its food; two courses will set you back about £18.

Newport

This town is the 'capital' of the Isle of Wight, with all facilities such as shops, supermarkets, post office and banks (most with ATMs). The town itself is nothing special but there are a few Roman remains on the outskirts, along with the very impressive **Carisbrooke Castle**, very close to the start of the Tennyson Trail and mentioned in the walk description. The TIC is in the Guildhall on the High St.

The Newport Quay Hotel (☎ 01983-528544) does B&B from £30; some rooms have four-poster beds. A little tattier but with much more character is *The Wheatsheaf Hotel* (☎ 01983-523865), on St Thomas Square, a 300-year-old coaching inn complete with low beams, historical ambience and B&B at £40/55 for singles/doubles. It also has a good pub and restaurant.

Alvington Manor Farm (☎ 01983-523463), on the western edge of Carisbrooke (a separate village but essentially a suburb of Newport), is an imposing and genuine working farm, surrounded by barns, tractors, dogs etc. It is very friendly, charging £20 for B&B. It's at the very end of Alvington Rd (a rough track), not far from Nodgham Lane – the starting point of the Tennyson Trail.

Yarmouth

There are plenty of places to stay in this pleasant little seaside town. Recommended B&Bs include *Meddlars* (☎ 01983-761541), on Hallet Shute, roughly 10 minutes' walk from the centre and up the hill towards Freshwater. A room in this converted barn, with friendly and enthusiastic management, has a tariff of £25. Also very welcoming is the more central *Rosemead* (☎ 01983-761078), on Tennyson Rd. Yarmouth TIC is on the Quay.

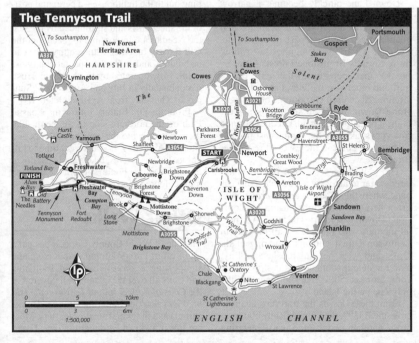

THE ISLE OF WIGHT

GETTING TO/FROM THE WALK

If you're staying in Freshwater, begin your day with a bus ride to Newport. It's only a mile from the centre of Newport to the official start at Carisbrooke.

From Alum Bay, at the end of the walk, buses will take you back to the starting point or Freshwater

THE WALK
Carisbrooke to Freshwater Bay
8.5mi (13.5km), 3–4 hours

The official start to the trail is at Nodgham Lane, Carisbrooke (a separate village but effectively a suburb of Newport these days). Nearby is **Carisbrooke Castle**, which dates from Norman times and was used to imprison Charles I in 1647–8, before his execution in London.

From the start, the trail goes up Down Lane; don't miss the turn-off with its slightly hidden sign pointing along the bridleway towards Freshwater Bay.

Down Lane quickly becomes a narrow path lined with trees and hedges, but it soon gives way to the field-side walking that characterises the first part of this route. There is a variety of signposts – follow those towards Brighstone Forest. A towering TV mast pops up to the north of the trail, but otherwise the views are relatively circumscribed until you emerge onto **Brighstone Down**. Its 214m summit is not the highest point on the island, but does provide fine views taking in the south coast from St Catherine's Point in the east to Freshwater Bay in the west.

The trail crosses the first road encountered so far to arrive at a National Trust car park, where there may be an *ice-cream van*. From here the trail climbs again to Mottistone Down, past a series of Stone Age burial mounds with fine views, all the way to Tennyson Down with its towering chalk cliffs, and west beyond Freshwater Bay. You can detour south down the slope to the **Long Stone**, a 5000-year-old megalith, the only one on the island.

From these downs the trail dips again to cross the B3399, then immediately climbs to cross another series of downs, teetering along the top of the ridge through a long and narrow golf course. The western end of the golf course ends at the beginning of Freshwater Bay, which is a good place for a lunch stop at one of the cafes or the bar in the *Albion Hotel*. Just beyond the bay is **Fort Redoubt**, built in the mid-19th century to forestall a feared French invasion. Today you can stroll the battlements or have a drink in the *tearoom* while keeping a weather eye to the south for the approach of hostile ships!

Freshwater Bay to Alum Bay
5.5mi (9km), 2–2½ hours

Alfred Lord Tennyson lived near Freshwater Bay for 16 years from 1853. It's recorded that he walked almost every day on the Tennyson Down, the next stage of this route. The **Tennyson Monument** marks the 145m high point of this coastal down, with its sheer cliffs tumbling straight into the sea.

At the western end of the downs are the Needles – a series of chalk outcrops stepping out to the lighthouse – a perennial postcard symbol of the Isle of Wight. At the foot of the sheer cliffs and surrounded by the sea, the Needles are impossible to reach, but the **Old Battery** (another 19th-century fort) can be visited and makes a spectacular view point. Now operated by the National Trust, it's open daily in July and August, and Sunday to Thursday from April to October.

From the Old Battery follow the Coastal Path on the northern side of the peninsula, then drop down to the amusement park and shops at **Alum Bay**. If you've got time to kill before the bus arrives, take a cable car down the cliff to see (or bottle) some of the famous, multicoloured sand.

Other Walks

The Isle of Wight County Council has put a lot of effort into designing, publicising and signposting a good network of footpaths and trails all over the island, well covered in the *Coastal Path & Inland Trails on the Isle of Wight* booklet (mentioned under Books earlier) and in several smaller leaflets. Most are linear and can be done in a day. Using the island's excellent bus service, you can always get back to your starting point. Try the **Shepherds Trail** (10mi) from Carisbrooke south over downland to the coast at Shepherds Chine; the **Bembridge Trail** (15mi) from Newport west to the coast, past villages, manor houses and Roman villas; or the **Worsley Trail** (15mi) from Brightstone over more downs to the holiday town of Shanklin on the east coast.

If you want a **circular walk**, a good route from Freshwater takes in part of the Coastal Path south to Alum Bay and the Needles, then follows a section of the Tennyson Trail over Tennyson Down to Freshwater Bay (for an early lunch), through Aston and along the eastern Freshwater Way to join the old railway track beside the Yar Estuary to Yarmouth (for a late lunch), then back to Freshwater via the coast and Fort Victoria Country Park.

And for the mile eaters there's the whole **Coastal Path** (77mi, 124km), which takes between four and eight days, although, as with the rest of the island, the western side is quieter and has fewer holiday resorts, so you might consider just doing part of it, eg, from Cowes or Yarmouth to St Catherine's Point.

Dartmoor

Dartmoor is a huge and spectacular, if frequently gloomy, expanse of moorland in the county of Devon, in south-western England. The rounded hills are dotted with piles of granite rocks called tors, looking for all the world like abstract sculptures or the remains of fantastical castles. Dartmoor is also covered by many genuine ancient remains, including prehistoric burial mounds and the largest concentration of Bronze Age hut circles in Britain. You'll also see 1000-year-old stone bridges and medieval crosses (from the days when monks would walk between surrounding abbeys), while abandoned mines and dismantled tramways are reminders of more recent, but now-forgotten, industrial days. The moor is also famous for its herds of semi-wild ponies.

Despite being heavily populated many centuries ago, Dartmoor today is the emptiest, highest and wildest area in Southern England. There is a great feeling of space and openness, and in some parts you can be farther from a road or village than anywhere else in Britain outside Scotland. For keen walkers this is, of course, its attraction but the notoriously fickle weather patterns (with mist, rain and even snow being common hazards) make some of the walking surprisingly challenging.

Most of Dartmoor is contained within the 365-sq-mi Dartmoor National Park. The north-western area is the highest, wildest part of the moor (peaking at the 621m summits of Yes Tor and High Willhays – the highest points in Southern England), while the eastern part is lower and more inhabited. The south-western area is also quite high (mostly between 400m and 500m) with a particularly good collection of ancient remains.

INFORMATION
Maps
The Ordnance Survey (OS) Outdoor Leisure 1:25,000 map No 28 *(Dartmoor)* covers the whole of Dartmoor with a lot of detail, including the ancient historical sites. For maps covering individual walks, see Planning in the introduction to each walk.

Books
The first walk includes part of the Two Moors Way, which is well described in *The Two Moors Way* by James Roberts, and also covers the Abbot's Way to Buckfastleigh. For more ideas, *Walking on Dartmoor* by John Earle is full of fascinating history but is very hard to use on the ground. More useful is the Pathfinder *Dartmoor* guide, published by Jarrold, with a good selection of routes and clear mapping. *Weekend Walks – Dartmoor & Exmoor* by Anthony Burton is ideal for keen walkers.

For background information, the *Dartmoor* official national park guide by Richard Sale is excellent and has beautiful photos. For archaeological information, local Tourist Information Centres (TICs) stock a huge range of books, covering everything from Bronze Age hut circles to the quarries that produced the London Bridge stone. Most useful as an introduction are the *Dartmoor Pocket Guides*, a series of inexpensive, weatherproof cards covering archaeology and many other subjects.

Information Sources
The South Devon area is a very popular tourist destination (although most visitors stick to the coast) and there are many TICs with information on the walks included in this chapter and on other routes. Some are run by local tourist boards, others by Dartmoor National Park Authority. These include Ivybridge (☎ 01752-897035) and Okehampton (☎ 01837-53020). The main park visitors centre is at Princetown (☎ 01822-890414). There are also many village information points; useful ones for the routes we describe are at Buckfastleigh and Sticklepath.

The free *Dartmoor Visitor* newspaper contains lots of useful information and addresses. You can also visit the national park Web site at Ⓦ www.dartmoor-npa.gov.uk.

DARTMOOR

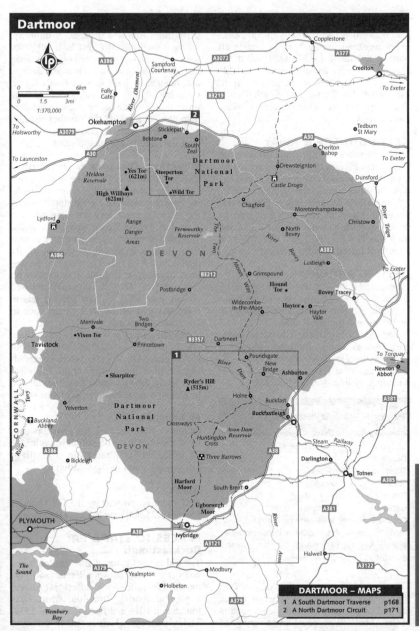

Dartmoor

To Holsworthy
To Launceston
To Exeter

Copplestone
Crediton
To Exeter

A386
A3072
A377
A30

Sampford Courtenay
B3219

Folly Gate
River Okement
Okehampton
A3079
A30

Tedburn St Mary
Cheriton Bishop
To Exeter

Sticklepath
Belstone
South Zeal
Drewsteignton
Castle Drogo
Dunsford

Meldon Reservoir
Yes Tor (621m)
Steeperton Tor
Wild Tor

D a r t m o o r   N a t i o n a l   P a r k

High Willhays (621m)

Chagford
Moretonhampstead
Christow
River Teign

Lydford

Range Danger Areas
Fernworthy Reservoir
North Bovey
Lustleigh
To Exeter

A386
D E V O N
The Teign
Two Moors Way
River Bovey
A382

B3212
Grimspound
Hound Tor
Bovey Tracey

Postbridge
Widecombe-in-the-Moor
Haytor
Haytor Vale

Merrivale
Two Bridges
B3357
Dartmeet

Vixen Tor
Princetown

To Torquay

Tavistock
Sharpitor

1
River Dart
Poundsgate
New Bridge
Ashburton
Newton Abbot

Yelverton
Dartmoor National Park
Ryder's Hill (515m)
Holne
Buckfast
Buckfastleigh
A381

C O R N W A L L
Buckland Abbey
D E V O N
Crossways
Avon Dam Reservoir
Steam Railway

River Tavy
A386
Bickleigh
Huntingdon Cross
Three Barrows
Darlington
Totnes
A385

A38
Harford Moor
South Brent
A381

PLYMOUTH
Ugborough Moor
Ivybridge
A3121
River Avon
Halwell
A3122

The Sound
A379
Yealmpton
Modbury
A379
Holbeton

Wembury Bay

0   3   6km
0   1.5   3mi
1:370,000

DARTMOOR

Guided Walks

The national park organises guided walks every weekend throughout the year in all parts of Dartmoor. Details are listed in the *Dartmoor Visitor* and on leaflets available from TICs. If you're in the area in April, ask about the Exeter and South Devon Walking Festival, which includes many guided walks.

GETTING THERE & AWAY

The main gateway cities for Dartmoor are Exeter and Plymouth – both are served by train and National Express coach from London and other parts of the country.

The Getting Around chapter lists several public transport inquiry lines that provide details of both national and local bus and train services: See the boxed text 'National Transport Information' on p92.

GETTING AROUND

From Exeter and Plymouth you can reach any of the 'border towns' around the moor by public transport – including Okehampton, Ivybridge and Buckfastleigh.

For specific information on public transport services around Dartmoor, pick up a copy of the *Dartmoor Public Transport Guide* from local TICs or phone the Devonwide inquiry line (☎ 01392-382800).

A South Dartmoor Traverse

Distance	14mi (22.5km)
Duration	7–8 hours
Standard	medium
Start	Ivybridge
Finish	Buckfastleigh
Gateways	Plymouth, Exeter

Summary A long walk over high ground, past many historical sites, including burial mounds, Bronze Age hut circles and a stretch of path established by medieval monks.

This route follows a section of the Two Moors Way (described in Other Walks at the end of this chapter) and then a section of the Abbot's Way, providing a very good taste of southern Dartmoor scenery. The early miles follow a dismantled tramway, where it's very hard to get lost, but problems can arise when you turn off west along the Abbot's Way as the route is less defined and landmarks hard to spot if it's misty. Consequently this walk should only be done on a clear day unless you're confident with map and compass. If the weather changes unexpectedly you should turn back rather than risk getting lost on the moor.

Direction, Distance & Duration

This linear route can be done in either direction but from Ivybridge clear waymarking ensures you make a good start. Once on the moor there are very few signs and you must rely on your own navigation skills. With this in mind you might prefer to start from Buckfastleigh and get the potentially difficult bit done first, knowing that the disused tramway will guide you home with few surprises. Your decision may be based on bus timetables, as you use the bus to reach the start of the walk or get back to your base afterwards.

Whichever way you go, this walk is 14mi, which requires a walking time of about seven hours. Allowing for lunch, map reading and investigating the various historical sites along the way, most fit people should be able to complete it in eight to nine hours.

PLANNING

Dartmoor National Park has a visitors centre at the walk's starting point in Ivybridge (☎ 01752-897035) and there is a village information point in Buckfastleigh.

Maps

This route is covered by the OS Outdoor Leisure 1:25,000 map No 28 *(Dartmoor)*.

PLACES TO STAY & EAT
Buckfastleigh

The old market town of Buckfastleigh lies just off the A38 between Exeter and Plymouth. Two miles north is **Buckfast Abbey**, a popular tourist attraction, which was founded in 1016 and flourished until 1539. Today's abbey, which is still in use, was rebuilt in the early 19th century in mock-Gothic style.

Campers can head for the pleasant little site at **Churchill Farm** (☎ 01364-642844), between Buckfast and Buckfastleigh, charging £3. The friendly owners are happy to advise on local walking routes. It's near a ruined chapel (marked on the OS 1:25,000 map) and can be reached on foot from Buckfastleigh up a steep path from the eastern end of the main street, much better than the long way around by road.

Of the pubs in town, **The White Hart**, in the town centre, is by far the most appealing, with a good beer and interesting bar food at reasonable prices. Just down the road, **The Globe Inn** (☎ 01364-642223) also does bar meals and has B&B for £20/32 per single/double. On the north-east edge of the village near the A38 off-ramp, **Furzeleigh Mill Hotel** (☎ 01364-643476) has en suite rooms for £24 to £29 in the summer (with discounts at quieter times of year), plus a quiet bar and evening meals served in the restaurant.

Apart from the pubs and hotels, your other eating options include cosy **Lorenzo's Pizza Restaurant**, in the town centre, open every evening except Sunday, and the rather frilly **Singing Kettle Tearoom**, nearby, open daily to about 5pm, plus Friday and Saturday evening. There's also a fish and chip **takeaway**, post office, **supermarket** and several smaller shops.

On the main road between Buckfast and Buckfastleigh, **The Abbey Inn** is a nice pub by the river with bar meals for around £7 and a smart restaurant where main courses cost £10 to £15. Nearby, the **Little Chef** motorists cafe is open every day until about 9pm in summer.

Ivybridge

Ivybridge is larger than Buckfastleigh, with more in the way of B&Bs, restaurants, cafes, pubs (one a Greek wine bar), plus shops, banks and other services. If you decide to stay here instead of in Buckfastleigh, the TIC (☎ 01752-897035), near the Town Hall south of the town's main street, can help with accommodation suggestions.

GETTING TO/FROM THE WALK

Bus An express bus runs twice each way between Exeter and Plymouth daily (except Sunday); it stops in Buckfastleigh by the entrance to the steam train station and on the main road about a mile outside Ivybridge (not in the town itself). A slower bus covers the same route five times per day (not Sunday). If you're staying in Buckfastleigh, the handiest bus to Ivybridge and the start of the walk comes through at about 9.30am and takes about 20 minutes.

There's also a local bus service hourly every day (not Sunday) between Newton Abbot (the nearest mainline train station) and Buckfastleigh.

Train The nearest mainline train stations to Buckfastleigh are at Newton Abbot and Totnes, both on the main line between London and Plymouth and served by regular trains. From Newton Abbot you can reach Buckfastleigh by local bus (see the previous Bus entry). From Totnes, buses to Buckfastleigh are not so handy but in the summer months steam trains run several times per day along the private South Devon Railway from Totnes all the way to Buckfastleigh.

Ivybridge is also on the main line between London and Plymouth but note that some express trains do not stop here; you may have to change in Exeter.

Car Both Buckfastleigh and Ivybridge are on the A38 between Exeter and Plymouth, although you have to turn off the main road to reach the town centres.

Taxi From Buckfastleigh, the C&M Cars company (☎ 01364-643171) will transport you to Ivybridge for £10.

THE WALK
Ivybridge to Crossways
8mi (13km), 4–4½ hours
The route starts at the TIC near the town hall in the town centre (it's signposted). From here head north along a footpath (look for the Two Moors Way waymarks on the lampposts) that becomes a narrow street called Costly St. On your right is a small

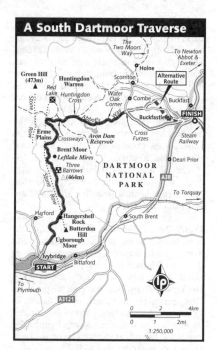

A South Dartmoor Traverse

The Two Moors Way

To Newton Abbot & Exeter

Green Hill (473m)▲

Huntingdon Warren

Red Lake

Huntingdon Cross

Holne

Scorriton

Water Oak Corner

Combe

Buckfast

Alternative Route

Erme Plains

Crossways

Abbot's Way

Avon Dam Reservoir

Cross Furzes

Buckfastleigh

FINISH

Steam Railway

Brent Moor

Leftlake Mires

Three Barrows

△(464m)

DARTMOOR NATIONAL PARK

Dean Prior

To Torquay

A38

Harford

Hangershell Rock ▲

Butterdon Hill

Ugborough Moor

South Brent

Ivybridge

START

Bittaford

To Plymouth

A3121

0   2   4km

0   1   2mi

1:250,000

The **tramway** was constructed in 1910 to carry china clay from a quarry on the moors at Red Lake to a factory near Ivybridge. The tramway was closed in 1932, but now provides a firm footpath for 6mi. It takes a rather circuitous route but apparent direct short cuts don't save much time.

Continue aiming mostly northwards, passing west of Hangershell Rock. Just beyond here the tramway intersects an ancient 'stone row' boundary, keeping roughly parallel to it for the next few miles. You pass **Three Barrows**, a cluster of huge burial mounds on a hill to the right, then reach Clay Bridge and the pool of **Leftlake Mires**. Over to your left (west) you can clearly see the hut circles on Erme Plains, the remains of an ancient settlement.

About 7.5mi from the start, the tramway curves west then east. To your left is the old **Red Lake** clay quarry and its volcano-like spill-heap. At this point, look for a path that branches off right (south), marked with a small 'TMW' (Two Moors Way) sign on a rock. The path is vague but swings round to aim east, crossing another tramway (running down from Red Lake) at a point called, naturally enough, Crossways. At this stage you're also on the Abbot's Way, a walking trail once used by monks to travel between the two abbeys of Buckfast and Buckland, near Yelverton.

supermarket; stock up here as there is nowhere to buy lunch on the walk.

Cross the main road in front of the supermarket and head north out of town, up a lane (signposted to Harford) that climbs steeply for about half a mile, continuing straight on at Cole Lane and immediately over the railway on Stowford Bridge. Look for the Dartmoor National Park and Two Moors Way signs. (If you've come by train, from Ivybridge train station you can walk west along the south side of the line to Stowford Bridge.)

Cross the bridge and continue for another 250m to Stowford Farm Cottage, then turn right onto a track signposted 'To the Moor'. After a few steps turn left (north) and continue along an old track, uphill between hedges. At the top, a gate leads onto the open moor. Follow a gradually climbing path through the grass and bracken towards the cairn on Butterdon Hill. Within half a mile of the gate you'll meet the old, dismantled tramway; turn left (north).

KELLI HAMBLET

Diagram of the internal structure of a Bronze Age hut, now a Dartmoor hut circle

Crossways to Buckfastleigh

6mi (9.5km), 3–3½ hours

From Crossways, the combined Two Moors Way and Abbot's Way aims north-east, but the path is hard to see in the long grass so you definitely need a compass. It becomes clear again as you drop into a valley to reach an ancient 'clapper' (stone slab) bridge, which you cross to the north bank of the River Avon. Follow the path (boggy in places) down the north side of the river to **Huntingdon Cross**, a standing stone used as a route and boundary marker in medieval times. To the north are the slopes of Huntingdon Warren, a former rabbit farm with the remains of artificial burrows and huts for the 'warreners' who looked after them.

Just after the cross you ford a small stream and the Two Moors Way heads off north-easterly, up Hickaton Hill. Stay on the Abbot's Way, following the north bank of the River Avon, then across the slopes above the Avon Dam Reservoir. To your left (north) are several more Bronze Age hut circles in good condition.

The path crosses Brockhill Stream. Keep heading east up the steep hillside (there's no clear path), then across a small, featureless plateau called Dean Moor and down to Water Oak Corner, where the open moor ends and you enter private farmland. There's a gate with a clear sign: 'Abbot's Way, Exit from Moor, to Cross Furzes'.

Keep to the path, following the marker poles through the fields. This leads to a stream, which you cross on a little clapper bridge, in a nice patch of woodland. Continue on a track to a junction of lanes in an area called Cross Furzes. The easiest way home is to turn right and follow the quiet lane south-east and east straight to Buckfastleigh.

There is another way from Cross Furzes to the finish at Buckfastleigh, which involves less walking on lanes. From the track junction go straight on (east) for 1.5mi, then turn right (south-east) through a farm called Button. Make sure you keep to the legal path through the fields, which leads to and through another lovely wood called Bilberryhill Copse. From here an old walled track leads down into Buckfastleigh.

A North Dartmoor Circuit

Distance	10.5mi (17km)
Duration	5–6 hours
Standard	medium
Start/Finish	Sticklepath
Gateways	Okehampton, Exeter

Summary A long walk through valleys and over high ground, into the heart of the moors. This is a very rewarding walk, although route finding is potentially difficult in bad weather.

This circular walk is an excellent introduction to the varied scenery of Dartmoor. It starts at a quiet village, with a beautiful section along a wooded river valley, then strides out across the moors, keeping mainly to high ground in an elongated horseshoe. The views are excellent and there's a tremendous feeling of space and openness.

Direction, Distance & Duration

This circular walk can be done in either direction, but we describe it clockwise so you get a chance to limber up in the valley before heading for the high ground. The total distance is 10.5mi (17km), which takes about five to six hours of walking. Allowing time for lunch and sitting in stone circles, the walk will take about six to seven hours.

PLANNING
Maps

This route is covered by the OS Outdoor Leisure 1:25,000 map No 28 *(Dartmoor)*.

Information Sources

In Sticklepath, at the village information point (the post office) or the National Trust Finch Foundry museum, look out for the excellent local walks leaflets describing short routes in the area, such as the Soil Trail, and local geology and ecology. There is also a Dartmoor National Park visitors centre in Okehampton (☎ 01837-53020).

PLACES TO STAY & EAT
Sticklepath

The delightful little village of Sticklepath is about 3mi east of Okehampton. On the

DARTMOOR

Warning

This route skirts the edge of Okehampton Range, used by the army for training with live ammunition. There is no firing in April, May, July, August and early September, nor at weekends, public holidays or Mondays all year, and you can walk here at these times. At other times, you can also walk in the range if no firing is taking place. If the range is being used, red flags fly at points where footpaths enter the danger area. You can also get the latest information from local TICs or by phoning (free) the Firing Information Service (☎ 0800-4584868). Even when there's no firing, you should beware of unidentifiable metal objects lying in the grass. If you do find anything suspicious, don't touch it. Make a note of the position and report it to the police after your walk.

Some unexploded shells may lie beneath the surface, so use common sense also if you need to relieve yourself in the open. While burying your excrement is recommended in most country areas, random digging around Dartmoor is not a good idea.

main street is **Finch Foundry** – a cottage-sized water-powered forge dating from the 19th century. Run by the National Trust, it's open to the public and has a small museum.

For budget accommodation there's a straightforward *camping barn* (☎ 01837-840359) attached to the village post office. It has showers, lounge and a kitchen, and charges £3.75 (plus £1.50 per dog), and you'll also need a few £1 coins for the electricity meter. *Tawside House* (☎ 01837-840183) is a walker-friendly, nonsmoking B&B, near the bridge on the main street, charging around £19 (but no dogs). The *Devonshire Inn* (☎ 01837-840626), a pub on the main street, offers a quiet atmosphere, good beer, meals and B&B for £15, but *only* for dog owners. (What is it about dogs in Sticklepath?)

There are more B&Bs in the nearby villages of South Zeal and Belstone, from where you can easily reach the walking route described here.

GETTING TO/FROM THE WALK

Bus There's a bus between Exeter and Okehampton via Sticklepath about six times daily (except Sunday) in each direction, and between Okehampton and Moretonhampstead via Sticklepath about four times daily (except Sunday).

Train The nearest train station is Okehampton. Trains run to/from Exeter six times daily on Sunday only, from late May to mid-September. From Okehampton you can reach Sticklepath by bus.

Car Sticklepath is just south of the A30 (a busy dual-carriageway) between Exeter and Okehampton.

THE WALK
Sticklepath to Steeperton Tor
5.5mi (9km), 2½–3 hours

From Sticklepath's main street, aim east over the bridge at the end of the village and then immediately right onto a path alongside the River Taw. The signpost says 'Tarka Trail' (see Other Walks at this end of this chapter). Follow this path, keeping close to the river (on your right), with gardens and the backs of cottages on the opposite bank. You then enter beautiful Skaigh Wood and cross a wooden footbridge, inscribed with a quote from *Tarka the Otter* by Henry Williamson.

Shortly afterwards you cross another footbridge to the north bank of the river, turning left to continue upstream along the north bank through a steep-sided valley called Belstone Cleve, quite possibly the inspiration for the quote on the bridge you crossed earlier. The path climbs diagonally up the valley side, skirts the village of Belstone and then crosses an open grassy area to meet a lane. Time for a breather and to admire the view – fortunately there's a choice of benches provided.

Continue south along the lane, taking the second rough track that forks off to the right, to reach a gate which leads to the open moor. There's a noticeboard here about firing days, so have a final check before you stride out.

The track leads south, with the River Taw to your left. At a suitable point (there's no set path), branch right off the track and go steeply uphill to the summit of **Belstone Tor**. Time for another look at the view: south across the open moorland and north across the farmland to the distant hills of Exmoor, with (on a clear day) the sea visible behind.

Aim south, down from Belstone Tor, through a gap in a huge dry-stone wall (called **Irishman's Wall** – a 19th-century job creation project) and up to Higher Tor. Then down again to meet a track coming up from the valley to your right. Near Winter Tor, you'll also notice the line of red-and-white poles marking the edge of the danger area.

The track follows the broad ridge southwards – a wonderful section with wide views on both sides. You pass just east of Oke Tor and enter the danger area, getting an increasingly clear view of Steeperton Tor, although it's marred slightly by the radio masts on the summit.

After another half-mile or so, with Steeperton Tor directly to the east, branch off the track on a path into a little valley called Steeperton Gorge. Just before you cross the stream there's a patch of grass on the left that makes a lovely sheltered picnic spot.

Once across the stream the path climbs up the other side of the valley, reaching a junction after 300m, where another path turns sharply back to reach **Steeperton Tor**. The summit offers great views of the ridge you've just followed from Belstone, and of the next section towards Cosdon Hill.

Steeperton Tor to Sticklepath
5mi (8km), 2½–3 hours

From Steeperton Tor it seems that Hound Tor is just a short hop across the valley, but don't be tempted – the valley floor is very boggy. Follow the path south-easterly for about 500m to cross Steeperton Brook by the ruins of an old hut. Turn north-east, passing some more red-and-white posts (you are now leaving the danger area). The path passes west of the rounded summit of Hound Tor, then just to the west of a **stone circle**, which is in good condition and well worth a stop.

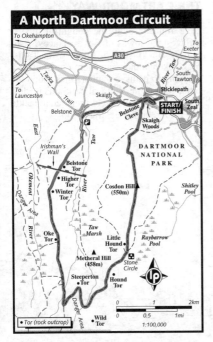

A North Dartmoor Circuit

Dartmoor Letterboxing

If you see the word 'Letterbox' marked on your map, don't expect to send your postcards home. Letterboxing is a peculiar (and typically British) pastime unique to Dartmoor, in which people hide small boxes in remote areas and other people try to find them. Each box has an owner, and inside is a rubber stamp with a unique pattern or picture that finders use to mark their logbook and a visitor book that the finder signs or stamps with their own personal insignia. The aim, quite simply, is to find as many letterboxes as possible. The craze goes back over a century, although it really became popular about 25 years ago, and there are several hundred such letterboxes all over Dartmoor. Only a few particularly old or important ones are marked on maps, and are considered 'too easy' by aficionados. You can get a leaflet with more information from TICs.

A path leads directly from the stone circle, over Little Hound Tor and then gradually up to the summit of **Cosdon Hill**, marked by a trig point, which has more excellent views north to where the moorland gives way, once again, to farming country.

It's all downhill now as you follow a path north from the summit. Take care as you descend; don't go too far east towards South Zeal but keep aiming north, straight towards Sticklepath and down into the corner formed by the moor boundary wall. In the corner are two gates. One leads to a path to South Zeal but take the other one, north, down an old sunken lane into Skaigh Wood. Turn right (north-east) and go over a stile to run along the top of the steep valley, then zigzag down to meet the path by the river that you walked along at the start of this route. Turn right to reach the village along the path or go over the small footbridge that takes you past a small graveyard into the car park at the back of Finch Foundry.

Other Walks

TWO MOORS WAY

Our South Dartmoor Traverse description in this chapter follows the early stages of a long-distance path called the Two Moors Way, which crosses the south-west peninsula via the national parks of Dartmoor and

Exmoor (described briefly in the Other Walks in Southern England chapter). If you get the urge to keep heading north, this route is 102mi long – most people take a week to do it – and passes through some of the finest (and wildest) scenery in Southern England.

THE TARKA TRAIL

Another LDP connecting Dartmoor and Exmoor is the Tarka Trail, inspired by the classic book *Tarka the Otter* by Henry Williamson. Our North Dartmoor Circuit description, earlier in this chapter, briefly touches the southern extremity of this route as it winds through the valley of the fledgling River Taw (Tarka's home) between South Tawton and Okehampton. The whole trail is much longer – a figure of eight based on Barnstaple in North Devon, which includes sections of walking, cycling and even a ride on a train along (inevitably) the Tarka Line.

THE DARTMOOR WAY

Another option is the Dartmoor Way, a circular route through the delightful moors, villages and towns of Bovey Tracey, Ashburton, Buckfastleigh, Princetown, Tavistock, Okehampton and Moretonhampstead. Keeping to paths and quiet lanes round the outer edge of the national park, this is ideal if you're not confident or prepared to tackle the wilder, higher central moors.

Norfolk

Norfolk is a large county in East Anglia, off the track for most foreign visitors, but popular with holidaying Brits – particularly the seaside resorts on the north and east coasts. Another attraction is the Broads, a vast network of navigable rivers and lakes between Norwich (the county capital) and the coast. The Broads Special Area is effectively a national park, although it's relatively (and thankfully) low-key and has limited visitor facilities once away from the waterways.

It has to be said that Norfolk is not a major walking destination: It's very flat, with the highest point, How Hill, only about 12m above sea level. Some parts of the Broads are so low that they're *below* sea level. Thus the Broads is not a place for peak baggers or seekers of wilderness; rather it should be walked through slowly and savoured.

The Norfolk coast is another area ideal for gentle walking, as it's mostly flat with wide sandy beaches, great expanses of salt marsh, a nature reserve rich in bird life, tiny villages and several busy seaside resorts.

In this chapter we describe a three-day walk along the north coast and a day walk through the Broads. These take in several highlights, with their accompanying crowds, as well as several quieter spots where your only companions will be cows, birds and great crested newts.

GETTING THERE & AWAY

Norwich (pronounced noh-ridge) is the main transport gateway to the Norfolk region. It is easily reached by National Express coach from all parts of the country, and is well serviced by rail.

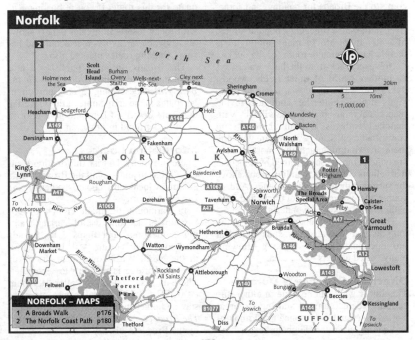

NORFOLK – MAPS	
1 A Broads Walk	p176
2 The Norfolk Coast Path	p180

For specific information on public transport services within Norfolk, try the Norfolk Public Transport information line (☎ 0500-626116). Alternatively, the Getting Around chapter lists several public transport inquiry lines that provide details of both national and local bus and train services: See the boxed text 'National Transport Information' on p92.

A Broads Walk

Distance	16mi (25.5km)
Duration	6–8 hours
Standard	easy
Start	Great Yarmouth
Finish	Potter Heigham
Gateways	Norwich, Great Yarmouth

Summary A walk on easy-to-follow paths alongside rivers and through villages, quiet meadows and farmland.

Most visitors (about 11 million each year) come to the Broads for boating, and sometimes in summer it seems like they've all arrived at the same time. On a popular stretch of water there are so many motor boats there's hardly enough room for the ducks.

However, back from the busy waterways is another world of quiet fields, woods, dykes and water meadows, home to many kinds of birds, butterflies and water-loving plants. There are picturesque villages with thatched cottages, ancient churches and comfortable pubs, and everywhere you look there are windmills (actually, most of them are wind pumps) – some ruined but others in marvellous condition, standing proud above the surrounding marsh and flatlands. And, of course, there's a network of tracks and footpaths which make for wonderful walking.

This walk mostly follows a section of the long-distance Weavers Way, and it's an ideal introduction to Broads walking, showing many varied aspects of the area.

Direction, Distance & Duration

This linear walk can be done in either direction. We recommend starting in Great Yarmouth (usually shortened to Yarmouth) and ending at Potter Heigham because the city skyline is better behind than in front, and if you stay in Potter Heigham it's easy to get into Yarmouth in the morning. For most of the route you can follow Weavers Way waymarks, but there are many signposts and markers for other paths. The route is 16mi, and you could do it in six hours nonstop, but allowing for lunch, photos, bird spotting or visiting windmills, you'll probably need about eight hours.

Alternatives The route can be finished at Acle, reducing the distance to about 10mi, or you can take the train from Yarmouth to Berney Arms, from where it's 11.5mi to Potter Heigham.

PLANNING
Maps & Books

The Broads and the southern half of the Weavers Way are covered by the Ordnance Survey (OS) Landranger 1:50,000 map No 134 (*Norwich & the Broads*), which is adequate for this route. If you're boating, *The Broads* map by GeoProjects (at 1:50,000, with many inserts in greater detail) shows all navigable areas in great detail and has some walking routes marked also.

The Broads Authority publishes a nice set of route cards called *Broad Walks in the Bure Valley*, describing several short circular routes in the area. Some of these overlap the route described here and give a lot of extra background information.

Information Sources

There are many Tourist Information Centres (TICs) in and around the Broads; some are run by local tourist boards, others by the Broads Authority.

In Yarmouth, the main TIC (☎ 01493-846345) stocks some useful leaflets, walking guidebooks and maps. The Broads Authority visitors centre (☎ 01493-332095), in the North West Tower near the River Bure road bridge, is open July to September. There is also a TIC at Potter Heigham (☎ 01692-670779). Local events, places to stay and other information can be found in *The Broadcaster*, a free tourist paper issued by the Broads Authority.

PLACES TO STAY & EAT
Great Yarmouth

Yarmouth is one of Britain's most popular seaside resorts, so there are endless places to stay and eat, along with all the tacky trimmings such as amusement arcades and gift shops. The *YHA Hostel* (☎ *01493-843991*) is on Sandown Rd, just north of the centre and very near the beach. Campers are better off at Potter Heigham, as Yarmouth's caravan parks are not aimed at passing backpackers. For B&B there's a huge choice. Spaces fill quickly at the height of summer, so it's easiest to contact the TIC (☎ 01493-846345) for suggestions. The main TIC is in the Town Hall and there's also a seasonal TIC on Marine Parade.

Potter Heigham

Unless you like busy seaside resorts, we'd recommend Potter Heigham. This place has two 'centres': the Village, which straddles

---

Just What Are these Broads?

In Norfolk, broads are open stretches of water – either separate lakes or ponds, or places where the rivers widen out. Drainage ditches, originally dug to turn marshes into agricultural land, are called dykes (or dikes). These empty into larger waterways called cuts. Larger canals (for boats) are called cuts, and the place where boats moor is called a staithe.

For many years the origin of the Norfolk Broads was unclear. The rivers were undoubtedly natural and the lakes seemed natural too, but how they had formed was unclear. The mystery was solved when records discovered in the remains of St Benet's Abbey showed that from the 12th century some areas were used for digging peat – a source of fuel.

Peat digging became a major industry and over the next 200 years approximately 2600 acres (about 1000 hectares) were dug up – leaving holes for water to gradually fill, causing marshes and lakes to develop. Eventually the peat-cutting industry died out, but in no other area of Britain has human effort changed the natural landscape so dramatically.

---

the main A149 road between Cromer and Yarmouth; and the Old Bridge, half a mile south. (The A149 bypasses to the east, crossing the river on, you've guessed it, the New Bridge.) Around the Old Bridge is the boat yard, supermarket, fish and chip shop, a pub, several cafes and shops, and even an amusement hall in case the natural scenery bores you. The TIC (☎ 01692-670779), next to the Old Bridge, is open April to October.

Between the Old Bridge and the main village, about 300m north of the bridge, is the *Causeway Cottage* (☎ *01692-670238*), where pitches (ie, a tent, car and up to four people) cost £9; this place is open summer only and you should be prepared for rather abrupt service.

The comfortable *Falgate Inn* (☎ *01692-670003*, ✉ *cypress@euphony.net*), about half a mile north of the Old Bridge, has B&B for £17 (£21 en suite), with bar meals at lunchtime and evening meals from £5.

Another B&B option, about a mile east of the village on the road towards Ludham, is the walker-friendly and very helpful *Red Roof Farmhouse* (☎ *01692-670604*) with double rooms for £55. The people here can assist with lifts, especially if you stay two nights, and can give advice on walking.

GETTING TO/FROM THE WALK

Bus Local buses run hourly between Norwich and Yarmouth, and between Potter Heigham and Yarmouth, five times daily each way, Monday to Friday. From Acle, there are seven buses daily (except Sunday and public holidays) to Yarmouth. There's no direct bus from Acle to Potter Heigham – you have to go via Yarmouth.

Train There are two railway lines between Norwich and Yarmouth. The main line goes through Acle, where trains stop about 10 times daily Monday to Saturday (six times on Sunday). A branch line goes via Berney Arms; you can shorten the walk by taking a train from Yarmouth, but there are only two trains daily Monday to Saturday (both in the afternoon), although four useful services on Sunday. Tell the conductor you want to get off here before the train leaves Yarmouth.

Car Yarmouth is reached by the A47 from King's Lynn and Norwich, the A12 from Lowestoft and the A149 from Cromer. Potter Heigham is on the A149 between Cromer and Yarmouth.

Taxi If your plans don't tie in with the bus times, a taxi between Yarmouth and Potter Heigham will cost about £12 (slightly less to or from Acle). Try Star Taxis (☎ 01493-443443) or Anglia Taxis (☎ 01493-855855).

THE WALK
Great Yarmouth to Berney Arms
4.5mi (7km), 1½–2 hours

The route starts at Vauxhall Bridge in Yarmouth, near the train station and the Asda supermarket. This is also the junction of the Weavers Way and Angles Way (for more details on these routes, see Other Walks at the end of this chapter).

Keeping the River Bure to your left, follow an embankment round the edge of the car park, under the swing bridge to reach the banks and salt marshes of Breydon Water. The path runs between the water and the railway line, then keeps to the top of a sea wall separating Breydon Water from the fields and marshes. To your left, boats of all sizes stream up and down the centre of the Water – a colourful sight – but little disturbs the tidal mudflats, so this is a good area for observing wading birds.

At Berney Arms, Breydon Water narrows to become the River Yare. Open to the public, **Berney Arms Windmill** is one of the largest remaining windmills in Norfolk, and offers great views from the 7th-floor balcony. Nearby, *The Berney Arms* pub is a convenient place to stop for morning coffee or an early lunch. The *shop* next door sells drinks and snacks.

Berney Arms to Acle Bridge
5.5mi (9km), 2–3 hours

Leave the river, aiming north-west over the railway line near the tiny Berney Arms train station and then across fields to **Halvergate**, which has several traditional houses and the *Red Lion* pub (a lunch possibility). From the village main street, turn right into Squires

Lane. This becomes a gravel track, which you follow through fields and over one of the highest points on the route so far – a dizzying 15m – with very good views over the marshes to the east.

In Tunstall the path meets a lane where you turn left and then right past the old church. Don't follow the concrete farm track, but head northwards instead on the footpath across the field to meet another lane. Keep on this, passing Staithe Farm to your left, until you reach a small junction where you turn left (west) on a track that leads towards Acle.

This is a very pleasant stretch through lush fields along the edge of **Decoy Carr**, a beautiful patch of woodland, past old dykes where reeds and lilies grow and (in summer) butterflies and dragonflies energetically do their stuff.

This idyll is suddenly truncated by the railway line and the main A47. Cross both (with care) to reach the Acle Cut boat yard.

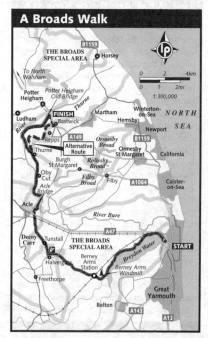

A Broads Walk

Go along the north side of the cut to meet the River Bure (pronounced byure), then turn left (north) and follow the towpath to reach **Acle Bridge**. On one side is the vast and busy ***Bridge Inn***, catering almost exclusively to the boat trade, with drinks at holiday prices and a not unreasonable range of bar food. On the other side of the bridge is a ***shop*** and ***snack bar***.

Acle Bridge to Potter Heigham
6mi (9.5km), 2½–3 hours

Cross to the north side of Acle Bridge, then head west along the path keeping the river to your left. About 45 minutes from Acle you reach Oby Cut. At the end of the cut, go through the car park and up the track towards Manor Farm, turning left down another track about 50m from the car park. (The signpost is hard to see.) Pass through the yard of another farm, then across fields, following signs, to reach a track just east of Boundary House. Go left onto this track, then (just before the gates into Boundary House) right onto a path that leads you to the **church** at Thurne. As with so many Broads villages, the church was built on high ground – an island in what would have been a 'sea' of marsh and river – once again giving excellent views of the route: west across the Bure and Thurne rivers, and south and east back towards Acle and the Halvergate Marshes, with Yarmouth still visible on the horizon.

Facing the church, go left round the corner into Thurne village, at the eastern end of Thurne Cut – a busy place, full of boats. There's a ***pub*** and ***shop*** here and the classic white **Thurne Mill**, a frequent feature on Broads postcards and brochures.

It's now an easy 3mi on the riverside path back to Potter Heigham, although after Repps your view of the river is blocked by holiday cabins.

A different route back to Potter Heigham from Thurne goes first northwards then through a lovely stretch of woodland across Shallam Dike. From here you turn north, passing to the right of the village of Repps, through fields to Bastwick. Turn left to reach the Potter Heigham Old Bridge.

The Norfolk Coast Path

Distance	46.5mi (75km)
Duration	3 days
Standard	easy
Start	Hunstanton
Finish	Cromer
Gateways	King's Lynn, Norwich

Summary A generally level route on good paths through rolling farmland and low-lying coastal areas. It's mostly firm underfoot, although stretches on soft sand and pebbles may slow down progress.

The Norfolk Coast Path, combined with the Peddars Way, is a national trail through East Anglia. The Peddars Way is a Roman road, originally built around AD 60 as part of a campaign against the legendary Queen Boudicca. Today much of the walking is on tracks and lanes, and – to be blunt – it's not the most interesting of routes.

So in this section we describe just the Norfolk Coast Path, which follows some of the finest stretches of sweeping, sandy beaches in Britain. Although in summer it can get pretty busy around the towns, walkers can easily avoid the crowds and enjoy spectacular vistas of sky and sea almost undisturbed. The route also offers plenty of history: Villages claim a maritime tradition that includes sending a number of ships to repel the Spanish Armada of 1588. Horatio Nelson, one of the greatest English admirals (Battle of Trafalgar, 'Kismet Hardy' and all that), was also a local lad.

The Norfolk Coast is the richest in Britain for birdwatching, with some internationally important reserves, including Cley Marshes Nature Reserve (for a description, see the boxed text on p181). You'll meet birdwatchers along the way who will be pleased to tell you what's new in the area. Even if you're not that keen on birds, it's worth packing a pair of binoculars.

Direction, Distance & Duration
The usual way is to start at Hunstanton and head east to Cromer; a distance of 46.5mi, which usually takes three days to complete.

NORFOLK

The path often follows beaches, but sometimes detours inland to avoid large salt marshes. You'll soon get the hang of a coastal walk that may not involve sea views for several miles.

The route is generally well waymarked with the standard national trail acorn symbol and straightforward yellow arrows. Stages for the three-day walk described here are:

day	from	to	mi/km
1	Hunstanton	Wells-next-the-Sea	23/37
2	Wells-next-the-Sea	Cley next the Sea	10.5/17
3	Cley next the Sea	Cromer	13/21

Day 1 is long but mostly flat and can be reduced by covering the 2mi from Hunstanton to Holme on the evening of the day before you start. Alternatively you could split Day 1 into two days (taking the walk total to four), giving you more time to amble along, paddle in the sea, eat ice cream and watch the birds.

If you're a strong walker, you could burn along in two long days, but you won't see much of your surroundings, which would be a shame given the remarkable sense of space that the landscape confers.

PLANNING
Maps & Books

The whole route is covered by the OS Landranger 1:50,000 maps No 132 *(North West Norfolk)* and No 133 *(North East Norfolk)*.

The official national trail guide *Peddars Way & Norfolk Coast Path* by Bruce Robinson is thorough and well presented, with extracts from OS maps, photos and plenty of interesting background information. Most useful is the inexpensive and regularly updated *Norfolk Coast Path, Peddars Way & Weavers Way Guide & Accommodation List*, produced by the Norfolk Ramblers. It's available at local TICs or direct from John Kent, Knights Cottage, The Old School, Honing, North Walsham NR28 9TR, for £3, including postage (in Britain).

Information Sources

TICs on the route include Cromer (☎ 01263-512497), Hunstanton (☎ 01485-532610), Wells (☎ 01328-710885) and Sheringham (☎ 01263-824329), but the latter two are open only in summer. For regional inquiries, the King's Lynn TIC (☎ 01553-763044) is open all year. Tourist information is also available on the borough council's Web site (W www.west-norfolk.gov.uk).

Practical route information is available in Wells-next-the-Sea from the experts at the Peddars Way and Norfolk Coast Path National Trail Office (☎ 01328-711533, e peddars.way@dial.pipex.com).

PLACES TO STAY & EAT

There are many places to stay on the coast, but advanced bookings are advisable as this is a popular holiday destination, even in spring and autumn, when the birdwatching is especially good. Most of the prices quoted here are for the high season (summer), but many places offer discounts at quieter times of year. Camping is also possible, but again there are not many places for walkers – most are larger places for caravans and big tents staying a week. The Hunstanton TIC (☎ 01485-532610) can book accommodation along the coast.

Places to stay are listed in the route description. For a wider choice, use *The Rambler's Yearbook & Accommodation Guide*, *Stilwell's National Trail Companion* (for details, see Books in the Facts for the Walker chapter) or the *Norfolk Coast Path, Peddars Way & Weavers Way Guide & Accommodation List*, mentioned under Maps & Books in the Planning section for this walk.

For food along the way, there are some excellent pubs and cafes on the coast. If you are self-catering, there are also shops where you can restock.

GETTING TO/FROM THE WALK

Bus King's Lynn and Cromer (at the end of the walk) are on the National Express coach network. Local buses run between King's Lynn and Hunstanton three times per day, but the service is drastically reduced in winter. There's also a very handy Coastliner bus service (again summer only) that runs along the coast between Hunstanton and Cromer, never too far from the route.

You can pick up a Coastliner timetable from local TICs, mentioned under Information Sources earlier. For more details, the Norfolk Bus Information Centre (☎ 0845-300 6116) is open 8.30am to 5pm Monday to Saturday, and staff are very helpful. They can also give local train information.

Train King's Lynn is the nearest train station to the start, with regular trains to/from London (via Cambridge). At the end of the route, Cromer is connected by rail to Norwich with regular services, although only a few operate on Sunday. Norwich is linked to London with frequent services.

Car Hunstanton is on the A140 and is easily reached from King's Lynn, which is at the junction of two major roads: the A10 to London and the A47 between Norwich and central England. Cromer is at the end of the A140, north of Norwich. The A149 runs between Hunstanton and Cromer, roughly parallel to the coast and within easy reach of several points along the route.

THE WALK
Hunstanton

Hunstanton is a busy seaside resort with a wide choice of hotels, cafes, pubs and B&Bs, although many close during winter. Central walker-friendly places include *Garganey House* (☎ 01485-533269, 46 Northgate), charging £20; and *The Gables* (☎ 01485-532514, 28 Austen St), charging £24. There's also a *YHA Hostel* (☎ 01485-532061), on Avenue Rd, charging £9.80. For details contact the TIC (☎ 01485-532610), in the Town Hall on the Green, near the sea.

Holme next the Sea

Holme next the Sea (usually shortened to Holme) is quieter than Hunstanton. If you arrive in the afternoon, a 4mi return stroll to Hunstanton is a pleasant limber-up and reduces your mileage next day.

Campers can go to *Inglenook* (☎ 01485-525598), a simple place on the main road,

charging around £3; or, a little farther east, to the friendly and similarly priced *Newholm Nurseries* (☎ 01485-525269). B&Bs in Holme include *Eastgates Cottage* (☎ 01485-525218), on the lane that loops off the main road north towards the beach, for £25. Nearby *Meadow Springs* (☎ 01485-525279) charges the same. Also nearby, *The White Horse* is a friendly pub serving good bar food from around £6.

Day 1: Hunstanton to Wells-next-the-Sea
23mi (37km), 7–9 hours
Today is a long walk with wide open vistas, empty sandy beaches, salt marshes and the sound of waves, gulls and the flap of rigging in the harbours as your soundtrack. Attractions include good swimming beaches and bird reserves, so you may want to do this stage in two days.

The route starts near the TIC. Leave Hunstanton along the promenade, past the old lighthouse, round a car park and then down a quiet street lined with holiday homes in Old Hunstanton. Continue beside a golf course and the River Hun to meet a small lane coming in from Holme. (If you stayed in Holme, you'll come this way from the village.) At this point you can either follow the track which leads to an isolated building called the Firs, or follow the signposted route on a boardwalk through the dunes. (The dunes themselves are fragile and shouldn't be walked on.) After a patch of pine trees, turn inland along the sea wall to avoid deep channels and enjoy the view.

Near Thornham the trail leaves the sea wall and follows a little footpath through the reeds, then cuts right along a lane into the village. Next comes an inland section to avoid impassable salt marsh and a long stretch along the main road: Take the main road through Thornham, then turn right along Chosely Lane. Follow this lane for a mile before turning left by a copse and continuing eastwards then northwards on tracks through flat featureless fields to Brancaster.

In **Brancaster**, *The Ship Inn* (☎ 01485-210333) has B&B from £45 per double, with a restaurant and bar serving meals.

NORFOLK

The Old Bakery (☎ 01485-210501) offers B&B from £18.

The path runs by the edge of the salt marsh behind Brancaster Staithe and into **Burnham Deepdale**. Here the very comfortable and attractive independent hostel, *Deepdale Granary (☎ 01485-210256, ⓔ info @deepdalegranary.co.uk)*, has small dorms of four or six beds, a twin room, showers, kitchen and lounge; you just need to bring a sleeping bag. It costs £9.50 to stay and groups get discounts. The friendly people who run this place can advise on walks and other activities in the area. Next door, there's a small *shop* at the petrol station.

From Burnham Deepdale, continue along the top of a sea wall once again, although the sea is now more than a mile away. Much of the marsh on your left is in Scolt Head Nature Reserve.

In **Burnham Overy Staithe**, the village pub, named *The Hero* in honour of Nelson, serves reasonable meals. B&Bs include *Domville Guesthouse (☎ 01328-738298)*, on Glebe Lane, charging £21 (£25 en suite).

Leave Burnham Overy Staithe by the sea wall and follow the path through the dunes onto the glorious beach of **Holkham Bay**. The view can only be described as 'big' here, and when the sand is firm underfoot (avoid high tides) it's a joy to walk on. With a huge nature reserve to your left, and the nudist beach near Holkham Gap, there's no shortage of interest. On a warm day the sea is very inviting.

About 2mi inland, **Holkham Hall** is a large and sumptuous 18th-century mansion.

If you're into stately piles, this could be another interesting diversion.

From Holkham Gap, you can either follow the path that runs along the inland edge of a clump of pines or walk along the beach. Both routes take you to the large car park near the lifeboat station at the end of a very straight road into Wells-next-the-Sea.

Wells-next-the-Sea

Wells-next-the-Sea is a lively resort in the summer months, with several cafes and takeaways. (It is also a working harbour, so the fish is always fresh.) The TIC (☎ 01328-710885) is in the town centre on Staithe St.

Walker-friendly B&Bs include *Brambledene (☎ 01328-711143)*, on Warham Rd at the village's edge, charging from £16; and the more central *Eastdene (☎ 01328-710381)*, at £20. Of the pubs in town, *The Crown (☎ 01328-710209)* is most appealing, with good beer and food, and B&B from £69 per double. You can camp at *Pinewoods (☎ 01328-710439)*, on the beach road.

Day 2: Wells-next-the-Sea to Cley next the Sea
10.5mi (17km), 4–6 hours
This day has few views of the sea, but away from the beaches and holiday-makers it offers a much wilder experience than Day 1, including the largest surviving areas of salt marsh in Britain. The going is firm underfoot and there's plenty of time to enjoy the wide open views.

Leave Wells by the road from the harbour. Where it starts to cut inland, the route goes

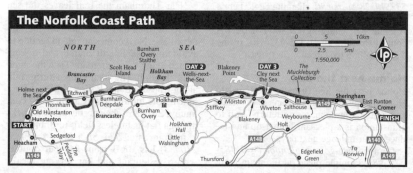

The Norfolk Coast Path

between some sheds and up onto the sea wall. After a couple of miles the trail passes north of Stiffkey, which has several B&Bs. The next feature is a car park near **Morston**, which has a National Trust visitors centre and a quay for the boats that take people out to the **seal colony** at Blakeney Point.

Another mile or so along the sea wall leads to **Blakeney**, where *The Kings Arms* (☎ 01263-740341) serves meals all day and has an interesting mix of show biz and local history pictures, should the art of conversation desert you. B&B costs from £55 per double. There's a *tea van* with tables in the car park, serving snacks and meals, although not to very nice views. Blakeney is another place to arrange **seal-watching trips**.

From Blakeney to Cley it's tempting to skip the three-sides-of-a-square walk along the top of the sea wall, but to do this would mean missing a particularly open (and in some weather, distinctly wild) stretch right on the edge of the marsh. Don't be tempted down onto the marsh, and even less to cross to the spit of land between you and the sea: There is no way through and the marshes can be treacherous.

Cley next the Sea

The village of Cley (pronounced to rhyme with eye) and its neighbours Blakeney and Wiveton were the richest towns in the area during the 15th century, when the coastal trade was at its height. Ships took fish to London and corn to Newcastle, returning with coal. But when 17th-century landowners built the sea walls to drain the marshes for pasture, the estuary of the River Glaven silted up and Cley's glory days were over. Today the village is famous for the **Cley Marshes Nature Reserve** (see the boxed text of the same name).

B&Bs include *Marshland* (☎ 01263-740284), in the old town hall, charging from £38 per double. *The George & Dragon Hotel* (☎ 01263-740652) does B&B from £42 per double (£62 en suite), and highly rated food and beer. For something different, you can stay in *Cley Mill* (☎ 01263-740209), a wonderfully restored and atmospheric 18th-century windmill on the edge

of the village overlooking the sea, with B&B from £54 to £76 per double on weekdays (£60 to £92 at weekends).

Day 3: Cley next the Sea to Cromer
13mi (21km), 5–7 hours
This is another relatively short and easy day, although quite a shock after the flat coastline – it actually involves some hills!

To leave Cley, the trail takes an unlikely path along the backs of houses, past the windmill, onto the sea wall running parallel to a lane, and out towards the sea. At the end of the lane, the path runs through a car park on the landward side of the shingle sea defence. You can walk along the beach but it's slow (walking along the sea defence is not encouraged as it's erosive), so you'll make better progress on the proper path. To the right is the Cley Marshes Nature Reserve, although you're a bit too far away to tell your redshanks from your greenshanks.

The path continues along the coast for a few miles. Just before Weybourne you might see signs of army activity at the **Muckleburgh Collection**, a military vehicle

Cley Marshes Nature Reserve

Managed by the Norfolk Wildlife Trust, Cley Marshes is one of the best-known bird reserves in Britain, and anyone with even a passing interest in our feathered friends should try to visit. Boardwalks allow you to get deep into the marshy reed beds, and there are several hides where you can watch the birds without disturbing them. This is a particularly popular place in spring and autumn, when migrating birds follow the Norfolk coast and species not normally seen here frequently pass through.

Although the Coast Path goes round the nature reserve, the only real way to see it is to walk through the village on the main road and find the visitors centre on the right, where you pay a small entry fee. The centre will also give you advice on what you may see and whereabouts to go.

museum, which is possibly worth a visit if you're into tanks and jeeps.

Weybourne itself is off the Trail, but has a *pub*, a *shop* and some places to stay. Beyond here the path climbs steadily onto the cliff tops. Signs now warn about the dangers of crumbling cliffs, and they mean it: You'll have to skirt round a line of old coastguard cottages, which are perched perilously close to the edge and destined one day to topple.

The route descends into **Sheringham** – a tourist town with any number of cafes and pubs to choose from, plus a *YHA Hostel* (☎ 01263-823215) and endless B&Bs should you want to break your journey. The TIC (☎ 01263-824329) is outside the station.

Leave Sheringham along the promenade and over **Beeston Hill**, with fine views of the surrounding caravan parks – this no doubt explains why the path turns inland. The trail crosses the railway line and then the A149, following a lane that turns into a track and then a path, going uphill through woods and past the fraudulently named **Roman Camp** (some earthworks are probably the work of medieval iron smelters).

The trail is well signposted into Cromer, which is lucky as it twists and turns a few times descending from the woods, then follows tracks and paths and finally a suburban street to meet the main A148 on the edge of Cromer, near the train station. The route seems to fizzle out here, but it's rewarding to continue down to the sea for a final paddle, to finish at the grand pier and celebrate with an ice cream on the prom.

Cromer

This seaside town has a TIC (☎ 01263-512497), on Prince of Wales Rd in the town centre, and a lot of places to eat, drink and stay, although most cater for holiday-makers staying at least a couple of days. Walker-friendly places include the central *Birch House* (☎ 01263-512521, 34 Cabbell Rd), which charges £18 (or £21 en suite); and *Morden House* (☎ 01263-513396, 20 Cliff Ave), on the east side of the centre, charging from £26.

If you're camping, on the way into town the trail passes *Seacroft Campsite* (open March to October), which charges from £3. Nearby, the Camping & Caravanning Club's *West Runton Site* (☎ 01263-837544) charges backpackers £6.

Other Walks

LONG-DISTANCE PATHS

In this chapter we've described walks that introduce you to the Broads and the coast. For another aspect of Norfolk, through farm country and areas of heath called the Brecklands, you could follow the **Peddars Way**. This former Roman road starts in Knettishall Heath, near Thetford, and aims straight as an arrow for Holme next the Sea, where it meets the Norfolk Coast Path. Together these two routes form a national trail and a six-day walk round the western and northern edge of the county.

Another option is the **Weavers Way**, which starts in Cromer (where the Norfolk Coast Path ends) and runs inland through the heart of north-eastern Norfolk to Yarmouth, where the Broads meet the sea. (The day walk we describe in this chapter follows a section of the Weavers Way between Yarmouth and Potter Heigham.) From Yarmouth, another long-distance path called the **Angles Way** runs through the southern Broads linking Yarmouth with Knettishall Heath – the start of the Peddars Way – thus completing a huge circular route around the county.

The whole 'Round Norfolk' route measures 230mi and could be done in two to three weeks. More information is available in the *Norfolk Coast Path, Peddars Way & Weavers Way Guide & Accommodation List* (see Books under Planning for the Norfolk Coast Path earlier in this chapter). There's also a booklet on *The Angles Way*, produced by the Ramblers' Association.

Alternatively, the very fit and historically motivated could continue heading west from Knettishall along the **Icknield Way** to Ivinghoe, then follow the ancient tracks of the **Ridgeway** to Avebury Stone Circle (as described in the Wessex chapter), taking in some fascinating historic sites on the way.

The Cotswolds

The Cotswold Hills are in west-central England, north of Bath, east of Gloucester and south of Coventry. This is classic English countryside, with neat fields, mature woodland, clear rivers flowing down grassy valleys, narrow hedge-lined lanes and a network of pretty villages, with houses, churches, cottages and farms all built with the famous honey-coloured Cotswold stone. Travel, particularly walking, here is a delight.

For walkers the main feature of the Cotswolds is the steep escarpment that runs along their western edge, running roughly parallel to (and offering fine views over) the Valley of the River Severn. The Cotswold Way, described in this chapter, follows the escarpment for much of its length. On their eastern side the Cotswolds slope off more gently, with streams and rivers that eventually lead into the River Thames.

The human landscape of the Cotswolds is all due to wool. In the 13th century there were half a million sheep here, producing a large slice of medieval England's wealth, and the fine stone houses and churches are symbols of that era. The wool trade died in the 17th century but the Industrial Revolution bypassed the Cotswolds, so the region has barely changed since. Having said that, although the wool trade may be gone, the Cotswolds are still a patch of England at its most affluent. The picture-postcard villages exude a heady aroma of solid bank accounts, and the area abounds with expensive public schools, new cars and golf courses.

INFORMATION
Maps
The whole area is covered by the Ordnance Survey (OS) 1:63,360 *Cotswold Touring Map* but this isn't really detailed enough for walking. OS Landranger 1:50,000 maps No 172 *(Bristol & Bath)*, No 162 *(Gloucester & Forest of Dean)*, No 163 *(Cheltenham & Cirencester)*, No 150 *(Worcester & the Malverns)* and No 151 *(Stratford-upon-Avon)* cover the area with more detail. The

OS Outdoor Leisure 1:25,000 map No 45 *(The Cotswolds)* covers only the northern part of this area (north of Cirencester and east of Cheltenham).

For maps covering individual walks, see Planning in the introduction to each walk.

Books
There's a huge number of books about walking in the Cotswolds, and the high density of places selling beer or hot drinks has not gone unnoticed. Try *Cotswold Teashop Walks* by Jean Patefield, *Pub Walks in the Cotswolds* by Nigel Vile or *Best Pub Walks in the Cotswolds* by Laurence Main. For a quieter atmosphere, *Discovery Walks in the Cotswolds* by Julie Meech avoids the honeypots, while *A Year of Walks: The Cotswolds* by Roy Woodcock deliberately seeks them out, with 12 circular routes to various highlights. For a range of walks, with good maps and route descriptions, *The Cotswold Pathfinder Guide* (published by Jarrold) is ideal.

Specific books for the routes we describe are listed in the relevant sections.

Information Sources
There are numerous Tourist Information Centres (TICs) in the Cotswolds. These include Bath (☎ 01225-477101), Bourton-on-the-Water (☎ 01451-820211), Broadway (☎ 01386-852937), Cheltenham (☎ 01242-522878), Chipping Campden (☎ 01386-841206), Painswick (☎ 01452-813552), Stow-on-the-Wold (☎ 01451-831082), Stroud (☎ 01453-765768), Winchcombe l(☎ 01242-602925) and Wotton-under-Edge (☎ 01453-521541).

Guided Walks
The Cotswolds Area of Outstanding Natural Beauty Partnership (☎ 01451-8620000) organises a series of guided walks – you can get details from local TICs. Several national companies organise walking holidays (these are listed in the Getting Around chapter) but one local specialist is Cotswold Walking

Holidays (☎ 01242-254353, **e** walking @star.co.uk, **w** www.cotswoldwalks.com), 10 Royal Parade, Bayshill Rd, Cheltenham GL50 3AY.

GETTING THERE & AWAY

The Getting Around chapter lists several public transport inquiry lines that provide details of both national and local bus and train services: See the boxed text 'National Transport Information' on p92.

To reach the Cotswolds from other parts of Britain, the main gateway cities and towns are Bath, Gloucester, Cheltenham, Oxford and Stratford-upon-Avon. These have good coach links with the rest of the country and are easy to reach by car if you're driving.

The most useful train service is the mainline railway between Worcester and Oxford (also to/from London), which runs through the northern part of the Cotswolds with a very handy stop at Moreton-in-Marsh, from where many other places can be reached by local bus. There are also train stations at Kemble and Stratford-upon-Avon. The Cotswolds are on the edge of London's upmarket commuter belt and all these stations are well served by regular trains to/from the capital.

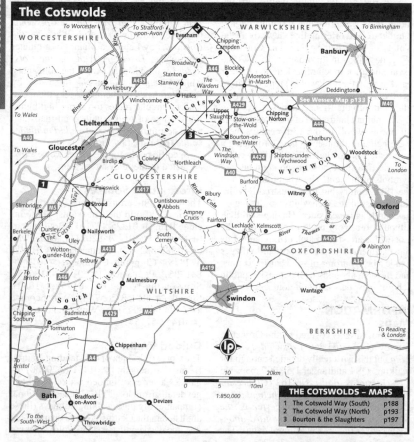

The Cotswolds

THE COTSWOLDS – MAPS

1	The Cotswold Way (South)	p188
2	The Cotswold Way (North)	p193
3	Bourton & the Slaughters	p197

1:850,000

GETTING AROUND

Once in one of these gateways, you can get deeper into the Cotswolds by local buses.

For specific information on public transport services within the Cotswolds, try the Gloucestershire County Council Transport Information Line (☎ 01452-425543). Local vistiors centres can provide you with the free *Explore the Cotswolds by Public Transport* leaflet (although this doesn't cover bus times) and *The North Cotswold Bus & Rail Timetable* (which does).

The Cotswold Way

Distance	103mi (165.5km)
Duration	7 days
Standard	easy-medium
Start	Bath
Finish	Chipping Campden
Gateways	Bath, Cheltenham, Evesham

Summary A fairly comfortable walk through picture-book English countryside. Long stretches of farmland are balanced by several sections of very attractive walking along the rolling edge of the escarpment.

The Cotswold Way runs along the western edge of the Cotswold Hills from Bath to Chipping Campden (just south of Stratford-upon-Avon), linking two of the most popular tourist towns in England. The Way is also a walk through England's history, passing prehistoric hillforts and burial mounds, Saxon and Civil War battlefields, reminders of the Romans, some fine stately homes and many other ancient monuments.

The Cotswold Way mainly follows the sharper western edge of the hills and, while it's a comfortable walk when compared with some of the wilder options described in this book, you underestimate it at your peril. The days are long and the walking often demanding, particularly if you are carrying a heavy backpack. There are some tiring ascents on many days and the weather can turn nasty very quickly. However, its greatest asset is the huge number of delightful pubs and B&Bs along the route, meaning a pint, a warm bed and good meal are never far away.

Direction, Distance & Duration

The walk can be done in either direction, although we describe it south to north (Bath to Chipping Campden), which generally gives you the sun and the wind at your back. It also offers greater satisfaction to finish at Chipping Campden, which is proud of being the end of the route, while Bath tends to focus on its mainstream tourism market.

The Cotswold Way is 103mi long but you can add a few miles by taking alternative routes to avoid roads or reduce the distance by using short cuts. With a few exceptions the waymarking is very good (generally small arrows with a white dot in the centre or beside the arrow) but it's still possible to miss turns simply because there are so many paths. It's wise to carry maps with you.

In January 1998 the Cotswold Way was approved as a national trail and will be officially opened in 2004. Between now and the opening the white dots will be replaced by the familiar national trail acorn symbol. Several minor changes will be made to the route before then, principally to improve road crossings and avoid sections on roads.

The following itinerary covers the route in seven days, in line with most trail guides. The most convenient places to start and finish each day are:

day	from	to	mi/km
1	Bath	Tomarton	16.5/26.5
2	Tomarton	Wotton-Under-Edge	14/22.5
3	Wotton-Under-Edge	Uley	10.5/17
4	Uley	Painswick	13/21
5	Painswick	Cheltenham	19/30.5
6	Cheltenham	Winchcombe	12.5/20
7	Winchcombe	Chipping Campden	17.5/28

Note that the hours given are walking times only. You should allow an extra hour or two for rests, lunch stops and so on. Except for the fifth night in Cheltenham or Charlton Kings, all of the overnight stops are right on the Way, although other possible stopovers are suggested throughout the text.

Alternatives If you're concerned about your fitness level or looking for a more leisurely walk, each of Days 1, 5 and 7 could be comfortably split into two days, with overnight stops at Cold Ashton or Marshfield, Birdlip and Broadway. A couple of additional days to rest and explore the many churches, manor houses, villages and monuments that litter the path would give you a relaxed and entertaining 12-day jaunt.

PLANNING
Maps
The OS Outdoor Leisure 1:25,000 map No 45 *(Cotswolds)* covers only about a quarter of the route (in the north) so needs to be supplemented by OS Explorer 1:25,000 maps No 155 *(Bristol & Bath, Keynsham & Marshfield)*, No 167 *(Thornbury, Dursley & Yate)*, No 168 *(Stroud, Tetbury & Malmesbury)* and No 179 *(Cheltenham, Gloucester & Stroud)*.

OS Landranger 1:50,000 maps provide less detail but are perfectly adequate given the reliable waymarking. You'll need map No 172 (Bristol & Bath), No 162 (Gloucester & Forest of Dean), No 163 (Cheltenham & Cirencester) and No 150 (Worcester & the Malverns), with the last few miles on No 151 (Stratford-upon-Avon). A good combination is Landranger map Nos 172, 162 and 163 with Outdoor Leisure map No 45.

Books
The one book you should not be without is *The Cotswold Way Handbook & Accommodation List* (£2), produced by and available from the Ramblers' Association (☎ 020-7339 8500) or TICs along the route.

Some general Cotswold books are mentioned under Books earlier in this chapter. For specific route guides *The Cotswold Way* by local expert Mark Richards is a brief and affectionate account of the walk but is light on detail. Another option is the Recreational Path Guide *The Cotswold Way* by Anthony Burton, which features 1:25,000 OS maps, detailed descriptions and a range of short circular walks along the route. Others include *A Guide to the Cotswold Way* by Richard Sale, which is engagingly written

but covers the route north to south; and *The Cotswold Way* by Kev Reynolds.

Information Sources
For specific route information, a good place to start is Spotlight Guides' Cotswold Way Web site at W www.cotswold-way.co.uk, which has lots of helpful information, including booking services for accommodation and luggage transport. Additional information is available from the Cotswold Way National Trail Office (☎ 01452-425637) in Gloucester.

Baggage Services
There are a number of companies and individual B&Bs that will take your luggage from stop to stop, generally for around £5 per bag, per section, but it's often cheaper for large groups. *The Cotswold Way Handbook* has contact details for both companies and B&Bs offering this service.

PLACES TO STAY & EAT
The Cotswold Way is admirably equipped with B&Bs, although these often cost well above the British average. Allow around £25 to £40 each night and be prepared to book early. Choice is more limited if you're trying to do it on a tight budget; the only hostel directly on the Way is in Bath. There are a number of farms that accept campers but these are mostly found outside the villages, so you'll have to plan your route accordingly. Recommended places are listed in the walk description. For more options, consult *The Cotswold Way Handbook & Accommodation List*.

Pubs, shops and cafes along the route make lunches fairly easy, although it's worth carrying some extra food, particularly during the first few days of the route. For evening meals you'll have no shortage of options in the bigger places, and most villages have at least a pub serving bar food.

GETTING TO/FROM THE WALK
Bus & Train Bath is very easy to reach; it's on the main line between London and Bristol, and is also linked by National Express coach to major points around the country.

From Chipping Campden there are a few local buses each day to Stratford and Evesham. Look out for the Cotswold Link express bus that runs twice a day between Bath and Stratford-on-Avon via Chipping Campden and several other Cotswold towns, although at the time of writing it was unclear if this service would continue. From Stratford or Evesham you can link up with trains and National Express coaches to other destinations.

Car Bath is south of the M4 motorway between London and Bristol, while Chipping Campden lies north of the A44 between Evesham and Oxford, about 12mi south of Stratford-upon-Avon.

THE WALK
Bath

Bath is one of Britain's most beautiful cities. The short-sighted approach to development that disfigured so many other rural towns and smaller cities in Britain left Bath relatively unscathed, and the splendid Georgian architecture is a delight to explore. You might be itching to hit the trail but try to build in at least a day to experience this lovely place.

The very good TIC (☎ 01225-477101) is in the Abbey Churchyard. Free walking tours of the town leave from here at 10.30am daily and 2pm Sunday to Friday. There's also the Guide Friday Tourism Centre (☎ 01225-444102) at the train station.

The best-known sites in and around **Abbey Courtyard** are always thronged with visitors but away from the centre there are many smaller museums well worth checking out, including the **William Herschel Museum**, the **Museum of East Asian Art** and the excellent **Museum of Costume**.

Places to Stay Bath is a popular tourist destination and has a wide range of options, but the cheaper places are snapped up fast during the annual Bath Festival (late May to early June) and during summer, so it's wise to book in advance.

The nearest campsite to Bath, *Newton Mill Touring Centre* (☎ 01225-333909), is

3mi west of town at Newton St Loe and charges £6. The popular and central *Bath Backpackers Hotel* (☎ 01225-446787, 13 Pierrepont St) is the best budget option available. B&B in a dorm costs £12 and singles/doubles are £20/30. The *YMCA International House* (☎ 01225-460471) is also central and often full in summer. The rooms are not particularly appealing but, with singles/doubles for £15/28 and dorm beds at £11, it's hard to be too critical.

The conveniently central *Henry Guest House* (☎ 01225-424052, 6 Henry St) remains one of the best-value B&Bs at £22.50, while *No 9 Charlotte St* (☎ 01225-424193) is a little more upmarket at £40 a double.

Across the river around Poultney Rd there's a cluster of B&Bs that all charge around £20 to £25 for singles and £40 to £50 for doubles. Check at the TIC for details and other options.

If you'd like to indulge in a little luxury before you head off, Bath also has several

Bath's Rebirth

For more than 2000 years Bath's fortune has revolved around its hot springs and the associated tourism. It was the Romans who first developed a complex of baths and a temple to Sulis-Minerva, on the site of what they called Aquae Sulis.

Throughout the 18th century Bath was the most fashionable and elegant haunt of English society. Aristocrats flocked here to gossip, gamble and flirt. Fortunately, they had the good sense and resources to employ a number of brilliant architects who designed the Palladian terraced housing, circles, crescents and squares that define the city.

During the 1980s, when Margaret Thatcher was prime minister, Bath lost a good deal of its gloss, with failed businesses and job losses emptying shops and bringing an increasing number of homeless people on to the streets. In recent years, however, new residents and new investment have allowed Bath to regain its reputation as the most fashionable and sought-after address in the region.

boutique hotels. With pleasant views of Parade Gardens, the *Abbey Hotel* (☎ 01225-461603), on North Parade, charges from £75/150. Around the corner on South Parade is *Georges Hotel* (☎ 01225-464923) with rooms from £50/65.

Places to Eat Bath's tourist trade means there's a huge number of eating options available for all budgets. Near the abbey, *Café Retro*, in York St, offers three-course meals for £12 and *Jamuna* has set lunch menus from £5.25, with a good selection of Indian vegetarian dishes. In Northumberland Place you'll find *Charlotte's Patisserie & Coffee House* and, directly opposite, *La Croissanterie*, which both offer a range of pastries and baguettes. In North Parade Passage there's *Tilley's Bistro*, with a three-course set menu for £9.50, and *Demuth's*, which serves tasty vegetarian and vegan meals from £4.50.

On Walcott Rd there are several restaurants upstairs in the modern Podium shopping complex, including American flavours at the *California Kitchen*, pub food at *Horse & Radish* and Italian at *Caffe Piazza*. Downstairs there are a juice bar, salad bar and the *Waitrose Organic Supermarket*, which has a good range of fresh food.

The central area has loads of good pubs, most of which offer meals. The best place for a pint is *The Old Green Tree*, in Green St, a cosy little place that exudes warmth and charm. *The Bell*, just past the unsightly Hilton Hotel on Walcott St, is also a good option and has bands on most nights. Others include the *Pig & Fiddle*, on the corner of Walcott St, which has outside tables; the tiny *Coeur de Lion*, in Northumberland Place; and the *Moon & Sixpence*, on Broad St.

Day 1: Bath to Tomarton
16.5mi (26.5km), 7–8 hours
Today's walk is a moderately hard introduction to the route, with a couple of steep ascents early on. There are also some interesting historical sites along the Way, so it's wise to get an early start.

From the abbey walk north-west past the beautiful Georgian architecture of **the Circle** and **the Crescent** before heading uphill

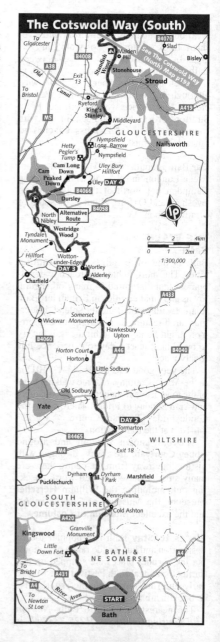

The Cotswold Way (South)

past a golf course and through a couple of suburbs. A short, sharp push up Penn Hill rewards you with fine views of Bath and the River Avon – and you're in the countryside proper at last.

For the next couple of miles there is good walking along tracks and to the first of several Iron Age hillforts that dot the route – **Little Down Fort**. After some more fields and one fine view point, you come across the **Granville Monument**, which commemorates a 1643 Civil War battle at this site.

Here, as the inscription notes, 'more officers and gentlemen of quality than private soldiers were slain'. Calamity indeed...

The Way continues along bridleways and through fields before a long, steep hill takes you up to the village of Cold Ashton, which features the fine but stern architecture of the rectory and manor house. If you wish to break for the night, Cold Ashton has a couple of B&Bs – *The Chestnuts* (☎ 01225-892020), which charges £25 and has camping for £2; and the larger *Tog Hill House Farm* (☎ 01225-891261) with rooms from £39. If these are full, a few places in nearby Marshfield offer a lift service, including *Knowle Hill Farm* (☎ 01225-891503), which has B&B from £18.

Leaving Cold Ashton you cross the A420, where the *White Hart* pub puts on a good lunch. Across a short field is Pennsylvania, where *The Swan Inn* (☎/fax 01225-891419) has B&B from £30 and a good menu. There are more fields and woods before you reach the pretty village of Dyrham, noted for its grand manor and deer park (although the main entrance to **Dyrham House** is on the A46, requiring a half-mile detour). You finish with a rather unpleasant crossing of the M4 motorway (although this will be bypassed by a new section of the route), to enter Tomarton from the south.

Tomarton

This tiny village is noted for its Norman church of **St Mary Magdalene**. The best place to stay is the *Portcullis Inn* (☎ 01454-218263), which charges £28/40, although there are a couple of other places, including *Noades House* (☎ 01454-218278) with B&B from £20, plus camping for £3.50. Two miles farther on, Old Sodbury has other options (see Day 2).

Day 2: Tomarton to Wotton-under-Edge

14mi (22.5km), 6–7 hours
This is a relatively easy day of undulating countryside, with plenty of farmland and a brace of hillforts. You pass several small villages but there are no shops, so bring lunch with you.

Leaving Tomarton you can either follow the path or take the easier road out of town and join the Way at Bath Rd. From here it's a pleasant and comfortable jaunt to Old Sodbury, where there are several B&Bs, including *1 The Green* (☎ *01454-314688*), at £21. The *Dog Inn* (☎ *01454-312006*) has tasty meals and B&B from £25, while *The Bell* also offers good lunches.

Leaving the village you pass a series of medieval stepped terraces before going up a steep escarpment to the prominent ramparts of the Iron Age **Sodbury hillfort** (you can avoid the steep bit by going straight ahead along a short stretch of public path) and down into the small town of Little Sodbury, where William Tyndale worked on the first translation of the Bible into English (see the boxed text 'William Tyndale – Martyr to the English Word').

From Little Sodbury, cross the fields and pass through the pretty village of Horton and on to **Horton Court**, the oldest house on the Way, dating from Norman times. A long stretch of muddy bridleway takes you to the fringe of Hawkesbury Upton (with a *pub* and a *shop)* and the grandiose 1846 **Somerset Monument**, commemorating Battle of Waterloo hero General Lord Somerset. After a stroll through some lovely woods to Alderly, the Way continues to the edge of Wortley, where the route then swings to the east of Wotton-under-Edge (usually called Wotton) and climbs to a view point. There's a sharp left at Blackquarries Hill before going down and then up to Coombe Hill and finally into Wotton.

Wotton-under-Edge

Wotton is another once-prosperous wool town, but it's retained its charm and boasts a host of fine buildings in its compact centre, plus an excellent array of pubs and eateries. The fine **St Mary the Virgin Church** dates from at least 1283, while the nearby **Hugh Perry's Almshouses** have a daunting list of regulations inside the entrance. There's a TIC (☎ 01453-521541) in the Heritage Centre.

The *Wotton Guest House & Coffee Shop* (☎ *01453-843158, 31a High St)* is a well-appointed B&B that welcomes walkers, charging £30/48 for singles/doubles, while the *Royal Oak* (☎ *01453-842316)* has rooms from £25, as well as good food. The *White Lion*, in the High St, and the *Falcon Inn*, on Church St, are also atmospheric if you're looking for a pint at the end of the day. Other places to eat include *The India Palace*, on Church St, with fine curries from £5.50, and, on the same street, the *Hong Kong Kitchen* with more than 200 choices on its menu.

Day 3: Wotton-under-Edge to Uley

10.5mi (17km), 4½–5½ hours
This is one of the best days on the route, although there are a few steep ascents to be negotiated. Accommodation is thin at the end of the day, so ensure you have a booking.

Leaving town you go steeply up Wotton Hill to a view point at the curious **Jubilee Clump**, a circular enclosure of trees planted in 1815 to commemorate the Battle of Waterloo. Next there's a delightful section of path through the cool and attractive Westridge Wood where the track is flat and bird life abounds. Passing the **Brackenbury hillfort**, you drop slightly to encounter the **Tyndale Monument**, erected in 1866 to commemorate William Tyndale's translation of the Bible into English (see the boxed text). You can go up to the top to take in the grand view but you need to go into North Nibley to get the key (50p). There's a plaque at the bottom of the hill with instructions on where to pick it up.

North Nibley is fairly unremarkable but has a few B&Bs, including *Nibley House* (☎ *01453-543108)* with rooms from £25 and camping for £3, plus the welcoming *Black Horse Inn* (☎ *01453-546841)* with singles/doubles for £30/45 and a good menu. The path descends to cross a stream next to an old mill and its ponds, before climbing steeply to the edge of a golf course that sprawls across Stinchcombe Hill. The route takes you round the edge of the golf course for a couple of miles but, apart from the breadth of views, there's little of interest. You can cut this section out by heading

William Tyndale – Martyr to the English Word

Born in the mid-1490s in North Nibley and educated at Oxford and Cambridge, William Tyndale is chiefly remembered as the man who first translated the Bible into English – and got himself executed for his trouble.

Tyndale started his work in England, but pressure from the Catholic Church forced him to move to Germany in 1524 to complete his translation. There he led a precarious existence, managing to stay one step ahead of vengeful church authorities, before the first edition of the New Testament was printed in 1526.

On its arrival in England later that year, Tyndale's translation was condemned by church leaders but proved immensely popular with congregations across the land. Fearing Tyndale's influence, Henry VIII sent emissaries to the continent to either persuade Tyndale to return to England or deliver him to local authorities. He was eventually located in the Netherlands and tried for heresy in Belgium in 1536. Despite pleas for clemency from the powerful English figure Thomas Cromwell, Tyndale was sentenced to be burnt at the stake. In a dubiously merciful gesture, he was spared the heat of the flames by being strangled before the fire was lit. His last words reportedly were: 'Oh Lord, open the King of England's eyes'.

Ironically, the Lord apparently did. A scant two years later Henry VIII passed a law requiring every church in England to hold an English language copy of the Bible. It must have been cold comfort to Tyndale's friends and family that it was based largely on his work.

for the clubhouse and then descending a steep hill into Dursley.

In the town centre, facing Dursley's 1738 Market House, is **St James' Church** – minus its spire. In January 1699 the bells were rung to celebrate the completion of major repairs but the vibrations brought the whole lot tumbling down, wrecking the end of the church and killing a number of spectators. Queen Anne, who helped pay for the repairs, was

rewarded with a singularly unattractive statue in a niche in the Market House.

There are several places to stay in Dunley, including the *Old Bell Hotel* (☎ 01453-542821), on Long St, with B&B from £25, plus a host of cafes along Parsonage Lane, the shopping street directly behind the Market House. For something more filling, try *Dil Raj Tandoori*, on Long St, or the *Old Spot Inn*, a popular pub on May Lane.

Leaving Dursley you follow a stretch of road before a short but very steep ascent to Peaked Down. (A route improvement is planned here, which will avoid the road and Peaked Down.) A further uphill section takes you to the bare ridge of Cam Long Down, which you follow for several hundred metres. This is possibly the only place on the whole Way where there are 360-degree views. You continue up once more to reach the **Uley Bury hillfort**; from here take the bridleway down to Uley rather than risk life and limb on the road.

Uley & Nympsfield

Uley is a tiny place nestled in a valley below the hillfort. The *Old Crown Inn* (☎ 01453-860502), on the main street, has nondescript singles/doubles for £25/40 but the food more than makes up for this. Other B&Bs include *57 The Street* (☎ 01453-860305), from £19; and *Hill House* (☎ 01453-860267), just out of the village on Crawley Hill, for £17.50. Apart from the pub, food options are limited, with *The Pumps* restaurant on the main street closing at 5pm.

If you can't get a place in Uley, there's also a lovely but expensive pub in Nympsfield, a couple of miles through Coaley Wood. The charming *Rose and Crown Inn* (☎ 01453-860240) charges £42.50/70.

Day 4: Uley to Painswick

13mi (21km), 5½–6½ hours
Today the Way includes woodland and an uninspiring section of town walking, with a thankfully scenic final section and picture-perfect village to finish.

Having hauled yourself out of Uley's valley, you descend into Coaley Wood and follow the contour for half an hour along a

THE COTSWOLDS

pleasant track. A detour to the impressive prehistoric burial site of **Hetty Pegler's Tump** is worth the climb, although a new section of path will soon take you even farther away to avoid a stretch of road walking. You soon pass the **Nympsfield long barrow**, before another long but enjoyable stretch through Buckholt and Stanley woods.

A section of dreary urban trudging follows through Middleyard and round King's Stanley, with its crossing of the busy A419, then you go across the disused Stroudwater Canal and into some farmland. (Another route option is planned here. The route through Middleyard will remain, but an alternative will take walkers over Selsley Common and along the Stroudwater Canal to Ryeford – a very attractive route.)

Beyond Maiden Hill you enter Standish Wood with its National Trust *campsite*, before skirting around the edge of the plateau on Haresfield Hill, taking in the views of the Severn Valley from Haresfield Beacon. Yet more woods – Cliff, Halliday's and Maitlands – precede a stretch of farmland that ushers you into the popular tourist town of Painswick.

Painswick

The compact town of Painswick attracts plenty of visitors and it's certainly a place with a history; New St was new in 1253 and the timber framing on the post office dates from 1428. The town is remarkably preserved, with the familiar Costwold stone almost the only building material used in the centre. **St Mary's Church**, dating from the 14th century, is the focal point and features a large collection of table-top tombs and 99 neatly trimmed yew trees – legend has it that no more than 99 will grow at any one time. On the same street is the welcoming TIC (☎ 01452-813552).

Painswick has a good range of places to stay, eateries and pubs, but be prepared to pay for the privilege. There are several good B&Bs close to New St, including the popular *Hambutt's Mynd* (☎ 01452-812352), on Edge Rd, for £27; *Madison House* (☎ 01452-813233), on New St, with rooms from £23; and *Thorne* (☎ 01452-812476), in Friday

St, for £25. There are plenty more B&Bs farther out of the village (check at the TIC for details). For the well heeled, the *Painswick Hotel*, in Kemps Lane, has a top-shelf restaurant with set menus for £16 (lunch) and £26 (dinner). Other places for a meal include the cosy and welcoming *Royal Oak*, in St Mary's St; and the *Thai Restaurant* (☎ 01452-813452), on the Cross. A better budget option is the *Chancellor's Tea Rooms*, on Victoria St, although it's only open for dinner at weekends.

Day 5: Painswick to Cheltenham
19mi (30.5km), 8–9 hours
This is a long and tough day, which is not helped by the fact that you have to leave the Way at the end to find a bed. However, the walking is attractive, dominated by woodland sections and featuring the by now familiar hillforts and golf courses.

From Painswick the path climbs steadily up to a golf course and enters a wood that takes you past the Painswick Beacon hillfort. Passing **Prinknash Abbey**, you follow the undulating terrain to the edge of Coopers Hill where there's an extremely steep, rolling field, which is the site of the annual Bank Holiday cheese-rolling contest – a rough and ready pursuit dating from medieval times.

A couple of miles along woodland tracks take you past the village of Birdlip – a short but steep climb away and good place to break for the evening if you have the time. B&Bs include the *Beechmount Guest House* (☎ 01452-862506), for £16; and the *Royal George Hotel* (☎ 01452-862506), charging £65/75 for singles/doubles.

Another sharp uphill section takes you to a view point before you make your way to a roundabout where *Air Balloon Inn* offers snacks and meals. Take care crossing the busy road here. You pass another hillfort just before the Crickley Hill Country Park and the well-preserved Neolithic **Shurdington Long Barrow**. Soon afterwards you reach Leckhampton Hill with its intriguing **Devil's Chimney** reaching for the sky.

At a confusing road junction close to the Seven Springs Inn, you have the option of a 1mi slog along the busy road or a 2mi country route, although a new and more direct section is planned through Chatcombe Wood. From here a hilly section through the pretty Lineover Wood takes you to the A40 by the Waterside Inn (formerly the Reservoir Inn), where you can walk, take the bus coming in from Burton-on-the-Water or catch a taxi (☎ 01242-523219) into Charlton Kings or Cheltenham for the night.

Places at Charlton Kings include the *Old Stables* (☎ *01242-583660, 239a London Rd*), charging £18 for B&B; or the upmarket *Charlton Kings Hotel* (☎ *01242-231061*) with single/double rooms from £61/92.

Cheltenham

An elegant Regency town, Cheltenham has not survived the 20th century as well as Bath, and its handsome squares and public gardens are interspersed with unappealing modern shopping areas. However, with much to see and a good selection of places to stay and eat, Cheltenham makes an ideal rest day and is also a handy 'escape' point as transport links to other parts of the country are good.

The helpful TIC (☎ 01242-522878) is on the Promenade – a wide street decorated with hanging baskets of flowers in summer, optimistically described as 'Britain's most beautiful thoroughfare' by the local council.

If you're on a tight budget, cheap places to stay include the *YMCA* (☎ *01242-524024, 6 Vittoria Walk*) with singles from £15. Over Easter and the summer holidays, *Cheltenham & Gloucester College* (☎ *01242-532774*) lets out student rooms from £18.

The best place to search out cheap B&B is the Montpellier area, just south-west of the centre. Along Park Place, cheery *Segrave* (☎ *01242-523606*), at No 7, charges from £16. Closer in is *Lonsdale House* (☎ *01242-232379*), from £21; and *St Michael's Guest House* (☎ *01242-513587*), for £28.

More expensive places include *Lypiatt House* (☎ *01242-224994*), in Lypiatt Rd, charging £55; and the *Beaumont House Hotel* (☎ *01242-578450, 56 Shurdington Rd*), south of the centre, with rooms from £42. There are loads more options; check with the TIC.

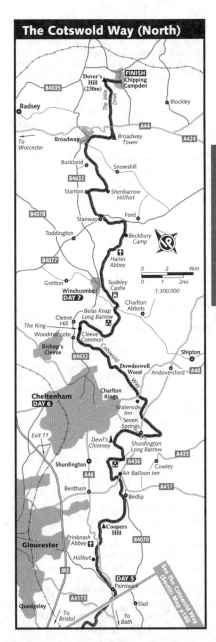

THE COTSWOLDS

For places to eat, Cheltenham has a very good choice for all budgets. South of the bus station along Montpellier St are several cheap cafes. On the parallel Montpellier Walk you'll find *Pizza Piazza* and *Shezan Indian Balti*, which offer reasonably priced meals. Other good places include *Café Rouge*, just north of the TIC, with two courses for £6.95; and the nearby *Bella Pasta* with meals from £5.99.

Day 6: Cheltenham to Winchcombe

12.5mi (20km), 5–6 hours

This is a comfortable day's walk through some fairly unexciting countryside, but the windswept views and a remarkable ancient site should keep your interest piqued.

From the Waterside Inn the path climbs fairly steeply up the edge of Dowdeswell Wood, then continues gently uphill through farmland for a couple of miles before reaching **Bill Smiley Reserve**, a conservation area alive with butterflies. A steady ascent brings you to the southern edge of **Cleeve Common**, where you can cut a couple of miles off the route by going straight ahead, but there are some good views to enjoy along with the relative wildness of the common.

The Way skirts the edge of the links, past the rugged ramparts of the hillfort (popular with climbers) and an Iron Age earthwork dubbed **the Ring**, and then to the golf course clubhouse. There are lots of crisscrossing paths both here and through Cleeve Common, so keep your eyes peeled for the waymarks. Cleeve Common is hardly rugged and desolate, but it is the only substantial section of unenclosed and wild land along the Way. There are several species of orchid and lots of bird life to spot, and it's a welcome change from fields and bridleways.

While the farmland returns too quickly, it does take you to **Belas Knap**, a 4000-year-old Neolithic long barrow (burial mound). With dry-stone walls at the false entrances on either side, it remains in remarkably good condition and is the perfect place for a rest stop.

From here its a steep descent through a wood, along a short stretch of road and

down past the ruins of a Roman villa, hidden by a dense copse. A few more fields and you're in Winchcombe.

Winchcombe

The small and engaging town of Winchcombe was once a medieval abbey but, after Henry VIII conducted his monastic land-grab in 1539, it almost completely disappeared. One exception is **St Peter's Church** (1465) with its outstanding collection of leering gargoyles. The other principal attraction is 19th-century **Sudeley Castle**, just to the south-east. The home of Henry VIII's sixth wife, Catherine Parr, it was deliberately damaged after the Civil War and not rebuilt for nearly 200 years.

B&Bs include *Gower House* (☎ 01242-602616), on North St, from £20; *Blair House* (☎ 01242-603626), on Gretton Rd, for £22; and the friendly *Plaisterer's Arms* (☎ 01242-602358), on the High St, from £30. Check at the TIC (☎ 01242-602925) in the old town hall for more options.

For meals, *Poachers*, on Hailes St, has two-course set menus for £16, while the upmarket *Wesley House Restaurant* does a similar deal for £23.50. More modest pub food can be found at the 15th-century *Old White Lion*, the *White Hart Inn* and the *Plaisterer's Arms*.

Day 7: Winchcombe to Chipping Campden

17.5mi (28km), 7½–8½ hours

It's another taxing day to finish the Costwold Way, but the route takes in some good views and another two hillforts before culminating with a stately finish along the Mile Drive.

Leaving Winchcombe via Puck Pit Lane, the path goes gently upwards to the ruins of **Hailes Abbey**, which once attracted streams of medieval pilgrims to see its famed sample of Christ's blood (later proven to be coloured honey). Nearby, the tiny **St Nicholas Church** pre-dates the abbey and has walls decorated with fading, but still discernible, 13th-century murals.

After *Hailes Fruit Farm* (☎ 01242-602123), where there are snacks, fruit and camping for £3, you enter Hailes Wood and go steeply up to **Beckbury Camp** – a large Iron Age fort and a good place for a breather. Dropping down again, the Way wanders into the pretty village of Stanton, where *The Mount Inn* has a splendid menu if it's time for lunch. It's another long climb out of town, this time to Shenbarrow hillfort, before you descend steadily to **Broadway**.

The kitsch village of Broadway started life as part of a nearby monastery and expanded during the 17th and 18th centuries to become an important stagecoach stop. Main street houses are constructed of golden stone with the typical Cotswold mix of tiled and thatched roofs. Unfortunately, Broadway has sold its soul to tourism and nowadays many of its buildings have been converted into tacky little knick-knack shops. If you wish to spend the night, book early – the TIC (☎ 01386-852937), at 1 Cotswold Court, can help out, but it's not open on Sunday or during January and February. Camping is available at *Leedon's Park* (☎ 01386-852423) for £5 per tent. You could also decide to splash out at the deluxe *Lygon Arms* (☎ 01386-852255) with singles/doubles starting from £135/183 and two pricey restaurants. B&Bs include *Olive Branch Guest House* (☎ 01386-853440, 78 High St), charging from £30; and the *Crown & Trumpet* (☎ 01386-853202), on Church St, for £40/52. Eateries include the *Swan Inn*, with the best-value meals in town; the *Horse and Hound*, on the edge of town, which offers similar fare; and *Oliver's Brasserie*, on the main street.

If you're continuing to the end it's another long ascent to **Broadway Tower**, an incongruous little folly dating from 1798. From here it's plain sailing as the path gradually descends to the Mile Drive, an extremely broad, grassed avenue that takes you quickly along to one last dogleg up **Dover's Hill** (it takes its name from Robert Dover who instituted a local 'Olympick Games' in 1612, featuring such fine sports as shin kicking), before you enter Chipping Campden.

Chipping Campden

The stonework in the houses of Chipping Campden is said to be the finest in the Cotswolds, and this attractive town is a fitting finale to the Cotswold Way. Buildings of interest include the medieval **town hall**, **St James' Church** and the 1627 **market hall**. Farther up the street, William Grevel's **late 14th-century house** can lay claim to being the oldest and finest in the village. Also worth a visit is the **Ernest Wilson Memorial Garden** with an international collection of plants from East Asia.

The TIC (☎ 01386-841206) is on the High St; staff here can help you book one of the town's many B&Bs. Those on Lower High St, near the Cotswold Way, include *The Volunteer Inn* (☎ 01386-840688) with rooms from £27.50, and *The Old Bakehouse* (☎ 01386-840979) with singles/doubles for £30/45. Others on the High St are *Badgers Hall* (☎ 01386-840839) with singles from £45, and *Dragon House* (☎ 01386-840734), from £38.

The village is well supplied with pubs that offer meals, including *The Kings Arms*, the *Red Lion*, the *Eight Bells* and the *Lygon Arms Hotel*, all of which are on the High St.

For a slap-up meal, go to the upmarket *Joel's Restaurant* or *Huxley's Restaurant & Bar*, where meals start from £8.95.

Bourton & the Slaughters

Distance	12mi (19.5km)
Duration	6 hours
Standard	easy
Start/Finish	Bourton-on-the-Water
Gateways	Cirencester, Stow-on-the-Wold

Summary Delightful walking through farmland and valleys, over rolling hills, along river banks and past chocolate-box villages.

No, Bourton & the Slaughters is not the name of a local rock band. The small town of Bourton-on-the-Water (usually shortened to Bourton) and the nearby villages of Upper and Lower Slaughter are among the prettiest places in the Cotswolds. All three are popular tourist destinations, especially Bourton, which can get busy on summer Sundays. The walk we describe shows you

THE COTSWOLDS

how to see these villages and the surrounding countryside, while escaping the crowds and enjoying the Cotswolds in idyllic peace and quiet.

Direction, Distance & Duration

This circular walk follows sections of two longer routes, the Windrush Way and the Wardens Way, both of which are quite well waymarked, although a map is very useful for when signs are missing. You could do it in either direction but we suggest visiting the Slaughters first and finishing along the the River Windrush valley. Allowing an extra hour or two for sightseeing, lunch and dangling your feet in a cool stream, your total day out will be about eight hours.

Alternatives The Windrush Way and the Wardens Way both link Bourton and Winchcombe. You could easily extend the route we describe here by following one of these linear options. A better choice is to walk the Windrush Way in one day, stay overnight in Winchcombe (for places to stay and eat, see Day 6 of the Cotswold Way) and then walk back on the Wardens Way to Bourton the next day.

If you want a shorter route you can cut south from Naunton and meet the Windrush Way just east of Aylworth.

PLANNING
Maps & Books

The route is on the OS Outdoor Leisure 1:25,000 map No 45 *(The Cotswolds)*. For local walks, a handy little booklet is *Country Walks around Bourton-on-the-Water*, available from local TICs.

PLACES TO STAY & EAT
Bourton-on-the-Water

The Bourton-on-the-Water TIC (☎ 01451-820211) is central and can provide leaflets on local walks, plus information on accommodation, public transport etc. If this is closed, contact the Stow-on-the-Wold (often shortened to Stow) TIC (☎ 01451-831082). You can also get information from the official Web site for Bourton-on-the-Water at Ⓦ www.bourton-on-the-water.co.uk.

In the centre of Bourton-on-the-Water, *Fairlie (☎ 01451-821842)*, on Riverside, is perfectly located with very good rooms and a friendly welcome for walkers; double rooms cost from £38. (If it's full, the owner, Mrs Morris, can advise on other places to try.) Nearby, on the High St, *Manor Close (☎ 01451-820339)* is also recommended and similarly priced. Just off the High St is *No 6 Moore Rd (☎ 01451-820767)*, neat, comfortable and well used to walkers, charging £19/25 for en suite singles/doubles. For more options, the street called Lansdowne is lined with B&Bs and small hotels. Campers can head for *Moor Farm*, a nice little site on the northern edge of the town. The TIC can advise on other seasonal camping options nearer the centre.

For food, Bourton has many choices – sandwich shops, fish and chip or Chinese takeaways, and several pubs and smart restaurants. *The Duke of Wellington* is a relaxed pub, serving bar food from £4 to £6 and main courses in the restaurant from £7 to £12. *The Bay Tree Restaurant*, near the TIC, is also recommended, with evening meals from £7 to £11.

GETTING TO/FROM THE WALK

Bus & Train The easiest public transport route is by train to Moreton-in-Marsh on the line between London and the Midlands, from where buses (which tie in with train times) run to Cirencester via Stow-on-the-Wold and Bourton-on-the-Water about 10 times daily Monday to Saturday. About six of these buses go on to Kemble (beyond Cirencester), which also has a train station. If coming from the West Country, you could get a train to Kemble (on a main line to/from London) and get the bus to Bourton-on-the-Water from there. This bus does not run on Sunday.

On summer Sundays (May to September) your only option is the bus that runs twice each way between Morton-in-Marsh and Cheltenham via Stow-on-the -Wold and Bourton-on-the-Water.

Look out also for the Cotswold Link express bus service between Bath and Statford-upon-Avon via several Cotswold towns, including Bourton-on-the-Water. At the time of writing, however, it was uncertain if this service would continue to operate.

Car Bourton-on-the-Water is on the main A429 between Cirencester and Stow-on-the-Wold. This road is called the Fosse Way, from the Roman road whose straight-line route it still follows.

THE WALK
Bourton-on-the-Water to Naunton
4mi (6.5km), 2 hours

The first part of the route follows the Wardens Way, which is signposted as starting in the centre of Bourton at the church. From the church a footpath leads along the back of some houses, heading east. This goes over an old railway embankment and across a field, then crosses the busy A429 main road.

From here you're out in the country; the route crosses fields, meets a lane and follows it for a short distance, before branching off again, downhill across more fields, to meet a track leading into the village of Lower Slaughter. (On some maps the Wardens Way is shown slightly farther north

than the route described but both ways lead you to Lower Slaughter.)

Lower Slaughter is a smaller version of Bourton, with a shallow river running between grassy banks through the heart of the village. In case you were wondering, the village name has nothing to do with killing but comes from Schlotre, the family name of the original Norman landowner. In the centre of the village, cross the river on a small stone-slab footbridge, passing some cottages on your right and the Old Mill (which has a *tearoom*), then leave the village by following the 'single file' footpath beside the river and across fields to cross another footbridge and enter **Upper Slaughter**. Here make sure you swing right (north) and then left round the church to follow a small path through a patch of woodland, then across fields and into woodland again.

After a mile or so you meet a road and turn left, following it for about 300m (take care, as there's no path) before turning right onto a track. Continue through a gate and across fields, then round a barn and along a track to meet another lane near Brockhill Farm, where you turn right (north-west). If it's quiet you can walk along the lane, but if it's

THE COTSWOLDS

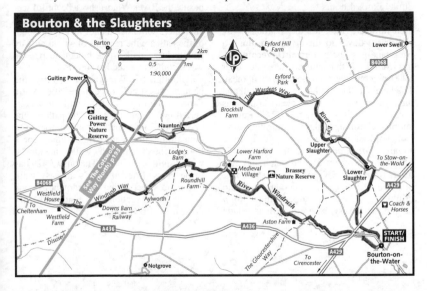

Bourton & the Slaughters

Thankful Upper Slaughter

Unlike most other places in the Cotswolds, and throughout Britain, Upper Slaughter has no war memorial; the village is almost unique in that the local men who fought in WWI and WWII all came home again. Such places are known as 'thankful villages', and a plaque in Upper Slaughter church thanks God for the protection. In contrast, of the 65 men from nearby Naunton who served in WWI, 13 were killed.

busy with cars look for the signs that show a path in the field running parallel to the lane.

You soon turn left (south) onto a track, which becomes a path and leads you through a patch of small fields, then steeply down into the quiet and not-too-cutesy village of **Naunton**. Turn back east a short distance along the village main street to reach the *The Black Horse Inn* pub, which serves coffees, teas, good beer, bar snacks from £5 and excellent lunches for around £8.

Naunton to Bourton

8mi (13km), 4 hours

Go westwards along Naunton's main street, then turn left (look for the Wardens Way waymark) down to the river and along a back lane past the historical **Dovecote** dating from the 17th century, where once over 1000 pigeons were farmed for their meat. The lane out of the village goes up a hill and then waymarks lead you clearly on paths across fields all the way to **Guiting Power**, another charming village featuring sturdy Cotswold stone houses around a little square. *The Farmers Arms* (☎ *01451-850358*) pub makes a good lunch and also offers B&B from £30/50 for singles/doubles, or you can buy cakes, chocolate and cold drinks from the time-warped village *shop* behind the bakery, where the friendly lady

also makes sandwiches to order (cheese or ham – that's the choice).

Here we say farewell to the Warden's Way. Leave Guiting Power the way you came in, then turn right in front of the school and along a lane. Follow this for a mile to a fork, where you go left (south). Just before a bridge, go through a gate on your right and across a field to reach a junction of footpaths, one of which is the Windrush Way and the route home.

Head south through a lovely patch of woodland then fields to meet the B4068, where you go right then almost immediately left into a field that runs along the back of some cottages. This path leads through the yard of Westfield Farm and down the driveway, then swings left (east) following a wonderful old track that winds beside hedgerows and through cornfields. Pass the settlement of Aylworth and then walk gradually downhill beside a stream (a tributary of the Windrush) to eventually meet a lane near Lower Harford Farm. Turn left, go down the lane for a 100m, then right onto the path and through a field. Bumps in the field are the remains of **Harford village** – which existed here in medieval times. Now the route runs beside the River Windrush – a beautiful section but all too short as the path turns uphill and enters some woodland. Just to the south of the path are the remains of an old railway and the large, dark bridge hidden deep in the wood comes as a sudden surprise.

Although the Windrush is nearby, the path crosses it only once more, after Aston Farm, on a bridge by the old mill – now converted into a smart house. The path climbs up to and follows the old railway for 100m then jumps down into fields again for a lovely finish through water meadows, within sight of the river. The busy A429 has to be crossed and then it's an easy walk down the street called Lansdowne (or via one final short section of riverside path) into the centre of Bourton.

Southern England Long-Distance Paths

This chapter covers two of the longest and best-known long-distance paths (LDPs) in Southern England – the South Downs Way and the South West Coast Path. At opposite ends of southern England, these walks are very different in length and character, and pass through very different types of scenery. They have their own chapter simply because they do not fit neatly into any other chapter in this book.

Other Southern England LDPs described fully in this book are the Ridgeway (in the Wessex chapter), the Cotswold Way (in the Cotswolds chapter) and the Thames Path (in the Wessex and London Region chapters).

The South Downs Way

Distance	100mi (161km)
Duration	8 days
Standard	easy-medium
Start	Winchester
Finish	Eastbourne
Gateways	Winchester, Brighton, Eastbourne

Summary An enjoyable eight-days of walking along well-maintained paths and tracks, over fine open rolling downland.

The South Downs Way (SDW) is a national trail through the heart of south-east England, mostly following a broad chalk ridge that divides the Channel coast from a lowland area called the Weald. This ancient route was first used by Neolithic people keen to avoid the marsh and dense forest below the downs. Later settlers all left their marks, including Bronze Age burial barrows and Iron Age hillforts.

For today's walker, the SDW takes in two types of countryside. Through Hampshire it threads from hilltop to hilltop on mostly open pasture, then in Sussex it follows the

edge of the Downs, dipping to cross river valleys that slice through the hills. At first plantations and natural woods sometimes restrict views, but later there are sweeping panoramas northwards over Weald's chessboard farmland and southwards to the sea. At the foot of the hills, following the 'spring line' where streams emerge from the porous soil, are picturesque villages and small towns well worth meandering through.

The South Downs is a farming area where crop growing and livestock rearing have co-existed for centuries. Traditionally, shepherds have driven their sheep off the sweet upland grasses to graze the harvested fields below, while in return the sheep fertilise the soil for the next year's crop. The recent advent of mega-agriculture means ancient hedges have disappeared and the land now resembles an Ohio cornfield in many areas. But most of the Downs still retain their gentle, small-scale charm, although walkers a generation from now may not be able to say the same thing.

Despite the influence of new farming practices, the Downs are within two Areas of Outstanding Natural Beauty – East Hampshire and Sussex Downs. Expect changes in the near future, though, as the South Downs are due to become a national park. Whether this will give the area any more protection against human ravages remains to be seen.

Direction, Distance & Duration

You can do this route in either direction. Most local guidebooks and maps suggest east to west, but we disagree. Our description goes west to east, with prevailing winds propelling you from the more enclosed part of the trail to open and dramatic scenery, with a spectacular cliff-top finish. Waymarking is generally excellent, although there are a few points in Hampshire where vigilance is required. Walkers share this national trail with bicycles and the occasional horse. With considerate use, there should be plenty of room for all.

Since the land is generally well drained and the climate mild, the SDW can be done at any time of year. The walk is 100mi long, but you should plan for an extra 10mi or so to/from overnight stops. Hours given in the walk description for each day are walking times only; you should add extra for lunch, rests, museums etc. The eight-day itinerary we suggest is:

day	from	to	mi/km
1	Winchester	Exton	12/19.5
2	Exton	Buriton	13/21
3	Buriton	Cocking	11/17.5
4	Cocking	Amberley	11.5/18.5
5	Amberley	Steyning	13/21
6	Steyning	Kingston-near-Lewes	15/24
7	Kingston-near-Lewes	Alfriston	13.5/21.5
8	Alfriston	Eastbourne	11/17.5

Alternatives Our itinerary is fairly gentle. If you're feeling strong, more challenging combinations are possible, for instance amalgamating Days 3 and 4, or Days 4 and 5. If you're short of time, you can omit the first two days and get the best of the route by joining at Buriton.

As with all LDPs, you can do just a single day linear section of the SDW, or a circular route taking in a stretch of the main route. See the boxed text 'The South Downs Way – Route Highlight' on p208 for suggestions.

PLANNING
Maps
The SDW is covered by Ordnance Survey (OS) Landranger 1:50,000 maps No 185 *(Winchester & Basingstoke)*, No 197 *(Chichester & the Southern Downs)*, No 198 *(Brighton & Lewes)* and No 199 *(Eastbourne & Hastings)*. Harvey produces an excellent *South Downs Way* strip map, which covers the whole route on one sheet at 1:40,000. Like all strip maps it's useless once you get

a few miles away from the trail but does include most of the off-route towns and villages where accommodation is available.

Books
Useful books include the official *South Downs Way* by Paul Millmore, which is clear and informative, and includes sections from relevant OS 1:25,000 maps. *A Guide to the South Downs Way* by Miles Jebb is more discursive, but still packed with practical, step-by-step information.

The South Downs Way Accommodation Guide is an invaluable resource, with a good list of B&Bs, hostels and campsites. It is available from local TICs, by post from the Sussex Downs Trail National Trail Office (☎ 023-9259 7618), Queen Elizabeth Country Park, Horndean, Hampshire PO8 0QE, or from the South Downs Conservation Board (☎ 01903-741234).

Information Sources
Tourist Information Centres (TICs) on or near the route include Winchester (☎ 01962-840500), where the staff can reserve accommodation along the trail; Arundel (☎ 01903-882268); Brighton (☎ 0906-711 2255); Lewes (☎ 01273-483448); and Eastbourne (☎ 01323-411400). You can also visit the South East England Tourist Board Web site at W www.seetb.org.uk.

For specific information on the South Downs Way, the South East National Trails Web site (W www.nationaltrails.gov.uk) covers the South Downs Way and the three other national trails in south-eastern England, with information on the route, accommodation (although it doesn't seem regularly updated) and links to public transport sites.

Also worth viewing is the South Downs Virtual Information Centre (W www.vic.org .uk), which covers many aspects of the Downs, including walking routes, books and maps, conservation, accommodation and links to other relevant sites.

PLACES TO STAY & EAT
There are three important things to note regarding places to stay on the Way. Firstly, there's very little accommodation *on* the

route – most villages with accommodation are a mile or two away, so build in extra time. Secondly, most B&Bs require advance bookings and don't take people turning up on spec. Thirdly, there isn't always much choice. The route is only partially served by YHA hostels, while campers struggle to find an official site every night. B&B options are also thin, as the people who can afford houses in this smug and comfortable part of Britain don't need to earn another few pounds providing beds for walkers (and many would rather you kept away completely). This contrasts strongly with areas that depend on tourism and have less cash to throw around – where outdoor enthusiasts are much more likely to find hospitality.

We provide some accommodation suggestions in the route description. For a wider choice use *The Rambler's Yearbook & Accommodation Guide* and the *Stillwell's National Trail Companion* (see Books in the Facts for the Walker chapter), or *The South Downs Trail Accommodation Guide* mentioned under Books earlier in this chapter.

GETTING TO/FROM THE WALK

The Getting Around chapter lists several public transport inquiry lines that provide details of both national and local bus and train services: See the boxed text 'National Transport Information' on p92.

Bus National Express coaches link Winchester with London (via Heathrow airport)

Water along the Way

Some days on the Downs can be long, hot and shadeless. You should always carry at least 1L of water, but note that you won't pass many villages or even streams for topping up (rain quickly percolates through the chalky soil). So important is water that taps are provided along the trail (and marked on some maps), but it's still worth carrying an extra bottle. Also worth considering is a filter and purifying tablets in case you need to use a dubious trough or other source.

and various other parts of the country with frequent services throughout the day. From Eastbourne, buses to London are not so frequent – trains are a better choice.

Train Fast trains run at least hourly between London's Waterloo train station and Winchester, and services between northern Britain, the Midlands and the South-West also pass through. At the end of the walk, an hourly service runs from Eastbourne to London's Victoria train station (via Gatwick airport). There's also a coastal line from west to east, parallel to the Downs, serving towns such as Chichester, Worthing, Shoreham, Brighton, Lewes and Eastbourne – all accessible by bus from points along the trail.

Car The route begins in Winchester, just off the M3 motorway, which links Southampton with London. It finishes in Eastbourne, from where the A22 leads to London. The A27 runs along the south coast between Eastbourne and Southampton.

THE WALK
Winchester

Allow yourself a good half-day's sightseeing in Winchester, once capital of Saxon England and now the county town of Hampshire. Don't miss the splendid **cathedral** (for details on Winchester, see the Clarendon Trail in the Wessex chapter). The TIC (☎ 01962-840500) is in the Guildhall on Broadway (the main street), near the cathedral; the friendly staff can reserve accommodation all along the trail. Before setting off, pause at the tomb of St Swithin to say a quick prayer for good weather; rain on his birthday, tradition says, means rain for the next 40 days.

Day 1: Winchester to Exton
12mi (19.5km), 4–6 hours
This is a good first day, not too hard, passing mainly through fields and woodland.

Leave Winchester by the end of Broadway (the main street), near the impressive **statue of King Alfred**, and turn right into Chesil St. After 200m turn left up East Hill, then bear right along Petersfield Rd, through leafy suburbs. After half a mile, where a street called

Chalk Ridge bears left, go straight on along an old road now a footpath. This leads to the footbridge over the M3 motorway and then, suddenly, you're in fields and at peace. Relax – there are no navigation problems for several miles, as the trail follows tracks and lanes through farmland.

Just past today's halfway stage (about 7mi from Winchester), *Milbury's* pub makes a pleasant lunch stop. From here more easy walking takes you to **Beacon Hill** (there are more such hills to come, each marking where fires were lit four centuries ago to warn of the approaching Spanish Armada) and a short stretch along a narrow lane, down into the Meon Valley and Exton.

Exton

About a mile south-west of this quiet and charming village, and less than a mile off the trail, *Corhampton Lane Farm* (☎ 01489-877506) is a very friendly B&B, charging around £25 for single rooms, £40 to £45 for

doubles, plus simple camping for £3. In the village *The Shoe* pub serves meals and bar snacks. Just across the main road (A32) in the village of Meonstoke, *The Buck's Head* (☎ 01489-877313, e *thebux.mac07@btinternet.com*) is a cosy pub with good beer and reasonable food, plus B&B at £32/50 for singles/doubles.

A mile or so east of Meonstoke, *Harvestgate Farm* (☎ 01489-877675) offers B&B between April and September, charging from around £20. There are further accommodation choices in the villages of Warnford and West Meon, 1mi and 2mi respectively north along the A32.

Day 2: Exton to Buriton
13mi (21km), 4–6 hours
This is a day of varied walking, mainly through pasture and fields, with a dash of woodland. It also includes the first steep ascents of the route – and the first of many spectacular vistas to come.

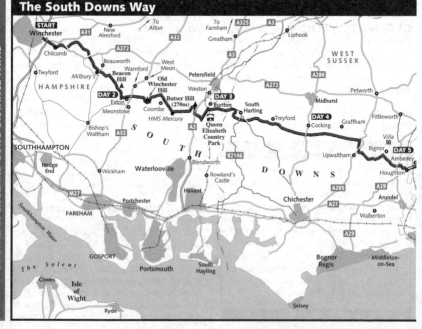

The South Downs Way

From Exton the trail climbs up to **Old Winchester Hill** – a good 11mi from Winchester as the crow flies – site of an Iron Age fort. It's an excellent viewpoint; you can look over the Meon Valley to the darker green of New Forest and the silver line of sea, which splits the Isle of Wight from the coast.

After Salt Hill, hurry past HMS Mercury, a landlocked naval station with grim razor wire fences and derelict outbuildings. Of more interest is the nearby **Sustainability Works**, the base of a charity that promotes sustainable living. open to visitors with a genuine interest.

Next comes **Butser Hill** – at 270m the highest point on the SDW, marking the beginning of the Downs. Savour a rolling descent, heading under the A3 to reach the headquarters of Queen Elizabeth Country Park with a *cafe*, toilets and visitors centre. Carefully follow the SDW signs (ignore the multicoloured waymarks for circular trails in the forest), mostly along a gravel track,

until you reach Hall's Hill Carpark, from where a lane drops down to Buriton and bed.

Buriton

This village (pronounced berry-ton) makes a great overnight stop, with cottages of sandstone and flint, a fine **Norman church** and a duck pond.

First stop for B&B should be *The Old Hop Kiln* (☎ 01730-266822), charging from £23; if this place is full the friendly owner can recommended other places in the village. Just outside the village is *Nurstead Farm* (☎ 01730-264278), charging from £17. A very walker-friendly place is *Well-stevens* (☎ 01730-261029, ✉ harrison@wellstevens.co.uk), in the village of Weston, 1.5mi north-west of Buriton on the west side of the A3, charging £24.

Buriton has two pubs. *The Master Robert* (☎ 01730-267275) is rather impersonal, with straightforward bar food and B&B at £35/45 for singles/doubles. Much better is

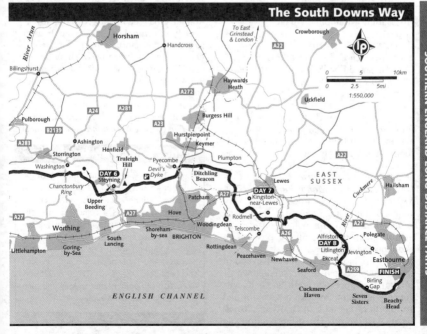

The Five Bells (☎ *01730-263584*), a friendly pub with good beer and lively atmosphere, charging £35 (single or double) in self-catering cottages (plus £10 for each extra person). Dinners are also very good, from £7 to £10, and with notice the pub will do breakfast for £5. Camping is free if you arrange it in advance and eat at the pub.

Day 3: Buriton to Cocking
11mi (17.5km), 4–5 hours
Today you reach the edge of the Downs proper and enjoy a wonderful rollercoaster route along the northern escarpment, with great views to the north and south.

Regain the trail from Buriton and then stride out over a succession of steep, rounded grassy domes, including Tower Hill and Harting Down. At Beacon Hill (yes, another one) and a place called Devil's Jumps, take care as the SDW switches back sharply on itself and it's easy to go striding straight on. Where the trail crosses the A286, to the north lies the neat village of Cocking. To avoid this busy road a footpath leads from Hill Barn down into the village.

Cocking & Around
Your first choice of accommodation in Cocking should be the *Moonlight Cottage* (☎ *01730-813336*, e *enquiries@moonligh tcottage.net*), where the friendly owners make a real effort to welcome weary walkers. B&B here costs from £23/40 to £30/46 for singles/doubles, and you can get snacks and meals until 5pm in the adjoining tearoom. When full they'll try and help you find alternative accommodation nearby; ask about *Cinque Port House* or *Carter's Cottage*. Also nearby is *Manor Farm* (☎ *01730-812784*) with B&B for around £20 and very simple camping for £1. Also in the village is *The Blue Bell Inn* with good evening meals for around £8, plus a post office *shop*, open daily.

There are more B&B options (several of which do pick-ups) in the small town of Midhurst, another mile north, and in the village of Graffham, 3mi east of Cocking and 1mi north of the trail. In Graffham, *Brook Barn* (☎ *01798-867356*) offers comfortable

walker-friendly B&B from around £25 and camping for £5.

Day 4: Cocking to Amberley
11.5mi (18.5km), 4–5 hours
This is another wonderful day along the escarpment, with some steep descents and ascents, but great views as always, and some historical features to provide atmosphere.

From Cocking regain the SDW as it runs through forest and farmland of the Cowdrey Estate. After a few miles you cross Slindon Estate, owned and managed by the National Trust, which is now reintroducing sheep ousted from much downland by intensive arable farming. Through it slices **Stane Street**, a Roman road that ran between London and the port of Noviomagus, today called Chichester.

Just to the south, the wondrously named *Gumber Bothy* (☎ *01243-814484*) offers bunk accommodation in a barn and camping for £6. Facilities include showers and a self-catering kitchen. This a handy spot to overnight if you want to visit nearby **Bignor Roman Villa** (see the boxed text below).

Onwards from here pause smugly as you negotiate the snorting traffic of the A29; you are now halfway between Winchester and Eastbourne. The SDW then drops into the Arun valley, passing near the village of Houghton, where the friendly *Houghton Farm* (☎ *01798-831327*) does B&B from £24 with good service and a swimming pool, and *The George & Dragon* pub does meals.

Bignor Roman Villa

Bignor Roman Villa is about 2mi north of the trail. For an entry fee of £3.50, you can still see parts of the original walls and underfloor heating system, plus a collection of tools, coins and domestic items. Best of all are the mosaics: Venus eyeing up a pair of gladiators, winter-snug in a warm cloak; a rasta-haired Medusa; and Ganymede, the androgynous shepherd boy. The villa (☎ 01798-869259) is open 10am to 5pm, March to May and June to September (closed Monday).

The trail crosses the River Arun on a footbridge to meet the B2139 north-west of Houghton Bridge, then contours along the escarpment past *High Titten Campsite* to meet a lane that drops down into Amberley.

Amberley

The quiet village of Amberley has houses of flint, brick and half-timber, all hiding behind trim gardens. There's a *shop* (open daily; mornings only on Wednesday and weekends) and two pubs. *The Black Horse* is a good, no-frills place with an equally straightforward selection of bar food; and the friendly *Sportsman*, just east of the village, has a fine selection of beers and home-cooked food from £5 to £8, served daily.

Roughly opposite The Black Horse is *Bacons* (☎ 01798-831234), offering B&B for £18; and near the Sportsman are two very walker-friendly places: *Woodybanks* (☎ 01798-831295), from £18; and *Simon's Lea* (☎ 01798-831321), from £20.

Back at Houghton Bridge, near the train station, you can eat at *The Bridge Inn*. Opposite, *Houghton Bridge Tearooms* serves snacks and lunches until 5pm.

There are more options in nearby Bury, including *Harkaway* (☎ 01798-831843), and in Arundel, 4mi off the route and linked to Amberley by hourly train. Arundel has a *YHA Hostel* (☎ 01903-882204) and several B&Bs. The TIC (☎ 01903-882268), on the High St, can advise.

Day 5: Amberley to Steyning

13mi (21km), 4–6 hours

This is a day of easy walking along the spine of the Downs. You only need to change your stride for one steepish ascent. If that doesn't take away your breath, the wrap-around views will.

Once you've puffed your way up from the Arun valley, cruise along the track through classic wide-open downland scenery – beautiful in clear weather but exposed in the wind and rain. At a fork by a barn (the first feature for several miles), make sure you keep left, nearer the edge of the Downs, before dropping down to scuttle across the A24 just south of Washington.

Amberley Museum

Between Amberley village and Houghton Bridge is Amberley Museum (☎ 01798-831370), 'the museum that works'. From 10am to 6pm Wednesday to Sunday, between 15 March and 4 November, you can meet a clay-pipe maker, blacksmith, wheelwright, broom maker, boatbuilder and other traditional artisans. Entry costs £6.50.

From here it's a stiff push up to **Chanctonbury Ring**, a coppice of beech trees planted in 1760 by a local landowner who, according to legend, climbed up the hill with bottles of water to nurture his young saplings. He must have turned in his grave when the 1987 storm took out the heart of his plantation, but it did reveal Iron Age and Roman remains that are still being excavated. This is a splendid spot for a rest, with superb views to the south and east towards Worthing, Shoreham and, for the first time, Brighton.

Then it's downhill all the way, either on footpaths that branch off direct to Steyning (if you're staying there) or on the main trail down into the valley of the River Adur, along which footpaths lead to Upper Beeding.

Steyning & Around

A proper town – the largest settlement since Winchester – although still characteristically trim and neat, Steyning (pronounced stenning) has a bank, shops and pubs. It's also famous for **Bramber Castle**, an impressive ruin on the edge of town.

Walker-friendly B&Bs include *Wappingthorn Farmhouse* (☎ 01903-813236, e ari anne@wappingthorn.demon.co.uk), outside the town on Horsham Rd (B2135, about half a mile beyond the junction with the A283), charging from £25/45 for en suite singles/doubles. *Miracles* (☎ 01903-812271), a shop on the High St in town, does B&B from £20. Also on the High St, the smart and highly rated *Springwells Hotel* (☎ 01903-812446) welcomes walkers with B&B from £30/52. Other B&Bs include *Ashburton* (☎ 01903-815265), just off the High St; and *Fir Croft*

(☎ 01903-816109), north-east of the centre, both charging from £20. Campers can aim for *The White House* (☎ 01903-813737), in the north-west of town.

For evening food there's a choice of recommended pubs on the High St, including *The White Horse* with good bar food for £5 to £7, and *The Star* with better food at slightly higher prices.

In Upper Beeding, south of the town near the roundabout, *The Rising Sun* (☎ 01903-814424) welcomes walkers, with B&B from £18/30 and bar food (not on Sunday evening). Or you can stroll into the centre to eat at the *Bramber Dragon* for Chinese food or the *Maharaja* for Indian.

Alternatively, push on for another 2mi to Truleigh Hill, which has a modern *YHA Hostel* (☎ 01903-813419) charging £9.80. Next door, on an organic smallholding, is *The Whiteley House* (☎ 07949-829799). Although the accommodation is not so smart, the owners are very friendly, flexible and welcoming (and guests must be a bit flexible too). B&B costs £20 to £25, and dinners or packed lunches are sometimes available.

Day 6: Steyning to Kingston-near-Lewes
15mi (24km), 5–7 hours
Today the trail sticks close to the ridge once again. Brief ups and downs are succeeded by long flat stretches through arable fields and sheep-cropped grassland.

After climbing from the Adur valley, your first highlight is **Devil's Dyke**, a deep valley cut into the edge of the Downs. Nearby is a car park and big touristy *pub* overlooking the tremendous view to the north. This is also a popular perch for hang gliders.

The next feature is less appealing: the A23 highway between London and Brighton. You cross the highway on a bridge to Pyecombe, where walker-friendly *Dolphin Cottage* (☎ 01273-843766, ⓔ pareeve@beathe mail.net) does B&B for £20, or you can camp at nearby *Pangdean Farm* (☎ 01273-843302). Nearby, *The Plough Inn* (☎ 01273-842796) does evening meals. From the stop behind the BP petrol station, buses run near-hourly to Brighton.

The route skirts a golf course and passes near **Clayton Windmills**, more popularly known as Jack & Jill. You then gradually gain height until **Ditchling Beacon**, where you can see, for the first time, the westernmost of the Seven Sisters cliffs – your treat in store for the final day.

Beyond here the trail is less trodden. Take care not to go straight on just after a hill called Plumpton Plain, but follow tracks zigzagging through the fields and a patch of wood to meet the A27 about 2.5mi west of Lewes (pronounced lewis). A short way

Brighton

BRYN THOMAS

Brighton's over-the-top Royal Pavilion

Holiday resort, university town and home to Europe's largest marina, Brighton (nicknamed 'London-by-the-Sea') can add a touch of metropolitan spice to your journey, with a host of bars, nightspots, hotels, B&Bs, hostels, pubs and places to eat. It differs from other South Coast towns in its unique blend of faded elegance and downright seediness, inherited when King George IV came down here on the original 'dirty weekend'. The Royal Pavilion, built when that same George was Prince Regent, is well worth visiting for its would-be oriental architecture and sumptuous furnishings. The Brighton TIC (☎ 0906-711 2255) is on Bartholomew Square, in the city centre.

east are several handy but uninspiring refuelling possibilities – a *tea van* in a lay-by, two petrol station *shops* and the *Little Chef* cafe (the former Newmarket Inn). It's far better to push on, down into Kingston-near-Lewes.

Kingston-near-Lewes

Is there no end to these trim villages? Apparently not! Kingston-near-Lewes is another one, where B&Bs include *Settlands* (☎ 01273-472295), charging from £20; and the smarter *Nightingales* (☎ 01273-475673), from £25. Very basic camping is possible at *Spring Bank Farm* (☎ 01273-472528), on the edge of the village, for £2. For lunch or dinner, *The Juggs* pub is a very good choice. In **Lewes** – a charming country town just 2mi away – there are many more B&B opportunities and some stirring reminders of home for American visitors (see the boxed text 'Lewes & the USA').

Day 7: Kingston-near-Lewes to Alfriston

13.5mi (21.5km), 5–7 hours
On this penultimate day of the walk, the route finally leaves the spine of the Downs behind. It's a simply spectacular farewell.

From Kingston-near-Lewes you stride along a gently undulating route, with a few short, sharp dips and rises, enjoying your last extensive views northwards over the Weald before dropping down to skirt the little village of Southease. In nearby Rodmell very comfortable B&B at *Barn House* (☎ 01273-477865, e *sharifin@gn.apc.org*) costs £30 (from May to September). On the main road, *The Abergavenny Arms* does good pub food. About 2mi south is *Telscombe YHA Hostel* (☎ 01273-301357), charging £9.

From Southease the trail follows a lane over flat floodplains then across the surprisingly large River Ouse on a bridge. Southease train station also comes as a surprise, but the hourly trains are handy for accessing Lewes or Brighton.

It's a tough haul up the east side of the valley, before a final stroll along the tops and a descent into Alfriston.

Alfriston

Sitting snugly at the foot of the Downs, Alfriston flaunts its flint and timber-framed cottages at the tourists who arrive by the coachload in high season. The **old church**, surrounded by a grassy moat, is another attraction. There are consequently many cafes, gift shops and places to stay, and a fine brace of characterful pubs.

In the centre, the friendly *George Inn* (☎ 01323-870319), dating from 1397, does B&B from £30/60 to £60/80 for en suite singles/doubles, of which some come with beamed ceilings, antique furniture and four-poster beds. Also on offer is good bar food at lunchtime and a la carte dinners in the evening from £10 to £14. Opposite, *The Star Inn*, only a few years younger and once frequented by pilgrims, has an old frontage but a slightly impersonal chain-hotel feel inside. Much better for a drink is *The Old Smugglers Inn* – also called The Market Cross – but obey the sign and take your muddy boots off first!

Going southwards down the High St, your B&B options include *The Greenhouse Effect* (☎ 01323-871399), above a florist, with cool airy rooms and Moroccan artefacts, charging £40 per room (single or double); and *Chestnuts* (☎ 01323-870298), above a good no-frills *cafe*, charging around £20. Nearby, *The Wingrove Inn* is a large pub with a garden and restaurant serving main courses from £7 to £11.

Farther out of the village, along the main road south towards Seaford, are some more choices, including the friendly *Dean's Barn*

Lewes & the USA

American visitors may want to visit Lewes. Tom Paine, a major intellectual inspiration for the American Revolution, lived at Bull House, 92 High St, and expounded his ideas to the Headstrong Club at the White Hart Hotel, where you can still see a copy of the Declaration of Independence. John Harvard, founder of the American university of the same name, also lived here.

The South Downs Way – Route Highlight

If you can only do a couple of days on the South Downs Way, the last two stages, Days 7 and 8, are highly recommended. You could base yourself in Eastbourne, take the train via Lewes to Southease and then follow the route described here back to the finish, overnighting in Alfriston on the way. Or you could do a circular walk, going out from Eastbourne on the northern alternative route, mostly used by mountain bikers. This route goes through Jevington (where the local pub claims to be the place where banoffy pie was invented) and over the top of the Long Man of Wilmington chalk figure, to overnight in Alfriston. To finish, follow the walker's route back to Eastbourne, with a grand finale over the Seven Sisters.

(☎ 01323-870274) with good-value doubles for £38 to £40. You can also stay in a separate flat for two or three people, which costs £40 if you self-cater, although breakfast can also be arranged. (Don't confuse this house with *Dean's Place* opposite, a big hotel). Also nearby is another friendly place called *Dacres* (☎ 01323-870447), which offers a separate en suite studio apartment with two beds for £25 with breakfast; self-catering is also possible. A little farther along (about 1mi from the village centre) is the *YHA Hostel* (☎ 01323-870423), charging £9.80.

Day 8: Alfriston to Eastbourne
11mi (17.5km), 4–6 hours
You have (if only in principle) a choice today. You could take the inland bridleway, but this is best left to mountain bikers. Or you could follow the walkers' route which, with an exhilarating finale along the cliff tops, is undoubtedly the better option.

The trail leaves Alfriston from the old Market Square and crosses the River Cuckmere. Where the bridleway goes straight on, you go right and south along the riverbank to Litlington, then through the woodland of

Seven Sisters Country Park to rejoin the Cuckmere at Exceat – the park visitors centre, with toilets and a *cafe*. The trail then continues south with views over the meandering river. You pass near *Foxhole Bottom Camping Barn*, administered by Seven Sisters Country Park (☎ 01323-870280, e *seven sisters@southdowns-aonb.gov.uk*), which charges £3.50. Bookings are essential. You can also camp here for £2.50 but it's walkers only as there is no access for vehicles. Under 18s get cheaper rates.

Route and river meet the open sea at Cuckmere Haven, where the home stretch lies before you. Turning east to follow the coast, the trail soon climbs steeply to the crest of Haven Brow, the first of the **Seven Sisters** cliffs (there are, in fact, eight but this doesn't alliterate so neatly). With staggering views over the English Channel, and the exhilaration of being so close to the sea, the Sisters can't fail to thrill.

About halfway along, at **Birling Gap**, there's a *hotel* and *pub*, a *B&B* and a row of houses about to fall into the sea, but you probably won't want to break your stride. Continue all the way to **Beachy Head** where the Downs finally tumble into the sea. Here the candy-striped lighthouse below makes a fine landmark for the end of the route, and the nearby large although uninspiring *pub* may tempt you for a celebratory pint or meal.

Savour all this because the official end of the trail, a couple of miles farther on at the edge of Eastbourne, beside a snack bar, is a complete anticlimax. For a proper finish, continue along the promenade and proudly put down your backpack at the end of Eastbourne's fine **19th-century pier**.

Eastbourne
A haven for the retired, and well past its own heyday, Eastbourne is an unexciting return to civilisation. Hotels and B&Bs line the seafront and most of the roads leading off it. Supply exceeds demand, so it's worth shopping around. The central TIC (☎ 01323-411400), on Cornfield Rd, can advise on the countless B&B options. There's also a *YHA Hostel* (☎ 01323-721081) and a multitude of snack bars, fish and chip shops, cafes

and tearooms, plus an even wider selection of pubs doing food, and restaurants offering Italian, Chinese, Indian and many other flavours, all ideal for a high-calorie splurge.

The South West Coast Path (Cornwall Section)

Distance	162.5mi (261.5km)
Duration	14 days
Standard	medium-hard
Start	Padstow
Finish	Falmouth
Gateways	Newquay, Penzance, Falmouth

Summary A continuously strenuous walk, with some extra tough bits thrown in. Includes cliff tops, beaches and resort towns, plus some rural inland sections.

The South West Coast Path (SWCP) is Britain's longest national trail and one of the longest continuous footpaths in the country. It follows the coast of the south-west peninsula from Minehead in Somerset, along the north Devon coast, around Cornwall via Land's End, then along the south Devon coast to Poole in Dorset. About two-thirds of the exceptionally beautiful coastline is designated Heritage Coast and one-third also belongs to the National Trust. On top of this, the trail passes several Areas of Outstanding Natural Beauty and Exmoor National Park. To balance this splendour, it also transits several large seaside resorts and working ports.

Experts disagree on the SWCP's total length, although the South West Coast Path Association (SWCPA), an active body that monitors path conditions and works with several other organisations to promote the interests of users, surveyed the path in 1999–2000 using GPS technology and gave it a total of 630mi (1014km). But the distance is only half the battle; the coast of the south-west peninsula is decidedly hilly and following the path involves a *lot* of steep descents into valleys where rivers meet the sea, then just as many steep ascents on the other side. The SWCPA calculates that if you did the whole route from end to end,

you'd actually ascend a total of 27,300m – three times the height of Everest!

To make matters more manageable, the SWCP is often divided into four sections, roughly related to the counties it passes through – Somerset and North Devon, Cornwall, South Devon and Dorset. Most popular is the Cornwall section, which is described here in detail. (The other sections are outlined briefly at the end of this chapter.)

Along the Cornwall section of the SWCP the views are rocky and dramatic, with steep cliffs, sandy beaches, secret coves, shipwrecks, castles, barrows, disused mines and engine houses, seals, dolphins and a wide range of bird life – it's well worth carrying a pair of binoculars. There's even some new words to learn as the trail passes *wheals* (mines), *porths* (bays or harbours) and *zawns* (gulleys) – reminders of the old Cornish language, akin to Welsh and Breton, which today is making a small comeback.

Direction, Distance & Duration

Although the SWCP can be walked in either direction, it seems traditional to do the northern coast first and we describe it this way. The trail is waymarked with national trail acorn symbols, although these have an irritating habit of vanishing just when the route is least clear. In theory, you can't go far wrong – except when transiting towns – because you keep the sea to your right (assuming you go anticlockwise). In practice, the number of other paths crossing the area can lead you astray if you don't keep a good eye on the map. As a rule of thumb, where paths divide and you're not sure, take the path closest to the sea as the aim of the SWCP is to keep as near to the coast as possible.

When researching this book, we measured the distance from Padstow to Falmouth as 163mi (262km). The recent GPS-based measurements from the SWCPA now have this as 168mi (271km). This may add up to half a mile on the daily distances in the table below. Fit walkers can cover the distance in two weeks, although you might want to add a few more days to spread the load, or for sightseeing. For a 14-day walk the most convenient overnight stops are:

day	from	to	mi/km
1	Padstow	Treyarnon	10.5/17
2	Treyarnon	Newquay	12.5/20
3	Newquay	Perranporth	11/17.5
4	Perranporth	Portreath	12.5/20
5	Portreath	St Ives	17/27.5
6	St Ives	Pendeen Watch	13/21
7	Pendeen Watch	Sennen Cove	9/14.5
8	Sennen Cove	Porthcurno	6/9.5
9	Porthcurno	Penzance	11/17.5
10	Penzance	Porthleven	13/21
11	Porthleven	Lizard Point	13/21
12	Lizard Point	Coverack	11/17.5
13	Coverack	Helford	13/21
14	Helford	Falmouth	10/16

Some of these distances look short and deceptively easy, but it's important to realise that the constant crossing of hills and valleys can really slow your progress. Don't overestimate your abilities. Many hardy hill walkers have come to grief on the SWCP, as those who usually walk at 3mph find they're only going at 2mph. That doesn't sound much until a planned eight-hour day turns into 12 hours, and you're walking in the dark or making dawn starts just to get to your next destination in time for dinner. If you're not fit or experienced, consider shorter stages; there are plenty of other overnight options. Take heed of one reader's hard-won experience:

I was far too ambitious in my original plan and completely underestimated the sheer hard work needed to walk down so many steep paths into coves and then up again on even steeper paths to reach the cliff tops on this scenic but difficult stretch of coastline. I was carrying a full backpack weighing about 18kg, including tent etc, and only managed to walk about half the total distance I had originally planned. For what it is worth my advice to anyone attempting this same walk with a fully loaded backpack is to plan about 10mi per day maximum unless you're super-fit. Without a backpack then probably a few more miles per day could be added. It was beautiful and worthwhile nonetheless and in spite of the bad weather I can say that I enjoyed every moment of it – now that I have finished!

Reg Tripp (UK)

Alternatives If your schedule is tight, consider a shorter section; the stretch from St Ives to Lizard Point lets you take in some of Britain's best known beauty spots in just five days. If your time is even more limited, see the boxed text 'The South West Coast Path – Route Highlight' on p220 for more ideas.

As with all LDPs, you can do just a single day linear section of the SWCP or a circular route, taking in a stretch of the main route.

PLANNING
Maps
The Ordnance Survey (OS) Landranger 1:50,000 maps needed for the Cornwall section of the South West Coast Path are maps No 200 *(Newquay & Bodmin)*, No 203 *(Land's End & Isles of Scilly)* and No 204 *(Truro & Falmouth)*. For further detail, which is recommended, you need OS Explorer 1:25,000 maps No 102 *(Land's End)*, No 103 *(The Lizard, Falmouth & Helston)*, No 104 *(Redruth & St Agnes)* and No 106 *(Newquay & Padstow)*.

Books
Without a doubt, the most useful book you can have is *The South West Coast Path Guide*, produced every year by the SWCPA. It contains a route outline, accommodation lists, transport information, planning tips and even tide tables, and is well worth the £6. For step-by-step details on the route, the SWCPA produces a series of *Path Description* leaflets (£1 each, including postage inside Britain). Both the guide and leaflets are available from the SWCPA Administrator (☎ 01364-73859, @ coastpath.swcpa@virgin.net, W www.swcp.org.uk), 25 Clobells, South Brent, Devon TQ10 9JW.

The official national trail guide is *South West Coast Path – Padstow to Falmouth* by John Macadam. As with other guides in this official series, the book combines good detailed descriptions with background information and relevant extracts from 1:25,000 OS maps (sufficient if you don't plan to go more than a mile or so off the route). Using maps that cover a wider area are useful if you do divert, and also help put your walk in context.

The National Trust publishes a series of *Coast of Cornwall* leaflets, available from TICs for around 80p, giving fascinating details about parts of the walk owned by the National Trust. Those of particular relevance to the Cornwall coast route are Nos 8 to 16.

Information Sources

Along the Cornwall section of the route are many TICs, including Padstow (☎ 01841-533449, ℮ padstowic@visit.org.uk), which offers a book-a-bed-ahead scheme for the coast path, Newquay (☎ 01637-871345), St Ives (☎ 01736-796297), Penzance (☎ 01736-362207) and Falmouth (☎ 01326-312300).

The indomitable SWCPA's very useful Web site (ⓦ www.swcp.org.uk) is full of information about all aspects of the route, and even includes a 'tour' of the entire trail using hundreds of photographs.

Baggage Services

Compared to routes in Northern England, there aren't many companies to transport your backpack from places to place along the SWCP. Those that do, tend to cover shorter stretches of the route, rather than the whole thing. The SWCPA produces lists of baggage services, which you can get for a small fee by post (see Books earlier for contact details). Several B&Bs along the route arrange baggage transport to your next destination (usually for around £10), so ask about this when you book.

PLACES TO STAY & EAT

As a prime tourist destination, Cornwall offers a wide range of facilities for all budgets. Places offering accommodation, food, tea or beer can be found usually (but not always) a short distance off the trail. Cornwall's main tourist season is from Easter to the end of September. Some B&Bs and cafes close outside this time. Over the Easter holiday and during July and August, particularly near the main tourist towns, it's essential to book in advance. In high season many places prefer to take guests for a week or at least for a few days and, as in all holiday places, prices fluctuate wildly according to season. We have tried to quote average prices in this section, but don't be surprised if places charge more if you pass by in August (or less in the depths of winter!).

A selection of places to stay is listed in the route description. For a wider choice, as well as the SWCPA's guide there is *The Rambler's Yearbook & Accommodation Guide* and *Stilwell's National Trail Companion* (see Books in the Facts for the Walker chapter for details).

The route is well served with campsites (some open only from Easter to October) and YHA hostels. There are also several independent hostels, plus cheap and cheerful backpacker joints.

GETTING TO/FROM THE WALK

General information about travel in Britain is given in the Getting Around chapter. For an outline of local options, contact the Cornwall County Council's Public Transport Information Line (☎ 01872-332142), but note this doesn't give detailed timetables

---

Warnings

As a coastal path, the South West Coast Path (SWCP) is cut by several river mouths. Some can be crossed by stepping stones or by wading – but only at low tide. Others are crossed by ferries, which may only run at high tide. Therefore, tides can greatly affect the timing of your walk. A simple tide table is available in local shops and is reproduced in the *The South West Coast Path Guide* (see Books earlier). Note that wading across rivers at low tide can save a lot of mileage but only when conditions are right; otherwise it can be fatal.

If you want to swim (for relaxation, *not* to cross river mouths), also note that many beaches have strong currents. Flags mark safe places and lifeguards are sometimes on duty. If in doubt, stay on dry land.

Note also that there's little shade on the SWCP, so in hot weather make sure you carry enough to drink. At the opposite end of the weather scale, hazards include coastal fog (especially dangerous near the edge of high cliffs) and driving wind (again dangerous on cliff tops when your backpack acts like a sail!).

for individual routes. For that you're better off phoning a TIC or the main bus company, First Western National (☎ 01208-79898, 01209-719988).

Bus National Express has regular coach services from London, Bristol and other parts of the country to Penzance, via Falmouth and Wadebridge, from where you catch a local bus to Padstow. There are about 10 buses daily Monday to Saturday, and five per day on Sunday.

Train The nearest train station to Padstow is Bodmin Parkway, from where buses go to Padstow. At the end of your walk, Falmouth is linked by a branch line to Truro, where you can get mainline connections to various parts of the country.

Car Padstow is reached from Wadebridge, a town on the A39 between Barstaple and Penzance. Falmouth is also on the A39.

THE WALK
Padstow
On the Camel Estuary, the small town of Padstow still clings to a fishing industry, making its harbour and surrounding twisty old streets a pleasant place to stroll. The TIC (☎ 01841-533449, e padstowic@visit.org .uk), on North Quay, offers a book-a-bed-ahead scheme for the coast path.

Walker-friendly B&Bs include *Rose Hill* (☎ *01841-532761*), charging from £17; *Estuary Views (☎ 01841-532551, 8 Treverbyn Rd)*, charging £22; and *Woodlands Close* (☎ *01841- 533109*) at Treator, 1mi outside Padstow, offering excellent accommodation from £20, plus long-stay parking. *Dennis Cove Camping (☎ 01841-532349)*, outside the town, has a swimming pool and cafe; it's mainly aimed at families, but walkers are welcome and get a special rate of £5.40 in high season.

For eats in Padstow, *The Seafood Restaurant* has been very popular since the owner-chef, Rick Stein, hosted a TV cookery show; a full dinner will cost around £30. Less expensive are its partner-eateries *St Petroc's Bistro* and *Middle Street Café*. All

also do accommodation from £65 to £140 per double. To reserve a table or room in any Stein property, phone ☎ 01841-532700.

For a more simple bite, Padstow is full of shops selling traditional Cornish 'pasties' – filled pastries, usually savoury, originally designed so miners could carry their food underground more easily, but now also a very handy lunch for long-distance walkers.

Day 1: Padstow to Treyarnon
10.5mi (17km), 4–6 hours
This stage makes a relatively easy introduction, although if you only got off the bus yesterday (or the plane the day before that!) you'll certainly feel the strain today.

The route leaves Padstow harbour near the TIC on North Quay and winds up to the headland and a granite war memorial. You drop to St George's Cove, from where at low tide you can cross the beach to Hawker's Cove. At high tide stick to the main path. From the Coastguard Station, the path then climbs up to **Stepper Point**; on a clear day you might just make out Bodmin Moor on the horizon.

The SWCP continues along the coast to Butter Hole Cove and Gunver Head, with views of the Merope Islands. Ahead you'll see **Porthmissen Bridge**, a multisided limestone and slate arch carved by the sea, where razorbills and guillemots nest in summer. Take care while walking round the collapsed Round Hole cave (especially when incoming waves from below turn it into a geyser!), then follow the path downhill to Trevone car park and nearby *cafe*.

Just inland, **Trevone** village is 5mi from Padstow. If you want to break here, the *Well Parc Hotel (☎ 01841-520318)* positively welcomes walkers, with rooms from £15 to £20 and B&B from £22 to £29.

From Trevone the trail follows the coastline round to the beach at Harlyn Bay. You can camp for £3.50 at *Higher Harlyn Park*, just off the western end of the beach, or stop for a drink or a meal at *The Harlyn Inn* (☎ *01841-520207*), which also does B&B from £21. Under the inn an Iron Age cemetery was excavated in 1900, but the finds have been removed to Truro Museum.

From Harlyn, you pass near the **Cellars**, where the pilchard harvest was once stored (see the boxed text 'Pilchards – Cornwall's Cod'), then continue round Cataclews Point, skirting Mother Ivey's Bay and Merope Rocks, where ravens nest. At Trevose Head lighthouse, the SWCP then turns south and passes Constantine Bay to reach Treyarnon.

Treyarnon

At this little beachside village, you can stay at the *YHA Hostel* (☎ *01841-520322*) for £9.80. The friendly *Treyarnon Bay Hotel* (☎ *01841-520235*) has a bar, restaurant and B&B from £20 to £27.50. There's also a *cafe* and *takeaway* on the beach, and camping at the *Treyarnon Bay Caravan Park* (☎ *01841-520681*). Note that swimming in the bay is dangerous. There are more B&B options in Porthcothan, a mile or so farther down the coast.

Day 2: Treyarnon to Newquay

12.5mi (20km), 5–7 hours
This day's walk is tougher than yesterday's 'warm-up', but the views are superb and there is plenty of interest to distract the weary along the way.

Pilchards – Cornwall's Cod

The days are long gone when shoals of pilchard 10 to 20 million strong were sighted off the Cornish coast, appearing like clockwork each July. 'Huers' would take up position along the headlands to watch for the tell-tale signs – a red tinge to the water and circles of screeching gulls. The fishermen would launch their boats and circle the fish with their nets, before pulling them ashore to be salted and stored for export to France, Spain and, particularly, Italy.

In 1870 there were 379 registered 'seines' (pilchard businesses consisting of three boats) but by 1920 the industry was dead, probably killed off by uncontrolled and excessive fishing.

In Newlyn, visited later on this route, Britain's last salt pilchard factory now houses a working museum, which tells the history of the now-gone pilchard trade.

From Treyarnon Bay the trail follows the headlands, bypassing an Iron Age fort chopped into three parts by erosion. Near **Porthcothan** you can get B&B at *Trelooan* (☎ *01841-521158*), a friendly and comfortable place, charging from £15.

From Porthcothan the SWCP dips steeply down to Porth Mear valley, then up again to reach Park Head, where you get a wonderful view of your next few miles south. Half a mile later the trail passes **Bedruthan Steps**, a series of rock stacks on the beach that have been a popular tourist attraction since the railway reached Newquay in 1875. Today crowds can still be dense in summer. There's a *shop*, toilets and *cafe* serving surprisingly good food, plus a viewing platform from where you can see other local rock formations, including the Queen Bess Rock (now minus its head) and Samaritan Island, named after a ship wrecked here en route to Russia with a cargo of satin.

The SWCP continues along the cliff top to **Mawgan Porth**, where *The Merrymore Inn* (☎ *01637-860258*) does B&B from £22, plus good cheap pub food. There are numerous other places to stay, plus shops and cafes, and two *campsites*; the one nearest the beach is basic and charges £3.50.

From here the trail heads inland and continues for 2mi along the cliff top (or on the beach at low tide) round **Watergate Bay**. The peace is likely to be shattered by jets flying into the nearby airforce base at St Mawgan.

Next you reach **Trevelgue Head**, which boasts remains of the most extensive Iron Age fort in Cornwall. The SWCP then continues round St Columb Porth Beach, then down some steps beside a bus shelter and under a road bridge before continuing along the cliff until it joins Lusty Glaze Rd and takes you into Newquay.

Newquay

The sprawling, brash and brazen town of Newquay (pronounced new-kee) is a working port, holiday resort and Britain's surfing capital, and likely to come as a nasty shock after the relative quiet of the countryside. The up side is an endless choice of B&Bs, although you'll still need to book ahead in summer – the TIC (☎ 01637-871345), in the Council Offices on Marcus Hill, can advise. Budget travellers can head for *Newquay Cornwall Backpackers* (☎ 01637-874668), on Beachfield Ave, charging £7 for a bed in the dorm; or *Fistral Backpackers* (☎ 01637-873146, 18 Headland Rd), charging around £10, or £18 in a double. *Trenance Caravan & Chalet Park* (☎ 01637-873447), at the southern end of Edgcumbe Ave, charges a mere £6.75.

Day 3: Newquay to Perranporth
11mi (17.5km), 4–6 hours

Today is probably the hardest walking so far. A potential problem is crossing the River Gannel, where the tide and the time of year decree how far upstream you have to go. Plan your day carefully.

The SWCP passes through Newquay on the main road and goes up the steps from the north side of the quay to Towan Head. You go above Fistral Beach to Pentire, then drop down to reach the River Gannel. The 'official' crossing (the one nearest the sea) is at Fernpit, where you go through a gate into the private gardens of a nice *cafe* (breakfast is £3) and use the bridge (free) at low tide or the ferry (70p) at high tide. If the cafe is closed (which it might be out of tourist season), you can't use this bridge or ferry, but there's another footbridge about half a mile upstream that is exposed for a few hours either side of low tide. If this is covered by water, walk another mile upstream to reach another footbridge, near a suburb of Newquay called Trenance. If that bridge is underwater as well, you have to go even farther upstream to the next bridge; this adds at least 6mi onto your distance, so it's well worth getting the tide times right and using the lowest possible crossing.

Once you have crossed the river, go along Crantock Beach and then round or across a bay called Porth Joke with a pretty, generally deserted beach. **Holywell** village can be bypassed if the tide is low, but a visit is a chance to have a drink or meal in the ancient *Treguth* pub, and to view the nearby well with reputed healing powers that gives the village its name.

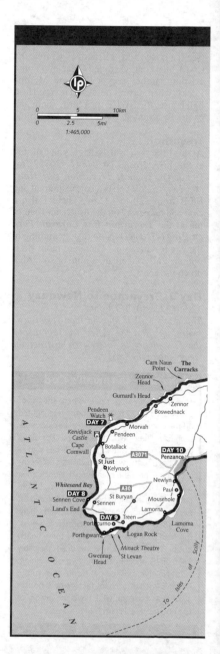

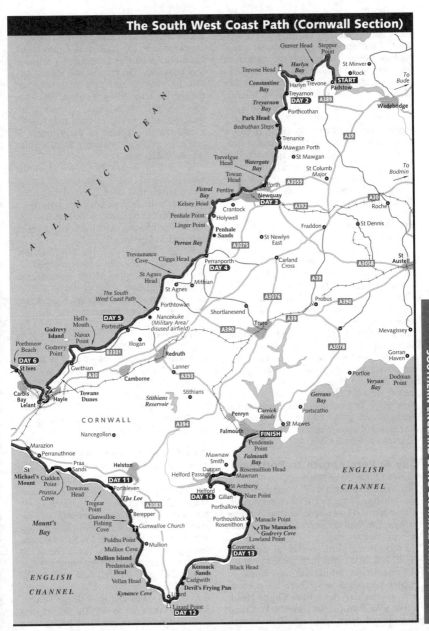

The South West Coast Path (Cornwall Section)

The trail continues southwards past Penhale Camp (a military property – keep seaward of the warning signposts) and across **Penhale Sands**, which cover the remains of 8th-century St Piran's Oratory, believed to be the oldest church in Cornwall but sadly reburied to protect it from erosion. Nearby, St Piran – who is also one of Cornwall's patron saints – has another ruined church named after him, this time dating from the 12th century, which can be seen and visited.

If the tide is out you can approach Perranporth along Perran Beach. At other times, however, you'll need to pick your way along the path between the cliff and the Perran Sands Holiday Centre.

Perranporth

This small and not very inspiring town has cafes, banks, a chemist and pizza takeaway among its facilities. Walker-friendly B&Bs include *Chy an Kerensa* (☎ *01872-572470*) and the *Perranova Guesthouse* (☎ *01872-573440*), both on Cliff Rd and both charging around £17 to £20. Also good is *The Seiners Arms Hotel* (☎ *01872-573368*), charging £20 to £31 depending on season. This is also the base for the village information point, where helpful Mrs Lawrence can advise on other places to stay.

At Droskyn Point, west of the village centre, the *YHA Hostel* (☎ *01872-573812*), costing £9, is a former coastguard station. Nearby is the proposed site of a huge sundial that will show Cornish Time – a good 12 minutes behind GMT.

Day 4: Perranporth to Portreath

12.5mi (20km), 5–7 hours
This stretch of the SWCP combines fairly easy walking along well-used cliff-top paths with stiffer sections where the trail dips into valleys. The final few miles to Portreath can be particularly tiring.

From Perranporth hostel at Droskyn Point, follow the cliff path, looking out for old mineshafts, which are now home to greater horseshoe bats. There are particularly spectacular views from **Cligga Head**.

The SWCP drops into Trevellas Porth and then up and down again into **Trevaunance**

Cove, which has a good *pub* and several B&Bs. The effort of going up from the cove is rewarded by the walk to **St Agnes Head**. Look out for nesting kittiwakes, guillemots and razorbills. Grey seals and sharks may also be visible. You may wish to divert through attractive **St Agnes** town, which has narrow streets of old miners cottages, a free museum and several good pubs and cafes for a mid-morning coffee or early lunch. If you're on a different itinerary, there are also several B&Bs here.

Beyond St Agnes Head you pass the ruins of Wheal Coates mine (one of a great many mines that once covered this area) and reach the bay of Chapel Porth, from where you can walk along the beach at low tide to **Porthtowan**, which has two *pubs*, a *cafe* and a *shop*.

Beyond Porthtowan, for the final few miles of this stage, the trail is wedged between the cliff top and the no-nonsense fence of a military area (shown on the OS map as a disused airfield) called Nancekuke. This leads you into Portreath.

Portreath

The little resort of Portreath has shops, a *takeaway* and two decent pubs – *The Basset Arms* and *The Portreath Arms*. Walker-friendly B&Bs include *Suhaili* (☎ *01209-842110*), charging from £16; *Cliff House* (☎ *01209-842008*), around £20; and *Fountain Springs* (☎ *01209-842650*), just off the trail at Glenfeadon House, from £19.

Day 5: Portreath to St Ives

17mi (27.5km), 8–10 hours
Today's walk is very long indeed. Strenuous at first, the walking gets easier around halfway, although the final stretch is not especially scenic. Either start early or consider taking two days to do this stage.

Leaving Portreath look for a narrow lane leading past houses at the south end of the harbour. The SWCP then climbs up to Tregea Hill and through 6mi of National Trust cliff-top property. The path crosses Carvannel Downs and Reskajeage Downs, with fine views out to sea. The B3301 runs close to the cliff here, but a path has been cut on the seaward side to keep walkers clear of the road. At **Hell's Mouth**, a striking (although not spectacular) cleft in the rocks, there is a small *cafe*, usually closed in winter. Look for grey seals as you walk towards Navax Point. The SWCP then continues around Godrevy Point where a lighthouse visible on Godrevy Island probably inspired Virginia Woolf's *To The Lighthouse*. Another small *cafe* is open here in summer.

After crossing the River Red (the colouring is caused by tin ore), the SWCP skirts the picturesque village of **Gwithian**, with many thatched cottages. The *Pendarves Arms* pub is worth a stop, and B&Bs include *Calize Country House* (☎ 01736-753268, e penny .bailey@talk21.com), at Prosper Hill, just under a mile off the trail, charging from £19.

You then follow waymarks for an exhausting 3mi slog through Towans Sand Dunes, although at low tide you can avoid it by walking on the beach.

At the end of the beach the SWCP swings inland and follows roads for a couple of miles through the town of Hayle, round the large bay of **Hayle Harbour** to Lelant. Birdwatchers can enjoy the waders on the mudflats, but most walkers hurry through. B&B options in Hayle include *Mrs Cooper* (☎ 01736-752855, 54 Penpol Terrace), from £18; and *Mrs Hoskings* (☎ 01736-754484, 34 Penpol Terrace), charging £14.

From Lelant it's another 2.5mi, round Porthkidney Sands and Carbis Bay, to St Ives, an altogether better place to stay.

St Ives

The delightful seaside resort of St Ives has narrow streets lined with cottages. Inevitably it gets packed in July and August, and prices are higher now than in most other places. The town has an artistic heritage, and it's well worth taking the time to enjoy the many art galleries – including the famous Tate (see the boxed text). The TIC (☎ 01736-796297) is in the Guildhall in the town centre.

For a place to stay, the main road into St Ives from Penzance, above Carbis Bay, is lined with B&Bs and guesthouses, and the part of the town overlooking Porthmeor Beach also has many options.

Campers can head for *Ayr Holiday Park* (☎ 01736-795855), half a mile from town, with good facilities and excellent views, charging £11 for two walkers and a tent in high season (£8.50 in spring and autumn).

Among the walker-friendly B&Bs are *Toby Jug Guesthouse* (☎ 01736-794250), on Park Ave, good value from £15; *Gowerton* (☎ 01736-796805, 6 Sea View Terrace), from £17; and *Kandahar* (☎ 01736-796183, 11 The Warren), right on the rocks by the water, charging £21 (£28 en suite).

The *Sloop Inn* (☎ 01736-796584), beside the harbour, charges from £35 and offers good seafood meals. Also near the harbour in the old part of town, *The Grey Mullet* (☎ 01736-796635) is an excellent guesthouse, charging from £20 to £24.

The best place to cruise for food is Fore St and the surrounding streets; there's a wide choice of pubs, cafes and restaurants.

Day 6: St Ives to Pendeen Watch

13mi (21km), 7–9 hours

This is one of the hardest stretches of the walk. The going is particularly tough because the trail is not only up and down

The Tate Gallery

The Tate in St Ives is an offshoot of the world-famous London galleries. It specialises, naturally, in paintings by members of the St Ives school of modern art – Ben Nicholson, Barbara Hepworth, Naum Gabo, Terry Frost, Patrick Heron and other local artists. The impressive building, designed by local architects Eldred Evans and David Shalev, replaced an old gasworks and has wide central windows framing the surfing scene on Porthmeor Beach below. The gallery's collection is small and exclusive, open 11am to 7pm Monday to Saturday, April to September (with shorter hours and different days in winter). Entry is £3, or £3.50 for the Barbara Hepworth Museum as well. The cafe on the roof is almost as popular as the gallery itself and does delicious crab salads and sandwiches.

but also exposed, uneven and boggy after rain. However, these difficulties are more than compensated for by the superb views out to sea and by the interesting flora, which includes orchids and royal fern. All possible lunch stops are inland (which adds to your mileage) so carry sandwiches if you don't want to divert.

To find the SWCP from St Ives, walk along Fore St and follow the signs for Porthmeor Beach. For a little way out of St Ives you share the trail with casual strollers but they quickly drop away as the going gets tougher. The trail keeps close to the cliff, with the steep dips into the coves keeping the pace slow. You can sometimes watch grey seals basking off the Carracks, twin offshore islets shortly after River Cove. The route then climbs steeply to Zennor Head where you can follow a path inland for half a mile to visit **Zennor** village.

If you want to break this stage, Zennor has a few sights (see the boxed text 'Zennor'). *The Old Chapel Backpackers* (☎ 01736-798307, ⓔ *zennorbackpackers@btinternet .com*) charges £10 for a bunk in a dorm and allows camping; facilities include a cafe and drying room. *The Tinners Arms* has bar food on the menu.

In nearby Boswednack, B&Bs include *Boswednack Manor* (☎ 01736-794183),

Zennor

Things to see in Zennor include the 60-year-old Wayside Museum, containing traditional everyday artefacts from the surrounding farms and cottage It's open from Easter to September (until 7pm during summer), allowing walkers plenty of time to visit at the end of the day. Also in the village, the 15th-century church contains a curious bench-end depicting a mermaid with a comb and mirror. Legend relates that the mermaid lured the local squire's son into the sea at Pendour Cove. On the wall outside, look for a memorial stone to John Davey of Boswednack (died 1891), 'the last to possess any considerable traditional knowledge of the Cornish language'.

charging around £18, with vegetarian food; and *Rosmorva* (☎ 01736-796722), similarly priced. A bit farther along the coast, *Treen Farm* (☎ 01736-796932) charges from £15.

From Zennor Head the SWCP continues along the cliff top and round assorted coves to Gurnard's Head, which is topped by remnants of an Iron Age fort. There are similar remains near dramatic **Bosigran Cliff** – today a favourite hangout for rock climbers. The last few miles to the lighthouse at the headland of Pendeen Watch are likely to be tiring, but don't relax when you get there – it's still another mile or so inland to the end of the day at Pendeen village.

Pendeen

Several places in Pendeen offer B&B, including *The Smugglers' Haunt* (☎ 01736-788310), from £18; and *The Radjel Inn* (☎ 01736-788446), a friendly pub charging from £18. Evening meals are served at *The North Inn* – a pretty, ivy-covered pub.

Day 7: Pendeen Watch to Sennen Cove

9mi (14.5km), 4–5 hours
Today's walk is relatively easy after yesterday's epic, but still with some tough and tiring sections. Although you will have seen mineshafts and ruined engine houses all along the path, the next few miles contain some excellent examples of Cornwall's great industrial heritage. Keen historians could spend two nights in this area and visit some of the sights. (See the boxed text 'Cornwall's Industrial Heritage'.)

From Pendeen Watch the SWCP follows the cliff top past **Levant Mine & Engine House**. Just inland is **Geevor Mine** and farther south are the twin towers of **Crowns Mine**, perched picturesquely on the rocks. Apparently, when the Princess of Wales visited in 1865, she was wearing a white flannel cloak and a white straw hat trimmed in blue. She, however, was not walking the coast path!

The trail then leads past two more picturesque engines – **Wheal Edward** and **Wheal Owles** – and skirts **Botallack** village, where you can cut inland for food and

Cornwall's Industrial Heritage

Some people find the detritus of past tin and copper mining unattractive, but as you pass the many ruined mineshafts and engine houses it's good to bear in mind that Cornwall was once much more than a tourist resort – it was an important industrial centre, producing valuable commodities that were exported to many parts of the world. Early customers of Cornish tin included Greeks and Romans some 2000 years ago, but the export trade really took off about 200 years ago with the invention of powerful steam pumps to efficiently drain the mines – many of which went under the sea.

Near Pendeen are two of the county's finest and most famous examples. **Geevor Mine** closed as recently as 1990 and is now open to visitors, with regular underground tours. The great pumping beam engine at **Levant Mine**, which closed in 1919 after an accident led to the death of 31 miners, has also been restored and can be visited. These, and many other historical sites, are managed by the Trevithick Trust. For more details see the Web site at W www.cornwall-county.com/trevithick-trust.

accommodation if required. Recommended B&Bs include *Llawnroc* (☎ 01736-788814), inland from Crowns Mine, from £16; and *Manor Farm* (☎ 01736-788525), charging around £23.

After Kenidjack Castle, with both Bronze Age and Industrial Age remains, you weave in and out to reach **Cape Cornwall** – once thought to be England's most westerly point before the title passed to Land's End. The SWCP doesn't go to the tip of the cape, but it's worth diverting for the views.

From Cape Cornwall the SWCP passes Carn Gloose, where a mysterious walled pit could be a Neolithic shrine, then heads inland along the Cot Valley. Where the trail switches back towards the sea you could continue to the village of **St Just**, which has several B&Bs. On the way you'll pass *Land's End YHA Hostel* (☎ 01736-788437), charging £9.80 for a bed and £5 for camping. Nearby *Kelynack Bunkbarn*

(☎ 01736-787633) costs £7. In the centre of St Just is a square, used in medieval times to perform miracle plays and now ringed with pubs, all of them offering food. The *Wellington* possibly has the edge for meals but the smaller *Star* is the most atmospheric drinking hole.

From St Just, the SWCP continues along the cliff to the mile-long **Whitesand Bay**, which is good for swimming and surfing. At high tide you'll have to skirt round the top of the bay where it's surprisingly easy to lose the trail altogether. Immediately afterwards you come to Sennen Cove.

Sennen Cove

The lively village of Sennen Cove has several cafes and pubs, including the *First & Last Refreshment House* and *The Old Success Inn* (☎ 01736-871232), which also does B&B from £26/39 for singles/doubles and dinner for £16. Friendly *Myrtle Cottage* (☎ 01736-871698) offers B&B for £20. If you want to sample the waves, Sennen Surfing Centre (☎ 01736-871404) offers lessons.

Inland, near Sennen Cove village, are two more options. *Whitesands Lodge* (☎ 01736-871776), also known as Land's End Backpackers, is a travellers hostel with dorm beds for £9 and a few more expensive guesthouse rooms (some en suite); facilities include a cafe, self-catering kitchen and bicycle hire, and you can also camp here. Nearby, *Homefields* (☎ 01736-871418) charges from £15 for B&B.

Before you leave Sennen Cove look out for the round house by the car park. This was an old capstan, created in 1876 from the winding gear of a disused mine, which was used to winch boats up from the beach. These days, predictably, it's a craft shop.

Day 8: Sennen Cove to Porthcurno

6mi (9.5km), 3–3½ hours

Today you pass a major milestone and your psychological halfway point – Land's End. The walking doesn't get much easier, although from here on you'll be heading east with more chance of the wind behind – but don't bank on it!

The South West Coast Path – Route Highlight

It's hard to pick a single section of coast which is better than the others but, if you've only got a day or two, the area around Land's End is among the best, and ideal for a short taster. OK, the paraphernalia around Land's End itself is tacky and commercial but what the hell, you're on holiday! Penzance is a good gateway, from where St Just can be quite easily reached by bus. From here it's a day's walk to Land's End. You can see the sights and return to Penzance by bus, or linger longer and overnight in Sennen Cove before returning to Penzance.

From Sennen Cove it's a quick scamper along the cliff tops to reach **Land's End**, completely dominated by a tacky theme park and a stack of souvenir stands, all dumped down with scant regard for this grand headland's iconic status. That said, the complex does provide 250 jobs in an unemployment black spot. You save on the £4 entrance fee by walking in, but can spend this and more on having your picture taken by the signboard showing the distances to John O'Groats (the other end of the British mainland), New York (across the Atlantic) and your home town. A bit vulgar, but everyone loves it.

Staying at the comfortable *Land's End Hotel* (☎ 01736-871844), the 'first and last hotel in England', costs £56/92 for singles/doubles, and gives you the chance to stroll around the headland in the evening after the crowds have gone. You can eat here too, or in the *Trenwith Arms*, a base for the Land's End–John O'Groats Association, whose members have made the 880mi end-to-end journey under their own steam – you might even see someone setting off on foot, bicycle or pogo stick.

But if enough is enough, you can leave Land's End behind and continue your journey along the well-marked but unsheltered path, soon also leaving the day trippers in your wake. After 3mi or so you reach the hamlet of Porthgwarra (with a small *cafe*)

and, just beyond here, another small place called St Levan. Here *Grey Gables* (☎ 01736-810421) offers B&B for £21 in an en suite room, plus evening meals for £11.50. It's another half-mile to the famous **Minack Theatre** (see the boxed text). Just north of here is Porthcurno village.

Porthcurno

The village of Porthcurno is a short distance inland. It is the rather unlikely site for a secret WWII underground communications centre, now an award-winning **museum**.

Places doing B&B include *Porthcurno Hotel* (☎ 01736-810119), charging around £20; and *Seaview House* (☎ 01736-810638), very friendly and welcoming, charging around £20, with excellent food (including evening meals and supper hampers to take to the theatre).

On Porthcurno beach *The Cable Station* pub isn't especially appealing, and the beach

The Minack Theatre

The Minack Theatre is an open-air auditorium built into the cliffs – one of the world's most spectacular settings. The audience sits on steep, curved rows of seats, while the actors' natural backdrop is the view across the sea. The theatre was built in the 1930s by Rowena Cade, an indomitable local woman who did much of the construction with her own hands, continuing until her death in 1983. She got the idea in 1935 after her family provided the local theatre group with an open-air venue for a production of Shakespeare's *The Tempest*, which proved so successful that annual performances were instituted. There are shows at the theatre most evenings from late May to late September; you can contact the box office (☎ 01736-810181) or a local TIC for details. Tickets cost £6.50. It's certainly worth taking in a performance if the weather's good (although gales have to be storm-force before a play is cancelled). Bring warm clothes and padding (the stone seats are hard), or you can hire a cushion. For more details see the Web site at ⓦ www.minack.com.

itself consists of broken shells rather than sand. The east end of the beach is used by naturists – seems they got a bit of a raw deal!

Day 9: Porthcurno to Penzance
11mi (17.5km), 6–8 hours
This day's walk is mixed, with some fairly easy sections to alleviate an otherwise tiring day. All along the route the views are very scenic.

From Porthcurno, follow the SWCP along the cliff top. In less than a mile you'll find a path leading off to **Logan Rock**, an 80-ton, once-rockable boulder owned by the National Trust. In 1824 Lieutenant Hugh Goldsmith pushed the rock clean off its perch, an exploit which was greeted with local outrage. The *Logan Rock Inn* in nearby Treen displays a copy of the bill for replacing the stone (£130 8s 6d), a sum which the lieutenant was forced to bear.

Beyond Logan Rock the walking is superb, although occasionally tough. At Lamorna Cove an excellent *café* serves delicious crab sandwiches, while *The Tremeneth Hotel* (☎ 01736-731367) charges from £18. Farther inland, *The Wink* pub was originally an illegal beer house. Nearby is *Dolphin Cottage* (☎ 01736-810394) with B&B for women only, from £22.

After Penzer Point you reach the edge of **Mousehole** (pronounced mowzl), a picture-postcard fishing village with several pubs, hotels and restaurants. It takes its curious name from either a cave mouth in the cliff south of the village or the narrow gap between its harbour walls. Like St Ives, it attracts artists, and crowds in summer. The excellent *Ship Inn* (☎ 01736-731234) does good seafood and B&B from £35/50 for singles/doubles.

The SWCP from Mousehole to Newlyn mostly follows the road, and is not that pleasant, although you can cut inland via the village of Paul, where a monument commemorates Dolly Pentreath, who died in 1778 – the last person to have spoken only Cornish. It's not particularly attractive, either, from Newlyn Harbour to Penzance, so you may prefer to catch one of the buses leaving regularly instead.

Penzance
The large town of Penzance spreads along the western side of Mount's Bay. It's an interesting place and worth reaching early enough for a stroll around. You might consider two nights here, with a rest and spot of sightseeing. Most interesting is the older part of town around **Chapel St**, lined with quaint shops selling (among other things) art, crafts and books, and some attractive Georgian and Regency buildings, as well as the exuberant Egyptian House. Look out also for the **Union Hotel**, where England's victory at the Battle of Trafalgar was announced, and the **statue of Humphrey Davy**, the local man who invented the miners' safety lamp. Other places to visit include **Penlee House Gallery & Museum**, the **Maritime Museum** and the **National Lighthouse Museum**. Penzance TIC (☎ 01736-362207) is on Station Rd.

The *YHA Hostel* (☎ 01736-362666), an 18th-century mansion in Alverton, on the town's outskirts, charges £10.85 (£5.50 for camping). *Penzance Backpackers* (☎ 01736-363844, e pzbackpack@ndirect.co.uk), also called The Blue Dolphin, is on Alexandra Rd, off the Promenade as you come into town from the west. Beds cost £9 and there's a kitchen for self-catering.

Penzance has a great many B&Bs and hotels, especially along Alexandra Rd, where the *Pendennis Hotel* (☎ 01736-363823), charging from £15 to £21, is a good cheap option. Morrab Rd also has many options, including *Kimberley House* (☎ 01736-362727), opposite the Penlee House Gallery, from around £18. Walker-friendly places include *Woodstock Guesthouse* (☎ 01736-369049, 29 Morrab Rd), charging £14 to £25; and *Trewella Guesthouse* (☎ 01736-363818, 18 Mennaye Rd), from £15 (or £17 en suite).

The Promenade is another happy hotel hunting ground. Just off the Promenade, *The Summer House* (☎ 01736-363744), on Cornwall Terrace, is highly recommended with stylish double rooms from £55 to £75 and a good restaurant. There are further choices on bohemian Chapel St, including the *Georgian House Hotel* (☎ 01736-365664), charging £18 (£21 en suite).

Also on Chapel St are two popular pubs serving food: the kitschy *Admiral Benbow*, crowded with figureheads and other nautical decor; and the *Turk's Head*, more sedate and cosy. Nearby, the more stylish (and more pricey) *Bar Coco's* serves tapas and cappuccinos. *Dandelions*, at 39a Causeway Head, is a vegetarian cafe and takeaway with daily specials like vegetable and cheese ratatouille for £3.25.

Day 10: Penzance to Porthleven
13mi (21km), 5–7 hours
Today is one of the easiest (or least tiring) sections, although the final few miles can be a nasty sting in the tail. If you didn't have time for sightseeing yesterday, you could spend a few hours in Penzance before setting out today.

Leave Penzance by following the path from the train station car park, which runs between the beach and the railway line. The trail then trundles along Mount's Bay beach to **Marazion**, another tourist honeypot with a selection of pubs and shops. Just offshore you can't miss **St Michael's Mount** – a rocky islet topped by an elaborate castle, which – despite ancient appearances – was mostly built only a century or so ago (see boxed text).

St Michael's Mount

In 1070 the island of St Michael's Mount was granted to a group of Benedictine monks, who built a priory here. (The same monks also built the similar Mont St Michel off Normandy.) It later became a castle, although remained a place of pilgrimage, and in 1659 was converted into the private house of the St Aubyn family – who still live here. Now a National Trust property, it's open to the public.

At low tide you can walk across the causeway to the mount from Marazion, but at high tide it's cut off, although in summer a ferry carries you over and lets you save your legs for the stiff climb up to the house. It's open 10.30am to 5.30pm Monday to Friday, April to October; entry is £4.40.

Beyond Marazion take the path along the cliff top. It's been eroded in places, but the path is just as regularly diverted. Prussia Cove is named after the King of Prussia Inn, which was run by a notorious 18th-century smuggler. In 1947 Cornwall's worst-ever shipwreck happened here when the *Warspite* battleship ran aground.

The SWCP rounds Hoe Point then follows the lovely beach of **Praa Sands** (with delicious cream teas at the first *cafe* you reach) and then climbs onto the spectacular cliffs and past the remains of the Wheal Prosper and Wheal Trewavas mines. The cliff edge here is dangerously crumbly, so the SWCP runs slightly inland to **Tregear Point**, where you pass a memorial cross set up by a vicar who decided shipwreck victims should be buried in consecrated ground (until then they'd been buried outside the churchyard).

Porthleven
The scenic fishing village of Porthleven has several pubs and shops dotted around the harbour, including the famous *Ship Inn*, which does excellent, good-value food. There's B&B at *Seefar* (☎ 01326-573778), from £16; *An Mordros Hotel* (☎ 01326-562236), from £17 to £25; and at *Pentre House* (☎ 01326-574493), for a similar price. All are beautifully situated on the hill above the harbour.

Day 11: Porthleven to Lizard Point
13mi (21km), 5–7 hours
The first part of today's walk is generally easy going and with spectacular scenery, but the last section can be tiring.

Leaving Porthleven, follow Loe Bar Rd and Mounts Rd from the far end of the harbour, passing the old coastguard station. Very soon you pass **the Loe**, Cornwall's largest natural body of freshwater, separated from the sea by Porthleven Sands. Legend says this was where King Arthur abandoned his sword Excalibur, so keep an eye out for mythical activity. You're more likely to see wading birds.

At low tide you can walk along the beach to Gunwalloe Fishing Cove. The SWCP then continues round Halzephron Cliff to Dollar Cove, before cutting across the headland and continuing beside the Towans golf course. It's well worth diverting onto the headland to examine **Gunwalloe church**, which has an unusual detached bell tower cut into the cliff-face. In the 11th century, when the Domesday Book was compiled, Gunwalloe had a large population, but the church now stands in splendid isolation with the sea threatening to cut it off from the mainland altogether.

South of Poldhu Point the SWCP passes a memorial from another era – the **Marconi Monument**, which commemorates the first transatlantic telegraphic communication in 1901. From here you drop to Polurrian Cove, then up and over to pretty Mullion Cove. Look out for nesting sea birds on Mullion Island, a short way offshore. Places to stay nearby include walker-friendly *Trenance Farm* (☎ 01326-240639), charging from £19 to £23.

Some excellent cliff-top walking follows, all the way to **Kynance Cove**, where coloured rock has been attracting tourists since the 18th century and is still busy today. The offshore islands – Asparagus Island, Sugarloaf Rock, the Bellows and the Bishop – can be reached on foot at low tide.

To return to the SWCP, cross a footbridge and pass a cafe to reach the top of the cliff. The route then wanders past old workings (where serpentine rock – a lustrous dark green or brown – was quarried) to reach **Lizard Point**, Britain's most southerly headland, famous for its mild climate, complex geology and associated unusual flora. Its name comes from the Cornish words *lis* (meaning 'palace') and *ard* (meaning 'high'). Today the highest feature of the point is the lighthouse (which can usually be visited during the afternoon). The nearby *cafes* are open year-round.

Lizard

Just inland from Lizard Point, in the village of Lizard, B&Bs include friendly *Green Cottage* (☎ 01326-290099), for £15. The famous Most Southerly House no longer does accommodation, so the most southerly

B&B is now at the most southerly farm, *Tregullas* (☎ 01326-290226), charging £20. For a taste of luxury, the *Housel Bay Hotel* (☎ 01326-290417), Britain's (you've guessed it) most southerly hotel, is right on the trail, charging from £60 per double.

Day 12: Lizard Point to Coverack
11mi (17.5km), 4–6 hours
This is another spectacular day along the cliffs. The trail begins quite easily for the first few miles, but after Cadgwith it gets tougher. Geologists will revel in the fine selection of rocks on display.

Just before Cadgwith you'll pass the **Devil's Frying Pan**, a vast crater probably caused by the collapse of a cave. Cadgwith itself is a particularly attractive Cornish fishing village with pretty thatched cottages. Stop for a pint and a crab sandwich at the *Cadgwith Cove Inn*, or clotted cream donuts at the *tearooms* in a former pilchard cellar.

Past Caerleon Cove and the ruins of another old serpentine works, **Kennack Sands** is popular with families in summer and there are several beach cafes. A final set of steep climbs over the headlands of Beagles Point, Pedn Boar, Black Head and Chynhalls Point brings you to Coverack.

Coverack
On the way into the old port of Coverack you pass a lot of modern bungaloid development, but this is a good place to overnight. The *YHA Hostel* (☎ 01326-280687) is up a steep hill and charges £9.80, and £5 for camping. Good B&Bs include the very walker-friendly *Mellon House* (☎ 01326-280482), just off the trail, charging £18; *The Croft* (☎ 01326-280387), a vegetarian nonsmoking place just north of the village, charging from £17 to £22; and the small but welcoming *Bakery Cottage* (☎ 01326-280474), similarly priced. *The Paris Hotel* is good for evening meals.

Day 13: Coverack to Helford
13mi (21km), 5–7 hours
This is a moderately easy day, following the coast for much of the way but heading inland for a stretch to avoid disused quarries.

From Coverack take the road past the beach and keep straight on past the houses to the fields, keeping to the path closest to the sea; this runs to Lowland Point, a raised beach. From here pick your way through quarry workings to Godrevy Cove, before turning inland to Rosenithon and Porthoustock.

Beyond Porthallow (pronounced pralla) you meet the coast again and an excellent pub, *The Five Pilchards*, right on the beach. Pictures on the wall tell the story of the many shipwrecks on the Manacles, a mile out to sea.

The SWCP then continues to Nare Head and Nare Point, with fine views of the mouth of the River Helford. In the tiny village of Gillan, *The Tregildry Hotel* (☎ 01326-231378) offers smart accommodation from £70, including dinner.

Your final obstacle is **Gillan Creek**, which can be crossed an hour either side of low water, although we heard from two walkers who still had water up to their waists. You're better off keeping to the official route: Go inland round the head of the creek and return to the coast for a final short stretch leading into Helford.

Helford

The picture-postcard village of Helford is the country retreat of such luminaries as Tim Rice and Pete Townsend. *The Shipwright's Arms* is a popular thatched pub, while B&B at the equally quaint *Pengwedhen* (☎ *01326-231481*) costs from £20. The next nearest B&Bs are *Landrivick Farm* (☎ *01326-231686)*, at Manaccan, about 20 minutes' uphill across fields from Helford, which offers a very friendly and comfortable service for £24, with evening meals by arrangement; and *Hideaway* (☎ *01326-221392)*, west of Helford towards Mawgan, charging from £16. Both places offer a pick-up from Helford if required. If these places are full, there are more options in the village of Mawnan Smith, on the north bank of the river.

Day 14: Helford to Falmouth

10mi (16km), 4–5 hours
The last lap from Helford to Falmouth is a breeze compared to the stiff up-and-down

stages you've encountered in the last two weeks – a relaxing finish to this finest of coast walks.

The day begins by catching the ferry from Helford Point across the river to Helford Passage, but this only operates from Easter to the end of October and is subject to weather and tidal conditions. Check departure times the night before. If the ferry isn't running, you're faced with an 8.5mi detour or a bus (weekdays only) to Falmouth.

Assuming the ferry is available, from the north shore of the Helford River the SWCP proceeds through Durgan, where a half-mile inland detour leads to **Glendurgan**, a tree-filled garden (with *tearoom)* open to the public Tuesday to Saturday through the summer (entry £3.50).

You then continue past a final collection of wonderfully Cornish names – Porthallack, Mawnan Shear, Parson's Beach, Rosemullion Head, Gatamala Cove, Maenporth – to round Pennance Point and reach Falmouth. Purists will notice the path does a loop round **Pendennis Castle** – an impressive fortress on a rocky buttress just east of the town. The SWCP then leads along the seafront to Prince of Wales Pier – which marks your journey's end.

Falmouth

Not Cornwall's most exciting town, Falmouth is nonetheless a tourist centre with plenty of services. As a port it came to prominence in the 17th century as the terminal for the Post Office packet boats that took mail to America. The dockyard is still important for ship repairs and building. The TIC (☎ 01326-312300) is on Killigrew St.

B&Bs include *Castle Crest* (☎ *01326-313572, 23 Castle Drive)* with views across Falmouth Bay, charging £18. Nearer the centre, Melvill Rd is lined with B&Bs, including *Ivanhoe* (☎ *01326-319083, No 7)*, large and comfortable, charging £20 to £24; *Melvill House* (☎ *01326-316645, No 52)*, charging £19 to £25; and the very walker-friendly *Clearwater Hotel* (☎ *01326-311344, No 59)*, a small family-run place with comfortable rooms from £18 and long-stay parking. Also good is the *Ambelside Guesthouse*

(☎ *01326-319630, 9 Marlborough Rd*), charging from £18.

For food, the central **Kings Head** pub is a perennial favourite. In the Old Brewery Yard, just off the High St, is **Cinnamon Girl**, a wholefood vegetarian cafe, and **Mavericks Café**, also open for dinner.

If you want a celebratory splurge (or have had enough of looking at the sea) you could do worse than stay at **Penmere Manor** (☎ *01326-211411*), on Mongleath Rd, a Georgian country house – allegedly haunted – in five acres of garden, 15 minutes' walk from the town centre, where B&B in the summer season costs £50 to £60.

Other Walks

We have described in detail the Cornwall section of the South West Coast Path. If you want to do more, these basic outlines of the other three sections will be useful.

SOMERSET & NORTH DEVON

The official start of the entire SWCP is the seaside resort of Minehead. With a large holiday camp and associated paraphernalia, this may not be your best introduction. However, you're very quickly free of the tackiness and walking through Exmoor National Park, with the chance to see wild red deer. The cliffs here are extremely high, which makes for strenuous walking. The highest point of the entire trail is Great Hangman (318m), near Combe Martin.

Lynton and Lynmouth are delightful villages linked to each other by a Victorian cliff railway, but very busy in summer. The scenery gets less dramatic as you head south for Ilfracombe and Mortehoe, passing some good sandy beaches, again very popular in summer. Farther south, there's fine cliff walking between tacky Westward Ho! (the only town in Britain – and possibly the world – with an exclamation point in its name) and tiny Clovelly, which is so 'chocolate-boxy' that it has had to start charging admission.

You cross into Cornwall and past another popular beach resort at Bude, but from then on the coast gets rockier and the villages

smaller. Tintagel's dubious connections with King Arthur have made it a popular tourist spot, but the section beyond to Port Isaac is very quiet and wild. This section ends at the village of Rock, from where a ferry crosses the River Camel to Padstow, the start of the Cornwall section described earlier.

SOUTH DEVON

The Cornwall section of this route ends at Falmouth, from where you can cross by ferry to St Mawes, after which the SWCP pushes through the delightful Roseland Peninsula and the villages of Portloe and Mevagissey. The town of St Austell is busy, although the old port can be a picture on a sunny day when the tall ships are in dock.

After St Austell you pass some immensely popular small Cornish resorts – Fowey, Polperro and Looe. Then you leave Cornwall, reach Devon and follow Whitsand Bay to Rame Head. You may wish to use buses to skip the conurbation of Plymouth (although the new waterfront walkway is pleasant and interesting). Pick up the trail on Plymouth's far side and continue to Bigbury-on-Sea, where Burgh Island boasts a wonderfully restored Art-Deco hotel, famously frequented by the likes of Noel Coward and Agatha Christie.

Next comes the South Devon Heritage Coast, through pretty Bantham to Salcombe, a medium-sized resort, and then on to delightful Dartmouth with a wide choice of gourmet restaurants and places to stay. A ferry crosses the River Dart to Kingswear, where you continue to Brixham. From there on, however, much of the coastline is one solid seaside resort, often with a railway line shadowing it, as you pass through Torbay, Teignmouth and Dawlish, with only occasional rural, and very beautiful, sections to provide contrast. This section ends just east of Dawlish at the mouth of the River Exe.

DORSET

From Exmouth this final section of the SWCP escapes into the Devon countryside, although Budleigh Salterton, Sidmouth and Seaton are all fair-sized resorts, busy throughout July and August.

Crossing into Dorset you pass Lyme Regis, famous for its fossils and for scenes in the film, *The French Lieutenant's Women*, where Meryl Streep stares out to sea a lot. East again is pretty thatched Abbotsbury with its unique swannery, best visited in May or June to see the cygnets.

The next feature is Chesil Beach, a huge curving bank of stones enclosing the Fleet Lagoon, which eventually leads you to Portland Bill and the large town of Weymouth.

East of Weymouth you can enjoy stunning coastal scenery at Lulworth Cove, Kimmeridge Bay and Chapman's Pool, before swooping round Durlston Head into Swanage, a mediocre seaside resort. A short hop north from here is Studland Point – official end of the SWCP – from where a ferry ride brings you to Poole. If you've walked the whole way at one go, and only the hardiest of long-distance walkers do, this will be the sweetest of journey's ends.

Other Walks in Southern England

In this book we have described a broad selection of walks throughout Southern England, from the eastern coasts of Norfolk and Kent, through the Isle of Wight and the Cotswolds, to Land's End at the country's south-west extremity. Of course, this part of Britain offers many more walking opportunities, and the following few pointers will help you get further and explore for yourself.

THE CHILTERN HILLS
The Chiltern Hills run in a broad band, south-west to north-east, from the banks of the River Thames between Goring and Reading to fizzle out near Aylesbury and Dunstable. These are the nearest 'proper' hills to London, covered in a mix of woods and farmland, and a very popular walking area, especially at weekends. There's an excellent network of footpaths, but don't expect wilderness: The area is also dotted with countless small villages and this is a very well-to-do part of the country, especially popular with wealthy London commuters.

THE NEW FOREST
Visitors to Britain love this name, as the area is more than 1000 years old (William the Conqueror christened it) and there aren't *that* many trees. But apart from these minor matters, it's a wonderful place with several good walking opportunities.

For many years the forest has been designated a Heritage Area, which gives it protected status. It should be a full national park by 2005. The towns of Lyndhurst and Brockenhurst make good bases, with Tourist Information Centres (TICs) and a choice of B&Bs and campsites.

EXMOOR
Exmoor is a wild area of grass and heather-covered hills cut by deep valleys, on the north coast of Devon in south-western England.

The whole area is contained within Exmoor National Park. On the coast itself are spectacularly high cliffs, great beaches, quiet villages and busy seaside resorts. The opportunities for walking are immense. The North Devon section of the **South West Coast Path** (described in the Southern England Long-Distance Walks chapter) runs through the national park from the resort of Minehead – a good place from which to explore the area.

Good bases for walking in the centre of Exmoor include Exford and Simonsbath. Popular bases on the coast are Lynton and Lynmouth, neighbouring villages at the end of the **Two Moors Way**, a long-distance path (LDP) across the south-west peninsula. The first section of the route is described briefly as A South Dartmoor Traverse in the Dartmoor chapter.

The **Tarka Trail** is another LDP that loops through Exmoor, inspired by the classic book *Tarka the Otter* by Henry Willamson. As with all long routes, you don't have to do it end-to-end; useful bases allow for circular walks over a day or weekend.

LONG-DISTANCE PATHS
In the London Region chapter we describe two sections of the **North Downs Way**, which runs south of the capital and into Kent – the 'garden of England'.

There are several other LDPs through this part of Britain, including the **Greensand Way**, which runs from Haselmere in Surrey to Hamstreet, near Ashford in Kent, through farmland, wooded hills and the area's famous hop gardens. The route runs parallel in many places to the North Downs Way but some walkers prefer the latter route – it's not quite as high, but still offers good views across Weald and manages to better escape the sight and sound of traffic. Guidebooks include *Along & Around the Greensand Way* by Bea Cowan.

Another good option is The **Saxon Shore Way**, a 160mi (257km) route round the coast of Kent from Gravesend to Hastings. The route is mostly flat or gently rolling, with some steeper bits along the south coast, through scenery varying from salt marsh to white cliffs, and several coast towns, including navy ports and seaside resorts. There are plenty of pubs and B&Bs along the way, and access by train is straightforward. The best guide is *The Saxon Shore Way*, once again by local specialist Bea Cowan, which includes extracts from Ordnance Survey (OS) 1:25,000 maps.

The route is well waymarked, and sections could be done as weekend excursions from London. I walked the Saxon Shore Way across a number of weekends, with a group of friends. The fitness and stamina requirements are not those of a young mountaineer.

Roger Slade (UK)

ACROSS SOUTHERN ENGLAND

If you're a real mile eater, it's possible to join up several different LDPs to trace a very long route right across Southern England.

In the Wessex chapter we describe the western section of the **Ridgeway**. This ends at Goring, where you could join the eastern section of the **Thames Path** (described in the London Region chapter), leading all the way to London to make a very varied nine- or 10-day walk through Southern England.

If you're searching for something even longer you could start walking at Avonmouth, a port town on the Severn Estuary near Bristol, and follow a path called the **Avon Walkway** through Bristol to Bath, then join the **Kennet & Avon Canal** – the first section of which, to Devizes, is described in the Wessex chapter. The canal path continues from Devizes to Pewsey, where you branch north to Avebury to join the **Ridgeway** and then the **Thames Path** all the way to London.

Another really long walk across the region starts on the South Devon coast at Lyme Regis and follows the **Wessex Ridgeway** path (described under Other Walks in the Wessex chapter) north to Avebury. Here, you could join the **Ridgeway** across the North Wessex Downs and the Chiltern Hills to its official end at Ivinghoe Beacon. This in turn is the start of the **Icknield Way**, which in turn links to the **Peddars Way** (described in the Norfolk chapter). Although only for the serious walker, this 370mi (595km) epic is an ideal way to follow Neolithic, Roman and medieval footprints all the way across Southern England from the Channel to the North Sea and could easily fill a month of your holiday.

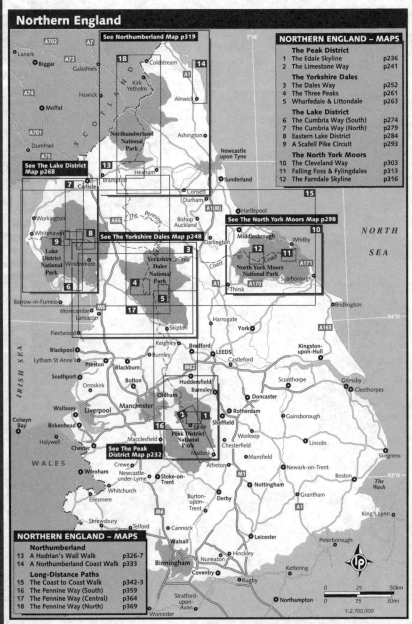

Northern England

See Northumberland Map p319

See The Lake District Map p268

See The Yorkshire Dales Map p248

See The North York Moors Map p298

See The Peak District Map p232

1:2,700,000

The Peak District

The Peak District is a broad area of moors and valleys in the northern part of central England (or the southern part of Northern England, depending on your point of view). Much of the area is contained within the Peak District National Park – one of Britain's largest – spread over much of Derbyshire and parts of Staffordshire, South Yorkshire, Lancashire and Cheshire. Despite often being called simply 'the Peak', this area is notable for its distinct lack of pointed mountain tops – the title actually derives from the name of some early inhabitants. Nevertheless, it is a very popular walking area with a limitless choice of routes of all lengths and standards.

Geologically the area is separated into two parts. The Dark Peak in the north is mostly high moorland covered in heather or peat-bog, sliced by gulleys known as 'groughs' and dotted with rocky outcrops of grey gritstone (a hard, course-grained sandstone), some eroded by the weather into unusual shapes. The White Peak in the south is lower and characterised by a less imposing landscape of pale limestone and fertile farmland.

Surrounded by large cities such as Manchester and Sheffield, the Peak is particularly popular over weekends and holidays when oxygen-starved urbanites invade its quiet serenity in pursuit of walking and other outdoor activities. Records show that the Peak is visited by 22 million people each year – putting the park among the busiest in the world, right up there with Mt Fuji in Japan.

As with other national parks in Britain, the Peak District is not state owned but made up of many different privately owned areas of land. Today, as for thousands of years, many people live and work in the park, engaged in farming and tourism, as well as more controversial industries like quarrying.

The Peak can be explored at any time of year, although in winter, when sunny days turn arctic in less than an hour, walking the upland areas can be a serious business. Even in summer, mist and rain can quickly turn an easy day into an epic adventure. Walking in the White Peak is far less hazardous.

In this chapter we describe two routes, one in the Dark Peak and the other in the White Peak, as samples of what the area has to offer. Use these as tasters and go on to explore for yourself. Some pointers for further walks are given at the end of the chapter.

INFORMATION
Maps
The Peak District is covered by the Ordnance Survey (OS) 1:63,360 *Peak District Touring Map* and OS Landranger 1:50,000 maps No 110 *(Sheffield & Huddersfield)* and No 119 *(Buxton & Matlock)*, but these are not really detailed enough for walking. Much better is the OS Outdoor Leisure 1:25,000 maps No 1 *(The Peak District – Dark Peak Area)* and No 24 *(The Peak District – White Peak Area)*. The latter is especially useful for walks in the White Peak.

Harvey maps also show all the detail you need (and none of the detail you don't). *Dark Peak South* and *Dark Peak North* are both available in the Harvey Walker's Map series at 1:40,000, while *Dark Peak* also comes in the Superwalker 1:25,000 format.

For maps covering individual walks, see Planning in the introduction to each walk.

Books
The Peak District is a popular walking area and very well covered by guidebooks. These can be bought in local Tourist Information Centres (TICs) or the many book and outdoor shops throughout the area. Try the specialist Scarthin Books in Cromford, near Matlock Bath, which also publishes *Family Walks in the White Peak* by Norman Taylor, containing 16 circular 'high interest, low mileage' walks. There's a similar *Dark Peak* guide, also published by Scarthin Books.

For a wider range, the area is comprehensively covered in a trilogy of books: *High Peak Walks*, *White Peak Walks – North* and *White Peak Walks – South* by

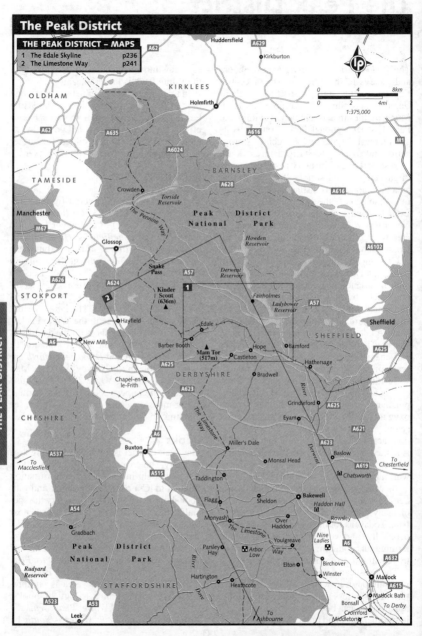

The Peak District

0   4   8km
0   2   4mi
1:375,000

Huddersfield
Kirkburton
KIRKLEES
Holmfirth
OLDHAM
A62
A635
A6024
BARNSLEY
A628
A616
TAMESIDE
Crowden
Torside Reservoir
Peak   District
National   Park
Manchester
The Pennine Way
Howden Reservoir
A6102
Glossop
Snake Pass
Derwent Reservoir
A624
A626
Kinder Scout (636m)
Fairholmes
Ladybower Reservoir
A57
STOKPORT
Hayfield
Edale
Sheffield
New Mills
Barber Booth
SHEFFIELD
A6
Mam Tor (517m)
Hope
Bamford
A625
Castleton
Hathersage
Chapel-en-le-Frith
DERBYSHIRE
Bradwell
Grindleford
A625
A623
Eyam
A621
CHESHIRE
The Limestone Way
Miller's Dale
A623
Baslow
Buxton
Monsal Head
To Chesterfield
A537
A515
Chatsworth
A619
To Macclesfield
Taddington
Flagg
Sheldon
Bakewell
Haddon Hall
Rowsley
A54
Monyash
Over Haddon
Nine Ladies
A6
Gradbach
Peak   District
Parsley Hay
Arbor Low
Youlgreave
Birchover
A632
Rudyard Reservoir
National   Park
Hartington
Heathcote
Elton
Winster
Matlock
River Dove
Bonsall
Matlock Bath
A523
A53
STAFFORDSHIRE
To Ashbourne
Cromford
Middleton
To Derby
A615
Leek

THE PEAK DISTRICT

Mark Richards. Alternatively, *Best Walks in the Peak District* by Frank Duerden is probably the most extensive and informative guide to the Peak District. Also with a good selection of varying lengths and standards is the *Peak District Pathfinder Guide*, published by Jarrold. Highly recommended is *Walks From the Hope Valley Line*, detailing routes from stations along this railway line, which runs through the park.

As in many national parks you can get *Pub Walks in the Peak District* and *Teashop Walks in the Peak District*, both published by Dalesman. Also useful is *The Peak District Youth Hostellers Walking Guide* by Martyn Hanks, which is available from most YHA hostels in the area. The same author also produces single-sheet maps of the area around each hostel with suggested walking routes.

A good bargain option is the handy *Walks About...* series of leaflets. Each covers a set of circular routes around a single area, such as the Hope Valley, Edale and Bakewell, with easy-to-read maps.

For background or maybe a souvenir of your visit, *The Peak District Official National Park Guide* is highly recommended – lavish and stylish without being expensive – with text by local expert Roly Smith and beautiful photos by Ray Manley.

Information Sources

There are many TICs in and around the Peak District. Some are run by local tourist boards, while others are run by the national park authority with exhibitions or displays about the park. These include Bakewell (☎ 01629-813227), Buxton (☎ 01298-25106), Castleton (☎ 01433-620679), Edale (☎ 01433-670207), Matlock (☎ 01629-583388) and Matlock Bath (☎ 01629-55082).

A useful Web site for the Peak District is [W] www.peakdistrict-tourism.gov.uk, which includes a weather forecast service. You can get specific information about the national park from the park authority (☎ 01629-816200, [e] aldern@peakdistrict-npa.gov.uk, [W] www.peak district.org), Aldern House, Bakewell DE45 1AE.

At TICs, shops and some hotels you can pick up *Peak District*, a free newspaper produced annually by the national park authority. It is full of tourist and background information, with a full list of guided walks and other local events.

TICs and many newsagents also sell *The Peak District Bus & Train Timetable*, which as well as public transport details is a pocket source of tourist information, covering places of interest, well-dressing dates (see the boxed text 'Well Dressing' on p242), market days, local services and places for bicycle hire – especially useful if you're planning to spend a few days in the area. It also contains a map showing all bus routes and long paths in the area, including the Limestone Way.

Guided Walks

National park rangers organise an excellent series of guided walks throughout the year. They're free of charge (although you might need to reserve a place) and range from gentle strolls to strenuous all-dayers. For more information, phone the Walks Information Line (☎ 01629-815185).

In summer Hope Valley Railway runs a program of guided walks starting at various train stations along the line (see Getting Around for more details); TICs have details.

The Peak District National Park's study centre at Losehill Hall (☎ 01433-620373), near Castleton, organises courses in subjects like photography and wildlife identification, and runs guided walks with an emphasis on improving skills such as map and compass navigation.

Derbyshire Dales Countryside Service organises guided walks in the White Peak area throughout the year; TICs have leaflets. The local Peakland Walking Holidays (☎ 01298-872801, [e] peakland@walkingholidays.org.uk) offers organised weekend breaks from £150, plus longer guided and self-guided options.

GETTING THERE & AWAY

The main gateway cities and towns to the Peak District are Derby, Sheffield and Manchester, all with good coach and train links to the rest of the country, and easily reached by car.

The Getting Around chapter lists several public transport inquiry lines that provide details of both national and local bus and train services: See the boxed text 'National Transport Information' on p92.

GETTING AROUND

Particularly useful public transport services within the Peak District are the TransPeak bus and the Hope Valley Railway line. The bus service crosses the area several times daily between Derby and Manchester via Matlock, Bakewell and Buxton. The Hope Valley Railway line runs between Sheffield and Manchester through the heart of the Peak, and stops at several train stations where you can walk off the platform and straight into the hills.

The Derbyshire Busline service supplies information for the whole of Derbyshire from two centres: Derby (☎ 01332-292200) and Buxton (☎ 01298-23098). For more information on bus and train times, *The Peak District Bus & Train Timetable* is available from local newsagents (for a more detailed description, see Information Sources earlier).

The Edale Skyline

Distance	11mi (17.5km)
Duration	6 hours
Standard	medium
Start/Finish	Hope
Gateways	Sheffield, Manchester

Summary A circular walk on ridges and across open moor and farmland, mostly on good paths with marvellous views.

The Edale and Hope Valleys, which mark the boundary between the gritstone Dark Peak and the limestone White Peak areas, are among the most attractive valleys in the national park. The geology also affects the human landscape: North of Edale lies heather-covered moor, while south of Hope the hills are covered in a patchwork of fields. This walk gives you a taste of both.

The Hope Valley is broad and contains several villages, including Hope and Castleton, a tourist honeypot famous for its nearby

underground 'show caves'. Another feature is the cement factory, the chimneys of which incongruously billow smoke amid this lush and tranquil scene. Aesthetically it's an eyesore but economically it's a lifeline that has prevented depopulation of the area.

The Edale Valley is more enclosed, less populated and seems more remote, flanked on its southern side by a steep grassy ridge and to the north by the notoriously boggy expanse of Kinder Scout. Much quieter than Castleton, the village of Edale, at the western end of its namesake valley, is the start of the Pennine Way (see the Northern England Long-Distance Paths chapter).

The traditional Edale Skyline route keeps to the high ground and makes a complete circuit of the Edale Valley. This is a very satisfying but very long route, so we suggest a shorter version here. You miss none of panoramic views over the Derbyshire hills but do avoid some of the longer, wilder, boggier sections. Paths are well defined but muddy in places. There are few signposts, so the ability to use a map and compass is crucial as weather conditions can change very rapidly. Nevertheless, in the right conditions this route is a beauty and enthusiastic walkers will find it a very satisfying day excursion.

Direction, Distance & Duration

We describe this circular route in an anticlockwise direction, so you can complete two-thirds of the distance before having a relaxed lunch in Edale village. If your timing is different you can easily do it the other way around. The total distance is 11mi. This will take about six hours of walking, not including lunch or other long stops, so you should allow seven to eight hours in total.

Alternatives An alternative start/finish point is Edale village, from where you could walk to Hope. For a shorter walk you can do the route as described from Hope to Edale (6.5mi), then get the train from Edale back to Hope. Information on places to stay and eat in Edale is included in the Pennine Way section of the Northern England Long-Distance Paths chapter.

You can also extend this route by staying on the Kinder Plateau longer and descending to Edale village via Grindsbrook Clough.

If you are feeling strong, the longest option (20mi) is to keep to the Edale Skyline for the whole walk, missing Edale village and continuing round the western end of the valley, over Bown Knoll, Rushup Edge and Mam Tor. This is best left for long, fine summer days.

PLANNING
Maps
For the Edale Skyline you will need either the OS Outdoor Leisure 1:25,000 map No 1 *(The Peak District – Dark Peak Area)* or the handy 1:40,000 Harvey Walker's *Dark Peak South* map.

Information Sources
The TIC at Edale (☎ 01433-670207) is the best source of information on all aspects of the area, including accommodation, food, transport and weather forecasts.

PLACES TO STAY & EAT
Hope
Among the walker-friendly B&Bs in Hope are *The Old Blacksmith's Cottage* (☎ 01433-621407, ✉ judith@woodbinecafe.freeserve .co.uk), next to the Woodbine Cafe on the main street, where double rooms are £38 to £45. *The Woodroffe Arms* (☎ 01433-620351), opposite, is a lively, friendly pub that welcomes walkers with bar snacks, meals from £6 to £9 and B&B at £59 per double. Nearby is the rather uninspiring *Old Hall Hotel* (☎ 01433-620160), where a double costs £40 for the room only – you'll have to go to the cafe for breakfast!

There are more choices on (or just off) Edale Rd, leading north out of the village. These include *Chapman Farm* (☎ 01433-620297), with just two guestrooms, charging from £25/40 for singles/doubles rooms; and *Mill Farm* (☎ 01433-621181), another small place well used to catering for walkers, charging from £22.50.

A bit farther up the road, *Underleigh House* (☎ 01433-621372, ✉ underleigh .house@btinternet.com) is friendly and good

quality, charging from £66 per double (£60 if you stay three nights), with singles from £30 on weekdays and £46 at weekends. Next door is *Moorgate* (☎ 01433-621219), run by Countrywide Holidays, catering specifically for walkers, with B&B from £22 or £25 en suite.

Also on Edale Rd is our favourite pub, *The Cheshire Cheese* (☎ 01433-620381), a no-frills place with an old countryside feel, a good range of beer and a selection of filling lunches from £5 and dinners from £7. It also does B&B in large en suite rooms for £60 per double.

The Woodbine Cafe, on the main road, is a very popular place among walkers and cyclists for breakfast, lunch and teas, with a sumptuous selection of home-made cakes and a roaring open fire on cold days. This is also a hang-out for roosting paragliders; the cafe has a direct radio link with a weather gauge on Rushup Edge, so the flyers can see if it's worth leaving their table. Next door is *Courtyard Cafe* with a nice sunny conservatory and an impressive menu of healthy soups, salads, baguettes and 'no chips' meals.

For food on the walk, Hope has a *shop* (open daily) and a *deli-bakery*, both selling picnic ingredients.

GETTING TO/FROM THE WALK
Bus Hope is very well served by frequent buses from Sheffield, which go on to Castleton, but your handiest service is the train.

Train Frequent and very convenient trains run between Sheffield and Manchester, stopping at Hope and Edale train stations – among others – about 10 times per day (slightly less on Sunday). Very few other national parks have such handy access. Make sure you get the stopping train though – otherwise you'll see the Peak at high speed from the Trans Pennine Express! Timetables are available from local TICs.

Car Hope is on the A625 between Sheffield and Chapel-en-le-Frith, which is linked to Manchester by the A6. The car park in the centre of the village is usually very busy on summer weekends.

THE WALK
Hope to Win Hill
1.5mi (2.2km), 45 minutes–1 hour

Leave Hope village by going north along Edale Rd. Continue for 300m, fork right onto a lane and follow this until you pass under a railway bridge. Turn immediately right onto a track, which leads you uphill to Twitchill Farm. (Now converted into holiday cottages, the farm is an attractive sight but also a reflection of recent developments in countryside economy – tourism makes more money than farming.)

Go through the yard and then through a gate into steep fields. The path is well signposted to Win Hill, although not always visible in the grass. Continue diagonally up to the ridge to a junction of paths on the ridge crest, where you turn right and walk for about 700m to reach the summit of **Win Hill** (462m). Stop to enjoy the views here and look across (west) to Lose Hill, which with Win Hill marks the entrance to Edale Valley.

(Lose Hill was once spelt Loose Hill but was changed after a battle many centuries ago when the victorious and the vanquished sides retired to a hill each.) While you are resting beware of the greedy (and fearless) sheep who try to snatch your sandwiches.

Win Hill to Edale
5mi (8km), 2½–3½ hours

Retrace your steps to the junction of paths and continue straight on (north-westerly) along the broad ridge crest. Up here you really get the feeling of being near the sky. Panoramic views and a fresh breeze will blow away any cobwebs in mind and body. Another path (a former Roman road) joins from the left, but keep going along the main ridge, with a plantation now on your right, to reach **Hope Cross** – an old stone marker built in 1737 and showing routes to Hope, Edale, Glossop and Sheffield.

Go through a gate and continue for about 300m to another gate. Here a signpost to

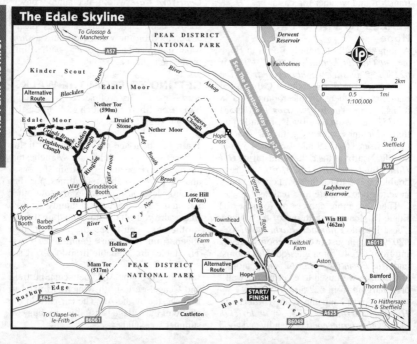

The Edale Skyline

Edale sends you left down a track into the small, steep-sided valley of Jaggers Clough. If it's been windy on the ridge, you can get a bit of peace down here and even listen to the birds.

Cross the stream and continue on the track leading towards Edale for about 50m until it bends up sharply to the left. Don't follow this but carry straight on along an overgrown path leading up Jaggers Clough itself. This path is not signposted and is easy to miss, so take care.

Warning

In spring or autumn, after rain, the stream may be full and the path up Jaggers Clough blocked. In winter it may also be icy and dangerous. To avoid this, either retrace your steps to the signpost near Hope Cross and continue north then west on clear paths round the head of the valley, or take the direct low-level path to Edale.

Assuming the Jaggers Clough path is passable, continue up this delightful valley past miniature waterfalls, crystal clear pools and clumps of hardy rowan trees. Remember to look back, too, for great views of Win Hill and your route so far. The path crosses the stream a few times. Sometimes it's so narrow you have to use the stream, climbing up the rocks or skirting along the edge. Just before the top it becomes quite steep and rocky.

When the gradient eases you meet a good path running along the southern edge of the Edale Moor, much more commonly called the Kinder Plateau after the high north-western part of the Kinder Scout moor. Turn left (south-west) and follow this path for about 1.5mi past an outcrop called the Druid's Stone, with great views down to your left (south) over the Edale valley to the ridge between Mam Tor and Lose Hill, which is your route this afternoon.

When you reach the top of a ridge called Ringing Roger, a path leads down towards Edale, but it's more enjoyable to continue on the high ground a little farther along the top of a beautiful valley called **Golden Clough**.

You'll join up with a path that leads straight down this valley to meet the path coming down Grindsbrook Clough at the head of a plantation. (Alternatively, you could also continue along the edge of Kinder Scout a little farther again and then come down Grindsbrook Clough itself.) Either way, the paths all lead downhill, finishing with a gentle, pleasant stroll through the trees, across a footbridge and into the northern end of **Edale** village, which is called Grindsbrook Booth.

Nearby is a famous pub called *The Old Nag's Head* and about a mile down the road, near the train station, is *The Rambler Inn*. Both pubs offer bar food and are worth visiting for lunch, although at both places the menu is surprisingly dreary and the atmosphere disappointing. As an alternative, try the basic *cafe* at the train station, which is popular with walkers, serving hot drinks, snacks and meals – mostly with chips.

Edale to Lose Hill
4.5mi (7km), 2–3 hours
From The Old Nag's Head walk south through the village to reach the church. From The Rambler Inn, retrace your steps northwards to reach the church. Opposite the church is an old cemetery. Turn left here, off the road and onto a footpath (signposted). The path crosses fields and skirts the *campsite* by the visitors centre, to go under a railway bridge and then meet the road that runs along the Edale Valley. Go straight across and onto a good farm track, which leads steeply uphill to meet a path that then leads even more steeply up to the ridge between Mam Tor and Lose Hill. You reach the ridge crest at a low point called **Hollins Cross**. Pause to savour the view over the next valley, with the village of Castleton below. To the west you can make out the collapsed sides of Mam Tor and, if conditions are right, the sky will be full of paragliders.

From Hollins Cross head east along the ridge path with excellent views down in both directions. It will take you about half an hour to reach **Lose Hill** summit (476m) for a final look at the panorama before descending. You meet a low path from Hollins Cross at a stile. Cross the stile and continue descending with a wall on your left to Lose-hill Farm. After the farm the path divides. The left branch (straight on) goes to Hope via Townhead, Edale Rd and *The Cheshire Cheese* pub. The right branch goes over another stile and then through fields directly to Hope, *The Woodbine Cafe* and the cream tea you've been waiting for all day.

The Limestone Way

Distance	26mi (42km)
Duration	2 days
Standard	easy-medium
Start	Matlock
Finish	Castleton
Gateways	Matlock, Derby, Sheffield

Summary A long but easy-going route on paths, tracks and lanes through valleys and farmland, neatly avoiding busy areas.

The Limestone Way was originally designed as a route through the White Peak from Matlock to Castleton in the Hope Valley – where White gives way to Dark. More recently, the route was altered slightly to pass west of Matlock, then extended southwards to Rocester, a village north of Uttoxeter, where it links with another route called the Staffordshire Way (see Other Walks at the end of this chapter). This section, however, describes the original route in a northbound direction.

The limestone country of the White Peak is characterised by steep-sided dales cloaked in ash woodland, while the higher land is crossed by narrow fields edged with dry-stone walls. Before the onslaught of modern intensive farming methods, these fields were multicoloured with some of the most flower-rich grassland in Britain. Commonplace plants mingled with rarer species and harboured a wonderful array of invertebrates that, in turn, attracted many birds. Although chemical fertilisers and uniform rye-grass have done away with much of this, some meadows of flowers do still exist and can be appreciated on the route. Look out for orchids in spring, particularly along the dales (see the boxed text 'Peak District Rarities' for more details).

Despite the natural beauty, the limestone dales of the Peak District also have a hard edge. The first part of the route follows tracks used by generations of lead miners, and centuries of small-scale industries have left a rash of shafts and spoil heaps that pockmark the hillsides. Although many are capped, some mines are still a potential hazard, so don't leave the path in these areas.

Direction, Distance & Duration

The Limestone Way can be walked in either direction but is described here south to north from Matlock to Castleton. Some of the route is signposted and waymarked (sporting a Derby Ram logo) but this is sporadic, and as the whole area is crisscrossed with a network of other paths, carrying a map is essential. The route described here is 26mi. We have described it as a two-day walk but it could be completed in a long summer day (10 to 14 hours).

day	from	to	mi/km
1	Matlock	Monyash	13.5/21.5
2	Monyash	Castleton	12.5/20.5

Alternatives The Limestone Way is never far from a bus route, so there are many options for doing just part of the route before returning to your start point. On top of this, the White Peak is covered with footpaths, so endless opportunities exist for shorter circuits incorporating parts of the Way.

If you want to tackle something longer, you could do the route north to south, from Castleton via Bonsall (near Matlock) all the way to Rocester, a total distance of 46mi.

PLANNING
Maps & Books

Most of the Limestone Way is marked on the OS Outdoor Leisure 1:25,000 map No 24 (*The Peak District – White Peak Area*). Castleton and the final 2.5mi are found on map No 1 (*The Peak District – Dark Peak Area*) of the same series.

Derbyshire Dales District Council publishes two leaflets: *The Limestone Way, Castleton to Matlock* and *The Limestone*

Peak District Rarities

In spring and summer many dales in the White Peak are full of flowers specially adapted to living on the thin limestone soil. One of these is Jacob's ladder, found almost exclusively in the dales of the White Peak, particularly in Lathkill Dale near Buxton – for a description of this area, see Other Walks at the end of this chapter. It has large blue flowers and ladder-like leaves, which give it its name.

Also rare, and especially enchanting, are orchids, flowering in April and May. Unfortunately, orchids have become rare due to generations of collectors flouting the law against picking rare flowers. This despite the fact that orchids need their own special soil fungi to grow, so won't germinate in people's gardens. As people are marginally better informed these days, you should see a few orchids if you walk here at the right time. Needless to say, these should be left in peace.

Way, Matlock to Rocester, both in a north to south direction with strip maps and useful background information. These are free of charge and available from local TICs.

For more detail, *The Limestone Way* by R & E Haydock and B & D Allen covers both directions, with several circular walks based on the route.

Information Sources

The TICs at Matlock Bath (☎ 01629-55082), Matlock (☎ 01629-583388) and Castleton (☎ 01433-620679) can advise on accommodation, public transport, local events and other walking options in the area.

GETTING TO/FROM THE WALK

Bus From Derby at least 10 local buses per day run to Matlock, at the start of the walk, via Matlock Bath. If you're coming from the other direction, the same bus service also runs between Bakewell and Matlock.

From Castleton, at the end of the walk, buses go to Bakewell (three times per day), from where you can get another bus back to Matlock. From Castleton buses also go to

Sheffield (at least 10 per day) via Hope, where you can switch to the train, but make sure you tell the driver you want the station (about a mile beyond the village centre). On summer weekends there's a regular shuttle bus between Castleton and Hope train station.

If you need to 'escape' along the route, buses go from Monyash to Bakewell on school days. Much better is the TransPeak Bus, which you can catch where the Limestone Way crosses the A6 near Taddington. This bus runs north to Buxton and Manchester or south to Matlock and Derby.

Train Local trains run regularly (except winter Sundays) between Derby and Matlock via Matlock Bath. From the finish at Castleton your nearest train station is at Hope village, 3mi east, from where you can reach either Manchester or Sheffield (for details, see Getting to/from the Walk in the Edale Skyline walk earlier).

Car Matlock is on the A6 north of Derby. There are two car parks near the train station; the long-stay one is free.

Castleton is on the A625 between Sheffield and Chapel-en-le-Frith; parking is expensive and limited.

THE WALK
Matlock

The country town of Matlock is easy to reach by public transport, with banks, shops and a good choice of places to stay. The TIC (☎ 01629-583388) is on Crown Square.

The excellent *YHA Hostel* (☎ 01629-582983) is on Bank Rd, just up the hill from Crown Square, charging £10.85.

B&Bs include the very friendly and flexible *Tuckers Guesthouse* (☎ 01629-583018, 48 Dale Rd), set back from the road, charging £23/37 for singles/doubles. Also good is *Kensington Villa* (☎ 01629-57627, 84 Dale Rd), from £20. Nearby, *Riverbank House* (☎ 01629-582593), on Derwent Ave (off Old Englishe Rd), charges from £23. A little farther along Dale Rd, beyond the railway bridge, *The Boat House Inn* (☎ 01629-583776) has rooms from £17.50 (£3 to £5 for breakfast); it also does evening bar food.

Along the road to Matlock are more B&Bs, including the walker-friendly **The Firs** (☎ 01629-582426, 180 Dale Rd), with a tariff of £20.

For food, Matlock has lots of options, mostly in Dale Rd, including **The Strand**, a stylish cafe-restaurant with main courses from £10 (or a two-course midweek set menu for the same price). Elsewhere in town you can get takeaway pizzas, kebabs, Chinese or Indian.

Good pubs include **The Crown**, on Crown Square, serving food; and **The Thorn Tree**, on Bank Rd.

Matlock Bath

Matlock Bath, a large village about 2mi from Matlock itself, is decked out somewhat bizarrely as a seaside town, complete with promenade, gift shops, ice cream, discarded fish-and-chip wrappers and a cable car. At the southern end of the main street is a grand old building from the Victorian heyday called **the Pavillion**, which now houses a small museum and the TIC (☎ 01629-55082). Other attractions include the famous 'illuminations', which delight crowds at weekends from late August to late October.

This appeal also merits many hotels and B&Bs. Those welcoming walkers include the cheap and cheerful **Wooodlands View** (☎ 01629-55762, 226 Dale Rd), from £15; and nonsmoking **Abraham House** (☎ 01629-583909, 216 Dale Rd), charging £18.50. On North Parade (the main street), smarter B&Bs include **Fountain Villa** (☎ 01629-56195, No 86) and **Ashdale Guesthouse** (☎ 01629-57826, No 92), both charging around £20 to £25.

Budget travellers should definitely head for **LettinGo Backpackers** (☎ 01629-580686, ⓔ n&j@lettingo.freeserve.co.uk), on the corner of Brunswood and Holme Rds, a very friendly and comfortable place where beds in small dorms cost £11.50 and a double is £26. There's a self-catering kitchen and the owners are keen walkers, so can advise on local routes.

Matlock Bath has many cafes and takeaways, but for a sit-down meal **The Balti** is a justifiably popular Indian restaurant with a good-value selection of meat and vegetarian dishes. Nearby, **Ell's Rib & Chop House** serves main courses for £8 to £10 and, despite the name, has a good range of veggie food too. The Italian **La Caverna** is another popular place.

Good pubs include **The Princess Victoria**, with good beer, and **The Fishpond**, centre of the local live music scene. Both pubs also do cheap and reasonable bar food.

For healthy picnic items go to **Beano's** wholefood shop.

Day 1: Matlock to Monyash
13.5mi (21.5 km), 6½–9 hours

From the car park near the train station go up Snitterton Rd. After 100m turn left onto a path, which goes steeply uphill crossing many fields. As you catch your breath, glance behind to views over Matlock and the Derwent Valley, with High Tor and Riber Castle (actually a Victorian sham) behind.

Pass to the right of Masson Lees Farm, then bear right along the edges of fields skirting **Masson Hill**, known locally as the 'first hill of the Pennines' – the area's southernmost hill over 1000ft. Follow a narrow track on the left to a junction where a left turn leads down a steep path to the stone market cross at the village of Bonsall. The **King's Head** pub is nearby but if it's not too early for eating or drinking, **The Barley Mow**, at the top end of the village, is a better choice.

(If you stayed in Matlock Bath, go up Holme Rd, then up Upperwood Rd, turning off on a path (still going up) that follows tracks and paths directly to Bonsall.)

Now you're walking on the Limestone Way proper and the signposting gets better. Keep the King's Head on your left, cross the village main street and follow the Way as it climbs a few steps between walls, then crosses a field to reach Upper Town. Where the path meets a lane, go straight on for about 200m to the next road junction. Go through a gate and follow the Way north across the field. By a small barn, ignore the path going straight on and keep left – the Way is the less obvious path along the wall.

This leads you to a track called Moorlands Lane, where you go left, then right through a stile and across the fields of Bonsall Moor. The Way crosses more fields and a few lanes and tracks before swinging more westerly. Just past an outcrop called Luntor Rocks, make sure you keep left and stick to the track that runs along the hillside above the village of Winster. Look out for the rather organic-looking bench made from wooden poles and strips of lead – a reminder of the industry that once thrived here.

The track meets a main road near a junction and the **Lead Ore House** – another relic from mining days (the history of this old building is explained on a plaque). From here you follow another track called the Portway (once a packhorse route, which in turn followed an even older trade route dating from prehistoric times), which meets the main street running through Elton on the eastern edge of the village.

Detour left (west) along the main street into the village itself. The classic *Elton Cafe* (☎ 01629-650217) does B&B for £21 and serves fine food such as home-made soup, things with chips (£2 to £4) and a selection of cakes, making it a mecca for cyclists and walkers. Unfortunately the cafe is open weekends only. There's also a *YHA Hostel* (☎ 01629-650394).

If you can resist the lure of cholesterol in Elton, cross the main street and continue north on the Portway, now called Dudwood Lane. At the bottom of the hill, just before meeting a main road, cross a stile on the left and head up a track before branching left onto a path passing between the prominent gritstone rock outcrops of Cratcliffe (on the right) and **Robin Hood's Stride** (on the left). This is a popular picnic site and a playground for local rock climbers. Robin Hood may well have been here as in medieval times Sherwood Forest (the legendary brigand's traditional Nottingham home) covered much of Derbyshire and would have been an ideal spot for wealth redistribution. Legend has him leaping between pinnacles on top of the outcrop, although this would have been quite a feat. (Incidentally, Robin Hood's trusty lieutenant, Little John, is buried at Hathersage, about 4mi east of Castleton – the end of the Limestone Way.)

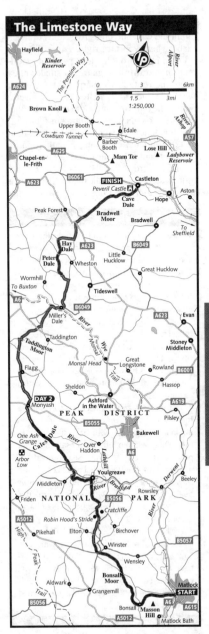

THE PEAK DISTRICT

Beyond Robin Hood's Stride go through a gap in the wall and cross two fields to reach a lane where you turn right. After 300m go left on a path through a nice patch of woodland, then down to a gate in a small valley where the route turns sharp right. Continue over fields downhill all the way to meet a lane on the outskirts of the old and traditional White Peak village of **Youlgreave**. Turn left onto this lane, cross over a bridge and then go left immediately along a path running through beautiful water meadows beside the River Bradford. After about 500m you cross a footbridge to the south bank. Nearby is a *cafe* and *ice-cream shop*. Just beyond is the village main street, which has a **YHA Hostel** (☎ *01629-636518*), B&Bs, shops and **The George Hotel** (☎ *01629-636292*), a walker-friendly pub that has good beer, excellent bar food and accommodation from £17 (£24 in en suite rooms).

The Way runs beside the river along another beautiful stretch with small weirs and pools, then crosses over an arched bridge and zigzags up to a road. Go right for 500m, then left over a stile by a gate and up an unclear path to another road above. Turn left along this road for 100m, then right through a squeeze gate, continuing diagonally uphill across fields and through a car park and picnic site to reach another minor road called Moor Lane.

Go left along Moor Lane to meet another road, where you go straight on, back into fields again, over several stiles and through several gates to skirt Calling Low Farm and reach **Cales Dale** (part of Lathkill Dale National Nature Reserve). Here the Way goes steeply down into the dale and then just as steeply up the other side.

After a few more fields you reach **One Ash Grange**, an old farm used in medieval times by the monks of Roche Abbey in Yorkshire as a penitentiary for rebellious brethren. It's still a working farm today, with a *camping barn* administered by the YHA *(bookings ☎ 01200-428366)* – a good cheap place to break your walk if you're doing it over two days.

Pass between the main farm on the left and the monks' former cold store and pigsties on the right. About 250m beyond the farm the track swings right, but you go straight on to follow a wall, then cross more fields, eventually to meet a track between old stone walls, which takes you down to Monyash.

Monyash

At roughly the halfway point of this route, the quiet village of Monyash makes a good place to stay. B&Bs include **Sheldon House** (☎ *01629-813067*, e *sheldonhouse@line one.net*), charging £30/42 for a single/double; the owners are keen walkers but only take bookings for two consecutive nights at summer weekends. Other places include **Cheney**

Well Dressing

Well dressing is a custom unique to the Peak District. It is the practice of decorating wells or springs in thanksgiving for a local supply of water. The practice may have started in pre-Christian times. It seems to have died out by the early 17th century but was revived by the inhabitants of Tissington in gratitude for their supply of pure water, which they believed protected them from the Great Plague of 1665.

Each year about 20 village wells are 'dressed' (decorated) with large, colourful pictures depicting scenes from the Bible, local history and events, or tackling more modern issues such as rainforest protection.

The pictures are produced by spreading a thin layer of clay over a wooden frame, then outlining the design with bark and filling in the colours with an intricate mosaic of flower petals and leaves. And in these conservation-minded days, the traditional practice of using slow-growing mosses and lichens as colour is beginning to decline, with seeds, acorn cups and coloured stones creating a textured background instead.

Well dressing takes place in Peak District villages from May to mid-September, with June and July being the main months. TICs will have a list of when village well dressings will be displayed. Wirksworth, Eyam and Youlgreave are three villages particularly renowned for this tradition.

Lodge (☎ *01629-815336*), charging £25/44 for en suite rooms; and a holiday cottage called *The Stables* (☎ *01629-814510*), usually hired by the week but with B&B also available at £18.50.

The only pub in the village is *The Bull's Head* (☎ *01629-812372*), a friendly no-frills place, popular at weekends, doing standard bar lunches from around £5 and filling dinners from £6 to £10. It also does straightforward B&B at £30 for double or triple rooms.

Monyash also has the *Village Store & Tearoom* and the *Old Smithy Cafe*; both welcome walkers. The latter is open every day from breakfast to evening (except on winter Mondays).

Day 2: Monyash to Castleton

12.5mi (20.5km), 5½–7 hours

Leave Monyash heading north along the lane past the **Pinfold** (where stray animals were once kept until their owner paid a fine and collected them), then left along a walled track by Dale House Farm. This leads to fields and skirts just south of Knotlow Farm before heading to the village of Flagg.

Beyond Flagg there are several miles of walking on lanes and tracks, over the fields of Taddington Moor and down to the Waterloo Inn on the A6 near Taddington – there's a YHA *camping barn* (*bookings* ☎ *01200-428366*) here.

The trail eventually leads down to **Miller's Dale**, lying at the bottom of a steep-sided gorge. Overhead two viaducts straddle the gap; they carried the railway between Manchester and Derby before short-sighted closures in the 1960s forced trains off the rails. Today one viaduct carries the Monsal Trail – see the boxed text 'The Monsal Trail' on p245. If you need refreshment, go up the hill to the small and basic *Wriggly Tin Cafe*, originally built by Victorian railway workers, now with good-value meals and snacks and a sign saying 'Boots, bags and bicycles always welcome'.

Go eastwards along the Miller's Dale main street, under the viaducts and past the church, before taking a minor road on the left up a hill (opposite the *Angler's Rest* pub).

After 100m turn sharp left on a rough track, which leads through the yard of Monksdale Farm and along a walled track. To the left (west) the fields drop into Monks Dales. The track leads you across a high area of fields to meet a lane at Monksdale House. Go left and down the hill, then turn right over a stile to thankfully regain paths leading northwards up **Peter Dale** and **Hay Dale**, a pair of delightful limestone valleys particularly famous for their wild orchids (see the boxed text 'Peak District Rarities' on p239).

At the end of Hay Dale go right on a track to reach a lane, then left to reach a main road (A623). Go left, then quickly right through a gate and down a walled track to meet a section of lane. Pass Cop Farm and then cross a field to join another walled track. After a small gate follow the path left between a wall and large pond.

Cross more stiles and gates as the route leads across the upland pasture of Bradwell Moor. Follow this path downhill to where it forks by a wall. Go through a small gate down into Cave Dale, where you can almost imagine yourself in the cavern system before it collapsed to form this steep-sided valley.

This dale leads you into the heart of Castleton through a narrow gap in the rocks beneath **Peveril Castle** (see the boxed text on p244). Turn left along Bargate and finish the Limestone Way in the village square. Nearby are several pubs and cafes where you can celebrate with a pot of tea or a pint of beer.

If you're not staying the night, go through the square to the main road, then turn right and continue round some sharp corners to reach the bus stop.

Castleton

The village of Castleton has a TIC (☎ 01433-620679) on Castle St, near the church, and a *YHA Hostel* (☎ *01433-620235*) on the village square, charging £10.85. Among several walker-friendly B&Bs are *Bargate Cottage* (☎ *01433-620201*, e *fionasaxon@bargate cottage78.freeserve.co.uk*), at £21.50 for en suite rooms; and *Bray Cottage* (☎ *01433-621532*), charging £22.50. Both are at the end of the footpath that brings you down into Castleton at the end of the day.

Also good and central is *Cryer House* (☎ *01433-620244*, 🖃 *fleeskel@aol.com*), on Castle St, charging £21 (with a fine teashop downstairs – open weekends and holidays only); and *The Ramblers Rest* (☎ *01433-620125*), on Mill Bridge, just north of the main road, charging £17.50 in standard double rooms, £22 for en suite and £27.50 if you've had a hard walk and want the room with the Jacuzzi!

Castleton also has several good pubs, all doing meals and most doing accommodation too. These include *The George*, next door to the YHA Hostel and first port of call for many walkers; and *The Castle* (☎ *01433-620578*), on the corner of Castle St and the main street, a central, large and atmospheric place with a wide range of food and B&B from £40/50 for singles/doubles. *Ye Olde Cheshire Cheese Inn* (☎ *01433 620330*), on How Lane (the main street heading out towards Hathersage), is not to be confused with the pub of the same name in nearby Hope, although it's just as good with cosy rooms, lots of historic pictures and artefacts, good beer and food, a welcome for walkers and B&B from £22.50 to £35.

As befits a major tourist spot, Castleton also has many cafes and tearooms. Try award-winning *Rose Cottage*, on the main street; walker-friendly *Three Roofs*, near

Peveril Castle

Peveril Castle was built more than 900 years ago, in 1080, for William Peveril, illegitimate son of William the Conqueror, when he was made Steward of the Royal Forest of the Peak. It was built on a rock bastion above the valley, and the village grew beneath (and took its name from) the castle. Henry II added more defences in 1176 and used the castle as a hunting lodge. Despite these regal connections, Castleton never became important. Its present status as a tourist honeypot is derived from the nearby show caves – source of Blue John, a semiprecious mineral – seen by several thousand visitors each year. If you come here in high summer, it'll seem like several million.

the car park; or *Peveril Shop & Cafe*, opposite the bus stop, which also does hot snacks and sandwiches to take away if your transport is just about to leave!

Other Walks

We have described just two walks in this chapter, which well represent the different landscapes of the Peak District, but the walking possibilities here are almost endless and the area has a very good infrastructure for visitors. There's a good public transport network, except in the south, and a wide choice of accommodation. The TICs listed under Information in the introduction to this chapter can provide details. For those on tighter budgets, the Peak District boasts no fewer than 16 YHA hostels, many campsites and several independent hostels, bunkhouses and camping barns. Contact the YHA headquarters in Matlock for more details (listed under Useful Organisations in the Facts for the Walker chapter), or phone ☎ 01200-428366 for YHA-administered camping barns.

NORTHERN PEAK DISTRICT

The northern part of the Peak District is called the Dark Peak, where the moors are high, wild and frequently featureless, a map and compass absolutely essential, and the walking rather 'specialised'. Sinking to your knees in a peat bog may not be your ideal day out, but for those who think this sounds like heaven, Kinder Scout, Bleaklow and the other moors offer endless possibilities.

Mile eaters could try the 40mi **Derwent Watershed Walk**. This tough two-day challenge should only be undertaken by fit and experienced walkers. It will take you from Yorkshire Bridge near Bamford, up Win Hill, along the ridge from Lose Hill to Mam Tor ridge, round the head of the Edale Valley to Kinder Low, Kinder Downfall and Mill Hill, then across the A57 to Bleaklow Head, Bleaklow Stones, Howden Moor and back south to where you started via Back Tor, Strines Edge and Stanage Edge.

A little less daunting is a 13mi circuit of Edale Moor, commonly called the **Kinder**

Plateau, which can be done from Edale, although even this has its wild moments. If you want to experience the high moor but prefer the comfort of a good path across the peat, the first day of the Pennine Way is a rewarding walk from Edale over to Crowden YHA Hostel. From here you can find transport to Sheffield or Manchester.

Another good idea would be to head for **Fairholmes**, near the meeting point of the Derwent and Ladybower Reservoirs, and quite easily reached by bus from Sheffield or Castleton, especially at weekends. A good circular walk takes you along the east side of Derwent Reservoir and up Abbey Brook onto the moors. The route then follows the ridge south over Back Tor and along Derwent Edge, past rocky outcrops with great names such as Cakes of Bread and Wheel Stones, ending back at Ladybower Reservoir.

CENTRAL PEAK DISTRICT

A good base for walking in the central area is the town of **Bakewell**, which has hotels, B&Bs, a YHA hostel, shops, restaurants, cafes and pubs (as well as several bakeries selling world-famous Bakewell puddings). The TIC (☎ 01629-813227) can advise on accommodation, walks and so on. The town also has good bus links to Buxton and Matlock, with onward connections to Manchester and Derby. The excellent bus service run by Virgin Trains connects (via Buxton) with the main railway line at Macclesfield, from where express trains run to London, the Midlands and the north of England.

The Monsal Trail

An excellent (and mostly flat) one-day option from Bakewell is to follow the Monsal Trail, the route of an old railway line that winds westwards through the heart of the central Peak District all the way to Buxton. From here you can get a bus back to Bakewell or simply stay the night in Buxton (the town has some interesting sights and a good choice of places to stay). To save clock watching, you could get an early bus from Buxton, have a look around and then walk back to Bakewell. The 13mi (21km) will take about five to six hours of walking; with stops it'll be seven to eight hours.

The route out of Buxton follows the A515 (the road towards Ashbourne) until just past the turn-off for the YHA hostel, then takes paths (and a short section of waymarks for the Midshires Way, a long-distance path between Buckinghamshire and Derbyshire) through the tiny hamlets of Steaden and Cowdale. It skirts north of King Sterndale, then drops down Deep Dale, circling a rather unsightly quarry to meet the main road (A6) between Buxton and Bakewell. Cross the road into a car park and continue down a woodland path beside the River Wye to meet the route of the old railway line and the Monsal Trail itself.

From here the going is easy and well signposted along the beautiful narrow valley of **Chee Dale**, leaving the old railway line (where it goes under a tunnel, now closed) to follow the river for a while, then back on the track and into **Miller's Dale**. The old train station has toilets and information boards about the surrounding nature reserve, and the nearby *Wriggly Tin Cafe* serves drinks, snacks and lunches (closed Monday), with a cosy fire when the weather's bad.

From Miller's Dale, go over the massive viaducts that once carried trains across the valley and continue along the Miller's Dale valley, leaving the railway path once again at Litton. *Barn House*, in the village, is a nice cafe also offering B&B. From here you follow delightful riverside paths to Cressbrook, where *D's Brewstop* cafe offers drinks and snacks.

A path goes up the hillside to rejoin the railway line once again, as you continue east with good views over the valley. Once again, the old railway goes under a tunnel, now closed, and the path climbs steeply up out of the valley to the small hamlet of **Monsal Head**, where there's a good *cafe* and the large walker-friendly *Monsal Head Hotel*, which offers good beer, lunches, dinners and B&B.

From Monsal Head, the route goes down the lane towards Great Longstone, then jumps back into the fields to follow the old railway line for a final spurt into Bakewell.

THE PEAK DISTRICT

Bakewell is surrounded by a network of footpaths (the TIC can provide leaflets or sell you local guidebooks). You could head eastwards along the disused railway line called the Monsal Trail (now converted to a path; see the boxed text 'The Monsal Trail' on p245) and continue along tracks and paths to the village of Rowsley, or to the famous stately home of Chatsworth. The bus run by Virgin Trains, mentioned earlier, also runs between Bakewell and Chatsworth in the summer months, so you could walk one way and bus back.

South from Bakewell takes you to the village of Over Haddon and into the wonderful and classic limestone valley of **Lathkill Dale**, protected as a nature reserve. Westwards, there's a host of circular walks through the lovely valleys of Monsal Dale, Miller's Dale and Chee Dale, and the dales radiating from them, combined with paths over the surrounding hills, crisscrossed with classic drystone walls. You can link several of these dales by following the Monsal Trail.

Farther south, similar routes also using long-gone railway lines, are the **Tissington Trail** between Ashbourne and Parsley Hay, and the **High Peak Trail** from Dowlow near Buxton all the way to Cromford near Matlock. Both trails provide effortless walking.

If you wanted something linear, but with a few views and gradients thrown in, from Bakewell you could also head for Baslow, either by foot on rights of way through the fields and Chatsworth Estate, or on the bus which goes towards Chesterfield. From here you can follow the famous **Derbyshire Edges** – a line of gritstone cliffs and a classic Peak District feature – north along Baslow Edge, Curbar Edge and Froggatt Edge, down to Grindleford, which has a classic walkers cafe and a train station on the Hope Valley Railway line.

If you want to stretch the walk or start from Grindleford, you can go up through the woods around Padley Gorge, past the ancient hillfort of Carl Wark, over Higger Tor and across to **Stanage Edge**. The edge can then be followed all the way down to the A57, where you can pick up a bus to Castleton, Manchester or Sheffield. That's a long

day walk but excellent on a fine summer day. Alternatively, from Grindleford you could head back south along the Derwent Valley, following its lovely river for most of the way to Baslow or back to Bakewell.

Another way of reaching the Derbyshire Edges is from Hathersage (which has a train station, B&Bs, pubs, cafe and a host of outdoor gear shops). You could even start at Grindleford and do a loop along the Edges then drop down to finish at Hathersage.

If you're looking for a really long route, try the **White Peak Way**, a week-long 90mi circular walk linking the villages of Bakewell, Hathersage, Castleton, Ravenstor, Hartington, Ilam and Youlgreave. All have YHA hostels as well as B&Bs. Each stage is between 9mi and 17mi. The walk is described in *The White Peak Way*, published by Cicerone. More information about this route can also be obtained from the YHA hostels along the way.

SOUTHERN & WESTERN PEAK DISTRICT

In the far south of the Peak District are some beautiful river walks along **Dovedale** and the **Manifold Valley**. These two can be joined to make an excellent day walk but they get very busy on summer weekends. Public transport is thin on the ground but a good base would be the YHA hostel at Ilam.

There is some good walking to be done in the western Peak District around **Gradbach**, along the River Dane and on the **Roaches**, a high gritstone outcrop popular with climbers. A long route, called the **Staffordshire Way**, skirts the south-western side of the Peak here – more details are given in the Other Walks in Northern England chapter.

Farther north the **Goyt Valley** is also well worth exploring but difficult to reach without your own transport. There is a useful bus service operated by Virgin Trains between Buxton and Macclesfield (connecting to the mainline railway), which goes over the surrounding high ground on the A537 – also called the 'Cat & Fiddle road'. It can drop you at the pub of the same name, from where you can walk down into the Goyt Valley or all the way back to Buxton.

The Yorkshire Dales

The Yorkshire Dales is an area of valleys and hills, roughly in the centre of Northern England. Some of the so-called hills are fairly mountainous, with steep sides, exposed cliffs and peaks over 600m, but most are lower, smoother and less foreboding. In fact most parts of the Dales are ideal for walkers and it's one of the most popular areas in England. Added to the natural landscape are human influences – remains of ancient settlements, scenic farms and villages, classic limestone walls and field barns, and the occasional eyesore quarry. There is no great wilderness here, but for many people that is the Yorkshire Dales' most important attraction.

The Yorkshire Dales are surrounded on three sides by other mountain areas. To the north extends the Pennine chain, to the west are the rugged fells of the Lake District and to the east lie the rolling North York Moors. South of the Dales are the great conurbations of Manchester, Burnley, Bradford and Leeds, looking close on the map but surprisingly distant when you're on open high ground or wandering through quiet valleys.

There is a traditional connection between the Dales and these industrial cities. In the early 20th century, and particularly since the end of WWI, factory workers would come to the Dales on Sunday, as a break from the drudgery of the 'dark satanic mills'. It's still something like that today. Every summer weekend the Dales' population probably doubles as visitors from the cities, and farther afield, come for walking, cycling, caving, rock climbing, fishing or just touring by car and coach. Despite, or perhaps because of, the influx of visitors, the people of Yorkshire seem to have the strongest 'national identity' of any county in England.

Much of the area lies within the boundaries of the Yorkshire Dales National Park. Like all national parks in England and Wales, this is not state land but made up of many privately owned farms and estates, administered by the national park authority. Conservationists question the authority's support for quarrying in the area, but this is very much a working park – with more than 60,000 people living here, many engaged in farming and an increasing number in tourism-related jobs.

Curiously, some parts of the Dales lie outside the county of Yorkshire (now actually three counties – North, South and West Yorkshire). Visiting the outer edges of the Dales, you may stray into the counties of Lancashire, Cumbria or possibly County Durham. Passports are not required for re-entry, although some Yorkshire folk may think otherwise!

INFORMATION
Maps
The Yorkshire Dales National Park is covered mostly by Ordnance Survey (OS) Landranger 1:50,000 maps No 98 *(Wensleydale & Upper Wharfedale)* and No 99 *(Northallerton & Ripon)*. For more detail, the park is also covered by OS Outdoor Leisure 1:25,000 maps No 2 *(Yorkshire Dales – South & West areas)* and No 30 *(Yorkshire Dales – Northern & Central Areas)*, plus map No 19 *(Howgill Fells and Upper Eden Valley)*. Harvey has Superwalker 1:25,000 maps *Yorkshire Dales Three Peaks* (west and central) and *Yorkshire Dales Bentham* (south), plus a *Howgill Fells* map. Footprint has an inexpensive and handy map guide called *Walks Around The Dales*, which includes several routes in the area around Settle, Malham and Ingleton.

For maps covering individual walks, see Planning in the introduction to each walk.

Books
General guidebooks to the Dales include the *Yorkshire Dales* Pathfinder Guide, published by Jarrold, *Complete Dales Walker – North* by Geoffrey White, *Complete Dales Walker – South* by Colin Speakman, and *Walks in the Yorkshire Dales* by Jack Keighley. If it all sounds too hilly, try *Yorkshire Dales Walking – On the Level* by Norman Buckley.

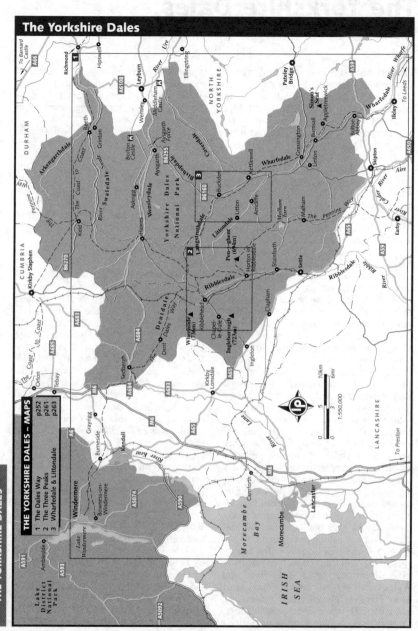

The Yorkshire Dales

THE YORKSHIRE DALES – MAPS

1 The Dales Way   p252
2 The Three Peaks   p261
3 Wharfedale & Littondale p263

The inspirational *Yorkshire Dales, Moors & Fells* by local enthusiast Paul Hannon describes 40 walks of various distances with maps and beautiful colour pictures. A good series to look out for is *Yorkshire Dales* by Terry Marsh, covering the whole area with long and short route descriptions.

The famous Settle-Carlisle Railway runs through the Yorkshire Dales, providing very handy access for walkers. A leaflet called *Settle-Carlisle Walks*, describing routes from train stations, is available from Tourist Information Centres (TICs).

Information Sources

There are many TICs in and around the Yorkshire Dales, selling walking maps and books, and able to provide information on places to stay and public transport. Most also provide the latest weather reports. Some TICs are run by the national park authority and include displays about the surrounding landscape. Useful TICs for visitors include those at Ilkley (☎ 01943-436200), Grassington (☎ 01756-752774), Malham (☎ 01729-830363), Hawes (☎ 01969-667450) and Settle (☎ 01729-825192).

For more information about events, transport and accommodation in the Dales area, check *The Visitor*, a free newspaper produced by the Yorkshire Dales National Park Authority (W www.yorkshiredales.org.uk).

Guided Walks

The national park authority organises guided walks in various parts of the Dales with different distances (easy to strenuous) and themes (wildlife, archaeology, local legends etc). TICs will give you the leaflet with all the details. Guided walks are also organised by the Settle-Carlisle Railway; all start and end at train stations along the line.

If you want to explore the northern Dales, the Swaledale Walking Guides Association leads walks around this area, weekly in the summer. You can get details from the Richmond TIC (☎ 01748-850252). The Yorkshire Dales Walking Company (☎ 01969-624699, e info@ydwc.co.uk, W www.ydwc.co.uk) organises an extensive program of day and weekend walks all over the area, guided and

self-guided Both organisations charge around £3 to £4 per day.

GETTING THERE & AWAY

To reach the Yorkshire Dales from other parts of Britain, main gateway cities and towns include Skipton and Kendal, which have good train and coach links, and can be reached by car. The Getting Around chapter lists several public transport inquiry lines that provide details of both national and local bus and train services: See the boxed text 'National Transport Information' on p92.

GETTING AROUND

The most useful public transport service for walkers is the railway line between Leeds, Settle and Carlisle, which runs through the western section of the Dales, providing easy access to many walking areas. Tied in with the trains on the Settle-Carlisle Railway are a series of tourist buses. For example, a bus runs from Settle train station to Malham and Grassington (both popular walking centres).

The very handy and comprehensive *Transport Times for Craven & The Yorkshire Dales* is available from local TICs.

The Dales Way

Distance	84mi (135km)
Duration	6 days
Standard	medium
Start	Ilkley
Finish	Bowness-on-Windermere
Gateways	Skipton, Kendal, Windermere

Summary An excellent walk on mainly good paths and undulating ground, through some of the most scenic valleys in Northern England.

The Dales Way winds through the heart of the Yorkshire Dales, leading to the foothills of the Lake District. These two national parks are among the most frequented walking areas in Britain, and this linking route is naturally very popular too. The major attractions are the scenery – traditional farmland, meandering rivers, ancient villages, rolling hills – and the relatively straightforward route – following clear paths, tracks and even a stretch of Roman road. The Dales Way is also particularly well served along its route by campsites, barns, B&Bs and a great many comfortable pubs.

Direction, Distance & Duration

The route can be done in either direction but we recommend going south-east to north-west. It's far better to leave Ilkley than to arrive, and Lake Windermere makes a very precise and satisfying finish.

The Dales Way is 84mi long. That's measured on the map, so it's a bit more with all the ups and downs. Despite its popularity, this route is not well waymarked so you have to keep an eye on the map to avoid following other footpaths.

Most people take six days to cover the route. We follow the same pattern and suggest the following stages as most convenient:

day	from	to	mi/km
1	Ilkley	Grassington	17/27.5
2	Grassington	Buckden	11/17.5
3	Buckden	Dentdale	16/25.5
4	Dentdale	Sedbergh	13/21
5	Sedbergh	Burneside	17/27.5
6	Burneside	Bowness-on-Windermere	10/16

Alternatives If you're a fast walker you could do the Way in five days but it would be a shame to rush. So, if your time is limited, start at Bolton Abbey and end at Sedbergh – the best bit of the route. If you really want to saunter, the route can be done in seven or eight days, eg, by splitting Day 1 at Burnsall and Day 3 at Cam Houses.

As with all long-distance paths (LDPs), you can do just a single day linear section of the Dales Way or a circular route taking in a stretch of the main path. Publications suggesting other routes are listed under Books following.

PLANNING
Maps

The Dales Way is mostly on OS Landranger 1:50,000 maps No 98 *(Wensleydale & Upper Wharfedale)* and No 99 *(Northallerton & Ripon)*, with the start on map No 104 *(Leeds & Bradford)* and the end on map No 97 *(Kendal & Morecambe)*. The southern and central parts (except the first few miles out of Ilkley) are also shown on the OS Outdoor Leisure 1:25 000 maps No 2 *(Yorkshire Dales – South & West)* and No 30 *(Yorkshire Dales – Northern & Central)*. The northern section of the route (north of Dent) is on maps No 19 *(Howgill Fells)* and No 7 *(The English Lakes – South Eastern)*.

Books

The Dales Way Route Guide by Colin Speakman & Arthur Gemmell is a very handy and inexpensive booklet, with details of the main route plus several circular day walks taking in sections of the Way. *The Dales Way Companion* by Paul Hannon is lovingly hand crafted in the Wainwright tradition, combining pen-and-ink text and illustrations, plus just enough background information to entertain without distraction. All these books have hand-drawn maps of varying quality but they should, nevertheless, be used with a proper survey map.

The exceedingly useful *Dales Way Handbook*, published annually by the Dales Way Association, contains accommodation listings, public transport details and other essential information. It's available in most TICs for £1.50 or by post from the Dales Way Association at 3 Moorfield Rd, Ilkley LS29 8BL. Membership of the association is only £4, which includes the handbook, and in this way you can support the people who support the route.

Information Sources

TICs on the Dales Way include those at Ilkley (☎ 01943-436200), which offers a Dales Way book-a-bed-ahead service; Grassington (☎ 01756-752774); Sedbergh (☎ 01539-620125); Kendal (☎ 01539-725758); and Windermere (☎ 01539-446499).

Guided Walks & Baggage Services

Most of the tour companies listed under Guided Walks in the Facts for the Walker chapter organise walking holidays on the Dales Way. Of these, Contours Walking Holidays and Brigantes also offer self-guided tours (complete with luggage transfer) along the Dales Way.

There are also several companies offering baggage services on this route. The main operators are Sherpa Van Project, which also operates an accommodation booking service, and Brigantes Baggage Services, which also serves the Herriot Way – described under Other Walks at the end of this chapter. For more details on baggage services, see the boxed text 'Baggage Services' under Clothing & Equipment on p50.

PLACES TO STAY & EAT

The Dales Way is well served by B&Bs, and there are also a few YHA hostels and bunkhouses along the route. We provide some suggestions in the route description. There are only a few organised campsites, although some farmers may allow walkers to pitch in a field for one night. For a wider accommodation choice, use *The Rambler's Yearbook & Accommodation Guide* or *Stillwell's National Trail Companion* (for details, see Books in the Facts for the Walker chapter), or the *Dales Way Handbook* (see Books in the introduction to this walk). If you prefer to camp and self-cater, there are several campsites on or near the route, and the Way passes many village shops for re-supplying. For meals along the Way, there are also numerous pubs, cafes and teashops; if you stopped in them all you'd never make it to Bowness-on-Windermere.

GETTING TO/FROM THE WALK

Bus At the start of the route, Ilkley is served by frequent buses from Leeds and Skipton, both easily reached from anywhere in the country by National Express coach.

The Dales Way ends at the small town of Bowness-on-Windermere, only 1.5mi from the larger town of Windermere itself. In the summer, local buses run between the two. From Windermere, buses go to all parts of the Lake District and other places in the north of England, while National Express coaches go to all parts of the country. (For

more details, see the Cumbria Way in the Lake District chapter.)

Train The nearest mainline station to the start of the walk is Leeds, linked to London and the rest of the country by regular services. From Leeds, local commuter trains run to Ilkley at least once an hour.

From Windermere there are hourly trains to Kendal, which is on a main line and from where you can reach the rest of the country.

Car Ilkley is on the A65 between Leeds and Skipton. Windermere is on the eastern edge of the Lake District, reached from the M6 motorway along the A591. To simplify transport, Scotts of Keighley (☎ 01535-602117, ℮ scottstim@aol.com) can provide long-term parking and a private-hire minibus from the end of the walk back to the start.

THE WALK
Ilkley

Originally established as a village on a packhorse route across the Dales, Ilkley grew in to a wealthy market centre in the Middle Ages, with much of the trade based on wool. Today Ilkley still exudes an air of quiet comfort, with hanging baskets and antique shops, reliable indicators of well-to-do towns, much in evidence.

Ilkley's TIC (☎ 01943-436200) is opposite the bus and train stations. There are many B&Bs in town and those used to walkers include *Belvedere* (☎ *01943-607 5982, Victoria Ave)*, charging from £17; *63 Skipton Rd* (☎ *01943-817542)*, from £25/36; *Archway Cottage* (☎ *01943-603399, 24 Skipton Rd)*, from £20/35; and *The Riverside Hotel* (☎ *01943-607338)*, in a quiet setting very near the start of the route, charging £40/55 for singles/doubles, and also with a bar and restaurant. Ilkley has a good selection of places to eat, including the famously genteel *Betty's Cafe* and some pleasant pubs.

Day 1: Ilkley to Grassington
17mi (27.5km), 6–8 hours
This day includes the section around Bolton Abbey, which gets crowded on summer weekends. If you're setting off to cover the whole

The Dales Way

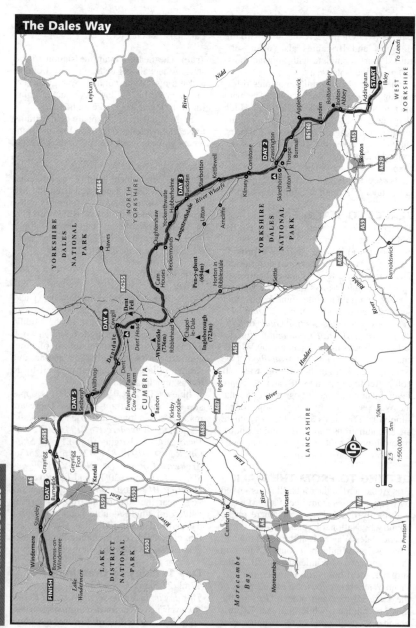

route, kitted out with boots and backpack, you feel a bit silly surrounded by people in beach wear, kids in pushchairs and grannies on Zimmer frames. Nevertheless, this is a really beautiful bit of the valley and a shame to miss. Try to do it on a weekday.

From the centre of Ilkley go down to the 'new' bridge (built in 1904) over the River Wharfe. Don't cross this bridge but go left down some steps and along the river to reach the attractive Old Bridge, the official start, marked by a single Dales Way signpost (which says, misleadingly, 'Bowness 73 miles').

Continue along the south bank of the Wharfe, then follow the path away from the river, through woodland, past a tennis club, then across flat meadows, to enter more woodland next to the river once again. Although the main road is nearby, it's surprisingly quiet; the sound of traffic is not enough to drown out the birdsong. The Way winds around the back streets of the village of Addingham, then follows the riverbank closely for 1.5mi, to suddenly pop out on a busy and narrow main road (the B6160). The Way used to follow this road but thankfully a new alternative route leads you diagonally back across the road and along the driveway of Lobwood House, before turning right (north) to follow a path through the fields, parallel to the road but separated from the traffic by a wall. Not quite far enough, though, as there's still a nasty few hundred metres along the edge of the road before you branch off onto a path back to the river. Go under another main road (the A59), then past old Bolton Bridge and across fields, following signposts to Bolton Abbey. Keep near the river to bypass the village of Bolton Abbey. just beyond here are the ruins of **Bolton Priory** – see the boxed text.

Near the priory cross the stepping stones (or the nearby footbridge) to the east bank of the river and head north. A short distance along, you could divert across another footbridge to reach *The Pavilion*, selling teas, snacks, ice creams and postcards. The route continues through delightful woods above a narrow gorge called **the Strid**, to reach Barden Bridge. From here you may want to divert to nearby Barden Tower, which has a good *teashop*.

Follow the river through farmland, passing close to Appletreewick – with a couple of *pubs* that get very crowded on summer weekends. Less frenetic is Burnsall, about 2mi upstream, where the comfortable *Red Lion* serves excellent food and offers B&B. But it's just a few more easy miles, through fields and patches of woodland, to Grassington, with a greater choice of accommodation.

Grassington

This very attractive village was once a lead-mining centre but today the major industry is tourism, with several pubs, cafes and craft shops, a small *supermarket*, a bank, an outdoor gear shop and heavy crowds on summer weekends. The TIC (☎ 01756-752774) is is at the large car park on the eastern edge of the village. The **Mining Museum** is worth a visit.

Places to stay include *Linton YHA Hostel* (☎ 01756-752400), just south of Grassington, charging £9.80. About one mile west, *Wood Nook Campsite* (☎ 01756-752412), at Skirethorns, is a good place with hot showers and a shop, where walkers pay £4.

Walker-friendly B&Bs include *Mayfield* (☎ 01756-753052), on Low Mill Lane, with rooms from £22; and *Lythe End* (☎ 01756-753196), on Wood Lane, charging £30/40 for singles/double rooms. At the upper end of

---

Bolton Priory

Bolton Priory is often mistakenly called Bolton Abbey (but that's the name of the village). The priory was built in the 12th century by Augustinian monks. During the dissolution of the monasteries under Henry VIII, all but the nave of the priory was destroyed. The surviving nave has now been converted into the parish church. The spectacle of these grand ruins in such beautiful surroundings has inspired poets and painters such as Wordsworth and Turner. The priory is open to visitors every day and contributions towards the upkeep are always welcomed.

THE YORKSHIRE DALES

the main street, *Craven Cottage* (☎ *01756-752205*) charges £25 and nearby *Grove House* (☎ *01756-753364*) charges £26.

A little out of the village centre, on Station Rd, is *Raines Close* (☎ *01756-752678*), which charges £56 for en suite doubles; and *Springroyd House* (☎ *01756-752473*), from £18 to £20.

In the heart of the village, *The Forresters Arms* (☎ *01756-752349*), an old coaching inn on the main street, charges from £25 for B&B, and serves good beer and bar meals. *The Black Horse* (☎ *01756-752770*) is another recommended pub, also doing B&B from £60 per double.

A smarter option is the *Grassington House Hotel* (☎ *01756-752406*), on Market Square, with good food and comfortable en suite rooms from £26, and evening meals in the £6 to £9 bracket. Another eating option is *Number Forty-seven* (☎ *01756-752069*), on the main street, a delightful little restaurant serving lunches and evening meals.

Day 2: Grassington to Buckden
11mi (17.5km), 4–5 hours
Today you continue up Wharfedale, but leave the valley floor to cross grassy fields and some beautiful sections of limestone pavement. You then drop again to wind through several picturesque villages, most with lunch or overnight possibilities.

From the centre of Grassington go up the main street, left into Chapel St, through the 'suburb' of Townhead and then through a farmyard; keep a careful lookout for the sign to Conistone.

The Way keeps high above the valley, passing some old lead-mine entrances (there are also many shafts in this area – take great care if you lose the path in mist), and crosses Bycliffe Road – an old packhorse route now a bridleway. On the other side of the valley is Kilnsey Crag – a rock climbers' test piece.

The route drops to meet a lane about 1mi south of the pretty little village of **Kettlewell**, then soon branches off right (north). If the lane is quiet you might as well head straight into the village – an ideal lunch stop with *pubs* and *tearooms*, a few *grocery*

stores, an outdoor gear shop and a post office. If you want to overnight here, details are given in the Wharfedale & Littondale walk later in this chapter.

Beyond Kettlewell the path follows the river, sometimes near the bank, sometimes a few fields away from it, but all the time through classic Dales scenery with stiles, dry-stone walls, ancient barns and a few patches of woodland, to reach Buckden.

Buckden
This small and scenic village has several B&Bs, including *West Winds* (☎ *01756-760883*), behind the pub, charging £17, which is also a nice quiet tearoom; *Birks View* (☎ *01756-760873*), next to the shop, charging £17; nearby *Long Barn Cottage* (☎ *01756-760866*), from £17; and *Romany Cottage* (☎ *01756-760365*), charging £18, with welcoming drinks and snacks, vegan options for breakfast and a lift service back from the pub in the next village if required.

The village *shop* stocks enough for lunch or overnight if you're camping. Attached is the friendly *Buckden Village Restaurant*, open daily until 8pm in summer (except Wednesday), which provides cakes, snacks and lunches for around £5, and dinners from £6 to £10. *The Buck Inn* (☎ *01756-760228*, e *thebuckinn@buckdon.yorks.net*) is a smart and quite comfortable pub with good meals from around £7 and B&B from £72 for a double room.

Hubberholme
Upstream from Buckden is the even smaller village of **Hubberholme** with more B&B options, including the friendly *George Inn* (☎ *01756-760223*, e *thegeorge.inn@virgin.net*), which has double rooms from £42 (£56 en suite) plus good beer and excellent bar meals; *Grange Farm* (☎ *01756-760259*), charging from £18, which also has a well-equipped bunkhouse barn for £6 but takes only groups at weekends; the smarter, non-smoking *Kirkgill Manor* (☎ *01756-760800*), which charges £27 for an en suite; and walker-friendly *Church Farm* (☎ *01756-760240*, e *gillhuck@hubberholme.fsnet.co.uk*), charging £20.

Day 3: Buckden to Dentdale
16mi (25.5km), 7–9 hours
This is a long day and potentially the most serious bit of the whole route. There are no shops or cafes on the Way – in fact there's not much at all, except wonderful, wild open hills. You could break the day into two and stay at Cam Houses.

After Hubberholme (where the old **church** is well worth a look around), the valley is called Langstrothdale but the river is still the Wharfe, getting more stream-like as it nears its source. The path crosses the river a few times, passing through the lonely farmsteads of Yockenthwaite and Deepdale. At Beckermonds take a lane north towards Hawes. Just after the hamlet of Oughtershaw, the Way branches off to the left (westwards). The names of these dispersed farmsteads – and many of the local names – are derived from the period when the Dales were inhabited by Nordic people.

The valley gets broader and the landscape more exposed. When the wind blows up here you really know about it and, even on calm days, there's a feeling of remote emptiness. The route climbs slightly to reach the remote settlement of Cam Houses, where *Camm Farm (☎ 07860-648045, 0113-271 1339)* is one of the most stylishly decorated B&Bs in Yorkshire – not a frill in sight – and well worth £29.95 for B&B with dinner. Reservations are essential. Even if you're not staying, the informative lady who runs this place often serves soups, hot drinks and home-made cakes from the kitchen. In bad weather this is a real haven. There are plans for a comfortable cottage-style bunkhouse.

If you're pushing on, follow the path through the farmyard and up the hill, round the northern corner of Cam Woods, across a farm track, then diagonally up a final slope to a cairn. Here you meet the Cam High Road, part of an old Roman road, where you turn south-west. Put the map away for a while and stride out like a centurion, taking in the splendid panoramas of Ingleborough and Whernside. This section is also followed by Pennine Way walkers (you'll find most walkers heading in the opposite direction).

At a second cairn the Pennine Way branches off left but you keep straight on, descending to the B6255 at Gearstones. Turn left and follow the road for 100m, then go up the first farm track on the right (signposted 'Dent Head'), past Winshaw House. From here the path leads through fields and the moorland edge to a lane. Turn left and follow the lane downhill into the top of Dentdale valley, under the arches of **Dent Head railway viaduct** – a fine example of Victorian engineering, which comes as quite a surprise in this quiet rural area. The Way continues along the lane. Traffic is light but take care.

Dentdale
Less than a mile from the viaduct you pass *Dentdale YHA Hostel (☎ 01539-625251)*, charging £9. As you go down the valley there are a couple of B&Bs, including *Scow Cottage (☎ 01539-625445)*, an old farmhouse charging from £17; the exceedingly pleasant *Sportsman's Inn (☎ 01539-625282, e info@thesportsmansinn.com)* with comfortable rooms from £20 (discounts in winter), log fires, fine beers and good bar food every day; and the walker-friendly *River View (☎ 01539-625592)*, near Lea Yeat Bridge and the settlement of Cowgill, charging from £18. Some B&Bs in Dent village, farther down the valley, will come to pick you up from here if you arrange it in advance.

Camping is possible at *Cow Dub Farm*, next to the Sportsman's Inn, and at *Ewegales Farm (☎ 01539-625440)*, farther down the valley, charging from £3.

If you're leaving the route here, Dent train station is also nearby – at the top of a very steep hill north of Cowgill. Trains head north to Carlisle or south to Settle and Leeds.

Day 4: Dentdale to Sedbergh
13mi (21km), 5–6 hours
This is a fairly easy day as the Way meanders through fields and woodland. The scenery is once again classic Yorkshire Dales (even though you're now in Cumbria).

From Cowgill the Dales Way winds down Dentdale, to begin with on the south side of the valley. At a farm called Low Laith, it descends to cross briefly to the north side of the valley to reach Mill Bridge. Nearby is the **Whernside Manor Bunkhouse** (☎ 01539-625213), charging £5, and also offering camping for £3 and breakfasts for £5.

From Mill Bridge you follow a delightful path beside the River Dee to the large village of **Dent** – an interesting place to look around with narrow, cobbled streets and a fine old church, plus pubs, teashops and a shop open daily. It's also an overnight possibility. You can camp at **High Laning Farm** (☎ 01539-625239), on the western side of the village. Walker-friendly B&Bs include **Little Oak** (☎ 01539-625330), small and stylish, from £18; **Smithy Fold** (☎ 01539-625368), similarly priced; and **Stone Close** (☎ 01539-625231), also similarly priced with an excellent teashop.

Village pubs include the **George & Dragon** (☎ 01539-625256) with B&B from £22/36, plus lunches and evening meals; and the **Sun Inn** (☎ 01539-625208), from £18.50, and bar meals for lunch or dinner.

From Dent return to the River Dee and continue on paths through fields. At a place called Ellers the Dales Way crosses the river on a footbridge and a new section goes up the valley side, through Hewthwaite Farm. There's one final hill, with fine views from the summit, before dropping through the village of Millthrop into the town of Sedbergh.

Sedbergh

This busy market town has food stores, banks, pubs, a TIC (☎ 01539-620125) on the main street and an outdoor gear shop. Walker-friendly B&Bs include **Homecroft** (☎ 01539-620754), on Station Rd, charging £18.50; and **Stable Antiques** (☎ 01539-620251), on Back Lane, from £18. **The Bull Hotel** (☎ 01539-620264) has B&B at £30/50 for singles/doubles and does lunches and evening meals.

The most convenient place for camping is **Pinfold Caravan Site**, on the east side of town, with plenty of facilities, including a laundrette, for £3. The well-equipped **Catholes Bunkhouse** (☎ 01539-620334) is just off the Way, before Sedbergh, and is best reached by turning off at Millthrop; the charge is from £6.

For food, stroll along the main street. **The Bay Tree** (☎ 01539-620627) does snacks and lunches during the day, and dinners in the evening, with main courses from £6 to £9. There's also the **White Rose** cafe serving takeaway fish and chips, or 'sit-down' fish, chips, tea, bread and butter for £4 (open until 7.30pm, closed Sunday and Monday). For tomorrow's picnic, stock up at **Fran's Bakery**.

Day 5: Sedbergh to Burneside
17mi (27.5km), 6–8 hours
This is a day of transition. The Way leaves the Yorkshire Dales and passes through the gently rolling landscape of the Eden Valley. The route is not well waymarked, so keep a close eye on your map as you encounter farmyards, old lanes and a great number of stiles and gates. There's no place to buy lunch, so bring a picnic.

The route leaves Sedbergh along the River Rawthey, which flows into the beautiful River Lune. This is followed through fields and meadows (and, at Hole House, almost through someone's kitchen!) for several miles. All morning the velvety humps of the Howgill Fells dominate the scene to your right (east) and the route is crossed by several splendid viaducts belonging to a disused railway, seemingly out of scale for what was a fairly minor branch line.

The handsome **Crook of Lune Bridge** is a good place for a rest, and maybe an early lunch, as the river, which you're about to cross, marks the boundary of the national park. Go over the bridge and bid farewell to the Dales. After another 2mi, the next bridge is quite a contrast – over the M6 motorway – but you soon enter farmland once again. A little farther along you also cross a major railway line at a level crossing. The signs say 'Beware Trains – Stop, Look and Listen'. You'd better – they fly along here.

The Way continues through the small settlement of Grayrigg Foot (1mi west of the slightly larger village of Grayrigg), where it crosses the main road (the A685) running south to Kendal, then continues through sleepy farmland. You go through the yard of **High Barn** (☎ 01539-824625, ⓔ hibarn @hotmail.com) at the hamlet of Shaw End, about a mile beyond Grayrigg Foot near Pattern Bridge. The B&B charges £25 in an en suite and includes dinner. With advance notice walkers can camp in the garden for £2.

Beyond here you pass the small lake of **Black Moss Tarn**. From here it's another 3mi or so along lanes, paths and farm tracks to finally reach the large village of Burnside.

Burnside & Around
On the edge of the Lake District, and overshadowed by the nearby town of Kendal, Burnside sees few visitors. It may be the better for that. There's a *shop*, post office, and (for those wanting to leave the Dales Way) a train station.

Just before Burnside there's very simple camping available at *Burnside Hall Farm*. On the main street, *The Jolly Anglers Inn* (☎ 01539-732552) is a friendly village local, charging £25/45 per en suite single/double, also serving bar food every evening (but only Thursday to Saturday in winter). Next door, *The Jolly Fryer* serves fish and chips to take away, but only on Tuesday, Thursday and Friday evening.

Just out of the village, across the railway line, is *Garnett House Farm* (☎ 01539-724542), a working farm with a hearty welcome, B&B for £21/37 in an en suite and dinner by arrangement. In the next village of Bowston, *Kentdene* (☎ 01539-724929) charges £18.

If these places are all full, some B&Bs in Kendal will come and pick you up. These include friendly *Bridge House* (☎ 01539-722041, e *sheila@bridgehouse-kendal.co.uk*), on Castle St, charging from £18 (£22 en suite). Guests are also offered a complimentary Kendal Mint Cake – a locally made, sugar-based traditional energy food, which has been keeping walkers fuelled up for decades. For more options, contact the Kendal TIC (☎ 01539-725758), in the Town Hall.

Day 6: Burnside to Bowness-on-Windermere
10mi (16km), 3–4 hours
This final day is pleasingly easy, alongside rivers and on through rolling farmland. Waymarking is generally good but there are still a few tricky bits. Rather than stopping en route, plan for a late lunch at Bowness-on-Windermere.

From Burnside the Way follows the River Kent for about 3.5mi – a very enjoyable stretch. Just south of Staveley village (with some good B&B options), the Way leaves the river, crosses a road, goes under a railway and then over the busy A591 between Kendal and Windermere on a small road bridge.

There's a short section along a lane and then the Way once again crosses peaceful farmland and some high ground near Hag End Farm, where a wide vista of Lake District mountains suddenly opens out before you. It's a wonderful sight but don't be distracted. Some paths branch off north to Windermere but keep going west towards Bowness-on-Windermere (usually shortened to Bowness). On these last few miles the route ducks and dives through gardens and narrow farm lanes, so it's easy to go wrong.

Just before the end, on Brant Fell, you're treated to the first view of Lake Windermere. Below this lookout is a slate bench with a plaque marking the 'official' end of the Dales Way. But it's more pleasing to continue down the path leading to Brantfell Rd, which then leads to the centre of Bowness – a busy tourist town that can be quite a shock after days of near-solitude in the Dales. Keep going downhill to the lake shore, where you can reach the water between crowds of holiday-makers and boats moored at the Pier, and dip your toe to ceremoniously mark the end of your walk. You can then enjoy a well-earned cup of tea or ice cream at one of the nearby snack bars overlooking the lake.

Bowness-on-Windermere & Windermere
Bowness is on Lake Windermere and the larger town of Windermere is a short distance inland, with the main train and bus station. The two towns merge; from the Pier to the station is about 1.5mi. Windermere's excellent TIC (☎ 01539-446499) is on the approach road to the train station. There is also a TIC in Bowness (☎ 01539-442895) by the Pier, which will help find you somewhere to stay if you haven't already booked.

When it comes to accommodation, if any house in Bowness or Windermere doesn't do B&B, it's probably abandoned. Or at least that's how it seems in this busy tourist honeypot. Having said that, in high season you may still have to do a bit of phoning around to find a bed for the night. Another point to remember is that many B&Bs here don't really cater for passing walkers but prefer to take tourists for a number of nights. We've listed the more walker-friendly ones. These include the smart and comfortable *Fairfield Hotel* (☎ *015394-46565*, e *ray &barb@the-fairfield.co.uk*), on Brantfell Rd – to your left as you come down the road at the end of the day's route. B&B here costs from £29 to £32. The nearby *Blenheim Lodge* (☎ *01539-443440*) charges around £39, while good-quality *Bellsfield House* (☎ *01539-445823, 4 Kendal Rd*), very near the end of Brantfell Rd, charges £25 in en suite doubles. Guests can use the sauna, massage and Jacuzzi facilities free of charge at a nearby hotel leisure centre – ideal for reviving tired legs after the walk! Also good are *Lingwood* (☎ *01539-444680*), on Birkett Hill about half a mile south of the Pier, charging from £19 to £25; and *Gillthwaite Rigg* (☎ *01539-446212*), on Lickbarrow Rd, just off the Dales Way near Matson Ground, about a mile before you reach Bowness, charging £25. The friendly people here will pick you up from the end of the route and run you back into town, if required, for an evening meal. If you've got your own car,

this place also offers long-term parking so you can leave it here while you're walking the Dales Way.

If you want a real blow-out at the end of your walk, try *The Old England (central reservations* ☎ *0870-400 8130)* overlooking the lake, where B&B ranges from £39 midweek in winter to about £75 on summer weekends. Take your boots off before checking in, though!

A good pub in the same part of town is *The Hole in 't Wall* (a reminder of all those squeeze gates you've pushed through on the Dales Way!), with good beer, lively atmosphere, bar food and music some evenings. There are other good pubs on the nearby streets, most doing food. For other eating options, Bowness and Windermere have more teashops, cafes and takeaways than you can shake a stick at, not to mention a batch of classy restaurants. Stroll around for 10 minutes and you'll soon find a place to suit your tastebuds and budget.

The Three Peaks

Distance	25mi (40km)
Duration	9–12 hours
Standard	hard
Start/Finish	Horton in Ribblesdale
Gateways	Settle, Skipton
Summary	A classic long and challenging walk through high, open dale country, with some lower farmland. Paths are mostly clear but there are some boggy sections. Only fit and experienced walkers should attempt the whole route.

Yorkshire Pride

A local poem reads, 'Whernside, Ingleborough and Pen-y-ghent – the highest hills twixt Tweed and Trent'. The River Trent is in Nottinghamshire and the Tweed is on the Scottish border. Some walkers point out that as the Lake District (which contains Scafell Pike – England's highest mountain) is only about 40mi away, the rhyme is a little misleading. Although Yorkshire people are known to be proud of their county, this might be just a tad too much hype!

The three highest peaks in the Yorkshire Dales are Whernside (736m), Ingleborough (723m) and Pen-y-ghent (694m) – the main points of this long, circular route, which has been a classic walk for many years. The first recorded completion was in 1887. Traditionally, walkers try to complete the whole route in under 12 hours, including stops. Others knock it off in six hours or less. Even faster are the fell runners in the annual Three Peaks Race, who do it in about 2½ hours. If you're looking for a challenge, this might be one for you. If you like to actually enjoy your walking, doing a section of this route is perfectly feasible and still highly recommended.

Direction, Distance & Duration

This circular route can be followed in either direction; we describe it anticlockwise. The traditional start/finish is the village of Horton in Ribblesdale (usually shortened to Horton). Another possible start is Ribblehead, if only to avoid the crowds that clog Horton on summer weekends. The route is signposted in places but not waymarked, so map and compass knowledge are essential.

The official total distance is 25mi, but with all the ups and downs, and twists and turns, it's better to reckon on 26mi. The route involves over 1500m of ascent, so this is no stroll in the park. Most people need between nine and 11 hours of walking time. With lunch and other stops, this still allows you to do it in under 12 hours.

Alternatives If 25mi is too far you can still enjoy a walk in this area by doing just one or two of the peaks. Pen-y-ghent and Ingleborough can be reached from Horton, while Whernside and Ingleborough can be reached from Ribblehead. All are fine walks in their own right, with circular routes of between 5.5mi and 12mi possible. The railway opens up more options. For example, from Horton you can walk via Pen-y-ghent or Whernside to Ribblehead, then catch the train back to Horton.

PLANNING
Maps & Books

The Three Peaks route is on the OS Landranger 1:50,000 map No 98 *(Wensleydale & Upper Wharfedale)*. For more detail use OS Outdoor Leisure 1:25,000 map No 2 *(Yorkshire Dales –South & West Areas)* or the Harvey Superwalker 1:25,000 *Yorkshire Dales Three Peaks* map.

Specific coverage of the route includes *The Three Peaks Map & Guide* by Arthur Gemmell, a handy little booklet that also describes other routes in the area, plus background on geology and history.

Guidebooks on the Three Peaks area include *Walks in the Three Peaks Country* by Paul Hannon, *Settle & the Three Peaks* by Mick North, and the *Rail Trail Guide to Settle & Carlisle Country*, published by Leading Edge – all with routes between 3mi and 10mi.

Information Sources

Horton's TIC (☎ 01729-860333), in the Pen-y-ghent Cafe, is also a national park information point. In between pouring mugs of tea, the friendly staff will help with route advice, recommend maps and guides (which they sell in the cafe), and offer a local accommodation booking service.

PLACES TO STAY & EAT
Horton in Ribblesdale

In the centre of Horton in Ribblesdale, *Holme Farm Campsite*, which has limited facilities, charges £2 per night. Another bargain is the camping barn at *Dub-Cote Farm* (☎ 01729-860238), about a mile south-east

---

Walkers' Clock-In Service

If you start and finish in Horton, at weekends and on some weekdays the Pen-y-ghent Cafe runs a clock-in-and-out service. You complete a card with your name and details, get the time punched onto it by the old factory clock in the cafe and leave the card. (If you want to get away quickly, the cafe runs an 'early bird' service – see the notice on their porch for details.) When you get back you punch in your finish time. Less than 12 hours earns you membership of the Three Peaks Club and a certificate. Note, however, that this is not a race. All you have to do is finish inside 12 hours – you don't get extra points for shorter times.

More importantly, the clock is a useful safety scheme in case anyone gets lost or injured. Although the cafe closes at 6pm, the staff wait on to check everybody back in. If by any chance you clock out and don't manage to get back to Horton, it is *essential* that you phone the cafe to tell them you're OK. Otherwise they'll report you missing and that wastes the time and resources of the police and mountain rescue team.

THE YORKSHIRE DALES

of the village, which offers straightforward self-catering facilities.

Nearly all the B&Bs in Horton cater for walkers. These include *The Knoll (☎ 01729-860283)*, an easy-going place charging from £17, with evening meals if required; *The Hikers Guesthouse (☎ 01729-860300)*, a terraced house on the main street (the owner lives next door), with singles/doubles from £20/36; *Studfold House (☎ 01729-860200)*, from £18; *Willows Guest House (☎ 01729-860373)*, from around £20; and *Rowe House (☎ 01729-860212)*, just north of the village, which has an excellent service for £22.

The village has two pubs. *The Crown Hotel (☎ 01729-860209)*, at the northern end of the village, has B&B from £21, a garden and a range of bar food. At the southern end of the village, *The Golden Lion Hotel (☎ 01729-860224*. e *the.golden.lion @kencomp.net)*, which can't be missed with its lurid green paintwork, offers a comfortable lounge, a lively hikers bar (wet boots welcome), B&B for £20/37 and a bunkroom (with rather exposed showers) for £7. You can also order breakfast, packed lunch, bar food and evening dinners.

The classic *Pen-y-ghent Cafe (☎ 01729-860333)*, on the main street in the centre of the village, serves filling meals, home-made cakes and pint mugs of tea. It's open from 9am to 6pm every day (except Tuesday) and from 8am at weekends. The friendly staff also sell maps, guidebooks and walking gear. There's also a *post office shop* selling groceries and takeaway food, which stays open in the evening during busy periods.

Ribblehead

An alternative start and finish for this route is the small settlement of Ribblehead, about 6mi north-west of Horton, where the *Station Inn (☎ 01524-241274)* does B&B in en suite singles/doubles for £25/44 (there are also some cheaper rooms without a bathroom), and has a bunkhouse charging £8 (but groups only at weekends). This place is proud to be a 'pub that sells food, not a restaurant that sells beer' with sandwiches, baguettes and bar meals (like Yorkshire

pudding with roast beef, chips and gravy, or veggie chilli con carne) for £3 to £6, and full meals like steak or chicken for £7 to £10. You can camp for free outside the pub and come inside to use the pub toilets (this is free, but you're asked to make a donation to a local charity).

GETTING TO/FROM THE WALK

Bus Buses run hourly between Skipton and Settle during the day (five buses each way on Sunday), but between Settle and Horton there's a single bus, which only runs on school days.

Train By far the best way to reach Horton or Ribblehead is on the trains that run between Leeds and Carlisle via Skipton, Settle, Horton and Ribblehead. This is the famous Settle-Carlisle Railway (see the boxed text on p266). From May to September there are about seven trains daily in each direction (five on Sunday). For details, see the official Settle-Carlile Web site at W www.set tle-carlisle.co.uk.

Car Horton is on the B6479, about 6mi north of Settle, which is just off the A65 between Skipton and the M6 motorway. The car park in the village often fills at weekends. The TIC will direct you to alternative parking places. Cars left on verges or in gateways may be towed away.

THE WALK
Horton to Pen-y-ghent Summit
2.5mi (4km), 1½ hours

Leave Horton southwards, down the main street past the church. Cross over the stream and turn left into a lane heading uphill to a farm at Brackenbottom. From here a path leads straight up the hillside, over several stiles and on boardwalks in places, to the southern shoulder of Pen-y-ghent. The cliffs look steep as you approach – and they are – but the path winds its way up between the worst bits, to flatten out near the top, just a few minutes from the **summit** trig point. Take a few moments to enjoy the view – hopefully the walk's other two peaks will be clearly visible.

Pen-y-ghent Summit to Ribblehead

7.5mi (12km), 3 hours

Cross the ladder stile over the wall, which runs across the summit plateau, and drop north-westerly downhill. Horton is over to your left. You'll also see the great hole of Hull Pot. Even more obvious is the board-walked route of the Pennine Way coming up to meet you. Do not take the Pennine Way back to Horton but continue north-west, dropping gradually down into the valley, over several streams and bogs. (In wet weather your route is likely to be blocked by Hull Pot Beck, in which case from the summit of Pen-y-ghent *do* follow the Pennine Way towards Horton to meet a track going up the west side of the beck. This will lead you back onto the path described above.)

The path finally meets a dirt track near a house called Old Ing. From here you continue downhill through fields to cross the River Ribble on a metal bridge to reach Lodge Hall Farm. Follow the farm lane to the B6479, then walk along this road (busy in summer so take care) north to Ribblehead junction. Meals and liquid refreshments are available in the *Station Inn*, while the *Fourth Peak tea van* may be parked nearby (summer and weekends only).

Ribblehead to Whernside Summit

4.5mi (7km), 2 hours

From east of Station Inn, a dirt road leads north-west towards the **Ribblehead Viaduct**. When the Settle-Carlisle Railway was threatened with closure, this viaduct became the symbol of the fight to keep the line open. The success of that campaign is commemorated by a plaque showing a Victorian navvy and a modern railway engineer 'shaking hands across the century'.

Do not go beneath the viaduct but go up-hill on the path running next to the railway line as it curves round to the north-east, to

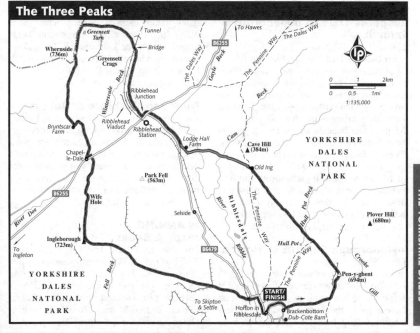

The Three Peaks

Greensett Tarn
Tunnel
To Hawes
Whernside (736m)
Bridge
Greensett Crags
Winterscale Beck
Ribblehead Junction
Greensett Beck
B6255
The Dales Way
Gayle Beck
The Pennine Way
The Dales Way
Beck
0   1   2km
0 0.5 1mi
1:135,000
Bruntscar Farm
Ribblehead Viaduct
Ribblehead Station
Lodge Hall Farm
Cam
Cave Hill ▲ (384m)
YORKSHIRE
Chapel-le-Dale
Old Ing
DALES
Park Fell △ (563m)
NATIONAL
Wife Hole
River Ribble
Ribblesdale
PARK
Selside
The Pennine Way
Pot Beck
Plover Hill ▲ (680m)
River Doe
B6255
Ingleborough (723m)
To Ingleton
Fell Beck
B6479
Ribble
Hull Pot
Hull Beck
YORKSHIRE
DALES
NATIONAL
PARK
START/FINISH
To Skipton & Settle
Horton in Ribblesdale
Brackenbottom
Dub-Cote Barn
Pen-y-ghent (694m)
The Pennine Way
Crooke
Gill

THE YORKSHIRE DALES

take a small bridge (also carrying Force Gill stream, so marked 'aqueduct' on OS maps) across the line. Continue upwards to the north of Greensett Tarn.

The path eventually reaches a wall that runs along the summit ridge of Whernside (738m). The path runs next to this wall all the way to the **summit trig point**. (The path is to the east of the wall and the trig point is to the west – you could miss it in mist.)

Whernside Summit to Chapel-le-Dale
3.5mi (5.5km), 1 hour

From the summit follow the path south-west down the ridge for about 1.5mi, before branching left (south) and heading steeply down the hillside and into fields to reach Bruntscar Farm. From here a track then a lane leads directly to the B6255, about 500m north of the small village of Chapel-le-Dale. Almost opposite where the lane meets the main road, the *Old Hill Inn* might be the place for a drink and a rest.

Chapel-le-Dale to Ingleborough Summit
2.5mi (4km), 1½ hours

From the Old Hill Inn head up the B6255 for about 200m to reach a gate and signpost on the right. The path goes through fields and a nature reserve of eroded limestone pavement, then past a large funnel-shaped depression called Wife Hole. Beyond here the path has been boarded. (Even though these boards are unsightly, they cross some severely boggy sections. The boardwalk turns into stone steps, which climb steeply up to the pathless **Ingleborough summit** plateau. In clear weather the trig point and large stone wind shelter are easy to see, but in the mist you could get lost here, so keep your wits (and compass) about you.

Ingleborough Summit to Horton
5.5mi (9km), 2 hours

From the summit retrace your ascent path for a short distance to reach a fork. Go right (left is where you came up), heading east on a clear path, then south-east. Keep descending, along limestone pavement, until

you see Horton down in the valley and the bizarre, turquoise lake in Maugham Quarry over to your right (south). You reach Horton near the train station. Cross the lines, go straight on, then over the river to reach the finish of the walk at the *cafe* where, no doubt, you'll deserve several mugs of tea.

Wharfedale & Littondale

Distance	13mi (21km)
Duration	5–6 hours
Standard	easy-medium
Start/Finish	Kettlewell
Gateways	Grassington, Skipton

Summary A good, hilly, but not too strenuous circular walk through classic scenery and two contrasting dales.

Wharfedale, cut by the River Wharfe, is one of the largest and best-known dales in Yorkshire. In contrast, the valley of Littondale, home to the River Skirfare, is small and hardly known. This walk takes in both dales, linking them by higher ground, which offers fine views of the surrounding landscape. This is the kind of walk to be done slowly, maybe with a picnic or pub lunch halfway, to properly absorb the Yorkshire Dales scenery and atmosphere.

Direction, Distance & Duration
This circular route starts and ends in Kettlewell. It can be followed in either direction; we describe it clockwise. Litton is a good place for lunch so what time you leave may decide which way round you go. The total distance is 13mi. This takes about five to six hours of walking, but you should allow an extra hour or two for stops.

PLANNING
Maps & Books
For this route use the OS Landranger 1:50,000 map No 98 *(Wensleydale & Upper Wharfedale)*. For more detail, the whole route, except a short section around Arncliffe, is also covered by the OS Outdoor Leisure 1:25,000 map No 30 *(Yorkshire Dales – Northern & Central Areas)*.

Books on this area are covered in the Three Peaks walk and under Other Walks at the end of this chapter.

Information Sources

The nearest TIC to the walk is at the town of Grassington (☎ 01756-752774).

PLACES TO STAY & EAT
Kettlewell

Campers can head for *Fold Farm (☎ 01756-760886)*, a simple place where the charge is £2.50. There's also a *YHA Hostel (☎ 01756-760232)*, charging £9.80. For B&B, on the edge of the village are two small walker-friendly places: *Lynburn (☎ 01756-760803)* and *Chestnut Cottage (☎ 01756-760804)*, both charging from £19. *Cottage Tearoom (☎ 01756-760405)*, on the main street, does luxurious 'four-poster B&B' for £21.50 mid-week (£24.50 weekends), plus breakfasts, snacks and drinks, and dinners in the cosy restaurant from £6 to £9.

Pubs in Kettlewell include *The Bluebell* and *The Racehorses* (also with a nice river-side beer garden), which both do bar food for around £7.

There are more places to stay in nearby Buckden and Hubberholme – described in the Dales Way earlier in this chapter.

Litton

The small village of Litton is about a third of the way along this route and makes a good lunch stop, or possible alternative start and finish. The friendly *Queens Arms Inn (☎ 01756-770208)* is open daily (except Monday) from noon to 3pm, 7pm to 11pm and all day on summer weekends. The inn does snacks and good bar food (including home-made pies for £6), and has a log fire when it's cold and a garden for when it's sunny. It does B&B from £50 per en suite double (or a bargain £30 midweek in winter).

GETTING TO/FROM THE WALK

Bus There are several buses each day from Leeds, Ilkley and Skipton to Grassington. Some continue to Kettlewell or you may have to change in Grassington. Services on weekdays during school holidays may be more limited but on summer weekends there are extra services.

Train The nearest train stations are at Skipton (from where you must get a bus to Grassington and Kettlewell, as described above) and Settle, on the Settle-Carlisle Railway (for details, see the Three Peaks walk).

Car Kettlewell is on the B6160, most easily reached via Grassington if you're coming from the south and via Buckden if you're coming from the north. There is a car park in the village.

THE WALK
Kettlewell to Arncliffe

2.5mi (4km), 1–1½ hours

From the centre of Kettlewell go west to cross the bridge over the River Wharfe. From the west side of the bridge, where the road bends round to the left, take a wide track on the right, which aims uphill away

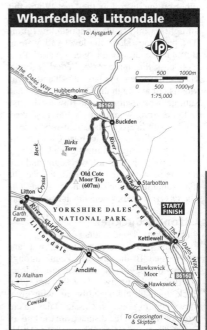

Wharfedale & Littondale

from the river path. You go through a gate and almost immediately branch left again and onto a footpath (signposted 'Arncliffe'). Keep heading up the fell, through a small, steep section of limestone cliffs, and then follow the path over a few stiles (which will confirm you're still on the path) as you cross the broad ridge. Behind you are fine views down over Kettlewell and Wharfedale.

After about an hour the path begins to descend into Littondale. You go through fields and then steeply down through woodland to reach the pretty little settlement of **Arncliffe**. Cross a lane and go through a small gate opposite and walk alongside the River Skirfare, with the church on the opposite bank.

Arncliffe to Litton
2.5mi (4km), 1 hour
In Arncliffe, cross the bridge over the river then turn immediately right, in front of a cottage and barns. After a few minutes you meet the lane again and turn right, over another bridge, to follow the lane. Where this lane bends left (signposted to Malham), go straight on into fields signposted to Litton. The path goes along the level valley floor, through meadows and over several stiles. You pass through **Scoska Wood National Nature Reserve** – the largest ash and rowan woods remaining in the Dales. In spring and summer a profusion of wild flowers flourish in the reserve, which is only lightly grazed.

The path keeps to the south-west side of the river all the way to East Garth Farm, where you go right to meet a track over the river. Look for the bridleway signs and follow the track round a few bends to meet the lane running through Litton, opposite *The Queens Arms* pub, where lunch may beckon.

Litton to Buckden
4mi (6.5km), 1½–2 hours
From the pub go left and uphill on a lane (signposted 'Bridleway – Buckden') through a farmyard. Beyond here a rough track drops briefly into the pretty little valley of **Crystal Beck**, then climbs steadily up, with great views behind you of a classic Dales patchwork of fields. In the distance are the bulk of Pen-y-ghent and its neighbour Plover Hill.

After about 30 to 45 minutes, where the gradient starts to ease, make sure you bear left to reach the broad top of the fell. As you cross the ridge, there's a trig point about 200m to the right. Unfortunately the top is too broad to allow views down into both valleys but, as you start descending into Wharfedale, a new scenery is revealed. You can see the villages of Buckden and Starbotton, and the edge of Kettlewell. The hills beyond include Buckden Pike.

The path down to Buckden is indistinct and sometimes boggy in places. There are a few blue-topped marker posts to keep you in line. Near the valley bottom, the path meets a track, which winds down round the edge of a wood and through fields near a farm, eventually meeting the lane just west of Buckden. Turn right and walk along the lane for 500m to reach the bridge over the River Wharfe.

Buckden to Kettlewell
4mi (6.5km), 1½ hours
If you need refreshment, go into Buckden village, where there are *pubs* and *teashops*. Otherwise, before crossing the bridge, go right over a stile and onto a riverside path heading south-east. You are now on the Dales Way, although heading against the direction most long-distance walkers take.

Keep to this flat and very pleasant path as it winds through a few patches of woodland, meadows and fields, past stone walls and barns, and over a rather tiring number of stiles, all the way back to Kettlewell. To reach the village cross back over the bridge; in summer months there's sometimes an *ice-cream stall* here. Otherwise the teashops or pubs in Kettlewell will provide any end-of-walk drinks and food required.

Other Walks

In this chapter we have described an LDP, a classic peak route and a less demanding circuit through two valleys, but there are many more opportunities for walking in the Dales. The following pointers describe areas roughly south to north.

THE SOUTHERN DALES

An interesting place with lots of walking potential is the area around the village of **Malham**, which has a good accommodation range (for details, see the Pennine Way in the Northern England Long-Distance Paths chapter) and can be reached by bus. The town can get very busy, however, so is best avoided at weekends and during holidays. The surrounding area is a geologist's paradise and fascinating for lay folk too – you can visit the precipitous cliff of **Malham Cove**, the remains of an ancient waterfall, topped by an area of classic limestone pavement complete with numerous grikes (narrow fissures) and clints (sections of rock between the fissures).

Nearby is picturesque **Malham Tarn** and the waterfall of Gordale Scar. These can all be linked on an excellent 8mi walk from Malham, which includes a scramble up or down Gordale Scar (not advisable when the river is high). Alternatively, you could walk here from Wharfedale along **Mastiles Lane**, an old drove road.

On the other side of the River Wharfe the hills are quieter. A good circuit goes from Bolton Abbey, northwards for a short distance along the river's east bank before climbing up through an area marked 'The Valley of Desolation' on OS maps (although it's very pleasant in reality) to reach the wide, flat moorland of Barden Fell and the impressive summit of **Simon's Seat**, with views over lower Wharfedale and the surrounding area. From here you have a choice of routes back to the Wharfe, which you follow all the way back to Bolton Abbey.

THE WESTERN DALES

In the western part of the Dales, the small town of **Ingleton** makes a good base, as it's quite easy to reach and has several places to stay. In the area to the north, the valleys of the Rivers Twist and Doe are popular, but the stunning scenery attracts many visitors, so come at a quieter time of year if you can.

Nearby is the village of **Clapham**, which has a TIC, a few places to stay and eat, including the quaintly anarchic Café Annie, and a train station 1.5mi away. From here

you can walk to the large and impressive Ingleborough Caves (£4 for a guided tour) and continue on to the high ground, even to the summit of Ingleborough itself – one of the famous Three Peaks.

To the north-west of Ingleton is **Ribblehead**, easily reached on the Settle-Carlisle Railway, which provides a great way for walkers to get into the heart of the Dales. As well as Ingleborough and Whernside (described in the Three Peaks walk earlier in this chapter), many other areas can be reached from here. If you've got an interest in history, you might want to go a few miles north of Ribblehead and walk part of the Roman road known as the **Cam High Road**. If you're fully prepared you could follow this ancient route all the way (12mi) from Ribblehead to Bainbridge in Wensleydale (described under Northern Dales following).

Another handy train station on the Settle-Carlisle Railway is Dent, providing easy access to **Dentdale**, another very beautiful valley (as described in the Dales Way walk) where many other circular routes are possible. See the boxed text 'The Settle-Carlisle Railway' on p266 for more information.

At the western end of Dentdale, and in the western reaches of the Yorkshire Dales National Park, is a group of very impressive, though often ignored, hills called the **Howgill Fells** – big, rounded and compact, sometimes likened to a group of squatting elephants. The best base is the town of Sedbergh (which is also on the Dales Way and described in detail in the walk description). A walk from Sedbergh over Calders to a summit called the Calf is an excellent introduction to these hills. There are not many paths and the tops are featureless, making navigation a serious test, even in good weather. However, the walking underfoot is easy and the hills are not crowded, with unsurpassed 360-degree views of the Lake District to the west, the Yorkshire Dales to the east and south, and the Pennines to the north.

THE NORTHERN DALES

The main valley in the northern part of the Dales is **Wensleydale**, famous worldwide for its cheese, and with plenty more walking

The Settle-Carlisle Railway

The Settle-Carlisle Railway – also called the Leeds-Settle-Carlisle (LSC) line – is one of the greatest engineering achievements of the Victorian era and takes passengers across some of the best country-side in England. The line was created by the Midland Railway Company (MRC). Legend has it that the company chairman looked at a map of Yorkshire, saw the big gap that was the Dales and drew a line across it with a pencil, saying 'That's where I'll have my railway'. It took 5000 men more than seven years to build, and cost over £3.5 million (a vast sum in those days) and 100 lives (an even greater cost) due to accidents and appalling conditions in the workers' camps.

It was the last major railway to be built using pick and shovel by gangs of navvies, and involved some amazing work. The Ribblehead Viaduct has 24 arches, the tallest almost 50m high, and the viaducts at Dent Head and Arten Gill are almost as impressive. The longest tunnel is under Blea Moor and is over 1mi long. Altogether there are 325 bridges, 21 viaducts and 14 tunnels.

In the 1970s British Rail decided the expense of repairing the line was unjustifiable and the line was threatened with closure, but the ensuing public outcry has ensured its survival, at least for the time being. During summer there are occasionally steam-hauled trains on the route but normally there are simply two-carriage diesels. Nevertheless, the views from the windows are amazing, and the railway is still one of the best ways for walkers to get to the heart of the Dales.

KELLI HAMBLET

The Ribblehead Viaduct, against the austere backdrop of the dales

opportunities on the wild fells to the north and south. The town of Hawes makes an excellent base, with a good TIC and several places to stay (described in detail in the Pennine Way). Other possible bases, farther to the east, are the villages of Askrigg (also with B&B options) and Aysgarth (with a **YHA hostel**) – handy for a visit to the spectacular Aysgarth Force waterfall.

Finally, don't forget **Swaledale**, a relatively remote but beautiful valley in the far north of the national park. A route along the length of this valley forms part of the Coast to Coast Walk and is described in more detail in the Northern England Long-Distance Paths

chapter, but there are many more circular options. Good bases include the village of Keld or the small town of Reeth, both described in the Coast to Coast Walk. Just beyond the far north-eastern tip of the park, the historic town of Richmond is another possible base.

Perhaps one of the best ways of exploring the northern Dales is to follow the four-day **Herriot Way**, named for James Herriot who wrote many popular books about his work as a vet in the farms of this area. The circular route links Hawes, Aysgarth, Reeth and Keld (which all have accommodation), thus combining two days of valley walking with two days of fell walking – a perfect Dales taster.

The Lake District

If anywhere is the heart and soul of walking in England, it's the Lake District – a wonderful area of high mountains, deep valleys and, of course, beautiful lakes. The reason for its popularity may be historical; this is where William Wordsworth and other 19th-century romantic writers were among the first people to take up walking for aesthetic reasons, rather than just to get from A to B. Or the reason may be to do with appearances; some national parks in England are mostly rounded dales and moors, but in the Lake District you find proper mountains – high, wild and rugged. One writer said the Lake District hills were so wonderful 'because they've got knobs on'.

Whatever the reason, it's true that the Lake District (often simply called the Lakes – but never the Lakes District) has an irresistible attraction to walkers. Although some people moan about crowded footpaths and notoriously unpredictable weather, many return year after year. And they're not all walkers – several million come for fishing, sailing, power boating (for a few more years at least) or to simply tour in cars and coaches. Over the years, various plans have been mooted to restrict the number of vehicles, but none have really been successful – if you're on the roads during summer, be prepared for a mighty crush.

Most of the area is contained within the Lake District National Park. Like all national parks in England and Wales, this is not public land but is rather made up of privately owned farms and estates, including many villages and even a few towns. It's very much a working park, not a trackless wilderness. Some people are employed in farming but many more depend on tourism for their income – so they welcome the annual influx.

The Lake District is traditionally divided into several smaller areas – the Central Fells, the Northern Fells, the Eastern Fells and so on. These high areas are separated by large valleys but are also based on divisions used by the famous writer Alfred Wainwright in

his series of classic guidebooks, which were first published in the 1950s and have inspired countless walkers ever since.

The Lake District is the remains of an old volcano, with the high ground roughly in the centre and the long ridges, valleys and lakes radiating out like the spokes of a wheel. Roads lead up to the end of several valleys but few go right across, so the central part of the park is still relatively remote and can only be reached on foot.

Of course, in a place like the Lakes, the choice of walking routes is endless. There are hundreds of high walks, peak walks, ridge walks, valley walks and (naturally) lake walks. Even a list of classic walks would run to several pages, so picking just a few to represent the whole area is particularly hard. We've made a brave attempt – the walks selected for this chapter are all different in flavour and include a batch of the area's most famous mountains, such as Scafell Pike, Fairfield and Helvellyn. Several routes can be done from the same base, so you won't have to move camp every night.

Also in this chapter we describe the Cumbria Way – a mainly lowland long-distance path (LDP) that runs right through the Lake District (parts of which can be incorporated into shorter one-day circuits). In the Northern England Long-Distance Paths chapter we have described the famous Coast to Coast Walk, which also crosses the Lake District and goes on to traverse the Yorkshire Dales and North York Moors.

INFORMATION
Maps

The Lake District is mostly covered by the Ordnance Survey (OS) Landranger 1:50,000 maps No 85 *(Carlisle & Solway Firth)*, No 89 *(West Cumbria)*, No 90 *(Penrith & Keswick)* and No 96 *(Barrow-in-Furness & South Lakeland)*.

If you want greater detail, which is recommended for most walks as the landscape is often complex, the area (except the far

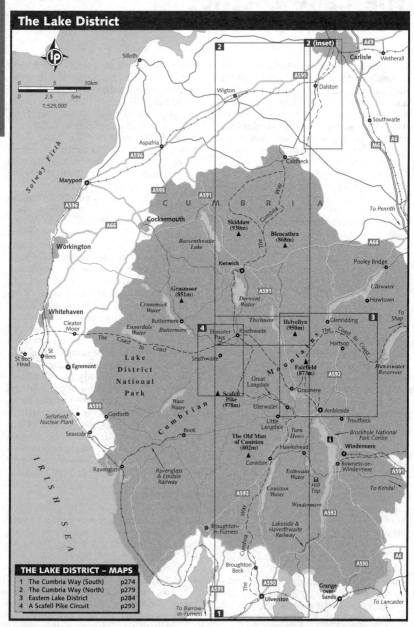

The Lake District

Silloth

Carlisle

Wetheral

Wigton

Dalston

Southwaite

Aspfria

Caldbeck

To Penrith

Maryport

C U M B R I A

Skiddaw
(930m)

Blencathra
(868m)

The Cumbria Way

Cockermouth

Bassenthwaite
Lake

Workington

Keswick

Pooley Bridge

Ullswater

Howtown

Grasmoor
(851m)

Derwent
Water

Whitehaven

Crummock
Water

Thirlmere

Helvellyn
(950m)

Glenridding

To
Shap

Cleator
Moor

Ennerdale
Water

Buttermere

Honister
Pass

Rosthwaite

The Coast to Coast

Hartsop

St Bees
Head

St
Bees

The Coast to Coast

Lake

Seathwaite

Fairfield
(873m)

Haweswater
Reservoir

Egremont

District

National

Grasmere

Park

Great
Langdale

Ambleside

Troutbeck

Scafell
Pike
(978m)

Elterwater

Wast
Water

Little
Langdale

Tarn
Hows

Brockhole National
Park Centre

Sellafield
Nuclear Plant

Gosforth

Boot

The Old Man
of Coniston
(802m)

Hawkshead

Windermere

Seascale

Coniston

Esthwaite
Water

Hill
Top

Bowness-on-
Windermere

Ravenglass

Ravenglass
& Eskdale
Railway

Coniston Water

Windermere

To Kendal

Broughton-
in-Furness

Lakeside &
Haverthwaite
Railway

Broughton
Beck

Ulverston

Grange-
over-
Sands

To Lancaster

To Barrow-
in-Furness

THE LAKE DISTRICT – MAPS

0   5   10km
0 2.5 5mi
1:525,000

Solway Firth

I R I S H   S E A

C u m b r i a n   M o u n t a i n s   The Coast to Coast

northern and southern sections) is covered by OS Outdoor Leisure 1:25,000 maps No 4 *(The English Lakes – North Western Area)*, No 5 *(The English Lakes – North Eastern Area)*, No 6 *(The English Lakes – South Western Area)* and No 7 *(The English Lakes – South Eastern Area)*.

Harvey also produces a large and excellent Superwalker series of maps of the whole Lake District at a scale of 1:25,000, and Footprint has several inexpensive map guides, such as *Walks around Ambleside* and *Walks around Keswick*, which are very useful for suggestions.

Alfred Wainwright fans will love the *Wainwright Maps of the Lakeland Fells*, published by Chop McKean and compiled from the tiny, intricate maps of his *Pictorial Guides* (see Books following) to cover wider areas. However, these are for armchair rambling – you'll need a proper survey map on the hills.

For maps covering individual walks, see Planning in the introduction to each walk.

Books

If you piled up all the books on walking in the Lake District there'd be another mountain to scale, so here are just a few. Specific books for the routes described are listed in the relevant sections.

The classic series of *Pictorial Guides to the Lakeland Fells* by Alfred Wainwright (or AW as he's known) is a set of seven pocket-sized volumes in a quaint, idiosyncratic and very attractive combination of hand-drawn text and pictures. However, these books were written in the 1960s and have been only slightly updated since. That's part of their charm but you should use them alongside a detailed map for route finding.

Modern guidebooks include *100 Lake District Hill Walks* by Gordon Brown, which covers every hill, fell and mountain in the area, including well-known classics and out-of-the-way rarities. The *Lake District Walks* and *More Lake District Walks* Pathfinder Guides, published by Jarrold, describe routes from a few miles to all-day treks, over high ground and along valleys, with extracts from relevant 1:25,000 OS maps.

For a few relaxing days, there's a choice of books covering shorter or easier routes, including *Teashop Walks in the Lake District* by Jean Patefield and *Lakeland Walking on the Level* by Norman Buckley. If you want to get away from the popular areas, *The Borders of Lakeland* by Robert Gambles describes 30 walks in the less-visited fringes.

The Lakes scenery naturally inspires a whole stack of picture books too. Again, AW is near the top of the pile. His *Wainwright's Favourite Lakeland Mountains* is a homage to several peaks, including Fairfield, Helvellyn, Scafell Pike, High Street and Glaramara (all on routes described in this chapter), with excellent photos by Derry Brabbs. There are more splendid photos plus good background information in *The Lake District* by Terry Marsh & Jon Sparks – the official national park guide.

Falling somewhere between a guidebook and a picture book is *Complete Lakeland Fells* by Bill Birkett. The highly acclaimed Bob Allen books, *On High Lakeland Fells* and *On Lower Lakeland Fells*, with colour photos and good descriptions, also contain sketch maps.

More books are suggested under Other Walks at the end of this chapter.

Information Sources

There are many Tourist Information Centres (TICs) in and around the Lake District. The main TIC for central Cumbria and the Lake District is at Windermere (☎ 01539-446499), next to the train station. Quite a few centres are run by the national park authority and provide additional information on the park. The main National Park Visitors Centre (☎ 01539-446601, fax 445555, **e** infodesk @lake-district.gov.uk, **w** www.lake-district .gov.uk) is at Brockholes, a few miles north of Windermere. You can also get information from the official Cumbria Board Tourist Web site at **w** www.cumbria-the-lake-dis trict.co.uk, or try the Go Cumbria Web site at **w** www.go-cumbria.co.uk.

Specific TICs, listed under Planning for individual walks, can provide accommodation and public transport information. Many also sell walking maps and books, or give away leaflets. Most TICs also provide the latest weather reports (usually pinned up on a door or window).

At TICs, hotels, shops and various other places you can pick up a copy of *Park Life*, a freebie newspaper produced by the National Park Authority. It's full of useful tourist information, background articles, and advertisements for places to stay and things to do.

The national park has a 24-hour Weatherline Service (☎ 01768-775757) for forecasts and information about mountain conditions.

Guided Walks

The South Lakeland District Council organises a series of guided walks around towns and villages, while the national park authority organises guided walks in the hills. Details are available from TICs. If these don't suit, the Lake District abounds with private mountain guides who can show you around on foot or arrange more energetic activities such as rock climbing. Most advertise in visitors centres, hostels and outdoor gear shops. Of particular interest to female visitors may be the company, Walking Women (☎ 01926-313321, e queries @walkingwomen.com, w www.walking women.com), which organises women-only guided walking holidays in the Lake District for three days or longer.

GETTING THERE & AWAY

The Lake District's main gateway cities and towns are Kendal, Windermere, Penrith, Keswick and Carlisle, which all have good coach links to the rest of Britain, and are easy to reach by car.

The main railway line between London and Scotland goes through Kendal (with a branch off to Windermere) and Penrith (where a Rail-Link bus ties in with trains and serves Keswick, Cockermouth and Workington on the northern side of the Lake District).

The Getting Around chapter lists several public transport inquiry lines that provide details of national and local bus and train services: See the boxed text 'National Transport Information' on p92.

GETTING AROUND

For specific information on public transport throughout the Lake District, or advice on planning a journey, contact the useful Cumbria County Council's Travelink service (☎ 01228-606000), or log onto the Web site at w www.travel cumbria.co.uk.

A very useful booklet, available free from TICs, is *Lakeland Explorer* – a complete list of all the bus services in the Lake District and surrounding areas, with details of buses that tie in with boats and trains. There's also a very good section on suggested linear walks using the bus to get back to your starting point at the end of the day. A leaflet called *Straight Line Walking in the Lake District* has other suggestions for walk-bus combinations.

A handy bus service is Stagecoach Cumbria's Lakeslink (No 555), running through the heart of the Lake District between Carlisle and Lancaster via Keswick, Grasmere, Ambleside, Windermere and Kendal. This route covers many of the bases for walking routes described in this book. The central portion between Keswick and Kendal has a frequent service roughly hourly from 8am to 5pm Monday to Saturday (with a

---

William Wordsworth

The unofficial poet laureate of the Lake District is William Wordsworth, a leading figure in the English Romantic movement. He was born in Cockermouth in 1770 and went to school at Hawkshead, near Ambleside. In 1799 (after he had begun work on his epic *The Prelude*), he and Samuel Coleridge began a tour of the Lake District, starting near Penrith and ending at Wasdale Head. Later the same year, Wordsworth and his sister Dorothy moved into Dove Cottage in Grasmere.

In 1802 Wordsworth married and, as his family and fame increased, Dove Cottage became increasingly crowded. In 1808 the family moved to Allan Bank, then to the Old Parsonage in Grasmere and, finally, to Rydal Mount between Grasmere and Ambleside, where he lived until his death.

few later buses between Kendal and Grasmere) and five times on Sunday. Most of the buses extend to Lancaster (only twice on Sunday), while the service extends to Carlisle three times daily (including Sunday). The *Lakeland Explorer* leaflet has all the details, or you can phone the Stagecoach Cumbria Information Line directly (☎ 0870-608 2608).

To reach the western side of the Lake District, the Cumbria Coast Railway is also very useful. It operates between Lancaster and Carlisle, which both have frequent train services to/from all parts of Britain.

The Cumbria Way

Distance	68mi (109.5km)
Duration	5 days
Standard	medium
Start	Ulverston
Finish	Carlisle
Gateways	Kendal, Ulverston, Keswick, Carlisle

Summary An excellent route through the heart of the Lake District, keeping mostly to valleys, plus a few high and potentially serious sections. Although some days are long, conditions are not too strenuous or difficult.

In the 1970s the county of Cumbria was created by joining the two ancient counties of Westmorland and Cumberland, with some parts of Lancashire and Yorkshire's west riding thrown in for good measure. For most visitors 'Cumbria' and the 'Lake District' are synonymous, although locals are often at pains to point out that there's more to their county than *just* lakes.

The Cumbria Way winds through the heart of the Lake District and rewards walkers with top-quality mountain views. However, it's essentially a valley walk and doesn't cross any summits, which makes this route ideal for less experienced or less hardy walkers.

Beyond the Lake District, the other parts of Cumbria are perhaps not quite as stunning as the high mountain areas, but they're scenic nonetheless and far less crowded.

The Cumbria Way goes through some of these areas too, presenting a true cross section of all the county has to offer.

Direction, Distance & Duration

The Cumbria Way can be followed in either direction, but we recommend starting in Ulverston and going north to Carlisle. This way you should have most of the wind behind you (although don't bank on it).

The Cumbria Way is 68mi long. That's measured on the map, so with the ups and downs it's probably 70mi or more. Although it's mostly a low-level route, it goes near several tempting mountain tops so the possibilities for diversions are numerous, which will, of course, add to your mileage (and time).

Many people take five days to cover the Way and we have divided the walk accordingly as follows:

day	from	to	mi/km
1	Ulverston	Coniston	15/24
2	Coniston	Great Langdale	11/17.5
3	Great Langdale	Keswick	15/24
4	Keswick	Caldbeck	13/21
5	Caldbeck	Carlisle	14/22.5

Note that the hours given for each stage in the route description are walking times only. You should allow an extra couple of hours for rests, photos, lunch stops and so on.

Alternatives If you're a fast walker, you could possibly do the whole route in four days. If you're simply pushed for time you could consider cutting the last day instead (see Day 5 for more thoughts on this). If you only have a day or two to spare, see the boxed text 'The Cumbria Way – Route Highlights' on p276.

Relaxed walkers could easily take six days, with breaks at Coniston, Elterwater, Borrowdale, Keswick or Skiddaw House, Caldbeck and Carlisle. With more days you could branch off the Way for some high-level add-ons. For example, you could stay two nights at Coniston, doing the nearby peak called the Old Man of Coniston on the day in between, or you could stay at Borrowdale two nights and bag Scafell Pike. (The latter route is described in this chapter.)

PLANNING
Maps

A good map is essential for this route as there are very few Cumbria Way signposts or waymarks. *The Cumbria Way* strip map by Harvey is good but has the weakness of all strip maps – if you go more than a mile or two off the route, you also go off the map. This can be a real bind if you're heading for an out-of-the-way hostel or you get lost. You're much better off with proper maps (especially if you plan to do any other walking in the Lake District). The extra expense of buying several maps is worthwhile when it saves you blundering around in the mist for several hours. If you go for Harvey maps, you'll need the Superwalker series 1:25,000 *South-West*, *South-East*, *Central* and *North Lakeland* maps (although the first and last sections of the route are not shown).

If you go for Ordnance Survey (OS) maps, the Cumbria Way is covered by OS Landranger 1:50,000 maps No 96 *(Barrow-in-Furness & South Lakeland)*, No 90 *(Penrith & Keswick)* and No 85 *(Carlisle & Solway Firth)*. If you want more detail, you'll need OS Outdoor Leisure 1:25,000 maps No 4 *(The English Lakes – North Western Area)*, No 5 *(The English Lakes – North Eastern Area)*, No 6 *(The English Lakes – South Western Area)* and No 7 *(The English Lakes – South Eastern Area)*. Note that only a small bit of the route is on map No 6, and No 5 doesn't quite stretch as far as Carlisle.

Books

A detailed guidebook for this route is not essential but can be very handy. The guidebook that created this route, *The Cumbria Way* by John Trevelyan, is out of print or hard to find. Several alternatives have filled the gap, including *The Cumbria Way* by Anthony Burton, which includes very detailed route descriptions placed opposite extracts from 1:25,000 OS maps. *The Cumbria Way* by Phillip Dubock has lovingly hand-crafted Wainwright-style maps and instructions, and is available by post from Miway Publishing, PO Box 2, Keswick CA12 4GA (£5.95 plus 60p postage within the UK). The same author also produces an accompanying *The Cumbria Way Accommodation Guide* (free with the guidebook or £1.25 on its own, including postage).

Information Sources

For specific information along the Cumbria Way, contact the local TICs – Ulverston (☎ 01229-587120), Coniston (☎ 01539-441533), Keswick (☎ 01768-772645) and Carlisle (☎ 01228-625600). Ulverston TIC has very friendly staff and, for a small charge, offers a booking service for B&Bs along the Cumbria Way.

Guided Walks & Baggage Services

There are annual walking festivals in Ulverston, Keswick and Cockermouth, which include guided walks; TICs have details. Several of the national companies listed under Guided Walks in the Facts for the Walker chapter organise walking tours on the Cumbria Way.

See the boxed text 'Baggage Services' on p50 for details on the Sherpa Van Project and Brigantes baggage-carrying services. Note that the Sherpa service may operate only between Ulverstone and Keswick. Another local company offering a baggage service is Contours Walking Holidays, listed under Guided Walks in the Facts for the Walker chapter.

PLACES TO STAY & EAT

On this route you're rarely more than a few miles from a hotel, B&B or campsite, and often much nearer. Specific places to stay are listed in the walk description, but for a wider choice use *The Rambler's Yearbook & Accommodation Guide* or *Stilwell's National Trail Companion* (details are given under Books in the Facts for the Walker chapter). For a local perspective, use *The Cumbria Way Accommodation List*, produced by South Lakeland District Council and available from TICs, or *The Cumbria Way Accommodation Guide* by Phillip Dubock, mentioned under Books in the introduction to this walk.

You can use YHA hostels the whole way and these can be booked in one go through the YHA Booking Bureau (☎ 01629-581061, e reservations@yha.org.uk).

The Way is also generally well served by comfortable pubs, cafes and restaurants. Finding something to eat in the evening is no problem, although lunch choices are sometimes nonexistent. For picnics or if you're cooking your own meals, there are several villages with shops.

GETTING TO/FROM THE WALK

Bus To reach the start, National Express coaches to Barrow-in-Furness go via Ulverston. National Express also goes to Windermere from many parts of the country, from where local buses run to Barrow-in-Furness via Ulverston about six times per day. At the end of the route, Carlisle is well served by National Express coaches.

Stagecoach Cumbria runs several local routes, including the very useful No 555 Lakeslink service between Carlisle and Lancaster. See Getting Around at the start of this chapter for details.

Train Ulverston is on the Cumbria Coast Railway, between Lancaster and Carlisle. To reach Ulverston, the local service runs every few hours Monday to Saturday, but only twice on Sunday.

At the end of the walk, Carlisle has frequent rail links with most parts of the country, including mainline services to London and Scotland, and the Cumbria Coast line back to Ulverston.

Car Ulverston is on the A590, which runs from the M6 motorway to Barrow-in-Furness. Carlisle is on the northern edge of the Lake District, just off the M6.

THE WALK
Ulverston

Not a typical Lake District town, Ulverston's cobbled streets have yet to be lined with gift emporiums and other tourist paraphernalia. There are shops, a supermarket and lots of pubs – some get lively on Thursday (market day) and at the weekend. Somewhat bizarrely, Ulverston also has a **Laurel & Hardy museum** (Stan was born here), which is worth a short visit before you get walking.

The excellent TIC (☎ 01229-587120) is in the town hall on County Square, a roundabout in the town centre. The friendly staff are particularly helpful in booking accommodation along the Cumbria Way. For last-minute purchases, the Furness Rambler on New Market St sells walking equipment, guidebooks and maps.

The nearest campsite is *Bardsea Leisure Park* (☎ 01229-584712), on the outskirts of town, which is mainly for caravans but walkers pay £6 per tent. If you prefer a roof over your head, *The Walkers Hostel* (☎ 01229-585588, e povey@walkershostel.freeserve .co.uk), on the edge of town as you come in from the east, is a recommended budget option. There's a range of double rooms and small, shared rooms, and other facilities include free tea, coffee and toast, a nice lounge with lots of books, and a garden. The owners can advise on the Cumbria Way and other routes in the area. Bed and breakfast is a bargain £10 and a four-course evening meal is £6. They also offer long-term parking.

B&Bs in town catering for walkers include *Church Walk House* (☎ 01229-582211), very near The Gill and the start of the walk, charging £22 (some are en suite); *Dyker Bank Guesthouse* (☎ 01229-582423), on Springfield Rd, with lower rates; and *Sefton House* (☎ 01229-582190, e roma@seftonhouse.co.uk), on Queen St, with en suite singles/doubles for £40/45.

For food in the evening there are at least three shops selling fish and chips in and around the centre. *The Rose & Crown* on King St and *The Farmers Arms* on the marketplace both do good pub food at reasonable prices. For slightly more stylish eating and drinking, *Laurels Bistro* (☎ 01229-583961) and *King's Cafe-Winebar*, both on Queen St, are recommended. Or try *Amigos* (☎ 01229-587616), a lively Mexican restaurant opposite the TIC.

Day 1: Ulverston to Coniston

15mi (24km), 6–7 hours

This first day is quite long, but undulating rather than steep, and not too hard. Keep a close eye on your map, though as it's a bit complex and not well signposted. There are no pubs or cafes for lunch. As you go along, the landscape changes from rolling farmland to rugged fells – a taste of greater things to come.

The start of the Way is in the corner of an open area (used as a car park) called the Gill, on the northern side of town. It's marked by an impressive steel Cumbria Way sculpture. There are also some public toilets – handy if you've just got off the bus and need to change into walking gear.

From the sculpture follow a footpath uphill, keeping close to the stream on your left. After five minutes go left across the stream on a small bridge and up another path to meet a lane. Don't cross the lane, but go sharply right through a very narrow gap in the wall called a 'squeeze gate' – the first of many you'll encounter on this route – and then across the fields towards Old Hall Farm.

From here the Way is mostly straightforward, winding through more fields and farmyards. Take care as you go through the village of Broughton Beck; take a small 'no through road' and, just *before* the stream, turn left (north) along a path. You also need to be alert at a large farm called Keldray, where the Way is diverted to the left (west) of the farmhouse but then seems to fizzle out. Once past the house go diagonally left and uphill to reach Gawthwaite. Here you enter the national park but, apart from a few more signposts and neater stiles, you won't notice much difference in the path itself.

Continue through fields and some craggy patches of moorland, passing a picturesque lake called Beacon Tarn (take care in the mist here as there's a bewildering choice of paths) before dropping to cross the A5084 and reach the shores of **Coniston Water**, a large lake – the first of several you will encounter on this walk. This final section through the lakeside woodland is a wonderful end to the day's walk. You hit civilisation at *Coniston Hall Campsite* (☎ 01539-441223),

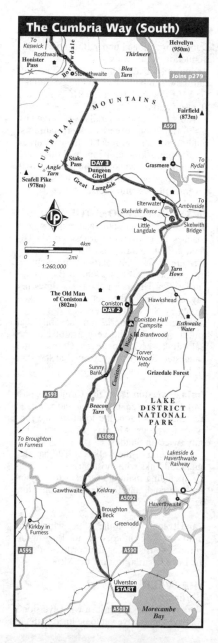

The Cumbria Way (South)

about a mile south of town, where walkers are charged £3 (but it's closed in winter). From here a clear path will take you into Coniston itself.

If you want to save a few steps, or you just enjoy boating, the Coniston Launch (☎ 01539-436216, W www.lakefell.co.uk) stops at Torver Wood jetty (about 2mi before the town) from 11am to 5pm, on the hour, during summer. For £2.40 you can cruise along to Coniston jetty, via the Brantwood jetty.

Coniston

The small town of Coniston has a manicured look, but the surrounding craggy hills give it an authentic edge. Attractions include the **John Ruskin Museum** (see the boxed text for details). There's also a TIC (☎ 01539-441533) in the large car park on Tilberthwaite Ave, just off the main street. On the main street itself is the *supermarket*, post office, bank, *cafes* and several shops, some of which sell walking gear, maps and books.

Holly How YHA Hostel (☎ *01539-441323)*, charging £9.80, is on the north edge of town; and *Coppermines YHA Hostel* (☎ *01539-441261)* is just over a mile away, charging £9.

B&Bs that welcome walkers include *Lakeland House* (☎ *01539-441303)*, which charges £16 to £20; and *Shepherds Villa* (☎ *01539-441337)*, from £18. Both are on Tilberthwaite Ave. Also recommended are *Beech Tree* (☎ *01539-441717)*, on Yewdale Rd, and nearby *Oaklands* (☎ *01539-441245)*. Both are nonsmoking and charge from £18.

The *Black Bull Hotel* (☎ *01539-441335)* offers 'olde-worldy' en suite B&B from around £30 and good, although rather expensive, bar food, plus meals in the restaurant from £9 to £15. Opposite, *The Yewdale Hotel* (☎ *01539-441280)* has similarly priced accommodation. *The Crown Hotel* (☎ *01539-441243)* was being completely renovated when we passed through, so might be worth a look; B&B is £25. Up the hill, just out of the village, *The Sun Hotel* (☎ *01539-441248)* does B&B from £25 and has a good bar serving food from £7 to £10.

Day 2: Coniston to Great Langdale
11mi (17.5km), 5–6 hours
This day is a wonderful mix of farmland, woodland, hills and river plains, leading to the top end of Great Langdale, a large valley penetrating into the heart of the high Lake District. Steep sections are rare, with just a few short sharp shocks at the end of the day.

The Way leaves from the east side of Coniston and can be tricky to find. From the TIC take Tilberthwaite Ave (towards Hawkshead) for 400m, go left (signposted to Ambleside) past the football field on the right, to reach a small, old stone bridge on the right. Go over this bridge and *immediately* left (not through the gate) over a stile to reach a path leading uphill through meadows and into woodland.

From here the Way is clear, past Low Yewdale Farm and Tarn Hows Cottages, then up a lane to reach Tarn Hows. The Way goes west of the tarn, then along a track to meet and cross the A593 main road.

After a short stretch near the road, the peaceful woodland theme continues as you follow lanes and paths, mostly downhill (with a possible diversion to view **Skelwith Force** – an impressive waterfall when the river is high). At Skelwith Bridge the Way goes through the yard of a slate factory. In

John Ruskin

John Ruskin (1819–1900) was a poet, writer, painter, philosopher, conservationist, social reformer and visionary, and a major influential figure of the 19th century. He lived in a house called Brantwood, on the east side of Coniston Water, from 1872 until his death. (Brantwood can be visited by boat from Coniston village.) The Ruskin Museum in Coniston village covers some aspects of Ruskin's life and work, and also includes exhibits relating to the lake and surrounding landscape. The Ruskin museum is open daily, but closed in winter. Brantwood is open all year but with reduced hours and access in winter. The TIC can provide more details.

the factory showroom (you'd be surprised how many things can be made from slate) is a *restaurant* with good home-made food at reasonable prices. Nearby *The Talbot* pub serves sandwiches and bar meals from £4.

Beyond Skelwith Bridge, the Way follows the north bank of the river upstream to **Elterwater**, a beautiful little lake. From here you get a fine view up Great Langdale, with rising fells on either side and the curiously conical Langdale Pikes dominating the end of the valley.

Follow the new path close to Great Langdale Beck to arrive at Elterwater village – a good spot for a late lunch or an early overnight stop. The charming *Britannia Inn* (☎ 01539-437210) does bar meals and has B&B for £31 (£35 en suite). At **Maple Tree Corner**, run by the inn, B&B is from £27. The village also has a *YHA Hostel* (☎ 01539-437245) and several other essentials – post office, *shop*, telephone, public toilet and bowling green.

The Cumbria Way – Route Highlights

The best section of the Cumbria Way is between Skelwith Bridge and Borrowdale, covered in the second half of Day 2, all of Day 3 and the first half of Day 4. If you're short of time you could do just this section by taking a bus from Ambleside to Skelwith Bridge, and then walk up to Elterwater and Great Langdale to overnight. An option from here if you're really short of time would be to go eastwards over the fells to Grasmere – famous for its Wordsworth connections – and return to Ambleside by bus. Alternatively, from Langdale follow the Cumbria Way over Stake Pass, with Scafell Pike and the other high peaks dominating your view to the west, before dropping down into Stonethwaite and Rosthwaite, which between them have a good choice of cafes, pubs and B&Bs. From here you can catch the bus (there's a few per day) or continue walking to Keswick, from where it's easy to get a bus back to Ambleside.

Great Langdale

Beyond Elterwater, the Way continues along Great Langdale. Near the head of the valley the *New Dungeon Ghyll Hotel* (☎ 01539-437213, @ enquiries@dungeon -ghyll.com) does B&B between £32 and £39, depending on time of year, while the bar serves snacks for around £3 and meals for around £5. Next door a very lively pub called *Sticklebarn* (☎ 01539-437356) serves bar food and also has a spartan bunkhouse (for £10). There are no cooking facilities but the pub serves breakfast. Beyond here the busy *National Trust Campsite* (☎ 01539-437668) charges £3.25. Nearby is the near-legendary *Old Dungeon Ghyll Hotel* (☎ 01539-437272), where the no-frills Hiker's Bar has good beer and large helpings of food for about £5. The hotel itself is a bit smarter and often full, but has been welcoming walkers for years with B&B from £33 (£37 en suite).

Day 3: Great Langdale to Keswick
15mi (24km), 6–8 hours
Until this point the Cumbria Way has mostly followed valleys, but today the route takes you into the fells proper. This is a harder day as you get a taste of the Lake District's splendid ruggedness. Alas, the 'taste' is only a tantalising one, as the Way soon returns to valleys.

Today's walk starts at the head of Great Langdale, where this valley splits into two branches. Take the right (north) branch, a valley called Mickleden, with a spur called the Band on your left (south) and the towering buttresses of Langdale Pikes on your right. At the end of Mickleden there's a fork in the path. Go right and up fairly steeply to **Stake Pass**. From the top you can see back down Mickleden, with a range of wonderfully named peaks spread out behind – Pike of Blisco, Crinkle Crags, Bow Fell – and on the other side the pointed top of the Pike of Stickle can also be seen.

All views briefly disappear as you cross the top of the pass, winding through grassy mounds and past the cairn that marks the highest point on this day's walk (about

480m). In misty conditions take a compass bearing at the top of Stake Pass to ensure you get the correct path down into Langstrath. Many people take the wrong path and arrive at Angle Tarn!

Another splendid view opens out as the Way drops into the quiet and narrow valley of Langstrath. This runs into another valley called Borrowdale, where the Cumbria Way crosses the Coast to Coast Walk (covered in the Northern England Long-Distance Paths chapter). You can divert briefly from the Way, across an old bridge, to have a look at the tiny and ancient farming village of **Stonethwaite**. If it's time for a break, there's a welcome *teashop*. There's also an *inn* and some B&Bs, with more options in nearby Rosthwaite, which makes this a possible overnight stop. (See the Scafell Pike Circuit later in this chapter for more details.)

From Stonethwaite the Way continues to Rosthwaite and then keeps fairly close to the River Derwent (one of many rivers in Britain with this name, so don't be confused) to reach the west bank of **Derwent Water** – one of the most scenic lakes in Cumbria. Make the most of the views because beyond Victoria Bay the Way leaves the lake and passes through woodland. Look out for **bears** in among the trees – don't worry, they're only big sculptures skilfully cut by chainsaw from local logs and sold at a nearby workshop.

Near Hawes End, branch off to the west if you are staying at *Catbells Barn* in Skelgill. Contacted through Lakeland Barns Booking Office (☎ 01768-772645, fax 775043, ⓔ keswicktic@lake-district.gov.uk), a night in the camping barn costs £3.50 (bookings essential). Beyond the woods, the Way goes through Pontinscale, from where you follow clear paths into Keswick.

If you want to cut the last few miles, the Keswick Launch (☎ 01768-772263, ⓦ www .keswick-launch.co.uk), a passenger boat, circumnavigates the lake (clockwise hourly in summer) via several jetties, including Hawse End and Nichol End (just before the route goes through Pontinscale). Cruising into Keswick is a splendid way to end the day's walk. You can get timetable details from TICs or the Keswick Launch Web site.

Keswick

The town of Keswick is the hub of the northern Lake District and often very busy, but it's been a market centre for centuries and on the tourist map for over 100 years, so it easily copes with the crowds. The TIC (☎ 01768-772645) is in the central market square. Keswick also has plenty of food stores, banks, a laundrette and main post-office, plus several outdoor gear shops.

Cheap places to stay include the *YHA Hostel* (☎ *01768-772484*), close to the centre, which charges £10.85. For camping, the *Keswick Camping & Caravanning Club Site* (☎ *01768-772392*) has back-packer pitches for £6.

For excellent value B&B, you can't go wrong at *Bridgedale Guesthouse* (☎ *01768-773914*), on Main St, just around the corner from the main bus stop. Single and double rooms cost from £14 (plus £2 for a light breakfast or £3 for the works). There are also some simple rooms with more beds that cost from £10. If you need to make an early start, breakfast is served from 7.15am. Other facilities include a drying room. The attached *tearoom* provides snacks and lunches, and Helen, the friendly and laid-back owner, can advise on local places for evening food.

The main cluster of B&Bs is just south-east of the town centre in the area around Southey and Blencathra Sts. On Eskin St several places cater for walkers, including *Allerdale House* (☎ *01768-773891*) with excellent rooms for £24, plus £11.50 for dinner; *Clarence House* (☎ *01768-773186*, ⓔ *clarenceho@aol.com*), from £21 to £28; and *Braemar* (☎ *01768-773743*, ⓔ *braemar @kencomp.net*), from £17 to £21. *Ander-dale Guesthouse* (☎ *01768-772578*), on Helvellyn St, is also recommended, charging £16 for standard singles and £32 for en suite doubles.

Crosthwaite Rd, north of the town centre, has another row of B&Bs, including *Hazel-mere* (☎ *01768-772445*), from £19.50 (£23 en suite); *Undereaves* (☎ *01768-772136*), from £17; and *Riverdale* (☎ *01768-772920*), from £25. At the top of the road, *The Pheasant Inn* (☎ *01768-772219*) does B&B for

£23/40 per single/double and has good food in the bar from £6 to £8.

If you want to reduce tomorrow's mileage, go to **Spooney Green** (☎ *017687-72601*), a very comfortable B&B on the northern side of town beyond the footbridge over the A66 bypass at the foot of the path up to Skiddaw. It charges £20.

Keswick has plenty of cafes and teashops. Recommended is the **Lakeland Peddlar**, which serves wholefood snacks and lunches, is also a bike shop and has an Internet service. In the evening, pubs are your best bet. The **Dog & Gun**, on Lake Rd, is justifiably popular but often crowded. The **Oddfellows Arms**, on the market square, and **The George Hotel**, on St John's St, are also recommended. **Greensleeves Restaurant**, also on St John's St, has good-value meat and veggie dishes for around £5, including a happy hour (6pm to 7pm) when pizzas and pastas are £3.50. Nearby, the **Square Orange Café-Bar** does healthy breakfasts, light lunches and evening meals. Opposite is **The Red Fort Indian Restaurant** with main courses for around £5 to £7.

Day 4: Keswick to Caldbeck
13mi (21km), 5–6 hours

This day is not especially long, but it's the most serious as it crosses the open moorland of Skiddaw where you're farther from civilisation than at any other point on the Way. This has benefits – a splendid feeling of space and airy isolation. But it also has its dangers – paths are not always clear and mist is a frequent possibility. You definitely need to know how to use your map and compass here. If the clouds are low or you're not feeling intrepid, you can take an alternative low-level route to the west of the main route following clear tracks and quiet lanes.

The official Cumbria Way leaves Keswick on the west side of town, along Crosthwaite Rd, then right into Brundholme Rd just before the petrol station. However, if you're in the town centre it's easier to take Station Rd across the bridge near the YHA hostel. When this road bears right, take a path straight on, past a swimming pool, to

Keswick & Lake District Pencils

By geological good fortune, some of the rock around Keswick happens to contain the finest graphite in the world. This is ideal for making pencils, and a pencil industry has existed here since the 15th century. The 160-year-old factory of the Cumberland Pencil Company is in the centre of Keswick, where the Cumberland Pencil Museum, also the world's largest pencil shop, is open daily (£2). It may not be for everyone, but I'll admit to a special fondness for this place. One of my most vivid childhood memories is a set of colouring pencils. On the lid was written *Lakeland by Cumberland* below a hand-drawn illustration of a range of mountains. My family lived in the south of England and I'd never seen a real mountain. What struck me about the illustration was that the mountains were not green but shaded in purple. This image (and the pencil box) stayed with me for a long time. For many years I wanted to go to Lakeland by Cumberland, which I assumed was a place in the north, to see those amazing purple mountains.

Maybe the pencil set planted subliminal seeds that got me into walking. These days I understand about artistic licence but still find Lake District mountains constantly attractive – even if they are mainly green – and I even find small, obscure museums quite interesting.

David Else

meet Brundholme Rd. Turn left, ignore a lane coming in from the right, then take a rough track on the right, up hill and over the A66 bypass on a footbridge. This goes up through pine plantation to meet the end of a lane that comes from Applethwaite.

From here the Way strides out across the open fells, ignoring the well-worn route up Skiddaw and taking instead a quieter path along the steep side of Glenderaterra Valley. On the route, the remote **Skiddaw House YHA Hostel** (*bookings* ☎ *01697-478325*) costs £7.35, although note that the hostel is closed in winter.

At Skiddaw House the alternative low-level route branches off north-west towards Bassenthwaite. The main route heads north-east and takes you down by Caldew Beck then up beside Graingsill Beck before going steeply up the valley side away from the beck to reach Lingy Hut – a mountain shelter.

Beyond the hut, paths go both sides of High Pike (at 658m, the summit of the Cumbria Way). The official route takes the path on the left, which runs just west of the summit. If you want to bag the summit, make your own way up **High Pike**. The top is marked by a cairn and a slate bench – an ideal place to rest and admire the view northwards to the Cheviot Hills and the silvery tongue of the Solway Firth, marking the border between England and Scotland. Below the lookout, the wild fells drop steeply and suddenly to farmland. The Lake District ends here, almost as if cut by a knife.

To leave the summit of High Pike use your compass to take a bearing on the hamlet of Nether Row, then drop to meet farm tracks, lanes and a short section of path that leads you into the village of Caldbeck.

Caldbeck

This peaceful village nestles below the fells. In the churchyard is the **grave of John Peel**, the famous huntsman. The village shop is open every day (but possibly closed on Sunday afternoon if it's raining). There's a bookshop, a museum and some other interesting little shops at Priests Mill, near the church.

There's no hostel or campsite, but *Hudscales Barn*, at Hudscales Farm about 1km east of Nether Row, is good and the people who run it very friendly. Book through the Lakeland Barns Booking Office (☎ 01768-772645, fax 775043, ✉ keswicktic@lake-district.gov.uk). As with all barns in the Lake District, it costs £3.50 to stay here. If you have your own tent, camping is also allowed on the farm for £3.

Whether you're in the barn or a tent, breakfast can be provided for £4. If you are staying here, make sure you take the footpath from Nether Row straight to the farm. Don't follow the signposts as they take you a very long way round on lanes and farm tracks.

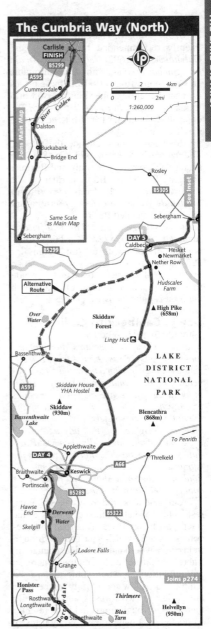

B&Bs in Caldbeck include *The Briars* (☎ 01697-478633), charging £19 and frequently recommended by walkers; and *Gatehouse* (☎ 01697-478092, ℮ ray@cald beckgatehouse.co.uk) with very comfortable en suite rooms from £19. Both these places are near the centre of the village. Also worth trying is *Grapes Barn* (☎ 01697-478128), opposite the church, where Mr Reed lets two single rooms for £18.

About half a mile outside the village, *Todcrofts Farm* (☎ 01697-478485) is a small place, but very friendly and flexible, charging £18.50 for B&B. Farther up the road (about a mile from the village) *Swaledale Watch* (☎ 01697-478409) is another recommended B&B.

In the village centre, *The Oddfellows Arms* (☎ 01697-478227) is a fairly smart but friendly pub with en suite rooms for £25/45. This is also the only place to get an evening meal, so prices are on the steep side (main courses around £8 to £10), although the food is undeniably excellent.

Day 5: Caldbeck to Carlisle
14mi (22.5km), 5–6 hours
After the long upland sections, this final day looks deceptively easy on the map. It's circuitous, however, with a more than generous helping of stiles and gates, and is surprisingly tiring. There are also some sections that are not exactly scenic, so it's tempting to cut this day completely. If you're short of time and weighing up this day against an extra one in the high fells then we'd definitely recommend the latter. But this is the Cumbria Way, not the Lakes Way, and this final bit of the route shows you parts of the county rarely seen by visitors.

From Caldbeck, the Way takes a quiet, residential road along the north bank of the river, past Briars B&B. This road soon becomes a track, which you follow through fields into woodland and pine plantation. There's a maze of paths and tracks here, so pay attention to your route. Don't be tempted to follow too closely to the river but go left at two forks, gradually uphill, then level through more fields to re-enter woodland on a wide track used by forestry

vehicles. About 2mi (about one hour of walking) out from Caldbeck, a path branches off this track to the right, marked by a small stone cairn, and goes steeply down to meet the river.

The Way now follows the river (rarely more than a few hundred metres from it), using faint paths, clear tracks and some sections of busy lane through farmland. At the village of Bridge End, about halfway between Caldbeck and Carlisle, the *pub* has food and the nearby garage has a small *shop* (closed Sunday). From here you cross to the east side of the river, through Buckabank, then cross back to the west side over a white footbridge (built in 1999 to replace its predecessor, which was washed away in a flood).

The Way then winds round the back of the small town of Dalston – with overgrown paths full of rubbish – then follows the river and the railway line to a bridge near Cummersdale, where you cross to the east bank for the final time. You might be able to avoid Dalston by keeping to the east side of the river between Buckabank and Cummersdale Bridge. Another option, if you're not a purist, is to catch a train from Dalston into Carlisle – or even back to Ulverston.

There's a final, semirural feel as the Way crosses flat meadows to reach the outskirts of Carlisle. Leave the fields and walk along a street called Boustead Grassing, with houses on your right and the river still on your left, passing between two large gas tank towers to meet a main road next to a pub called the Cumberland Wrestlers. Don't go into this unappealing pub but turn left along the main road, then swing right over a railway bridge. Take the third left, leading to a pedestrian shopping street, where you'll see the old town hall (now the TIC) and the famous **Carlisle Cross**, a fitting and welcome end to the Cumbria Way.

Carlisle
The city of Carlisle is the capital of north Cumbria, with all facilities and a surprisingly pleasant atmosphere. Historically it's fascinating, with **Roman remains**, a **cathedral**, city walls and a fine **castle**. The **Tullie House Museum**, where you can see and

touch Roman finds and replicas, is one of the best in Britain.

The *YHA Hostel* (☎ *01228-597352*) is part of the university residences, on the edge of the city centre, with single rooms in flats for £12.50 (self-catering only).

The main drag for B&Bs is Warwick Rd, stretching for 2mi from the centre to the eastern outskirts. Good places include *Howard Lodge* (☎ *01228-529842, No 90*), from £20; *Cornerways Guest House* (☎ *01228-21733, No 107*), from £16; *Craighead* (☎ *01228-596767*), on a side street opposite Cornerways, from £16.50; and *Warwick Lodge* (☎ *01228-523796, No 112*), from £18. A long way from the centre, but good and

friendly, *The Warren* (☎ *01228-533663, No 368*), charging from £18, is also definitely worth trying.

For food, there are several cheap *cafes* and *takeaways* around the train station. For an after-walk splurge, try *Francos Pizzeria* on Town Hall Square near the TIC (☎ 01228-625600), with pizzas and pastas for £5 to £6, or all for £3.20 during the 5.30pm to 6.30pm happy hour. In the nearby streets are several pubs and other places to eat. For unusual surroundings try the *Priory Restaurant* in the old vaults of the ruined cathedral.

Carlisle

The city of Carlisle has a long history and several sights of interest. The Romans first built a military station here, probably on the site of a Celtic camp. Later, Hadrian's Wall was built nearby and Carlisle became a Roman administrative centre (see the Hadrian's Wall Walk in the Northumberland chapter). Even the mighty Roman Empire was hard-pressed to maintain control, however, and the Picts ransacked the town in AD 181 and 367.

The town survived into Saxon times, but was under constant pressure from the Scots and was also sacked by Danish Vikings in 875. The Normans seized the town from the Scots in 1092 and began construction of the castle and town walls, although the Scots regained control between 1136 and 1157. Sixty years later the city withstood a siege by the famous Scottish hero William Wallace during the Scottish War of Independence.

Under the constantly shifting powers of English and Scottish forces, this area was called the 'Debateable Lands', ungoverned and ungovernable from the late 13th to the mid-16th century. Local warlords and their armies were known as reivers, appropriately remembered in the word bereaved. Carlisle was in the middle of this unstable territory, and the city's walls and the great gates that slammed shut every night served a very real purpose.

The Fairfield Horseshoe

Distance	10mi (16km)
Duration	5–7 hours
Standard	medium
Start/Finish	Ambleside
Gateways	Windermere, Ambleside
Summary	A classic mountain circuit with fine, open walking and wonderful views. It's relatively straightforward in good weather, but potentially serious if conditions are bad.

Fairfield is the name of a large mountain close to the centre of the Lake District. By Wainwright's definition (see Books under Information in the introduction to this chapter) it's in the Eastern Fells. At 873m it's one of the highest peaks in the area, along with neighbours Helvellyn (950m) and the wonderfully named Dollywaggon Pike (858m). When viewed from the south or west, the Eastern Fells appear more rounded than many parts of the Lake District. The Fairfield Horseshoe provides fine, open walking over a rolling landscape, which is relatively straightforward in good weather. (A more serious walk from the other, more rugged, side of the mountain is described later in this chapter as the Fairfield & Dovedale walk.)

This walk is a classic circuit, going up one ridge and down another on either side of a valley, with the summit of Fairfield at the highest point of the route, where the two ridges meet. When the weather is kind, the views are excellent. To the west you can see

Scafell Pike and to the east the long ridge of High Street (both covered in this chapter). The view south is dominated by the vast lake of Windermere, which is usually dotted with sailing boats looking like scattered confetti from this distance.

Often, however, you'll get no view at all. The weather can be awful with wind, rain and mist making a walk unpleasant and (even on this clear path) navigation skills necessary. As with anywhere in the Lakes, the conditions can change very quickly so, even if it looks fine, take warm, waterproof clothes, plus a map and compass that you know how to use.

The route starts and ends in Ambleside – a small but busy town and a very popular base for walkers. There are plenty of accommodation options and about a million outdoor gear shops to explore if there's too much rain on the hills.

Direction, Distance & Duration
The route is not waymarked. We suggest going clockwise as this way the walk ends in the centre of Ambleside. The route we describe is 10mi. However, you gain around 800m in height so the walking time is five to seven hours. Allowing for lunch and photo opportunities, your overall time will probably be around six to eight hours.

PLANNING
Maps & Books
If you're using OS Landranger 1:50,000 maps, Ambleside and the Fairfield Horseshoe are on No 90 *(Penrith & Keswick)*. With OS Outdoor Leisure 1:25,000 maps you need No 7 *(The English Lakes – South Eastern Area)* and a small but important section is on No 5 *(The English Lakes – North Eastern Area)*. The route is also on Harvey Superwalker's 1:25,000 *Lakeland Central*.

Wainwright's classic *Pictorial Guide to The Eastern Fells* includes a section on Fairfield, and is good for further inspiration, to admire the detail of his work and to share his love for the area. The Footprint map guide *Walks Around Ambleside* covers the Fairfield Horseshoe and several other routes in the area.

Most of the shops selling outdoor clothing and equipment also sell maps and local guidebooks. The Adventure Traveller bookshop on Compston Rd has a particularly good stock.

Information Sources
Ambleside's central TIC (☎ 01539-432582) is open daily April to October, and on Friday and Saturday for the rest of the year.

PLACES TO STAY & EAT
Ambleside
Ambleside is a compact town with supermarkets, shops, banks (with ATMs), a laundrette and a range of outdoor gear shops. The TIC (☎ 01539-431576), on a street called Market Cross, can answer queries and charges £3 to book accommodation.

The *YHA Hostel* (☎ *01539-432304)* is 1mi south of the centre, overlooking the lake, charges £12.95 for beds in small rooms and dorms. For camping, things are not so handy; the nearest is the National Trust site at *Low Wray* (☎ *01539-463856)*, 3mi south of Ambleside on the western shore of Windermere, charging £3.25.

There are plenty of B&Bs in the centre of town. On Church St these include *3 Cambridge Villas* (☎ *01539-432307)* charging from £16 to £20; *Croyden House* (☎ *01539-432209)*, from £19; *Hillsdale* (☎ *01539-433174)*, from £16 to £25; and *Norwood* (☎ *01539-433349)*, from £17 to £23. Norwood is run by a member of the local mountain rescue team who is very knowledgeable about the surrounding area. Nearby, the *Smallwood House Hotel* (☎ *01539-432330*, e *enq@smallwoodhotel.co.uk)*, on Compston Rd, is very comfortable and welcomes walkers, with en suite rooms at £27.50. Evening meals are £13. Lake Rd (the one towards Windermere) is another happy hotel hunting ground.

For food there are several good places, including *Apple Pie*, a bright and cheerful bakery and cafe with good food and a nice atmosphere (it also does sandwiches to take away); *Daisy's Café*, near the TIC, frequented by walkers and climbers; and under the cinema on Compston Rd, *Zeffirelli's*

Pizzeria, offers pizza and pasta dishes for around £5.

For something more substantial try **Sheila's Cottage** (☎ *01539-433079*), in a back street called the Slack, with meals around £6 to £10. For more serious food try **Stampers** (☎ *01539-432775*), on Church St, with mains for £8 to £12. Opposite is **Lynch Christies**, billing itself as a '16th-century cafe-bar', with lunches around £4 and good evening meals around £8. Also good is **Walkers Bistro** (☎ *01539-431234)*, on Compston Rd, with snacks and lunches during the day and a huge choice of grills, fish and vegetarian dishes in the evening for around £9 to £12. A three-course early evening special is £11.95. On Keswick Rd, **Spice of Bengal** serves Indian food in the £5 to £9 bracket.

Most of Ambleside's central pubs do lunch and evening bar meals but, strangely, none we found were particularly appealing.

GETTING TO/FROM THE WALK

Bus Ambleside is easy to reach from Windermere and Keswick, which are well served by National Express coaches from all parts of the country and by local buses from other towns around the Lake District. Most useful is the Lakeslink service No 555 between Lancaster and Carlisle via Ambleside (see Getting Around in the introduction to this chapter). There's also the Coniston Rambler service No 505, running eight times per day (less on Sunday and in the winter) between Bowness and Coniston via Ambleside, Rydal, Grasmere and Hawkshead; and the No W1, which operates two or three times per hour between Windermere train station and Grasmere via Ambleside. For more details on these or any services in the area, pick up the *Lakeland Explorer* timetable from any TIC.

Your other option between Windermere and Ambleside (or any other town with a hostel in this part of the Lakes) is the YHA Shuttle Bus (☎ 01539-432304).

Train Frequent train services link Windermere with the rest of the country, but between Windermere and Ambleside you'll have to take the bus.

Car The usual route into the Lake District from the south is via Windermere. Ambleside is just 5mi north along the A591, although in summer it can take an hour or more to do this bit due to traffic jams. From the north you can approach Ambleside by the A591 from Keswick or the A592 from Penrith. This latter route goes over the Kirkstone Pass, making it the highest A-road in England. It is very dramatic but, as the road hasn't been widened much since horse and cart days, it is also frequently jammed so is best avoided in busy times.

THE WALK
Ambleside to Rydal
1mi (1.5km), 30–45 minutes
Walk along the busy main road (the A591) north-west out of Ambleside towards Grasmere. After about half a mile the road crosses over a stream on a small bridge. Immediately after this, turn right through some gates onto a track signposted to Rydal Hall. Follow the track through parkland, ignoring various tracks branching off left and right, to reach the outbuildings of Rydal Hall. There is a *teashop* here if you need early sustenance. Go between the buildings and leave the grounds of Rydal Hall by a gateway to meet a steep lane leading up from the main road.

Rydal to Fairfield summit
4mi (6.5km), 2½–3½ hours
Go right (north) up the steep lane, past an old house called **Rydal Mount** (Wordsworth's home until his death in 1850) on your left. Continue up the zigzags. Beyond the houses, at the top of the lane, go through a gate. The track goes straight on but you strike off left (north-west) on a path, steeply up over a few stiles and then up the ridge through open fell, on a clear path, swinging round to the north to reach the first peak of the day, Heron Pike (612m). From here the path undulates (although the ups are less steep than the first bit) over a few more peaks, including **Great Rigg** (766m). The views to the left (west) are fabulous. Across the valley you can see the back of Langdale Pikes, Bow Fell and Scafell Pike. There's a final ascent to the top of the ridge and the broad **summit of Fairfield**.

Don't expect a peak here. The summit is actually more like a plateau. There are cairns all over the place but the largest one, which marks the highest point, is to the north side of the plateau. The views to the north-east, down into Deepdale, are good but this plateau is so broad that you don't get a 360-degree view from just one spot; you have to walk a few hundred metres south-east to get the best view of Windermere, the same distance north-west to see Helvellyn, and so on. If it's misty there won't be any views and you should take great care where you wander. Do not go too far to the north-east as the cliffs at the top of Deepdale are, as the name suggests, precipitous. If the wind is strong you can sit behind one of the dry-stone shelter walls to stop your sandwiches blowing away.

Fairfield Summit to Ambleside
5mi (8km), 2–2½ hours

From the summit retrace your steps slightly, tending left (south-east) to reach the main ridge between the top of the Rydal Valley, to your right (south), and the top of the Deepdale Valley, to your left (north). If the mist is down take great care here. Do not go

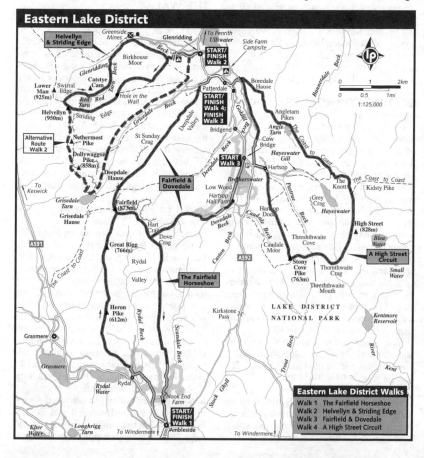

Eastern Lake District

too far left (east) towards the unforgiving cliffs at the top of Deepdale.

Once on the ridge, head east and then south-east to go up slightly, passing just to the east of Hart Crag summit and over **Dove Crag** (792m), before swinging to the south and heading straight down the ridge with Ambleside and Lake Windermere spread before you. A wall runs down the crest of this ridge with paths on both sides. According to the OS map the path on the west side is the right of way, so keep to this as you descend, passing the Low Pike summit (508m) 1½ to two hours from the top of Fairfield.

About 500m beyond Low Pike, at High Brock Crags, follow the right of way through the gap to the east side of the wall. The path continues downhill through fields and over several stiles. You cross Scandale Beck at Low Sweden Bridge and pass Nook End Farm; from here a lane runs down into the centre of Ambleside, where cafes, teashops and pubs await.

Helvellyn & Striding Edge

Distance	7.5mi (12km)
Duration	5–6 hours
Standard	medium-hard
Start/Finish	Glenridding
Gateways	Glenridding, Penrith

Summary A top-quality route up a classic peak. The paths are well worn but the gradients are steep, and one section of scrambling requires the use of hands.

Helvellyn (950m) is the second-highest peak in England and dominates the Eastern Fells of the Lake District. Although this mountain can be reached relatively easily via its smooth western slopes from near Grasmere, the walking is far more rewarding – albeit harder – on the rugged eastern slopes overlooking the Patterdale Valley. It is this harder option we describe here.

The classic Helvellyn route starts and ends at Glenridding. The route goes up the Mires Beck path and includes a traverse of Striding Edge, a precipitous ridge adorning countless postcards and picture books, and

a favourite walkers' challenge. In contrast, the summit of Helvellyn itself is broad and flat, forming part of a long spine running north to south through the area.

This route descends via the subsidiary peak of Catstye Cam and the Red Tarn path.

Direction, Distance & Duration

It is infinitely more satisfying to reach the summit of Helvellyn by an ascent of Striding Edge, so the route is described this way round. This 7.5mi route involves an ascent of about 830m and requires about five to six hours' walking. Allowing for stops, you should take six to seven hours.

Alternatives If you're feeling strong and the weather is fine, we describe a longer, alternative descent via Dollywaggon Pike (worth it just for the name) and the valley of Grisedale. This alternative descent is 5.5mi (9km), instead of 4mi (6.5km) on the main route, and if you go this way the whole circuit will take about one to two hours longer.

If the legs are still strong and the spirit is willing, you can extend this walk even further by going from Grisedale Tarn, via Grisedale Hause, up to the Fairfield summit, then returning to Patterdale or Glenridding via St Sunday Crag (as described in the Fairfield & Dovedale walk following). A combination of all these grand summits makes for a truly fabulous Lake District walk.

PLANNING
Maps & Books

The route we describe here is on OS Outdoor Leisure 1:25,000 map No 5 *(The English Lakes – North Eastern Area)* and on Harvey's Superwalker 1:25,000 *Lakeland Central* map.

Wainwright's classic *Pictorial Guide to the Eastern Fells* includes a good section on Helvellyn, as well as Fairfield and all the other peaks in this area. Another good local book is *Fifteen Walks from Patterdale* by Paul Buttle.

Information Sources

The very efficient and informative Glenridding TIC (☎ 01768-482414) offers stacks of information, maps and guidebooks, money-changing, local weather bulletins and an accommodation booking service.

Guided Walks

In summer there are about three guided walks per week, all organised from the TIC in Glenridding.

PLACES TO STAY & EAT

In the Patterdale Valley is the long lake of Ullswater, with the busy village of Glenridding at the southern end. Glenridding is the area's main centre for walking and climbing, with several places to stay, pubs, shops and cafes. South of Glenridding is the smaller village of Patterdale, which also makes a good base. The villages are about a mile apart along the main road (A592). It's not too bad a walk as the footpaths cut through woods on either side of the road for much of the way, keeping you a safe distance from the traffic.

Glenridding

There's an excellent selection of accommodation in and around Glenridding. Campers can try *Gillside Farm (☎ 01768-482346)*, on the western edge of Glenridding, open March to October and charging £3 and £1 for a tent. There's also bunkhouse accommodation for £6. Nearby is *Helvellyn YHA Hostel (☎ 01768-482269)*, on the fell side in a former mine building about a mile from the village, charging £9.80. Also in the old mine area is *Swirrel Barn*, where a bunkroom space costs £3.50. Bookings are essential and are made through the Lakeland Barns Booking Office (☎ 01768-772645, fax 775043, e keswicktic@lake-district.gov.uk).

B&Bs in Glenridding include *Cherry Holme (☎ 01768-482512)*, near the petrol station, which charges around £22 for en suite rooms; the very walker-friendly *Beech House (☎ 01768-482037, e reed@beech house.com)*, next to the Glenridding Hotel, with simple rooms from £18 (£24 en suite); the charming and efficient *Moss Crag Tearoom (☎/fax 01768-482500, e mosscrag @talk21.com)*, near the village shops, from £19.50 to £27.50, plus snacks and three-

course evening meals for £15; and *Fairlight (☎ 01768-482397)*, near the TIC, which is a straightforward cafe charging £18 for rooms (£20 en suite).

At the top end of the price range is the *Glenridding Hotel (☎ 01768-482228)* at £53/78 for singles/doubles, with discounts if you stay for two nights or more. Facilities include a comfortable residents bar-lounge, swimming pool and sauna, plus lunches, flasks, maps and advice for walkers. Downstairs is the lively *Ratcher's Bar*, open to all, with TV, pool table and good bar food for around £5. For the same food in quieter surroundings, there's *Ratcher's Restaurant* and next door is *Kilners Coffee Shop & Internet Cafe*. For a pint and a bite *The Travellers Rest*, up the hill from the village centre, serves bar food and is always busy.

In the centre of the village there's the informative TIC (☎ 01768-482414), which is open on winter weekends and every day during the season (two weeks before Easter until 5 November). There's also an outdoor gear shop and two *general stores*. A favourite is *Glenridding Minimarket*, which is open daily and offers sandwiches, cakes and groceries, plus a very impressive range of traditional English bottled beers.

Patterdale

There are more accommodation options in the nearby village of Patterdale. Campers should head for *Side Farm (☎ 01768-482337)*, on the eastern side of the valley next to Ullswater, charging £4.50. There's also a *tearoom* at the farmhouse, serving breakfasts and snacks, and selling maps.

In the village the *YHA Hostel (☎ 01768-482394)* is very comfortable and charges £10.85. B&Bs include small and welcoming *Grisedale Lodge (☎ 01768-482084)*, charging £18; and *Glebe House (☎ 01768-482339)* with en suite rooms, charging £22.

About a mile south of the village, the very walker-friendly *Greenbank Farm (☎ 01768-482292)* charges from £17, with evening meals for £7 and packed lunches. Patterdale's pub, *The White Lion Inn (☎ 01768-482214)*, on the main road in the village centre, has good bar food and B&B for

£26.50 in en suite rooms. Almost opposite is *The Patterdale Hotel* (☎ 01768-482231), which caters largely for coach tour groups and is rather uninspiring, with B&B from £30 plus meals and bar food. Patterdale also has a *shop* at the post office.

GETTING TO/FROM THE WALK

Bus It's easier (but not essential) to approach Glenridding and Patterdale from the north side of the Lake District, ideally from Penrith: There are four or five buses daily during the summer months (but fewer in the winter) from Penrith to Glenridding and Patterdale. If you're coming from the south or central parts of the Lake District, public transport is not so handy. From Windermere, a bus runs over the Kirkstone Pass and down to Botherswater, Cow Bridge, Patterdale and Glenridding, but this goes only at weekends in June and July and daily throughout August. During the rest of the year there's no bus service this way.

Car Glenridding is on the A592 between Windermere and Penrith. From Ambleside you can join the A592 at the top of the Kirkstone Pass by taking the steep, narrow minor road to the west (labelled 'The Struggle' on the map, so give it a miss if there's 10 of you in a campervan!). There is a large car park in Glenridding next to the TIC.

THE WALK (see map p284)
Glenridding to Hole-in-the-Wall
2.5mi (4km), 1½–2 hours
From the small row of shops in Glenridding village centre, keep Glenridding Beck to your right (with the TIC on the other side of the stream) and follow the track signposted to Helvellyn. After Gillside Farm (10 minutes from Glenridding) turn left up a track (still signposted to Helvellyn). After 100m a path to Grisedale goes off left – ignore this, and the path branching off right to Greenside Mines. After another 100m another track branches off right and goes through a gate in a wall marking the boundary of the open fell – follow this. Once through the gate the path divides; go left (right goes to Red Tarn), following the path beside Mires Beck and keep

going uphill. The clear path now climbs steadily, with a few large zigzags, to reach a ridge top at a point east of Red Tarn, marked on the OS map as **Hole-in-the-Wall**. From here you get a great view of the rest of the route: Helvellyn at the head of the valley, overlooking Red Tarn, with Striding Edge to the left (south) side and the pointed peak of Catstye Cam to the right.

Hole-in-the-Wall to Helvellyn Summit
1mi (1.5km), 1½–2 hours
Continue following the clear path uphill. After about 300m the ridge narrows to about 2m in width and you're on the jagged teeth of **Striding Edge** proper, with precipitous slopes on either side. You'll need to use your hands in places and less experienced hill walkers may feel decidedly vulnerable. However, much of the exposed area is optional as there are paths on the right (north) side of the ridge that avoid some of the most vertiginous sections. Note that at the end of the ridge there is a 2m vertical rock face to descend, which definitely requires the use of all hands and feet.

From the end of Striding Edge the path climbs steeply through rough ground, strewn with loose rocks, to the summit of **Helvellyn**. As with Fairfield (described earlier), there is no lofty pinnacle here but a wide summit plateau – so wide, in fact, that in 1926 someone managed to land a plane here and the spot is marked by a plaque. Near the centre of the plateau is a cross-shaped wind shelter, but the highest point is marked by a trig point 100m farther on.

The views from the summit of Helvellyn, if the weather is clear, are tremendous. To the west loom the great peaks around Scafell Pike, while to the east the broad summit ridge of High Street can be seen. Both of these mountains are described later in this chapter and looking at them from here should provide plenty of inspiration!

Helvellyn Summit to Glenridding
4mi (6.5km), 2 hours
The usual descent from Helvellyn is via Catstye Cam. Walk 100m north-west beyond

the trig point and then descend to the right (east), following another dramatic narrow ridge called **Swirral Edge**. Great care is needed to locate the correct place – in bad weather a wrong move can be potentially fatal. Scramble down the crest of the ridge until, after 200m or so, the steepness eases. From this point you can divert up to the dramatic summit of **Catstye Cam** itself or continue descending the ridge, passing north of Red Tarn, then swinging north-east round the base of Catstye Cam, following the stream from Red Tarn (Red Tarn Beck). Follow this down to meet Glenridding Beck and continue along the south side. The route passes the old lead mines at Greenside (to reach the YHA hostel, cross the footbridge above the weir) and continues on the southern slopes of Glenridding Valley. Keep to the path beside the wall to meet your outward path and retrace the last mile or so back to Glenridding.

Alternative Route: Dollywaggon Pike

5.5mi (9km), 3–4 hours
This is a longer but more interesting descent from Helvellyn. From the summit to Glenridding by this route is 5.5mi (9km), instead of 4mi (6.5km) on the main route, and if you go this way the whole circuit will take about one to two hours longer.

From the summit aim southwards along the ridge – one of the finest broad ridges in the Lakes. The views here are even better than from the summit, with the smooth slopes of the Thirlmere Valley to your right (west) and the steep cliffs falling away to your left (east), as well as views of the Scafell and High Street mountains.

The path skirts the summit of **Nethermost Pike** (891m) – it's littered with a jumble of small rocks but you might want to bag it anyway – and then heads for the summit of **Dollywaggon Pike** (858m), although again you have to branch off the path if you actually want to reach the summit.

The path then zigzags steeply down to **Grisedale Tarn**. Just before the stepping stones over the stream (Grisedale Beck), the path curves away to the north-east and leads all the way down the Grisedale Valley,

keeping north of the beck. Near the end of the valley, paths branch off to Gillside (if you're camping) and Glenridding. If you're staying in Patterdale, cross to the southern side of Grisedale Beck: The path turns into a track and then eventually into a lane that leads you into Patterdale.

Fairfield & Dovedale

Distance	7.5mi (12km)
Duration	5–7 hours
Standard	medium-hard
Start	Cow Bridge, near Hartsop
Finish	Patterdale
Gateways	Glenridding, Penrith

Summary A hard but varied and very rewarding walk. Some ascents are very steep. It's a difficult route in bad weather.

The mountain of Fairfield (873m) lies to the north of the town of Ambleside and to the west of the large Patterdale Valley. The most popular walk up Fairfield (see the Fairfield Horseshoe earlier in this chapter) starts and ends at Ambleside, and is probably the least serious approach to the summit. The ascent of Fairfield from the Patterdale Valley is very different. It leads initially through farms and woodland in the picturesque Dovedale Valley (not to be confused with another famous valley of the same name in the Peak District), then forces its way up a craggy fellside before finally reaching the open tops and the Fairfield summit. The return is via the splendid long ridge of St Sunday Crag. This option is undeniably harder than the Fairfield Horseshoe, but it's a gem of a walk and well recommended.

Direction, Distance & Duration

This route starts at Cow Bridge, near the northern end of a small lake called Brotherswater (1.5mi south of Patterdale), where the main road (the A592 between Windermere and Penrith) crosses the river running between Brotherswater and Ullswater. If you're staying in Patterdale, the best way to reach Cow Bridge is to walk along the side of the road, which is quite busy – so take care.

Detail of a Peak District well dressing, an intricate mosaic of flower petals, moss and leaves

TONY WHEELER

Green Yorkshire Dales countryside dissected by a maze of dry-stone walls

CHRIS MELLOR

In the shade of the Strid gorge, near Bolton Abbey on the Dales Way, Yorkshire Dales

DAVID TIPLING

EOIN CLARKE

Heading down Swirral Edge off Helvellyn

HUGH WATTS

Looking across Lake Windermere, Lake District

EOIN CLARKE

Airy views on High Brock Crags, Lake District

The route can be followed in either direction but it's better to walk on the main road earlier in the day (when the traffic is quieter). Also, going up Dovedale is better than coming down, and finishing on St Sunday Crag leads you straight back to Patterdale.

The distance covered is about 7.5mi, but the route includes at least 700m of ascent, so will take an absolute minimum of five hours to walk, and probably nearer seven for most people. In reality, with stops, lunch and so on, you should allow at least eight hours. And don't forget the 1.5mi along the road between Patterdale and Cow Bridge to get to the starting point of the walk. Your total day out will probably be nearer nine hours.

PLANNING
For details on guided walks, books and maps, see the Helvellyn & Striding Edge walk earlier in this chapter.

PLACES TO STAY & EAT
Hartsop
There are a couple of accommodation options near the tiny village of Hartsop and the start of this walk. In Hartsop, *Fellside Farmhouse* (☎ 01768-482532) offers B&B from £17 and, near Brotherswater, the *Brotherswater Inn* (☎ 01768-482239) offers simple B&B for £14 (room only) and a bunkroom for £8.50, plus food and beer. Camping is also available at the attached *Sykeside Campsite*.

GETTING TO/FROM THE WALK
For information on transport to Cowbridge and Patterdale, which are both on the A592, see Getting to/from the Walk in the Helvellyn & Striding Edge walk earlier in this chapter.

THE WALK (see map p284)
Cow Bridge to Fairfield Summit
4mi (6.5km), 3–4 hours
On the west side of the A592 road, near Cow Bridge, is a small car park. Go through the gate at the back of the car park and take the rough vehicle track along the western shore of Brotherswater. After a mile or so you pass **Hartsop Hall Farm**, which dates

back to the 16th century. Here the path goes uphill beside a wall, through some old oak woodland, and then runs alongside a stream to open hillsides beneath the imposing cliff of **Dove Crag**, at the head of the valley.

The path then climbs steeply to the right of the crag and then round the back to the summit. From here follow the ridge top north-west for half a mile to **Hart Crag** and then to the **summit of Fairfield**. For a description of the summit itself see the earlier Fairfield Horseshoe walk.

Fairfield Summit to Patterdale
3.5mi (5.5km), 2–3 hours
From the summit of Fairfield head north over the minor summit of Cofa Pike, then descend about 200m to the broad pass of Deepdale Hause. To your right the ground drops very steeply into Deepdale, while to the left (west) you can see the steep side of Dollywaggon Pike, with Grisedale Tarn at its foot and the broad flat top of Helvellyn behind.

From Deepdale Hause the path climbs to the top of **St Sunday Crag** (you'll be glad to know it's not as steep as the descent from Fairfield) and then follows the crest of the ridge – a very enjoyable section of gradual downhill. Near the end of the ridge the path keeps to the left (north) and then drops quite steeply, with excellent views along Ullswater. There's a nice final section through a small patch of wooded farmland before you meet the lane leading down to Patterdale.

A High Street Circuit

Distance	12.5mi (20km)
Duration	6–8 hours
Standard	medium
Start/Finish	Patterdale
Gateways	Glenridding, Penrith

Summary A long, high mountain day out, with fine views and generally easy paths. As with all Lake District peaks, you should also be prepared for bad conditions and limited visibility.

High Street (828m) is an unusual title for a mountain but it gets its name from a Roman road that once ran across the long, flat summit ridge. Since the days of the legion-naires, this route has been tramped by hill walkers and fell runners, not to mention the odd motorcycle and a lot of sheep. The walk along High Street is very satisfying because once you gain height you can stay up and enjoy great views all day. It's a long but not difficult route, although thick mists are not uncommon and the wind can really pick up speed over the summit, so you must go properly prepared.

Direction, Distance & Duration

This route starts and ends at Patterdale. The circuit can be followed in either direction, but clockwise is more pleasant as the ascent is more gradual. The total distance is 12.5mi, with at least 800m of ascent, so a minimum walking time is six to eight hours. Allowing for stops, most walkers will take between seven and 10 hours to do this route.

PLANNING

For details on maps, books, guided walks and places to stay and eat, see the Helvellyn & Striding Edge walk earlier in this chapter.

GETTING TO/FROM THE WALK

For information on transport to and from Patterdale, on the A592, see Getting to/from the Walk in the Helvellyn & Striding Edge walk earlier in this chapter.

THE WALK (see map p284)
Patterdale to High Street Summit

5.5mi (9km), 3–4 hours
From the main road that runs through Pat-terdale, about 50m north-west of the pri-mary school, follow a track that leads east to Side Farm. Go through the farmyard (there's a *cafe* here, which is open most days during summer) and turn right (south-east) along a farm track. About 250m from the farm, go through a gate and turn sharp left up a path. (You can also reach this point by following a lane from just north of the YHA hostel.)

The path climbs steeply across the open fellside to a gap called Boredale Hause, then keeps aiming south-east, past Angle

Tarn, to finally skirt the summit of a small peak called the **Knott**. This section between Patterdale and the Knott follows the route of the Coast to Coast Walk (described in the Northern England Long-Distance Paths chapter) and you'll inevitably see more walkers than usual along here.

About 500m south of the Knott, the Coast-to-Coasters turn left (heading for Kid-sty Pike and distant Shap), but our path con-tinues southwards, aiming for the summit of High Street. The main right of way shown on the maps aims just west of the ridge along the line of the Roman road, but an-other path keeps slightly farther to the east, close to a dry-stone wall that runs across the mountain. This latter path has better views and also has the advantage in bad weather of taking you directly to the trig point that marks the **summit of High Street**.

High Street Summit to Patterdale

7mi (11.5km), 3–4 hours
South of High Street the ridge broadens and the crest swings west to **Thornthwaite Crag**, marked by a splendid dry-stone pillar, which is labelled as a 'beacon' on the OS map. From Thornthwaite Crag the main path des-cends steeply to a pass called Threshthwaite Mouth. (If time is short, you can go north from here, down into Threshthwaite Cove and along Pasture Beck to Hartsop.)

Continue west from the pass, climbing steeply to reach **Stony Cove Pike** (763m). From the summit, paths are not clear but you need to aim north-west, keeping to the west side of a dry-stone wall that runs along the summit of the ridge towards a small peak called Hartsop Dodd. From here a steep path zigzags down to a bridge over Pasture Beck and into the tranquil little vil-lage of **Hartsop**, with its old stone houses tucked away behind solid walls and neat gardens. Hartsop means 'valley of the deer' but you won't see any here these days.

Follow the lane down through Hartsop. Just before the main road turn right into a small lane, which soon becomes a track and then a path, and leads past the farms of Beckstones and Crookabeck to Patterdale.

A Scafell Pike Circuit

Distance	8.5mi (13.5km)
Duration	5–6½ hours
Standard	medium-hard
Start/Finish	Seathwaite
Gateway	Keswick

Summary The hardest and most serious walk described in this chapter, but with the right conditions it's one of the finest and most rewarding. Be fully prepared for bad weather.

Although not quite at the centre of the Lake District, Scafell Pike (978m) dominates the Southern and Western Fells. It is also the highest peak in England and a natural magnet for walkers.

In this part of the Lake District the peaks are rugged and steep-sided. Consequently, conditions are harder and the paths steeper and more circuitous. There's far less room for error here if the mist comes down and you have to rely on your map and compass to get home. Conditions can change quickly anywhere in the Lake District, but particularly so here. Even if it looks fine, take warm, waterproof clothes, plus a map and compass that you know how to use.

There are several routes up Scafell Pike, including those from the surrounding valleys of Langdale, Eskdale and Wasdale. We've chosen one from Borrowdale simply because we think it's the nicest. However, the route we describe is quite long and should only be considered in spring, summer or autumn. In winter the days are too short to do it comfortably, while weather and ground conditions may make it dangerous for the inexperienced.

At any time of year, if the weather does turn bad while you're out, there are a number of short cuts and diversions that avoid the highest and potentially most dangerous section of this route. Having said that, in fair weather an ascent of Scafell Pike is an absolutely marvellous walk. It goes right to the heart of the high Lake District with dramatic scenery that seems, at times, to engulf you, while the summit offers some of the finest views you could wish for.

Direction, Distance & Duration

This circular route starts and finishes at Seathwaite – once a tiny settlement, now just one farm. You could do the route in either direction but we have described it anticlockwise. The route is not waymarked and there are very few signposts, so you need to be competent with a map and compass.

Measured on the map, the distance to/from Seathwaite is 8.5mi. It doesn't seem far but, with all the steep ups and downs, your walking time will be five to 6½ hours. One or two extra hours for lunch, photos and map reading brings the total for the route up to seven to nine hours. On top of this you may have to allow more time for

Scafell & Scafell Pike

In his book, *Wainwright's Favourite Lakeland Mountains*, the old sage of the hills comments: 'It is remarkable that the highest mountain in England should suffer a confusion of names'. He's right! It is not uncommon for visitors to assume that Scafell Pike and Scafell are the same thing, or to go up one instead of the other, not only reaching the top of the 'wrong mountain' but often getting into difficulties in the complex landscape of the high ground.

Wainwright explains that the whole mountain massif was originally called Scaw Fell (this pronunciation is still used locally and by Lakes aficionados) and early maps of the area marked three summits called the Pikes of Scawfell. Later this title was altered to Scawfell Pikes. Then two of the summits got their own names, Broad Crag and Ill Crag, leaving the highest to be singularised into Scafell Pike. (Scafell is sometimes written Sca Fell, although that seems still to be the name of the whole massif.)

Scafell (964m) is now the name given to a separate summit on the same massif, some 800m directly south-west of Scafell Pike (978m). Scafell is a mere 14m lower, but a much more serious mountain to tackle. Keep a close eye on your map and make sure you go up the right mountain!

getting to the start from wherever you stay (eg, Seatoller or Rosthwaite).

Alternatives If you have the time and energy, and the weather is kind, you can extend this walk by taking an alternative route back to Stonethwaite via a peak called Glaramara. This extends the main circuit by about half a mile and adds an extra hour of walking.

Another option from Esk Hause and Glaramara is to continue down the ridge to meet the main road between the villages of Seatoller or Rosthwaite. This is longer and harder than going down the valley, but it's more enjoyable, and especially useful if you're staying in either of these places. From Esk Hause back to the main road is 4.5mi (7km), which will take about two hours.

PLANNING
Maps
The Scafell Pike route described here is on the OS Landranger 1:50,000 map No 90 *(Penrith & Keswick)*. If you want more detail (highly recommended for this route), you'll need OS Outdoor Leisure 1:25,000 maps No 4 *(The English Lakes – North Western Area)* and No 6 *(The English Lakes – South Western Area)*. Harvey (1:40,000 or 1:25,000) *Lakeland West* map has the whole route on one sheet, including an enlargement of the immediate Scafell Pike area.

Information Sources & Guided Walks
There's a very friendly and well-stocked TIC in Seatoller (☎ 01768-777294). The staff can help with local accommodation and also organise a series of guided walks around Borrowdale through the summer. The TIC is closed in winter; during this time the staff at Keswick TIC (☎ 01768-772645) can help with inquiries.

PLACES TO STAY & EAT
Seathwaite
In the hamlet of Seathwaite, close to the start of this walk, *Seathwaite Farm (☎ 017687-77284)* offers all you could wish for – camping for £3 with hot showers, a camping barn for £3, B&B for £20, a packed

lunch service and a very good *cafe* (summer only). Seathwaite also has public toilets and a phone box.

Seatoller
There are more options in and around the village of Seatoller, about 1.5mi from Seathwaite. Seatoller TIC (☎ 01768-777294) is on the main street running through the village. Simple camping is available in the fields of Seatoller Farm, and B&Bs include the charming and walker-friendly *Seatoller House (☎ 01768-777218)*, charging £28.50. Nearby, *The Yew Tree (☎ 01768-777634)* is a very stylish but welcoming cafe-bar-restaurant with low ceilings, some garden seating, drinks, snacks, bar meals and a smart restaurant. It also sells outdoor gear. Just outside the village, *Glaramara (☎ 01768-777222)* is a large old country house and walking centre, offering B&B for £18 plus evening meals and a series of guided walks at weekends. About a mile away, *Thornythwaite Farm (☎ 01768-777237)* offers B&B from £18 (summer only).

About 2mi west of Seatoller (up a very steep hill) is *Honister Hause YHA Hostel (☎ 01768-777267)*, which charges £9.

Rosthwaite
In Rosthwaite, 2mi north-east of Seatoller, *Dinah Hoggus Camping Barn (☎ 01768-772645, fax 775043, e keswicktic@lake-district.gov.uk)* charges £3.50; bookings are essential.

B&Bs include *Nook Farm (☎ 01768-777677)*, which is good value at £17 to £21, and *Yew Tree Farm (☎ 01768-777675)*, in a lovely position overlooking the valley, with doubles for £45. Nearby is the *Flock-In Tearoom* (offering 'drinks if you're flock-in thirsty and food if you're flock-in famished') with big mugs and hearty portions.

On the main road, *The Royal Oak Hotel (☎ 01768-777214, e royaloak@ukgateway.net)* has rooms from £30 to £45, including dinner. It also serves good hearty pub food (around £6 to £7) in the bar at the back. Nearby, *The Scafell Hotel (☎ 01768-777208, e scafellhtl@aol.com)* has a hikers bar, which serves good food and charges

£40 for B&B. The hotel also offers 'Fell Break Weekends' (combining fine food and comfortable accommodation with guided walks) for £124 all-inclusive and two-night midweek special deals for £83, with even more discounts in winter.

Rosthwaite has a small but well-stocked village *shop*.

Longthwaite

In Longthwaite, 1mi north-east of Seatoller, is *Borrowdale YHA Hostel* (☎ 01768-777257), which charges £10.85. *Gillercombe* (☎ 01768-777602) also provides accommodation, charging £18. The friendly people here also run nearby *Chapel Farm Campsite*, which costs £3.

Stonethwaite

In Stonethwaite, B&Bs include *6 Chapel Howe* (☎ 01768-777649), in a small row of modern houses, charging £17; and the more cottage-like *Knotts View* (☎ 01768-777604), which charges £19 and offers dinner for £9. At the end of the lane, *The Langstrath Hotel* (☎ 01768-777239) is quite smart but welcomes walkers and charges £24 for B&B (£27 en suite). It also provides good beer, packed lunches and snacks, and has a very interesting range of evening meals (how about wild boar and duckling pie?) from £7 to £10. Beyond here simple camping is available in the fields belonging to *Stonethwaite Farm*. Also in Stonethwaite is *The Peathouse Cafe*, serving teas and snacks.

GETTING TO/FROM THE WALK

Bus Keswick is well served by National Express coaches from all parts of the country, and by buses from other towns around the Lake District. To reach Seatoller from Keswick, the very handy 'Borrowdale Bus' (No 79) runs eight times per day in each direction on summer weekdays (six on Sunday and less in winter). Two of these buses go all the way to Seathwaite. Otherwise you'll have to walk from Seatoller to Seathwaite (1.5mi). For timetable details check with the TIC in Keswick or Seatoller, or phone one of the information services listed under Getting Around at the start of this chapter.

Car Seathwaite is 1.5mi from the village of Seatoller, which is about 8mi south of Keswick. Parking at Seathwaite and Seatoller is limited, so you should consider taking a bus from Keswick.

THE WALK
Seathwaite to Scafell Pike
4mi (6.5km), 2½–3½ hours

Walk through the farm and past the cafe. Follow the bridleway (this was once a pack-horse route into Wasdale) to Stockley Bridge, then directly up the valley of Styhead Gill to pass the small lake of Styhead Tarn and reach **Styhead Pass**. In the days before road transport (and before walking became a leisure activity), packhorses carried goods across the mountains of the Lake District. Styhead Pass was on one of the busiest routes and a major junction for traders heading between the western, northern and southern parts of the area. Today you won't see any horses – just walkers and

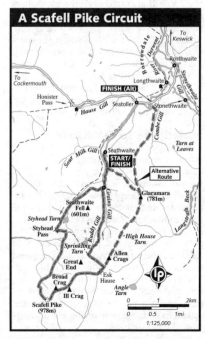

A Scafell Pike Circuit

a large wooden box marked 'Mountain Rescue First Aid Kit'.

From Styhead Pass take the path branching to the left (south-east). About 300m from the rescue kit another path branches off right (south-west then south). This path is called the Corridor Route and it leads you – always heading roughly south-west – through the very broken and complex landscape that surrounds the high peaks. You pass above the southern end of a very large and deep gully called **Piers Gill**, and shortly afterwards the path becomes indistinct, eventually fizzling out completely as you reach the rocky outcrops below the summit. You need to take very great care here if the mist is down. Eventually the gradient eases and you reach the **summit of Scafell Pike**. After the broad summits on some other mountains (like Fairfield and Helvellyn, described earlier in this chapter), this one feels like a real mountain top. A trig point and large cairn mark the highest point in England. You'll also find several rock shelters dotted around the summit area, which are most welcome when the weather is bad. When conditions are good you'll get spectacular views over the whole Lake District: Derwentwater and Keswick; Crinkle Crags and Bowfell, with a glimpse of Windermere; Great Gable and Buttermere; and lots more. On a clear day you can even see the coast and Sellafield Nuclear Power Station!

Scafell Pike to Esk Hause
1.5mi (2.5km), 1 hour
From the summit aim north-east. Take care here, especially when the weather is bad, as the route is not obvious across the rocks. A path descends steeply on a rocky ridge, with cliffs and buttresses on either side of the path, to reach a small pass between Scafell Pike and it's neighbour Broad Crag. The path climbs up again, passing to the right (east) of the summit of Broad Crag and north of another neighbour called Ill Crag. The path curves down and to the right (east) below another peak called **Great End** to finally reach a pass and junction of paths called Esk Hause, where there's a cross-shaped wind shelter.

For peak baggers it's possible to go on a quick detour up and down **Great End** for some more wonderful views. On long summer days this will be quite easy, but take care at other times of the year, as it will add about 45 minutes onto your day.

Esk Hause to Seathwaite
3mi (5km), 1½–2 hours
This is slightly shorter and easier than the alternative route, and ideal if the weather looks like it might deteriorate.

From Esk Hause take the path west towards Sprinkling Tarn. After about 500m, before you reach the tarn, a path on the right (north) goes down beside a stream called Ruddy Gill, which turns into Grains Gill a bit farther down. At Stockley Bridge you'll meet the bridleway you came up on. Retrace your steps to Seathwaite.

Alternative Route: Seathwaite via Glaramara
3.5mi (5.5km), 2½–3 hours
This is a longer, harder, but much more enjoyable return route to Seathwaite. (It's also very useful to go via Glaramara if you're heading back to Seatoller or Rosthwaite.)

From Esk Hause aim north-east, over the top of a small peak called Allen Crags and then along a broad ridge with several ups and downs, to reach the fine summit of **Glaramara** (781m). Beyond the summit the path divides: left (north-west) takes you back to Seathwaite and straight on takes you steeply down the fellside to Seathwaite and the finish.

If you're staying at Seatoller or Rosthwaite, you can continue heading northerly from Glaramara along the ridge, descending through pleasant woodland on the lower section to finally reach Strands Bridge on the main road between Seatoller and Rosthwaite.

Other Walks

LONG-DISTANCE PATHS
Apart from the Cumbria Way (which is described in this chapter) and the Coast to Coast Walk (in the Northern England

Long-Distance Paths chapter), several other LDPs go through the Lake District. Even if you don't have the time or inclination to do them end-to-end, you can follow a section for a day or two, or even for a few hours, tying in with a circular walk.

The Cumberland Way

Whereas the Cumbria Way crosses the Lake District north to south, the Cumberland Way (80mi, 128km) goes west to east. It starts at Ravenglass and goes mainly via valleys through Wasdale, Black Sail Pass, Buttermere, Keswick and near Penrith, to finish at Appleby-in-Westmorland. At the finish there's a very handy train station on the Settle-Carlisle Railway to take you onwards to Northumberland or the Yorkshire Dales. The route is described in *The Cumberland Way* by Paul Hannon.

The Cumbria Coastal Way

On the far western side of the Lake District is the 'forgotten' Cumbria Coast, completely overshadowed by the nearby Lake District mountains when it comes to tourist destinations. For some, however, this comparative emptiness is the attraction. The Cumbria Coastal Way (125mi, 201km) follows the coast from Roa Island, near Barrow-in-Furness in the south, via quiet farmland and the River Esk estuary round Ravenglass and the slightly more dubious attraction of Sellafield Nuclear Power Station, through St Bees Head (the start of the Coast to Coast Walk) and Whitehaven, and round the shore of the Solway Firth to end at Carlisle. From here you can return to your starting point – or elsewhere in the Lakes – on the Cumbria Coast Railway. The route is described in a free *Cumbria Coastal Way* leaflet, published by Cumbria County Council and available from local TICs.

Wainwright Memorial Walk

Another one for Wainwright fans! This is a 102mi comprehensive tour of the finest mountains in the Lake District, based on a route taken by AW himself over a long weekend in 1931. It has been split into 11 stages for today's softie walker. The route is described in *The Wainwright Memorial Walk*, published by Michael Joseph, which includes maps and text from Wainwright's famous *Pictorial Guides*.

MOUNTAIN WALKS

In this chapter we have described the high-profile mountains of Fairfield, Helvellyn, High Street and Scafell Pike. These are all in the Southern, Eastern and Far Eastern Fells (as defined in Wainwright's *Pictorial Guides* – see Books under Information in the introduction to this chapter for more on these influential volumes). In the same area are several more major mountains which, although we don't have the space to describe them in full, make excellent days out for experienced walkers.

To the north of Scafell Pike is **Great Gable**, with scree-ridden sides that always look so sheer, while to the east lies the impressive peak of **Bowfell**, at the head of the Great Langdale Valley. Great Gable can be approached from Seatoller (covered in the Scafell Pike section) and Bowfell can be approached from Langdale (covered in the Cumbria Way section of this chapter).

Great Gable can also be reached from **Wasdale**, one of the Lake District's more remote and hard-to-reach valleys. This valley also makes a good gateway to the **Western Fells**, which are usually much quieter than the popular central parts of the Lakes and worthy of a few days' exploration if you have the time, skills and inclination. The *Wasdale Head Inn*, with B&B and camping, has been a popular base for walkers and rock climbers for almost a century; early photos in the bar show leading climbers of the day limbering up on the inn's stable wall!

In the Eastern Fells are the peaks of **Great Dodd** and **Stybarrow Dodd**. These can be approached from the east from Patterdale or Glenridding (described in the Helvellyn & Striding Edge walk earlier) or from the west from the settlement of Legburthwaite (near *Thirlmere YHA Hostel*) in the Thirlmere Valley. Probably the most pleasing way to bag these peaks is as part of a spectacular long-ridge walk, along the **Backbone of the Eastern Fells** between Clough Head (south-east of Keswick) and Grisedale Tarn (north of Grasmere), which also includes Helvellyn and Dollywaggon Pike. You can even continue southwards and do Fairfield as well, to finish at Ambleside (where a bus takes you back to your starting point). The route can also be done south to north, but either way it's long and potentially serious – it's one to leave for the fine days of summer.

This 'Backbone' route is described fully in *Walking the Ridges of Lakeland* by Bob Allen. This is an inspiring book, which also describes three other long linear routes and about 20 circular routes of varying lengths in the Central, Eastern and Far Eastern Fells, linking sets of peaks in a series of spectacular ridge walks. Each route has a map and the whole book is illustrated with colour photos.

VALLEY & LAKESIDE WALKS

There are many other high peaks in the Lake District to explore but, if the weather is bad or you just want to stay on flatter ground for a while, there's also a whole set of valley and lakeside walks. The **Cumbria Way**, which we describe in this chapter, is an LDP that winds through the Lake District via Coniston, Elterwater, Great Langdale, Borrowdale, Derwentwater, Keswick, Skiddaw and Caldbeck, skilfully keeping to low ground for much of the way. Any of the stages of this route can be followed as a day walk or used as part of a circular route if you base yourself at, say, Coniston, Elterwater, Keswick or anywhere in the Langdale or Borrowdale valleys. (Places to stay and eat are listed under the Cumbria Way earlier in this chapter.)

Other places for short or flat walks include the west bank of **Lake Windermere**. For example, from Bowness-on-Windermere you can take the ferry across the lake and follow the shore northwards on paths and tracks through woodland. You can either continue northwards to Ambleside (from where you can return to Windermere by bus

or lake steamer) or you could return through the woods on the higher ground slightly farther to the west. A small hill called Letterbarrow has surprisingly good views.

You could even base yourself on this side of the lake. There are many B&B, camping and hostel options in and around Hawkshead. If you did stay here, another place for easy walks is **Grisedale Forest**. There is a good network of marked routes, including a Sculpture Trail, which takes you past about 25 large and imaginative outdoor works of art. You can also reach Grisedale Forest from the village of Coniston – also described in the Cumbria Way walk description.

Tying in your walk with a ride on a lake steamboat is always an enjoyable way to travel. In the Cumbria Way description there's information on the Coniston and Derwentwater boats. As well as these, and the Windermere boats mentioned above, there's a boat service on Ullswater between Glenridding and Pooley Bridge via Howtown. A good walk from Glenridding goes round or over Place Fell to Howtown, from where you can return on the steamer to Glenridding. The TICs have boat timetables or you can visit their Web site at W www.ullswater-steamers.co.uk. This is an ideal walk if you're based at Glenridding for the Helvellyn & Striding Edge and A High Street Circuit walks described earlier in this chapter.

In between the large lakes in the valleys and the high peaks of the fells lie the many tarns (small upland lakes and ponds) that are so characteristic of the Lake District scenery. Many people include a tarn or two during their walk as it gives the satisfaction of a definite point to aim for (and is usually nice for a picnic). One outdoor magazine has even suggested that 'tarn bagging' might become as popular as 'peak bagging'. All the Wainwright *Pictorial Guides* include coverage of tarns, and for more modern guidance you could get *The Tarns of Lakeland* by J & A Nuttal.

The North York Moors

The North York Moors are in north-eastern England – an area of wild and empty rolling hills cut by dales (valleys) that shelter woods, fields and small villages, plus the occasional ruined abbey or castle. The western and northern sides of the Moors are buttressed by steep hills and escarpments, while on the southern side gradients are more gradual. On the eastern side is the North Sea coast, with high cliffs, quiet bays and not too many caravan parks. Much of the area is contained within the North York Moors National Park, covering just over 550 sq mi. The coast is also protected as Heritage Coast. The southern part of the park, and the area just south of the Moors, is known as Ryedale.

One of the principal glories of the North York Moors is the heather – the largest continuous area of this hardy upland plant in Britain. It blooms spectacularly, in an explosion of purple, from July to early September. Even outside the flowering season, the brown-tending-to-purple on the hills, in vivid contrast to the green of the dales, gives the park its characteristic appearance.

Although the heather-covered landscape might appear to be wilderness, it was, in fact, created by human activity. In the Bronze Age this area was relatively densely populated and the inhabitants cleared the forest, their domestic animals prevented regeneration and the soil's nutrients were leached away, leaving it to the hardy heath plants. Today, the remains of ancient settlements and burial mounds are scattered right across the region.

Later North York Moors inhabitants included James Cook, the great explorer, who led pioneering expeditions to far-flung places around the world but most famously Australia. You will find many buildings in Whitby and other towns claiming to be his birthplace, home, school, pub etc.

In this chapter we describe the Cleveland Way, a long route and excellent overview of the Moors, plus two single-day walks, which also give a good introduction to the area.

INFORMATION

Maps

The area is covered by the Ordnance Survey (OS) 1:63,360 *North York Moors* Touring Map. For more detail, the OS Landranger 1:50,000 maps No 93 *(Middlesbrough)* and No 94 *(Whitby & Eskdale)* show most areas. The best choice for walkers are OS Outdoor Leisure 1:25,000 maps No 26 *(North York Moors – Western Area)* and No 27 *(North York Moors – Eastern Area)*. For maps covering individual walks, see Planning in the introduction to each walk.

Books

Specific guidebooks for the routes we describe are detailed in the Planning section of each walk. Books covering the whole area include the stylish *North York Moors Official National Park Guide* by Ian Sampson. Walking guidebooks include *The North York Moors* Pathfinder Guide, published by Jarrold, and *Longer Walks on the North York Moors* by V Grainger. The national park produces a very good range of booklets and leaflets on walks in most parts of the Moors; these cost from 30p to about £2, and are an excellent introduction.

Information Sources

There are many Tourist Information Centres (TICs) in and around the North York Moors, all with information about local places to stay, public transport and so on. TICs run by the national park authority also provide exhibitions and additional information about the park. The Moors Centre (☎ 01287-660540) at Danby, 5mi west of Grosmont, offers an excellent range of information, as does the Sutton Bank National Park Centre (☎ 01845-597426).

Other TICs in the area include Helmsley (☎ 01439-770173), Pickering (☎ 01751-473791), Scarborough (☎ 01723-373333) and Whitby (☎ 01947-602674).

Around the park are several Information Points, in shops or post offices, where you

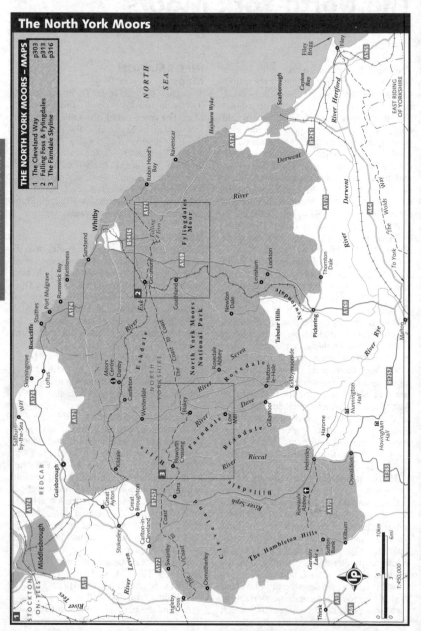

The North York Moors

can get a more limited range of leaflets and information. Specific TICs are listed in the Planning section for each walk. You can also get information from the tourist board Web site (W www.ryedale.gov.uk) or from the national park Web site (W www.north yorkmoors-npa.gov.uk).

At TICs, hotels, shops and other places you can find the annual *Moors* newspaper – a free publication full of useful tourist information, background articles and advertisements for places to stay or things to do.

Guided Walks

Details on guided walks organised by the national park authority are available from TICs. The historic North Yorkshire Moors Railway (☎ 01751-472508, e nymr@herbert2 .demon.co.uk, W www.nymr.demon.co.uk) organises guided walks in the summer from its train stations. Harebrained (☎ 01947-896048, e harebrained@talk21.com), a Goathland-based company, organises guided walks on request; it has a particular interest in environmental subjects.

GETTING THERE & AWAY

To reach the North York Moors from other parts of Britain, the main gateway cities and towns are Middlesbrough, Thirsk, Whitby, Scarborough and York, all with good train and coach links to the rest of the country, and easily reached if you're driving. The Getting Around chapter lists several public transport inquiry lines that provide details of both national and local bus and train services: See the boxed text 'National Transport Information' on p92.

GETTING AROUND

A particularly handy public transport service is the Esk Valley Railway, which has regular trains running through the northern part of the Moors between Middlesbrough and Whitby, with intermediate stops including Glaisdale, Egton and Grosmont – all overnight bases for walking routes described in this book. Some trains on this line run direct to/from Darlington, which is on the main east coast line between London and Scotland.

Local TICs can provide you with *Transport Times for Ryedale & the North York Moors*, a free and useful booklet. You can also get useful local public transport information from the Moorsbus Web site at W www.moorsbus.net.

The Cleveland Way

Distance	109mi (175.5km)
Duration	9 days
Standard	medium
Start	Helmsley
Finish	Filey
Gateways	Middlesbrough, Thirsk, Whitby, Scarborough

Summary A national trail through upland and coastal areas. Some moorland sections involve significant ascents and descents, and much of the walk crosses exposed country, but overall conditions suit the intermediate walker.

The Cleveland Way National Trail is the second-oldest long-distance path (LDP) in Britain, skirting the western, northern and eastern edges of the North York Moors, passing through varied landscape dominated by heather moorland and coastal scenery. The route is also rich in visible history, offering striking insights into the stewardship of the Moors from prehistory via the Vikings to the Victorian age and today. Views are plentiful, with grand panoramas and exhilarating seascapes that intoxicate the spirits and make you glad to be alive.

Direction, Distance & Duration

Traditionally the Cleveland Way is walked clockwise, so that the wind is predominantly behind you. Going the other way, foul weather on the North Sea can make the journey northwards up the coast rather more of a trial than it ought to be. Also, although generally good all along the route, the signposting is clearer for the clockwise walker. As the trail grows in popularity it may be worth reversing this, especially in summer when competition for B&Bs is at its fiercest.

Officially the trail is 109mi in length. Nine days is a sensible timetable given the wealth of historical and natural features along the way. The itinerary suggested averages 12.25mi per day. There are also two minor deviations from the official route to reach suitable accommodation.

day	from	to	mi/km
1	Helmsley	Sutton Bank	10.5/17
2	Sutton Bank	Osmotherley	11.5/18.5
3	Osmotherley	Clay Bank Top	11/17.5
4	Clay Bank Top	Kildale	9/14.5
5	Kildale	Saltburn-by-the-Sea	15/24
6	Saltburn-by-the-Sea	Sandsend	17/27.5
7	Sandsend	Robin Hood's Bay	10/16
8	Robin Hood's Bay	Scarborough	14/22.5
9	Scarborough	Filey	11/17.5

Alternatives Strong walkers can trim the walk down to seven days by combining Days 3 and 4, and by shrinking the Saltburn to Scarborough section to two days with a stay in Whitby. If you can only do one day on the route, a circuit incorporating the segment from Whitby to Robin Hood's Bay gives a good taster (see the boxed text 'The Cleveland Way – Route Highlight' on p309 for details).

Some walkers choose to complete the circuit back to Helmsley by making use of the Tabular Hills Link (not described here), which leaves the Cleveland Way at Scarborough. This circular walk measures 158mi; figure on 12 days.

PLANNING
Maps
For complete coverage of the route, you need OS Outdoor Leisure 1:25,000 maps No 26 *(North York Moors – Western Area)* and No 27 *(North York Moors – Eastern Area)*, and OS Explorer 1:25,000 map No 301 *(Scarborough, Bridlington & Flamborough Head)*. Another option is the OS Touring

Map 1:63,360 *North York Moors*, but you'll need to supplement this with OS Landranger 1:50,000 maps No 94 *(Whitby & Esk Dale)* and No 101 *(Scarborough)* for full coverage. The most manageable map you can get away with is Footprint's very handy strip map, *The Cleveland Way*, complete with trail notes and suggested stopover points.

Books
The official national trail guide, *The Cleveland Way* by Ian Sampson, is the best guide to the route, not least because it contains extracts from OS 1:25,000 maps. Except for the odd circumstance when you must leave the route in search of accommodation, this is a good stand-alone guide, although it doesn't have specific accommodation information. For that you need the indispensable *Cleveland Way National Trail Accommodation & Information Guide*, published annually and well worth the small price.

Other walking guides (some might be hard to find) include *The Cleveland Way plus the Tabular Hills Link* by Martin Collins, and *The Cleveland Way Companion* by Paul Hannon. *The Cleveland Way* by Bill Cowley is an interesting read with some insights into local history. More academic and better suited to an armchair, *The North York Moors Landscape Heritage*, edited by DA Spratt & BJD Harrison, is nonetheless a fascinating reference that adds much to the understanding and enjoyment of the local countryside.

Information Sources
Vital information on accommodation and transport along the Cleveland Way is available from the Sutton Bank National Park Centre and the various TICs dotted about the route. Helmsley TIC carries a wide range of publications. Spotlight Guides' commercial Cleveland Way Web site (W www.cleveland-way.co.uk) is also very useful indeed.

Baggage Services
If you want your backpack carried, several Coast to Coast Walk baggage services (listed under Planning in the Northern England Long-Distance Paths chapter) and Sherpa Van Project (listed in the boxed text

'Baggage Services' on p50) cover this route, making a seven-day itinerary more viable.

PLACES TO STAY & EAT

It is fairly easy to find accommodation along the route, although booking ahead during summer is advisable. B&Bs are scattered liberally, although less so along the section from Osmotherley to Kildale, where it may be necessary to make a detour of a few miles to find a bed. There are five YHA hostels on the route, three of which (Helmsley, Osmotherley and Scarborough) coincide with breaks in the route as described. Camping is possible, with provision on or near the route at least every 10mi. In addition to the accommodation booklets mentioned earlier, both *The Rambler's Yearbook & Accommodation Guide* and *Stilwell's National Trail Companion* contain detailed sections on the Cleveland Way. Except on the Clay Bank Top to Kildale section, there are places to stop for lunch. Selected places to stay and eat are mentioned in the route description.

GETTING TO/FROM THE WALK

Bus From York Stephensons of Easingwold buses (☎ 01347-838990) run to Helmsley four times daily, except Sunday. On Sunday York Country Buses (☎ 01904-707008) and the Moorsbus Network (contact Sutton Bank National Park Centre on ☎ 01845-597426, W www.moorsbus.net) operate two buses, although the Moorsbus service only runs during the summer. The Moorsbus Network also has a Sunday summer service from Thirsk. From Malton to Helmsley there are RW Appleby buses twice daily, except Sunday. Scarborough and District (☎ 01723-369331) has hourly services daily between Scarborough and Helmsley.

Train The train stations most convenient for Helmsley are York, Scarborough, Malton and Thirsk. Buses link these towns with Helmsley (see Bus earlier). York is the recommended gateway, as it is on the east coast main line and has relatively regular bus services to Helmsley, but Scarborough has the most frequent bus connections to the start.

At the end of the walk there are regular trains from Filey to Hull and Scarborough, where you can change for York and further connecting services. The Cleveland Way also crosses the Esk Valley line (with services to Darlington) at Kildale and Whitby.

Car From the A1, take the A61 north-east to Thirsk, continuing east on the A170 to Helmsley. Scarborough is farther east along the A170. For Filey take the A165 south-east out of Scarborough and then the A1039.

THE WALK
Helmsley

The centre point in the wealthy, prim market town of Helmsley is its marketplace (Friday is market day) and the monument to local nobleman William, second Earl of Feversham, which stands at the start of the Cleveland Way. The town thrives on the tourists that flock to see **Helmsley Castle** (☎ 01439-770442), run by English Heritage, and **Duncombe Park** (☎ 01439-771115), a large estate just west of the centre. Also of interest is **Helmsley Walled Garden**. Try to visit either the castle or estate before striking out on your walk as, although they're passed by the trail, you won't have time to do them both justice in a morning.

Helmsley TIC (☎ 01439-770173) is on the west side of the marketplace. Accommodation and good food is all around. Among the recommended places to stay are *Ashberry* (☎ *01439-770488, 41 Ashdale Rd*) with B&B from £17; and *Feathers Hotel* (☎ *01439-770275*), on the marketplace, with B&B at £33. *Gepetto's* (☎ *01439-770479, 8 Bridge St*) serves fine Italian food, while *Hunter's*, also on the marketplace, is perfect for any picnic preparations.

Day 1: Helmsley to Sutton Bank
10.5mi (17km), 4–6 hours
The first day's walk is short on distance but long on history, a gentle stroll through croplands and plantations broken repeatedly by sites of archaeological interest.

Setting off from the monument in Helmsley, head north-west away from the town centre on the road to Stokesley, leaving the church to your right. A few yards after the church you encounter the first Cleveland Way signpost directing you to Rievaulx, 3mi away. Follow the stony track as it rises out of Helmsley, through fields and woodland, and past **Griff Lodge**, where you get your first view of the Rye Valley, covered in a mantle of conifers. Just prior to entering the next patch of woodland at Quarry Bank, there's a short detour to the right, leading up to the remains of the medieval village of **Griff**, a field now consigned to grazing sheep, criss-crossed by ancient earthworks. Once back on the trail descend through Quarry Bank Wood past overgrown limestone scars to reach a minor road. Turn left and follow the road to the junction at pretty **Rievaulx Bridge**. A right turn here takes you up the road to **Rievaulx Abbey** and village.

Return to the junction at Rievaulx Bridge to rejoin the trail. Cross the bridge and continue along the minor road past Ashberry Farm for half a mile, where you turn right onto a track that follows a series of ponds towards the head of **Nettle Dale**. Watch out for adders here basking on the banks of the path. Follow signposts with care as you cross a stream on stepping stones and pass through a thicket to join a gravel track paralleling the stream up Nettle Dale. After negotiating this segment the track soon leaves Nettle Dale by way of a valley to the left, shortly turning right up a narrowing gully to emerge on the open plateau of the Hambleton Hills. A straight track leads you into **Cold Kirby**, where *Mount Grace Farm* (☎ 01845-597389) does B&B for £25 to £30. Climb through the village past generously proportioned properties, turning left after the last building on the left and following the track as it zigzags across fields to the edge of a plantation. At the plantation turn right and take the track past the stables at Hambleton House, turning left at the driveway, which takes you through the woods to the A170 and the *Hambleton Inn* (☎ 01845-597202). Here you can get excellent meals for between £7 and £13. Two doors up from the pub, *Cote Faw* (☎ 01845-597363) does B&B from £17. While Sutton Bank is the official end of today's stage, accommodation is only available here or roughly 2.5mi south at Kilburn.

If you decide to stop here but still have time to make the excursion to the White Horse of Kilburn chalk figure (for a general discussion of chalk figures, see the boxed text 'Wessex Chalk Figures' on p158), drop the bags and enjoy an unfettered stroll via Sutton Bank.

From Hambleton Inn take the A170 west towards Sutton Bank, branching diagonally left at the road to the White Horse and following a straight path through trees to Sutton Bank, an expansive precipice, from where you can catch a stunning sunset over the distant Pennines. At a trail junction (T-intersection), turn left to follow the escarpment past Roulston Scar and the gliding club to the **White Horse of Kilburn**, about a mile from the trail junction. Keep an eye out for the remains of a hillfort on outlying Hood Hill. The horse, when reached, is singularly unimpressive from above. If you want a proper look you'll have to drop down the hill another mile into the village of Kilburn.

In Kilburn, B&B is available at *Church Farm* (☎ 01347-868318), a working farm, from £18; and *Forresters Arms* (☎ 01347-868386), from £38/48 for singles/doubles. *Singing Bird Tea Rooms* does very edible sandwiches but is usually only open during the daytime.

Rievaulx Abbey

Rievaulx Abbey is in a beautiful setting that is at once pastoral and powerful. Henry VIII's dissolution of the monasteries in the 1530s doomed this site, the 'mother ship' of the Cistercian order; it is today the largest monastic ruin in Britain. English Heritage (☎ 01439-798228) charges £3.40/1.70 for an adult/child and opening times are 10am to 6pm April to September, closing at 5pm in October and at 4pm during the rest of the year. From the entrance follow the road up through Rievaulx village to the National Trust's elegant Terrace and Temples property (☎ 01439-798340), which affords views of the abbey from above. It's open daily from 10.30am to 5pm April to October; admission costs £3/1.50.

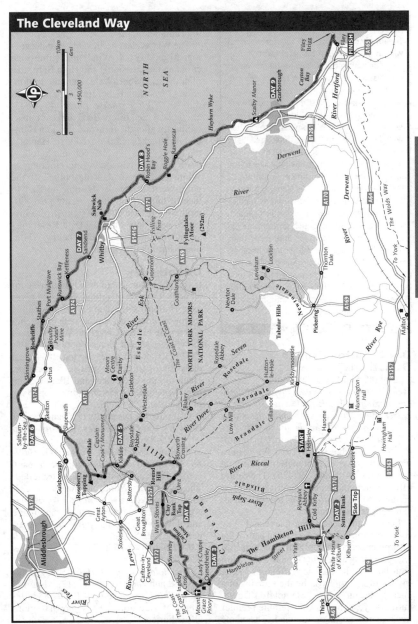

The Cleveland Way

THE NORTH YORK MOORS

The Hambleton Drove Road

The route north from Sneck Yate (pronounced yat, an old local term for gate) takes you up onto the high moor, following the course of Hambleton Street, part of an ancient network of drove roads that ran from Scotland to Southern England. All sorts of livestock were driven along this track: cattle, sheep and even geese, which were, by some accounts, fitted with felt 'shoes' to protect their feet! Early drovers were regarded as little more than rogues and vagabonds, something akin to the image of the cowboy in the American West, but later, under the reign of Henry I, the profession succumbed to government regulations and the drovers had to be licensed. Hambleton Street continued to flourish even after the development of improved roads along the floor of the Vale of York because, while these newer roads charged tolls, access to the old upland ways remained free. It took the coming of the railways in the mid-19th century to spell the end for the Street as a commercial route.

Day 2: Sutton Bank to Osmotherley

11.5mi (18.5km), 5½–7½ hours

Today's stretch may seem barren and desolate, but in fine weather it has one significant redeeming quality: a grand landscape is your constant companion throughout the day.

From Sutton Bank head north, maintaining the cliff edge to meet the A170 once more, this time at Sutton Bank National Park Centre (☎ 01845-597426). The centre offers much the same material found at Helmsley TIC. A *cafe* serves tea (of course) and light refreshments.

Leaving the centre, the Cleveland Way continues north along an enclosed path at the escarpment edge. A footpath soon branches left, providing access to Gormire Lake. Turn your back to the lake at vertiginous White Mare Crag; before you lie the remains of a once-proud racecourse, **Hambleton Down**, until 200 years ago considered the premier track in the north of England. The name

survives today in the form of a titled race – the Hambletonian.

The Way is clear northwards, past the geological oddity of Windypits (limestone caves and depressions) and High Barn, to a minor road at **Sneck Yate**. Here the trail re-enters woodland before climbing out through *High Paradise Farm* (☎ 01845-537033), which offers B&B and camping.

Shortly after the farmyard you join **Hambleton Street** (see the boxed text 'Hambleton Drove Road'), which you join to follow north for approximately 5mi, climbing to White Gill Head, then dropping off the north-western edge of Hambleton End to meet a minor road at a parking area. Osmotherley is a welcome sight in the distance, with only the Oak Dale Reservoirs and a small but steep valley below Whitehouse Farm left to negotiate.

Osmotherley

If you have time to explore Osmotherley for an hour it can be diverting. Everyone raves over **Thompson's**, a curious shop that time forgot. Standing in a similar state of dereliction a mile off the Cleveland Way, north of the village, **Mount Grace Priory** (☎ 01609-778132) is worth an excursion. It is open daily 10am to 6pm, April to September, 10am to 5pm in October and 10am to 1pm from November to March. Admission to the priory costs £2.80/1.40.

Osmotherley has plenty of amenities. For B&B try the *Osmotherley Walking Shop* (☎ 01609-883818) with rooms for £22.50; or inviting *Oak Garth Farm* (☎ 01609-883314) north of town, with views back across the countryside you've travelled. The owner, Mrs Wood, charges £20 to £23. *Cote Ghyll Caravan Park* (☎ 01609-883425) is farther north, out of the village and down a lane to the right, charging £4 per tent. On the same lane is *Cote Ghyll YHA Hostel* (☎ 01609-883575), which has beds for £10.

The Golden Lion (☎ 01609-883526) has upscale pub food for £8 to £12, while the *Three Tuns Restaurant* (☎ 01609 883301) aims for fine-dining at somewhat more refined prices.

Day 3: Osmotherley to Clay Bank Top

11mi (17.5km), 6–8 hours

This is a strenuous day's walk, more difficult than yesterday but more rewarding, with views opening out to the north and east this time. There are a lot of steep climbs and descents, and the land can be quite exposed. Only two spots en route present themselves as suitable candidates for breaks, well placed to coincide with lunch and tea.

From Osmotherley set off northwards for a few hundred metres, turning left at Rueberry Lane. Follow the track as it meanders round the brow of a hill, passing Chapel Wood Farm and the detour to Mount Grace Priory. Requiring less effort to get to than the Priory, **Lady's Chapel**, off to the right of the trail, is worth a peek.

The Cleveland Way then traverses Beacon Hill (with its fearsome array of radio masts) and Scarth Wood Moor, crossing a minor road into Clain Wood before dropping down to a road leading into Swainby. This village, a mile off the trail, is a good place for lunch. *The Blacksmiths Arms (☎ 01642-700303, Black Horse Lane)*, with a large adventurous menu, is a good bet. *The Black Horse Inn (☎ 01642-700436, 23 High St)* also does lunches daily.

Resuming the trail, head south-east for about half a mile before dropping out of the woods through fields to Scugdale Beck, crossed on a small road bridge. Climb the road past Hollin Hill Farm, over a road junction and by a phone box to start the ascent onto Round Hill. This is the first of four tough ridges. The glider strip and facilities on Carlton Moor are still used, but only when winds are favourable. A steep drop off the eastern end of the moor lands you in the lush, wide saddle in front of Cringle Moor, where the trail crosses a lane coming up from the village of Carlton-in-Cleveland. The *Lord Stones Cafe*, a few yards southeast of the lane crossing (and easy to miss), makes a good tea break; it serves food from 9.30am to 5pm daily in summer.

Cringle Moor, Broughton Bank (more commonly known as Cold Moor) and Hasty Bank lie ahead, and with them further scars on the landscape, including a disused alum mine and jet workings. Jet, a carbonaceous substance, was tremendously popular during Victoria's reign (she wore it in mourning for her dead husband, Albert) but its role as a fashion accessory did not endure. Alum had a more solidly prosperous life as an important ingredient in the dying of textiles and leathers. Alum mines also went the way of the dodo due to a technological innovation allowing for the derivation of alum from coal mines' waste materials. The focus of the day's final big ascent, up Hasty Bank, are the **Wain Stones**, giant blocks of a coarse, hard sandstone called gritstone, scattered about the hillside. A welcome final but sharp descent brings you to the Clay Bank Top, where the trail crosses the B1257. A *campsite*, set in a meadow here, is open from May to October. The caretaker comes around in the evening and collects £2. For other accommodation options you need to head to Urra or Great Broughton.

Urra & Great Broughton

To reach Urra, head up the road from Clay Bank Top and turn left as signposted, or avoid the road by taking the footpath which leaves the trail a little beyond Clay Bank Top. In this tiny hamlet is *Maltkiln House (☎ 01642-778216)*, definitely the most sensible option for accommodation and food, but you need to book ahead as it's a popular choice. Run by Gerry and Wendy Broad, it offers unpretentious luxury from £17 to £19, and a welcome evening meal in the convivial dining room for an extra £10.

Other options are in Great Broughton, 2.5mi north on the B1257 (although this is better avoided by taking footpaths from just west of the Wain Stones, before you reach Clay Bank Top). B&Bs include *Ingleby Hill (☎ 01642-712449)*, on Ingleby Rd, from £17.50. Mr Robinson at *Holme Farm (☎ 01642-712345, 12 The Holme)* charges the same; as with most other walker-friendly B&Bs in this town, he'll drop you back at Clay Bank Top next day. *The Jet Miners Inn (☎ 01642-712427)*, on the main street, does decent evening meals and welcomes campers for £2.

THE NORTH YORK MOORS

Day 4: Clay Bank Top to Kildale
9mi (14.5km), 4–6 hours

A short day and a welcome one given the earlier taxing terrain. Heather, grouse, ancient milestones and a disused incline railway are the discernible features overlying otherwise undistinguished country.

Beginning at Clay Bank Top, there's a steep approach up Carr Ridge to the gently rising summit of **Round Hill**, the highest point on the walk at 454m. From the trig point an easy walk across featureless moorland merges with a disused railway and then doubles back dramatically at Bloworth Crossing, where traces of railway workers' dwellings exist. At this point the Coast to Coast Walk, which has overlapped the Way from near Osmotherley, parts company and heads eastwards.

Proceeding north you pass stones near Burton Howe that indicate this track was once a main route between Helmsley and Stokesley. The gentle descent continues after Tidy Brown Hill, to the point where you meet the Baysdale Abbey to Kildale road. Just over a mile along this minor road and you are down into the valley of Battersby, near the village of Kildale.

Battersby & Kildale
Places to stay in the Battersby valley include *Low Farm*, the residence of Mr and Mrs Cook (☎ 01642-722145), who, in addition to running a B&B (prices from £17) in their farmhouse, also tend *Kildale Camping Barn* at nearby Park Farm, charging £3.50. Both places are under a mile south-south-west of Kildale.

The 17th-century *Dudley Arms*, a farther 2mi away in Ingleby Greenhow, is worth the extra walk; it serves meals with massive portions for £6 to £10.

Glebe Cottage (☎ 01642-724470), in Kildale proper, is open daily for lunch and tea, and does evening meals by prior arrangement only. Another welcoming B&B choice is *Bankside Cottage* (☎ 01642-723259). The cottage stands on the far side of Kildale from your approach, overlooking the village from the side of Coate Moor; rooms start at £18.

Day 5: Kildale to Saltburn-by-the-Sea
15mi (24km), 7–10 hours

Today the trail gradually leaves its namesake hills behind and, after the landmark peak of Roseberry Topping, makes a beeline for the sea. The industrial influence of Middlesbrough, with conurbations and fiery refineries, comes into startling focus, weighing steadily heavier on the landscape like a spectre from Tolkien as you march towards the coast.

From Kildale cross the nascent River Leven east of the road leading to St Cuthbert's Church and the train station, then climb Coate Moor on a lane. At the top, cut left through the plantation to reach **Captain Cook's Monument** on Easby Moor summit, complete with rousing epitaph on the side of the 51ft-high obelisk. The hill here is sometimes used by paragliders as a launching point and its appeal is obvious; the slope drops sharply away to the south-west, with 5mi of valley floor before Carlton Moor rises up to match Easby's elevation.

From Easby you nip down the hill into Gribdale, across a road and up the other side onto Great Ayton Moor. The tiring official 1mi detour to the last challenging knoll of **Roseberry Topping**, a popular peak known as the 'Matterhorn' of North Yorkshire (unlike the original it has stone stairs built into its side), is next but the views are rewarding. Drop east off the Topping, then back up onto heather moorland, past a farm and into **Guisborough Forest** (pronounced giz-boruh). Follow logging tracks for a few miles, past the junction with the Tees Link path. This section can be quite muddy and, despite signs prohibiting them, horses and mountain bikers add further to the mire.

The scenic low point of the day comes at the descent to **Slapewath** and the busy A171 main Middlesbrough to Whitby road. Just before crossing, take care as the wooded hillside here is used by off-road motorcycles. Once across the A171 turn left, following the right-hand side of the road 200m to the *Fox & Hounds* (☎ 01287-632964), off to the right. This pub, despite its godforsaken location, does hearty lunches.

When leaving the pub be careful not to confuse the signs for Cleveland Street with those of the Cleveland Way. The Street is a different path. Instead head north-west from the pub up a short rise leading to the end of a residential street. Turn right beyond the last driveway. A sharp climb round a quarry rim puts you back up onto higher ground and leads you mercifully away from the sound of traffic. The walk is easy from here as you cross fields to a farm and down Airy Hill Lane to Skelton Green, continuing in a straight line through encroaching suburbia and Skelton proper. Cross the main road in Skelton and head off downhill, turning right at Ullswater Drive, then left at a T-junction. Go down to the end of the road and into a small subdivision on the right, which leads to fields and a path once more.

The approach to Saltburn-by-the-Sea diverts slightly from the course given on the Ordnance Survey map to accommodate the recent Skelton to Brotton bypass, but it's a well-marked section. After an underpass a descent through woods deposits you at **Skelton Beck**, at the foot of an impressive railway viaduct, which still carries freight. The sign warning of danger from falling bricks doesn't instil confidence, although the bridge certainly looks a sturdy construction. A footbridge leads you back up the other side of the valley; follow its steeply wooded banks into Saltburn-by-the-Sea (commonly called Saltburn).

Saltburn-by-the-Sea

A millionaires' retreat in Victorian days, Saltburn is now sadly forgotten. Campers should head for the *Saltburn Caravan Park* (☎ 01287-622014), in Milton St, where you can pitch a tent for £3.50 from March to October. *Albany Guest House* (☎ 01287-622221, 15 Pearl St) has B&B from £15, or you could splash out at *Spa Hotel* (☎ 01287-622544), Saltburn Bank, with views over the newly renovated Victorian pier, the largest such structure on the east coast. Rooms at the Spa are £25 to £35; there is a restaurant and a buffet breakfast is served.

Alessi's (☎ 01287-625033, 10 Dundas St), straight out of Sicily, is a real find. Dishes cost £6 to £13. *The Ship*, on the waterfront, is a great stop for a pint.

Walkers in need of equipment can find solace at Coast & Country, 14 Milton St.

Day 6: Saltburn-by-the-Sea to Sandsend

17mi (27.5km), 7½–10 hours

The trail from Saltburn hugs the coastline pretty closely all the way to Filey. Route finding is straightforward, but chances are you'll come across a few areas where waymarks disagree with the OS map. Usually this is due to coastal erosion, which makes it necessary to divert sections of the trail on an annual basis. You are now on some of the most unstable coastline in Britain. Watch your step in wet and windy conditions and stay well away from the cliff edge as landslips can occur without warning. Today's walk also takes you onto the headland at Rockcliffe (more commonly known as Boulby Cliff), the highest point on the east coast at 213m.

Crossing the beach at Saltburn to reach the cliffs to the east you'll spot cobles (pronounced cobbles), a local variety of fishing boat, and their attending tractors, which drag them up the sands from the sea. From here to Skinningrove the trail describes a tangent with the marvellously engineered Saltburn to Whitby railway line, now only used as far as Boulby by goods trains.

Three miles along the cliff top from Saltburn, past the first of a series of **Roman signal station sites** – used to warn of attacking fleets – and down a cliff scarred by industry, you arrive in Skinningrove. This is a curious village that grew with the discovery of iron seams in the 1850s from a quiet fishing cove to a crowded mining community. Today Skinningrove's economic future lies very much in the hands of the steel mill overlooking the bay. The **Tom Leonard Museum** (☎ 01287-642877) up the hill shows what life was like for the miners.

A considerable climb sets you atop the high cliffs at **Rockcliffe**, where things get easier. If the chimneys at Cleveland's potash mine to the right look tall, consider that the shafts over which the complex is built are a dozen times as deep, the deepest mines in Britain. They extend laterally as well, reaching some 3mi or more out to sea, with working temperatures exceeding 40°C.

Cut across Cowbar Nab and drop down into justifiably touristy **Staithes**, where you can grab a bite to eat at the ***Cod & Lobster*** (☎ 01947-840295), on the seafront. Nearby and also on the water, ***Sea Drift*** serves light meals all day. ***Greystones*** (☎ 01947-841694, 🅔 tonyrd@lineone.net), on the High St, provides B&B from £16.

Back up on the cliffs, continue by Port Mulgrave and unspoilt **Runswick Bay** (with its pub, the ***Royal Hotel***), along the beach to a well-hidden inlet leading to winding steps that regain the cliff path to Kettleness. Only a few farms and houses remain here; in 1829 a landslip claimed the village. Pass the next Roman signal station at Goldsborough and cross fields. After a steep and muddy descent through trees you emerge just in front of the looming mouth of an abandoned rail tunnel. From here it's level walking along the disused railway line into Sandsend.

Sandsend

The village of Sandsend has plenty of places to stay, including ***Pat Coakley's*** (☎ 01947-893202), on the hill leading out of town. B&B here costs from £17, with (if you're lucky) a pot of freshly made tea brought to your room in the morning. The ***Bungalow Hotel*** (☎ 01947-893272), just next door, is a good choice if you're a group; B&B costs from £25 to £32. The nearest campsite is at ***Sandfield House Farm*** (☎ 01947-602660), on Sandsend Rd, open from April to October and charging from £3.50.

For a meal in the evening, try the ***Hart Inn*** (☎ 01947-893304) with main courses from £5 to £10. Family-run ***East Row Restaurant*** (☎ 01947-893424) is the place to go for an after-walk treat.

Day 7: Sandsend to Robin Hood's Bay

10mi (16km), 5–6½ hours
The shorter distance today should allow you to spend a bit of time in bustling, historic Whitby. But don't linger too long:

later in the day, the coastline is undulating and tiring.

Start out on the uninspiring Whitby Rd, turning left at the golf course to meet the sea bluffs and the western suburbs of Whitby. Continue down to the harbour past amusement arcades and the fish market, crossing the swing bridge to the old town, where countless nooks and crannies lead to tiny shops and pubs. The ***Duke of York***, at the foot of the 199 steps to the abbey, is well placed for food. Up the steps, the foreboding dark stone of **Whitby Abbey** surveys the town and coast. Its decline in the 16th century closely mirrors Rievaulx's later history. Admission costs £1.70/90p. Next door is ***Whitby YHA Hostel*** (☎ 01947-602878) with beds from £9.80.

From the abbey entrance, turn away from Whitby to follow a minor road, turning left soon after at a signpost for the Cleveland Way. Head out of Whitby through a holiday home and watch for the exclamation mark of rock that is **Saltwick Nab**. Again, the integrity of the cliffs along this stretch is questionable; take care. A few miles' walk funnels you into the upper part of Robin Hood's Bay.

Robin Hood's Bay

The small town of Robin Hood's Bay clings to cliffs on the edge of the coast and is often crammed to the gills with ramblers and tearoom junkies. Romantics may be disappointed to find out that the link between Robin Hood's Bay and the heroic outlaw is only legendary, and extremely tenuous. Nevertheless, while roaming the steep and narrow cobbled lanes, with miniature cottages and tiny gardens glued to the steep slopes of the bay, there is nothing to stop you from imagining the bustling fishing community of earlier centuries – a haven for smugglers, shipwrecked sailors and, of course, heroic outlaws.

The best place for camping walkers is ***Hooks House Farm*** (☎ 01947-880283), about half a mile before the edge of town on the main road towards Whitby, charging £3.50 in the high season. You can also head inland along the disused rail trail towards

Fylingthorpe and the *Middlewood Farm* (☎ *01947-880414*), where you can pitch for £5 from April to October. The nearest *YHA hostels* (☎ *01947-602878*) are at Whitby, to the north, and at the delightfully named Boggle Hole, to the south (see Day 8).

Ravenswood (☎ *01947-880099*), right on the trail, does good B&B for £18.50. On the outskirts of town, just as you come off the cliffs, *Meadowfield* (☎ *01947-880564*), on Mount Pleasant North, is recommended, with B&B from £16. Nearby is the similarly priced *Rosegarth* (☎ *01947-880578*). In the heart of the village is the quaint and secluded *Orchard House* (☎ *01947-880912*), from £22.50 for an en suite. Also recommended is *The White Owl Guesthouse* (☎ *01947-880879*), from £18.

The Bay Hotel (☎ *01947-880278*), overlooking the slipway, has B&B for £40 per double (£50 en suite) and a popular hikers bar. Back up the hill and more upmarket is *The Victoria Hotel* (☎ *01947-880205*), with great sea views and single/double B&B for £40/66. There's also good bar food, including vegetarian, and a restaurant serving a la carte.

The Cleveland Way – Route Highlight

The trail from Whitby to Robin Hood's Bay offers a good introduction to the coastal section of the Cleveland Way. This 7mi (11.5km) stretch will take you about 2½ to 4 hours of walking, but allow longer to look around Whitby and Robin Hood's Bay.

Whitby is accessible by train from Darlington and by car from York via the A64 and A169. There's a parking area next to Whitby Abbey. From the train station walk across the swing bridge over the harbour and through the old town up the steps to the abbey. Refer to the description in Day 7 for notes on the trail to Robin Hood's Bay. Tees & District (☎ 01947-602146) run hourly buses back to Whitby, stopping near the train station.

Day 8: Robin Hood's Bay to Scarborough

14mi (22.5km), 7–9 hours

The character of the coastline changes today, most noticeably at Hayburne Wyke, a nature reserve and renowned beauty spot, where hardwood deciduous trees still flourish. This is a rare haven that gives a glimpse back to a time before settlement and industry caused radical change to the natural environment of North Yorkshire.

On leaving Robin Hood's Bay you have two options. At low tide you can walk the length of the wide beach to Boggle Hole, or you can follow the waymarked trail along the cliffs above the bay. *Boggle Hole YHA Hostel* (☎ *01947-880352*) charges £9.80. At the far end of the wide, sweeping bay, climb through mixed woodland and scrub to **Ravenscar**. The National Trust has a small visitors centre here that's open daily in the spring and summer. Go on to the road and turn left for *Raven Hall Country House Hotel* where, if you're not feeling too scruffy, you can get some refreshment at the bar. At the end of Station Rd, *Foxcliffe Tearooms* (☎ *01723-871028*) is a popular halt for teas or light lunches.

A pleasant ramble straight along the cliff edge for 3.5mi gets you to the 'pocket beach' at **Hayburne Wyke**, strewn with rounded stones. If you don't fancy a picnic lunch by the water, head up the wooded valley to *Hayburne Wyke Inn* (☎ *01723-870202*) for lunch in peaceful surroundings.

Beyond Hayburne Wyke the countryside opens out and affords a sweeping prospect over the last stage of the walk. On a clear day Flamborough Head, just north of Bridlington, is visible and, as you approach Scarborough, its castle shines like a beacon in the setting sun. If you're camping, down your pack at *Scalby Manor* (☎ *01723-366212*), in Field Lane, just off to the right of the trail before you hit Scalby Mills. The charge is about £5 per tent.

Scarborough

This bustling seaside town offers a wide choice of accommodation. Hotels with sea views are £25 to £40 but cheaper B&Bs can be had if you look on North Marine Rd, where prices range from £17 to £25. The TIC (☎ 01723-373333), at the junction of Westborough and Northway, can help.

For those on a tight budget, try the *Kerry Lee Hotel* (☎ *01273-363845, 60 Trafalgar Square*), where rooms go from £12. *Cliffside Hotel* (☎ *01723-361087, 79–81 Queen's Parade*) offers good views from £19. Or splash out at the *Clifton Hotel* (☎ *0173-375691*), in Queen's Parade, where rooms start at £35/50 per single/double.

The town centre offers a variety of restaurants and fast-food joints. *Raj* (☎ *01723-506199, 37 Dean Rd*), an excellent Indian place, does sit-down and takeaway meals for £4.50 to £7.

Day 9: Scarborough to Filey
11mi (17.5km), 5½–6½ hours
The final day is an easy cliff-top walk, a fittingly enjoyable end to the trail.

The first hour or so is spent getting clear of Scarborough. The route round the headland and along the beach to the Spa (a complex dating from the Victorian era, nestled beneath a steep, Italianate garden) is a bracing start that systematically introduces you to the typical elements of a British resort town. You leave grand northerly hotels behind and pass the beachfront amusement arcades and the harbour, and finally climb past even grander hotels overlooking South Bay.

Beyond the Spa you come to the spot where, in 1993, the Holbeck House Hotel and the land on which it stood gave way and crumbled into the sea. Not many clues to its existence remain, but the disaster is a reminder of the coast's flighty geology.

The trail runs along fields and subdivisions to a fine view over Cayton Sands, a surfer's hangout. There's a *cafe* midway down the beach, which you can reach either by the beach or from the road above. From here caravan parks give way to wheat fields on the breezy track out to Filey Brigg. The seas around the Brigg are a favourite haunt of seals, who know when the salmon nets are out. If the tide is favourable you can make it out to the tip of the Brigg by descending steps on its south side. The area is

a nature reserve and it's common to find interesting sea creatures trapped in the many rock pools around the point.

Then it's back on the track, where one final mile brings you into Filey. The official completion book kept at the Filey Country Park Stores provides an excellent opportunity for giving feedback on the route just completed.

Filey
The subdued seaside resort of Filey has plenty of B&Bs. Near the beach, *Downcliffe Hotel* (☎ *01723-513310*) is expensive at £35 to £40 but worth it if you have the money to spoil yourself. Or try *Abbots Leigh Guest House* (☎ *01723-513334, 7 Rutland St*), with rooms from £20. *The Star*, on the way up to the train station in Mitford St, is a welcome pub.

Falling Foss & Fylingdales

Distance	16.5mi (26.5km)
Duration	5–7 hours
Standard	easy-medium
Start/Finish	Grosmont
Gateways	Whitby, Pickering

Summary A fairly long circular walk on clearly defined tracks and paths, so not too arduous. Some parts are muddy in winter. The route undulates but gradients are mostly gentle.

This walk is an excellent North York Moors introduction, covering a rich variety of scenery and terrain, with several points of interest. There are some fine open sections across Fylingdales Moor, complete with North Sea views, plus a stretch of lovely wooded valley around May Beck and Falling Foss – a fairly impressive waterfall.

This route also passes through the typical North York Moors villages of Grosmont (pronounced growmont) and Goathland, which are linked by lovingly restored steam trains on the North Yorkshire Moors Railway. The line, one of the first in Britain, was built by none other than George Stephenson, way back in 1836. Goathland is quite busy because a popular TV series called *Heartbeat* was filmed in the village, which did wonders for the local tourist trade. When we passed through, news was breaking that a forthcoming *Harry Potter* film would also be made here, doing even more to put Goathland on the tourist map.

Direction, Distance & Duration

The best place to start is the village of Grosmont. This circular route can be done in either direction, but clockwise gets the steep section over with early and allows for a final train ride back to base, if required. If you have a car, you could start at May Beck and have lunch at Goathland or Grosmont.

The whole distance is 16.5mi. If you walk fast you could do it in five hours, but six to seven would be less of a rush. Also allow an extra hour or so for lunch, train spotting and, of course, the excellent views. Using the train on the final section reduces the walking distance to 13mi.

PLANNING
Maps & Books

Maps and books covering the North York Moors are described under Information in the introduction to this chapter. This route is on OS Outdoor Leisure 1:25,000 map No 27 *(North York Moors – Eastern Area)*.

Information Sources

In Grosmont a shop called the Trading Post sells books and maps, and also has a tourist information point – basically a leaflet dispenser. For other inquiries you should contact the TICs in Pickering (☎ 01751-473791) and Whitby (☎ 01947-602674).

PLACES TO STAY & EAT
Grosmont

If you're camping, head for *Fairhead Farm*, east of the village and up the hill, where a space in the field, with just toilets and hot water wash basins, costs £2; there's no need to book. For B&B *Eskdale* (☎ 01947-895385) is perennially popular and well used to walkers, with rooms from £17. Another good, friendly choice is *Hazlewood House* (☎ 01947-895292), on Front St, just downhill from the train station, charging around £19; it comes with a tearoom, garden seating and good home baking. Also recommended is *Grosmont House* (☎ 01947-895539, ℮ admin@linton.co.uk), a large and well-organised place next to the train station, charging from £20 (or £45 for an en suite double). Family rooms are available. The dining room, also open to nonresidents, has main courses from £7 to £15; the affable host is happy for walkers to phone ahead to discuss the menu or place orders.

For snacks and lunches, *Signals Tearoom* at the train station is good. The *Station Tavern*, also near – you've guessed it – the train station, is basic but friendly and serves standard bar food. Continuing the railway theme, for a splurge, every Thursday, Friday and Saturday the *North Yorkshire Moors steam train* does evening trips with a full 'Orient Express-style' dinner served on board. Ask at the train station for details, or try the headquarters in Pickering (☎ 01751-472508).

Goathland

In Goathland you can get hot drinks, snacks and meals at the *Station Buffet*, and in the village there are teashops and two pubs

Heather & Grouse

The North York Moors have the largest expanse of heather moorland in England. Three types can be seen: ling is the most widespread, has a pinkish-purple flower and is most spectacular in late summer; bell heather is deep purple; and cross-leaved heather (or bog heather) prefers wet ground, unlike the first two, and tends to flower earlier. Wet and boggy areas also feature cotton grass, sphagnum moss and insect-eating sundew plants.

The moors have traditionally been managed to provide an ideal habitat for red grouse – a famous game bird. The shooting season lasts from the 'Glorious Twelfth' of August to 10 December. The heather is periodically burned, giving managed moorland a patchwork effect – the grouse nests in mature growth but feeds on the tender shoots of new growth.

doing accommodation, plus several B&Bs in and around the village.

GETTING TO/FROM THE WALK

Bus & Train You can reach Pickering easily by bus, with regular services from Leeds, York and Scarborough. But after that, local services become a bit erratic and the train is by far the best way to reach the start. There are five trains per day (including Sunday) in each direction between Middlesbrough and Whitby via Grosmont. You can also approach Grosmont from Pickering by steam train on the North Yorkshire Moors Railway (phone ☎ 01751-473535 for the talking timetable), which is an excellent journey at around £9 for the return trip. There are several intermediate train stations, and five to eight services per day in each direction, depending on the season.

Car Grosmont lies between the A171 and A169, south-west of Whitby. There is a car park by the train station (£1.50 all day) and another on the edge of the village.

THE WALK
Grosmont to Falling Foss

5.5mi (9km), 2–2½ hours

From the train station head east on the road through the village, up the steep hill. There are two forks in the road; at both go right, signposted to Goathland. You'll also see 'Coast to Coast' (CtoC) signs, as the first section of this walk follows this famous long-distance route.

The road continues steeply, across a cattle grid, to reach a point near the top of the hill where a track and a footpath branch off left (north-east). Take the footpath, uphill slightly, heading to the right of a small, disused quarry and then swinging to the east. This is a nice little section of moorland, with good views down to Whitby and the coast. The path is not well defined, however, so if you get lost, keep just to the left of the small hill's summit (marked by a trig point) until you meet another path running west to east. Take this path eastwards down to meet the A169 next to a large blue road sign warning drivers of a steep hill ahead. (If the cloud is

low, or this bit sounds too tricky, keep going on the road and branch off about a mile later onto a narrow path signposted 'Littlebeck' that takes you to the A169 near the big blue road sign mentioned above.)

Cross the A169 (with great care) and go through the gate on the east side of the road. Follow the track downhill, turning left at a junction, then joining a lane leading down into the hamlet of **Littlebeck**. Cross the river, continue on the lane for 30m, then go through a gate on the right, onto a footpath signposted 'CtoC'.

The path winds through a delightful patch of woodland, with the gurgling waters of the stream down to your right. There are several forks, but keep following the 'CtoC' signs to reach **the Hermitage** – which looks like a cave but is actually a hollowed-out boulder. Just beyond here keep left at the fork, then right (to pass alonside a wall), then left and down to reach a point overlooking **Falling Foss** waterfall. We're not talking Niagara here but it's quite impressive after rain.

Falling Foss to Fylingdales summit

4.5mi (7km), 1–1½ hours

From Falling Foss take the path to the left of Midge Hall (an old house) over a footbridge, then up to meet a track near a large stone bridge. Do not go over this bridge, but follow the 'CtoC' signs through a final section of woodland to reach the car park at May Beck. A *van* usually sells teas and snacks here between April and September.

> ## Possible Route Changes
>
> Between May Beck and Eller Beck Bridge this route follows paths and tracks that are regularly used by walkers but are not rights of way. The landowners are Forest Enterprise, a private estate, and the Ministry of Defence. Although not very likely, walkers should be prepared for route diversions or closures in the case of, for example, logging, grouse shooting or military activity.

At the far end of the car park, ignore the lane that doubles back on itself to the left (north) and take the track southwards uphill into a plantation. After 300m, as this track bends round to the right, you drop down left, over a stream and then uphill in a straight line, following a little valley and a wide gap in the conifers, where rowans and other deciduous trees have been allowed to grow.

At the top of this valley the path meets a track. Turn right (west), past a pond, and follow the track uphill, turning left (south) at another junction. Keep on the main track, ignoring any temporary tracks that might have been made by logging vehicles, always going uphill. Suddenly the woods give way and with great relief you're on top of the wide, open expanse of **Fylingdales Moor**, with good views of the other surrounding moors – quite a contrast after being enclosed by trees.

At its highest point the track passes through a gate. About 50m to the left (east)

a trig point marks the summit of Fylingdales Moor. It's the highest point but don't expect a lofty peak here! The views are good, though, of Fylingdales Moor. Across the valley to the south-west is a large square building – a military listening station – which, although you can see it for miles around, isn't marked on any maps, but the surrounding 'Danger Area' (closed to the public) is shown.

Fylingdales summit to Goathland
3.5mi (5.5km), 1–1½ hours

From the gate and trig point, aim south on the track for 400m until you reach a junction, where you take another clear track heading off to the right. (To your left a path leads to an ancient stone cross on the hillside.) Continue on this track for 200m, then it's very important that you take a small path forking off right (at a small marker peg with 'LWW' written on it – see the boxed text 'The Lyke

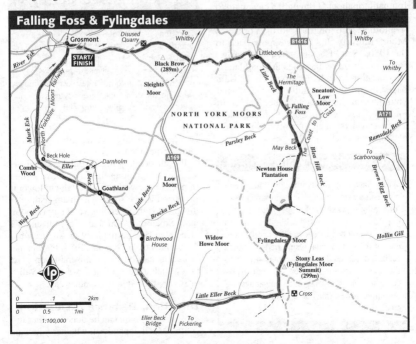

Falling Foss & Fylingdales

Wake Walk' below). Look out for the clear 'Keep Out' signs and ensure that you do not enter the 'Danger Area'. Follow this narrow path through the heather and west across the moors, running parallel to Little Eller Beck. Sometimes it seems the beck and the path are one, and these sections can be boggy.

At Eller Beck Bridge you meet the busy main road (the A169 again) – a rather unwelcome intrusion after the peacefulness of the moors. Turn right across the bridge, go uphill and take the first left down a minor road back to quieter climes. Follow this road for about a mile. To your left is the railway (look out for steam trains). Just before the road goes under a railway bridge, take a lane on the right, signed to Birchwood. This skirts to the right of Birchwood House and becomes a rough track, with good views of the valley (and more steam trains). After passing through a farmyard the track becomes a lane again, then meets a road. Cross straight over, following the footpath for about 500m until a clear path to the left cuts down to **Goathland** train station – another stop on the North Yorkshire Moors Railway. It's like stepping back to the 1950s. See Places to Stay & Eat earlier for information on facilities in Goathland.

An option from here is to catch the train back to Grosmont – quite a good idea if your legs are starting to ache. The short journey gives a glimpse of the golden era of steam travel (soot in your eye, dirty face, hacking cough etc).

The Lyke Wake Walk

While walking in the North York Moors you may come across signposts and marker pegs for the Lyke Wake Walk (LWW), a challenging 40mi route across the high ground. In days gone by it was followed by people from east of the Moors, near Osmotherley, as they carried deceased family members across to the coast at Ravenscar for burial at sea. Walkers who complete this route nowadays are presented with a small badge in the shape of a coffin.

Goathland to Grosmont

3mi (5km), 1–1½ hours

Go uphill from the train station towards the village, then take the first small road to the right (Mill Green Way), which leads onto another road. Turn left here and onto a footpath on the right, signposted 'Grosmont Rail Trail'. This follows the route of a steep incline (downhill), which was the original railway route. Keep to the line of the old railway (rail trail deviations add extra distance), and this final stretch leads you quickly but pleasantly through woods and fields.

Just before Grosmont the path crosses over to the east side of the railway as it runs through a small tunnel and brings you out on the main street by the train station. After crossing the railway you can divert south for 100m or so for a look around the engine shed (if it's open to visitors) and a final farewell to the trains.

The Farndale Skyline

Distance	16mi (25.5km)
Duration	6½–8 hours
Standard	easy-medium
Start/Finish	Low Mill
Gateways	Kirkbymoorside, Pickering
Summary A long route of easy walking, mostly on wide tracks on level ground across moors, with a section of valley at the end.	

Farndale is a large valley in the heart of North York Moors. This route keeps mainly to the surrounding high ground and finishes with a section along the River Dove – most famous for its wild daffodils, which flower in profusion every April. The main feature of this route is the open, high and empty moorland expanse – wild and beautiful under a clear blue sky, particularly in August when the purple heather blooms. But if the weather is bad, it can be really miserable up here; you're better off staying down in the valley or saving this walk for another day.

Direction, Distance & Duration

This circular route can be done in either direction. Much depends on whether you want lunch at the Lion Inn at Blakey, and if you want it early or late. Clockwise, as described, the inn is about three-quarters of the way along. The 16mi takes six to seven hours of walking, so you should allow eight to nine hours in total. You could also base yourself at Blakey and do the circuit from there.

PLANNING
Maps & Books
This route is on OS Outdoor Leisure 1:25,000 map No 26 (North York Moors – Western Area).

Information Sources
The nearest TICs are at Helmsley (☎ 01439-770173) and Pickering (☎ 01751-473791). They can advise on local accommodation and public transport up to Low Mills. In Hutton le Hole, at the Rydale Folk Museum (☎ 01751-417367), is a park information point with leaflets, maps and guidebooks.

PLACES TO STAY & EAT
Low Mill
The facilities in this small hamlet are limited to a post office and some public toilets in the car park. Nearby, *Keysbeck Farm* (☎ 01751-433221) offers straightforward B&B and a friendly welcome for £14. A short distance farther south, *Olive House Farm* (☎ 01751-433207) charges from £12.50.

Church Houses
North of Low Mill, this hamlet is about half a mile off the route. *The Feversham Arms* (☎ 01751-433206) does B&B from around £20, plus lunches and dinners. Just south of here and only 200m off the route is *Daffy Caffy*, open 10am to 5pm in summer, serving breakfasts, lunches and teas. At Oak House (about a mile north of Church Houses) there's a *camping barn*, which costs £3.60; to reserve a bunk contact the YHA Camping Barns Reservations Office (☎ 01200-420102, e campbarnsyha@enterprise.net).

Gillamoor
This village is 3mi south of Low Mill. B&B options include friendly and welcoming *Manor Farm* (☎ 01751-432695), charging

from £17 for an en suite; and *The Royal Oak* (☎ 01751-431414), a good traditional pub charging £25 for rooms and also doing food, with a menu featuring mainly (and proudly) British beef and lamb – a deliberate statement in this staunchly pro-farming area.

The well-stocked village *shop* (open every day in summer) also sells sandwiches.

Blakey
The miniscule hamlet of Blakey consists of just two buildings – fortunately both offer accommodation. *The Lion Inn* (☎ 01751-417320) offers snacks, lunches and dinners, plus B&B and camping. Opposite, *High Blakey House* (☎ 01751-417186) also does B&B. For full details on Blakey, see Day 11 of the Coast to Coast Walk in the Northern England Long-Distance Paths chapter, but note that rooms are sometimes hard to get, precisely because the Coast to Coast comes through here.

Hutton-le-Hole
The village of Hutton-le-Hole, 4mi south-east of Low Mill, also has several B&Bs, pubs and cafes.

GETTING TO/FROM THE WALK
Bus The only time a bus goes to Low Mill is when the daffodils are out! It's a shuttle minibus to/from Hutton-le-Hole, connecting with the Moorsbus Network service, running every Sunday in April and over the Easter holiday.

The excellent Moorsbus Network service operates every Sunday and Bank Holiday from April to the end of October, and every day between late July and early September. There is a service to Gillamoor (3mi south of Low Mill) on bus No M2 from Pickering, via Kirbymoorside. Another option is to get the bus to Blakey and start the route there. Moorsbus No M1 goes from Pickering and No M3 goes from Helmsley, both via Hutton-le-Hole and Blakey, both at least five times each way. You can get more details from the Web site at ☒ www.moorsbus.net.

Car Low Mill is best reached from the main A170 Thirsk to Pickering road via Kirkby

Mills, Hutton-le-Hole and several miles of narrow lane. There's a free car park, but you will be asked for a donation.

THE WALK
Low Mill to Blakey
12mi (19.5km), 5–6 hours

From Low Mill car park turn right to head north up the lane for 300m, then left on the track towards Horn End Farm. This track becomes a path and leads across fields. About 200m past a ruined barn, the path drops to cross a stream then climbs out of the Farndale valley, straight up the hillside, before swinging more northerly and ascending at an easier gradient. There are several vague forks in the path, and the path itself is indistinct, but it's important not to go too high too soon. Keep climbing gradually until you meet a wide, straight track running northwest to south-east across the moors. This ancient route is called **Westside Road**, and the broad ridge it follows is Ruddland Rigg.

Turn right (north) and follow this track as it cuts effortlessly across the rolling moorland for 3mi, to a junction of tracks, including a former railway, at **Bloworth Crossing** (6.5mi and about three hours of walking from Low Mill). This is where this route coincides with two LDPs – the Coast to Coast and the Cleveland Way.

Turn right to follow the former railway line, which winds its way along the crest of the hills, with great views down to the right into the Farndale valley. For more details on the railway and other aspects of this route, see the Coast to Coast Walk in the Northern England Long-Distance Paths chapter.

About 5.5mi (about 2 to 2½ hours) from Bloworth Crossing, a small path cuts off left up to **The Lion Inn** for a late lunch or early evening drink. The pub is not signposted; look for the LLW marker peg. Note, however, that this small 'concessionary' path is not a right of way so it may be closed to walkers in future, in which case continue for

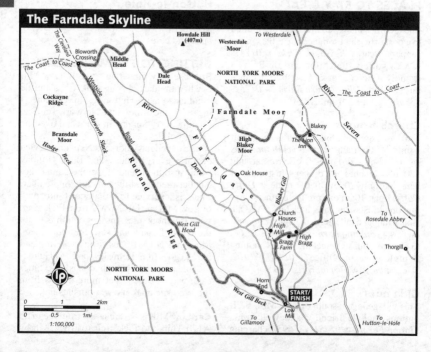

The Farndale Skyline

half a mile to the point where a track forks right off the old railway, just before a closed-off bridge, to meet a lane running down into Farndale. Turn left and left again, back along the main road, to reach the Lion Inn.

Blakey to Low Mill
4mi (6.5km), 1½–2 hours

From the Lion Inn retrace your steps to the point where the lane to Farndale turns off the main road and the old railway goes under a closed-off bridge. (In bad weather you could head straight down the lane into Farndale.)

It looks tempting to continue following the route of the old railway but this is not a right of way. So follow the main road, which leads south towards Hutton-le-Hole, for about half a mile until you see a small footpath signpost on the right (west) side of the road. There's no path on the ground but head diagonally through the heather towards the end of the low railway embankment clearly visible 200m away. From here a small line of cairns and then a path leads southwards through several gates (look out for yellow footpath arrows), across rough pasture and then fields, downhill all the way into Farndale, to meet a lane near some buildings called High Bragg. As you drop down the views along the valley are beautiful.

Take a rough track past High Bragg, round the edge of Bragg Farm and through fields. The path round the farm is confusing, so make sure you keep to stiles and gates marked with yellow footpath arrows. You meet another path running alongside the River Dove between Low Mill and Church Houses, and can branch off north to reach the *Daffy Caffy* (marked as High Mill on the map) or *The Faversham Arms* at Church Houses.

To get to Low Mill aim south. This final section along the sheltered fertile valley floor is in sharp contrast to the open moorland that has been your backdrop for most of the day, and it's a very nice finish to the walk. You pass through rich meadows, a little section of woodland and next to a pond full of noisy ducks, before crossing a footbridge that brings you out by Low Mill car park.

THE NORTH YORK MOORS

Northumberland

Taking its name from the Anglo-Saxon kingdom of Northumbria (north of the River Humber), Northumberland is one of the largest, emptiest and wildest of England's counties. There are probably more castles and battlefield sites here than anywhere else, providing vivid reminders of long and bloody struggles between the English and Scots. The castles all have fascinating histories; most changed hands several times as the border was pushed back and forth over the centuries. In the south of the county are older remains and reminders of even earlier battles from the time of Roman occupation – villas, forts and roads, plus Hadrian's Wall, one of Britain's most famous ancient monuments.

For walkers, Northumberland has two main attractions: the starkly beautiful hills and valleys of Northumberland National Park (which takes up much of the west of the county); and the Northumberland Coast, the eastern side of the county between Berwick-upon-Tweed and Alnmouth, an Area of Outstanding Natural Beauty.

In this chapter we describe a three-day walk along Hadrian's Wall (easily reduced to individual day walks if you prefer), at the southern edge of Northumberland National Park, and a walk along one of the finest stretches of British coast, taking in two most splendid castles.

INFORMATION
Maps
Northumberland is a big county covered by several Ordnance Survey (OS) Landranger 1:50,000 maps. The maps most useful to walkers are No 74 (*Kelso & Coldstream*), No 75 (*Berwick-upon-Tweed*), No 79 (*Harwick & Eskdale*), No 80 (*Cheviot Hills & Kielder Water*) and No 86 (*Haltwhistle & Brampton*), so decide where you're going before buying them all.

OS Outdoor Leisure 1:25,000 maps No 16 (*The Cheviot Hills*), No 42 (*Kielder Water*) and No 43 (*Hadrian's Wall*) cover most of Northumberland's hill and mountain areas (the Cheviot Hills, the area east of Kielder Water and the central Hadrian's Wall area). Additional OS Explorer 1:25,000 maps should fill in the gaps – notably the coast – by 2001.

Harvey produces a very handy twin set of maps *Cheviot Hills* at 1:40,000.

For maps covering individual walks, see Planning in the introduction to each walk.

Books
A general guidebook on the whole of Northumberland is *Walks in Reiver Country*, produced by the Northumberland National Park. For a more relaxing ambience, try *Pub Walks in Northumbria* by Stephen Rickerby. The *Northumbria Walks* Pathfinder Guide, published by Jarrold, also has a good selection of routes of varying lengths, combined with extracts from OS maps.

Information Sources
There are many Tourist Information Centres (TICs) in Northumberland. Those most useful for the walks described in this chapter are listed in the relevant sections. These can provide you with information on places to stay and public transport, and many also sell walking maps and books or give away leaflets. Some TICs are run by the national park authority and provide additional information about the park.

For general tourist information, you can also visit the following Web sites: W www.northumberland.gov.uk and W www.ntb.org.uk. The Northumberland National Park Web site is at W www.nnpa.org.uk.

Guided Walks
Look out for a little booklet called *Discover Northumberland*, free from TICs, which lists guided walks and other outdoor activities or countryside events around the county.

GETTING THERE & AWAY
To reach Northumberland from other parts of Britain, the main gateway cities and towns

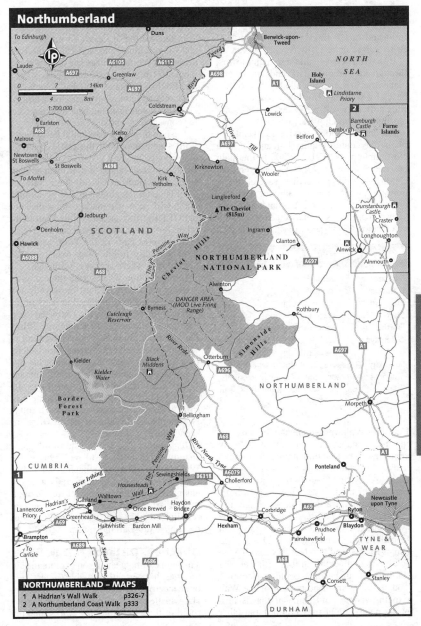

Northumberland

To Edinburgh

Duns

Berwick-upon-Tweed

NORTH SEA

Lauder

A6105

A6112

Greenlaw

A698

A697

A697

Holy Island

Lindisfarne Priory

0   7   14km
0   4   8mi
1:700,000

Coldstream

Lowick

Bamburgh Castle

Bamburgh

Farne Islands

Earlston

A68

Kelso

River Till

A697

Belford

Melrose

Newtown St Boswells

St Boswells

A698

Kirknewton

Wooler

To Moffat

Kirk Yetholm

Langleeford

▲ The Cheviot (815m)

Ingram

Dunstanburgh Castle

Craster

Jedburgh

Denholm

SCOTLAND

The Pennine Way

Cheviot Hills

Glanton

Longhoughton

Alnwick

Hawick

A6088

A68

NORTHUMBERLAND NATIONAL PARK

A697

Alnmouth

Alwinton

Byrness

DANGER AREA (MOD Live Firing Range)

Rothbury

Catcleugh Reservoir

River Rede

Simonside Hills

A697

A1

Kielder

Black Middens

Otterburn

A696

Kielder Water

NORTHUMBERLAND

Border Forest Park

Bellingham

River North Tyne

Morpeth

A68

A1

CUMBRIA

River Irthing

The Pennine Way

Sewingshields

B6318

A6079

Ponteland

Housesteads Wall

Chollerford

Newcastle upon Tyne

Lanercost Priory

Gilsland

Walltown

Once Brewed

Haydon Bridge

Corbridge

A69

Ryton

Greenhead

A69

Haltwhistle

Bardon Mill

Hexham

Prudhoe

Blaydon

Brampton

A689

River South Tyne

Painshawfield

TYNE & WEAR

To Carlisle

A686

A68

Consett

Stanley

NORTHUMBERLAND – MAPS
1   A Hadrian's Wall Walk   p326-7
2   A Northumberland Coast Walk p333

DURHAM

NORTHUMBERLAND

are Newcastle upon Tyne, Carlisle, Alnwick and Berwick-upon-Tweed. All have good train and coach links with other parts of Britain and can be easily reached by car.

Buses run between all these major towns, through the national park and via several places that are recommended in this book as bases for walking. Northumberland's local transport network pages are at W www .northumberland.gov.uk/jplanner.

For details on local services, you can also phone the central inquiry bureau of Arriva Northumbria (☎ 0191-212 3000), the main bus operator for the area. Alternatively, the Getting Around chapter lists several public transport inquiry lines that provide details of both national and local bus and train services: These are summarised in the boxed text 'National Transport Information' on p92.

A Hadrian's Wall Walk

Distance	22mi (35.5km)
Duration	3 days
Standard	easy-medium
Start	Once Brewed
Finish	Lannercost Priory
Gateways	Carlisle, Haltwhistle, Hexham, Newcastle upon Tyne

Summary The route is not strenuous and daily distances are not long, but there are many sights of interest along the way. Paths are mostly clear and easy to follow.

Hadrian's Wall was built by the Romans during their occupation of Britain in the early centuries of the first millennium. It crosses a neck of Northern England, virtually from coast to coast, for about 74mi (about 120km) between the modern-day cities of Newcastle upon Tyne and Carlisle. An amazingly impressive feat of military engineering, the Wall marked the outer limit of the great Roman Empire, which at its zenith stretched across Europe and into North Africa. To the south was civilisation; to the north were the 'barbarians' that Rome could not control. Today only a small proportion of the Wall remains visible (and some of that is in a pretty poor state of preservation), but other sections have survived the ages remarkably well and are a fascinating sight.

In recognition of the area's important archaeology, culture and landscape it has been declared a World Heritage site under the auspices of Unesco, the Countryside Agency and English Heritage. This has been a controversial process, with some local farmers and landowners resisting wide-ranging plans for conservation and development.

Despite this latter-day battle between the Wall's guardians and the restless natives thereabouts, the best way to experience the Wall is to walk along it – Roman-soldier-style. The Hadrian's Wall Path National Trail is under development and by summer 2002 will be a waymarked long-distance path (LDP) from one end of the Wall to the other. For now, although you can keep fairly close to most parts of the Wall, some sections currently follow busy roads or cross private land where access is forbidden.

In this section we describe three days of walking that take in the best-preserved, most accessible and most interesting parts of the Wall, from Sewingshields (between Hexham and Haltwhistle) to Lannercost Priory (east of Brampton). As well as the Wall itself, this route takes in various turrets, temples and forts, including Housesteads and Vindolanda, some excellent museums and several historical sites from other ages, including Thirlwall Castle and Lannercost Priory. This section also passes through Northumberland National Park, where the scenery is at its finest.

By 'marching in the footsteps of bygone shadows' it's possible to really enjoy the Wall and its unique atmosphere. You can look out across the austere landscape, unchanged for millennia (except for the addition of a few farmhouses and the lack of rebellious tribes), just as the centurions must have done all those years ago.

Direction, Distance & Duration

To avoid carting gear as you explore the antiquities, it's perfectly possible (in fact, recommended) to base yourself at one place (eg, Haltwhistle or Once Brewed) and cover this route in three separate day walks, making

DAVID TIPLING

Visitors to Bamburgh Castle no longer meet a hostile welcome party, Northumberland coast

ANDREW MARSHALL & LEANNE WALKER

Like battle-ready centurions, walkers stride out along Hadrian's Wall

MANFRED GOTTSCHALK

The remains of the Roman forts reveal much about life on the Wall many centuries ago

TONY WHEELER

A warm welcome in Edale

TONY WHEELER

The sweeping valley of High Cup Nick, on the Pennine Way

TONY WHEELER

The Pennine Way winds above the natural amphitheatre of Malham Cove

DAVID ELSE

The civilised way to negotiate a dry-stone wall

TONY WHEELER

Easy going on the Pennine Way

use of the good local public transport system. If you prefer linear walks, though, there are places to stay along the route – mostly in and around Greenhead.

This combination of day stages can be done in any order or direction, but history dictates a westbound route. The Wall was built from east to west, the milecastles and turrets are numbered from east to west and most guidebooks to the Wall also proceed this way. We go with the flow.

The total distance of the route described here is 22mi, spread over a relaxed three days. If you're a mile eater, you could cover it in two, although your schedule may often need to be adjusted to mesh with the opening and closing times of the various historical distractions. The days start and end at the following places:

day	from	to	mi/km
1	Once Brewed	Once Brewed	7.5/12
2	Once Brewed	Greenhead	7/11.5
3	Greenhead	Lannercost Priory	7.5/12

Alternatives Each stage of the three-day route could be done as a single day walk. Each walk is not long, as there's much to see along the way, but could be shortened further by using taxis and buses. For example, on Day 1, instead of beginning from Once Brewed, you could take the bus to Vindolanda and start there.

PLANNING
Maps

OS's *Historical Map & Guide – Hadrian's Wall* covers the Wall in strip-map format at scales of 1:25,000 and 1:50,000, and is adequate for finding your way. It includes the route of the original Wall superimposed on the modern information. If you want to get beyond the strip, OS Landranger 1:50,000 map No 86 *(Haltwhistle & Brampton)* covers the route we describe.

Books

There are numerous general books on the Wall and its history, including Stephen Johnson's excellent illustrated *Hadrian's Wall*. Walking guides that cover the Wall and the surrounding area include *Exploring from Hadrian's Wall* by John Barker and *Hadrian's Wall – Wall Country Walks* by local expert Mark Richards. Look out too for *Walks in Hadrian's Wall Area*, a selection of walks of between 3mi and 8mi long, produced by Northumbria National Park.

Hadrian's Wall Code of Respect

The Hadrian's Wall National Trail Officer, along with several organisations representing walkers, archaeologists, farmers, traders and other local inhabitants, has developed the following Code of Respect for visitors. Please abide by its principles.

• Avoid walking *on* the Wall; you may cause it to collapse

• Consider circular walks instead of an out-and-back along the Wall; this reduces path damage, especially in winter months when the ground is waterlogged

• Keep to signed paths at all times

• Respect private land and livestock

• Keep dogs on a lead

• Visit organised sites (forts, museums etc) as these can handle larger visitor numbers

• Use local shops, restaurants and other facilities

• Take public transport where possible

Note that all the land next to the Wall and in the surrounding area is privately owned. Some of it is owned by the National Trust and open to the public. Other land belongs to local farmers and you are not allowed to cross it, apart from on legal rights of way. If you keep to paths, follow signs and use only stiles to cross walls and fences you should be OK. If you start climbing over things and walking across untracked farmland, the chances are you're breaking the law and likely to be chased by angry rangers or farmers (and their dogs). Play the game and everybody has an easy life.

Hadrian's Wall

KELLI HAMBLET

Hadrian's Wall milecastle

The Romans occupied and dominated Britain for about 350 years from AD 44, but the island remained a constant headache for the invaders. The Pict peoples of the north (today's Scotland) constantly rebelled against the Romans, and vast military expenditure was required to ensure the safe exploitation of the mineral-rich territories.

Eventually the costs could not be justified – about 10% of the empire's entire army was committed in Britain, probably the least important colony – so in 122 the Emperor Hadrian decided that rather than conquer the Picts he'd settle for simply keeping them at bay. Accordingly he ordered a great wall to be built across the country. To the south would be civilisation and the Roman Empire; to the north would be the savages.

His plan became the Roman Empire's greatest engineering project – and took over six years to build. The Wall followed the course of an already-established coast-to-coast military road, the Stanegate, and incorporated the north-facing cliffs of the Whin Sill, a geological feature that also crossed the country at this point, providing extra natural defences.

The Wall follows a standard pattern for its entire length of 80 Roman miles – about 74 modern miles (120km). At every Roman mile there was a milecastle, and in between every two milecastles were two turrets. These are numbered across the country, starting with Milecastle 0 at Wallsend (now a suburb of Newcastle upon Tyne) and ending with Milecastle 80 at Bowness-on-Solway, west of Carlisle. The intermediate turrets are tagged A and B, so Milecastle 37 is followed by Turret 37A, Turret 37B and then Milecastle 38.

KELLI HAMBLET

A line of turrets were spaced at regular intervals between milecastles along the Wall

Hadrian's Wall

After the Wall's completion it was decided that larger forts were also necessary and 16 of these were built. The prime remaining forts include Vercovicium and Banna (more commonly known today by their English names: Housesteads and Birdoswald). In addition there are several other forts that predate the Wall and stand some distance behind it, including Vindolanda (Chesterholm).

The Wall also followed a standard pattern in cross section. It was intended to be about 10ft (about 3m) wide at the base and somewhere between 12ft (roughly 4m) and 20ft (6m) high, although budgetary constraints later forced parts to be built with a narrower 8ft (2.5m) width. Immediately to the north a protective ditch was dug, except where the Wall runs along the top of the Whin Sill cliffs. To the south of the Wall is a wider ditch known as the *vallum* with embankments on each side. This sometimes runs close to the Wall, and sometimes some distance away. In many places where all traces of the Wall itself have disappeared (it made a fine source of stone for later generations), the ditch or the vallum still remains as clear as ever. Wall walkers soon develop a keen eye for signs of these irregularities in the landscape.

After completion, the Wall brought stability to this area of Britain and settlements sprung up around the forts. Over the following centuries the garrisons steadily became more British and less Roman. Meanwhile, the remote outposts were gradually forgotten by Rome, busy fighting fires closer to home. Pay came less frequently and farming began to replace soldiery as a source of income. It's generally accepted that Britain was abandoned by Rome around 410 and the Wall and its settlements went into steady decline. The population dropped and the region became unstable and dangerous, a situation that went unchanged for more than 10 centuries.

The borderlands between Scotland and England continued to be a bitterly contested battlefield until the start of the 17th century, after the unification of the two countries. There can be few bloodier frontiers on the planet; certainly few where the struggles continued for 1500 years.

Before you visit the Wall, if you're coming from Newcastle you can orientate yourself by visiting the Museum of Antiquities, which is off King's Walk in the University of Newcastle upon Tyne, to the north-east of the city centre (not to be confused with the University of Northumbria). This museum contains many items found along the Wall and a reconstruction of a Roman temple. One of the most interesting exhibits is a model of the Wall at a scale of 6 inches to 1mi, neatly reducing the whole walk to 36ft (about 10m). Entry is free.

If you're coming from Carlisle, the award-winning Tullie House Museum, on Castle St in the centre of Carlisle, has a good Roman collection, including a reconstructed section of the Wall. It also has exhibits and reconstructions from the 1000-year period of clan warfare and general unrest after the Romans pulled out, when the border country between England and Scotland became the 'Debatable Lands'.

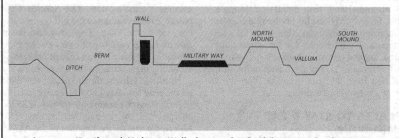

A cross section through Hadrian's Wall, showing details of the Roman fortifications

Tyne Valley Train Trails lists a selection of walks, including to the Wall, from train stations on the railway line between Carlisle and Newcastle upon Tyne. *Hadrian's Wall – The Wall Walk* by Mark Richards enthusiastically describes an LDP, mostly along the Wall, that includes the best bits and avoids the worst bits by taking pleasant detours through the surrounding countryside via villages and other historical sites. Many of the books and maps listed here are available by mail order from the Hadrian's Wall Tourism Partnership, listed under Information Sources following.

Information Sources

The main TIC for the central portion of Hadrian's Wall and the surrounding area is in Haltwhistle (☎ 01434-322002, e info @hadrians-wall.org), at the train station, just on the southern edge of the town centre. Nearer to the Wall itself, there's another excellent TIC at the tiny settlement of Once Brewed (☎ 01434-344777), although it's closed in the winter months. The friendly staff at the TICs never get tired of explaining how to reach the Wall by foot or public transport, and at Once Brewed there's also a small exhibition. Both TICs can advise on local accommodation and you can pick up the timetable for the very handy Hadrian's Wall. There's also a range of leaflets about the Wall, including *Hadrian's Wall Where to Stay for Walkers* (free), which also contains some general tourist information; and the comprehensive *Essential Guide to Hadrian's Wall*, showing the route through Northumberland with details of things to see, buses, taxis, useful phone numbers etc (an absolute bargain at 20p). Both TICs sell maps and guidebooks for the surrounding area, and the one at Haltwhistle runs a mail-order service. You can get even more information from the local tourism Web site at w www.hadrians-wall.org.

PLACES TO STAY & EAT
Haltwhistle

The market town of Haltwhistle lies 3mi south of the Wall and makes a good base, with neat transport connections, banks, shops, cafes, pubs and a wide selection of places to stay and eat. The informative TIC (☎ 01434-322002) is at the train station, just south of the town centre. The town claims to be at the central point of Britain, and there's a signpost on the main street pointing to the far (and equidistant) corners of the land.

B&Bs include *Hall Meadows* (☎ 01434-321021), a quiet and pretty cottage on the main street well used to walkers, charging £17 (single or double). Just off the main street, *Ashcroft* (☎ 01434-320213) is large, smart, well equipped and nonsmoking, with singles/doubles from £25/45 (mostly en suite). Farther along the main street, *Chase Close* (☎ 01434-320042) is small but welcoming, charging £32 per double.

The central and friendly *Manor House Hotel* (☎ 01434-322588), on the town's main street, does B&B from £15 and bar food for around £5; it also has a smarter restaurant where the food is good but takes a long time coming. *The Grey Bull Hotel* (☎ 01434-321991), on the main street, has basic B&B from £16.50 and plans for a budget bunkroom.

Top of the range is the *Centre of Britain Hotel* (☎ 01434-322422, e centreofbritain @aol.com), also on the main street, with the smartest rooms from £40 to £50 and cheaper but very comfortable 'lodge' rooms from £35. If you want to take a chance, all rooms have 'stand-by' reductions of £10. The Scandinavian decor is unexpected but very stylish. Meals in the restaurant are £13 for two courses and £15.50 for three.

For food in Haltwhistle, all the hotels do evening meals, as does *The Spotted Cow* pub at Town Foot, down the hill on the eastern side of the town. The town also has a *fish and chip cafe* (open every evening), a *Chinese takeaway* and an *Indian takeaway*, all on the main street in the town centre.

North of Haltwhistle and nearer the Wall on the road towards The Milecastle Inn, the friendly *Doors Cottage* (☎ 01434-322556) charges £22/34. An easy walk away, *The Milecastle Inn*, on the junction of the A6318 and the road down into Haltwhistle, has a lively mix of tourists and locals, and good evening food.

Campers can head for the Camping & Caravanning Club's (CCC's) well-equipped *Haltwhistle Site* (☎ 01434-320106) at Burnfoot, about 2mi south-west of Haltwhistle. It charges £4.15 for walkers.

GETTING TO/FROM THE WALK

Bus Haltwhistle is easily reached using the Arriva Northumbria bus, which runs several times a day (three times on Sunday) between Carlisle and Newcastle upon Tyne. This bus also goes through Hexham, Bardon Mill and Greenhead. If you're heading for Once Brewed, change at Hexham or Haltwhistle for the Hadrian's Wall Bus, or walk or get a taxi for the 2.5mi from Bardon Mill.

Most useful for walkers and other visitors is the Hadrian's Wall Bus, which cruises up and down the roads parallel to the Wall between Carlisle and Hexham, stopping at all the important places such as Brampton, Birdoswald, Greenhead, Once Brewed, Vindolanda and Housesteads about five times per day in each direction. This makes it easy to do a linear walk and get back to your starting point. Fares are very reasonable: As a sample, Lannercost Priory to Once Brewed costs £2, and Lannercost Priory to Brampton costs 65p. An all-day unlimited travel ticket is £5.

The Hadrian's Wall bus timetable, available from TICs, contains two-for-the-price-of-one vouchers to various historical sites.

Train There are several trains each day between Carlisle and Newcastle upon Tyne along the Tyne Valley railway line. These stop in Brampton (the train station is about 2mi south-east of the town centre), Haltwhistle and Bardon Mill (about 2.5mi from Once Brewed).

Car Haltwhistle is on the A69, which runs between Carlisle and Newcastle upon Tyne, roughly parallel to the Wall. The B6318 follows the Wall more closely (sometimes it runs *over* the Wall) and is still known as the Military Road.

Taxi If your perambulations don't fit in with the bus, or you don't want to walk from Bardon Mill to Once Brewed, local taxis to be contacted include Sproul's (☎ 01434-321064) and Turnbull's (☎ 01434-320105); both are used to dropping walkers at remote points along the Wall, or carrying backpacks to onward destinations.

THE WALK
Once Brewed & Around

The settlement of Once Brewed, on the B6318 north-east of Haltwhistle, is a good base; it's within a mile of the Wall and several other attractions. Once Brewed consists of only three or four buildings, so the TIC (☎ 01434-344777) is easy to find; it's also clearly signposted. Next door, the large *YHA Hostel* (☎ 01434-344360) charges £11. Nearby, the rather drab *Twice Brewed Inn* (☎ 01434-344534) has uninspiring B&B from £17 to £22 and mediocre bar food from £2 to £5, although it is always worth trying in case there's a change of management.

About half a mile to the east in East Twice Brewed, there's friendly and good-value B&B at *Craw's Nest* (☎ 01434-344348), a former farmhouse just off the main road, from £17.

About half a mile to the west, in (you've guessed it) West Twice Brewed, are some more B&B options, including *Vallum Lodge* (☎ 01434-344248), a fairly modern country hotel charging from £22 to £28, and £15 for dinner; and *Sunningdale* (☎ 01434-344460) with bright and cheerful rooms from £18 (£20 en suite). There's also a family room where children pay £10.

About 250m farther west along the main road, *Winshields Farm* (☎ 01434-344243) charges £3.50 for camping.

Day 1: Circuit from Once Brewed via Vindolanda & Housesteads

7.5mi (12km), 3–4 hours
Today's circular outing starts and ends at Once Brewed. The first part of the walk is on lanes instead of paths, but they're not very busy. For lunch, Vindolanda and Housesteads both have cafes.

Your walk should start at the excellent Once Brewed TIC, where you can get leaflets, maps and the bus timetable. That done, head south on the lane from Once Brewed for just under half a mile, then turn left onto a lane that leads for another mile straight to the western entrance to **Vindolanda Fort** – see the boxed text for details.

Leave Vindolanda by the eastern entrance (near the museum and shop) and turn right onto a lane that heads uphill to join another lane heading north-east. At a T-junction veer right and keep walking eastwards along the lane. To your left (north) you'll get your first proper views of the Whin Sill, the rocky ridge with a sharp north face that crosses England at this point, adding its natural defences to the battlements of Hadrian's Wall. After half a mile turn left onto a farm track that leads past Crindledykes Farm, over a small hill, across a large ditch (this is the *vallum,* built in Roman times as part of the defences) and down to the main road (the B6318), which runs parallel to the Wall. Cross the road, then go through a gate with National Trust signs

and up a track to reach the museum and ticket office for **Housesteads Fort** – and your first meeting with the Wall itself. (For details of the fort, see the boxed text 'Vindolanda & Housesteads Forts' on p328.)

From Housesteads, you can add a mile or so to today's route by doing an out-and-back branch east along a fine section of Wall past the remains of Turrets 33B, 34A and 35A to the impressive lookout at **Sewingshields**, beyond which the Wall meets the B6318 and disappears. (This road was first constructed in the 18th century as a military highway by troops under the infamous General Wade. They flattened the Wall and used the stones to provide an excellent road foundation.)

From Sewingshields return to Housesteads, then continue west along this finest section of the Wall, with superb views to the north and along the Wall in both directions. Don't forget to look back as well as forward, as the view of the Wall from Housesteads Crags and Milecastle 37 is superb. A

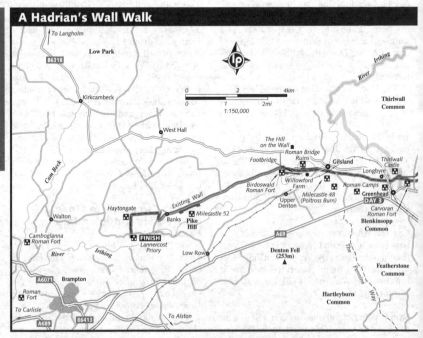

A Hadrian's Wall Walk

mile beyond Housesteads the Pennine Way joins the Wall and shares the route for the next 8mi, so you may see weary walkers going in the other direction.

Our walk along the Wall drops down to Milking Gap, then up and over the dramatic cliffs of **Steel Rigg** to Turret 39A, which has superb views. Before the next turret a lane crosses the Wall, running south. Take this southwards back to Once Brewed.

Day 2: Once Brewed to Greenhead
7mi (11.5km), 3–4 hours
Today's walk is linear, so to get back to your base make sure you have the Hadrian's Wall Bus timetable. You could bring lunch as well, although there's a cafe at the Roman Army Museum and a teashop at Greenhead.

From the Once Brewed TIC, cross the B6318 and retrace yesterday's final stage back up to the Wall near the site of Turret 39B. From here head west following the

Wall as it strides over the impressive Winshields Crags – at 375m the highest point along the Wall.

The Wall crosses another road (which runs south down to the appropriately named *Milecastle Inn*) and continues on to the remains of the **Aesica Fort** (this is also Milecastle No 43), now partly occupied by a farmhouse called Great Chesters. The next section is particularly fine as the Wall rollercoasts up and down a line of cliffs called the **Nine Nicks of Thirlwall**, past Turret 45A, where it ends abruptly at **Walltown** – a former quarry, now a nature reserve, with a sculpture park, visitors centre and toilets.

Just beyond Walltown, there's no sign of Magnis Fort, which once stood here, but instead the **Carvoran Roman Army Museum** (☎ 01697-747485) gives an excellent impression of life on the Wall for the troops. It's open 10am to 4pm, 5pm, 5.30pm or 6pm depending on the time of year, but closed from mid-November to mid-February. Entry

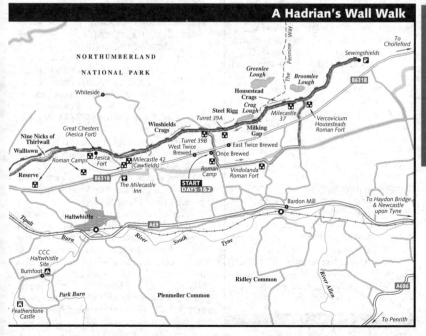

A Hadrian's Wall Walk

is £3.80; combined tickets with Vindolanda (see the boxed text) are available.

If you've run out of time, it's about 2.5mi back to Haltwhistle. If you're continuing,

---

Vindolanda & Housesteads Forts

At **Vindolanda Fort** (occasionally known by its English name, Chesterholm) you can see the impressive remains of walls and buildings spread over a wide area. There are also reconstructions of a stone turret, an earlier wooden turret, and houses from the Romano-British period. Most interesting is the museum, which contains pristine pottery, some early travel gadgets (including a portable comb and a midge net) and some extraordinary written records – the Roman equivalent of stray memos that escaped the office shredder. The evocative fragments include a birthday party invitation to the commander's wife, an officer's complaint that his men didn't have enough beer, a soldier's mention of the 'wretched British', a note accompanying a parent's present of warm socks and underpants, and a child's piece of school work with the teacher's acidic comment: 'sloppy'.

The fort (☎ 01434-344277, e vindolanda trust@btinternet.com, w www.vindolanda .com) and museum are open from 10am to 4pm daily, later in high season. Entry is £3.80 (or £5.60 for combined entry to Vindolanda and the Roman Army Museum at Carvoran – also on the route we describe).

Housesteads Fort, correctly but rarely called Vercovicium, is the finest fort along the Wall. It certainly has the most impressive location, perched atop the ridge, and the long stretches of Wall leading to it from either direction add to its importance. The fort's huge flushing latrine is a prime attraction but there are a host of other buildings, including the hospital and four fine gateways.

This English Heritage site (☎ 01434-344363) is open 10am to 6pm daily, April to September, and to 4pm during other months. Entry is £2.80.

---

from the museum go back to the lane and turn left to pick up the route of the path along the Wall, which drops down rather circuitously to Thirlwall Castle Farm. Here is the charming, friendly *Holmhead Guesthouse* (☎ 01697-747402, e holmhead @hadrianswall.freeserve.co.uk) with comfortable B&B from £28 and a basic camping barn for £3.50; evening meals can be ordered. Nearby are the ruins of **Thirlwall Castle**, from where you cross a field, a river and the railway to reach Greenhead.

Greenhead & Around

If you decide to do Hadrian's Wall as a linear route, you will find Greenhead a very handy place to stay. Accommodation includes the *YHA Hostel* (☎ 01697-747401), in a former Methodist chapel, charging £8.10. *The Greenhead Hotel* (☎ 01697-747411) nearby charges from £22.50 for B&B, with evening pub food also available; it's rather drab and basic, although walkers get a friendly welcome. Opposite the pub, *The Olde Forge Tearoom* serves snacks and meals from lunchtime to 5pm, sometimes later in the summer.

In Longbyre, just north of Greenhead, *Four Wynds* (☎ 01697-747330) has good en suite rooms for £20 but a smoky atmosphere. Free lifts and packed lunches are available. Between Longbyre and Greenhead, near the golf course crossed by the Pennine Way, *Wall End Farm* (☎ 01697-747339) offers B&B from £19.

Two miles west of Greenhead is the village of Gilsland where walker-friendly B&Bs include *Howard House* (☎ 01697-747285), on the north side of the village, charging £20 to £24. Also in Gilsland, *The Samson Inn* does good beer and filling bar food.

Another mile west is *The Hill on the Wall* (☎ 01697-747214, e thehill@hadrians -wall.demon.co.uk), a large airy house with big gardens and a peaceful and comfortable atmosphere. Rooms start at £26. This is also the base for Walking Hadrian's Wall (see Guided Walks). Mike Swan, the friendly owner, is knowledgeable about routes in the area; even if you're not staying, he's happy to give advice.

Day 3: Greenhead to Lannercost Priory

7.5mi (12km), 3–4 hours

This is another linear day. If you stayed at Haltwhistle or Once Brewed, start the day once again with a bus or taxi ride back to last night's finishing point at Greenhead. Today's best lunch stop is the cafe at Birdoswald Fort.

Leave Greenhead on the road north towards Gilsland, then turn left up a path that crosses the golf course. Cross over a stile back into fields; the Pennine Way route branches off left (south) but our path goes right, down to and through the yard of Wall End Farm, then west across fields, beside the remains of the vallum, round Chapel House Farm and down into Gilsland. Just past the Station Inn (an uninspiring pub – the nearby *Sampson Inn* is much better), the path leads down to the very fine **Poltross Burn Milecastle 48**, wedged up against the railway embankment.

The path runs next to the railway, then crosses it and skirts the western end of Gilsland by the primary school. Cross the road and follow another well-preserved section of Wall down to **Willowford Farm**. In days gone by the Wall was seen as a handy source of construction material, and locals simply used the Roman stonework to build their own farms and houses. Willowford Farm was no exception: Look closely for the Roman inscriptions on the bricks that now form part of a barn.

From the farm another stretch of Wall leads down past Turret 48B to the remains of a large bridge built by Roman engineers across the River Irthing. The river has since shifted its course and today there's a modern, graceful and multi-award-winning **footbridge** to take you to the north bank.

Beyond the footbridge a stiff uphill section takes you to Milecastle 49 and then to **Banna Fort**, more commonly known by its English name, Birdoswald. This fort has a *cafe* and an interesting little museum, which contains a reproduction of a section of the Wall as it would have looked, complete with watchtower and guards plus numerous fascinating finds. If the weather's fine its principal delight is the picnic area at the southern edge of the fort, with fine views over the River Irthing valley. The museum is open 10am to 5.30pm daily, late March to November, and the fort ruins are open all year. Entry is £2.50 (free for English Heritage members).

Beyond Birdoswald the Wall follows a lane westwards. To be blunt, it's a bit of a trudge as there are few stone remains to be seen for several miles until you reach Milecastle 52 and the nearby turrets at Pike Hill. You can see the route of the vallum and turf wall, which was originally built here – probably as a cost-saving exercise – before the stone model was introduced along a different line. **Turret 52A** is a fine example of a turf wall turret, later remodelled when the stone Wall was completed.

Beyond here fork right and drop down through the hamlet of Banks, then up a track past a short but quite high chunk of Wall and Hare Hill House. The path crosses fields, still following the line of the ditch, now almost buried under a hedgerow. From here most traces of the Wall disappear, so at a house called Haytongate turn left (south), bid farewell to the Romans and descend on a track to **Lannercost Priory** – a sudden change of style and era, but a fascinating end to this walk through history. After a

Lannercost Priory

Lannercost Priory was built by Augustinian monks in 1166. As you walk around you won't quite forget Hadrian's Wall, as the monks were not at all averse to a bit of recycling and made liberal use of building material from the Wall and thereabouts – including a number of Roman altars, which needed only minor modifications for Christian ceremonies. After Henry VIII's dissolution of the monasteries in 1539–40 the priory fell into ruins. Today many splendid arches and windows survive intact; the nave was converted into a parish church in 1740 and is still in use today. The ruins (not the church) are managed by English Heritage; entry is £1.

stroll around the priory (see the boxed text on p329 for more details), you can take the bus back to Once Brewed or Haltwhistle, or onwards to Brampton, which has B&Bs and connections to Carlisle.

A Northumberland Coast Walk

Distance	13mi (21km)
Duration	5–6½ hours
Standard	easy
Start	Bamburgh
Finish	Craster
Gateways	Alnwick, Berwick-upon-Tweed, Newcastle upon Tyne

Summary A beautiful coastal route via pretty fishing villages and imposing medieval castles. The walk isn't too strenuous, although cold sea winds can make it tiring. The paths are mostly of a reasonably standard.

This day walk takes in the finest section of the Northumberland Coast and neatly links two of the county's most spectacular castles: Bamburgh and Dunstanburgh. This coast also includes many long, sandy beaches but they never get very crowded, and there are no large resort towns anywhere nearby. The reason for this is the weather – probably one day in three the coast is shrouded by a sea mist, known locally as a 'fret', so the sun and fun seekers go elsewhere leaving the beautiful, wild and windswept shore relatively untouched for walkers to enjoy. As a sign of its importance, this section has been declared the Northumberland Heritage Coast and is protected as an Area of Outstanding Natural Beauty.

Bird life here is particularly impressive: You'll see cormorants, shags, kittywakes, fulmars, terns, gulls and guillemots, either on the beach or on the rocky islets and points along the route. You are also likely to see seals. The offshore Farne Islands are world-famous for their seabird colonies. They can be reached by boat from the small port of Seahouses, on the walk route, so with a full day you could combine walking, boating and birding.

Direction, Distance & Duration

This linear route could be done in either direction, but we describe it north to south. The total distance by coastal footpath between Bamburgh and Craster is 13mi, but this can sometimes be a bit shorter if you walk on the firm sand of the beach (only possible at low tide). Walking time is five to 6½ hours but you should allow extra for looking around castles, lunch, swimming and bird spotting.

Alternatives There are no short cuts and doing only part of this route would involve missing one of the castles. However, good local transport gives various options for reducing the distance without missing the highlights. For example, you could walk from Bamburgh to Seahouses, then go by bus to Embleton and walk the final stretch to Craster, reducing the route to about 6mi.

You could also extend this walk by continuing south from Craster to Alnmouth, adding another 7mi (11km) and three to 3½ hours, bringing the total walk up to 20mi (32km) or eight to 10 hours. This is possible for fit walkers on a long and fine summer's day, but the walk could also be split into two days.

PLANNING
Maps & Books

The coastal walk described here is covered on OS Landranger 1:50,000 maps No 75 *(Berwick-upon-Tweed)* and No 81 *(Alnwick & Morpeck)*.

The Northumberland Coastline by Ian Smith, published locally by Sandhill Press, is available from TICs; it describes the whole coast from the Scottish border to Newcastle upon Tyne, with Wainwright-style text and hand-drawn maps. Another local book is *Walks on the Northumberland Coast* by Tony Hopkins & David Haffey, which describes 10 short walks in the area. Most useful is the *Exploring the Northumberland Coast* pack of six leaflets published by Northumberland Countryside Service, covering areas such as Bamber, Craster and Alnmouth, with colour illustrations and notes on history and wildlife. All are available from local TICs.

Information Sources

At Alnwick, a large town near Alnmouth, the main TIC (☎ 01665-510665) can help with information on transport and accommodation. The TIC in Berwick-upon-Tweed (☎ 01289-330733) is also very helpful. On the route there are seasonal (closed in winter) TICs at Seahouses (☎ 01665-720884) and Craster (☎ 01665-576007). All TICs stock walking leaflets and maps and also have bus timetables.

Guided Walks

The National Trust organises walks on the Northumberland coast about twice a month. They're free, and you can get details from local TICs.

PLACES TO STAY & EAT
Bamburgh

The small village of Bamburgh is just inland from the beach, overlooked by the giant walls of its famous **castle**. It has a good range of accommodation, so might make the best base for this walk, although places farther down the coast are sometimes a bit cheaper.

There are several B&Bs and hotels on the wide square called Front St, including *The Greenhouse* (☎ *01668-214513*), also a good restaurant and tearoom, charging from £20 for en suite rooms and up to £26 for larger rooms; *Greengates* (☎ *01668-214535*), a small and quiet place with rooms from around £20; *The Victoria Hotel* (☎ *01668-214431*), a large, smart hotel with B&B from £35, a bar serving meals from around £7 and a brasserie serving main courses for £11 to £13; and *The Lord Crewe Arms* (☎ *01668-214243*), the best of the hotels, offering B&B from £60 per double room with private bathroom (or £75 en suite), also with a bar and restaurant.

On Lucker Rd, just off Front St, are several other possible options, such as *Glenander* (☎ *01668-214336*), which is unassuming on the outside but good inside, charging from £25.

For food, apart from the pubs and hotels, *Blackets Tearoom*, on Lucker Rd, serves meals like fish and chips for £6 until 8pm.

Beadnell & Embleton

These two villages in between Bamburgh and Craster provide several accommodation options – especially useful if you intend going all the way from Bamburgh to Alnmouth and splitting the route over two days.

At Beadnell, B&Bs include *Low Dover* (☎ *01665-720291*), near the harbour, charging from £26; and the smarter *Beach Court* (☎ *01665-720225*), also near the harbour, charging from around £30. *Beadnell Bay* (☎ *01665-720586*) is a good Camping & Caravanning Club (CCC) campsite, charging walkers £5.70 in the high season.

In Embleton there's *The Blue Bell Inn* (☎ *01665-576573*) with B&B from £16; and *The Sportsman* (☎ *01665-576588*), overlooking the beach, charging from £20. Both pubs have bar food. Campers can go to another good CCC site, *Dunstan Hill* (☎ *01665-576310*), about half a mile inland from the coast in between Embleton and Craster, charging £6.25.

Craster

At the walk's end, the small and picturesque fishing village of Craster is on the coast south of Beadnell and Bamburgh. The TIC (☎ 01665-576007) is at the car park on the landward side of the village. It's closed in winter, so for information at this time, contact the TIC in Alnwick (☎ 01665-510665).

Campers can head for *Proctors Stead* (☎ *01665-576613*), which charges from £8 per tent for two people. B&Bs include *Stonecroft* (☎ *01665-576433*), just outside the village, charging from £18; and *Howick Scar Farm* (☎ *01665-576665*), from £17.

Alnmouth

If you decide to extend the route all the way to Alnmouth, this small, quiet town has several places to stay. Walker-friendly B&Bs include *Bilton Barns* (☎ *01665-830427*), a working farm about 1.5mi west of Alnmouth on a hill with views of the sea, charging £26, with small reductions if you stay more than one night. Good, large evening meals are £14.

For more sea views, plus tartan carpet, try the *Marine House Hotel* (☎ *01665-830349*,

NORTHUMBERLAND

e *tanny@marinehouse.freeserve.co.uk)*, just off the main street, which has B&B with en suite rooms from £47 and serves an evening meal. For a bit more atmosphere, the friendly *Hope & Anchor Hotel* (☎ *01665-830363*) is a traditional pub on the main street with B&B from £22 to £26 and good bar food. Also on the main street, *The Famous Schooner Hotel* (☎ *01665-830216*, e *john@schooner.freeserve.co.uk*) is a large, welcoming pub (reputedly haunted) with B&B from around £30, plus good beer and bar food, and a smarter restaurant. There are a couple of other pubs nearby, also doing food and accommodation. For information on places to stay in Alnmouth, contact the TIC (☎ 01665-510665) in nearby Alnwick.

GETTING TO/FROM THE WALK
Bus The gateway towns for this walk are Newcastle upon Tyne and Berwick-upon-Tweed, along with Alnwick, which can all be reached from other parts of the country by National Express.

An exceedingly useful local bus service (Nos 501 and 401) operates between Alnwick, Craster, Beadnell, Seahouses, Bamburgh and Belford five times per day in each direction (four on Sunday). This means you can base yourself somewhere for two nights, do the walk on the day in between and easily get back to your accommodation by bus. It might be best to catch the bus to the start of the route and walk back, so you have no worries about keeping time. At Alnwick and Belford these buses continue (or there are connecting services) to/from Newcastle upon Tyne and Berwick-upon-Tweed. To go by bus to/from Alnmouth and Alnwick, there's a service roughly hourly every day. This bus also runs to/from Newcastle upon Tyne via Amble and Morpeth.

Train The nearest train station is at Alnmouth, at the end of the walk, about 1.5mi to the west of town on the line between Newcastle upon Tyne and Berwick-upon-Tweed, which is also the main line between London and Edinburgh. Long-distance express trains stop at Alnmouth about six times per day. Alternatively, you can change at Newcastle upon Tyne or Berwick-upon-Tweed and get a more regular local stopping service.

Car Bamburgh, Craster and Alnmouth are all lined along the coast to the east of the main A1 between Newcastle upon Tyne and Berwick-upon-Tweed.

THE WALK
Bamburgh to Beadnell
5.5mi (9km), 2–2½ hours
After looking around Bamburgh Castle (see the boxed text for details), go down to the

Bamburgh Castle

This impressive fortress rising from the sea dominates the coast for miles around. It stands on an outcrop of intrusive basalt that makes up part of the great Whin Sill, a natural barrier that stretches across the county and continues east out to sea where it forms the Farne Islands. For obvious defensive reasons, this site has been occupied since prehistoric times. It is thought that both early Britons and Romans had forts here.

Bamburgh was the capital of the Anglo-Saxon kingdom of Northumbria from the 6th to 9th centuries, but the oldest part of the castle visible today is the 12th-century Norman keep, built in the reign of Henry II with walls more than 3m thick. Probably the most famous battle to take place here was during the War of the Roses in 1464, when Yorkist Edward IV defeated Lancastrian Henry VI.

Much later, at the end of the 19th century, the castle was bought by wealthy industrialist Lord Armstrong who did a major rebuild; just about everything you see today dates from this time or later. It is still the home of Lady Armstrong, his descendant. Tours of the castle take in various halls, the armoury and exhibitions of later weapons and machinery from Lord Armstrong's time. Views from the upper castle walls out to the islands and along the coast to Dunstanburgh provide inspiration for the walk to come. The castle is often floodlit at night. It is open from 11am to 5pm daily, April to October, and entrance costs £4.

beach, turn right and stride out southwards. To your right are large sand dunes and to your left is the sea, with the island of Lindisfarne (or Holy Island), topped by the castle-like Priory, visible to the north-west, and the Farne Islands clearly visible to the north-east. This is a beautiful section of beach with a wonderful feeling of space – unless you hit one of Northumberland's notoriously unpredictable sea mists, which will completely spoil your view.

After an hour or so, you'll reach the outskirts of **Seahouses**, where it's easier to join the road for the last half-mile into town. This is a strange place; half traditional fishing port, half tacky seaside resort. It does have a good supply of shops selling fish and chips – with fresh fish – so this is probably one of the better places to try the traditional English dish. Less greasy is *Koffee & Kream*, a cafe selling drinks, snacks and meals. The harbour is interesting and usually busy, as this is where you find boats for the Farne Islands. Seahouses' TIC (☎ 01665-720884), in the car park just inland from the harbour, can provide more details.

Work your way out of the north-east side of town, past the caravan park, round the golf course, along some strange parallel ridges and back onto the beach again (you may possibly be forced onto the road for a short distance to cross a small river that flows in here). These obstacles overcome, you can once again enjoy fine, open walking along the beach for another mile to Beadnell.

At the northern end of the village is a small *grocery* selling hot drinks and takeaway snacks. From here follow the small road through the village, past holiday homes and fishermen's shacks, all the way to the **harbour**, where there's usually some activity, with fishing boats or scuba divers and some interesting old lime kilns.

Beadnell to Craster
7.5mi (12km), 3–4 hours
From Beadnell Harbour continue southwards round the wide curving beach of Beadnell Bay down to Snook Point, a spit of exposed rock sticking out into the sea. Beyond here is Newton Point. Our route does not go to the

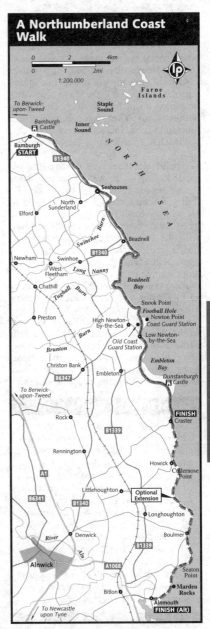

A Northumberland Coast Walk

NORTHUMBERLAND

end of the point itself, but continues straight on, to the left (north and east) of an old coastguard station up on the hill, to meet a lane which goes down into the tiny fishing village of **Low Newton-by-the-Sea**. This village consists of three rows of houses in a square, with the fourth row to the sea so boats could be pulled up in bad weather. One of the houses is now *The Ship* pub, which does lunchtime food, including very good crab sandwiches. (Incidentally, the bay between Snook Point and Newton Point is called Football Hole. It seems a modern title, but the 1850 map on the wall of the pub shows it with this name, so it can't be *that* new.)

If you want a change from the beach, a pleasant footpath runs through a National Trust nature reserve round Embleton Bay, with the ruined tower of **Dunstanburgh Castle** (see the boxed text) now large on the opposite headland – standing like a jagged tooth waiting to be pulled.

After visiting the castle, it's only a mile or so to **Craster**, another picturesque fishing village, particularly famous for its kipper (smoked fish) factory, although the crab sandwiches served at lunchtime in *The Jolly Fisherman* pub are pretty legendary too. The pub also does bar meals in the evening. Your other eating options are the *village shop*, which sells picnic supplies; *Robson's*

Dunstanburgh Castle

Dunstanburgh Castle dates from the 14th century. It was built in a strategic position, protected to the north and east by the sea and to the west by the cliffs of the Whin Sill. On the vulnerable south side a large wall was constructed. It was home to John of Gaunt and his son Henry IV and, like neighbouring Bamburgh, was a Lancastrian stronghold during the War of the Roses. The castle was abandoned in the 16th century. Today the impressive gateway still survives, as well as a tower and some of the wall, so the castle is still well worth a visit. It's open all year (until 6pm in summer, and to 4pm or 5pm during other seasons) and entrance is £2.

Restaurant & Coffee Lounge, connected to the famous kipper factory (open lunchtime and evenings only) with meals from £5 to £8; and *Bark Pots Tearooms*, near the TIC, serving drinks, snacks, breakfasts and lunches – including 'kipper crumblie' – for £3 to £5 in a friendly nonsmoking atmosphere (open daily April to December, but weekends only from January to March). It also sells a small selection of local maps and guidebooks. (Incidentally, the tearooms are named after the solution of tree bark in which fishing nets were traditionally soaked to prevent rotting.)

Optional Extension: Alnmouth
7mi (11.5km), 3–3½ hours

This optional extension from Craster turns the whole walk into quite a lengthy enterprise. With good weather, a following wind and a late lunch at Craster, it could be done in a day. Alternatively you can split the whole walk from Bamburgh into two days, possibly overnighting in Beadnell or Embleton (see Places to Stay & Eat earlier).

From Craster, continue south along the path that runs along the top of the cliffs overlooking the rocky, wave-cut platform. You can't miss the noisy groups of sea birds nesting on the cliffs. From Cullernose Point, you can either keep to the inland path or walk on the beach or over the rocks past the outcrops of Longhoughton Steel and the small fishing village of **Boulmer**.

The route passes Seaton Point, a sandy beach and the Marden Rocks outcrop, and then passes a last stretch of beach to Alnmouth, set dramatically on a steep ridge overlooking the estuary of the River Aln – a striking finish to this walk along the coast.

Other Walks

Most walking opportunities in Northumberland (apart from the coast) are in Northumberland National Park, one of the largest yet least visited parks in the country and often billed as 'the loneliest park in England'. It covers 398 sq mi of high ground inland from the coastal plains, between

Hadrian's Wall in the south and the Scottish border in the north. There are few roads and the landscape is characterised by high, windswept grassy hills cut by streams and valleys, almost empty of human habitation.

Multi-day routes that cross this wild and remote area include the infamously tough

---

Northumberland – A Short History

A significant part of Northumberland National Park is used by the army as a training ground. This may seem strange to visitors from countries where national parks are carefully preserved areas virtually untouched by human interference, but it happens in Britain (where all national park land is privately owned), and while you're walking you may hear the bangs and thuds of live ammunition carried on the wind from nearby valleys.

The involvement of the army here is not completely inappropriate, as this was once the most war-torn region of England. The Romans built Hadrian's Wall in an attempt to control rebellious tribes and, after they left, the region remained a contested zone between Scotland and England – home to warring clans and families lead by ruthless warriors called 'reivers', from where we get the modern word 'bereaved'.

Few buildings from this time remain. Most families lived in simple structures of turf that could be quickly and cheaply built and just as quickly abandoned. A few larger farms were more solidly constructed and better fortified. Known as 'bastle-houses', one of the best remaining examples is at Black Middens, between Bellingham and Byrness, west of the Pennine Way.

Peace came in the 18th century, but coincided with new farming practices so that the tenant farmers were dispossessed, leaving large estates. Unlike much of the rest of England, the high ground of Northumberland has no scattering of villages, no stone walls and only a few small farms. Scenically, it has a bleak grandeur with wide horizons and vast skies.

Pennine Way (described in the Northern England Long-Distance Paths chapter) and the increasingly popular St Cuthbert's Way (described in the Scotland Long-Distance Paths chapter).

Apart from Hadrian's Wall, the best areas of the park for day walkers are the central area around Bellingham and the northern section, including the Cheviot Hills, which we outline briefly here. In the western area around Kielder Water are huge pine plantations, which have less appeal. North of Otterburn is a military training area where access to the public is restricted (for more details, see the boxed text 'Northumberland – A Short History').

CENTRAL NORTHUMBERLAND

The small town of **Bellingham** is a good place to base yourself in the central part of the park. There are bus connections to/from Otterburn and Hexham, where you can connect with services to/from Carlisle and Newcastle upon Tyne. It's surrounded by beautiful countryside, which you could begin to explore by following a section of the Pennine Way that passes through Bellingham. You could even get here on foot by walking from Once Brewed, on Hadrian's Wall, about 18mi south. For information on places to stay, see the Pennine Way in the Northern England Long-Distance Paths chapter, or contact the Bellingham TIC (☎ 01434-220616).

Another good base is the charming town of **Rothbury**, which provides relatively easy access to the Simonside Hills on the eastern side of the park. The hills have some of the widest views in Northumberland, from the Cheviots to the coast. In summer months you can reach Rothbury by direct bus from Newcastle upon Tyne. The town also makes a good base for circular walks in the hills to the north (which are outside the park and not so 'wild' but still well worth a visit). For a place to stay, there are several B&Bs on and around the wide main street, plus teashops and a couple of nice pubs doing evening meals. Rothbury TIC (☎ 01669-620887) can give information, and stocks books, maps and leaflets on walks in the surrounding area.

The tiny settlement of **Byrness** also lies in splendid countryside, particularly to the north, and is also on the Pennine Way. Straddling a main road, access is quite easy and includes the National Express coach between Newcastle upon Tyne and Edinburgh that passes through three times per day. You could walk here along the route from Bellingham (15mi), or head up into the Cheviot Hills – for more details on the route and places to stay and eat, see the Pennine Way section of the Northern England Long-Distance Paths chapter.

NORTHERN NORTHUMBERLAND

The best place to base yourself for walks in this area is the market town of **Wooler**, which is easy to reach by bus from Newcastle upon Tyne, Berwick-upon-Tweed or Alnwick. The town has a TIC (☎ 01668-282123), which can provide more information on walking routes, accommodation and transport in the park and surrounding area, plus several good places to stay, shops, banks, cafes and pubs, along with a very nice second-hand bookshop that specialises in guidebooks to the area. Good walker-friendly B&Bs include *Southgate* (☎ 01668-282004), *St Hilliers* (☎ 01668-281340) and the delightfully chintzy *Loreto Guesthouse* (☎ 01668-281350). Many of Wooler's pubs also provide accommodation, which can be cheaper than the B&Bs, although somewhat less appealing.

There are several circular day walks possible in this area. You can walk up the quiet and beautiful **Harthorpe Valley** into the Cheviot foothills, and some walks even deeper into the heart of the park become viable if you tie in with the local postbus that goes up this valley to Langleeford.

Another option from Wooler for hardy walkers is to go up the Harthorpe Valley and continue to the summit of the Cheviot itself (815m), the highest point in the county and the remains of an ancient volcano. From here you could descend to Kirk Yetholm in Scotland, 14mi away, the second half of the route following the Pennine Way. (Only consider this if you've got enough time and the right equipment – the weather can be terrible up here, the area is not so well frequented and paths are often faint on the ground.) There are less energetic options in the area north of the Harthorpe Valley and south of the road between Wooler and Kirknewton.

Also near Wooler is the **Breamish Valley**, with the village of Ingram at its eastern end. Here there's a very good TIC and visitors centre (☎ 01665-578248), with leaflets on suggested local walks in the valley or up onto the high ground. Many of these take in the remains of Bronze Age settlements that once covered this area.

Northern England Long-Distance Paths

This chapter covers two of the longest, and most famous, long-distance paths (LDPs) in Northern England – The Coast to Coast Walk and the Pennine Way. Each route crosses several different parts of Britain – including the Lake District, Peak District, Yorkshire Dales and the North Pennines – most of which are famous walking areas in their own right. These routes have a chapter of their own because they are too long to fit anywhere else!

Other LDPs in Northern England are described in their own chapters. These are the Cumbria Way (in the Lake District chapter), the Dales Way (Yorkshire Dales) and the Cleveland Way (North York Moors).

The Coast to Coast Walk

Distance	191mi (307.5km)
Duration	12 days
Standard	medium
Start	St Bees Head
Finish	Robin Hood's Bay
Gateways	Whitehaven, Ambleside, Richmond, Whitby

Summary A classic route incorporating the finest scenery in England. Despite this route's popularity, signposting is minimal, especially in the early stages, so map-reading experience is very important.

Some walkers say the Coast to Coast Walk should be called the 'Wainwright Way'. The route was first described in a book published in 1973 by the prolific writer Alfred Wainwright. Although AW (as he is known) produced most of his books in the 1960s and 1970s, he remains one of Britain's most famous walker-writers. He combined a romantic devotion to wilderness and solitude with a scientific attention to detail in his unique, hand-crafted text, maps and illustrations.

Wainwright was careful to call his creation *A* Coast to Coast Walk, implying that it was only one of many ways of crossing the country. However, most people doing Wainwright's route call it *The* Coast to Coast, and follow the description very closely. Purists refuse to deviate even a few steps from AW's incredibly precise instructions.

Although the route has been realigned in some places (mainly so it follows legal rights of way – less of an issue when AW wrote the first edition), it still keeps pretty much to the original and certainly follows it in spirit. It passes through the finest landscape in England and can be covered in around two weeks, so it's now the most popular LDP in Britain.

The route falls into three main sections, each a traverse of a national park – the Lake District, the Yorkshire Dales and the North York Moors. Of these, the rugged mountains of the Lake District are the hardest challenge and you need some outdoor experience. Beyond here the terrain is less arduous and the paths easier – through the rolling hills and picturesque valleys of the Yorkshire Dales, over farmland and down quiet lanes, finally crossing the haunting emptiness of the North York Moors. Between the Lakes and the Dales you cross the rolling Eden Valley area, and between the Dales and the Moors you cross the flat Vale of Mowbry.

Some sections include several miles of forestry tracks and sealed roads, which are, frankly, tedious at times. However, for the most part it's an imaginative and exciting journey though a slice of British geography, history and society. There are ancient farms, dry-stone walls and barns, and fields of sheep and cattle; there are the mines and railways, reminders of a once flourishing industrial age; there are lonely inns on windswept hilltops, once busy medieval travellers' haunts; there is the legend of

Robin Hood, the brigand who stole from the rich to help the poor; and, above all, there is the wilderness, the space and the sheer, beautiful bleakness of the mountains and moors that cover the north of England.

Direction, Distance & Duration

The Coast to Coast Walk can be followed in either direction. We recommend going west to east, with the wind and sun behind you (mostly, anyway). Although this provides steep terrain at the beginning of the walk, you can tackle it while you're still fresh and raring to go.

The route is not a national trail and has no official recognition. Thus signposting and waymarking is often minimal or non-existent, although you will see some 'Coast to Coast' signs (often shortened to 'C to C', 'CtoC' or 'C-to-C'). The route follows one path that is part of a network of thousands, with frequent junctions, so you need to keep a very close eye on your map to keep going in the right direction.

The route is 191mi long and traditionally tackled over 12 days, an itinerary originally devised by Wainwright. We have kept with tradition and split the route thus:

day	from	to	mi/km
1	St Bees	Ennerdale Bridge	14/22.5
2	Ennerdale Bridge	Rosthwaite	14.5/23.5
3	Rosthwaite	Patterdale	17.5/28
4	Patterdale	Shap	16/25.5
5	Shap	Kirkby Stephen	21/34
6	Kirkby Stephen	Keld	13/21
7	Keld	Reeth	11/17.5
8	Reeth	Richmond	11/17.5
9	Richmond	Ingleby Cross	23/37
10	Ingleby Cross	Clay Bank Top	12/19.5
11	Clay Bank Top	Glaisdale	18/29
12	Glaisdale	Robin Hood's Bay	20/32

There is no doubt that this itinerary is a demanding undertaking if completed in one go, particularly if you're not fit, or if you are camping and carrying your own gear. Note that most days have some serious ascents. Note also that the hours given for each stage in the main route description are walking times only; you should allow an extra hour or two for rests, lunch stops etc.

Alternatives Many walkers decide that Wainwright's 12-day itinerary is simply too tough and add a few extra overnight stops. This shortens some daily distances and spreads the walking over a more manageable 13 to 15 days. One of the best places to add an extra overnight stop is at Grasmere, between Rosthwaite and Patterdale. Days 4 and 5 could be turned into three days by staying one night each at Bampton and Newbiggin-on-Lune, instead of at Shap. Another option is to turn Days 11 and 12 into three, overnighting at Blakey and Grosmont, instead of Glaisdale.

If you're short of time, some days could be combined but this would turn the walk into quite a march (although the whole route has been done as a run in around 39 hours!). You're better off just doing a section in a week; for ideas, see the boxed text 'The Coast to Coast Walk – Some Route Highlights' on p344.

PLANNING
Maps

Deciding what to take is tricky. To cover the whole route you need Ordnance Survey (OS) Landranger 1:50,000 maps No 89 *(West Cumbria)*, No 90 *(Penrith & Keswick)*, No 91

Baptism of Fire!

The Coast to Coast is, justifiably, one of the most popular LDPs in Britain, but many people overestimate their own capabilities before setting off. The first few days on the steep, rough paths of the Lake District can be a real baptism of fire for the unwary, but perfectly possible if you're fit and prepared. Just make sure you are!

(*Appleby-in-Westmorland*), No 92 (*Barnard Castle & Richmond*), No 93 (*Middlesbrough*), No 94 (*Whitby & Esk Dale*) and No 99 (*Northallerton & Ripon*) – quite a load. For more detail (which is recommended) the route is covered by, going from west to east, OS Outdoor Leisure 1:25,000 maps No 4 (*The English Lakes – North Western Area*), No 5 (*The English Lakes – North Eastern Area*), No 19 (*Howgill Fells and Upper Eden Valley*), No 30 (*Yorkshire Dales – Northern & Central Areas*), No 26 (*North York Moors – Western Area*) and No 27 (*North York Moors – Eastern Area*). These appear more useful but there's a gap between maps No 30 and No 26, so (most annoyingly) you'll also need the OS Landranger 1:50,000 maps No 93 and No 99 to get across.

The problem of too many maps is partially solved by two OS *Coast to Coast* strip maps, which cover the whole route with extracts from relevant 1:25,000 sheets. Footprint Maps also produces two *Coast to Coast* strip maps, which are lighter and cheaper than the OS maps, have a wider coverage and are easier to read, but are not quite as detailed.

In theory using strip maps means no other maps are needed, but in practice navigating is difficult, especially in bad weather, because these maps only show a limited part of the area you're passing through. If you wander off the route you may wander off the map too and then you're lost.

We recommend using a combination of strip maps plus 'proper' maps of the Lake District, where the possibility of bad weather and the complicated route means you really need more coverage.

Books

The original 'pictorial guide' to this route, *A Coast to Coast Walk* by Alfred Wainwright, is a classic and has been reprinted often. Since 1994 it has been slightly revised, describing alternatives to Wainwright's route where it had strayed from public rights of way, although still faithfully keeping the original text for historical completeness.

The Coast to Coast Walk by Paul Hannon is a practical, pocket-sized paperback. It describes the Wainwright route in similar style, with hand-drawn illustrations, but with printed text. This means it is a little more clearly presented and easier to read. There's also *The Northern Coast to Coast Walk* by Terry Marsh, which has adjusted the original route in consultation with conservation officials, keeping to rights of way, avoiding eroded areas and reducing time spent walking on roads.

The Coast to Coast Accommodation Guide is an invaluable booklet produced by Doreen Whitehead (☎ 01748-886374), Butt House, Keld, North Yorkshire DL11 6LJ, available by mail order for £3, including postage (overseas visitors can send a US$5 bill). Mrs Whitehead also offers accommodation in Keld – see Day 6 for details.

Another *Coast to Coast Accommodation Guide* is produced by Ewen Bennett from the North York Moors Adventure Centre (☎ 01609-882571, 🅦 www.coast-to-coast .org.uk), Park House, Ingleby Cross, Northallerton DL6 3PE (£4 including postage inside UK, plus £1 for overseas). Coast to Coast badges, T-shirts and certificates are also available.

Wainwright's Coast to Coast Walk is a picture book celebrating the route with AW's characteristic prose and splendid photos by Derry Brabbs. Use it to whet your appetite or as a souvenir after the walk.

Information Sources

The main Tourist Information Centres (TICs) on or near the actual route are at Whitehaven (☎ 01946-852939), near St Bees; Seatoller (☎ 01768-777294), near Rosthwaite; Grasmere (☎ 01539-435245); Glenridding (☎ 01768-482414), near Patterdale; Kirkby Stephen (☎ 01768-371199); and Richmond (☎ 01748-850252). For additional information on the Yorkshire Dales, contact Grassington TIC (☎ 01756-752774). The route does not pass any towns with visitors centres through the North York Moors, so you will need to contact the TICs at Helmsley (☎ 01439-770173) and Whitby (☎ 01947-602674). All TICs can provide information on local accommodation and services. Some are run by the Lake District, Yorkshire Dales and North York Moors national park authorities, and include additional information about the parks the route goes through.

A good source of information is Coast to Coast Guides (☎ 01748-821111, W www.coasttocoastguides.co.uk), which provides a free on-line advice service with answers from professional walking guides. It also sells guidebooks, accommodation lists and maps covering the route, and will send them anywhere in the world.

The Web site (W www.coast-to-coast.org.uk) run by the North York Moors Adventure Centre (see Books for contact details) is another useful reference point.

Guided Walks & Baggage Services

Several national companies organise walks along all or part of the route, notably Contours Walking Holidays and Discovery Travel; these are listed under Guided Walks in the Facts for the Walker chapter.

Because the Coast to Coast is so popular, there are several baggage transfer services. The charge is usually £3.50 to £5 per bag per stage. Some companies pick up and deliver to/from the B&B where you are actually staying, while others use a central point (usually another B&B or hotel) in that town or village. Check this carefully when you book. Coast to Coast Packhorse, listed below, offers an all-inclusive package of

Avoiding the Bulge

If at all possible you should avoid starting the Coast to Coast on a weekend, which is when most British walkers begin (as they aim to do the walk within a two-week holiday). If you start midweek you'll have a bit more space on the hills. You'll also be out of sync with the 'bulge' of high demand for accommodation that follows these walkers along the route, and thus have more chance of finding a place to stay.

long-term parking, baggage transfer, B&B along the route and lifts to/from the start or finish for £750. The main players are Brigantes Baggage Couriers and Sherpa Van Project, whose contact details are listed in the boxed text 'Baggage Services' on p50. Others include:

Coast to Coast Packhorse (☎ 01768-371680, e packhorse@cumbria.com) This company runs a minibus along the route every day, April to September. You can book in advance for a slightly cheaper rate but the service is flexible – ideal if you don't want luggage transported every day or make on-the-spot decisions. It also carries passengers.
Coast to Coast Baggage Services (☎ 01642-489173, e coasttocoastbaggage@lineone.net) This is a flexible and reliable door-to-door service – phone them in the evening and they'll pick up your bag next day. Book in advance for a discount.

Most baggage services can also arrange safe car parking at either end of the route, and will transport you between the start and finish as required.

PLACES TO STAY & EAT

The route is well served by hotels and B&Bs, although this is a popular route through three popular areas and the prices reflect this. The route is also well served by campsites, usually on farms, and there are some bunkhouses and camping barns.

There's also a good supply of YHA hostels (apart from the last few days), although some are away from the overnight stops recommended here. The YHA Booking Bureau (☎ 0870-241 2314, e reservations@yha.org.uk) can book the hostels for you in one go.

For more accommodation options consult the route accommodation guides listed under Books, or *The Rambler's Yearbook & Accommodation Guide* and *Stillwell's National Trail Companion* (see Books in the Facts for the Walker chapter).

For a meal at the end of the day, you'll usually have no trouble finding pubs serving meals or restaurants in bigger places. Some B&Bs also offer evening meals (although you must order these in advance) and packed lunches. If you're camping, the route passes shops only on some days, so being completely self-sufficient is a logistical headache. For lunch, some days include a midway cafe or pub, but you'll often need to provide your own food. Details are given in the route description.

GETTING TO/FROM THE WALK
The Getting Around chapter lists several public transport inquiry lines that provide details of both national and local bus and train services: See the boxed text 'Public Transport Information' on p92.

Bus To reach the start of the walk, National Express coaches run from various parts of the country to Penrith, from where Stagecoach Cumbria (☎ 0870-608 2608) buses run via Keswick to Whitehaven about five times per day (less on Sunday). Twice a day this bus continues to St Bees.

From Robin Hood's Bay, at the walk's end, there are buses to Whitby about every hour. From Whitby buses go to Middlesbrough or York, from where you can reach the rest of the country.

Train St Bees is on the line between Carlisle and Barrow-in-Furness, both of which are linked to mainline services and the rest of the country. There's a train between Carlisle and Barrow-in-Furness several times per day, except Sunday when trains run between Carlisle and Whitehaven only.

At the end of the walk, the nearest station to Robin Hood's Bay is Whitby, from where trains go to Middlesbrough with connections to the rest of the country.

Car St Bees is reached from the M6 at Penrith, by the A66 to Cockermouth, the A5086 to Egremont and from there along a small country road.

Robin Hood's Bay is off the A171 between Whitby and Scarborough.

THE WALK
Although it's traditional to do the Coast to Coast in 12 days, this is a suggested itinerary only – there are several variations possible with longer days or additional stops. Some of these are detailed under 'Alternatives' in the introduction to this walk.

St Bees
The unpretentious village of St Bees could easily be a more lively tourist location if it wasn't for three things – Sellafield nuclear power station to the south, Whitehaven chemical works to the north and the Lake District to the east, which attracts most of the tourists who come to this part of Britain. However, St Bees bravely stands up to the challenge and proudly boasts a beach, a large **bird reserve** (the only place in the country where black guillemot breed) and the historic **Priory Church of St Bega** – St Bees' original name. The village post office is also a tourist information point.

There are plenty of B&Bs (many full on weekdays with Sellafield workers) and some pubs with accommodation. Most of them can be found on Main St, including *Stonehouse Farm* (☎ 01946-822224) with good B&B from £16 to £20, plus camping in the back garden for £2.50; the attractive and friendly *Outrigg House* (☎ 01946-822348), from £16; and basic *Fairladies Barn Guesthouse* (☎ 01946-822718), also from £16.

The Oddfellows pub, opposite Fairladies Barn, serves reasonable bar meals, and the food at *The Queens Hotel* has been recommended. For something more exotic, *French Connection* in the station building offers a special ambience and a more varied menu, with main courses from £9 to £13. You can get sandwiches for the walk from *Hartley's Tearoom* down on the beach.

Day 1: St Bees to Ennerdale Bridge
14mi (22.5km), 6–7 hours
This first day introduces the contrasts and variety to come. From the foaming Irish Sea you cross industrial and agricultural plains, patches of forest, quiet valleys and some high ground with absolutely marvellous views.

On the beach of St Bees dip your toe into the water, a ritual to repeat at the end of the walk, marking your passage 'from sea to shining sea'. That done, head for the foot-bridge at the end of the concrete promenade, going up steps to the cliff path leading to St Bees Head and Fleswick Bay. 'C to C' signposts and yellow arrows are easy to follow until Bell House Farm.

Continue past the farm, through a gate and follow the right-hand path. At a fork, confusing arrows point in both directions. Go left, down the field, underneath the railway line and immediately left to zigzag through several fields (and under another railway – now dismantled), passing through the villages of Moor Row and Cleator – the latter with a *shop*.

The route continues through fields, then follows a forestry track. Look for a sign on the left to 'Dent Fell' and exchange, with a sigh of relief, the hard track for a soft grassy path, leading up to the summit of **Dent Fell**. The views from this summit make you feel like the journey really starts here. Everything that you are leaving behind and

that you are about to enter is laid out at your feet. Behind is the glinting sea, the hazy, haunting silhouette of the nuclear reactors and the billowing clouds of the chemical works, while ahead rises the imposing, almost intimidating, skyline of the mountains of the Lake District.

This is the best part of the day. After descending through a patch of eerie, silent forest, you enter the enchanting limestone vale of Nannycatch Beck, which is like an oasis after the windswept fell. Keep a close eye on the map in this area as there are numerous path junctions. (Many walkers take a wrong turn and mistakenly head back towards Cleator.) The path leaves the beck and meets a lane, which continues for about a mile to the main road and the village of Ennerdale Bridge.

Ennerdale Bridge

Places to stay include the peaceful *Old Vicarage* (☎ *01946-861107*) with B&B from

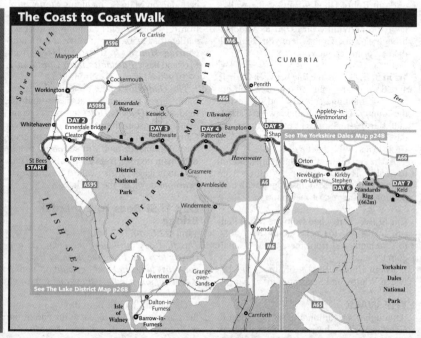

The Coast to Coast Walk

£18 plus camping for £3, although it's a very small area that may be full. Camping is also available at **High Bridge Farm** (☎ 01946-861339), just outside the village, for the same price. Better is **Low Moor End Farm** (☎ 01946-861388), farther up the road towards Ennerdale Water, with camping for £2.50. Another good option for B&B is the friendly **Shepherds Arms Hotel** (☎ 01946-861249), from £27. After a rough day on the hills, this place feels like heaven. To add to your comfort it also serves afternoon tea and the restaurant is highly recommended, with delicious meals around £9 to £12. For tomorrow's lunch (or supper if you're camping) the village **store** is open daily.

Day 2: Ennerdale Bridge to Rosthwaite

14.5mi (23.5km), 6–7 hours
This is a long but easy day, with a pleasant section along your first Lake District lake – leave plenty of time to savour this.

From Ennerdale Bridge follow the signs to Ennerdale Water, turning right as you enter a plantation along a quiet lane that zigzags to the lake. The path leads along the southern side of the lake for over a mile, level with the water line, except for a short, easy scramble below the cliffs of **Angler's Crag** – queues can form here on busy days!

At the end of the lake, stiles lead to a footbridge across the River Liza and you go up the valley, passing the very simple (no electricity) **Ennerdale YHA Hostel** (☎ 01946-861237), which charges £8.10. Just past here a high-level option over Red Pike and Hay Stacks goes off left, but this is long, hard, demanding and requires mountain experience. The usual low-level route follows 4mi of flat and fairly boring forestry track along the valley to the remote and even simpler **Black Sail YHA Hostel** (☎ 07711-108450), which also charges £8.10.

About half a mile past here the path swings north and heads steeply upwards beside Loft

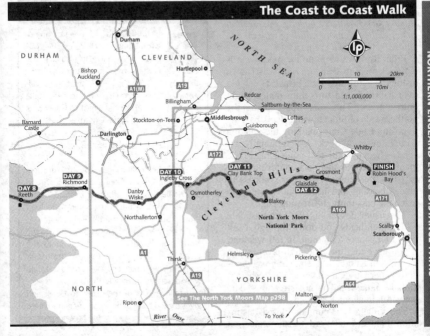

The Coast to Coast Walk

Beck. At the top of the fell, there's a misleading collection of cairns and paths, so you may need your compass to ensure you go in the right direction, contouring round below a peak called Brandreth to reach some disused mine workings. Follow the old, straight tramway (which used to carry slate) down to the road at Honister Pass – now the site of **Honister Hause YHA Hostel** (☎ 01768-777267), charging £9. Descend eastwards on the road into the valley of Borrowdale, then through the village of Seatoller to reach the larger village of Rosthwaite.

Rosthwaite

There's a wide choice of places to stay in Seatoller and Rosthwaite. For details, see Places to Stay & Eat in the Scafell Pike Circuit walk in the Lake District chapter.

Day 3: Rosthwaite to Patterdale
17.5mi (28km), 7–10 hours
This is a very long, hard and potentially serious day through the heart of the Lake District. It can be broken into two days by staying at Grasmere, making this section easier and much more fulfilling with time to enjoy the wonderful scenery.

From Rosthwaite go up the road towards Keswick for 50m, then turn right (east) down a stony lane towards Hazel Bank Hotel. Go over a bridge and turn immediately right onto a track. This runs uphill along the northern side of Stonethwaite Beck, past the imposing **Eagle Crag** (marking the junction with Langstrath Beck), and gradually ascends Greenup Gill to Lining Crag. Take great care here as there's a confusing maze of paths and cairns. Use your compass to take a bearing and head south-easterly to reach the pass through **Greenup Edge**.

The usual descent is via Far Easedale Gill, which leads you down through a fell called Grasmere Common. In fair weather, if you have the time, the high-level option via Gibson Knott and Helm Crag is a wonderful alternative; it makes use of the height already gained and is not strenuous. The paths rejoin about 1.5mi outside Grasmere.

The village is a popular tourist destination thanks to its Wordsworth connection

– see the boxed text 'William Wordsworth' on p270. You may have lunch here or stay overnight; there are plenty of B&Bs, cafes and pubs, and a TIC. **Butterlip How YHA Hostel** (☎ 01539-435316), charging £9.80, is just north of Grasmere centre. Most B&Bs that cater for walkers are also on this side and along the A59, which bypasses the village. These include the rather twee but comfortable **Fairy Glen** (☎ 01539-435620), charging £20; the walker-friendly **Dunmail House** (☎ 01539-435256), charging £20 to £25; and **Chestnut Villa** (☎ 01539-435218), charging around £25. The nearby **Swan Inn** serves lunches and evening meals.

To skip Grasmere follow the Coast to Coast path as it turns left (northwards) before the village, near the **Thorny How YHA Hostel** (☎ 015394-35316), which charges £12. The route then crosses the main road at Mill Bridge. Here **High Broadrayne Farm & Grassmere Hostel** (☎ 01539-435733,

The Coast to Coast Walk – Some Route Highlights

It's difficult to pick out just one or two highlight sections on this truly excellent and incredibly varied route. Perhaps the most impressive days are those through the Lake District. An excellent walk goes from Grasmere to Patterdale, or follow this part of the Coast to Coast on a circular walk tying in the Grisedale valley with the fells of St Sunday Crag. See the Helvellyn & Striding Edge walk in the Lake District chapter for more details.

For a softer, rolling landscape, the Yorkshire Dales offers several circular walks around Swaledale, using Reeth as a base to follow part of the Coast to Coast along the high ground and return along the valley floor.

Yet another type of landscape awaits on the North York Moors. A good section of the Coast to Coast runs northwards from Osmotherley. Alternatively, the Farndale Skyline walk described in the North York Moors section follows part of the Coast to Coast and gives a good taste of the wide open moorland.

e *jodennisondrake@broadraynefarm.fre eserve.co.uk)* offers comfortable B&B in the old farmhouse from £23.50. The separate hostel has small bunkrooms for £12.50, a well-equipped self-catering kitchen, showers, washing machines, free tea and coffee, drying room, central heating, a wonderful lounge with even more wonderful views, and friendly and helpful management, making it one of the finest hostels along the whole route. Nearby, the busy *Travellers Rest Inn (☎ 01539-435604)* offers teas, lunches and good evening meals, plus B&B from around £30.

Continuing on you ascend to Grisedale Hause, with the picturesque little lake of **Grisedale Tarn** just beyond. From here the low-level option leads you down the valley of Grisedale, which is like a dream brought to life – meadows teeming with wild flowers, a melodious stream cutting a silvery trail along the foot of the fellside and lonely barns hiding secrets of days gone by. It's plain sailing now into Patterdale.

If you broke this day at Grasmere you should be refreshed and maybe ready to consider a high-level alternative. From Grisedale Tarn walk up to Deepdale Hause (just north of the summit of Fairfield – described in the Lake District chapter of this book) and then over St Sunday Crag, with great views of Ullswater as you descend again into Patterdale. If you are feeling really fit, from Grisedale Tarn you could go up to the path to Dollywaggon Pike and then to Helvellyn, descending via Striding Edge and Glenridding, still with enough energy left to saunter into Patterdale. This latter option is also described (in reverse) in the Lake District chapter and could be the highlight of your route, but it's very serious and not to be undertaken lightly.

Patterdale

As you come down the path from Grisedale, *Grassthwaite How (☎ 01768-482230)* is uphill on the left (if you can still make it). It is basic but quaint with B&B from £15. The only drawback is lengthening tomorrow's distance, and you'll have to walk into Patterdale for an evening meal. Farther down

the hill in a beautiful position is *Home Farm (☎ 01768-482370)*, charging £17 for B&B and £1.75 for simple camping.

It's another half-mile into the village of Patterdale itself, which has several places to stay. At the nearby village of Glenridding, about a mile to the north, there are more accommodation options, plus shops and a TIC. Full details on Patterdale and Glenridding are given under Places to Stay & Eat in the Helvellyn & Striding Edge walk in the Lake District chapter.

Day 4: Patterdale to Shap
16mi (25.5km), 6–7 hours
Today you may feel pangs of nostalgia and melancholy, for you are leaving the lovely Lake District. But comfort yourself! Today you're also rewarded with magnificent views over Ullswater and the Helvellyn ranges, and by the afternoon, excitement at the prospect of a new landscape will prevail.

From Patterdale, south of the White Lion pub, turn east off the main road onto a small lane. Follow it to its end where a wall marks the beginning of the open fell. Go through a gate and take the path that climbs diagonally up the fellside to Boredale Hause, from where you follow a glorious, airy path with wonderful views over the valley and surrounding mountains. Go to the north of Angle Tarn and skirt a peak called the **Knott**. Alternatively you can divert briefly to the summit, where the views are excellent.

From the Knott aim south beside a wall for about 300m, then turn left (north-east) at a junction of paths (straight on leads to a peak called High Street). Take great care here, especially in the mist. Even on clear days some walkers miss this path and end up on top of High Street by mistake. The path swings round to aim east, continues over **Kidsty Pike** (780m), traditionally the last Lakeland summit on this route, and then drops down to the southern end of a lake called Haweswater. In bad weather precise compass bearings are called for to avoid missing Kidsty Pike. You then follow the path along the bonny banks of Haweswater to its northern end.

An alternative, high-level route (if you have time, good weather and a proper map, plus a compass you can use well) goes from just before Kidsty Pike over High Raise and Wether Hill, down to Haweswater at its northern end.

From Haweswater the route continues east. You could branch off to stay in the villages of Bampton or Bampton Grange, but if Shap is your aim you'll enjoy a lovely stroll via Haweswater Beck and the River Lowther, passing the remains of 12th-century **Shap Abbey** before entering the village.

Shap

While Shap is not the most attractive village on this walk, it has several B&Bs, including the very reasonably priced *Pleasant View* (☎ *01931-716336*), at £15; *Fell House* (☎ *01931-716343*), charging from £16.50; *The Rockery* (☎ *01931-716340*), charging £18; *Brookfield* (☎ *01931-716397*), from £18 and also offering evening meals; and *The Hermitage* (☎ *01931-716671*), a lovely old house, from £18 (£22 en suite).

Shap also has a brace of pubs. *The King's Arms Hotel* (☎ *01931-716277*) has rooms from £20 and good food. *The Bulls Head Inn* (☎ *01931-716678*) is straightforward with B&B from £18, camping for £2 and meals from around £5 served in the bar or restaurant. *The Crown Inn* (☎ *01931-716229*, e *crow-innshap@totalise.co.uk*) does B&B from £18.50 and offers comfortable bunkhouse accommodation for £6.50. You can get food in the bar and a slightly fancier selection, including good vegetarian options, in the nonsmoking restaurant. Bunkhousers can get a full breakfast for £4. Another cheap and basic option is *Rest Easy Bunkhouse* (☎ *01931-716538*), charging £8.

Day 5: Shap to Kirkby Stephen

21mi (34km), 8 hours

After the exhilarating experience of crossing England's highest mountain region, this day will feel tame but will be a welcome respite from the windswept desolation of upland fells. However, the day is also long and quite tiring, so ancient stone circles and other prehistoric remains are welcome distractions along the way. It is important to note that some sections of the route have *been revised, so it is crucial to keep strictly to the authorised paths.*

The route leaves Shap, turning off the A6 opposite the King's Arms Hotel and crossing the railway line, taking you straight to the M6 motorway – an unfortunate reminder of 'civilisation'. Cross the footbridge and make a quick escape to the moors.

Just past the secluded hamlet of Oddendale, slow down for **Oddendale Stone Circle**, a superb lookout, and get back in touch with the serenity of ancient sites that abound in this area. These include Robin Hood's Grave, about 2mi farther along the route, one of several resting places dedicated to the legendary brigand.

The route bypasses the village of Orton (which has a pub and B&Bs), winding through open country. The next highlight is **Sunbiggin Tarn**, a Site of Special Scientific Interest, which is protected as a breeding ground for birds; its shores out of bounds for human feet. Just past here the route runs north of the village of Newbiggin-on-Lune, which is a possible overnight stop if you're turning Days 4 and 5 into three days. One option is **Bents Barn** with simple facilities for £3.50, which must be booked in advance through the Lakeland Barns Booking Office (☎ 01768-772645, fax 775043, e keswick tic@lake-district.gov.uk).

The route crosses a small river called Smardale Gill and goes over Smardale Fell. From **Lime Kilne Hill**, the views of the Eden Valley to Nine Standards Rigg will help take your mind off your aching feet and whet your appetite for tomorrow's jaunt. Beyond here it's a couple of miles to Kirkby Stephen.

Kirkby Stephen

The ancient, but still bustling, market town of Kirkby Stephen is the largest settlement reached so far. It has supermarkets, shops, banks, outdoor gear shops, post office and a Holistic Health Centre (☎ 01768-372482) offering remedial massage for weary walkers. The TIC (☎ 01768-371199) is in the centre of town on Market St.

You can camp at *Pennine View Caravan Park* (☎ *01768-371717*), on the southern edge of the town, for £3, with showers. Nearby, *The Croglin Castle Hotel* does pub food.

The central **YHA Hostel** (☎ 01768-371793), on Market St, charges £9. Next door is *Fletcher House* (☎ 01768-371013) with B&B from £20. Other B&Bs include *Old Court House* (☎ 01768-371061), on the High St just outside the town centre, which is tastefully furnished, comfortable and friendly, and charges from £15. Next door is *The Jolly Farmer* (☎ 01768-371063), also very good although a touch impersonal, with B&B from £16. Farther down the same street, now called South Rd, *Lockholme* (☎ 01768-371321) is also very friendly, charging from £16. On the other side of town, *Redmayne House* (☎ 01768-371441), in Silver St, is an excellent choice with a large garden, charging £16. More upmarket is *The King's Arms Hotel* (☎ 01768-371378) with B&B from £25/45 for singles/doubles, although walkers sometimes get discounts. The food served in the bar is varied and good value (from around £5) and there's a pleasant, lively atmosphere.

Other pubs doing food include the straightforward *Pennine Hotel* and the slightly smarter *White Lion*. For a change from pubs, *The Old Forge Restaurant*, on North Rd, serves evening meals from £6, including 'cock and bull' – chicken stuffed with beef in peppercorn sauce – for £9. The town has several cafes serving standard 'with chips' meals, or try *Mulberry Bush Tearoom* for healthier options. Stock up for tomorrow's lunch at *Megabites* sandwich shop or visit the *Indian takeaway* just behind the TIC, which will make up a lunch pack of samosas and other portable delicacies.

Day 6: Kirkby Stephen to Keld
13mi (21km), 6 hours
Today's walk is a gem, leading you into the picturesque landscape of the Yorkshire Dales via the Pennine watershed. Bring food as you pass no cafes today.

From Kirkby Stephen's marketplace head north, over Frank's Bridge, for a short but pleasant riverside stroll to the delightful village of Hartley. From the main street take

a path down to a footbridge, and then a lane that bears left uphill to Hartley Quarry. It's a stiff uphill push for a few miles as you enter the hills of the Yorkshire Dales. The lane ends at a fork; go left, through a gate and uphill over Hartley Fell.

The sweating finishes at the summit of **Nine Standards Rigg** (662m) – the highest you'll be for the rest of the walk. The origin of the Nine Standards is a matter of imagination. Are they a stone army to ward off invaders or merely boundary markers? The choice is yours. One thing is certain, the views are magnificent – east to Swaledale, west to the Lake District, north to the Pennines and south to the long grassy ramp of Wild Boar Fell (reputedly the last place in this country where wild boar were hunted).

From the summit head southwards briefly and, a short distance past the view indicator (dedicated to Lady Di's wedding), a signpost points you south across the moor to Ney Gill. This was the original Wainwright route but because the fragile moorland vegetation has been damaged under thousands of Coast to Coast boots, the route has since been revised. Instead it veers left (east) into Whitsundale and on to the hamlet of Ravenseat. This new path is beginning to suffer erosion as well, so a system of seasonal rotation has been introduced. You can use the traditional route from May to July, and the Whitsundale route from August to November. In winter Nine Standards Rigg and the moors thereabouts should be avoided altogether in favour of a low-level route from Hartley Fell, via Lamps Moss and Ney Gill, to Ravenseat.

From Ravenseat, the last section along Whitsundale Beck is a delight. A final stretch of road takes you into the village of Keld – the halfway point.

Keld
The tiny village of Keld is unspoilt, traditional and purely residential, with few facilities for the traveller – except some public toilets. There's no restaurant and no pub (it was turned into a Methodist chapel many years ago), so apart from spiritual nourishment you'll go hungry unless you

book a meal at the hostel or your B&B. The Pennine Way also comes through here, so accommodation is at a premium.

Campers have two choices. *Park House* (☎ 01748-886549, **e** *parkhouse@global net.co.uk*), near the bridge about 1mi west of Keld, has friendly owners, camping for £1.50 and a small *shop* selling enough to make an evening meal or tomorrow's sandwiches. *Park Lodge Farm*, in the village, always has plenty of room (no booking required); camping costs £3, including hot showers. The *YHA Hostel* (☎ 01748-886259) has space for 40 people, including some double rooms, and charges £9.

Keld has only a few B&B options. The first of these is *Butt House* (☎ 01748-886374), home of the legendary Mrs Whitehead – compiler of the *Coast to Coast Accommodation Guide* (mentioned under Books in the Planning section for this walk) – who is very welcoming, a fount of knowledge on local history and society, and even numbers senior politicians among her friends and confidants. En suite B&B costs £17, including a first-class breakfast with real coffee, and dinners are £10 with beer and wine available. *Prospect House* (☎ 01748-886495) is another friendly, welcoming place, where Mrs Cox charges £16 for B&B and £9 for excellent dinners.

Greenlands (☎ 01748-886576), just over half a mile south of Keld on the road towards Thwaite, with views over the valley, charges £19.50 for B&B and £10 for dinner.

Frith Lodge (☎ 01748-886489, **e** *mary .pepper@virgin.net*), about 1mi north of the Coast to Coast and bang on the Pennine Way, charges £15 and provides dinner for £8. To get there, turn north before Keld and go up through the settlement of West Stonesdale, from where a path leads diagonally across the valley to the lodge.

Day 7: Keld to Reeth
11mi (17.5km), 5 hours
The main feature of today's walk is Swaledale – an enchanting, verdant valley, winding a course through a backdrop of grey and austere moorlands. On the upper slopes you'll see industrial waste from the lead mines, which flourished here 300 years ago. In mist and rain the surroundings will either fuel a romantic taste for mystery or simply turn your day into a tedious trot across bleak and barren nothingness.

The Coast to Coast leaves Keld down a path to a footbridge over the Swale. This is a junction with the Pennine Way where you might want to swap experiences with other long-distance walkers. From the footbridge, the path takes you up to the top of Swinner Gill and then follows a wide dirt track to the steepsided river valley of Gunnerside Gill. You cross the gill and go up the other side, to pass through the ghostly **ruins of lead smelting mills**, empty mine shafts, stark chimneys and mounds of debris. The ruins evoke the blood, sweat and tears of the men and women who toiled in the bowels of the earth for a meagre subsistence, and the names are evocative. You pass near Old Rake Hush and descend by Old Gang Beck to Surrender Bridge. Beyond here the route winds through farmland – a welcome change after the harsh moorland – and leads you into Reeth.

Reeth
The 'capital of Swaledale' is a small and charming town, which is popular with tourists and has several pubs, teashops and stores, a post office (selling guidebooks and maps), a TIC and a museum, all dotted around the main square.

Walker-friendly B&Bs include *Walpardoe* (☎ 01748-884626), a cottage just off the square, charging from £17.

The *Arkleside Hotel* (☎ 01748-884200) is a bit expensive at £33, but it's definitely worth it if you fancy some luxury. About 150m down the lane is the delightful and good-quality *Arkle House* (☎ 01748-884815, **e** *info@arklehouse.com*), charging from £22. Just off the main square, *2 Bridge Terrace* (☎ 01748-884572) is very welcoming, with single/double rooms for £16.50/20. Next door, *Hakney House* (☎ 01748-884302) is also good, charging from £16.

For food, *The Old Temperence*, on the square, serves teas and a large and interesting selection of meals, while *The Copper*

Swaledale Miners

The Yorkshire Dales were formed during the ice age by glaciers cutting through the rocks and the mineralised faults, which revealed seams of lead beneath. Mining for lead probably began here as early as 1000 BC, but by the 17th and 18th centuries lead mines dominated the scenery and the whole social fabric of the area. The miners either worked for themselves or were employed by companies in groups or 'gangs'. The work was arduous, dangerous and very poorly paid. Child labour was common and diseases like scarlet fever and typhoid were rife. When cheaper foreign ore was imported into Britain in the late 19th century, the mines of Swaledale had to close. Many miners, desperate in their search for a livelihood, emigrated to Australia and America, while the Yorkshire mines and mills gave way to the farming communities found in the area today.

Kettle does lunches and evening meals from £4 to £6.

The King's Arms Hotel (☎ 01748-884259) has a roaring fire on cool evenings, good beer and bar meals for around £6 to £8, plus B&B from £20 and sometimes live music. Next door, and also very good, is *The Black Bull* (☎ 01748-884213) with bar food plus B&B from £20 to £25.

Grinton Lodge YHA Hostel (☎ 01748-884206), 1.5mi south of Reeth, charges £9. The nearby *Bridge Inn* does good food. There's camping for £2 at *Low Whita Farm* (☎ 01748-884430), about 2.5mi west of Reeth and 1mi south of the route. There is also a *bunkhouse* here (all you need is a sleeping bag), which costs around £5. Book through the central camping barns reservation office (☎ 01200-420102, Ⓔe campbarns yha@enterprise.net).

Day 8: Reeth to Richmond
11mi (17.5km), 5 hours
After the bleak moors, this is a day of sauntering through picturesque, sleepy villages, fields of cows, sheep and horses, and meadows and woodlands, which – in spring and summer – explode with wild flowers.

From Reeth the route keeps north of the swirling River Swale, following lanes to **Marrick Priory**. The nearby woodlands were enjoyed by nuns in the 12th century. If the sun is shining and the birds singing, with the flowering garlic smelling sweet, and carpets of bluebells and primulas covering the ground, heaven could certainly be within reach.

From Marrick village the route embarks on a waymarked journey, with fabulous panoramic views over rolling farmland. Along the way, *Nun Cote Farm* serves teas, cakes and is famous for hot apple pie. (It also does B&B.) Beyond the village of Marske, life is easy. It's a stroll across to Applegarth Scar, through Whitcliffe Wood and down a quiet lane into Richmond.

Richmond
One of the most intact historic towns in England, Richmond is unspoilt by modern architectural eyesores. The wide marketplace is the lively central point, with cobbled streets leading past elegant Georgian housefronts, all overlooked by the powerful Norman **castle**. Facilities include cafes, pubs, shops, supermarkets and a TIC (☎ 01748-850252), next to a small park called Friary Gardens, on Victoria Rd. Castle Hill Books (☎ 01748-821111) specialises in books on Yorkshire and the Coast to Coast.

On your way into town you pass some B&Bs, including the very small and also very welcoming *8 West Terrace* (☎ 01748-825418), charging £18 (or £20 if you want a full breakfast); and the friendly *West Cottage* (☎ 01748-824046, Ⓔe kay.gibson@tesco.net), on Victoria Rd, which is small, non-smoking and good value at £22 in en suite rooms. Just down Victoria Rd is the smart and comfortable *Nun's Cottage Guesthouse* (☎ 01748-822809, Ⓔe alanparks@bt internet.com), charging £22 to £25. Nearby, the small and cosy *27 Hurgill Rd* (☎ 01748-824092) charges from £18. Another recommended place is *Pottergate Guesthouse* (☎ 01748-823826), charging from £19. There are many more B&Bs along the street called Frenchgate; those at Nos 58, 66 and 70 are all good.

Just off the central marketplace, on Finkle St, *The Black Lion* (☎ *01748-823121*) is a good, old-style, no-frills pub doing B&B for £17, with bar food for around £5. Also on Finkle St, *The Continental Bistro-Café* does lunches and evening meals Thursday to Saturday. Other pubs doing food include *The Golden Lion* and *The Bishop Blaize*. These are both on the marketplace, where you'll also find several cafes, teashops, fish and chip takeaways, and a pizzeria.

The nearest place for camping is *Village Farm* (☎ *01748-818326*), in Brompton-on-Swale, east of Richmond, charging £2. It also has a camping barn for £3.50 and bookings can be made through the central reservation office (☎ 01200-420102, e camp barnsyha@enterprise.net).

Historic Richmond

Richmond boasts many historic buildings and no less than three museums. These are the 18th-century Georgian Theatre & Museum, the Richmondshire Local History Museum and the Green Howards Museum. Green Howards is a military history museum set in a 12th-century church in the marketplace, where many exhibits relate to the 900-year-old Catterick Barracks nearby.

CHRISTINE OSBORNE

The Richmond riverside

Day 9: Richmond to Ingleby Cross
23mi (37km), 8 hours

Today is a long walk across the flat and pastoral Vale of Mowbray. It's the least attractive section of the route; the walking is often monotonous through working farmland or along country lanes. To skip it, you can go by bus to Northallerton and Osmotherley.

The start of today's walk is pleasant enough, leaving the marketplace and crossing Richmond Bridge for the south bank of the River Swale and a splendid view of the castle. You follow the course of the river, with sections of woodland and meadow to savour, to the small town of Catterick and then cross back to the north side. You then bid the lovely Swale farewell and embark on a long trot for about 2½ hours along country lanes, with only sleepy villages and occasional plantations breaking up the dull flatness of the scenery. Eventually, at Oaktree Hill, those who prefer to feel the earth under their feet, not asphalt, can sigh with relief.

The next few miles are still flat and fairly boring, but all stupors are shattered when the quiet lane you're following suddenly ends at the very busy A19 dual carriageway. If you need sustenance there's a petrol station *shop* and *Little Chef* restaurant on your left.

Cross the road (with great care) and duck down another lane, which leads through the small village of Ingleby Arncliffe to the even smaller settlement of Ingleby Cross.

Ingleby Arncliffe
In Ingleby Arncliffe, B&Bs include the efficient and walker-friendly *Ingleby House* (☎ *01609-882433*), charging £18.50. If this place is full, the owners can recommend other people locally who also take guests.

Ingleby Cross
The handful of buildings that form Ingleby Cross include a post office shop and *The Blue Bell Inn* (☎ *01609-882272*), a popular Coast to Coast watering hole which has B&B for £20, reasonable pub meals from £5 and camping facilities for £2.

Also at Ingleby Cross, *The North York Moors Adventure Centre* (☎ *01609-882571*) offers B&B for £15 and camping for £2. They also sell Coast to Coast badges and certificates (but no cheating, you've still got three or four days to go!) and are happy to give guests a free lift to the pub.

About 1mi north-east of Ingleby Cross, on the main A172, *Ox Hill Farm* (☎ 01609-882255) offers straightforward but very welcoming and comfortable farmhouse B&B for £15. The nearby *Black Horse* in Swinby does excellent food.

There are more accommodation options in the picture-postcard village of Osmotherley, just to the south of the route about 2mi beyond Ingleby Cross. For more details on Osmotherley, see the Cleveland Way in the North York Moors chapter.

Day 10: Ingleby Cross to Clay Bank Top
12mi (19.5km), 4–5 hours
This day will more than compensate for yesterday's tedium. It's a hard but very enjoyable rollercoaster stomp on easy paths, through heather moor and gorgeous woodlands. In hot weather take enough water to last the day.

From Ingleby Cross aim south-east then north-west uphill through woodland. Beyond Osmotherley, the Coast to Coast is joined by the Cleveland Way and together they follow the edge of the North York Moors. Views to the north are dominated by the industrial chimneys of Middlesbrough, while to the south are the moors themselves, hiding secrets of a barren but engaging wilderness.

After a few miles the little valley of **Scugdale** provides a surprisingly lush interlude to the empty moors, with its delightful mixed woodlands, abundant wild flowers and twittering birds. Then it's upwards and onwards, crossing a lane that comes up from Carlton-in-Cleveland. At this point *Lord Stones Café* (so well landscaped you could miss it) is a welcome oasis if the weather's hot, and a refuge if it isn't.

Three miles on from the cafe you reach Clay Bank Top where the route crosses the B1257 road, which is surprisingly busy with cars, trucks and caravans, plus illegally racing motorcycles.

Clay Bank Top
Accommodation at Clay Bank Top is limited to a *campsite* – the route passes straight through it. Set in a meadow, it is open from May to October. The caretaker comes round in the evening and collects £2.

Your nearest B&B is *Maltkiln House* in the hamlet of Urra, about 1mi south of the route. There are more places at Great Broughton, 2.5mi north. For details on all these options, see Day 3 of the Cleveland Way walk description in the North York Moors chapter.

Day 11: Clay Bank Top to Glaisdale
18mi (29km), 6–7 hours
The first half of today's walk is mostly level, along a dismantled railway. The second half of the day is more varied – across heather moor and an old horse track leading down to the Esk Valley.

From Clay Bank Top follow a wide track up to Urra Moor and across appropriately named Round Hill. Just past here the path joins the route of the legendary Rosedale Ironstone Railway, which served mines in the area during the 19th century. At Bloworth Crossing you cross an ancient track called Westland Road and can still see old, wooden sleepers buried in the shale.

At this point say goodbye to any fellow walkers who may be doing the Cleveland Way; they turn sharply north but you stay on the old railway (also the route of the Lyke Wake Walk – see the boxed text on p314) for the next 5mi. The walking is fairly straightforward but clear weather and good views make this day special. As you stride along, thinking of all the railway songs you've ever known, you may wonder where in the world you might find a similar feeling of space and infinity, of lightness and light. If you are unlucky, enveloped by a void of mist and rain, let your imagination create the hustle and bustle of the iron-ore mines and the whistle of the trains steaming through blizzards, gales and storms.

Don't get too carried away, though, or you may well miss the 'LWW' marker peg on the left, which leads up a narrow path to

The Lion Inn (☎ 01751-417320) at Blakey. (This concessionary path is not a right of way, so it may be closed to walkers in future. If this is the case, continue for half a mile to where a track forks right off the old railway line, just before a closed-off bridge, to meet a lane. Turn left and left again, back along the main road to reach the Lion Inn.) This legendary pub – possibly more legendary than the railway – is just about the highest point of the North York Moors (400m) and the fourth-highest pub in Britain (who can name the first three?). It's a formidable place for lunch with a welcome fire and plenty of space, except on summer weekends. Many walkers come to grief here, calling in for a quick lunchtime drink or to shelter from the rain, and then staying in the warmth and comfort all afternoon. Fortunately the pub caters for such tardiness and offers B&B in small rooms from £17 to £32 or basic camping for £1. Opposite, High Blakey House (☎ 01751-417186, e highblakey.house@virginnet.co.uk) is very comfortable, with excellent views and good facilities, and charges from £19 to £22 for B&B.

From Blakey walk along the main road northwards (left as you step out of the pub door). After about 1.5mi a right turn brings you to an ancient stone called White Cross (also called 'Fat Betty' – you'll see why). Pause for a minute to enjoy panoramic views over a sea of endless moorland. You are now bound east, following lanes and tracks, skirting south of the head of Fryup Dale and then veering north-east to stride along the incredible, endless ridge of Glaisdale Rigg, with wonderful views into the valleys on either side, to finally reach the village of Glaisdale.

Glaisdale

The village is quite spread out, from the shops and post office on the hill, down past the church to two pubs and the train station in the valley.

There's a good choice of B&Bs at several of the farms in the Glaisdale valley, west of the village. (If you stay here, make sure you come down (south) off Glaisdale Rigg at the right place, without going into the village,

otherwise it's a long tramp back along the road.) These include (from west to east) Hollins Farm (☎ 01947-897516), which is small and quaint but very friendly, with B&B for £16 and camping for £2 with shower; Red House Farm (☎ 01947-897242), which is quite smart and has very friendly owners, charging £25; and Hart Hall (☎ 01947-897344), another small and very friendly place (there must be something good in the water at Glaisdale), charging £20.

At the valley's end, in Glaisdale village, B&Bs include Sycamore Dell (☎ 01947-897345), charging around £17. Pubs in Glaisdale include, from west to east (from the top of the hill that runs through the village to the bottom), The Mitre, a smart place offering good quality meals; The Moon & Sixpence (☎ 01947-897261), formerly The Anglers Rest, which offers B&B for £17, bar meals for £5 to £10 and camping for £3.50; and The Arncliffe Arms (☎ 01947-897209), which also offers a selection of bar food and B&B.

Down at the bottom of the village, at the train station, Beggars Bridge Tearoom opens from about 9am to 5pm daily in summer and sells breakfasts, snacks, lunches and sandwiches.

About 1mi north of the village, Egton Banks Farm (☎ 01947-897289) is very welcoming, with B&B from £16, evening meals from £8, and lifts to and from the farm.

At the village of Egton Bridge, about 2mi along the route east of Glaisdale, there are more B&B choices. The very highly recommended Postgate Inn (☎ 01947-895241) has friendly management, B&B for £17.50 and a range of straightforward, good-value lunches and dinners from £5 to £8. The Inn also serve sandwiches and baguettes all day. If you're staying in Glaisdale and want to eat here, just phone and they'll pick you up free of charge. Now that's service!

Day 12: Glaisdale to Robin Hood's Bay
20mi (32km), 7–8 hours
And now for the grand finale, exchanging bleak, rugged moorland for sweet-smelling woodlands, ancient trees, rolling pastures

and gurgling rivers. This day also means the abandonment of wilderness and loneliness, as we join bands of holiday-makers near the coast. Don't relax yet, though! Today is a surprisingly long haul, so make sure you leave Glaisdale early.

Leave Glaisdale on the road past the train station and, at the bottom of the hill just before the railway bridge, turn right, across a footbridge and into delightful Arncliffe Woods – half an hour of luscious indulgence and peaceful calm. (Before entering the woods, go under the railway briefly to see **Beggar's Bridge**, built in the 17th century and still standing proud – a beautiful witness to travelling days gone by.)

On leaving the woods (far too soon) a quiet lane carries you downhill, across the River Esk and into the pretty village of Egton Bridge, where a coffee on the terrace of the ***Postgate Hotel*** may be called for. Onwards from here your acquaintance with the River Esk is prolonged on a pleasant track along its course, which takes you into the village of Grosmont.

Grosmont has a robust charm and is most famous for its delightful, 1950s-style station on the North Yorkshire Moors Railway, complete with steam trains. This is a good place to stay if your previous overnight was the Lion Inn at Blakey. There are B&Bs, cafes and a pub – see the Falling Foss & Fylingdales walk in the North York Moors chapter.

After a rest and a touch of train-spotting, you must follow the Coast to Coast up a very steep hill out of Grosmont. (The route is well signposted on this stretch.) Keep to the road, which isn't too busy, across the heather-covered Sleights Moor and, to your left (north) beyond the port of Whitby, you'll get your first view of the sea since leaving St Bees.

Before reaching the busy A169 main road, opposite a car park, a sign to Littlebeck leads you along a narrow path across the moor. This continues north-east, farther than indicated on the OS map, to meet the A169 by a large blue road sign warning drivers of the steep hill ahead. You go virtually straight across the road (take care crossing!) and

onto a grassy track, which joins a lane and leads you on down to the tiny settlement of Littlebeck.

Beyond here the path goes through some beautiful woodland along the banks of May Beck – a last sylvan feast on the Coast to Coast. It harbours treasures like an 18th-century hermitage hollowed out of a boulder and **Falling Foss**, a waterfall that plunges 20m into a leafy ravine.

At May Bank car park (which has a ***tea van*** in summer) you turn sharply up a sealed lane and leave the beauty of nature behind. There's a disappointing couple of miles, mostly along roads and through caravan sites, then all is forgiven as the route ends with a final hour of wonderful, cliff-top walking overlooking the sea, depositing you rather unceremoniously in the suburbs of Robin Hood's Bay.

Keep going until you meet the main road and go left and downhill to descend the final stretch of steep cobbles to the water's edge at the slipway. Naturally you'll want to dip your boot in the sea, to mark the official end of your walk. Beware of waves that wash up here when the wind's in the right direction. Total immersion would be a tragic end to this otherwise most marvellous of long-distance walks.

View of Robin Hood's Bay, on the dramatic cliff edge of the North York Moors

NORTHERN ENGLAND LONG-DISTANCE PATHS

Robin Hood's Bay

The Bay Hotel (☎ 01947-880278) has a hikers bar where you can have a celebratory pint, sign the Coast to Coast log book and get yourself awarded with a certificate (£2); there's good beer, and bar meals cost around £6. For further details about the town, see Day 7 of the Cleveland Way in the North York Moors chapter.

The Pennine Way

Distance	259mi (416.5km)
Duration	16 days
Standard	medium-hard
Start	Edale
Finish	Kirk Yetholm
Gateways	Sheffield, Manchester, Skipton, Penrith, Berwick-upon-Tweed

Summary A national trail along the central mountain spine of Northern England. It's long and hard, but very rewarding and not the fearsome undertaking it once was.

The Pennine Way is the oldest and second-longest national trail in Britain. It follows a north-south line of mountains and upland areas in the centre of Northern England – some of the highest, wildest (and bleakest) countryside anywhere in Britain south of Scotland. The trail passes through the Peak District, the South Pennine moors, the best of the Yorkshire Dales (including one of the famous Three Peaks and beautiful Swaledale), the highest pub in England, the stunning High Cup Nick valley, tranquil Teesdale and the North Pennines, the history-rich Hadrian's Wall and the windswept Cheviot Hills. It is undoubtedly a classic walk.

For many years the Pennine Way had a reputation for being extremely hard, with bad weather and notorious moorland bogs. In truth the weather is bad only *some* of the time – that's the nature of mountains – and many sections of the route have been improved, with lines of rough flagstones laid across the most difficult stretches.

So in recent years the Pennine Way has become a bit of a paper tiger, but its fearsome reputation is somewhat overstated. This doesn't mean you should underestimate it – swift weather changes can still bamboozle even the most experienced walker – but tales of people struggling for hours through thigh-deep slime are ancient history. While the Pennine Way remains a serious challenge, the rewards are great, and the walk is now more enjoyable than it's ever been.

We did the Pennine Way in one go (a bit rushed at 13 days) but had several days where we never saw another person from start to finish, and mostly an average of three or four – in the middle of summer. You don't get the camaraderie of the Coast to Coast, but you get a real sense of isolation and escape. Having walked the route pre- and post-paving, although it's harder on the feet and detracts from the challenge of the bogs, the dramatic reduction in erosion is fantastic to see. A thin line of natural stone undisturbed on either side is much better than the great swathes of mire that existed before.

Richard Hollis (UK)

Direction, Distance & Duration

The Pennine Way is traditionally walked from south to north, with the prevailing winds at your back. The route is waymarked with arrows and national trail acorn symbols, but not uniformly. Some stretches will have indicators every few steps, while others will leave you standing bewildered at unclear junctions. You definitely need a map.

There are lots of alternative distances quoted for the Pennine Way, complicated by the many short variations along the

Warning

Pennine Way weather conditions can be very changeable and occasionally dangerous. Even in summer, rainfall can be high, and strong winds force temperatures down. Mist is common and signposts irregular, so you must be confident with a map and compass. And just in case you do hit a hot patch, there is very little shade and water is often hard to find on the high ground. You should be well equipped, carry emergency supplies, be aware of escape routes and check local weather forecasts.

route. The route as we describe it measures 260mi, while the official national trail distance is 268, the Wainwright guidebook (see the Books section below) insists it's 270mi and the permanent-looking sign at the very start of the walk announces there are 275mi to go. You'd be safer allowing for the largest figure – that way you won't be disappointed. Forays off the route (sometimes essential to reach a place to stay) will also extend the distance.

You can sprint the way in less than two weeks or stroll it in three. In this description we suggest covering the walk in 16 days, averaging 16mi each day with just one long day right at the end (which can be split into two more manageable stages).

day	from	to	mi/km
1	Edale	Crowden	16/25.5
2	Crowden	Standedge	11.5/18.5
3	Standedge	Hebden Bridge	15/24
4	Hebden Bridge	Lothersdale	19/30.5
5	Lothersdale	Malham	15/24
6	Malham	Horton in Ribblesdale	14/22.5
7	Horton in Ribblesdale	Hawes	14/22.5
8	Hawes	Tan Hill	16/25.5
9	Tan Hill	Middleton-in-Teesdale	17/27.5
10	Middleton-in-Teesdale	Dufton	20/32
11	Dufton	Alston	20/32
12	Alston	Greenhead	18/29
13	Greenhead	Once Brewed	7/11.5
14	Once Brewed	Bellingham	15.5/25
15	Bellingham	Byrness	15/24
16	Byrness	Kirk Yetholm	26/42

Alternatives There are numerous alternatives for reducing or increasing the total number of days spent walking. Some suggested extra places to stay are listed in the route description.

As with all Long-Distance Paths, you can do just a single-day linear section of the Pennine Way or a circular route taking in a stretch of the main route. See the boxed text 'The Pennine Way – Some Route Highlights' on p358 for suggestions.

PLANNING
Maps
Footprint's two handy little *Pennine Way* strip maps cover the walk in two sections. These may not be detailed enough for tricky navigation and suffer the complaint of all strip maps (if you go to far away from the route you're off the map) but many people find them very useful.

If you want to be fully equipped with Ordnance Survey (OS) maps you will need OS Landranger 1:50,000 maps No 110 *(Sheffield & Huddersfield)*, No 109 *(Manchester)*, No 103 *(Blackburn & Burnley)*, No 98 *(Wensleydale & Upper Wharfedale)*, No 91 *(Appleby-in-Westmorland)*, No 86 *(Haltwhistle & Brampton)*, No 80 *(Cheviot Hills & Kielder Water)*, No 74 *(Kelso & Coldstream)* and No 92 *(Barnard Castle & Richmond)*.

The OS Outdoor Leisure 1:25,000 maps are recommended as they show more detail. Listed south to north, these are: No 1 *(The Peak District – Dark Peak Area)*, No 21 *(South Pennines)*, No 2 *(Yorkshire Dales – South & West Areas)*, No 30 *(Yorkshire Dales – Northern & Central Areas)*, No 31 *(North Pennines – Teesdale and Weardale)*, No 43 *(Hadrian's Wall)*, No 42 *(Kielder Water)* and No 16 *(The Cheviot Hills)*.

Books
The classic book is *The Pennine Way Companion* by Alfred Wainwright. It's fun and part of Pennine Way tradition, although very idiosyncratic – for a start it goes backwards! As with all Wainwright guides, the text is (neatly) handprinted and the intricate maps show every stile, gate and cow pat along the way – wonderful if you're on track, but useless once you're five steps off it. It's now out of print and second-hand copies are collectors' items, so you'll be lucky to find one.

Far more useful are the official national trail guides, *Pennine Way South* and *Pennine Way North* by Tony Hopkins. They combine text with extracts from OS maps, which you can *almost* use without needing other maps.

Also good, and neater to carry, is *Pennine Way* by Martin Collins, with black-and-white strip maps, route descriptions and cartoons, or *Pennine Way* by Terry Marsh.

Information Sources

The main TICs on or near the route are (north to south) Edale (☎ 01433-670207); Hebden Bridge (☎ 01422-843831); Malham (☎ 01729-830363); Horton in Ribblesdale (☎ 01729-860333); Hawes (☎ 01969-667450); Alston (☎ 01434-381696); Once Brewed, near Hadrian's Wall (☎ 01434-344777); Bellingham (☎ 01434-220616) and Kelso (☎ 01573-223464). They can all provide information on local accommodation and services in their surrounding area. Those run by national park authorities offer additional information about the parks the route passes through.

For specific information about the route, contact the Pennine Way National Trail Officer. This position was unfilled at the time of writing, so there is no address or telephone number to contact. However, emails sent to ⓔ info@pennineway.demon.co.uk should get a response. When the post is filled, the address, along with other information, will be on the Pennine Way's official Web site ⓦ www.pennineway.demon.co.uk.

Most visitors centres can give you the free *Pennine Way Accommodation & Services*

Pennine Way History

The Pennine Way has a long and chequered history, and is held in great regard by many British walkers – even those who have never walked it. First proposed by the walkers' campaigner Tom Stephenson in 1935 and inspired by the national trails established in America, the idea played a key part in the public access struggles of the 1930s, which finally led to hikers and ramblers being allowed to cross private land. It was not until 1949, however, that Parliament approved the concept and it took until 1965 for the Pennine Way to be officially opened – the first of Britain's long-distance paths and, later, national trails.

leaflet, which lists some places to stay. More comprehensive is *The Pennine Way Accommodation & Camping Guide*, a very handy booklet by John Needham, available along the route or from the Pennine Way Association, 23 Woodland Crescent, Hilton Park, Manchester M25 9WQ. Send £1.50 and a stamped, self-addressed envelope.

Guided Walks & Baggage Services

Companies organising walks along the route are listed under Guided Walks in the Facts for the Walker chapter. Several of the baggage companies listed in the Coast to Coast section also cover the Pennine Way. Contact details for Brigantes Baggage Couriers and Sherpa Van Project, which also offer an accommodation booking service, are listed in the Facts for the Walker chapter.

PLACES TO STAY & EAT

With the odd compromise and short diversion it's possible to use YHA hostels along the route. They can be booked in one go through the YHA Booking Bureau (☎ 0870-241 2314, ⓔ reservations@yha.org.uk). There are also plenty of B&Bs, campsites and hotels. For more options, as well as the accommodation guides listed in Information, consult *The Rambler's Yearbook & Accommodation Guide* and *Stillwell's National Trail Companion* (see Books in the Facts for the Walker chapter). It's wise to book accommodation, especially in summer or over the Easter holidays.

Most overnight stops have pubs or restaurants for evening meals. Lunch can be more problematic, however, and it's often wise to bring sandwiches or other sustenance. Most B&Bs will provide packed lunches and many also offer an evening meal (although you must order this in advance). Details are given in the route description.

GETTING TO/FROM THE WALK

The Getting Around chapter lists several public transport inquiry lines that provide details of both national and local bus and train services: See the boxed text 'National Transport Information' on p92.

Bus You can reach Edale circuitously by bus, but the easiest transport for walkers is the train – see below.

At the end of the route there's a bus between Kirk Yetholm and Kelso, where you change for Berwick-upon-Tweed. The last bus from Kirk Yetholm leaves at around 6pm. If you miss it (the last day's walk is long), a taxi to Berwick is around £20.

Train A very regular train service runs between Sheffield and Manchester, stopping at Edale 10 to 15 times a day. Either way it takes around half an hour and costs £4.50. (Make sure you get the stopping service – not the express!)

Near the route's end, Berwick is on the main line between Edinburgh and London.

Car Edale lies north of the A625 between Sheffield and Chapel-en-le-Frith. Pennine Way walkers can leave their car at the Ramblers Inn – where it's guarded by a friendly Rottweiler for £1 per day.

THE WALK
Edale

The pretty village of Edale has two pubs, a post office shop, a handful of B&Bs and a good National Park Information & Visitor Centre (☎ 01433-670207). It's about half a mile north of the train station on the main street and is open daily. Campers can use *Fieldhead Campsite* (☎ 01433-670386), next to the visitors centre, which costs £3.25 with showers another 50p. Also in the village, near the Nag's Head, is *Cooper's Camp* (☎ 01433-670372), charging £2.50. Another option is *Ollerbrook Farm* (☎ 01433-670235), just east of the village, which offers camping for £2 and a bunkhouse for £8. Nearby, *Cotefield Farm* (☎ 01433-670273) offers B&B from £20 and basic camping for £3. There's also a *camping barn* here, which costs £3.50 but must be booked separately through the YHA Camping Barns Reservation Office (☎ 01200-420102, e campbarns yha@enterprise.net). It's the same deal for the *camping barn* at Upper Booth, about 2mi west of Edale – the Pennine Way goes through the yard.

The large and busy *YHA Hostel* (☎ 01433-670302), about 2mi east of the village, costs £10.85. It's very popular with schools and youth groups.

Good walker-friendly B&Bs in Edale village include *The Old Parsonage* (☎ 01433-670232) and *Mam Tor House* (☎ 01433-670253), both from around £15. Also good is *Stonecroft* (☎ 01433-670262), from £23 to £25. *Brookfield* (☎ 01433-670227), in Barber Booth, about a mile west, charges around £17.

The Ramblers Inn (☎ 01433-670268) does B&B for £24, and straightforward bar meals for £5 to £7 at lunchtime and in the evening, although this pub is fairly uninspiring. Edale's other pub is *The Old Nag's Head*, the traditional start of the Pennine Way, but again it has only standard pub food and is disappointing – tacky and often busy, yet impersonal and soulless. Your final option is the cheap and cheerful chips-with-everything *cafe* at the train station, but it closes at 5pm.

Day 1: Edale to Crowden
16mi (25.5km), 6–7 hours

This first day is not too demanding, but it can be tough if you have not limbered up. After the first steep ascent, it's mainly across rolling moors. There's nowhere for lunch so bring supplies.

The Pennine Way starts at the northern end of Edale village, which is called Grindsbrook Booth, opposite The Old Nag's Head pub. From here it aims west out of Edale across fields to Upper Booth. Go up the lane to Lee Farm then follow the track to, and steeply up, the impressive staircase of **Jacob's Ladder**. You are now on Edale Moor, usually called the Kinder plateau (from Kinder Scout, the highest part of the moor), and the trail sticks close to the edge. At **Kinder Downfall**, when the River Kinder is in full flow, an impressive waterfall tumbles down. The trail keeps to the plateau edge before dropping and then climbing to the cairn and post at Mill Hill. Here you turn north-east and strike out over Featherbed Moss – once a Pennine Way horror story through sticky mud, now a doddle along flagstones all the way to the A57 road at Snake Pass.

Cross the road and continue along Devil's Dyke and Hern Clough. The trail then wanders across the frequently bleak area called, appropriately, Bleaklow Hill. Here several waymarks have disappeared and paths lead in all directions, so you'll need a compass. You pass the interesting **Wain Stones** outcrop, then join a little stream called Wildboar Grain.

Towards the end of the day you leave the plateau, descend steeply to Torside Reservoir, cross the dam to the north shore and walk east on a path that avoids the main road to the small settlement of Crowden.

Crowden & Around

For camping, the well-equipped *Crowden Camping & Caravanning Club (CCC) Site* (☎ *01457-866057*) charges £3 to £5, depending on the season. The town *YHA Hostel* (☎ *01457-852135*) charges £8; breakfast and dinner are available to nonresidents,

> ## The Pennine Way – Some Route Highlights
>
> The Pennine Way has many excellent highlight sections, which are ideal if you only want to sample a day or two of the whole trail. The sections through the Yorkshire Dales are very attractive, and at Haworth many walkers divert from the trail to pay homage to the Brontë sisters. There are several good circular walks in the area tying in parts of the Pennine Way. Malham is another major Dales tourist centre, again with numerous circular walk possibilities that go in one direction along the Pennine Way and then loop back on other paths. In the North Pennines, the section along Upper Teesdale, via several waterfalls, is very scenic. For a taste of the Pennine Way where it coincides with Hadrian's Wall and the numerous Roman ruins nearby, base yourself at Once Brewed and do a circular walk (as described in the Hadrian's Wall Walk in the Northumberland chapter.)

which is handy if you're camping and don't want to cook, as the nearest pub is 4mi away in Padfield (more details following).

Crowden has no B&Bs. Your nearest option is in Padfield, a village about 2mi southwest of the Pennine Way, just east of the small town of Hadfield and about 2mi north of the larger town of Glossop. (You can reach Padfield by turning off the Pennine Way before you cross the dam and following the Trans-Pennine Trail). In Padfield, *White House Farm* (☎ *01457-854695*) charges £20/34 for singles/doubles, plus £2 each way for lifts if you book in advance. Nearby, *The Peels Arms* (☎ *01457-852719*) does B&B for £25/40 and bar food. With notice, the people here can also usually pick walkers up from Crowden.

There are more B&B options in the town of Glossop, 2mi beyond Padfield, several of which offer lifts.

Holmefirth

In and around the town of Holmefirth, 8mi north-east of Crowden, are some more places to stay. Some walkers use *Holme Castle Hotel* (☎ *01484-680680*) but it's not a cheap option, charging from £25 for B&B, plus £8 for a lift and £2 for tea and coffee. The walker-friendly *Valley Guesthouse* (☎ *01484-681361*) charges £25/28 for singles/doubles in an en suite or with private bathroom, and also offers lifts for a nominal fee.

Day 2: Crowden to Standedge
11.5mi (18.5km), 5–6 hours
This is a short, pleasant day over the wild moors squeezed between Manchester and Huddersfield. If you're a mile eater, you could extend the day by heading for Mankinholes or Hebden Bridge, described on Day 3.

The trail starts by climbing steeply beside Crowden Brook and emerges on the edge of **Laddow Rocks**, with fine views down to the reservoir. Up on the plateau a 'yellow-brick road' of flagstones winds across the soggy moors to the broad, peaty summit of Black Hill. There's a break in the slabs near the very top of the plateau, but 50m beyond the trig point a line of cairns leads you to the descent path, which is paved once again.

The trail heads north-east before bending north-west and dropping down to Dean Clough. It then climbs back up to cross the A635 at Wessenden Head. A *food van* is sometimes parked nearby.

The next stretch passes several reservoirs, with a picturesque climb up from Wessenden Reservoir along Blakely Clough and across the northern edge of Black Moss moor, then past the Swellands and Black Moss Reservoirs to reach the A62 at Standedge.

Standedge

Globe Farm (☎ 01457-873040), on the main road about half a mile west of where it's crossed by the trail, looks uninspiring but is a welcoming haven for walkers, with en suite B&B for around £20 and camping for £2.50. Evening meals are also available. Nearby, *The Floating Light* pub used to do B&B and bar meals, but it was closed and boarded up when we came through; it might open again in the future.

East of the trail, also on the main road, are some more options. *The Great Western* pub is less than half a mile away and serves a good range of bar meals from £5 to £8 every evening. A little farther east, *The Carriage House* (☎ 01484-844419) is a large pub with friendly owners, lunches and evening meals daily, and free *camping* for walkers out the back, as long as you eat and drink in the pub.

Your next nearest option for accommodation is *Forest Farm* (☎ 01484-842687), about 1.5mi north-east of the trail towards Marsden (you can walk here by turning off the Pennine Way before the A62 and following the Standedge Trail), where you'll get a good welcome and B&B for £18/32, a bunkhouse for £8.50 and very simple camping for £2. Evening meals can be ordered in advance, or you can walk the mile up to The Carriage House or a mile down into Marsden, which has a few more *pubs* as well as a fish and chip *takeaway*, but don't forget the mile back, which seems much longer after a day's walking!

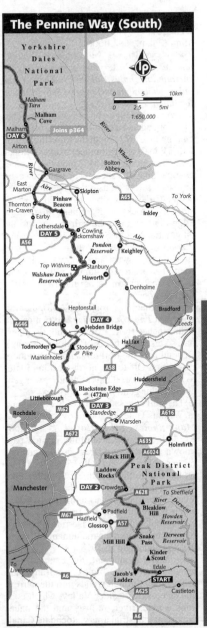

NORTHERN ENGLAND LONG-DISTANCE PATHS

Day 3: Standedge to Hebden Bridge

15mi (24km), 6–7 hours

Today's walk takes you over several moors and past many reservoirs, which supply the surrounding industrial cities. There's one pub or you might prefer to be self-sufficient for lunch.

From Standedge you cross some patches of moorland and a couple of main roads – including the A672 – with the towering Windy Hill TV mast as a prominent marker. Hidden away in a cutting, the M62 motorway comes as something of a shock. The trail, however, crosses it safely on its own, elegant bridge.

Then it's up Redmires, tamed by flagstones, to rocky and dramatic **Blackstone Edge** (472m). From here drop down to the enigmatic Aiggin Stone, an ancient route marker where the trail turns 90 degrees from north to west and follows a 'Roman road' for a short distance, although this road's real origin is as uncertain as the marker stone's.

At another main road (the A58), the trail goes past *The White House Inn* (a nice pub with lunches from £5 but without a hikers bar, so take your boots off before entering). Beyond here the trail turns north past more reservoirs. Off to the north-west, and later to the north-east, stands of wind-power generators whir gently on the horizon.

The trail edges around Coldwell Hill and at Withins Gate, if you're overnighting at *Mankinholes YHA Hostel* (☎ 01706-812340), take the beautifully crafted path known as the 'Long Drag', a 19th-century famine relief project. Otherwise, continue on the trail to the prominent **Stoodley Pike Monument**, built during the Napoleonic Wars. Construction was temporarily halted when Napoleon escaped from Elba and it was completed in 1815. Despite its monolithic construction, the monument collapsed in 1854 and again in 1918.

From the monument, the Pennine Way wanders across the high ground and then drops down through woods into the narrow and steep-sided Calder Valley, which contains a road, river, railway and the once-important industrial artery, **Rochdale Canal**, as well as the towns of Todmorden and Hebden Bridge.

The trail crosses the canal (past a noticeboard with local information) and the river to meet the main road (the A646). If you're continuing north, go right and then left, up a lane called Underbank Ave. Alternatively, if you're heading into Hebden Bridge, it's about 1.5mi to your east. You can get there along the canal towpath – it's a bit industrial but has several interesting locks, wharfs and boats, and is much nicer than walking along the road.

Hebden Bridge

For some reason Hebden Bridge is frequently overlooked, but it's a surprisingly attractive, slightly 'trendified' town with lots of pubs, B&Bs and hotels, some interesting little shops, a TIC (☎ 01422-843831) on a major street junction called Bridge Gate in the centre of town, and an **alternative technology centre** beside the canal. It's definitely worth arriving early enough to wander around.

As you go towards town from where the Pennine Way meets the road and canal, after about half a mile you pass *The Stubbing Wharf* pub; it's pleasantly relaxed with good food, good beer and sometimes live music. Nearby is Savile Rd, where *Prospect End* (☎ 01422-843586) offers walker-friendly B&B in en suite rooms for £20/£37 per single/double.

It's another 15-minute walk along the towpath into town (leave the canal at Blackpit Lock No 9, which brings you out by a crossroads and the TIC). Just north of the centre, *Myrtle Grove* (☎ 01422-846078), on Old Lees Rd, charges £20 for B&B.

Places to eat include *The White Swan*, a busy no-frills pub serving bar food, while just up the road *The White Lion* is quieter and also does food. There are several *takeaways* selling fish and chips, Chinese and Indian (also a restaurant). *Crown Fisheries* does a filling Yorkshire 'fish supper' (fish, chips, bread and butter, and a pot of tea). More upmarket are *Il Mulino Italian Restaurant* with meals from around £5 to £10, and *Kittie's Restaurant* (☎ 01422-842956) with interesting main courses for around £10 to £13.

A half-mile walk uphill from Hebden Bridge is the delightful village of Heptonstall, with cobbled streets and several good pubs, and a couple of B&B options. There are also places to stay in and around Colden, 2mi farther along the Pennine Way – see Day 4 for details

Day 4: Hebden Bridge to Lothersdale
19mi (30.5km), 8–10 hours
Today's long walk leads across wild and empty northern moors, leaving the industrial cities behind. Today also has a bookish theme as you pass Wuthering Heights and the setting of a popular British children's book, The Railway Children. Pubs for lunch come too early or too late, so bring something to eat.

From Hebden Bridge walk back to the point where the Pennine Way crosses the A646 and go up Underbank Ave, beneath the railway bridge and up a steep switchback to cross a lane east of the village of Blackshaw Head. Just on the other side of the lane is *Badgerfield Farm* (☎ 01422-845161), a very friendly place with B&B for £20 and free camping, although a small charge is made for showers. Campers can order breakfast and guests can get a lift to the nearby pub for a nominal fee.

The trail continues, crossing another lane near the hamlet of Colden. East of here, *Poppyfields House* (☎ 01422-843636) does B&B from £18.

Between Backshaw Head and Colden is a friendly pub called *The New Delight*, which serves meals every evening and offers camping in the garden for £3. A little farther along the trail, *High Gate Farm* has very simple but free camping for Pennine Way walkers, and a good *shop* for supplies.

Beyond Colden the trail heads north-west across a stretch of moor, until a sharp right (north) turn takes you down past a reservoir channel and steeply down to a stream called Graining Water, then back up the other side and along a road for a short distance. The trail leaves the road and after about 1mi

passes between two Walshaw Dean Reservoirs before heading north-east across moors, again by easy paths or flagstone walkways, to the ruins of **Top Withins** – also called Withens. You are now in 'Brontëland', for this tumbledown building is thought to have inspired descriptions of the Earnshaw house in *Wuthering Heights* (see the boxed text 'The Brontës of Howarth') – although the claim is tenuous. Regardless, it makes a place to aim for. If the weather is fine you can have your lunch on the bench outside. If the weather's really bad, you can shelter in the grimy outhouse.

The trail continues north-east on a wide track and, about 200m after a farm called Upper Heights (another inspiration?), the Pennine Way turns left (north). If you want to follow the literary theme, keep on the track (north-east) to **Haworth**, 2.5mi off the trail. This was the home of the Brontës and is also a stop on the Keighley & Worth Valley Railway, where steam trains pull in big

The Brontës of Haworth

The three Brontë sisters lived in Haworth in the 19th century – daughters of the town parson – and remain major figures in English literature. Emily Brontë's best-known novel is *Wuthering Heights*. Published in 1847, it's an epic tale of obsession, revenge and passion; much of the action takes place at the remote farmhouse supposedly inspired by Top Withins, passed on today's walk. Charlotte Brontë's most famous book, *Jane Eyre*, revolves around the central character's dilemmas over a choice of husband and, by using techniques of melodrama and exaggeration, explores the themes of emotion, love, and – again – passion, and is a celebration of the independent female spirit. Anne Brontë wrote *The Tenant of Wildfell Hall*, yet another novel of melodrama, mystery and love. In all of these novels, the landscape surrounding Haworth had a great influence, and throughout the Brontë sisters' work the austere Yorkshire moors have a presence as strong as any of the leading characters.

crowds. As a popular tourist centre Haworth has many accommodation options. The numerous signposts on this stretch are in Japanese as well as English – the Brontës are big in Japan!

If you want to break your journey before Lothersdale, there are two good places to stay near the trail. East of the route, between Ponden Reservoir and the village of Stanbury, *The Old Silent Inn* (☎ 01535-647437, e enquiries@old-silent-inn.com) oozes history with log fires, low beams and comfortable B&B from £28 in en suite rooms. There's also good beer, lunches and excellent evening meals from £4 to £12. The owner is a keen walker and especially welcomes people doing the Pennine Way. A little farther along the trail, at Ponden Reservoir, *Ponden Guesthouse* (☎ 01535-644154) has B&B from £18 and basic camping for £2. Snacks and hot drinks are sometimes available for passing walkers (look for the sign).

If you're pushing on, at the west end of the Ponden Reservoir the trail turns north, climbs up past some houses to meet and briefly follow a road, then heads confidently north-west across a wide expanse of moorland, eventually dropping down to a busy main road between the villages of Ickornshaw and Cowling. Near where the trail crosses the road, *Winter House Farm* (☎ 01535-632234) does B&B for £17.50 and camping for £2. The nearby *Black Bull Inn* in Ickornshaw does bar food, while Cowling offers a smart *restaurant*, several more *pubs*, and *fish and chips*.

The trail goes through Ickornshaw and follows a mix of country lanes and field paths for another 2mi, down into the picturesque little mill town of Lothersdale.

Lothersdale

On the main street that runs through Lothersdale is the friendly and good-value *Old Granary Cottage* (☎ 01535-636075) with B&B from £16 or £25 with dinner. Nearby, *Burlington House* (☎ 01535-634635) charges £15 and, right next door, *The Hare & Hounds* serves fine food and beer. Just along from the pub is *Lynmouth*

(☎ 01535-632744) with B&B from £16 and camping.

Day 5: Lothersdale to Malham
15mi (24km), 7–8 hours
On today's green and pleasant walk, you enter the Yorkshire Dales National Park, heralding a change in scenery and an increase in good lunch opportunities.

From Lothersdale, the trail runs across open and surprisingly high moors over the hill of Pinhaw Beacon, before dropping across fields. Aim for Brown House Farm and look for the stile on the left, just as you approach the farmyard itself, and follow a track for the rest of the way to Thornton-in-Craven on the busy A56. A mile south is *Earby YHA Hostel* (☎ 01282-842349).

From Thornton-in-Craven you cross fields again before emerging on the **Leeds & Liverpool Canal** towpath. At **East Marton** an unusual double-arch bridge crosses the canal and the *Cross Keys* pub offers refreshment. Alternatively you can continue along the canal to the very pleasant little **Abbot's Harbor** restaurant and cafe. The trail then leaves the canal and heads through a small wood and fields to Scaleber Hill, with the church in Gargrave a useful target ahead.

If you're breaking your journey in **Gargrave**, walker-friendly B&Bs are *2 Westfield Gardens* (☎ 01756-748084), from £17; and, on the way out of the village, *Old Hall Cottage* (☎ 01756-749412), for around £20. For food try *The Mason's Arms*, opposite the church, or *The Old Swan Inn*, on the main street, which serves good bar food for £6 to £7. There's also the *Dalesman Café* and a *takeaway* selling fish and chips.

Leave Gargrave northwards, cross the canal again and go straight on up Mark House Lane, before turning off across fields, dropping gently to a bridge over the River Aire.

The trail follows the river for the next 4mi, a very pretty and gentle stroll. At the village of Airton, *Lindon Guesthouse* (☎ 01729-830418) is highly recommended, with B&B for £21 and dinner for £12. There's also the simple *Quaker Hostel* (☎ 01729-830263) for £5, which is self-catering (you need your own sleeping bag).

Leave the river by Hanlith Hall and Badger House (look for the weather vane), go up a lane, then turn off across fields, above the river, before dropping down into Malham.

Malham

This busy village has lots of places to stay and eat. The TIC (☎ 01729-830363), in the large car park on the southern edge of the village, is open daily from Easter to October. Shops include the *Cove Centre*, which sells walking equipment and has a cafe. In the village centre, the *YHA Hostel* (☎ *01729-830321)* charges £10.85. Nearby, as you enter the village on the trail, *Miresfield Farm* (☎ *01729-830414*, @ *chris@miresfield .freeserve.co.uk)* offers B&B in en suite rooms for £24 and camping for £3.50. On the other side of the village, on Cove Rd, the well-equipped *Hill Top Farm Bunkhouse* (☎ *01729-830320)* charges £7. Opposite, you can camp at *Town Head Farm*.

B&B options include *Malham Café & B&B* (☎ *01729-830348)*, near the hostel, charging £42 for en suite doubles; the central *Eastwood House* (☎ *01729-830409)*, charging £18; *Town End Cottage* (☎ *01729-830487)*, also central, charging £17; *Dale House* (☎ 01729-830664, @ *dalehouse@ma lhamdale.com)*, on Cove Rd, charging £20 or £25 for an en suite; and *Beck Hall* (☎ *01729-830332)*, just off Cove Rd by the river, charging £17 or £24 for an en suite.

For a little taste of luxury, *The Buck Inn* (☎ *01729-830317)* has singles/doubles for £33/57, a lounge bar with standard pub food and a fancy dining room with pricier meals. If you want to keep your boots on, there's a stone-floored hikers bar too.

Old Barn Café does snacks and lunches, and sandwiches to take away. *The Listers Arms* does interesting bar food for around £6, plus good meals in the restaurant for £9.

Day 6: Malham to Horton in Ribblesdale

14mi (22.5km), 7 hours
Today's enjoyable walk winds through the heart of the Yorkshire Dales, finishing with Pen-y-ghent, a famous landmark. You pass no cafes or pubs, so bring your lunch.

Leaving Malham the trail climbs steeply up the west side of the curved amphitheatre of cliffs that make up **Malham Cove**, then edges right across the top of the cliffs – a textbook stretch of limestone pavement with wonderful views back down to Malham.

At the east end of the pavement, go sharp left and head for Malham Tarn – a real, honest-to-God lake after so many artificial reservoirs! The trail edges round the east side of the tarn before heading into woods past Malham Tarn House, now a field studies centre, and turns north just before some houses. For 1mi the trail crosses fields, then turns east to cross a road by the prominently signposted Tennant Gill Farm.

Leaving green fields for darker moor, the trail climbs up to Fountains Fell (668m) over a series of ridges, each hinting that maybe it's the top, and past a scattering of disused mineshafts to a bleak stone-walled summit called In Sleets – maybe a reference to the weather! As you drop steadily downhill to meet a lane called Silverdale Rd, you can look across at what you'll shortly have to climb on the other side, the long hump of **Pen-y-ghent**. The trail almost circles the hill before moving in, marching alongside it for about a mile, as if to give walkers plenty of time to contemplate the ascent, before turning west past Dale Head Farm, then north across to the base of Pen-y-ghent. After all this foreplay the peak turns out to be a bit of a disappointment. A couple of short, sharp efforts and you're on top, crossing a wall at the summit (694m). The views are splendid, though – look to the northwest for the nearby hills of Whernside (736m), and Ingleborough (724m) to the west, which with Pen-y-ghent make up the famous 'Three Peaks'.

Drop swiftly down the other side, along a winding but extremely clear path, and in less than an hour you're in the busy little village of Horton in Ribblesdale.

Horton in Ribblesdale

The village is on a major railway line, so it's a good place to join or leave the Pennine Way

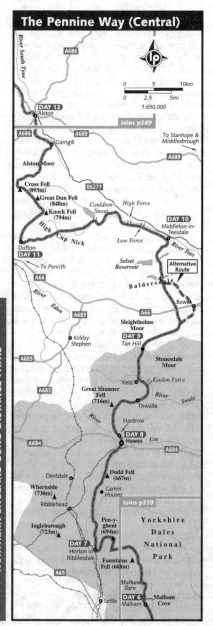

The Pennine Way (Central)

River South Tyne

A686

0   5   10km
0   2.5   5mi
1:650,000

DAY 12 Alston

Joins p369

A686   A689
Garrigill

To Stanhope & Middlesbrough

A689

Alston Moor

Cross Fell (893m)
Great Dun Fell (848m)
Knock Fell (794m)

Couldron Snout   High Force

DAY 10 Middleton-in-Teesdale

Low Force   River Tees

Dufton
DAY 11

High Cup Nick

To Penrith

Selset Reservoir   **Alternative Route**

A66

River Eden   Baldersdale

Bowes

A685   A66

Sleightholme Moor
DAY 9   Tan Hill

Kirkby Stephen

A685

Stonesdale Moor

A683   Keld   Kisdon Force

Great Shunner Fell (716m)   River Swale

River   Thwaite

Hardrow

DAY 8 Hawes   Ure

A684   A684

Dentdale   Dodd Fell (667m)

Whernside (736m)   Camm Houses

Ribblehead   **Joins p359**

Ingleborough (723m)   Pen-y-ghent (694m)   Yorkshire Dales National Park

DAY 7 Horton in Ribblesdale

A65   Fountains Fell (668m)

Malham Tarn

DAY 6 Malham   Malham Cove

Settle

---

if you're doing the walk in sections. There's also a good range of accommodation, plus a village *shop* and post office. The local TIC is in the ***Pen-y-ghent Cafe*** (☎ *01729-860333*), one of the Pennine Way's most popular refuelling points. For details on places to stay and eat, see the Three Peaks walk in the Yorkshire Dales chapter.

Day 7: Horton in Ribblesdale to Hawes
14mi (22.5km), 6 hours
This is another wonderfully wild Dales day, through country riddled with limestone caves – a mecca for potholers. Once again there's nowhere to get food, so bring supplies.

The trail departs Horton in Ribblesdale through the yard of the New Inn, at the north end of the village, and follows a drove road that climbs up onto Birkwith Moor. Three miles north of Horton the trail turns sharply to the west and, shortly afterwards, back north again, passing Old Ing Farm. As it's hidden behind a stone wall, you could easily miss the attractive stream tumbling into the mouth of **Calf Holes cave**. Only another quarter of a mile along the trail, a short excursion past the barn to the left of the road will bring you to Browngill Cave, from where the stream emerges. Potholers revel

The Pen-y-ghent Cafe & the Three Peaks

The Pen-y-ghent Cafe is a classic feature of the Pennine Way. Walkers stop here to swap Pennine Way stories, enjoy a meal, perhaps buy new socks and the next map, and to sign the Pennine Way log book, which goes back to 1966.

The cafe is also the start and finish point for a piece of local masochism – the Three Peaks walk. All you have to do is go out the front door of the cafe, pop up to the top of Pen-y-ghent, and the 'neighbouring' hills of Whernside and Ingleborough (a total distance of around 26mi), and walk back in again within 12 hours. For full details, see the Three Peaks walk in the Yorkshire Dales chapter.

in this watery underground route, but Way walkers may feel wet enough already.

Your next feature is pretty little **Ling Gill Gorge**. You cannot enter this steep-sided valley, but the riverbank makes a pleasant picnic spot and there's an interesting old bridge at the head of the gorge. The trail then climbs up to the Roman road route of Cam High Road, and starts a lonely trudge north-east, coinciding for a spell with the Dales Way, before turning north to edge around Dodd Fell. At the settlement of Cam Houses, down in the valley to the south, *Camm Houses* is a possible B&B stop – see the Dales Way in the Yorkshire Dales chapter for details.

The trail follows the northern shoulder of Dodd Fell, and overlooks a wide, deep valley, which is popular with paragliders, before finally dropping down through fields and farms, following Gaudy Lane and a circuitous route through the village of Gayle to reach the town of Hawes.

Hawes

The surprisingly bustling little town of Hawes has a wide variety of shops, a supermarket, banks with ATMs, outdoor gear shops, half a dozen pubs, even more cafes, a couple of smart restaurants and some basic fish and chip takeaways. There's also a wide choice of B&Bs and hotels, plus a Wensleydale cheese factory starring Wallace and Grommet. The TIC (☎ 01969-667450) is in the fascinating **Dales Countryside Museum** at the old train station just off the main street on the north-east side of town. Nearby, *The Old Station House* (☎ *01969-667785*) does B&B in singles/doubles for £30/42. In the centre, *Laburnum House* (☎ *01969-667717*) charges £20 for B&B, and offers snacks and meals in the busy *tearoom* downstairs.

The *YHA Hostel* (☎ *01969-667368*), on the west side of town, charges £9.80. Nearby is *Steppe Haugh* (☎ *01969-667645*), charging from £18 for B&B.

There are plenty of pubs ready to feed hungry walkers, including *The Fountain* (☎ *01969-667206*) with bar food for around £5 and B&B from £30; and *The White Hart* (☎ *01969-667259*) with meals around £6 and walker-friendly B&B from £18. The real

surprise is *The Bulls Head*, which is not a pub anymore but a stylish restaurant offering some of the most interesting dishes you'll find along the Pennine Way.

Campers can aim for the well-organised *Bainbridge Ings Caravan & Camping Site* (☎ *01969-667354*), on the eastern side of town, which charges from £2.

Day 8: Hawes to Tan Hill

16mi (25.5km), 7 hours
Today's route takes you over more lonely high ground, through the quieter northern reaches of the Dales. If you're tired of sandwiches, there are a couple of lunch options.

From Hawes it's only a mile to the village of Hardraw, where the rather uninspiring *Green Dragon Inn* (☎ *01969-667392*) does B&B for around £24 and allows camping. You can divert to see **Hardraw Force**, the highest waterfall in England (but you have to go through the pub to reach it and pay 80p).

From Hardraw the trail abandons green fields for moorland, often following stone-slabbed paths up to the famous peak and viewpoint of **Great Shunner Fell** (716m). From the summit the trail drops down, through moorland and fields, to the small village of Thwaite where the *Kearton Teashop & Country Hotel* (☎ *01748-886277*) makes an excellent lunch break and offers B&B from £24 for an en suite or £31 with dinner.

From Thwaite the path climbs high above the **River Swale** with wonderful views across this beautiful section of the upper valley, and then drops to cross the river on a wooden footbridge, briefly coinciding with the Coast to Coast Walk. Grassy riverbanks overlooking small waterfalls make this an ideal picnic spot. Nearby Keld has a *teashop* and several good B&Bs, which you may need to use if today's objective, the Tan Hill Inn, is full. (See Keld at the end of Day 6 in the Coast to Coast Walk earlier in this chapter.)

From Keld you say farewell to Swaledale as the trail climbs back onto the moor, with a possible short diversion to **Kisdon Force** waterfall. Then, although the road is never far to the west, the next 4mi can be a lonely trudge across the moors (take care in mist, there are numerous, unfenced mineshafts nearby) to Tan Hill.

Tan Hill

At 528m the highest pub in England, the justifiably famous *Tan Hill Inn* (☎ *01833-628246)* is your reward for persevering on today's long walk. It has good beer, a roaring fire, a wide choice of food (soups, sandwiches and bar meals for around £5), plus B&B at £32/50 for singles/doubles or simple, windswept camping for £1. There's no other place to stay anywhere nearby, so phone ahead.

Day 9: Tan Hill to Middleton-in-Teesdale

17mi (27.5km), 7 hours

Today is another long walk as the trail enters the North Pennines, an Area of Outstanding Natural Beauty. The next few days of wild, high fells – eerie and empty under big skies – epitomise the very essence of the Pennine Way. As befitting wilderness, there are, of course, no places to buy lunch, so it's back to the sandwiches.

From lonely Tan Hill the trail slouches across equally lonely Sleightholme Moor for 5mi. If the weather is dry the walk along the stream can be quite pleasant. In the wet it can be a dishearteningly muddy experience; following the lane and rejoining the trail later may be preferable. As you leave the moor the trail divides. Going right (north-east) is a longer option into the attractive old market town of **Bowes** – an overnight possibility with a *pub*, *B&B* and *shop*. Going left (north) is considered to be the main route and it crosses the River Greta on a natural stone slab called **God's Bridge**, before a short detour leads to a tunnel under the busy A66. Less than a mile to the west, wildlife fans may want to visit the **Otter Trust Reserve** (☎ 01833-628339), where otters, deer and other animals can be seen.

North of the road you return to bleak moorland. After 3mi or so, the path from Bowes rejoins the main route at **Baldersdale** – a valley full of reservoirs – marking the halfway point of the Pennine Way. Nearby is *Baldersdale YHA Hostel* (☎ 01833-650629),

which charges £9 and has camping for £4.50; plus *Clove Lodge* (☎ *01833-650030,* 🖃 *ann@heys70.freeserve.co.uk),* offering B&B for £20 and with a warm bunkbarn for £5. You can hire a sleeping bag (£1.50) and get breakfast for £3 to £4.50 or a three-course home-cooked dinner for £9.

Beyond here the trail climbs up, then drops down to more reservoirs, before climbing again and meandering through a maze of fields into Middleton-in-Teesdale.

Middleton-in-Teesdale

The River Tees flows past this handsome little grey-stone town. There are shops, a supermarket, pubs and B&Bs. Campers can head for *Daleview Caravan Park* (☎ *01833-640233),* passed as the trail comes into town, for £3. In the town centre B&Bs include *Bluebell House* (☎ *01833-640584),* on the marketplace, which is very friendly and welcoming, and excellent value at £17. Across the road, *Brunswick House* (☎ *01833-640393)* charges £22 to £30. Nearby, the *Marketplace Guesthouse* (☎ *01833-640300)* charges from £17.

For real luxury you might want to look at the *Teesdale Hotel* (☎ *01833-640264)* with single/double rooms for £38.50/60.50, although discounts are often available. It also has a fancy restaurant, a cheaper tapas bar and good pub food (from £5 and up to £12 for specials). Also in town, *The Kings Head* bistro has very good-value food and wine.

Day 10: Middleton-in-Teesdale to Dufton

20mi (32km), 8 hours

Today's long but varied walk is one of the most interesting on the trail, through classic North Pennine landscape and past a couple of impressive waterfalls.

For the first 8mi the trail runs along beautiful Teesdale, following the peaty amber waters of the River Tees, past **Low Force** waterfall, and then the larger and more impressive **High Force**, where a short detour could be made to the *High Force Hotel* if an early lunch is needed.

Beyond the waterfalls the trail briefly abandons the Tees to pass close to Langdon

Beck, with a *pub* and *YHA Hostel* (☎ 01833-622228), but soon returns to the north bank and follows a beautiful stretch of rocky valley (although the rocky path can be dangerously slippery if wet) to reach **Cauldron Snout** waterfall – an impressive sight spoilt only slightly by the large, concrete dam upstream. You cross the Tees here and say goodbye to it, aiming south-west (yes, south-west on this northbound path) across wild, empty moors for several miles. The trail is bordered by signs warning of an adjacent army artillery range, then for a couple more miles it follows the sparkling waters of Maize Beck. The route crosses the beck soon after meeting it but, if the water is running high, there is a detour that continues along the right-hand side of the beck and leads you to a bridge. However, this is a long way round and very boggy, so you might just prefer to get your feet wet crossing the beck at the proper place.

All thoughts of damp socks are forgotten as, with a shock, you arrive at **High Cup Nick**, a stunning valley cut deep into the high country with a steep drop shelving down, down, down to a silvery stream in the distance. This would be a breathtaking view from any angle, but the sudden arrival makes it even more superb.

From here it's just a few more miles downhill (remembering all the time that all this downhill will be paid for tomorrow) into the bright and sturdy little village of Dufton.

Dufton

The Dufton *YHA Hostel* (☎ 01768-351236) charges £9 and there's camping at *Brow Top Farm* for £2. On the main street of the village, the *Ghyll View* (☎ 01768-351855) charges £17 for B&B, while *Dufton Hall Farm* (☎ 01768-351573) does B&B from £18 and camping for £2.50. Also on the main street, *The Stag Inn* (☎ 017683-51608) is a classic old pub with a warm and friendly welcome for walkers. It has B&B for £20 and very good bar food from £5 to £7 (with king-size desserts). *The Village Stores* is very well stocked and also has hot drinks and snacks.

Day 11: Dufton to Alston
20mi (32km), 8 hours

Today's route over remote Cross Fell is one of the most serious sections encountered so far – weather conditions can be notoriously bad. Garrigal, the only place for supplies, is reached quite late, so make sure you've got enough to survive the day.

The trail wanders out of Dufton along farm lanes and then starts to climb, first to Knock Fell (794m) and then to Great Dun Fell (848m), with its air traffic control radar station (including a giant golf ball) visible from far away. The trail drops, then climbs, often along stone-slabbed pathways, to Little Dun Fell and finally **Cross Fell** (893m), the highest point along the entire Pennine Way. An 18th-century article commented that Cross Fell was covered in snow for 10 months of the year and cloud for 11. You may think things are much the same now! You may strike a good day, however, and be able to rest happily on the Pennine Way's summit, under a clear North Pennine sky, with almost two-thirds of the trail done and some fabulous sections still to enjoy.

A series of tall and wobbly-looking cairns leads across this bleak summit before the trail drops down to the Corpse Road (this was once a lead-mining area and the bodies of dead miners were carried along the track) and then to *Greg's Hut*, a mountain refuge that could be useful in one of those sudden, midsummer snowfalls.

From here it's six weary miles across the moors along a rough track, which is easy to follow but uncomfortably covered in awkward, sharp stones. Reaching Garrigill is a considerable relief. *The George & Dragon* pub may detain you, and this village also has several B&Bs, a camping barn and a small *shop*, but it's less than 4mi along a pleasant path beside the River South Tyne to Alston.

Alston

This little town (handsome rather than pretty) has many places to stay, plus a selection of pubs, shops, banks (with ATMs) and a TIC (☎ 01434-381696) in the town centre. The modern *YHA Hostel* (☎ 01434-381509), on the outskirts of town, charges £9. Campers can head for **Tyne Willows Caravan Site** (☎ 01434-381318), which charges £3 and has drying facilities.

Walker-friendly B&Bs include **Blueberry Teashop & Guesthouse** (☎ 01434-381928), on the marketplace in the town centre, charging from £16. A few steps farther up the road is **The Victoria Inn** (☎ 01434-381194) with B&B for £14.50 (£18 en suite); it also does bar food.

Other good places include **Nentholme** (☎ 01434-381523) at the Butts, just out of the town centre, charging from £15 to £20; **Albert House** (☎ 01434-381793), charging from £20 to £30, including a three-course dinner; and **Highfield** (☎ 01434-382182), at Bruntley Meadows just outside the town centre, charging from £15 and offering remedial massage for weary walkers.

In the town centre, pub food is available at the cosy **Angel Inn** and the pleasant **Turks Head**, among others. For a change of diet, consider Chinese at nearby **Ho's House**.

Day 12: Alston to Greenhead
18mi (29km), 7 hours
This is another transition day, mostly along the scenic South Tyne Valley as you approach Northumberland. Roman remains remind you that Hadrian's Wall is nearby.

Leaving Alston the trail makes a pleasant start with a long stretch through green farmland, passing the distinct embankments of a Roman fort. These are soon followed by reminders of a more recent era as the trail keeps close to an abandoned railway line that once transported lead ore from the area's mines. A number of spectacular viaducts remain from this time – imposing examples of Victorian engineering.

About 5mi from Alston, the village of Slaggyford has a *campsite* and some B&Bs. Another 2mi farther north in the village of Knarsdale you'll find the pleasant **Kirkstyle Inn** (☎ 01434-381559), offering reasonable lunches and B&B. Here the Pennine Way follows the route of an old Roman road before embarking on a series of field crossings and a brief section of moorland. Late in the day the walk becomes a bit tedious as it wanders under electricity pylons, over the A69, around a golf course and along an almost imperceptible section of the Hadrian's Wall defence line, before finally reaching the small settlement of Greenhead.

Greenhead
The **YHA Hostel**, the **Greenhead Hotel** and the **Olde Forge Tearoom** are all central, and there are more choices in nearby Gilsland and Haltwhistle. For details on all these places, see the Hadrian's Wall Walk in the Northumberland chapter, which also gives more information on the wall itself. If you're staying at **Greenholm Guesthouse**, don't go into Greenhead; stay on the Pennine Way, over the railway line and a river, and the trail goes through the guesthouse yard.

Day 13: Greenhead to Once Brewed
7mi (11.5km), 3 hours
Today's short walk follows a rollercoaster route along Hadrian's Wall. There's plenty to see, including a museum and the remains of a large fort. If you visit the sites there are tearooms, so you won't need to bring along sandwiches today.

From Greenhead you regain the trail at the ruins of **Thirlwall Castle**. Constructed with blocks purloined from Hadrian's Wall, the 700-year-old castle is a stark reminder of how this border region remained perilously unstable for 1000 years after the Roman departure. Beyond here the paths are confusing and inadequately signposted, but a stiff uphill bit alongside the wall brings you to the site of Carvoran Fort, where the **Roman Army Museum** is well worth a visit.

The Pennine Way keeps following the route of Hadrian's Wall, through Walltown Quarry – now a nature reserve and sculpture park – and then along an excellent section of wall, built high on cliffs with great views to the north. You pass Aesica or **Great Chesters**, a Roman fort now overlapped by a farm building, then reach Cawfields, a picnic site and car park (maybe with an *icecream van*). From here the Cawfield Crags and Winshields Crags sections comprise one of the best-preserved and most impressive stretches of the wall, and you can stride out centurion-style.

Near Steel Rigg a lane crosses the line of the wall. Turn right (south) to reach the settlement of Once Brewed.

Once Brewed

At Once Brewed there's an excellent TIC (☎ 01434-344777) with very friendly staff. Nearby is a *YHA Hostel* and several B&Bs. For details, see the Hadrian's Wall walk in the Northumberland chapter – which also describes a circular walk to the Roman remains at Housesteads and Vindolanda. If you have plenty of time, you could park your pack at Once Brewed and do this walk, or at least part of it.

Day 14: Once Brewed to Bellingham
15.5mi (25km), 7 hours

Today's route enters Northumberland National Park and the wilds of Wark Forest. In midge season (June to August), this is where they start to be a nuisance.

From Once Brewed regain the trail and head east along some more well-preserved and impressive sections of the wall's ridgetop route. You pass high above Crag Lough – a small lake acting as a natural moat – and shortly afterwards turn left (north), leaving the protection of the wall and entering the former land of the barbarians. **Housesteads Fort** is less than a mile farther east and warrants a visit if you did not make it yesterday.

The trail drops down from the Wall, crosses some marshy country between two larger loughs and enters the southern portion of the giant Wark Forest conifer plantation, before finally emerging to cross farmland, dropping down to Warks Burn and climbing up to Horneystead Farm.

Another mile brings the trail to **Lowstead**, a fine example of a fortified 16th-century building called a 'bastle-house' and a reminder of that unsettled era when families had to be prepared for outlaw onslaughts. The trail goes right through the yard, emerging onto a lane.

From here your route alternates between path, track and lane, passing *Shitlington*

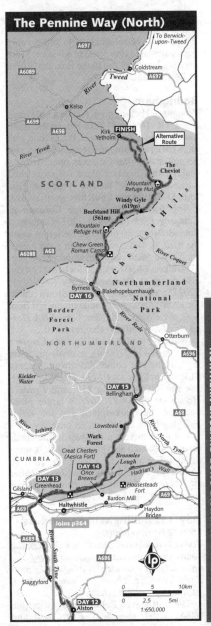

The Pennine Way (North)

Crag Farm Bunkhouse (☎ 01434 230330), which charges around £6.50, with breakfast (home-made bread and honey) and evening meals available if ordered in advance. From here it's less than 3mi to the final day's goal of Bellingham.

Bellingham

Pronounced belling-jum, this neat little town has a TIC (☎ 01434-220616), in the small town hall on the main street, banks (one with an ATM), two pubs, an excellent bakery and several shops (the Co-op is open daily) – making this the last place for more than basic supplies until the end of the trail. Historic **St Cuthbert's Church** is worth a visit.

The friendly **Brown Rigg Caravan & Camping Park** (☎ 01434-220175), about a mile south of town on the trail as it runs along the road, is well equipped with good toilets, showers, a small shop and laundrette, charging walkers £4.50 (or £7.50 for two). You can also camp at **Demesne Farm** (☎ 01434-220258), a simple site nearer the town centre, for £2.50. About half a mile up the hill from here, the elderly and rather basic **YHA Hostel** (☎ 01434-220313) charges £8.10.

Walker-friendly B&Bs include **Crofters End** (☎ 01434-220034), a small place on the trail as you come into town, charging £15; **Lynn View** (☎ 01434-220344), opposite the TIC, charging £17; and **Lyndale House** (☎ 01434-220361), a larger place between the marketplace and the river, charging from £22 for an en suite.

For food there's a **teashop** in the small town hall (which also houses the TIC), open to 5pm. For an evening meal **The Rose & Crown** is reasonable, but **The Cheviot Hotel** (☎ 01434-220696) is much better, with bar food from £5 and B&B for £25.

Day 15: Bellingham to Byrness
15mi (24km), 6 hours

Today is a relatively easy walk through the contrasting moorland and forest of the national park – an ideal rest before the final day's long slog. There's no place for food, so stock up in Bellingham.

The trail leaves Bellingham passing the YHA hostel, then leaves the road and crosses a wonderfully lonely sweep of heather moor for about 5mi before dropping down to the start of a forest plantation. Sheltered by a wall, the trail climbs steeply, and muddily, up the edge of the plantation before levelling out and marching resolutely along with forest to the left, moor to the right. A succession of marker stones along the fence line bear the letters 'GH'. Gabriel Harding was the High Sheriff of Northumberland and these reminders of the extent of his lands have stood on this remote moor for nearly 300 years.

The trail dives into the forest and most of the remaining miles are through fir plantations. You leave the trees near the tiny settlement of Blakehopeburnhaugh, where you can go through a gate and across the burn to **Border Forest Caravan Park** (☎ 01830-520259), where the friendly owners charge walkers £3.30 for camping. They also offer a self-catering bunkhouse for £7 and comfy, motel-style B&B at a rate of £20/36 for a single/double.

From here it's a mile along the valley to Byrness, where the trail crosses a footbridge and brings you to the busy A68 next to a little church.

Byrness
The small and scattered settlement of Byrness straddles the A68. Turn left (west) to reach the **YHA Hostel** (☎ 01830-520425; for bookings over a week in advance ☎ 01629-581399), which charges £7.35. If you turn right and walk along the main road for

Blakehopeburnhaugh

Blakehopeburnhaugh is the place with the longest name along the Pennine Way. Although at first appearing unpronounceable, things get easier if broken down into four components. In the Wainwright guide, the old sage usefully explains that Blake might be a personal name, Hope means 'sheltered valley', a Burn is a stream, and Haugh means 'flat land beside a river'. Despite these explanations most walkers say 'near Byrness'.

100m, you'll reach Border Park Services petrol station, which has a *cafe* and small shop open 8am to 6pm daily in winter (later in summer). Opposite, *The Byrness Hotel* (☎ 01830-520231) is slightly run down but very friendly, with B&B for £20 (£25 en suite), decent food and free *camping* (a shower in a hotel room costs £2). Campers can also order a full breakfast for £5. Nearby, *The Old Rectory* (☎ 01830-520818) offers B&B in big, comfortable and airy en suite rooms – very good value at £15 – plus a baggage service to Kirk Yetholm for a nominal fee.

East of here, along the main road between Byrness and Blakehopeburnhaugh, is *Middle Byrness Cottage* (☎ 01830-520294), a small place charging £15/26 for a single/double. East again and almost back in Blakehopeburnhaugh, *Low Byrness* (☎ 01830-520648, 🖂 pdq@globalnet.co.uk) costs from £22/36 for an en suite, with a baggage-carrying service on request.

Day 16: Byrness to Kirk Yetholm
26mi (42km), 10 hours
Today's grand finale is the longest and loneliest stretch on the whole Pennine Way, and can be very hard going – especially if the weather is bad.

From Byrness the trail goes past The Old Rectory, then heads uphill on a sharp 150m ascent, which gets the early morning circulation going. The next few miles are gentle along the wide ridge overlooking the valley of Cottonshope Burn. After 4mi you reach the border fence between England and Scotland, which you'll follow for much of the day, although staying on the English side.

The trail passes Chew Green Roman encampment and the first *mountain refuge hut*, climbing over Beefstand Hill and other moorland bumps, which rejoice in names like Mozie Law (something to do with controlling the midges?) and Windy Gyle (no comment needed). This latter peak (619m) is topped by **Russell's Cairn**, a huge pile of stones, once a Bronze Age burial mound, marking the halfway point on today's walk. About a mile farther on, a track turns off down to *Uswayford* (see the boxed text

'Byrness to Kirk Yetholm – Lightening the Load' for an easier option to the otherwise long day).

After more rising and falling moor, the trail climbs up to the head of a valley at Cairn Hill, where the border fence and the Pennine Way make a sharp left turn. From this point an official out-and-back diversion off the trail ('not an option', say the purists) leads to the summit of the **Cheviot** (785m) – a 2.5mi return trip. The ascent is quite straightforward in good weather, but the view is rather dull and nonexistent in mist. ('Stuff it', say tired realists.)

Back at Cairn Hill the trail drops northwest to spectacular Auchope Cairn and then

Byrness to Kirk Yetholm – Lightening the Load

The 26mi stretch over the Cheviot Hills from Byrness to Kirk Yetholm is a cruel sting in the tail for Pennine Way walkers, but alternatives to doing it in one long slog are rather limited.

In the summer months, long daylight hours give you plenty of time to cover the distance. But with 10 hours' walking, plus extra for lunch and viewing stops, you'll need around 12 hours, so an early start is essential. You can lessen the hardship by arranging to have your pack transported to Kirk Yetholm, either by one of the operators listed under Guided Walks & Baggage Services or by one of the B&Bs in Byrness, which also offer this service.

Your other option is to split this stage into two. If you have camping equipment you can spend the night under canvas, and with a sleeping bag and some supplies you can overnight in one of the two mountain refuges along the trail. However, the first refuge (at 9mi) is probably too early and the second (at 19mi) is probably too late. For more comfort you could use a farmhouse B&B, although this will add distance and entail some descent and ascent. The most convenient halfway stop is *Uswayford* (☎ 01669-650237), which is only 1.5mi off the trail from about the 15mi mark. It offers single/double B&B and an evening meal from £23/34.

steeply to the second ***mountain refuge hut***. (Look back to see the glacial hanging valley at Hen Hole.) From here it's almost easy street. There's one final slog up the Schil before the trail finally abandons the border fence and crosses decisively into Scotland.

Four miles from the end, there's a choice of routes. One stays low in the valley while the other goes through the hills for the final stretch. You may not want to be bothered with decisions at this stage, but the high route doesn't take much longer. The two routes meet a mile from the end to follow a lane into the village of Kirk Yetholm and you've reached your journey's end.

Kirk Yetholm

The traditional finishing point of the trail is the bar of ***The Border Hotel*** (☎ 01573-420237, e theborderhotel@tinyonline.co.uk), on the village green. Have a drink here to celebrate – you've probably earned it! Many years ago, walkers who'd completed the whole route in one go used to get a free drink in the bar – on Wainwright's tab. These days the hotel sometimes revives the tradition with sponsorship from a local brewery, so it's always worth asking – if you're a genuine case! This place also does good-quality B&B for around £35 on summer weekends, although with lower rates (around £20 to £25) midweek and in the quiet season, and sometimes a discount for Pennine Way walkers. The hotel also serves excellent food; ideal for a further grand celebratory splurge.

The cheapest accommodation is at ***Kirk Yetholm SYHA Hostel*** (☎ 01573-420631), which charges £8.25. For B&B, ***Valleydene*** (☎ 01573-420286) is friendly, comfortable and stylish, and costs £20. Another place to try is ***Blunty's Mill*** (☎ 01573-420288), also from £20. There are a few other B&Bs in the village and more at Town Yetholm, half a mile west, which also has a small shop. At Kelso, 30 minutes away by bus, there's a bank, a TIC (☎ 01573-223464) and more accommodation options.

Other Walks in Northern England

THE NORTH PENNINES

To the north of the Yorkshire Dales and south of Northumberland is an area of hills and mountains called the North Pennines. The landscape is high, wild and impressive, the weather is often severe, the population is thinly dispersed and there are relatively few visitors. It is not a national park but it is an Area of Outstanding Natural Beauty. The tourist board bills it as 'England's Last Wilderness' and cynics say it has probably remained wild precisely because it *isn't* a national park.

Whatever the arguments, the North Pennines area undeniably has some marvellous walking opportunities. One of the best is **Teesdale**, the valley of the River Tees. The stretch from Barnard Castle to Langdon Beck offers some excellent walking and is easily accessible, lying on the bus route between Barnard Castle and Alston. A good place to base yourself would be Middleton-in-Teesdale or at the YHA hostel at Langdon Beck, from where the impressive waterfalls of High Force and Cauldron Snout are within striking distance. The Pennine Way, described in the Northern England Long-Distance Paths chapter, also passes through this section of the valley.

Another long-distance option is the **Teesdale Way**, a 90mi (145km) route that officially starts at Middleton-in-Teesdale. An alternative start would be to follow the Pennine Way east from Dufton up to High Cup Nick and over to Maize Beck, which runs into the River Tees. Leaving the Pennine Way at Middleton, the Teesdale Way proper follows the Tees through Barnard Castle and east to finish at Teesmouth on the coast. The first half of the walk is particularly good and doesn't hit urban developments until it reaches Middlesbrough. Guidebooks include *The Teesdale Way* by Martin Collins.

The other major river valley in the North Pennines is **Weardale**, also lovely and less frequently visited than Teesdale. Upper Weardale offers more excellent walking, combining riverside paths and wild moorlands with evidence of the area's industrial heritage – old mining sites and disused railways. It will come as no surprise to learn that another long route, the **Weardale Way**, runs along this valley from Allenheads to the North Sea coast.

Books on the area include *Walking in the North Pennines* by Paddy Dillon and *Teesdale* by Paul Hannon. There's also the useful Ordnance Survey (OS) Outdoor Leisure 1:25,000 map No 31 *(North Pennines – Teesdale and Weardale)*.

THE WOLDS WAY

Billed as 'Yorkshire's best kept secret', the Wolds Way is one of the least trod of Britain's national trails. This 80mi (128km) route starts at Kingston-upon-Hull (always shortened to Hull) on the River Humber and curves north through the rolling farmland, quiet villages and deep chalky valleys of the Yorkshire Wolds, to end at Filey Brigg, a peninsula on the east coast south of Scarborough. This is also the end of the Cleveland Way – described in the North York Moors chapter.

This is an ideal beginners' walk and is usually possible in five days. It can be done at any time of year as the landscape is not high or strenuous and the area gets surprisingly little rain, although (as with any part of eastern England) in winter cold winds and snow can blow in from the east.

The route is covered in *The Wolds Way* by Roger Ratcliffe, and you can get more information from the National Trail Officer at The Wolds Way Project (☎ 01439-770657), c/o North York Moors National Park, The Old Vicarage, Bondgate, Helmsley, York

YO62 5BP; or from the trail's official web site at **W** www.woldsway.gov.uk.

If you want a shorter taste of the Wolds, look out for the excellent series of *Railway Walks* leaflets available (free) at stations served by the Northern Spirit train company. The leaflets list suggested routes of different lengths, all of which are accessible from the line between Hull and Scarborough.

THE STAFFORDSHIRE WAY

This long-distance route runs for just over 90mi (145km) through rural and semirural parts of the county of Staffordshire, between Mow Cop (near the town of Congleton) and Kinver Edge (near the town of Stourbridge, south-west of Wolverhampton). As well as farmland, the route passes through the woodlands of Cannock Chase and also skirts the edge of the Peak District National Park. Local Tourist Information Centres (TICs) can provide you with the leaflet produced by Staffordshire County Council.

We decided on the Staffordshire Way because it was described as 'showing the walker as many aspects of English scenery as possible along its length'. The route also provided easy access to villages and suitable accommodation – namely, old inns. The walk provided us with a truly marvellous experience. Views from around Alton will long be remembered. There was not one moment that could be described as boring.

Phillip Crampton (Australia)

THE TRANS PENNINE TRAIL

This is not a wilderness walk. The Trans Pennine Trail is a coast-to-coast recreational route across Northern England, mainly through urban landscapes, following disused railways, canal towpaths and other tracks, but with surprisingly frequent frolics into rural areas. If you want to see all aspects of Northern England, not just the beautiful areas we concentrate on in this book, then this is the route for you. It runs from Southport, near Liverpool on the Irish Sea, to Hornsea, near Hull on the North Sea. That's a total length of 200mi (322km) and much of the route can be covered by bicycle as well as on foot. Several spurs off the main route – to cities like York, Sheffield and Leeds – have also been developed. The Trans Pennine Trail is also part of an even longer route – see the boxed text 'Istanbul Here We Come!'.

Istanbul Here We Come!

If you've covered all the routes in this book and want to stretch yourself a little further, you'll be pleased to know that the Trans Pennine Trail (TPT) forms part of a much longer route running right across Europe. Called the Atlantic to Black Sea Path (or the E8), the route starts by traversing southern Ireland, before crossing Britain on the TPT and extending eastwards through Holland, Germany, Poland and Bulgaria – all the way to Turkey.

And if that isn't enough, the E8 is just one of 11 proposed trans-European walking routes known as E-Paths, set up by the European Ramblers' Association (ERA). Many combine existing long-distance paths in various countries. The other E-Path that crosses Britain is the E2 Atlantic–Mediterranean route, which runs through Scotland and England via the Pennine Way, and then through Holland, Belgium and France to end at Nice.

For more details, see the ERA Web site at (**W** www.era-ewv-ferp.org).

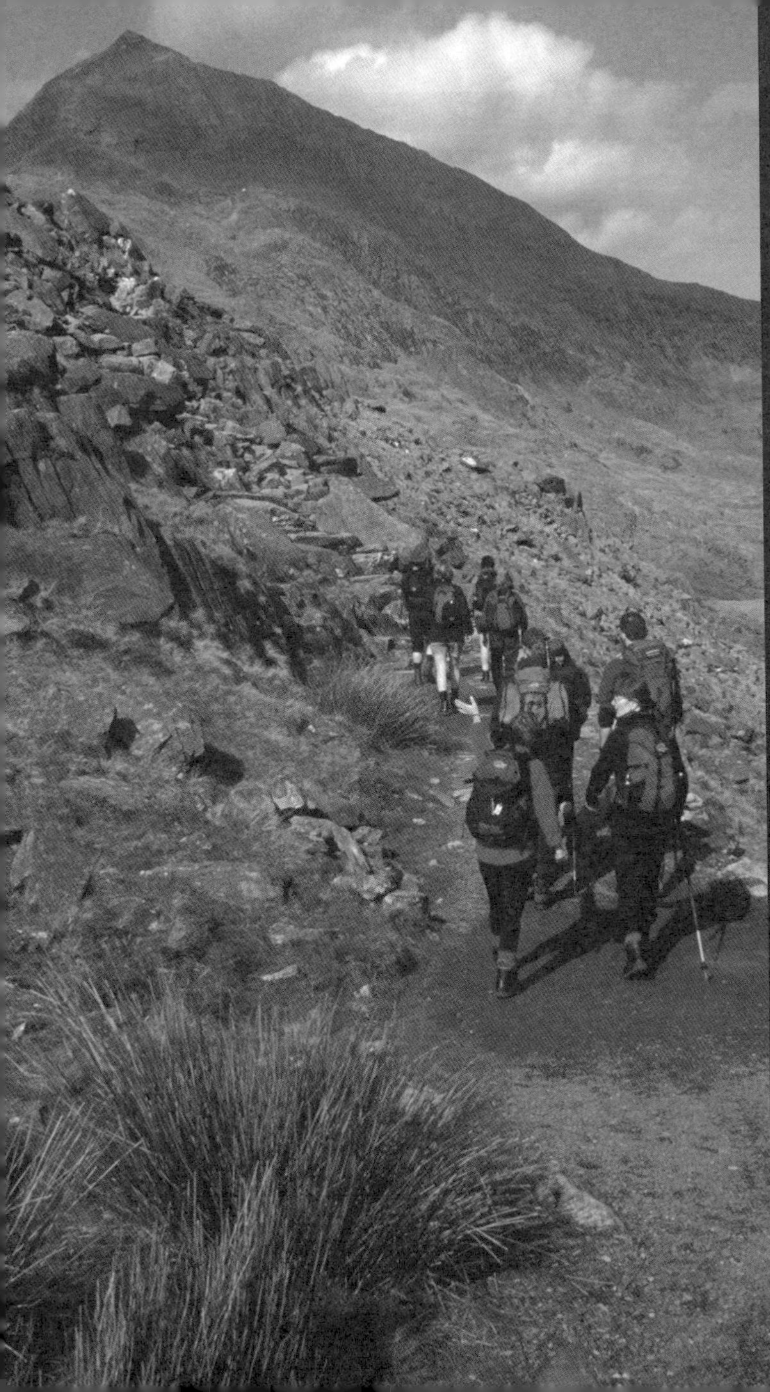

Wales

Wales

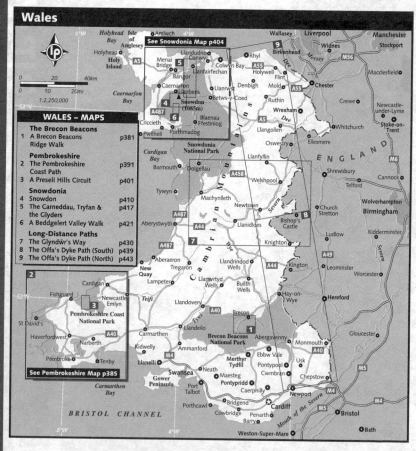

The Brecon Beacons

The Brecon Beacons is the name of a large group of mountains in South Wales, running west to east, forming the natural border between the central and southern parts of the country. The mountains and surrounding foothills are contained within the Brecon Beacons National Park (Parc Cenedlaethol Bannau Brycheiniog in Welsh) and the whole area is also known as Brecknockshire.

There are four separate mountain ranges within the national park: In the west is the Black Mountain, which is wild and relatively remote, and Fforest Fawr, which is lower and less austere. Over to the east are the confusingly named Black Mountains (plural), and in the centre are the Brecon Beacons themselves, the highest range and most favoured by walkers, giving their title to the whole park.

Although the Beacons cannot compare in dramatic terms with Snowdonia, they are the highest mountains in southern Britain. Forming a range of gigantic rolling whalebacks with broad ridges and table-top summits, they are cut by deep valleys with sides falling so steeply the grass has often given up the ghost to expose large areas of bare rock.

Within this area is a fantastic choice of day walks. The route we describe is along one of the most frequented sections but it's justifiably popular and provides an excellent introduction to the Beacons' beauty and walking potential.

INFORMATION
Maps & Books
Most of the park is covered by Ordnace Survery (OS) Landranger 1:50,000 maps No 160 *(Brecon Beacons)* and No 161 *(Abergavenny & The Black Mountains)*, and OS Outdoor Leisure 1:25,000 maps No 12 *(Brecon Beacons – West & Central Areas)* and No 13 *(Brecon Beacons – Eastern Area)*.

Harvey has a 1:40,000 Walker's map *Brecon Beacons* that covers most of the park, and two Superwalker 1:25,000 maps, *Brecon Beacons East* and *Brecon Beacons West*; the route described here is on *Brecon Beacons East*.

Guidebooks covering walking in the Brecon Beacons include *Best Walks in Southern Wales* by Richard Sale, which has a section on the Brecon Beacons ridge route.

Information Sources
Visitors centres in the Brecon Beacons are run by both local tourist boards and by Brecon Beacons National Park. You can find centres at Abergavenny (☎ 01873-857588), Brecon (☎ 01874-622485) and Llandovery (☎ 01550-720693).

The national park headquarters (☎ 01874-624437, e enquiries@breconbeacons.org) can also help with information about the park, as can the National Park Visitor Centre (☎ 01874-623366), not far from the village of Libanus, 5mi south-west of Brecon. The visitors centre has frequent slide shows and exhibitions but is hard to reach without your own wheels, although there's a shuttle bus from Brecon on Sunday. All visitors centres stock a good range of leaflets, a series of walking booklets covering the main areas, plus other books and maps.

The national park also produces *Beacons Bannau*, a free newspaper for visitors, full of information about the local environment, special events, guided walks etc.

Guided Walks
The national park runs a very good series of guided walks and other active events during the summer, usually at places that can be reached by the Beacons Bus (see the Getting There & Away section). You can get details from Tourist Information Centres (TICs) or the National Park Visitor Centre.

GETTING THERE & AWAY
The Getting Around chapter lists several public transport inquiry lines that provide details of both national and local bus and train services: See the boxed text 'National Transport Information' on p92.

Bus The main gateway to the Brecon Beacons is the town of Brecon, which can be reached from other parts of Britain by National Express coach, usually via Cardiff or Birmingham, where you may have to change.

Brecon can also be reached by bus from Newport via Abergavenny, and from Hereford via Hay-on-Wye (both have about five services per day each way, except Sunday), or from Swansea (three per day, except Sunday). All buses are run by Stagecoach Red & White (☎ 01633-266336). Most buses leave and arrive at the Bulwark, in Brecon's centre, although some depart from the car park adjacent to the canal basin on Canal Rd.

If you're coming from Cardiff, you can get a bus to Merthyr Tydfil (hourly except Sunday). Buses to Brecon (via Storey Arms) run every two hours, Monday to Saturday. The last one leaves at around 7pm.

On summer Sundays and public holidays the Beacons Bus network is very useful. Centred on Brecon town it has interconnecting services to/from Hereford, Abergavenny, Merthyr Tydfil, Cardiff and Swansea, most with at least two services each way per day. Phone ☎ 01873-853254 for details or get a timetable from a TIC.

Train The nearest train stations are at Abergavenny (via Newport) and Merthyr Tydfil (via Cardiff), from where you can get one of the buses mentioned above. Abergavenny and Merthyr Tydfil have regular trains to/from the main line, which runs between London and West Wales.

Warning – Jazz Festival

Some years ago, a few musicians got together in a pub for a bit of jamming. This developed into Brecon Jazz – now one of Europe's leading music festivals, held over three days in early or mid-August and attracting crowds of literally thousands. If you're into jazz, or just into good times, it's great – but note that accommodation is almost impossible to find. For more details, phone ☎ 01874-625557 or see the Web site (**W** www.breconjazz.co.uk).

Car Brecon is beside the A470 (between Cardiff and Conwy) and the A40 (between Gloucester and West Wales).

A Brecon Beacons Ridge Walk

Distance	14mi (22.5km)
Duration	7½–9½ hours
Standard	medium
Start	Storey Arms
Finish	Brecon
Gateways	Brecon, Merthyr Tydfil

Summary A walk mostly through high, open country where weather conditions can be demanding, with steep ascents and descents and some final flat sections of farmland.

This route follows the most impressive section of the Brecon Beacons' central ridge, taking in the summit of 886m Pen y Fan (pronounced pen-er-van, which means 'Top Peak'), plus three other high summits. On either side of the ridge are vast bowl-like corries, with U-shaped valleys beyond, all formed by glaciers some 10,000 years ago. It's classic textbook geography and you may see groups of school kids struggling along the path, pens and soggy notebooks in hand, gamely attempting to take it all in.

This route also passes through tranquil farms and woodland and finishes along the banks of a canal near the meandering River Usk – an interesting contrast to the peaks, ridges, *cwms* (valleys) and *bwlchs* (passes) of the high ground.

The rounded nature of the Beacons belies their seriousness. It can get wet and cold, with winds strong enough to blow you over. Take appropriate clothing, plus a map and compass. You see day trippers with none of these, but you also hear horror stories of people who get lost, sometimes fatally. Don't be one of them.

Direction, Distance & Duration

The walk starts at Storey Arms, a high point on the main road, about 7.5mi south of the town of Brecon. It ends at Brecon. You could do it in reverse, but this involves a lot more ascent. The total distance is just under 14mi. There are a lot of ups and downs on this route, so it requires about seven to nine hours of walking, but with stops you should allow eight to 10. The route is not waymarked and there are no signposts on the high ground.

Alternatives You can shorten this route by dropping off the main ridge earlier and aiming north to Brecon. The easiest route to follow is the old road that leaves the ridge at Bwlch ar y Fan, making the total distance about 10mi.

PLANNING
Maps
The walk route is covered by OS Outdoor Leisure 1:25,000 map No 12 *(Brecon Beacons – West & Central Areas)*.

PLACES TO STAY & EAT
On the route itself there's no cafe or pub for lunch, so take all you need from Brecon (which has several shops). Near the end of the walk, in Llanfrynach, there is a pub and also a couple of B&Bs if you'd prefer to stay outside Brecon (see the route description for details).

For other budget accommodation options in the area, a very useful Web site at **W** www .hostelswales.com lists about 20 bunkhouses, barns and backpacker hostels in the Brecon Beacons area, many in excellent walking locations, with plans to expand coverage to the whole country in the future.

Brecon
The town of Brecon, on the northern edge of the park, makes a good base for this walk. Its Welsh name is Aberhonddu (pronounced aber-hon-thee), and you'll see this on road signs. As a tourist centre it's busy in the summer, while Friday and Saturday nights are always lively as pub crowds become reinforced by soldiers from the nearby barracks. The TIC (☎ 01874-622485) is in the large car park in the centre of town.

The *YHA Hostel* (☎ 01874-665270) at Ty'n-y-Caeau (tin-er-kaye), a large country house near the village of Groesffordd, 2.5mi east of Brecon, costs £9. There is also

Llwyn-y-Celyn YHA Hostel (☎ 01874-624261), on the main road (A470) south of Brecon towards Storey Arms, charging £9, or £4.50 for camping. Campers can also head for *Neuadd Farm* (☎ 01874-665247), 2.5mi south of Brecon near the small village of Cantref, charging backpackers from £1 per night. A bit nearer, with full facilities including free hot showers, is *Brynich Caravan Park* (☎ 01874-623325), about 2mi east of Brecon, where walkers pay £4.50.

For bargain accommodation in Brecon, *Bike & Hikes* (☎ 01874-610071, **e** bikes -hikes@brecon.co.uk), on the Struet, has twin rooms, family rooms and small dorms, all for £12.50. It's basic but very comfortable, and you can also hire maps or arrange other outdoor activities.

Also cheap and central is *Canal Barn* (☎ 01874-625361), near the canal on the edge of the town centre, with many good facilities, including a self-catering kitchen and small dorms, for £10.

Most B&Bs are a few minutes' walk outside the centre. Along a street called the Watton (towards Abergavenny) are *Paris Guesthouse* (☎ 01874-624205), from £18; the smarter *Lansdowne Hotel* (☎ 01874-623321) with single/double en suite rooms from £28/48; and the walker-friendly *Brecon Canal Guest House* (☎ 01874-623464), at the end of the walk, charging £17 to £20.

On Bridge St, west of the river, *Beacons Guest House* (☎ 01874-623339) has rooms from £18, or £22.50 for an en suite. The restaurant is also open to nonresidents and the food is highly recommended (main dishes from £5.50).

For pricier accommodation, *George Hotel* (☎ 01874-623421, **e** enquiry@george-hotel .com), in the town centre, costs £40/65 and in comfortable rooms and has a good-value restaurant with main courses from £7 to £11.

Brecon has several cafes, teashops and a surprising number of takeaways, including Chinese, Indian and fish and chips. The smart bistro, *Welcome Stranger* (☎ 01874-622188), on Bridge St, is open for evening meals with main courses between £7 and £12. The town also has a good selection of pubs, with most doing bar food, including

THE BRECON BEACONS

The Sarah Siddons and *The Bull's Head*, both in the town centre.

GETTING TO/FROM THE WALK

Bus From Brecon there are buses to Merthyr Tydfil via Storey Arms (the start of the walk). Buses leave at two-hourly intervals from around 9am, Monday to Saturday. On Sunday only, the Beacons Bus (see Getting There & Away earlier) covers the same route, with five services. Ask the driver to shout when the bus reaches Storey Arms as it's easy to miss.

Car To reach Storey Arms by car is easy, and there are car parks nearby. However, if you park here and do the whole route, you have to get back afterwards. Buses don't run after late afternoon, so leave your car in Brecon and catch a bus to Storey Arms before starting the walk.

Taxi If you miss the bus, a taxi from Brecon to Storey Arms costs roughly £10. Taxi Companies include Captains Cabs (☎ 01874-625108), Ace Taxi (☎ 01874-625522) or Ron's Cab (☎ 07771-900559).

THE WALK
Storey Arms to Pen y Fan
3mi (5km), 1½–2 hours
The route starts at Storey Arms, about 7.5mi south of Brecon. There was once a pub here, on the highest point of an ancient drove route, and later the turnpike road (now the A470), crossing the mountains between South and Mid-Wales. Today the building is an outdoor centre and there's not a beer in sight.

Near the phone box, on the north-east side of the road, a gate leads to a footpath that goes steeply uphill onto the moorland. After about 20 minutes, at the crest of a broad ridge, there's a fork. Straight on leads you into the Blaen Taf Fawr *(blaen* in Welsh means 'valley') and up again but it's easier to skirt north then east round the head of the valley to meet the ridge just below Tommy's Obelisk (see the boxed text), overlooking Llyn Cwm Llwch *(llyn* in Welsh means 'lake'). From the obelisk, the route is clear:

Go up the path (pitched with stones to prevent further erosion) south-east to the **summit of Corn Du** (which fittingly translates as the Black Horn), about 1¼ hours from Storey Arms. The summit rewards you with fine views north to Brecon, west over Fforest Fawr and – most spectacularly – eastwards along the ridge, with Pen y Fan and the other table-top summits lined up for inspection.

Once again the route is clear: Go down the ridge and steeply up again, with Llyn Cwm Llwch to your left (north-west) and the Blaen Taf Fechan valley to your right (south). A few steep rock steps at the top of the path bring you to **Pen y Fan** (886m), marked by a large cairn and trig point. Here the views are even better: To the east, beyond Cribyn and Fan y Big, you can see the Black Mountains.

Pen y Fan to Llanfrynach
7mi (11.5km), 4–5½ hours
Take care leaving the summit of Pen y Fan, especially in mist. The path does not aim straight for Cribyn but goes south 'off the back' of the table top, with a view ahead (south) of the Upper Neuadd Reservoir far down in the valley, before it curves round on the ridge crest once again. The Blaen Taf Fechan valley is still to the right (south), but to the left a new valley, Cwm Sere, opens out, overlooked by steep cliffs on the north-east face of Pen y Fan. About 20 to 30 minutes from Pen y Fan you reach the **summit of Cribyn** (795m).

The path continues south then south-east, dropping over grassy slopes with yet another

> ## Tommy's Obelisk
>
> The obelisk on the ridge below Corn Du is dedicated to the memory of a young boy called Tommy Jones, who died here in 1900 – a plaque tells the sad story. Lost in the valley while walking with his father, Tommy somehow made his way up to this exposed spot, where his body was found some weeks after he went missing. A newspaper had offered a reward but the money instead was used for this memorial.

spectacular corrie (the head of Cwm Cyn-wyn) to your left. At the low point called Bwlch ar y Fan, between Cribyn and Fan y Big, an old road crosses the ridge. It's popular with mountain bikers and you may also see 4WDs churning it up. This is also a short cut to Brecon – useful in bad weather. But if you're pushing on, from here it's a steep slog up to **Fan y Big** (719m), the final summit, and last chance to take in the wraparound views before descending.

From Fan y Big, a broad grassy ridge leads south curving east then north round the head of the Cwm Oergwm. The path becomes boggy round the right-angled bend at Bwlch y Ddwyallt, but the going is not too bad.

Several other paths join from the right, coming up from the Talybont Valley. Ignore these and continue north-east down the grassy ridge, with Cwm Oergwm on the left and great views back up the valley to Fan y Big and the other summits dominating the skyline. The path drops off the ridge into an area of scattered bushes, small trees and a few walls, although you don't cross any of them yet. Pay close attention to the map, aiming for the right side of a line of wind-swept trees in the valley. On reaching these trees, drop steeply downhill, keeping the tower of Llanfrynach church ahead and to your left as you descend to reach a stile (with a yellow footpath marker) in the corner formed by two walls. Cross the stile and head north downhill past some woodland marked on the map as Coed Cae Rebol.

Footpath markers lead you near to the ruined farm of Tir-hir along the edge of a field, over a stream and then along a track to a lane near Tregaer Farm. Turn right and follow the lane into Llanfrynach village.

This is your first brush with civilisation, so a pint in *The White Swan*, in the centre of the village, may be called for. If you'd like a B&B, try *Ty Fry Farm* (☎ *01874-665232*), costing £15; or *Llanbrynean Farm* (☎ *01874-665222*), for £20. Both lie just out

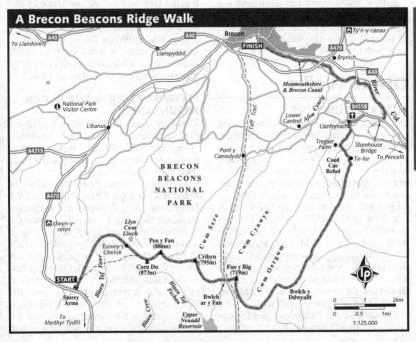

THE BRECON BEACONS

of the village. There's also a bus to Brecon every two hours, Monday to Saturday. The last ones leave at around 5pm and 7pm.

Llanfrynach to Brecon

4mi (6.5km), 2 hours

From Llanfrynach church follow the lane out of the village past The White Swan. At a forked junction with a road (marked on the map as the B4558), turn right and continue for 400m to reach Storehouse Bridge, which crosses the Monmouthshire & Brecon Canal. Go over the bridge and through the gate onto a towpath, heading north-east towards Brecon. The towpath is a section of the Taff Trail, a long-distance path from Cardiff (for further details, see the Other Walks in Wales chapter). Very close to the bridge is the Water Folk Canal Museum, with horse-drawn canal trips, and *Cambrian Cruisers* (☎ 01874-665315), which offers boat hire as well as B&B from £25/40 for singles/doubles.

Follow this towpath for about 3mi – a nice section of flat, easy walking – over an aqueduct and past a lock to the canal basin in Brecon, where the waterway and this walk both terminate.

Other Walks

BLACK MOUNTAINS

The Black Mountains are the easternmost section of Brecon Beacons National Park. You can use Abergavenny as a base but even handier is the small town of Crickhowell, which is on the bus route between Brecon and Abergavenny and gives excellent access to the mountains and valleys. One recommended place to stay is *The Dragon Hotel* (☎ *01873-810362*, e *dragon-hotel @crickhowell10.freeserve.co.uk*), where B&B costs from £40/52 for singles/doubles. The friendly owner organises guided walks and holidays (from a day to a week) and can advise on local routes. There's also a *YHA Hostel* and a wide choice of B&Bs. The TIC (☎ 01873-812105) can provide more details.

The Offa's Dyke Path (described fully in the Wales Long-Distance Paths chapter) runs north along the eastern fringe of the Black Mountains from Pandy to Hay-on-Wye, and this section could be followed as a day walk. The views are spectacular but the route is along a high, exposed grassy ridge that can be very windy. Pandy is on the A465, on the bus route between Abergavenny and Hereford. If you follow all or part of this route, it's definitely worth dropping down to visit the ruins of Llanthony Priory, where the remaining buildings now house a *pub* and a delightfully atmospheric *hotel*. Farther north up this valley is the *Capel-y-Ffin YHA Hostel*. As a less strenuous alternative to walking along the ridge, you could follow the River Honddu from Llanvihangel, lower down in the valley. TICs stock leaflets that cover walks in this area.

The highest point in the Black Mountains is Waun Fach (811m). Reaching this on foot is a serious proposition. If you've got a car, it's best to drive via Patrishow (an interesting 13th-century church in an idyllic location) to the end of the track in the Mynydd Du Forest. Follow the old railway track up to Grwyne Fawr Reservoir, where a path runs up Waun Fach. Alternatively, the peak can be reached from Llanbedr (where there's a *bunkhouse*) up to the ridge that runs north via Pen-y-Gadair Fawr.

FFOREST FAWR & THE BLACK MOUNTAIN

These areas are in the western part of the Brecon Beacons National Park. Neither is visited as often as the main Beacons range, but they both have great scenery and several good walking opportunities.

To explore Fforest Fawr, the village of Ystradfellte is a good base. There's a *YHA Hostel*, and along the rivers and streams to the south there are a number of attractive waterfalls, including Sgwd-yr-eira (which means 'spout of snow'). There are other falls at Pontneddfechan and Coelbren. Look out for the *Waterfall Walks* leaflet at local TICs.

The Black Mountain is the westernmost part of the park (not to be confused with the Black Mountains in the east). The repetition of the name is not surprising – when the weather is bad any piece of bare high ground in the Brecon Beacons deserves to be called 'black'. This western section of the park contains the wildest and least visited walking country. The park's highest point, **Fan Brycheiniog** (also known as Camarthen Van; 802m), can be reached from the village of Glyntawe, between Sennybridge and Ystradgynlais, north of the industrial towns of Neath and Swansea.

On the north side of the range, the town of Llandovery is a nicer place to stay but farther from the high ground. There's a *YHA Hostel* at Llanddeusant, deeper into the hills. Another good base is *Llanerchidda Farm* (☎ *01550-750274*, e *nick@cambrianway .com)*, a very comfortable and award-winning guesthouse, whose proprietor is a keen and knowledgeable walker.

THE BLACK TO BLACK

For a long walk in the Brecon Beacons, you could consider the 'Black to Black', a 50mi, five-day route that crosses the park from east to west, from Chapel-y-Ffin near Crickhowell to Llanddeusant near Llandovery, keeping to the high ground and mountain watershed wherever possible. This walk is just one section of the Cambrian Way, a coast-to-coast route described briefly in the Other Walks in Wales chapter.

An organised self-guided option is available from The Dragon Hotel in Crickhowell and Llanerchidda Farm near Llandovery (both listed earlier). For one price you get accommodation, meals, food, maps, guidebooks, pick-ups, drop-offs and even a mobile (cellular) phone in case of emergency.

Pembrokeshire

Pembrokeshire is a county in the far southwest corner of Wales. Its name in Welsh is Sir Benfro, and the original inhabitants were Celts, who left their mark on the landscape in the form of ancient standing stones and other remains over 2000 years old. Even before this time, the 'bluestones' of Stonehenge were quarried here, then transported to their present resting place in Southern England.

English incomers first arrived in the 11th century (and still pour over the border each summer, usually as holiday-makers). Despite this, the Welsh language is alive and kicking, especially north of an ancient division called the Landsker Line, which separates northern Pembrokeshire from the more anglicised south.

For many visitors, Pembrokeshire's main attraction is its dramatic coastal scenery. Without doubt this is one of the most beautiful parts of Britain – an array of beaches, cliffs, rock arches, stacks, buttresses, islands, coves and harbours. You have to go to Cornwall to get anything like this, or to North-West Scotland for anything better.

This scenery is contained within Pembrokeshire Coast National Park, as are the offshore islands of Skomer, Skokholm, Grassholm and Ramsey (named by 10th-century Viking invaders). The park also features an impressive array of wildlife, including some of the world's largest populations of sea birds, such as shearwaters and gannets, as well as puffins, kittiwakes, cormorants and gulls, plus rarer choughs and peregrine falcons. Out at sea, seals, porpoises and dolphins are common, and there's even the odd shark. Paradise indeed.

The area is well known for its relatively mild climate, which means you can walk here year-round, although the coast gets hammered by some spectacular gales, especially in winter.

Inland, and still within the national park, are the little-known Preseli Hills (Mynydd Preseli in Welsh), the secluded Gwaun Valley (Cwm Gwaun) and the Milford Haven Waterway, one of the world's largest natural harbours, which upstream becomes the tranquil Daugleddau Estuary. These areas have just as much to offer as the more famous coastline, but they're often overlooked by visitors, so if you're after solitude they could well be the place for you.

INFORMATION
Information Sources
Pembrokeshire Tourist Information Centres (TICs) are run either by the local tourist board or by the national park authority. Most open daily in summer, with shorter hours and Sunday closing in winter. TICs include Cardigan (☎ 01239-613230), Fishguard (☎ 01348-873484), Milford Haven (☎ 01646-690866), Newport (☎ 01239-820912), Pembroke (☎ 01646-622388), Tenby (☎ 01834-842404), and St David's (☎ 01437-720392). Online, Ⓦ www.pembro keshire-holidays.com is the main tourist information Web site.

It's worth noting that the county is often separated by the TICs into South and North Pembrokeshire (divided by the Milford Haven Waterway), and it's surprisingly hard to get information on the north from a TIC in the south (and vice versa).

The national park authority publishes a free newspaper called *Coast to Coast*, which is full of information on local events and public transport, plus tide tables and

Kittiwakes squabbling over territory

GRAHAM BELL

adverts for places to eat, stay or visit; it's available from TICs. The national park Web site (**W** www.pembrokeshirecoast.org) also covers the coast path.

GETTING THERE & AWAY

Pembrokeshire is easy to reach from other parts of South and West Wales, and also very easy to reach from England. The Getting Around chapter lists several public transport inquiry lines that provide details of both national and local bus and train services: See the boxed text 'National Transport Information' on p92.

The main gateway town, Haverfordwest, in the centre of Pembrokeshire, is served by trains (a few per day) and National Express coaches (at least once daily) from London via Bristol, Cardiff, Swansea and Carmathen. There are also coach and train services to/from Birmingham and the Midlands.

From Haverfordwest you can reach the other main Pembrokeshire towns of Tenby, Pembroke, Miford Haven and Fishguard by local bus or branch-line train. There are also local buses between Carmarthen and Cardigan (a gateway town to the north of Pembrokeshire).

Pembrokeshire

PEMBROKESHIRE – MAPS
1 The Pembrokeshire Coast Path p391
2 A Preseli Hills Circuit p401

The Pembrokeshire Coast Path

Distance	186mi (299.5km)
Duration	15 days
Standard	medium-hard
Start	Amroth
Finish	St Dogmaels
Gateways	Haverfordwest, Pembroke, Fishguard

Summary This cliff-top trail includes some of the finest beaches and coastal scenery in Britain, with some strenuous walking as the path frequently rises and falls.

The Pembrokeshire Coast Path is quite simply one of the most beautiful routes in Britain – or, to be more precise, most sections of it are beautiful. This national trail includes sections of rugged coastline, passes through tiny fishing villages, skirts secluded coves, and crosses some areas surprisingly empty of people. Distractions along the way include St David's (with its fine cathedral) and Tenby (a charming seaside town), plus Iron Age forts, ruined castles, superb beaches and tranquil nature reserves – not to mention the pubs, many of which are conveniently situated right by the trail. The rocks here are amongst the world's oldest, and the spectacular patterns and colours of the strata in the cliffs are another constant attraction. But this route also shows you the other side of Wales – ugly towns, oil refineries and a power station. This may be authentic and necessary, but it ain't scenic, so we suggest ways to avoid the blight and enjoy the coast with your memories unblemished.

Direction, Distance & Duration

Although you can go in either direction, we suggest going from south to north. The wildest walking is in the north, so you can limber up in the tamer south, and this way you'll have the sun and the wind (usually) behind you.

The official length of the trail is 186mi, but in reality the actual distance walked will be over 200mi to include detours when the tide is high or to reach your accommodation.

We describe a 15-day itinerary, but you should add extra days for side trips to nearby islands or to visit places of interest. Note that the hours given for each stage in the main route description are walking times only; you should allow an extra hour or two for rests, lunch stops, seal watching, swimming etc.

day	from	to	mi/km
1	Amroth	Tenby	7/11.5
2	Tenby	Manorbier	8.5/13.5
3	Manorbier	Bosherston	15/24
4	Bosherston	Angle	15/24
5	Angle	Pembroke	13.5/21.5
6	Pembroke	Sandy Haven	16/25.5
7	Sandy Haven	Marloes	14/22.5
8	Marloes	Broad Haven	13/21
9	Broad Haven	Solva	11/17.5
10	Solva	Whitesands	13/21
11	Whitesands	Trefin	12/19.5
12	Trefin	Pwll Deri	10/16
13	Pwll Deri	Fishguard	10/16
14	Fishguard	Newport	12.5/20
15	Newport	St Dogmaels	15.5/25

Some distances look deceptively short and easy, but you must remember the endless steep ascents and descents where the trail crosses river valleys. This is undoubtedly a challenging walk. Having said that, if you're a strong walker some stages can be doubled up, eg, Amroth to Manorbier in a day. An option at the start is staying two nights in Tenby: Arrive the evening before your walk, find accommodation, then next day get the bus to Amroth and walk back.

Along the route there are several possibilities for short cuts, but most involve cutting across headlands away from the coast, which is a shame because that's the trail's whole point. If you're tight on time and can only do one part of the route, we'd recommend sticking to the northern section: Sandy Haven or Marloes to St Dogmaels.

It's worth noting that Days 4, 5 and 6 might be worth skipping completely. Some ways of doing this are given in the boxed text 'South Coast to Sandy Haven Direct' on p392.

If your time is really limited, see the boxed text 'Pembrokeshire Coast Path – Some Route Highlights' on p394.

PLANNING
Maps & Books
The route is covered by Ordnance Survey (OS) Outdoor Leisure 1:25,000 maps No 35 *(North Pembrokeshire)* and No 36 *(South Pembrokeshire)*. This is very handy, as most long-distance paths (LDPs) require many more maps.

For specific route information, the national park publishes *Coast Path Accommodation* and *Public Transport Guide* booklets. The park also produces a very good range of cheap booklets and leaflets covering sections of the coast path, or circular walks incorporating part of the route. A series of single-sheet *trail cards* covers the route in 10 sections, with a simple map, listing points of interest along the way (40p each). These are available from local TICs, or by post from the National Park Information Centre (☎ 01437-764636, [e] pcnp @pembrokeshirecoast.org), Winch Lane, Haverfordwest SA61 1PY.

The official national trail guide *Pembrokeshire Coast Path* by Brian John includes detailed route descriptions (north to south), OS map extracts and colour photos. More useful is *The Pembrokeshire Coastal Path* by Dennis Kelsall, which describes the route in the preferred south to north direction, and includes detailed route descriptions, background information, line maps and an accommodation list.

Information Sources
TICs can be found along the route in Tenby (☎ 01834-842404), Pembroke (☎ 01646-622388), Milford Haven (☎ 01646-690866), St David's (☎ 01437-720392), Fishguard (☎ 01348-873484), Newport (☎ 01239-820912) and Cardigan (☎ 01239-613230).

Guided Walks & Baggage Services
National park rangers lead walks along parts of the path, across islands, up estuaries and over inland areas between April to October.

In May/June, they lead a 14-day walk of the entire path. See the *Coast to Coast* newspaper or contact a TIC for details. National companies operating on the Pembrokeshire Coast Path include Contours Walking Holidays (see Guided Walks in the Facts for the Walker chapter for details), which offers self-guided tours, including accommodation and baggage transfer.

Of the local companies, Pembrokeshire Walking Holidays (☎ 01437-76664, [e] wal king@menterpreseli.freeserve.co.uk) offers self-guided tours, mainly along the Pembrokeshire Coast Path, with accommodation, meals, transfers and baggage support, for four nights (from £130) or seven nights, or according to your own itinerary. Landsker Countryside Holidays (☎ 01834-860965, tourism@sparc.org.uk) organises coast path

Warning
The Pembrokeshire Coast Path, you won't be surprised to hear, follows the coast for much of its length, and there are some specific potential dangers you need to be aware of. The path often goes close to the top of steep and high cliffs, where you must take great care, especially in fog (when you can't see how close the edge is) or in high wind (when your backpack acts like a sail!).

In many places you can walk along beaches below the cliffs, but don't relax here either as it's possible to get cut off when the tide comes in. In some areas the sea comes right up to the base of the cliffs and, if you get trapped, drowning is a distinct possibility. To avoid this danger, it's very useful to carry a local tide table showing the times of high and low water.

A tide table is also very useful for the occasions where you can cut distance by crossing river mouths on bridges or stepping stones, which are only exposed at low tide.

If you want to swim (for relaxation, *not* to cross river mouths), also note that many beaches have strong currents. Flags mark safe places and lifeguards are sometimes on duty. If in doubt, stay on dry land.

PEMBROKESHIRE

tours and also specialises in the quieter, hidden inland areas, with short walking breaks including transport and B&B from £20 per day, or walking holidays over six nights from £170. This helpful organisation can also assist with other services for walkers such as accommodation booking and baggage carrying.

PLACES TO STAY & EAT

There's a wide range of places to stay and eat in this popular holiday area, although from November through February most YHA hostels and B&Bs are closed. In high summer (June to August) you must book ahead, and many B&Bs won't take single-night walkers; understandably they're looking for longer stays. The best months for good weather and lack of crowds are May and September.

B&Bs and hotels are listed in the route description. Some B&Bs arrange transport to meet you, taking you back to the path the next day. For a wider choice, use *The Rambler's Yearbook & Accommodation Guide* or *Stilwells's National Trail Companion* (see Books in the Facts for the Walker chapter), or the *Coast Path Accommodation* guide listed under Maps & Books earlier.

The path is well served by YHA hostels; you can book your needs all in one go through the central booking bureau (☎ 0870-241 2314, fax 01629-581062, 🄴 reserva tions@yha.org.uk, 🆆 www.yha.org.uk), PO Box 67, Matlock, Derbyshire DE4 3YX. There are also many places for camping; some are large and cater mainly for big tents and caravans, while others offer basic facilities for walkers. Camping on beaches is not officially allowed and all farmland is private.

Welsh Language

One thing making Wales so distinctive is the survival of Welsh as a living language. Welsh, with its weird-looking and seemingly unpronounceable chains of consecutive consonants, is an Indo-European language and is part of the Celtic group of languages, which also includes Scots Gaelic, Irish, Manx, Cornish and Breton. The language as it is spoken today, although later influenced by French and English, seems to have been more or less fully developed by the 6th century, making it one of Europe's oldest languages.

From around the 13th century, English attempts to colonise Wales (and their eventual success) had a detrimental effect on the language. Following the Act of Union in 1536, it was forbidden for people to hold high office unless they spoke English as well as Welsh. Bishop Morgan's translation of the Bible into Welsh in 1588 is thought to have played an important part in keeping the language alive.

The decline of Welsh continued into the 19th century, when the Industrial Revolution brought a new class of industrial landlords and employers, few of whom spoke Welsh. By 1901 only 50% of the population spoke Welsh, and by 1991 this figure dropped to 19%, most of whom (75%) lived in North and north-west Wales.

Since the 1960s, the importance of Welsh has been officially recognised, and in 1967 the Welsh Language Act ensured that Welsh-speakers could use their own language in court. Since then an increasing number of publications have been bilingual, Welsh-language TV and a radio station have been established, and it's rare nowadays to see a road sign in just one language.

In 1988 a Welsh Language Board was set up to advise the Secretary of State for Wales on everything to do with the language, while in 1994 a new Welsh Language Act gave equal validity to Welsh as a language for use in public-sector businesses – it's now illegal to discriminate against Welsh-speakers, in employment for example.

To those English visitors who get very hot under the collar when they have difficulty communicating in some areas, the Welsh-speakers point out that it's no different from going to any other country where, naturally, everybody speaks their own language. For non-British visitors it's a fascinating subject, but it's probably not wise to express strong opinions without first getting a good grip on the facts.

GETTING TO/FROM THE WALK

Bus The daily National Express coach between London and West Wales goes via Kilgetty, 3mi from Amroth. There's a local bus link but it's often quicker to walk. Alternatively you can get off this coach at Tenby, from where local buses run regularly to Amroth. The National Express coach also stops at Carmarthen, Pembroke, Pembroke Dock, Milford Haven and Haverfordwest.

From one end of the route at St Dogmaels it's 2mi to Cardigan, from where local buses run to Carmarthen and then the same National Express service returns to London, with links to other parts of the country. The local bus between St Dogmaels and Cardigan extends to/from Poppet Sands in summer (but not on Sunday).

For travel between intermediate points along the route, some local bus and train details for South Pembrokeshire are given in the boxed text 'South Coast to Sandy Haven Direct' later in this chapter. In North Pembrokeshire by far the most useful service is the Puffin Shuttle, specially designed for walkers and other tourists, running between Milford Haven and St David's, twice in each direction every day in summer, via Dale, Marloes, Broad Haven, Newgale and Solva. It'll stop anywhere safe to pick up or drop off passengers. All TICs have timetables.

Train Mainline trains from Swansea, Cardiff and England go to Carmarthen, from where services run to Milford Haven, to Fishguard, and to Pembroke Dock via Tenby and Kilgetty (3mi to Amroth).

At the end of the route, the nearest train station to Cardigan is at Fishguard. You can get there by bus, or take a bus to Carmarthen and join the train there.

Car Amroth is south of the A477, about 10mi by road from Tenby. At the end of the route, St Dogmaels is 2mi north of Cardigan, which is on the A487.

THE WALK
Amroth

Amroth is a little seaside resort straggling along a sandy beach. If you need sustenance

before setting out, very near the start *The New Inn* offers drinks and crab sandwiches. Farther along, *Beach Haven Guesthouse* (☎ 01834-813310), at the village post office, charges from £15 for B&B. At the far end of the beach, *Ashdale Guesthouse* (☎ 01834-813853) is similarly priced. The uninspiring *Amroth Arms* serves lunches and dinners, and the well-stocked village *shop* sells maps, guidebooks and takeaway hot snacks and drinks. *Pentlepoir YHA Hostel* (☎ 01834-812333) is 1.5mi inland from Saundersfoot, about 4mi from the start of the trail.

Day 1: Amroth to Tenby
7mi (11.5km), 3½–4 hours
This fairly easy section can be walked in a half-day, and is a good limber-up.

The path begins at the far eastern end of Amroth beach near *The New Inn*, where a stream marks the national park boundary and a plaque commemorates the opening of the trail in 1970. Follow the road westwards, parallel to the beach. As the road turns inland, the trail branches off left and climbs steeply up onto the cliffs, with good views back along the beach. You can stride out now for a few miles. In the jolly seaside village of **Saundersfoot** there are several lunch options. The path then runs along the edge of Rhode Wood to round Monkstone Point, then rises and falls, crossing small valleys, to follow a track, which turns into a lane then a street that leads you down into Tenby, to a point overlooking the bay, next to the TIC.

Tenby

The Welsh name for this seaside town, Dinbych y Pysgod (Little Fort of the Fishes), is as charming as Tenby itself. Elegant Georgian houses, most of them now hotels, rise above the beach and harbour. The most interesting building to look around is the late 15th-century **Tudor Merchant's House**. Tenby TIC (☎ 01834-842404) is on a street called the Croft, overlooking the harbour.

The town is surrounded by caravan and campsites; nearest is *Windmills Camping Park* (☎ 01834-842200), about 1mi north of the town centre, where two walkers and a tent pay about £8.

In the town itself there's a line of smart hotels along the Esplanade, with several smaller guesthouses and B&Bs on the streets behind. These include *Myrtle House* (☎ 01834-842508), on St Mary's St, friendly and proud of its nonsmoking record, and the nearby *Ripley St Mary's Hotel* (☎ 01834-842837), pleasantly old-fashioned with wonderful flowers, both charging around £25; *Boulston Cottage* (☎ 01834-843289, 29 Trafalgar Rd), similarly priced; and *Weybourne Guesthouse* (☎ 01834-843641, 14 Warren St), near the train station, plain but cheap, with rooms for around £15. Also recommended is *Glenholme Guesthouse* (☎ 01834-834909), on Picton Terrace, with B&B from £20; the people here are keen walkers and can advise on route information, maps etc.

For a different atmosphere, *The Normandie Inn* (☎ 01834-842227, steve@normandie-inn.demon.co.uk) is a lively and colourful place on Frog St, with double rooms for around £60, good food and live music some evenings.

Tenby has numerous places to eat, including countless takeaways selling fish and chips, burgers etc. If you want to sit down for a straightforward refuel, *Candy Restaurant* does snacks from £2, breakfasts for £3 to £4 and lunches for £4 to £6 (all with great views over the bay). Next door, *The Bay of Bangal* (☎ 01834-843331) is open every day serving Indian food; a full meal will cost about £10. Also good for an evening meal, *The Bay Tree*, on Tudor Square, is recommended, with main dishes from £6 to £10.

Most pubs in Tenby cater for the lively holiday crowd. For a quieter atmosphere, no-frills decor and decent beer, try *The Hope & Anchor*, down by the harbour, and *The Crown*, on Frog St, which also does bar food for around £4.

Day 2: Tenby to Manorbier
8.5mi (13.5km), 3½–4½ hours
This is another short enjoyable day; the walking is quite easy, the scenery varied and there are several places for food.

If the tide is out the first mile can be walked along the sands of **South Beach**.

When the red flags fly at Giltar Point (a military firing range) you'll have to make a detour through the village of Penally. The path soon regains the cliffs, dotted with caves and blowholes, passes the sandy beach of Lydstep Haven (half of which is covered by a caravan site), and the headland **Lydstep Point**, buttressed by high cliffs, which are favoured by rock climbers. If you need refreshment, up the lane is the *Lydstep Tavern*.

One mile beyond and 200m from the beach is *Manorbier YHA Hostel* (☎ 01834-871803), charging £10.85, or £5.50 for camping; with its futuristic grey and yellow cladding, this place looks like a cross between a 1960s-style space station and a motorway diner.

From Skrinkle Haven, the trail heads inland, round an army camp, and across the cliffs to Manorbier Bay.

Manorbier
In pretty Manorbier village the **castle** is well worth a visit.

At *East Moor Farm* on the trail, just 2mi west, there's simple camping (£2 per tent for walkers) and a teashop open from lunchtime to 6pm.

B&Bs include *Fernley Lodge* (☎ 01834-871226), very friendly and stylish, charging £22; and *The Old Vicarage* (☎ 01834-871452, ℮ oldvic@manorbier-tenby.fsnet.co.uk), which charges £25 for en suite rooms and welcomes walkers.

Also worth a try for B&B is *Honeyhill* (☎ 01834-871906), on Warlows Meadow (a modern bungalow estate on the edge of the village).

The village also has a *shop*, open daily, *The Chives Tearoom* and *The Castle Inn*, which does good pub food.

Day 3: Manorbier to Bosherston
15mi (24km), 5½–7 hours
You should be getting into your stride now, as this is a longer day, with excellent cliff-top walking. There are not many places to get lunch, though, so consider carrying food.

From Manorbier it's 3.5 easy miles to Freshwater East, a busy little seaside resort. At the western end of the beach there are some public toilets, and a *shop* selling drinks and snacks. After another great rocking and rolling section you reach the tiny harbour of **Stackpole Quay**, (where a *tearoom* offers lunches for around £5) and then pass some more spectacular rock formations to reach the headland of **Stackpole Head**, where you can proudly look back over your walk so far.

About 2mi beyond Stackpole Head you reach a bay called Broad Haven (note, there's another Broad Haven later on the route), where the trail goes inland slightly and crosses a footbridge on the edge of

Stackpole Estate National Trust Nature Reserve. West of here is another military firing range, and the trail divides. If there's no red flag flying the range is open to walkers, and you take the path along the coast, past several natural rock arches, to round **St Govan's Head** (the most southerly point in Pembrokeshire) and visit the tiny **St Govan's Chapel**, set into the cliffs, which dates from the 6th century. From the chapel you follow a lane 1.5mi north to reach the little village of Bosherston.

However, if the red flags *are* flying, the coast route is closed. Instead, you follow

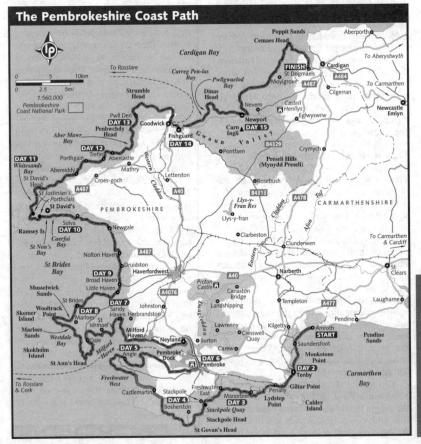

The Pembrokeshire Coast Path

the path inland through the nature reserve (a very nice route in its own right), over footbridges and round long thin lily pools to reach Bosherston.

Bosherston

About half a mile outside the village, there's simple camping at *Glebe Farmhouse* for £2 per tent.

In the village, *St Govan's Inn* (☎ *01646-661311*) does B&B from £20, plus good beer and fine home-made food, including venison for £6.50, cawl (thick soup) for £3 and several veggie dishes. Next door, *The Olde Worlde Cafe* serves lunches and snacks in a nice garden. Opposite the church, *Cornerstones* (☎ *01646-661660*) does very comfortable B&B from £20 to £21; rooms are en suite or come with a private bathroom.

Also called Trefalen Farm, *Trevallen Farm* (☎ *01646-661643*, e *trefalen @aol .com*), south-east of the village and very near the trail, is another option, with welcoming service and comfortable rooms for £18.50. Simple camping and baggage transfer is also available.

Day 4: Bosherston to Angle
15mi (24km), 5½–7 hours
There's wonderful coastal scenery on the first and last bits of this day's walk, but also a tedious 9mi road walk. If you're tempted to cut days, this could be one – see the boxed text 'South Coast to Sandy Haven Direct'.

From St Govan's Chapel, if the range is open, the trail continues along the coast – a beautiful 3.5mi stretch with numerous caves, blowholes and natural arches. At Stack Rocks you must turn inland and follow the road to Castlemartin. With ear-splitting detonations from the range, this is not a peaceful section, while across the fields to the north loom the signs of industry around Milford Haven. Some maps show a pub outside Warren but it's closed. Things are grim all round.

You reach the coast again (with relief) at Freshwater West, and the trail loops round the Angle Peninsula – another beautiful section with caves, tiny islands and little bays. At West Angle Bay there's a popular beach

and the *Wavecrest Cafe*. It's just a few miles now to Angle Point.

Angle

At Angle Point, you swing south and pass the quirky tumbledown *Old Point House* pub, definitely worth a stop, although opening hours are vague. Just down the track is

South Coast to Sandy Haven Direct

Day 4 has some beautiful coastal sections but is marred by a lot of road walking, while Days 5 and 6 pass through a mainly urban industrial setting. Purists may follow the trail but you'll probably be happy to skip these three days completely (hence details here are very limited). There are various ways of doing this.

From Manorbier village there's a bus to Pembroke and Pembroke Dock hourly (five daily on Sunday); this goes through Lamphry, which is 2mi inland from Freshwater East. Alternatively, you can walk inland 1.5mi to Manorbier Station, on the railway line between Tenby and Pembroke Dock. Or from Freshwater East you can walk to Lamphry Station, on the same line. There are trains six times a day to Pembroke and Pembroke Dock.

From Bosherston, things are a bit harder. There's a bus only twice a week (in the late afternoon) to Pembroke and Pembroke Dock. You could try hitching (with the usual precautions), or phone for a taxi from Pembroke to come and pick you up; Fred's Cars (☎ 01646-682226) will charge about £7.

You might overnight in Pembroke or continue onwards. There are several buses daily until about 4pm (although none on Sunday) from Pembroke and Pembroke Dock to Milford Haven, sometimes continuing to Herbrandston. The Puffin Shuttle bus (see Bus under Getting to/from the Walk earlier) runs from Milford Haven (at around 11am and 4pm daily in summer) to Herbrandston and St Ishmael's. Alternatively, consider a taxi from Pembroke to Milford Haven. Beyond Herbrandston, you can pick up the trail again in Sandy Haven.

a small *campsite*. Angle itself is not a pretty village, although *Mrs Watkins* B&B, on the main street, welcomes walkers, charging £20, and *The Hibernia Inn* has very good beer and food. There's also a village *shop*.

Day 5: Angle to Pembroke
13.5mi (21.5km), 5–6 hours
Today the scenery is unattractive and there's nowhere to get lunch.

The trail runs around Angle Bay and along the south bank of the estuary, always in the shadow of the vast oil refinery, past (or even under) several tanker jetties. Your next highlight is the demolished power station, beyond which tracks, lanes and roads lead into Pembroke.

Pembroke
The pleasant market town of Pembroke is built around a well-preserved 500-year-old castle, seat of the Tudor dynasty and birthplace of King Henry VII. If you're not hurrying through, there are several B&Bs and some good pubs. The TIC (☎ 01646-622388), on Commons Rd in the centre of town, can help with suggestions.

Day 6: Pembroke to Sandy Haven
16mi (25.5km), 6–8 hours
If you thought yesterday was bad, today is even worse.

The path takes you across the Pembroke River and round the backstreets of Pembroke Dock (a separate town), then over the large Cleddau Bridge, which does at least provide some views. There are more streets through Neyland, then another bloody oil refinery, before you reach the suburbs of Milford Haven. Beyond the docks there's a final section of grey suburban streets and, just for luck, one more oil works (dismantled) and – hurrah! – you're back to the national park and the beautiful coast again. From here it's a short hop to Sandy Haven.

Sandy Haven
The little estuary of Sandy Haven can be crossed (using stepping stones) two hours either side of low tide (a tide table is posted

by the slipway on each side). At high tide it's a 4mi detour via Herbrandston and Rickeston Bridge.

At Herbrandston, the *Sir Benfro Country Inn* (☎ 01646-694242) is a small, walker-friendly hotel offering B&B for £38/48 per single/double in en suite rooms, a range of bar food and full meals in the restaurant.

Above the river crossing, friendly and relaxed *Sandy Haven Caravan Site* (☎ 01646-698844, in July and August ☎ 01646-695899) has good facilities and charges walkers £3.50; bookings are preferred.

On the west side of the estuary, close to the trail, *Skerryback Farm* (☎ 01646-636598) welcomes walkers with B&B for £20 to £25, and three-course evening meals for £12 (or you can get a lift to the pub). A bit farther off the path is similarly priced *Bicton Farm* (☎ 01646-636215), another good option. There are more B&B options in the nearby village of St Ishmael's.

Day 7: Sandy Haven to Marloes
14mi (22.5km), 5–6½ hours
Today is a joy, with beautiful scenery, mostly level ground and a great pub lunch stop.

From Sandy Haven there are 4mi of fine, cliff-top walking to Gann, another inlet that can be crossed only two hours either side of low tide (otherwise it's a 2.5mi detour via Mullock). A lane leads into the holiday village of Dale, where *The Griffin Inn* does bar meals for £5 to £7. If you want to break here, *The Post House Hotel* (☎ 01646-636201) offers smart B&B at £26/48 for singles/doubles, and evening meals for £10.

From Dale it's 5mi round beautiful St Ann's Head to Westdale Bay (where you could almost pop back to Dale for another beer), then 2mi along the cliffs above Marloes Sands, from where Marloes village is about 1.5mi inland.

Marloes
West of Marloes, just off the path near Martin's Haven, *West Hook Farm* (☎ 01646-636424) offers simple camping – walkers pay £1.50. Nearby, *East Hook Farm* (☎ 01646-636291) charges £3 for one camper, £4 for two and offers simple B&B for £16, plus

evening meals for £6; you can also hire a caravan (sleeps six) for £25 per night.

Marloes Sands YHA Hostel (☎ *01646-636667*) is outside the village, near the beach and path, charging £7.35.

In Marloes village B&Bs include the very well-organised *Foxdale* (☎ *01646-636243*), from £18.50, with good camping facilities for around £3; the more relaxed and walker-friendly *Red Rails* (☎ *01646-636380*), also an art studio, from £17.50; and *Marloes*

Minimarket (☎ *01646 636365*), from £16 – also the village shop, open daily for groceries and packed lunches.

The Lobster Pot Inn (☎ *01646 636233*, *e* *lobsterpot@tinyworld.co.uk*) does lunches and dinners, including local fish, from £6 to £9, and B&B. New on the scene is the smart and trendy *Clock House* (☎ *01646-636527*, *e* *info@clockhousemarloes.co.uk*), where the coffee shop serves genuine lattes and cappuccinos, and B&B costs £20 to £25.

Pembrokeshire Coast Path – Some Route Highlights

If you've only got a day or two, we highly recommend the section of coast path between Dale and Martin's Haven, near Marloes. This is a particularly scenic stretch and all three points are easily reached from Milford Haven or Haverfordwest, and on the route of the excellent Puffin Shuttle bus service – see Getting to/from the Walk earlier for more details.

You could base yourself at Marloes and walk southwards, round St Ann's Head to Dale, before coming back on the Puffin Shuttle. Or from Marloes you could walk northwards along the coast to St Brides, then get the shuttle back. If that doesn't fit your timing, get the shuttle to St Brides, then walk back to Marloes from there.

Alternatively, a lovely circular day walk from Marloes takes you southwards to the east end of Marloes Sands beach, then round the wonderful headland to Martin's Haven, where you can branch off to reach Wooltack Point for great views, then along to Musslewick Sands and inland back to Marloes village (total distance 8mi/13km).

Another route highlight is the stage from Solva to Whitesands, especially recommended if you want to visit St David's, as there are good transport links here. You can stay in St David's for two nights and do an out-and-back route via Porthclais to St Justinian (9mi/15km), or get the Puffin Shuttle to Solva or Newgale, then walk back to St David's along the coast from there.

Day 8: Marloes to Broad Haven
13mi (21km), 4½–6 hours
This is another wonderful scenic stretch – a mix of beach and woodland, but there's no lunch place.

Retrace to Marloes Sands, then continue round the gorgeous Marloes Peninsula. Near the tip is the bay of **Martin's Haven**, from where you can reach the nature reserve islands of Skomer and Skokholm (you'll need a day off from walking, and the trip is highly recommended). From Martin's Haven it's just 2mi to **Musselwick Sands**, and another 2mi to **St Brides**, which has a beach and an interesting 13th-century church just inland.

From St Brides it's a reasonably easy 5mi stretch to **Little Haven**, a pretty village, although crowded in summer. *The Swan Inn* does excellent food, with crab sandwiches, cawl or ploughman's lunches for £2 to £4. *The St Brides Inn* (☎ *01437-781266*) also does food, and has B&B from £25/43 for singles/doubles. There's also a *shop* and *tearoom* by the harbour.

Outside the village, on the road (which is also the trail) from Little Haven towards Broad Haven, *Whitegates* (☎ *01437-781552*, *e* *welshhaven@aol.com*) offers B&B for £20 to £27; all rooms are en suite or have a private bathroom, there's a small swimming pool, great views and a small bar-restaurant that serves (among other things) pizzas, tapas, and organic ostrich steaks!

Broad Haven
This is a popular holiday centre with pubs, shops and B&Bs. The *YHA Hostel* (☎ *01437-781688*), beside the TIC, costs £10.85.

B&Bs include *Lion Rock* (☎ *01437-781645)*, up on Haroldson Hill, from £20; and *Anchor Guesthouse* (☎ *01437-781051)*, charging from £17.50.

Day 9: Broad Haven to Solva
11mi (17.5km), 4–5½ hours
Today offers more classic coastal scenery and varied walking – cliff paths, sandy beaches and some stiff ascents.

From Broad Haven the trail follows the cliff tops for 2mi, then joins the road near Druidston (where the rambling old *Druidston Hotel* (☎ *01437-781221)* is in a fabulous position, with B&B for around £35). The trail then runs above Druidston Haven beach and along the cliffs to the attractive little beach of Nolton Haven.

The trail climbs onto the cliffs again and offers good views north along **Newgale Sands**, one of the best beaches in Wales, especially popular with surfers. Should you feel the urge to try the waves, Newsurf (☎ 01437-721398) rents boards and wetsuits, and has showers and changing rooms. There's also a *pub*, *shop* and *cafe* here, and two cheap places for camping. About 2.5mi inland, the small modern *Penycwm YHA Hostel* (☎ *01437-721940)* charges £9.80.

From Newgale the trail climbs onto the cliffs. The 5mi walk to **Solva** is along a rugged section with impressive rock formations – a grand finish to a marvellous day.

Solva
Solva is unlike many other Pembrokeshire seaside villages; it's got slightly more style and a little less tackiness. Maybe it's the nearby yacht marina or maybe it's the influence of the National Trust. Whatever, it's good to be here.

The Harbour Inn (☎ *01437-720013)* does good beer and food, and also B&B from £27 (£38 en suite). Other B&Bs include *Caleb's Cottage* (☎ *01437-721737)*, a smart and friendly place charging £20; homely *Gamlyn* (☎ *01437-721542)*, from £20; and *The Smithy* (☎ 01437-721337), £20.

For something to eat take a stroll along Main St. *The Ship Inn* has good atmosphere, real ale and fine food; *The Old Printing*

House (☎ *01437-721603)* is a tearoom with B&B for £20; *The Old Pharmacy* (☎ *01437-720005)* is a cafe with seating in the garden out the back and a restaurant highly rated for its fish (main courses £13 to £19).

Day 10: Solva to Whitesands
13mi (21km), 5–7 hours
Much of this section of coast is owned by the National Trust and it's a beautiful area. There's nowhere for food; you could detour into St David's for lunch from Caerfai or Porthclais. If you haven't got a spare day to visit St David's, you might spend the afternoon and night here, and rejoin the route tomorrow at Whitesands.

From Solva, the trail climbs onto the cliffs and the superb coastal scenery continues – interesting rock formations, natural arches, caves and small islands. It's 4.5mi to Caerfai Bay, with a busy sandy beach and camping at *Caerfai Farm* (☎ *01437-720548)*, from £3. Half an hour's walking brings you to **St Non's Bay** – named after the mother of St David (see the boxed text 'St David's). The holy well has long been a pilgrimage site and there's a modern chapel nearby.

Another half-hour brings you to Porthclais, with a landing stage and some lime kilns. You can camp at nearby *Rhos Y Cribed Farm* for £2. Continuing round the headland there are good views across to Ramsey Island, a nature reserve that can be visited from the bay at St Justinian's (marked on the map as Porthstinian).

In just over two easy miles you reach the busy beach of **Whitesands Bay**; there's a large car park, *cafe*, telephone and public toilet here.

Whitesands & St David's
Half a mile uphill from Whitesands Bay is *St David's YHA Hostel* (☎ *01437-720345)*, a small and simple converted farmhouse with great views, charging £8. There are also a couple of campsites nearby, but these are not aimed at passing backpackers.

Most other accommodation options are in St David's, 2mi farther inland. The TIC (☎ 01437-720392) is in the large car park on the eastern edge of town, open daily, and worth a visit to see the interesting mix of ancient and modern architectural styles. Nearby is **Bryn Awel** (☎ *01437-720082, anthiny@stdavids71.freeserve.co.uk*), with a friendly laid-back atmosphere and B&B for £20. Alternatively, the main strip of B&Bs is Nun St, where walker-friendly choices include **Glendower Guesthouse & Restaurant** (☎ *01437-721650, No 7*), charging around £19, with all rooms en suite; **Y Glennydd Hotel** (☎ *01437-720576, No 51*), at £20/25 for singles/doubles; and **Y Gorlan** (☎ *01437-720837, No 77*) with excellent views from the lounge, charging £24.

A smarter option is **The Old Cross Hotel** (☎ *01437-720387*, **e** *enquiries@oldcrosshotel.co.uk*), on Cross Square, which is well used to walkers, with B&B from £48/82, snacks in the bar, evening meals from £10 and teas in the garden during the day. If you think it's time for a rest day, a two-night deal costs £63/113 with dinner.

Other smarter eating places, both with main courses from around £10, are **Cartref Restaurant**, on Nun St, and **Coxes Restaurant**, on the High St (the latter with a very interesting menu, including East Asian specialities). Around Cross Square are many cheaper cafes, teashops, and snack takeaways. **The Farmer's Arms**, Goat St, is a perennially popular pub, and deservedly so, with good beer and bar food.

St David's

This small country town is named after St David, the patron saint of Wales (his name is Dewi Sant in Welsh and St David's is called Tyddewi, literally David's House). He was born in AD 462, where the ruined chapel now stands in nearby St Non's Bay, and was inspired by the surrounding scenery to found a monastic community here in the early 6th century. Even today there's something very special about St David's that the crowds of holiday-makers fail to extinguish. His relics are kept in a casket in the magnificent cathedral. This cathedral makes St David's technically a city, the smallest in Britain.

If you want a break from walking and would like to try another coastal activity such as surfing, kayaking or rock climbing, TYF (☎ 01437-721611, **e** info@tyf.com), on Cross Square in the centre of St David's, seems to have the outdoor scene sewn up, and offers a range of courses from a few hours to a week.

Day 11: Whitesands to Trefin
12mi (19.5km), 4½–6 hours
Most of this section is straightforward walking with superb views; Porthgain is a good place for lunch.

If you stayed at St David's, regain the trail at Whitesands and head north along a wonderfully wild, heather-covered section round **St David's Head**, with an Iron Age fort at the end of the promontory. From here it's 7.5mi of excellent cliff-top hiking to Abereiddy, which has a small beach, then another mile or so to **Porthgain**, a former brick works and slate centre, now a quiet village with a picturesque harbour. If you want to view the wonderful cliffs from the sea but kayaking sounds too energetic, local skipper Rob Jones (☎ 01348-831518) offers boat trips. At **Harbour Lights** you can buy teas, sandwiches from £3 or a crab salad for £7.50, and every Thursday, Friday and Saturday evening a three-course meal of local specialities costs £25. **The Sloop Inn**, in an age of theme pubs, is highly recommended for its old-fashioned ordinariness and for its food – sandwiches from £2.50 and main meals from £5 to £7. Sit on the terrace and try a plate of mussels washed down with local ale. Relax! Good job it's only 2mi to Trefin this afternoon.

Trefin
The village of Trefin (pronounced treveen) is just inland from the path, with a post office, **shop** and some good accommodation options. The **YHA Hostel** (☎ *01348-831414*), in the old school, costs £8, while campers can aim for **Pendergast Caravan Site** (☎ *01348-831368*), on the south side of the village, charging walkers £2.50.

B&Bs include **Cranog** (☎ *01348-831392*), friendly and genteel, charging

£17.50; *The Old Court House* (☎ *01348-837095*), a comfortable vegetarian guesthouse, charging from around £21, also offering self-guided walks, with lifts provided; and *Bryngarw Guesthouse* (☎ *01348-831211*, e *a.r.johnson @dial.pipex.com*), on the east side of the village, charging £24 to £27, with all rooms en suite.

In the village, *The Ship Inn* does good beer and food, and *Melin Trefin Craftshop* offers teas and snacks. Nearby, *The Gallery* does highly rated evening meals.

Day 12: Trefin to Pwll Deri
10mi (16km), 3½–4½ hours

Today's walk is yet again a wonderful experience, with cliffs, rock buttresses, pinnacles, islets, bays and beaches. St David was right – this is heavenly country. It's tempered only slightly by the choice of places to stay being thin on the ground. You might consider stopping early, and then pushing all the way to Fishguard on the next day.

From Trefin it's an easy 3mi to Abercastle, where there's a small beach. A mile beyond here, at the tiny bay of Pwllstrodur, you can branch off inland to reach *Carnachenwen* (☎ *01348-831636*), on a farm halfway between the coast and the village of Mathry. This is a very walker-friendly place with B&B for £21. Packed lunches and evening meals are available to order, anything from a snack (for a few pounds) to a four-course blow-out for £14. Camping costs £3 and campers can also order breakfast or dinner. The welcoming owner is an experienced walker and can advise on maps, the surrounding coast path, circular routes, local guides etc. If this place is full, other local people who take guests on an occasional basis can be recommended. There are also a couple more B&B options in Mathry.

Two more miles brings you to the larger beach at Aber Mawr. Just inland, luxurious *Tregwynt Mansion* (☎ *01348-891685*, *annsayer@tesco.net*), marked as Tregwynt Farm on the map, offers hotel-style B&B for £43/66 per single/double; evening meals are not available, but the helpful owners can advise on local taxis or loan you a bicycle to reach the pub at Mathry.

Preseli Venture (☎ *01348-837709*, e *info @preseliventure.com*), is another choice, inland and south from Aber Mawr at Parcynole Fach, a small outdoor activities centre, which also offers very comfortable 'ski-lodge-style' bunk accommodation from £23. The restaurant-bar serves dinners, lunches and drinks. This may be a spot to consider staying two nights and have a break from walking. You can go kayaking on the sea or 'coasteering' along the cliffs to explore the beautiful coast from another angle. Coasteering, a recognised British pastime, is intended to include everything from climbing to scrambling and swimming, but should be attempted with caution. If you combine activities with accommodation you get a better deal.

But if you're a dedicated walker, you'll push on to reach the headland of **Penbwchdy**, the western end of one of the most impressive stretches of cliffs on the whole path. If the weather is good you can see all the way back to St David's Head. If it's windy you may be thankful for the circular dry-stone shelter here. Either way, it's a wild 40-minute walk to join the road above the bay of **Pwll Deri**. There's another stunning view from here back along the cliffs.

Pwll Deri
The *YHA Hostel* (☎ *01348-891385*) must have one of the finest locations of any hostel in Britain, worth every penny of the £8.10 charge. You can also camp here. There are no B&Bs nearby, so consider stopping early near Aber Mawr. If you're continuing on, there's a tea garden at *Tal-y-Gaer Farm*, near the hostel, and at a house called *Trethro*, about half a mile north.

Day 13: Pwll Deri to Fishguard
10mi (16km), 3½–4½ hours

There's excellent cliff scenery and reasonably easy walking on this section, but nowhere for lunch.

From Pwll Deri the trail leads you along the cliffs for 3mi to the impressive promontory of **Strumble Head**, marked by its famous lighthouse. Inland at *Tresinwen Farm* (☎ *01348-891238*) there's camping for £2.

PEMBROKESHIRE

About 3mi farther on you reach **Carregwastad Point**, where the last invasion of Britain occurred some 200 years ago (see the boxed text 'The Fishguard Invasion').

An hour later you round the headland and with a sudden jolt see Fishguard – the largest town since Milford Haven. The trail drops down to the port of Goodwick to come out by the ferry quay, then past a roundabout at the bottom of the hill. Nearby, there's a TIC and the **Ocean Lab exhibition centre**. From here the trail climbs steeply up into Fishguard, but keeps to the cliff edge and skirts the town. Stay with it until you reach a viewpoint overlooking Lower Fishguard, then go up the street called Penslade, which will bring you out on West St, very near the town centre.

Goodwick & Fishguard

Goodwick has the train station, the beach and the port for ferries to Ireland. Fishguard is larger, with a wider choice of places to stay and eat, and a TIC (☎ 01348-873484), which is in the town hall in the town centre.

The Beach House (☎ 01348-872085), just off New Hill in Goodwick, has B&B from around £15. Just along Quay Rd, *Sirole Guesthouse* (☎ 01348-872375) and *Stanley Guesthouse* (☎ 01348-873024) both do B&B from £15 and offer bed-only deals from £13. Pubs in Goodwick include *The Hope & Anchor* (☎ 01348-872314), which also does walker-friendly B&B from £20, and *The Rose & Crown* with good beer and good-value food.

In Fishguard, *Hamilton Guesthouse & Backpackers Lodge* (☎ 01348-874797, e ste phenism@hotmail.com, 21 Hamilton St) is a good budget choice, with beds in dorms or double rooms from £10, a self-catering kitchen and a friendly manager who knows the coast path well.

Good walker-friendly B&Bs include *Cri'r Wylan* (☎ 01348-873398), on Penwallis St, which does B&B from £18; and *Mrs Wheat* (☎ 01348-873592, 55 West St), similarly priced. Up a grade is *Three Main Street* (☎ 01348-874275), primarily an award-winning restaurant (three courses for £28), also with stylish double rooms from £60.

Other options for food include several fish and chip takeaways, cafes and pubs: *The Royal Oak* on the Square has good beer and recommended bar meals. On the High St, *The Ship* and *Bennet's Navy Tavern* both do good cheap pub food.

Day 14: Fishguard to Newport
12.5mi (20km), 5–6 hours
There are superb views from the cliffs on this section, but only one lunch option.

Leaving Fishguard you follow the trail round picturesque Lower Fishguard, the old part of town (and location for the 1971 film *Under Milk Wood*, starring Richard Burton and Elizabeth Taylor), and then out along the cliff tops once again.

About 4mi from Fishguard, at the small bay of Pwllgwaelod, *Old Sailors* offers seafood snacks and lunches for £4 to £8. It's possible to take a short cut to Cwm-yr-Eglwys through the valley that almost divides **Dinas Head** from the mainland, but don't be tempted – it's a wonderful walk around the headland and on to Newport.

The Fishguard Invasion

The last invasion of Britain occurred in 1797 at Carregwastad Point, a few miles west of Fishguard. The invaders were a group of about 1500 French mercenaries and bailed convicts, led by an American who'd been expelled from his homeland by George Washington for being too radical. This hotch-potch army's main purpose was to divert English troops then occupying Ireland, so France could seriously invade Ireland instead. But after a few days of pillage in the surrounding area, the French were seen off by local volunteer 'yeoman' soldiers, with help from the people of Fishguard, including most famously one Jemima Nichols, who single-handedly captured 12 mercenaries in the main street with nothing more than a pitchfork.

The whole story is told in the Fishguard Tapestry, a 100m-long Bayeux-style project made by local craftworkers, which can be seen (free) in an exhibition hall in the town centre.

Newport

Newport (its Welsh name is Trefdraeth) is a charming, compact little town and a good base for exploring the area. A route up the rocky outcrop of **Carn Ingli** overlooking the town is described in the Preseli Hills Circuit later in this chapter. If it's raining, there are plenty of good cafes, and the **West Wales Eco-Centre** is worth a brief visit. Newport TIC (☎ 01239-820912) is on Long St, just off the main street.

The modern *YHA Hostel* (☎ *01239-820080*), in the town centre, charges £9, while *Morawelon Caravan & Camping Park* (☎ *01239-820565*), on the beach outside the town, charges £3.

Newport has many B&Bs, pubs and cafes along (or just off) East St and Bridge St, which together form the main drag, including *Llysmeddyg Guesthouse* (☎ *01239-820008*), popular and walker-friendly, charging around £20; *Hafan Deg* (☎ *01239-820301*), on Long St, walker (and cat) friendly, charging from £18 (£21 en suite); *Cnapan* (☎ *01239-820575*), a smarter place with good quality rooms, charging £35/56 for singles/doubles, and also a highly regarded restaurant; and *The Golden Lion Hotel* (☎ *01239-820321*), with B&B from £20/35, plus bar food and a restaurant.

For food, *The Llwyngwair Arms* serves real ales and bar food. *Fronlas Cafe* does lunches and cream teas; *Café Fleur* is similar, and open evenings too. *Beehive Cafe* (☎ *01239-820372*) does good snacks and lunches, and dinners in the evening from £6 to £9.

Day 15: Newport to St Dogmaels

15.5mi (25km), 6–7½ hours
This is quite a long day, but it finishes the trail with a flourish and offers some of the best walking of the whole route. Again there's nowhere nearby for lunch, so bring food and drink.

East of Newport Sands the coast along the first half of this section is wild and uninhabited, with numerous rock formations and caves. **Pwll-y-Wrach**, the Witches' Cauldron, is the remains of a collapsed blowhole.

You may see seals on the rocks nearby. At Ceibwr Bay you could branch inland to Moylgrove, which has several B&B options. Onwards from here the route is quite tough, but it's a wonderful rollercoasting finale, through stunning cliff scenery.

At **Cemaes Head** stop and take stock. The end of the trail is nigh but, aesthetically, this headland is the finish, as the last few miles are something of an anticlimax.

So, having fully savoured the last few days or weeks, from here you turn inland, and follow the lane towards St Dogmaels and Cardigan. If you're in no rush there are some places to stay nearby. There is cheap camping at *Allt-y-goed* (☎ *01239-612673*), less than half a mile from Cemaes Head. A mile farther on is simple *Poppit Sands YHA Hostel* (☎ *01239-612936*), charging £9 or £4.50 for camping.

A mile past the hostel, the road swings sharp right by the lifeboat station. Just beyond here you leave the national park and a plaque on a wall marks the end of the trail. Time for some congratulations, and maybe a cup of tea in the nearby *cafe*. (There's also a phone box here, from where you could call a taxi from Cardigan.) But the map disagrees and has you walk another mile, where the trail fizzles out on the edge of St Dogmaels village; maybe they think the nautically decorated *Ferry Inn* is the place for a celebratory pint instead – the beer's certainly good and so is the food (bar meals £5 to £7), but service can be a bit abrupt. Another mile brings you to the *Teifi Netpool Inn*, larger, friendlier and with cheaper food.

If you want to stay locally, B&B at the *Princess Villa* (☎ *01239-612224*), a family home with just one guest room, costs £15. Another choice is the rather plain *Webley Waterfront Hotel* (☎ *01239-612085*) with B&B in en suite rooms from £30. Otherwise, it's 2mi from St Dogmaels to Cardigan.

Cardigan

Although the official end of the Pembrokeshire Coast Path is at St Dogmaels, most walkers continue for 2mi into the small town of Cardigan, either for a place to stay or for transport home. This town (outside the national park and actually just over the border outside Pembrokeshire) was once an important seafaring and trading centre but things are quieter now. The TIC (☎ 01239-613230) is in the foyer of the theatre (which also has an excellent *cafe*), just off the town's main street.

There are several good places to stay on Gwbert Rd, north of the centre, including *Maes-a-Môr* (☎ 01239-614929) from £16; and *Brynhyfryd* (☎ 01239-612861), similarly priced. Nearby, *Garth Guesthouse* is another option.

Your food options include several fish and chip takeaways and at least two Indian restaurants. On the main street, the *Black Lion Hotel* (☎ 01239-612532) has bar food and B&B in comfortable en suite singles/doubles for £30/40.

A Preseli Hills Circuit

Distance	15mi (24km)
Duration	6–8 hours
Standard	medium
Start/Finish	Newport
Gateways	Haverfordwest, Fishguard, Cardigan

Summary A circular walk over open moorland and through wooded valleys. Paths are generally well marked, although indistinct in places (and boggy after rain).

The Preseli Hills (also spelt Presely) are the highest landmass in West Wales, and the views from the summits are exceptional – as far as the Gower Peninsula to the southeast and to the mountains of Snowdonia in the north. In extremely clear conditions you may even see the Wicklow Hills in Ireland. Other notable features include the abundance of Neolithic monuments – burial chambers, hillforts and standing stones.

The route we describe gives you a taste of this magical mystical area. From the small coastal town of Newport it goes across the moorlands around Carn Ingli, dips into the tranquil Gwaun Valley, then rises again to wilder moors, before looping back to the start via the woods of Sychbant.

Although the hills are not particularly high, they can be exposed, and they occasionally get a covering of snow in winter, so take appropriate clothing.

Direction, Distance & Duration

This circular route starts and ends at Newport. It can be done in either direction, but an ascent of Carn Ingli is best done near the beginning so that you get a preview of the splendours to come. This route is not way-marked, so a map should definitely be carried. The total distance is 15mi. There's a reasonable amount of ascent and descent, but nothing very serious, so you should allow around six to eight hours of walking, plus an hour for lunch or looking at ancient monuments (longer if you're a big eater or historian).

Alternatives From Llanerch you can cut across to Sychbant, straight down the Gwaun Valley, and miss out the southern part of the route, making a total of around 8mi.

PLANNING
Maps & Books

The OS Landranger 1:50,000 map No 145 (*Cardigan/Aberteifi & Mynydd Preseli*) covers this area. For more detail use the OS Outdoor Leisure 1:25,000 map No 36 (*South Pembrokeshire*).

Guidebooks specifically covering the Preseli Hills include *Walking in the Presely Hills* by Brian John (published by the national park), which describes seven circular walks. The same author and publisher also

Which Newport?

It's important to note that the start of this walk is in Newport, a small town between Fishguard and Cardigan in West Wales. It shouldn't be confused with the much larger town of Newport, in Gwent, which is near Cardiff, nor with the town on the Isle of Wight, which we also describe in this book, nor with the dozen or so other places in Britain that also share this common name.

The Brecon Beacons from Pen y Crug Hill Fort; Fan y Big (left), Cribyn, Pen y Fan and Corn Du (right)

For Gothic atmosphere, walkers can overnight at the ruins of Llanthony Priory, Brecon Beacons

NICHOLAS REUSS

NICHOLAS REUSS

Looking along heath-covered cliffs to Strumble Head, Pembrokeshire

A worthwhile detour from the trail – St David's Cathedral, dedicated to the patron saint of Wales

Tenby, a blend of fishing tradition and lively tourism, on the Pembrokeshire Coast Path

have the *Upper Gwaun Valley Walks Pack* and *The Carningli Walks*.

Information Sources
Newport TIC (☎ 01239-820912) can assist with information on the area and accommodation options.

Guided Walks
National park rangers run guided walks in the Preseli Hills. You'll find details at Newport TIC, or in the free visitor newspaper *Coast to Coast*.

PLACES TO STAY & EAT
Newport
For information on places to stay and eat in Newport, see Day 14 of the Pembrokshire Coast Path, earlier in this chapter.

GETTING TO/FROM THE WALK
Bus See Getting There & Away earlier in this chapter for details on National Express coaches from outside the region. There's a local bus almost hourly (twice each way on Sunday) between Fishguard and Cardigan via Newport.

Train The nearest train station is Fishguard, which has two trains a day to/from London. From there get the local bus – see Getting to/from the Walk under the Pembrokeshire Coast Walk earlier.

Car Newport is on the A487 between Fishguard and Cardigan. There is a car park on Long St, opposite the TIC.

THE WALK
Newport to Llanerch
3mi (5km), 2–2½ hours
From the centre of Newport, take Market St then Church St uphill, past the castle on your right. Keep on this road for about a mile to reach a phone box, where you take a track on the right – still uphill. After 300m you fork left to join a path running alongside a wall. Go right (west) at the next path junction and work your way up to a peak called **Carn Llwyd**, before heading south, and still steeply up, to **Carn Ingli** summit.

This is the site of an Iron Age hillfort, which fully exploits the precipitous hillsides as defence – it's still a tough scramble to the top, so take time here to catch your breath and admire the marvellous views.

From Carn Ingli take the path down the south-east side of the hill to the lane. Turn right and follow the lane, which becomes a dirt track, past the farms of Dolrannog Isaf and Dolrannog Uchaf, and through the woods to reach the farm at Llanerch and the lane that runs down the Gwaun Valley.

If you are taking the short cut, turn right along the valley road to reach Sychbant.

Llanerch to Sychbant
7.5mi (12km), 3–4 hours
If you are going for the southern part of this route, follow the road straight on (south-east) for 200m then turn right onto a path where the lane swings round to the left. This path leads through some lovely woodland, alongside pools and waterfalls, to meet a

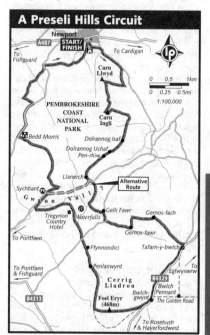

lane at Gelli Fawr. Turn right and go along this lane for 300m, then turn left onto a signposted bridleway. Follow this through the abandoned farm of Gernos-fawr, then up through fields to go through the yard of Gernos-fach (still a working farm, so close the gates!). From here a dirt track leads across the moor to Tafarn-y-bwlch.

At Tafarn-y-bwlch you meet the B4329. Turn right and follow it for about 1mi to Bwlch-gwynt. This road is fairly traffic-free, but if you want to avoid it, a bridleway (the old road) forks off to the left (south) and meets another bridleway at Bwlch Pennant (*bwlch* in Welsh means 'pass'), where you turn right (west) to reach Bwlch-gwynt. (This second bridleway is part of 'The Golden Road', which runs across the crest of the Preseli Hills.)

From Bwlch-gwynt a permissive path leads up to the summit of Cerrig Lladron, which is called Foel Eryr ('Hill of the Eagle') and certainly offers bird's-eye views. Then you descend again to meet a bridleway, which leads over rough moorland eventually down to the farms of Penlanwynt and Ffynnondici. Cross the lane and go down the drive of Tregynon Country Hotel, where you *must* keep to the footpath markers. These guide you through the edge of the hotel garden and past another Iron Age fort, before going down into the densely wooded Gwaun Valley once again. After a long descent you reach a footpath, which crosses the boggy valley floor on a footbridge, and again meets the lane which runs down the Gwaun Valley. Turn right along this for about 300m to Sychbant, or left to reach Pontfaen, 1mi west of the route, where the *Duffryn Arms* is a single room in the landlady's rather tumble-down house, which hasn't changed for about 50 years. Beer is served in jugs through a hatch, and food is limited to chocolate, crisps and pickled eggs.

Sychbant to Newport
4.25mi (7km), 2–2½ hours
Sychbant is the name of a patch of woodland with some short walking trails, a picnic site and public toilet. From here follow the track up through the woodland into the forestry plantation, to finally emerge on the west side of the plantation from where a path leads to a lane at a standing stone called **Bedd Morris**. Local myth tells of a highwayman called Morris who was buried here, but it is in fact a Bronze Age marker stone, still used as parish boundary today.

Turn right (northwards) onto the lane. You can follow it all the way to meet the A487 on the western edge of Newport, or leave it for a short while by turning left about 500m from Bedd Morris onto a rutted old track, which leads to a new farm track, where you turn right and follow another narrow lane, to rejoin the main lane down towards Newport.

After 100m on this lane, turn right (east) onto a bridleway and follow this for about half a mile, past Hill House, traversing the hills above Newport. This eventually meets the top of Mill Lane, which leads straight down into the town centre.

Other Walks

THE DAUGLEDDAU ESTUARY
For walkers the best parts of Pembrokeshire are the coast and the Preseli Hills – both covered in this chapter. But another part of the national park that is often overlooked is the Daugleddau Estuary – a tranquil wetland area where four large rivers meet. So few people come here that it's been dubbed the 'Secret Waterway' by the local tourist organisation. For walkers there are several short routes called **Secret Waterway Trails** along the eastern side of the river and into the surrounding farmland.

Good points to aim for include the villages of Landshipping and Lawrenny, which can both be reached by public transport from Haverfordwest, Pembroke or Tenby. Carew Castle is also well worth a visit, there are some historic shipbuilding sites, and several of the villages have pleasant pubs and teashops, which make good lunch stops. The birdwatching is also excellent.

To tie in a lot of these options, you could take the bus between Pembroke and Tenby, get off at Carew, visit the castle, then walk north on one of the Secret Waterway Trails to Cresswell Quay, through Lawrenny and Landshipping, to finish at Canaston Bridge, on the bus route between Haverfordwest, Narberth and Tenby. This is over 20mi, so it would be a long day, but you could always shorten it by getting the bus to/from Lawrenny or Landshipping, or splitting it in two by staying overnight in the area; Lawrenny and Cresswell Quay both have a selection of local farmhouse style B&Bs.

You can get a lot more information on this area, plus a range of good free leaflets covering walks, places to stay and things to see, from any TIC in South Pembrokeshire, or direct from Greenways, part of SPARC (☎ 01834-860965, ⓔ tourism@sparc.org.uk), a tourism promotion organisation. The friendly people here are very keen to help with all aspects of your visit.

HIDDEN HERITAGE WALKS
A series of short circular walks has been developed to take visitors away from the more popular and crowded areas. Many of these can easily be reached from the Pembrokeshire Coast Path, and make interesting diversions away from the main route. They include the **All Saints Walks** south of the town of Pembroke, the **Ritec Walk** between Penally and St Florence, and the **Lampeter Vale Walk** east of Narberth and Haverfordwest. Good leaflets with maps and route descriptions are available from local TICs or direct from Greenways/SPARC (☎ 01834-860965, ⓔ tourism@sparc.org.uk).

LANDSKER TRAILS
If you're looking for something longer, the **Landsker Borderlands Trail** is a 50mi circular route taking in the best of the Secret Waterway and other 'Hidden Heritage' sites mentioned earlier. You can follow this route at your own pace, staying at local B&Bs along the way, or get a package organised for you by Landsker Countryside Holidays, another arm of the active Greenways/ SPARC organisation (☎ 01834-860965, ⓔ tourism @sparc.org.uk). Tours include accommodation, packed lunches, maps and route guides, baggage transfer and transport to/from train stations. The same outfit also organises walking tours on the **South of the Landsker Trail**, an excellent 60mi walk combining the Secret Waterway, the coast and the hinterland, and is keen to assist with any aspect of your visit to South Pembrokeshire. Its informative Web site (ⓦ www .southpembrokeshire-holidays.co.uk) has more details.

Snowdonia

Snowdonia is the mountainous region of North Wales, taking its name from the highest peak in England and Wales, Mt Snowdon (1085m), which dominates the area. The area is contained within the Snowdonia National Park, which covers an area of over 800 sq mi (approximately 2000 sq km). Its name is Parc Cenedlaethol Eryri in Welsh; Eryri means 'home of the eagles', although these days you're more likely to see falcons

and buzzards flying around the region's mountainsides.

The mountains around Snowdon are the remains of volcanoes, subsequently eroded by ice age glaciers. This mix has bequeathed a striking landscape of sharp ridges and steep cliffs, while beneath the summits are smooth bowl-shaped valleys called *cwms*. East towards the Carneddau mountains or south towards Cadair Idris,

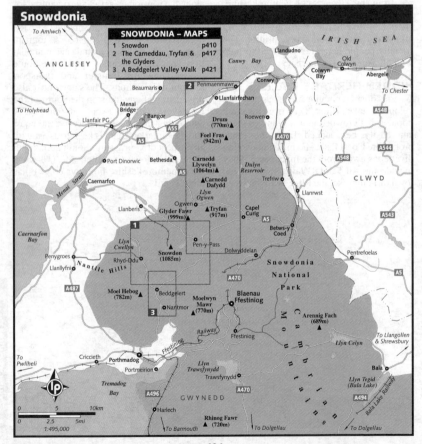

SNOWDONIA – MAPS	
1 Snowdon	p410
2 The Carneddau, Tryfan & the Glyders	p417
3 A Beddgelert Valley Walk	p421

the hills are more rounded although they still retain a ruggedness that differs from the uplands of England.

Snowdonia is varied not only visually but socially. In the west are mainly Welsh-speaking people, from farming and slate-mining backgrounds. In the east the communities are closer to the anglicised flatlands of Clwyd, and mainly English speaking. This contrast has a historical thread, the remains of frustrated English attempts to occupy Wales in the 13th and 14th centuries, on the heels of the Romans who had similarly failed several centuries earlier.

The survival of the Welsh language is a testament to the Welsh spirit and determination, and when you read, scratched on a rock, 'You English can visit Wales, but please don't come and live here', you'll see that for some the division is alive and kicking. However, Welsh people are generally hospitable (especially if you're not English!) and Snowdonia offers some of the best mountain walking in Britain, so a visit here is highly recommended. If you don't have time to reach Scotland for the big mountains, then North Wales goes a long way towards supplying the goods.

In this chapter we describe in detail four separate day walks over three different mountain groups in the northern part of Snowdonia. Because they're of such high quality, some of these routes are popular and are likely to be busy in the high season. Early starts will help you avoid the crowds.

Warning

Unless you have the appropriate mountain skills, the high-level routes described in this chapter are not recommended in the winter (between December and March) as they may be partly covered by snow or ice. Even in summer, it's important not to underestimate weather conditions on the summit as they are often very different from conditions lower down. Check the weather forecast at Tourist Information Centres (TICs), or phone the Mountaincall Snowdonia weather information service (☎ 0891-500449).

We also describe a valley walk – ideal if the weather is bad or you don't have a head for heights. At the end of this chapter we outline other options in Snowdonia, and also suggest how some walks can be linked together to form a longer route.

GETTING THERE & AWAY

The Getting Around chapter lists several public transport inquiry lines that provide details of both national and local bus and train services: See the boxed text 'National Transport Information' on p92.

The main gateway towns for northern Snowdonia are Llandudno, Bangor and Caernarfon, all transport hubs. Farther south, Porthmadog is accessible by train, while Llanberis and Betws-y-Coed, on the edges of the national park, are useful walking bases.

Bus Snowdonia's gateway towns are all easily reached by National Express coach from Manchester and London.

Train The mainline stations for northern Snowdonia are Llandudno Junction and Bangor, with regular services to/from Crewe in England, where you can connect with trains to the rest of the country. South of Snowdon is Porthmadog, which is linked by train to Birmingham via Machynlleth.

Car If driving to Snowdonia, the main approach route from England is along the A55, an extension of the M56, which branches off the M6 near Manchester. Other main roads are the A5 from Birmingham and the A470 from Cardiff.

GETTING AROUND

Bus There are local buses to Llanberis six times per day (no service on Sunday) from Bangor, and half-hourly (every hour on Sunday) from Caernarfon.

Most useful for transport within Snowdonia are the Snowdon Sherpa buses. These follow routes from Llandudno, Betws-y-Coed, Porthmadog, Pwllheli, Caernarfon, Llanberis and Bangor, and crisscross the main Snowdon area via Beddgelert, Capel Curig and/or the Pen-y-Grwyd Hotel.

At Llanberis and Bethesda you can connect with regular local buses to/from Bangor. There are also services between Llanberis and Caernarfon.

On the Snowdon Sherpa service, you sometimes have to change bus to get where you want, but all-day rover tickets are available. Get a timetable from a TIC and it all falls into place. Note that this service is also used to take children from villages down to schools in the main towns, so in school holidays some services are limited; they are also reduced in winter (November to March).

The *Gwynedd Public Transport Guide*, an essential booklet covering all bus, train and coach services in the area, is also available from TICs.

Train The main line between London, the English Midlands and Holyhead (Anglesey) runs along the northern side of Snowdonia, while branch lines run along the eastern and southern sides of the national park through several small towns and villages, including Betws-y-Coed, Blaenau Ffestiniog, Minfford and Porthmadog, which can be used as gateways or ends to the walks described in this section.

PLANNING

The information in this section is relevant to all the walks in this chapter.

Maps

The Ordnance Survey (OS) Landranger 1:50,000 map No 115 *(Snowdon/Yr Wyddfa)* covers all the walks described in this chapter, as does Outdoor Leisure 1:25,000 map No 17 *(Snowdonia – Snowdon and Conwy Valley)*. For wider coverage of the rest of Snowdonia, you'll need Outdoor Leisure maps No 18 *(Snowdonia – Harlech, Porthmadog & Bala)* and No 23 *(Snowdonia – Cadair Idris & Bala Lake)*.

Harvey maps cover the area in three sheets, each at 1:40,000 or 1:25,000. The routes described in detail in this section are on *Snowdonia West*, which covers Snowdon, the Glyders and Llanberis, and *Snowdonia North*, which covers the Carneddau, Tryfan and the Glyders.

Books

Snowdonia is very well covered by guidebooks for walkers. *Hill Walking in Snowdonia* and *Scrambles in Snowdonia* by Steve Ashton are both very popular (but beware – some of the scrambles included are rock climbs!). The technical definition of scrambling is discussed under Place Names & Terminology in the Facts for the Walker chapter.

Less outrageous are *Walks in Snowdonia Mountains* and *Walks in North Snowdonia* by Don Hinson, the former covering the summits, the latter covering low-level walks. Footprint Maps produce a handy combined *Snowdonia* map and guide, while *Snowdonia, Anglesey & the Lleyn Peninsula* Pathfinder Guide, published by Jarrold, describes a good range of routes. An inspiring picture book that also has good route information is *On Foot in Snowdonia* by Bob Allen, although this is harder to find these days. *The Ridges of Snowdonia* by Steve Ashton is a worthy successor.

Information Sources

There are several TICs in and around Snowdonia. Some are run by the Gwynedd Tourist Board and some by the Snowdonia National Park Authority. Most open daily in summer, but have shorter hours or close from October to April. There are centres in Beddgelert (☎ 01766-890615), Betws-y-Coed (☎ 01690-710426), Caernarfon (☎ 01286-672232), Llanberis (☎ 01286-870765), Llandudno (☎ 01492-876413) and Porthmadog (☎ 01766-512981). The TIC in Llanberis is particularly useful as some staff members are keen local walkers and can advise on routes, maps etc. There's also a central office (☎ 01341-423558, e tourism @gwyneddgov.uk, w www.gwynedd.gov .uk) for all Snowdonia tourist inquiries.

Useful information leaflets (free), available from TICs, include *Walking in Snowdonia* and *Enjoy Your Visit to Snowdonia*. Most TICs also display weather forecasts, as do several outdoor gear shops in the area. If you're only interested in Snowdon itself, look out for the handy series of Footpaths on Snowdon leaflets, each covering a single path to the top, with a map and route notes (for a very reasonable 40p). There's a similar series for Cadair Idris.

For specific information about the park, contact the Snowdonia National Park Authority (☎ 01766-770274), Penrhyndeudraeth, Gwynedd LL48 6LF. The park authority also produces *Eryri Snowdonia*, a free annual newspaper, available from TICs, with details of organised events, local places of interest and lots of useful ads for activities and places to stay.

Guided Walks

The Snowdonia National Park Authority organises a series of guided walks throughout the year; you can get details from any local TIC and the *Eryri Snowdonia* newspaper. If you want something more specific, Guided Walks Snowdon (☎ 01690-720240, **e** bron.eryri@lineone.net), based at Capel Curig, offers high- or low-level day walks, charging £50 for two people. Turnstone Tours (☎ 01286-677059, **e** turnstone@tours23.freeserve.co.uk), based at Caernarfon, charges around £100 per day for small groups, but rates are negotiable according to the route.

Several larger companies provide tuition courses and weekend holidays for individuals or small groups, involving climbing, scrambling or hill walking. These include Wild Wales (☎ 01492-582448, **w** www.travel-quest.co.uk/wild-wales), which organises walking weekends from £95; Snowdonia Adventures (☎ 01286-871179, **w** www.suckalemon.com), with its base at the Heights Hotel; High Trek Snowdonia (☎ 01286-871232, **e** high.trek@virgin.net), with walking weekends and longer walking holidays, including a strenuous seven-day trans-Snowdonia for £445; and Pathfinder (☎ 07897-416632).

Plas-y-Brenin National Mountain Centre (☎ 01690-720214, **e** info@pyb.co.uk), in Capel Curig (see the Tryfan & the Glyders walk), runs a comprehensive range of courses, including rambling, hill walking, scrambling and navigation, lasting from a few hours to a few days. Many of the YHA hostels in the area also offer activity courses.

The Snowdon Horseshoe

Distance	8mi (13km)
Duration	5½–7½ hours
Standard	hard
Start/Finish	Pen-y-Pass
Gateways	Llanberis, Caernarfon

Summary A classic route, including a very exposed mountain scramble requiring the use of hands! Must be treated with caution, especially in wet conditions, and not to be attempted in heavy rain, high wind, ice or snow. For experienced walkers only.

Snowdon (1085m) is the highest mountain in Wales and arguably the most spectacular. It's also higher than anything in England. Its Welsh name, Yr Wyddfa, means 'burial place' – reputedly of a giant slain by King Arthur. The beauty of the peak lies along its fine ridges, which drop away in great swooping lines from the summit. Beneath these ridges are cliffs and airy pinnacles, falling to deep lakes and sheltered cwms, which are home to birds of prey and rare alpine plants.

But Snowdon also has great ugliness. The mountain railway chugs noisily from Llanberis to the station and summit cafe, and on the southern slopes a hydroelectric pipeline cuts an angular scar through the surrounding greenery. Even paths stand out like veins, suffering from the impact of over half a million visitors each year.

Despite all this, Snowdon is still a wonderful mountain, and we thoroughly recommend a walk on its ridges and slopes. The Snowdon Horseshoe route takes in the famous Crib Goch ridge, plus the main summit and three other major peaks. This route is universally reckoned to offer one of the best mountain days in Britain, but it's also one of the most serious bits of walking included in this book – only for those who enjoy very sharp ridges with steep drops on either side. The Snowdon Traverse, described later, is a less serious option.

Direction, Distance & Duration

This circular route starts at Pen-y-Pass, 6mi from Llanberis. By beginning with the Crib

Goch ridge and going anticlockwise you tackle the scrambling when you are fresh.

The total distance is 8mi on the map, but with the stiff ascent and scrambling will seem longer: Allow 5½ to 7½ hours, plus an extra hour for stops. In bad conditions it could take twice that. In fact, if the weather's bad you shouldn't be here! If you're caught in a sudden storm halfway, a possible escape is the Miners Track (described below). Another option is to take the train from the summit (if you can bear the shame!), or simply to follow the path beside the railway to Llanberis. Any one of these descents will take about two hours.

Alternatives If the Horseshoe route sounds a bit too airy, Snowdon can be sampled on a circular walk from Pen-y-Pass by going up the Pyg Track (described in the Snowdon Traverse following) and down the Miners Track (described as an escape route in this section). Although easier than the Snowdon Horseshoe, this route should still be treated with respect in the event of less than perfect weather.

PLACES TO STAY & EAT
Llanberis
This small town, the capital of walking and climbing in North Wales, is a good base for any Snowdonia visit. It was once a slate-mining centre (see the boxed text 'Slate Mining in Llanberis') and now thrives on tourism with a vast range of hotels, B&Bs, pubs, cafes, food shops, a bank (with ATM) and several outdoor gear shops, plus plenty of visitor attractions. The TIC (☎ 01286-870765), on the High St in the town centre, is particularly useful.

Llanberis YHA Hostel (☎ 01286-870280) charges £9.80. Another cheap option is the *Heights Hotel* (☎ 01286-871179, ⒺＥ climbing@heightshotel.demon.co.uk), on the High St, a long-standing favourite for walkers, climbers, backpackers and layabouts, offering beds in small dorms for £12.50 with breakfast. Good-value B&B in en suite doubles costs £40, or £50/60/75 for three/four/five people; it's cheaper for a bed-only deal. There's a bright, noisy bar

with food-like burgers at £3, pizzas at £5 and main meals for up to £7. There's also a quieter lounge bar, which becomes a restaurant at weekends, with meals at the same prices. This hotel also has laundry and drying facilities, and arranges local music sessions. The flexible and friendly management can set you up with walking guides or just about anything else required.

Most other B&Bs are also on the High St. Good walker-friendly places include *Dol Peris Hotel* (☎ 01286-870350), charging £19 (£22.50 en suite); *Glyn Afon Guesthouse* (☎ 01286-872528, ⒺＥ reception@glynafon.com) with standard singles/doubles/triples for £17/32/£42 (or en suite doubles for £35); and *Maesteg* (☎ 01286-871187, ⒺＥ hilarymaesteg@hotmail.com), charging £16 to £22 (nonsmoking). The latter can arrange local guides and reflexology sessions – everything you could need during and after a walk!

Slate Mining in Llanberis

While in Llanberis you cannot fail to see the huge (and we mean really huge) piles of slate that dominate the valley opposite the village. Llanberis had been a major slate quarrying centre for centuries, with most slate used on house roofs, but when demand dried up in the 1970s the quarries closed. The railway, which once transported slate to the coast, now functions as a tourist attraction along the lake.

Today a new industry occupies the old quarry area. A power station has been constructed underground, which uses surplus energy to pump water from Llyn Peris through underground pipes to Marchlyn reservoir, about 600m higher up the mountain. When electricity is needed quickly the water in the upper lake is released to fall down the pipes and power enormous turbines also buried inside the mountain.

Guided tours of the 'Electric Mountain' power station are run daily; details are available from the TIC. If you are unlucky with the weather it's a good alternative to walking on the tops.

On the edge of the village *Snowdon Cottage* (☎ 01286-872015) is a small welcoming place, charging £16. Nearby, for luxury try the large *Royal Victoria Hotel* (☎ 01286-870253) with B&B from around £40 (and special offers at quiet times down to £25). The bar used to be a popular walkers' and climbers' hang-out but it's been smartened up now and has become a bit soulless – the food is quite good, though, and costs £5 to £9.

For food, top of the list is *Pete's Eats*, on the High St, a classic cafe where tea comes in pint mugs and you can easily top up your cholesterol for under £5 (open to 8pm in summer). Other cheap options include the three *takeaways* on the High St, serving burgers, pizzas and fish and chips. Apart from the hotels already listed, another good choice is *The Balti Raj* (☎ 01286-871983), serving the finest Indian food in North Wales, where a good meal will cost about £10. The bar food at the *Padarn Lake Hotel* is also OK, at around £5 to £6. In a different league, and very highly recommended, is *Y Bistro*, on the High St, with fine Welsh and European cuisine. Main courses cost from £8 to £13, while a three-course set menu can be enjoyed for £15.50.

About half a mile north of Llanberis towards Bangor, *Gallt-y-Glyn Hotel* (☎ 01286-870370, e sales@gallt-y-glyn.co.uk) has good B&B at £30/40, a bunkhouse for £11.50 (all you need to bring is a towel), food in the bar and a recommended restaurant with pizzas and pastas from £4 to £6 and main courses for around £8.

Nant Peris

About 2mi east of Llanberis, this village has some more options. *Pritchard's Farm Campsite* is open all year, charging £2.50, plus 50p for showers. There's no need to book as even in high summer it's never too full – they just open another field. Next door is *Cae Gwyn Campsite*, which costs the same. Next door the other way *Cerrig Drudion* (☎ 01286-871327) offers walker-friendly B&B from £15. Very nearby, *The Vaynol Arms* has bar food and is popular with walkers and climbers.

Pen-y-Pass

At the start of the route, Pen-y-Pass (about 5mi south-east of Llanberis) consists of a large car park, a *YHA Hostel* (☎ 01286-870428), charging £9.80, and a *cafe* with some wonderful old photographs of Snowdon in the early 20th century. A mile farther south-east towards Capel Curig, the *Pen-y-Gwryd Hotel* (☎ 01286-870211) has B&B from £23 (or £28 with private bathroom), lunches from £3 to £6, evening dinner for £17 and a very cosy bar full of climbing memorabilia, including a ceiling signed by members of the successful 1953 Everest Expedition.

GETTING TO/FROM THE WALK

Bus From Llanberis, the best way to Pen-y-Pass is on the excellent Snowdon Sherpa bus service, which runs regularly up and down the valley. For more details, see Getting Around in the introduction to this chapter.

Car Pen-y-Pass can be approached from Llanberis on the A4086 or from Capel Curig and Betws-y-Coed on the A5. The car park at Pen-y-Pass costs £4 per day – less after 1pm – but often fills in summer, when a 'park and ride' system operates between Nant Peris and Pen-y-Pass. It's also possible to hitch between Llanberis and Pen-y-Pass, as most people in cars are walkers too (but you should always take precautions).

THE WALK
Pen-y-Pass to Crib Goch
2mi (3km), 1–1½ hours

From the car park two paths lead towards Snowdon. With your back to the cafe, take the path in the back-right corner. This is the Pyg Track, paved with stone slabs, which leads after about 45 minutes to a pass in the ridge called **Bwlch-y-Moch**. ('Pyg' is sometimes written 'PyG' because it's named after the nearby Pen-y-Gwryd Hotel, although Bwlch-y-Moch means Pass of the Pig – so it's sometimes spelt 'Pig'. Got that?)

At the pass you get your first spectacular view into the great bowl-shaped valley holding Llyn Llydaw and the smaller lake of Glaslyn, which this route is about to circuit.

Don't take the path downwards, but turn right (east) to follow a path steeply up the ridge crest. It zigzags a little and there are some short rock steps to scramble up, but if the rock doesn't look as though thousands of boots have scuffed it smooth then you're off-route! The last part of this section of the ridge is quite steep and exposed, with steep cliffs down to your right. With some relief you reach the cairn on the **summit of Crib Goch** (921m). Time for a breather and a chance to admire the tremendous views: up to the main summit of Snowdon, down into the valley or across to the opposite ridge and the other side of the 'horseshoe'.

Crib Goch to Snowdon Summit
1.5mi (2.5km), 2–2½ hours
This is where the fun starts! If you didn't like the ascent to Crib Goch summit then the next bit will finish you off completely. (In which case, crawl back down the way you came up.)

From Crib Goch summit the route follows the Crib Goch ridge, an absolute knife-edge less than a half a metre wide in places, with precipitous drops on both sides, especially to the right. The best technique is to keep to the left side of the crest and use your hands to hold onto the top! It is also possible to follow a narrow path about 3m down on the left (south) side of the ridge.

If you're not used to scrambling this ridge will seem to go on for ever, while if you revel in such escapades it will finish all too soon. The ridge is about 250m long, and at the end you have to negotiate the **Pinnacles**, although each has a small escape gangway around it. After the last pinnacle you descend steeply (still with hands in places) to **Bwlch Coch** – a wide pass of red scree. In an emergency it's possible to descend steeply north from here into Cwm Uchaf.

From Bwlch Coch continue upwards along the next section of ridge called Crib-y-Ddysgl. It's steep and there are one or two

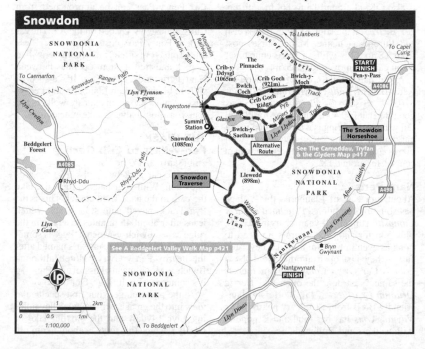

short rock steps, but eventually it widens and you arrive at the delightfully flat and broad summit of **Crib-y-Ddysgl** (1065m), marked by another trig point.

Next comes the middle, fairly straightforward, section of the horseshoe. Follow the broad ridge from Crib-y-Ddysgl down its west side to **Fingerstone** – a standing stone about 2m high that marks the point where the Miners Track and Pyg Track join the summit ridge. In bad weather you can descend directly from here (see the Alternative Descent: The Pyg Track & Miners Track at the end of the walk description for details).

A few metres beyond the Fingerstone the tracks of the Snowdon Railway come as a surprise. Try not to be run over by steam trains and follow the tracks to the **summit station**, which has a *cafe* and *shop* (most incongruous on a mountaintop, and the cause of much debate), where you can buy anything from a pint of beer to a 'Snowdon the Hard Way' T-shirt. You can even post your mail from the highest postbox in Britain. Purists will note that the actual **summit of Snowdon** is about 100m to the east of the cafe, marked by a cairn. Go here to savour being on the highest peak in Wales.

Snowdon Summit to Pen-y-Pass
4.5mi (7km), 2½–3½ hours

The next peak to aim for is Llewedd, southeast of Snowdon's summit. To find the path, it's important to first head south-westerly

down the crest of the ridge from the terrace at the back of the cafe. After about 150m, by a cairn and standing stone, you turn left (east) and zigzag down through steep broken scree to eventually reach the pass of Bwlch-y-Saethau. This is a popular lunch stop for people keen to avoid the cafe, with great views over the two lakes in the valley and across to the Crib Goch ridge – the site of this morning's fun and games.

The path is level for a while, then reaches a junction: Right (south) is the Watkin Path down to Nantgwynant, but we go straight on up the ridge path to the west peak of **Llewedd** (898m). You are now above the huge, sweeping cliffs on the north side of Llewedd. Ground-breaking climbs were made here in the early 20th century by mountaineers, such as George Mallory, who later disappeared on Everest in 1924.

From the west peak of Llewedd the path drops down to a tiny pass, where a steep gully cuts into the north face, continuing up to the east peak (893m).

From the pass, you think you're nearly home and dry, but the descent path is surprisingly rough and steep in places (although maintenance work was in progress when we passed, which might smooth out the bumps in future). Leave the ridge where it flattens out slightly, and take another steep path (north) down to the edge of Llyn Llydaw, where you join the Miners Track, which is wide and clear all the way to Pen-y-Pass.

Llyn Llydaw, backed by the Snowdon Horseshoe and the peak of Mt Snowdon

GRANT DIXON

Alternative Descent: The Pyg Track & Miners Track

If you need to escape in bad weather, you can descend from the Snowdon summit directly to the start. From the Fingerstone (where the path between Crib-y-Ddysgl and Snowdon summit meets the railway track) a clear zigzag path descends south towards the small lake of Glaslyn. This is the Pyg Track. Keep descending to the lake shore, from where the Miners Track leads you down to Pen-y-Pass.

Alternative Descent: The Snowdon Railway

If you're feeling really tired or the mist is really awful, you can get the train down the mountain railway to Llanberis. Tickets on standby cost £8 but don't rely on this service: Priority is given to passengers who come up on the train, and it doesn't run when weather conditions are bad.

A Snowdon Traverse

Distance	7mi (11.5km)
Duration	5–7 hours
Start	Pen-y-Pass
Standard	medium-hard
Finish	Nantgwynant
Gateways	Llanberis, Beddgelert

Summary A high but relatively straightforward mountain walk on clear paths. Conditions can potentially be very serious in bad weather.

In the Snowdon Horseshoe walk we outline the nature of the mountain and describe a serious 'hands-out-of-pockets' walk around the main summits, but there are several other routes on the mountain that are less serious and strictly walking only. These include: the Llanberis Path, which runs roughly parallel to the railway; the Pyg Track and the Miners Track, which start at Pen-y-Pass; the Rhyd-Ddu (pronounced reed-thee) and Snowdon Ranger paths, on the west side of the mountain; and the Watkin Path to Nantgwynant, south of the summit. Any two of these can be joined to form a traverse of the mountain. For a varied and full day out we recommend the taverse described in detail here,

which combines the Pyg Track (the most efficient summit route) and the Watkin Path, then descends into a valley above Beddgelert.

Direction, Distance & Duration

The traverse is a linear walk and can be done in either direction. We recommend going east to west, as starting from Pen-y-Pass means you're already a good way up the mountain. In fair conditions this 7mi (11.5km) route will take between five and seven hours of walking, plus an hour for stops, making six to eight in total. If conditions are bad, however, you should allow more time. Because paths are good, don't be lured into complacency.

PLACES TO STAY & EAT

This route starts at Pen-y-Pass, 6mi southeast of Llanberis. For details of accommodation in these places, see Places to Stay & Eat in the Snowdon Horseshoe walk earlier.

Nantgwynant

The tiny settlement of Nantgwynant, in the valley of the same name, is at the end of the walk. Places to stay include *Bryn Gwynant YHA Hostel* (☎ 01766-890251), about a mile north-east of where the Watkin Path meets the main road, charging £9.80. Nearby, and nearer the end of the Watkin Path, *Bryn Dinas Bunkhouse & Hostel* (☎ 01766-890234, e *vince@bryndinasbunkhouse.co .uk*) is another bargain option, charging £8 for a bunk in the main house, which has a self-catering kitchen, and £6.50 (plus £1 for heating) in timber cabins, which have a separate cookhouse. You need to bring your own sleeping bag, and if you don't want to cook, simple meals and breakfasts can be ordered. This old place got quite run down a few years ago, but the new management are gradually upgrading things.

Beddgelert & Around

Beddgelert TIC (☎ 01766-890615), on the main street near the car park and Royal Goat Hotel, can provide assistance with accommodation options.

If you want to camp, the roomy *Forest Holidays Campsite* (☎ 01766-890288) is about a mile north of Beddgelert on the A4085; prices vary from £4.60 in the high season to £3.40 in the low. This includes the good showers, and there's a well-stocked shop on site. Nearer is *Cae Du Campsite*, just off the A498, about half a mile northeast of Beddgelert.

In town, walker-friendly B&Bs include *Emrys House* (☎ *01766-890240*, e *gauler @lineone.net)*, a nonsmoking place charging £17; and *Plas Tan-y-Graig* (☎ *01766-890310, eay.b@virgin.net)* with a range of rooms from £17.50 (£22.50 en suite), plus some cheaper family rooms. Nearby are three places with confusingly similar names: *Plas Colwyn Guesthouse* (☎ *01766-890458*, e *plascolwyn@hotmail.com)* is a very walker-friendly nonsmoking place, charging £21. The owners can assist with local guides or weather forecasts. The guesthouse also has a good small restaurant (open to nonresidents) specialising in Welsh dishes, where three-course meals start at £12. *Colwyn Guesthouse* (☎ *01766-890276*) and *Plas Gwyn* (☎ *01766-890215*) charge £20 in en suite rooms and have rooms with shared bathroom at cheaper rates.

There are three pubs in the village, all with accommodation and bar food, including the smart and cosy *Tanronnen Inn* (☎ *01766-890347*) and the more straightforward *Saracen's Head* (☎ *01766-890223*).

More upmarket options in Beddgelert include the *Royal Goat Hotel* (☎ *01766-890224*), in the village centre, and *Sygun Fawr Country House Hotel* (☎ *01766-890258*), about a mile to the north-east.

For food, apart from the pubs, *Lyn's Cafe* is consistently good and wholesome, serving meals, snacks and drinks. Try the *Glyndŵr Café* for pizzas and ice cream. For an evening meal, *Beddgelert Bistro & Antiques* (☎ *01766-890543*) is good, with main courses for £10 to £13; it also offers B&B. Beddgelert has a couple of small shops and an outdoor gear shop.

GETTING TO/FROM THE WALK

Bus To reach Pen-y-Pass by bus, see Getting to/from the Walk in the Snowdon

Horseshoe walk earlier. At the end of the route, the Snowdon Sherpa Bus passes through Nantgwynant and Beddgelert regularly, with connections to Porthmadog and Caernarfon, and to Pen-y-Gwryd where you can connect to Llanberis or Capel Curig.

Train The nearest train station to Beddgelert is Porthmadog. For more information on trains, see Getting There & Away in the introduction to this chapter.

Car To reach the start of this route, see Getting to/from the Walk under the Snowdon Horseshoe walk. To reach the end of the route, you can approach Beddgelert from Caernarfon on the A4085, or from Porthmadog on the A498. If you're coming from the A5 and Capel Curig, take the A4086 to reach Pen-y-Pass, branching onto the A498 for Beddgelert.

THE WALK (see map p410)
Pen-y-Pass to Snowdon Summit
4.5mi (7km), 3–5 hours

From the car park two paths lead towards Snowdon. With your back to the cafe, take the path in the back-right corner: This is the Pyg Track, paved with stone slabs, which leads you after about 45 minutes to a pass in the ridge called **Bwlch-y-Moch**. The path crosses the pass and traverses beneath (south of) the great ridge of Crib Goch, with great views down to Llyn Llydaw below. After an hour or so, this path is joined by the Miners Track coming up from the left. You then follow a steep set of switchbacks that lead up to the ridge, marked by the **Fingerstone** (a standing obelisk). Turn left here and follow the path parallel to the railway track for a final 500m up to the **summit station**, where there's a *cafe* (for further details, see the Snowdon Horseshoe walk description earlier).

Snowdon Summit to Nantgwynant
3.5mi (5.5km), 2–3 hours

From the summit it's important to head first south-westerly, down the crest of the ridge from the terrace at the back of the cafe. After about 150m, by a cairn and standing stone, turn left (east) and zigzag down through steep broken scree to eventually reach the **pass of Bwlch-y-Saethau** – a popular view point and lunch stop. The path is level for a while, then reaches a junction. Straight on goes up the ridge path to the west peak of Llewedd (898m). For this walk, however, we go right (south) onto the Watkin Path, which descends steeply and swings south-west into Cwm Llan. From here follow the stream past the old quarry buildings and along the overgrown tramway to the large valley of Nantgwynant, which holds two lakes, Llyn Gwynant and Llyn Dinas, and is thick with rhododendron bushes (see the boxed text 'Rhododendrons – Invasion in Pink'). Below nestles the picturesque village of Beddgelert.

gorge cutting deeply into the surrounding cliffs. It's a place of Celtic aura and fantasy that befits a landscape steeped in legends of King Arthur. The National Trust protects this delicate and valuable environment. The RAF (Royal Air Force), by contrast, uses the area as a fighter-jet training alley, so on weekdays prepare to be dive bombed!

The route we describe starts with an ascent of Tryfan, then joins the main Glyder ridge and descends via the Devil's Kitchen. Experienced scramblers will enjoy picking

Tryfan & the Glyders

Distance	5mi (8km)
Duration	5–7 hours
Standard	hard
Start	Llyn Ogwen (east end)
Finish	Ogwen, Llyn Ogwen (west end)
Gateways	Bangor, Betys-y-Coed

Summary A classic mountain walk, if a bit rough and slow on the high ground, especially in the wet. Navigation is tricky in cloud, so map and compass skills are required; some avoidable scrambling is involved.

The peak of Tryfan seen in profile looks like a huge dinosaur, with a prickly back curved in a huge arc, rising to a dramatic rocky summit (915m). It's one of North Wales' most famous sights. South of Tryfan (pronounced tre-van) are the more rounded peaks of Glyder Fawr (999m) and Glyder Fach (994m). Bordered on the north and east sides by steep cwms and cliffs, these form a long, broad ridge strewn with shattered boulders, moved by ice to form eerie towers and otherworldly shapes. A walk combining the three summits is a classic Snowdonia outing.

At the foot of Glyder Fawr is the nature reserve of Cwm Idwal. Central to this cwm is the Devil's Kitchen, a dark and austere

Rhododendrons – Invasion in Pink

Walking in Snowdonia in May, you can't fail to notice the profusion of beautiful pink flowers all over the hillsides. You will probably stop to marvel at this amazing floral display, but don't be deceived – these are rhododendrons, the scourge of the hills.

Rhododendrons were introduced to Britain about 200 years ago as an ornamental shrub in the estates of large houses. They thrived in British weather conditions, but it wasn't until this century, with the break-up of many estates, that they started to spread unchecked. Their environmental impact is devastating, and they now threaten the existence of many indigenous plant and animal species in Snowdonia, and even the very nature of the landscape.

Rhododendron leaves and roots are poisonous, while the dense foliage means that no plants can grow beneath them. This deprives plant-eating animals, birds and insects of a vital food supply, which in turn leads to the decline of carnivorous animals and birds of prey.

So why don't the locals just get rid of them? Not so easy. These plants are almost indestructible. They tolerate all extremes of weather, require minimal daylight for survival, grow back rapidly after cutting, and each bush produces several million seeds every year. They are, in short, a conservationist's nightmare. Their single redeeming feature is the spectacular flowers, but if it wasn't for those, they wouldn't have been imported into Britain in the first place.

a route up the rocks, but there are easier options, although the this range is distinctly rocky and everyone must use their hands in places. For those who are inexperienced or like to keep their hands in their pockets there is also an alternative route on Tryfan that manages to avoid the ridge (and the summit) completely.

This whole route is also notoriously tricky in bad weather, and not recommended unless you have some skill at using a compass and map.

Direction, Distance & Duration

We recommend a clockwise circuit, starting with the ascent of Tryfan, because the scrambles are best approached in an uphill direction. The walk measures only 5mi on the map, but because of the ascents and rough ground, this takes five to seven hours of walking time. With stops, about six to eight hours is more likely.

PLACES TO STAY & EAT
Ogwen & Around

Ogwen is a tiny settlement at the western end of the lake of Llyn Ogwen, and the site of *Idwal Cottage YHA Hostel* (☎ 01248-600225), ideally situated for this route. It is self-catering only but there's a good modern kitchen and you can buy food supplies. In the nearby car park a *snack bar* is well placed to serve reviving hot food and drinks when you come down off the mountain.

Along the A5 towards Capel Curig are two farms. The nearest one to Tryfan is *Gwern Gof Uchaf* (☎ 01690-720294) with simple camping facilities for £2 and a new bunkhouse for £5.

Just 300m farther east is *Gwern Gof Isaf* (☎ 01690-720276), which has camping for £2, a very basic concrete-floored camping barn for £4 and a more comfortable bunkhouse, which is much better value at £5 (all plus 50p for showers). In the barn and bunkhouse you still need your camping kit (except the tent).

Capel Curig & Around

This village, 5mi south-east of Llyn Ogwen, has several good options. The *Plas-y-Brenin*

National Mountain Centre (☎ 01690-720214) is an activity centre, catering mainly for groups, which provides B&B for £20, available even if you're not doing a course. Reservations are not accepted far in advance in the summer months as course participants have priority. It's worth noting that members of the British Mountaineernig Council (BMC; see Useful Organisations in the Facts for the Walker chapter) pay only £12.50; to join the BMC is £15. There's also a bar serving meals and free lectures each evening, and you can get a weather forecast here. Nearby is small and simple *Llugwu Guesthouse* (☎ 01690-720218), charging £17.50.

Also in Capel Curig, going south along the main road towards Betws-y-Coed is *The Bryn Tyrch Hotel* (☎ 01690-720223), which is popular with walkers and climbers, and so can get away with charging £20.50 at the weekend for B&B in faded and basic rooms (£24.50 with private bathroom). Rates are slightly cheaper midweek, and food is available in the bar but is not especially good value. Nearby is *Capel Curig YHA Hostel* (☎ 01690-720225), charging £9.80. A good accommodation choice is comfortable and welcoming *Bron Eryri Guesthouse* (☎ 01690-720240, e bron.eryri @lineone.net), charging £21 for an en suite; it has a cosy (nonsmoking) lounge. Also nearby is the smart but friendly *Cobdens Hotel* (☎ 01690-720243, e info@cobdens .co.uk) with B&B from £29.50 and a pleasant 'brasserie' restaurant; and the slightly plainer but equally friendly *Tyn-y-Coed Hotel* (☎ 01690-720331, e res@tyn-y-coed .co.uk), charging £27.50 for B&B, also with some cheaper bunkrooms for five people, and a hikers bar open to all.

On the road junction near the Llugwu Guesthouse is the *Pinnacle Café* and a local *shop*. Near the Bryn Trych Hotel are the *Snowdonia Café* and a petrol station with a *shop* selling basic supplies and outdoor gear.

The town of Betws-y-Coed, about 5mi beyond Capel Curig, has a wider range of places to stay and eat (plus two large outdoor gear shops).

GETTING TO/FROM THE WALK

Bus The nearest towns to Llyn Ogwen are Bangor to the west and Betws-y-Coed to the east. From Bangor there are regular local buses to Bethesda. A Snowdon Sherpa bus service runs between Bethesda and Betws-y-Coed about five times per day (three on Sunday) via Idwal Cottage (at the western end of Llyn Ogwen), the eastern end of Llyn Ogwen and Capel Curig. See Getting Around in the introduction to this chapter for more details.

Car Llyn Ogwen is beside the main A5 road about halfway between Bethesda and Capel Curig. The best car park for this route is at Idwal Cottage, at the western end of Llyn Ogwen, where the route ends. You can also park in the lay-by (free) at the eastern end of the lake near the start of the route.

THE WALK
Llyn Ogwen to Tryfan Summit
0.5mi (1km), 1½–2 hours

Start from the lay-by on the main A5 road near the eastern end of Llyn Ogwen, below the North Ridge of Tryfan, where a wall runs down to meet the road. Go through a small gate and follow the wall southwards uphill to where it meets a large cliff. This is Milestone Buttress, so called (surprise!) because there used to be a milestone on the London to Holyhead road here.

It's important to realise that you don't follow the North Ridge from its base, but work your way up to meet the crest about a quarter of the way up the ridge.

From the foot of Milestone Buttress, climb steeply up leftwards (south-east) over loose rocks. A maze of paths weaves through heather and scree. Keep going until you can see down into the valley on the east side of the ridge, then you can turn more to the right (south) and start going up the crest of the ridge proper. (Some old hands say the trick is to look for the building in a small patch of woodland way down in the valley, and line yourself up exactly with the apex of the roof!)

Even when you start climbing properly, keep in mind that this ridge does not have a sharp and well-defined crest, and you shouldn't expect a single easy-to-follow route. In fact, a confusing set of vague paths lead uphill round cliffs, buttresses and boulders. You'll have to use your hands a bit, but if it gets serious you're off-route. (If you don't like using your hands, a precipitous path called Heather Terrace runs along the east side of Tryfan, missing the summit.)

After one to 1½ hours of steady ascent you reach the foot of an imposing rock buttress. Follow the path round its left (east) side, to reach a small pass below a fine amphitheatre after another 15 minutes. Descend a little from the pass into the amphitheatre, then go up the first deep and obvious gully (west), under a boulder at the top and back onto the ridge. About 100m farther up the ridge is the **summit of Tryfan**, with the standing stones of Adam and Eve marking the spot. Daredevils can leap from one stone to another, to get 'the freedom of Tryfan', but remember that help is a long way away if you break a leg trying. Better enjoy a rest and the view instead (although one walker we know reports having his lunch disturbed by a rescue helicopter balancing its wheels on the stones – so be prepared).

If you haven't already noticed, the lake of Cwm Bochlwyd down to your west looks like a map of Australia. Farther away, to the south-west, the summits of the Snowdon Horseshoe appear as distant giants, while to the north the view of the classic U-shaped Nant Ffrancon valley leads the eye out to the Anglesey coast.

Tryfan Summit to Glyder Fawr
2mi (3km), 2–3 hours

Once you've torn yourself away from the view, descend southwards from the summit of Tryfan. It's a steep, rough and rocky path, with a few cairns along the way, keeping to the right (west) side of the ridge, especially down lower. This leads down to **Bwlch Tryfan**, a wide pass crossed by a large dry-stone wall (handy for sheltering behind in bad weather).

South from Bwlch Tryfan a very steep ridge rises up in a series of rocky needles. This is affectionately known by walkers as

Bristly Ridge – a wonderful outing for happy scramblers – although you won't see this name marked on maps. If you prefer not to use your hands, the steep and stony path goes to the left of the ridge. It is a bit loose underfoot but it brings you out at the top of the ridge, where it flattens into a plateau covered with a manic jumble of huge sharp blocks, some lying flat and others pointing skywards like jagged pinnacles.

The path is marked by cairns as it continues across this plateau, aiming southwest. Look out for the **Cantilever Stone**, a huge monolith suspended on its side over a drop, a bit like a diving board (with a very bad landing). About 100m beyond is the rock tower that marks the **summit of Glyder Fach** (994m).

From Glyder Fach summit, the path descends slightly, passing a particularly large and impressive, and unbelievably spiky, outcrop called Castell-y-Gwynt (castle of the wind) on its left side, and then drops to a pass, from where an escape route descends to Llyn Bochlwyd in Cwm Bochlwyd.

The main path continues south-west and then west, clearly at first and then over rocks (if there is mist, pay close attention to your navigation), to the summit of **Glyder Fawr**, one of several rock towers standing on the broad summit plateau.

Time for rest, and for a final look round in this fantastical landscape, before heading towards home.

Glyder Fawr to Idwal Cottage
2.5mi (4km), 1½–2 hours

The path leaves the summit of Glyder Fawr heading south-west. Take special care here in bad weather as it's easy to go too far south. The path is marked by a few cairns as it curves and descends over very steep and loose scree, heading generally northwest, down to a flat pass near the small lake of Llyn-y-Cwn.

Once again, care is called for to avoid getting lost. Don't go to the lake (unless you want to stop here for a picnic) but aim right (north-east) away from it, to follow a path that takes you to a rocky gap through the cliffs. This path gets steeper, but is paved

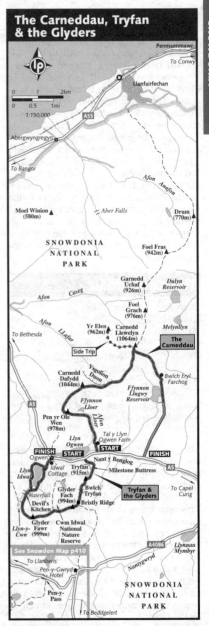

The Carneddau, Tryfan & the Glyders

with rough stone steps. Make sure you find the proper path; any other apparent descent will soon lead you over precipitous cliffs.

As you descend on the path, to your left (north) is the **Devil's Kitchen** – a steep gorge with a waterfall and surrounding cliffs covered with ferns and mosses constantly fed by the mist and dripping water. (The mist sometimes looks like smoke from a cooking fire – hence the name.)

Beyond the gorge, the path divides, taking you either west or east of Llyn Idwal. There's hardly any difference in distance but the western path is worth taking after heavy rain as there's a deep and fast stream on the eastern route. Beyond the lake, the easy paved path takes you down to Idwal Cottage car park, at the west end of Llyn Ogwen, where the *snack bar* can provide a welcome ice cream or hot coffee – depending on the weather.

The Carneddau

Distance	8mi (13km)
Duration	4–6 hours
Standard	medium
Start	Llyn Ogwen (east end)
Finish	Nant y Benglog (Ogwen Valley)
Gateways	Bangor, Betws-y-Coed

Summary A long classic route with straightforward walking on mostly good (if faint) paths through a relatively quiet area.

The group of mountains called the Carneddau (pronounced car-neth-aye), in the north-eastern section of the national park, take their name from the two main peaks – Carnedd Dafydd and Carnedd Llewelyn. This area has a more isolated atmosphere than many others in Snowdonia because its mountains are broad and open, although hidden among the grassy slopes are cliffs of a scale more often seen in the Highlands of Scotland. The northern similarities continue further, as in winter the Carneddau attract more snow than other areas, and even in summer the weather can become atrocious on the tops.

The circular route we describe starts near the eastern end of the lake of Llyn Ogwen, between Bethesda and Capel Curig; it takes in the main summits and returns to the main road in the valley of Nant y Benglog (universally called the Ogwen Valley), about 1.5mi east of the start point.

A longer linear route is described under Other Walks at the end of this chapter.

Direction, Distance & Duration

This circular walk can be walked in either direction, but clockwise is recommended, as the ascent of Pen yr Ole Wen is better early in the day. On top of the Carneddau you can cover quite a lot of ground fairly quickly, so the total distance of 8mi (13km) takes about four to six hours of walking. Add at least another hour for lunch and photo stops.

Alternatives An alternative start to the walk is from the Idwal YHA Hostel or the Ogwen car park at the west end of Llyn Ogwen. From here a path leads straight to the summit of Pen yr Ole Wen, but be

The Welsh Threes

The Carneddau summits make up seven of 14 peaks in Wales that are over the magical 3000ft (914m) contour. The whole round of these mountains is known as the Welsh Three-Thousanders, or more simply the Welsh Threes. The route starts with an ascent of Snowdon (some people say it starts at the *top* so use the train to get up there), then descends the Llanberis Path to Nant Peris. From here the route goes up Elidir Fawr, over Y Garn, and then takes in the Glyders and Tryfan. That's all before you nip across to the Carneddau peaks that stretch in a line northwards to Llanfairfechan. The whole route can be completed by fit walkers in a very long day, and the record is about five hours. Doesn't it make you sick? For more casual walkers, the 14 peaks can be split over a few days and enjoyed at leisure. Possible walk options are discussed under A Snowdonia Coast to Coast in Other Walks at the end of this chapter.

warned that this is a steeper and definitely more serious ascent.

PLACES TO STAY & EAT
For details of accommodation and eating options around Llyn Ogwen, see Places to Stay & Eat in the Tryfan & the Glyders walk earlier.

GETTING TO/FROM THE WALK
Bus See Getting to/from the Walk in the Tryfan & the Glyders walk earlier.

Car Llyn Ogwen is beside the main A5 road between Bethesda and Capel Curig. The handiest car parking is at the farms of Gwern Gof Uchaf and Gwern Gof Isaf (for more details, see Ogwen & Around under Places to Stay & Eat in the Tryfan & the Glyders walk earlier); parking costs £1 for a day.

THE WALK (see map p417)
Llyn Ogwen to Pen yr Ole Wen
2mi (3km), 1½–2 hours
From the eastern end of Llyn Ogwen take the track towards Tal y Llyn Ogwen farm. Just before the farm gate, the path strikes north uphill, then follows a stream called Afon Lloer continuing north and uphill. This leads you to a large bowl-shaped valley, Cwm Lloer. Don't go into this valley, but turn left (west) and continue going up along the ridge that curves round towards the north and leads to the summit of **Pen yr Ole Wen** (978m). This is the first of the Carneddau summits. Time for a rest and a breather. There are great views to the south over to the Glyders with Snowdon behind, and north-west to Bangor with the Isle of Anglesey beyond.

Pen yr Ole Wen to Carnedd Llewelyn
3mi (5km), 1–2 hours
From the summit of Pen yr Ole Wen, follow the ridge north, over a bump called Carnedd Fach, then north-east to the **summit of Carnedd Dafydd** (1044m). Once again the views are good; among other summits, you can see Carnedd Llewelyn, your next objective, to the north-east.

From this summit it's important not to head straight for Carnedd Llewelyn. First you must head east, along the ridge, with the fittingly titled sheer cliffs of Ysgolion Duon ('Black Ladders') dropping down to your left (northwards) at the head of the Afon Llafar valley.

Continue for about one mile then swing northwards, now with a steep drop down to your right (south-east) as well, for a final ascent up to the **summit of Carnedd Llewelyn** (1064m) – the highest in the Carneddau range. Time for another break, and to marvel at the views. Looking south, the aspect across to Tryfan is now truly magnificent, while in the other direction the Carneddau summits of Foel Grach, Foel Fras and Drum stretch away to the north. (If you're tempted to follow the broad ridge that links these rounded giants, see the 11.5mi linear extension, called the Carneddau Three-Thousanders walk, discussed under Other Walks at the end of this chapter.)

Side Trip: Yr Elen
1.5mi (2.5km), 1 hour return
If you want to bag another Carneddau top over 3000ft you can take an out-and-back detour to the summit of Yr Elen (962m) – very worthwhile if you have the time and the energy. There is a dramatic drop down into Cwm Caseg from the summit, so make sure you come back the same way.

The Carneddau & the Glyders

The mountains around Carnedd Dafydd and Carnedd Llewelyn are known as the Carneddau. *Carnedd* means 'mountain', and the plural is *carneddau*, which means literally 'mountains' – not very helpful if you translate as there are a great many mountains hereabouts. Strangely, although Carnedd Dafydd and Carnedd Llewelyn are known by the Welsh plural name, the nearby mountains of Glyder Fawr and Glyder Fach are nearly always anglicised to the Glyders, rather than the Glyderau, which is the correct plural form in Welsh.

Carnedd Llewelyn to Ogwen Valley

3mi (5km), 1½–2 hours

From the summit of Carnedd Llewelyn the path leads south-east down a steep, narrow ridge, with some near-sheer drops on either side. This is tricky in mist, so take care.

About 45 minutes from Carnedd Llewelyn you reach the steep-sided pass of Bwlch Eryl Farchog. Do not go through the pass, but turn right (south) and follow the steep zigzagging path that takes you down to the Ffynnon Llugwy reservoir, nestling in the horseshoe of steep mountainsides. Follow the path along its east bank to join the service road which carries you swiftly down the hill. It's an eyesore but at least you can't lose the way! This brings you you down to the A5, where this route ends, opposite the farm and campsite of *Gwern Gof Isaf*.

If you need to get back to the start, turn right (west) and follow the main road for 1.5mi to reach the east end of Llyn Ogwen.

A Beddgelert Valley Walk

Distance	5.5mi (9km)
Duration	3–4 hours
Standard	easy
Start/Finish	Beddgelert
Gateways	Beddgelert, Porthmadog, Caernarfon

Summary A straightforward hill walk past several interesting features, mainly on good paths but with a spot of tricky riverside rock hopping.

Beddgelert (pronounced beth-gel-ert) is a village on the south-west side of Snowdon, where the main roads from Caernarfon and Capel Curig meet and head south towards Porthmadog. It's quite easy to reach, and there's a wide choice of places to stay and eat, so it makes a good base. This walk starts and finishes in Beddgelert and keeps mainly to low valleys – ideal if the weather is bad on the higher peaks. You're not completely enclosed, though, and there are several interesting features from North Wales' early industrial era, including an old railway track (complete with tunnels) and several copper mines (some disused, one reopened). Signposting is good, paths are clear and it's almost impossible to get lost on this route.

Direction, Distance & Duration

This circular walk can be done in either direction, but a start along the old railway is better, as the ascent this way is more gentle. The total distance is 5.5mi, which will take about three to four hours' walking time, although you should allow extra for visiting Gelert's Grave, having lunch etc,

The Beddgelert Story

Beddgelert is Welsh for 'Grave of Gelert'. Historians report that a saint from Ireland, called Celert, is thought to have founded a small church here during the early years of Christianity in Britain. When he died and was buried, the settlement took its name from his grave. By medieval times the site was covered by a large Augustinian monastery, although there is very little remaining today except some windows that have been reused in the church.

Another story goes back to the 13th century, when Prince Llewelyn of Wales had a hunting lodge here. Apparently the prince went hunting one day without his faithful dog, who was called Gelert. Returning later he found the dog covered in blood and the bed of his baby son empty. Llewelyn thought Gelert had savaged the little boy, so in a rage he killed the dog. Then the prince heard a cry – his son was hidden but unharmed, and nearby was the body of a wolf that the faithful hound had killed to protect the baby. Naturally, Llewelyn was rather upset about this misunderstanding and buried his dog in the fine grave that can still be visited today.

A third story dates from early 19th century, when trade at the Royal Goat Hotel was a bit slack. The enterprising landlord resurrected the 'faithful dog' legend, with its catchy 'look before you leap' moral, and built a grave of Gelert where it could easily be reached by visiting gentry. The ploy worked and a steady stream of romantic visitors came to Beddgelert. They've been arriving ever since.

and at least another hour if you want to visit the working copper mine at Sygun.

PLACES TO STAY & EAT
For information on food and accommodation, see Beddgelert under Places to Stay & Eat in the Snowdon Traverse earlier.

GETTING TO/FROM THE WALK
For details on transport to and from Beddgelert, see Getting to/from the Walk in the Snowdon Traverse earlier.

THE WALK
Beddgelert to Bwlch-y-Sygun
3mi (5km), 1½–2 hours

Leave the bridge over the river in the centre of Beddgelert village and walk down the lane eastwards along the river's south bank, following a clear path signposted to 'Gelert's Grave'. Follow this path and branch off to the **grave** (a few hundred metres from the river) when you see the sign. For the story of its unverifiable origins, see the boxed text 'The Beddgelert Story'. After looking (it won't take long), retrace your steps almost back to Beddgeleret, then cross a footbridge near some cottages and aim south down the east bank of the river. You should be heading downstream with the river on your right.

After 500m the riverside path joins the track of a disused railway, which used to cross the river here on a small bridge (you can still see the parapets). This was once the Welsh Highland Railway, which hugged the steep valleyside running between Porthmadog and Caernarfon. It opened in 1922 but closed in 1937, leaving the pleasant (and flat) footpath for walkers to enjoy. Note, however, that there are plans for this railway to re-open, linking in with other tourist-orientated railways to the west and east; if this happens, a new path will probably be created nearer the river.

But for now, keep walking along the railway track as it enters the scenic and steep-sided **Pass of Aberglaslyn**. Just before the old railway goes through two old tunnels carved out of the rock (and a third tunnel, which is very long and closed off to walkers), signposts point you down to a

lovely path that follows the bank of the river as it tumbles over rapids and waterfalls. Walkers must hop from rock to rock, which are slippery after rain, so take care, although a few metal handles are provided on the trickiest sections. If the river is high, this path may be submerged and impassable, so be prepared to turn back.

Assuming all is well, follow the riverside path through the woodland. Very near a road bridge called Pont Aberglaslyn the path divides. The right branch goes to the bridge, but our route goes left and uphill through trees to skirt the western edge of a village called **Nantmoor**, at the foot of the Cwm Bychan. Down to your right is a small car park, some public toilets and an information board about the area's wildlife and history.

From the car park, a path goes through a small pedestrian tunnel under the railway and aims north uphill through trees, past the remains of an old copper-processing works to your right.

A Beddgelert Valley Walk

Soon the path leaves the trees and enters open moorland, climbing steadily past old mine workings and pylons, the remnants of an aerial runway that once carried copper ore down to the works at Nantmoor. (Don't be tempted to enter any of the old mine shafts – they haven't been maintained for decades and are very unsafe.)

Continue up the valley, to finally reach the pass of Bwlch-y-Sygyn at the top. Cross a fence by a ladder stile and go left for 100m to reach a junction. This is a good spot for a breather. There are fine views down to Llyn Dinas and up the Nantgwynant valley, with the great bulk of Snowdon behind.

Bwlch-y-Sygyn to Beddgelert
2.5mi (4km), 1½–2 hours

From Bwlch-y-Sygyn junction, take the right turn northwards downhill on a clear path of grey slate chippings, through a splendid section of open rocky moorland (although rhododendrons are beginning to take over here – see the boxed text 'Rhododendrons – Invasion in Pink' on p414) and then steeply down to Llyn Dinas.

Go over the stile here and follow the path along the river flowing out of the lake downstream (with the river on your right). This leads to a track, which soon brings you out to the car park of Sygun Copper Mine, which has been reopened as an award-winning visitor attraction. (Now is your chance to go underground in safety. You can even try gold panning here.)

From the mine rejoin the track as it leads through fields to become a sealed lane near *Cae Du Campsite* and eventually meets a bridge over the river, with the A498 just beyond. Do not cross the bridge but go left over a stile and follow another path beside the river, past a splendid row of cottages, over the footbridge you crossed at the start of the walk and into Beddgelert.

Other Walks

The routes already described in this chapter are well known and well trodden. But Snowdonia has a lot more to offer, and this section will give you a few ideas for further exploration. More ideas for walks in the areas around Snowdonia are given in the Other Walks in Wales chapter.

Particularly rewarding is southern Snowdonia, with wonderful and rarely visited mountains, such as Moel Hebog, the Moelwyns, the Rhinogs, the Arans and Cadair Idris. Some of these are crossed in our final suggestion in this section.

CARNEDDAU THREE-THOUSANDERS

Earlier in this chapter we described a circular route across several high summits in the Carneddau mountains. Also possible in this area is an excellent linear option that initially follows the circular route and then strikes out northwards, taking in seven summits, all in a line and all over the magic 3000ft (914m) contour, to finish by the sea at the small town of Llanfairfechan.

The route can be walked in either direction, but if you start from Llyn Ogwen you have the advantage of being already at 300m, whereas Llanfairfechan is at sea level. The total distance for this route is 11.5mi (18km), but the going is fairly good and in fine weather it will take about six to seven hours' walking (seven to eight in total).

This route starts at Llyn Ogwen (places to stay are described in the Tryfan & the Glyders walk earlier) and follows the circular route over the summits of **Pen yr Ole Wen** (978m), **Carnedd Dafydd** (1044m) and **Carnedd Llewelyn** (1064m), and detours out to **Yr Elen** (962m). The linear route carries on northwards along the fine broad ridge to **Foel Grach** (976m).

The broad, flat and grassy ridge continues northwards, with gentle rises to **Carnedd Uchaf** (926m) and **Foel Fras** (942m), and eventually to **Drum** (770m), the final top. From here you descend a broad ridge in a north-westerly direction on a vehicle track to Llanfairfechan.

THE NANTLLE RIDGE

The Nantlle (pronounced nant-clee) area lies west of the main Snowdon massif, and is relatively seldom visited. It has the stark character of a place that is depressed, and the mountains appear grey and foreboding on a typical autumn afternoon. But in summer, when the grass shines and the clouds throw bright shadows across the slopes, it looks alive, awake and vibrant with colour. The central feature (indeed, the backbone) of the area is a narrow ridge that provides an exhilarating walk with splendid views of the surrounding mountains and across the Irish Sea, although if bad weather comes from the south-west these hills get the worst of it.

The usual access point to the Nantlle Ridge is from **Rhyd-Ddu**, a village on the A4085 main road about 3mi north of Beddgelert. If you stay in Beddgelert (as described in the Beddgelert Valley Walk), Rydd-Ddu is quite easy to reach on the Snowdon Sherpa bus. Alternatively, Rhyd-Ddu has a couple of B&Bs and the *Cwellyn Arms* (☎ *01766-890321*), which offers good food, B&B, a bunkhouse, camping and an open fire in the bar to welcome the most weary of walkers. Nearby, the *Tan y Craig* (☎ *01766-890202*) is a very walker-friendly B&B, while *Snowdon Ranger YHA Hostel* is 1mi north.

A complete east to west traverse of the ridge is most rewarding, with a finish at the farm of Maen-llwyd, near the villages of Llanllyfni and Penygroes. The walk is 8mi from Rhyd-Ddu to Llanllyfni, but the number of passes along the ridge mean quite a few ups and downs, which slows progress a bit, so you should allow five to seven hours. You can get a bus from Penygroes to Cearnarfon, and thence back to Beddgelert. With a car, you can arrange for someone to pick you up at Maen-llwyd, although cars shouldn't be left unattended in this area as there have been break-ins.

Alternatively, an out-and-back walk along the ridge means you can turn round at any point, according to the day's weather or your own preference, and don't have to worry about arranging transport back to the start.

To reach the ridge from Rhyd-Ddu, take the minor road (B4418) west – signposted to Penygroes – for 300m. On a bend there is a stile and two gates; take the narrower gate and follow the path onto open grassy slopes. The paths may be confusing, so make sure you stick to public rights of way in this area. A path leads steadily but steeply to the summit of **Y Garn** (633m), the first peak on the ridge, about one to 1½ hours from Rhyd-Ddu.

From Y Garn follow the ridge southwesterly. It is exposed in places – you can avoid the hardest bits on their left (east) side. The section finishes with a steep and sometimes greasy scramble to the summit of **Mynydd Drws-y-coed** (695m).

The ridge swings west and continues over the summit of **Trum y Ddysgl** (709m) to reach **Mynydd Tal-y-mignedd** (653m), where the huge summit cairn is marked as an obelisk on some maps. From here the ridge swings south-west and descends to the obvious pass, Bwlch Dros Bern. From the bwlch you ascend again the highest point on the ridge (734m), which strangely appears nameless on maps (although it's just to the east of **Craig Cwm Silyn**). This is best approached by initially following the path skirting rocky outcrops on the right, then a path to the left that zigzags up to the summit.

From Craig Cwm Silyn you cross another wide bwlch to reach **Garnedd Goch** (700m), the final summit, before descending grassy slopes (no path) to the north-west, to eventually meet a track that runs between Llynau Cwm Silyn and the Maen-llwyd farm, which turns into a lane leading into Llanllyfni.

A SNOWDONIA COAST TO COAST

If you want a longer walk in Snowdonia, several options exist for crossing the whole area from the north coast to the south-west coast. Perhaps surprisingly, there is no established waymarked multi-day route, as in many other national parks. However, the following suggestion (which links parts of three of the day walks already described in this chapter) is a very popular route, because it crosses some of the finest scenery in the country, and because there are options to take in all the mountains in Wales that rise above 3000ft. Most of the stages on this route are also followed by the long-distance **Cambrian Way** and **Snowdonia to** the **Gower** routes, outlined in the Other Walks in Wales chapter.

This route starts in Llanfairfechan, goes over the Carneddau, then Tryfan and the Glyders, then Snowdon. Beyond here there are several choices. The walk is best split into four or five stages, each of a day's duration (although you can just do two or three stages if you want). The route can be walked in either direction, but walking north-east to south-west is the usual way. Only the barest directions are given here; the walking is mostly on good paths, but to do this whole route you need to be a fit and experienced walker, confident of your navigation skills in poor weather.

Stage 1
The first stage starts at Llanfairfechan, going via a small hill called Garreg Fawr to the summit of Drum, from where you cross the Carneddau Three-Thousanders of **Foel Fras**, **Carnedd Uchaf**, **Foel Grach**, **Carnedd Llewelyn**, **Carnedd Dafydd** and **Pen yr Ole Wen,** before descending to Llyn Ogwen.

Stage 2
On the second stage you have two main choices. The first choice is a long one: From Llyn Ogwen, follow the route described in the Tryfan & the Glyders walk earlier to Llyn y Cwn, then continue north-east to **Y Garn** (947m), then north to **Foel Goch** (831m). From here the ridge descends to Bwlch y Brecan, from where you can descend to Nant Peris, 3mi west of Pen-y-Pass.

Your second main choice is much shorter and can be combined with Stage 3. From Llyn Ogwen take the Miners Track (not to be confused with the track of the same name on Snowdon), which leads past Llyn Bochlwyd

to Bwlch Tryfan. From here the track continues down to the Pen-y-Gwrdd Hotel.

Stage 3
This will be your third day if you took the long route yesterday, or can be combined with the short version of Stage 2 into a single day. From **Pen-y-Pass** take the Pyg Track to the summit of **Snowdon** (as described in the Snowdon Traverse earlier). From the summit you have more options: You could either descend on the Rhyd-Ddu Path to Rhyd-Ddu or via the Watkin Path into Nantgwynant, near Beddgelert. This all depends on your choice for the next day.

Stage 4
For the final stage you have several options. If you descended yesterday on the Rhyd-Ddu Path, then you could follow the **Nantlle Ridge** (as described in the section earlier), eventually dropping down to finish at Llan-llyfni, near the village of Penygroes.

If you descended the Watkin Path to Nantgwynant, then for Day 4 you could go from Beddgelert south over the **Moel Hebog** (782m) and **Moel Ddu** (552m), eventually to reach the seaside town of Porthmadog.

A much longer option (requiring two days) leads you south from Nantgwynant via the summits of **Moelwyn Mawr** (770m) and **Moelwyn Bach** (711m), or through the valleys between these peaks and Mowl-yr-Hydd, down to the villages of Maentwrog and Trawsfynydd. The final day is through the rough, tough and little visited Rhinogs mountain range. You can proceed either via the summit of **Rhinog Fawr** (720m) or by skirting the peaks to the west, following tracks and paths that lead eventually down to Barmouth, on the coast of the Irish Sea.

Wales Long-Distance Paths

Neither Glyndŵr's Way nor Offa's Dyke Path can be easily categorised. Unlike other walks in Britain, which are generally found in national parks or some other distinct geographical area, these two paths have evolved from the exploits of two individuals – Welsh hero Owain Glyndŵr and King Offa of Mercia.

Glyndŵr's Way is the more coherent of the two, following historically significant sites from Glyndŵr's life through the beautiful rolling hills of Mid-Wales. Offa's Dyke, however, follows this 8th-century engineering marvel from coast to coast, taking in an extraordinary array of terrain as it crosses and re-crosses the Wales–England border.

Glyndŵr's Way is also the easier and prettier, but Offa's Dyke's rugged beauty and sheer variety has its own charm. If you have the time and inclination, you could combine both routes by walking from Chepstow to Knighton, turning west to follow Glyndŵr's Way through Machynlleth to Welshpool, before heading north again to complete Offa's Dyke Path. This challenging route will take you the best part of a month, but it's an immensely rewarding way to experience this friendly and attractive part of the world.

The Glyndŵr's Way

Distance	132mi (212.5km)
Duration	9 days
Standard	medium
Start	Knighton
Finish	Welshpool
Gateways	Shrewsbury, Newtown, Machynlleth, Welshpool

Summary A national trail mainly on good paths and farm tracks through the quiet, rolling hills and pretty valleys of Mid-Wales. Some sections pass through bleak but beautiful moorland where conditions are more difficult.

Glyndŵr's Way National Trail is named after Owain Glyndŵr, the Welsh warrior-statesman who led a spirited but ultimately ill-fated rebellion against English rule in the early 15th century (see the boxed text following). The route passes many sites connected with the rebellion, including the town of Machynlleth where Glyndŵr convened Wales' first ever parliament.

Glyndŵr's Way was granted national trail status in 2000 and was officially opened in spring 2001. During this process, the route underwent some radical but also welcome changes, mostly to eliminate the 25 or so miles of unpleasant road walking that spoilt the original version. Almost one-third of the old path has been replaced and the trail is almost 4mi longer than the original.

The area along the trail is sandwiched between the well-known walking regions of Snowdonia to the north and the Brecon Beacons to the south. The landscape is predominantly low moor and farmland, with lakes, gentle hills and beautiful valleys. Although undulating, the route never rises above about 500m and rarely drops below 200m. A particular highlight is the impressive range of bird life, including buzzards, kingfishers, woodpeckers, red kites, peregrine falcons, flycatchers and wrens. This is a quiet part of Wales but the route's new status means it will attract a lot more attention in the future.

Direction, Distance & Duration

The trail can be followed either way but we describe it in the more popular Knighton to Welshpool direction. Most people tackle the walk in eight to 10 days; we have described it in nine, although the hilly terrain and multitude of paths crossing the trail can add up to pretty slow going, so it's wise to allow a little more time than you would for more established trails. Hours given in the route descriptions are approximate walking times only. You'll need to add more for lunch stops, map reading (a lot on this route) and sightseeing. If you don't intend to camp, plan your time around accommodation availability; it's extremely scarce on some sections of this route.

The route has dual waymarks – the national trail acorn symbol and a white disc with a red Welsh dragon designed for this route. The waymarking is being improved but it will take a couple of years to bring it up to the standard of other national trails.

For a nine-day walk, as described here, the most convenient places to start and end each day are:

day	from	to	mi/km
1	Knighton	Felindre	15/24
2	Felindre	Abbeycwmhir	14/22.5
3	Abbeycwmhir	Llanidloes	15.5/25
4	Llanidloes	Dylife	16/25.5
5	Dylife	Machynlleth	14.5/23.5
6	Machynlleth	Llanbrynmair	14/22.5
7	Llanbrynmair	Llanwddyn	17.5/28
8	Llanwddyn	Pontrobert	12/19.5
9	Pontrobert	Welshpool	13.5/21.5

Alternatives Nine days is pretty comfortable but Day 7 is long and could be split into two, with an overnight stop in Llangadfan. Llanidloes, Machynlleth and Lake Vyrnwy are all worth exploring during rest days, and there's plenty to keep you occupied in Welshpool, so you could conceivably turn this into a leisurely 14-day holiday.

If you don't wish to tackle the walk in one go, Machynlleth is the halfway point, so you can catch a train to Shrewsbury (via Welshpool), from where you can get to most other parts of Britain.

INFORMATION
Maps
A good set of maps is essential and the Ordnance Survey (OS) Explorer maps are the best option here. At a scale of 1:25,000 they provide the level of detail required in the absence of a trail guide. Maps No 201 (*Knighton & Presteigne*), No 214 (*Llanidloes & Newtown/Y Drenewydd*), No 215 (*Newtown/Y Drenewydd & Machynlleth*) and No 239 (*Lake Vyrnwy, Llyn Efyrnwy & Llanfyllin*) cover the entire route, except the last half-mile as you enter Machynlleth. You could purchase the OS Outdoor Leisure map No 23 (*Snowdonia – Cadair Idris &*

Bala Lake) for this tiny section but you'll be able to get by using the *Glyndŵr's Way Section 9* leaflet map (see Information Sources for details).

In general, the OS Landranger series lacks the detail required for this route but, if the OS Explorers aren't available, they'll do. You'll need No 148 (*Presteigne & Hay-On-Wye/Llannandras a'r Gelli Gandryll*), No 136 (*Newtown/Y Drenewydd & Llanidoes*), No 135 (*Aberystwyth & Machynlleth*), No 125 (*Bala & Lake Vyrnwy/Llyn Efyrnwy*) and No 126 (*Shrewsbury & Oswestry*).

Books
Owain Glyndwr's Way by Richard Sale is the route's only dedicated guidebook but it's now both out of print and out of date.

Otherwise, you'll have to get by with the leaflets, waymarks and a good set of maps. An official national trail guide is planned for 2003. Like others in the series, it will feature extracts from OS Explorer maps.

Information Sources
Tourist Information Centres (TICs) along the trail include Knighton (☎ 01547-529424), Llanidloes (☎ 01686-412605), Machynlleth (☎ 01654-702401), Lake Vyrnwy (near Llanwddyn; ☎ 01691-870346) and Welshpool (☎ 01938-552043). They can supply you with the *Glyndŵr's Way Accommodation List* plus a series of 16 leaflets called *Glyndŵr's Way*, which describe the route. Published by the Powys County Council, the leaflets outline the history of the route and surrounding area, contain some wildlife notes and have been updated to take in new sections of the route. The full set costs £4 and includes the accommodation list.

There is a full-time Glyndŵr's Way National Trail project manager (☎ 01654-703376) who can answer queries or provide advice and information on the new route.

Baggage Services
There's currently no service that covers the entire route but many B&Bs are happy to take your bags on to the next stop. Budget on £10 to £20 per section and request the service when booking your accommodation.

PLACES TO STAY & EAT

You can cover the entire Glyndŵr's Way staying in B&Bs, pubs and guesthouses but the options are extremely limited in some places so it's important to book ahead, particularly during summer.

This situation has not been helped by the fact that only certified accommodation appears in the annual *Glyndŵr's Way Accommodation List* (see Information Sources) from 2001. Many smaller operators are refusing to pay the hefty fee levied by the Wales Tourist Board for this service, so the list doesn't reflect the breadth of options along the route. We've included as many of these places as possible in the route descriptions, while *The Rambler's Yearbook & Accommodation Guide* and *Stillwell's National Trail Companion* (see Books in the Facts for the Walker chapter) may also help fill the gaps.

Knighton, Llanidloes, Machynlleth and Welshpool are the only towns of any size along the route and offer a good range of services, accommodation and restaurants. Elsewhere, your options are pretty limited and you'll need to plan around what is available.

If you wish to camp, several of the B&Bs in *Glyndŵr's Way Accommodation List* offer camping facilities. As the route is generally remote you can easily pitch a tent almost anywhere, although you must get permission when on private land (ie, outside campsites or farms offering camping facilities).

There are several pubs along the way for lunchtime stops, but on some days you will need to be self-sufficient. Although there are shops on the route where you can stock

---

Owain Glyndŵr

Owain Glyndŵr is a Welsh hero but surprisingly little is known about him. Some of the most detailed but often highly embellished stories of his life emerge from the writings of the Welsh bards. We know that Owain Glyndŵr was the son of a wealthy landowner, descended from the royal houses of Powys and Gwynedd, and lived in Wales in the second half of the 14th century. As was common in those times, he became a squire to the English nobility, in particular to Henry of Bolingbroke, later King Henry IV. Glyndŵr fought for the English army in mainland Europe and Scotland, and then settled in Mid-Wales with his wife and children. Little may have ever been heard of him had his neighbour Reginald Grey, Lord of Ruthin, not stolen some land from him.

Glyndŵr decided to fight Grey in court but the Welsh people were regarded as barbarians by most of the English and the case was dismissed, apparently with the words, 'What care we for barefoot Welsh dogs?' At around the same time Henry IV was engaged in a military campaign in Scotland. Glyndŵr refused to take part and was labelled a traitor by the king. He was forced to flee his home for some time but it is recorded that on 16 September 1400 Glyndŵr met his brothers and a few close associates at Glyndyfrdwy, on the banks of the River Dee. He was proclaimed the Prince of Wales – a deliberate stand against English rule – and so began a long, drawn-out fight for Welsh independence.

Several skirmishes followed and by the end of 1403 Glyndŵr controlled most of Wales and, secure in his position as the Prince of Wales, he called the first Welsh parliament at Machynlleth. Events began to turn sour as a new protagonist appeared on the English scene: Prince Henry, son of Henry IV, and hero of the Battle of Agincourt. He delivered shattering blows to the Welsh army at Grosmont and Usk. The people of South Wales began to renounce the rebellion and Glyndŵr's position started to look shaky.

Welsh fortunes declined further in 1406. With Prince Henry wreaking havoc in the south, Glyndŵr was forced to retreat to the north. His hopes and plans for a Wales free of its English oppressors were shattered, and gradually the English regained control. There was no last glorious stand and around 1406 Glyndŵr simply disappeared. Theories have him dying anonymously in battle or spending his last years wandering in the mountains, living quietly among friends. The Welsh bards paint a more romantic picture of him sleeping in a hidden cave with his followers, waiting for the right moment to rise again against the English. The only sure thing is that nobody knows.

up on snacks and lunch ingredients, they are far from plentiful, so do plan ahead. Also note that in this part of Wales most pubs keep traditional hours; lunchtimes and evenings only. If you are staying at a remote B&B, check that they offer an evening meal and request one when you book.

GETTING TO/FROM THE WALK

The Getting Around chapter lists several public transport inquiry lines that provide details of both national and local bus and train services: See the boxed text 'Public Transport Information'.

Bus There is only one bus service each week to Knighton, running on Tuesday from Newtown. The D75 bus service runs every two hours, Monday to Saturday, from Welshpool to Shrewsbury. Contact the Welshpool TIC (☎ 01938-552043) for timetable details.

Train The easiest way to get to and from the walk is by train. Knighton is on the *Heart of Wales* line between Shrewsbury and Swansea, with four trains a day (three on Sunday). Welshpool is served several times a day by the *Cambrian Coaster* between Pwllheli and Birmingham via Machynlleth and Shrewsbury.

Car The route starts in Knighton, which is on the A4113 and links with Shrewsbury, Leominster and Hereford by the A49. From Welshpool the A458 leads to Shrewsbury.

THE WALK
Knighton

Set on a hill around a central clock tower, the small and austere border town of Knighton lacks the charm of many villages later in the route but it has a good selection of services, pubs and shops. As well as being the start of the trail, Knighton (Tref-y-clawdd in Welsh, meaning 'town on the dyke') is the halfway stage of the Offa's Dyke Path, which explains why the TIC (☎ 01547-529424) is in the refurbished Offa's Dyke Centre.

Offa's Dyke House (☎ 01547-528634), near the clock tower, is the best option for walkers. Welcoming and comfortable, with

B&B from £18, it's run by walking enthusiasts who are knowledgeable about the route and can suggest good day walks in the area. Other options include *The Red Lion* (☎ *01547-528231*), on Broad St, from £17; *Larkspur* (☎ *01547-528764*), near the train station, for £15; and *The Fleece House* (☎ *01547-520168*), on Market St, from £23.

The pubs all offer meals, with the *George & Dragon*, on Broad St, having a particularly good menu (£2.95 to £9.95). You can also enjoy a tasty meal at *Nosebag's Brasserie*, next to the Horse & Jockey pub, Station Rd.

There isn't much to see or do in Knighton, so if you arrive early enough in the day it may be worth considering an immediate

---

The Glyndŵr's Way – Route Highlight

8.5mi (13.5km), 4–5 hours
This walk takes you round the three main peaks that surround Knighton. With the clock tower at your back, go left up Broad St and take the Offa's Dyke Path signpost to the right. It takes you past a picnic area by the river, which you cross via the footbridge next to the railway line. Strike steeply uphill and where the Offa's Dyke Path turns left, head right instead to enter the trees of Kinsley Wood. Take the path that drops down to follow the edge of the plantation and circle round to finish at the train station.

From here head back into town and pick up Offa's Dyke again by taking the lane that goes straight ahead at the T-junction. Follow signs out of Knighton and climb up Ffridd hill to enjoy the views and one of the best-preserved sections of the Dyke in Wales. At the gentle saddle about a mile out of town, take a very sharp right down the side of a fence and follow it down to a minor road. Where the road meets the A488, turn left and follow it for a quarter of a mile to Brookhouse Farm, before turning right onto a minor road to partly circumnavigate Garth Hill. Go straight on at Little Cwm-gilla farm and complete the circuit by following the Glyndŵr's Way waymarks round the slopes of Garth Hill and back into town.

start. There's accommodation around Llan-gunllo (5mi along the trail) and this makes a nice, late-afternoon walk. Alternatively, try the loop outlined in the boxed text 'The Glyndŵr's Way – Route Highlight'.

Day 1: Knighton to Felindre
15mi (24km), 6–7 hours

This is a relatively comfortable day intro-ducing you to many features typical of the trail – rolling hills, rich green farmland, open moor and tiny villages.

The official start of the route is the clock tower in the town's centre. From here you go up the picturesque 'narrows' (a street of houses dating from Tudor times), through the back streets of Knighton and on to a track that takes you round the northern side of leafy Garth Hill (346m). This is the first of two new sections of the route on today's walk and avoids a mile or so of road walking.

Rejoining the old Way at Little Cwm-gilla, there's a testing little climb through farm-land for more than a mile before another new section swings south towards Llangun-llo, taking you through the attractive and welcoming *Cefnsuran Farm* (☎ 01547-550219), which offers B&B for £23. Another couple of miles of pleasant farmland and you descend into the village of Llangunllo.

The trail used to pass 1.5mi to the north of Llangunllo, but the new section happily takes you through the village. Apart from a 13th-century church, its chief attraction is *The Greyhound*, a broken-down but friendly little pub at the back of the village *shop*. Places to stay include *Rhiwlas* (☎ 01547-550256), a mile to the north, and *Craig Fach* (☎ 01547-550605), in the village it-self. They offer B&B for £16 and £15 re-spectively, as well as evening meals.

From Llangunllo, the trail heads north on a road before you head into farmland again via a path on the left. After crossing a small stream, you pass under the railway line and take a path up to Nayadd Fach farm. An-other few miles of pastoral walking in un-dulating terrain brings you back to the original path just past Ferley.

The next few miles provide the first taste of open moorland – one of the real attractions

of the trail. These windswept hills are cov-ered in bracken, heather and grasses, and while the walking is undeniably more enjoy-able in good weather, even in the cold and rain it's beautiful. Gradually the hills give way to more farmland as you near Felindre.

Felindre
This village is even smaller than Llangunllo, so book accommodation early. It has a *shop* that keeps irregular hours and a friendly pub, *The Wharf Inn* – only open at weekends. B&B is offered by the excellent *Trevland* (☎ 01547-510211), for £17.50; and *The Brandy House Farm* (☎ 01547-510282), for £19. Both offer camping and evening meals.

Day 2: Felindre to Abbeycwmhir
14mi (22.5km), 5½–6½ hours

Not the best day of the route but the later stretches of moor, mountain and forest easily make up for the early trudge through fields.

From Felindre the route is well way-marked through gently rising farming coun-try to a short section of road. Where the road turns to the north, you head south in-stead along a byway – another new section of path that replaces 3mi of road walking. The trail takes you steadily uphill past an old earthwork known as Castell-y-Blaidd and on to a lane and into Llanbadarn Fynydd. Here *The New Inn* (☎ 01597-840378) of-fers comfortable B&B from £20, as well as meals throughout the day.

From Llanbadarn Fynydd the trail gently climbs to open moor, skirting woods to reach *Bwlch Farm* (☎ 01597-840366), a friendly B&B for £21.50 that offers great food, par-ticularly for vegetarians. The remainder of the walk to Abbeycwmhir is a delight. It be-gins with a fine ridge walk rising to a 450m summit, before dropping through Neuadd Fach wood into the valley of Bachell Brook.

Abbeycwmhir
Abbeycwmhir has a *shop* and a pub, *The Happy Union*, but it doesn't offer meals. *Home Farm* (☎ 01597-851666) has B&B from £14, plus camping facilities and even-ing meals. The lovely little St Mary's Church (1870) is worth a look if open.

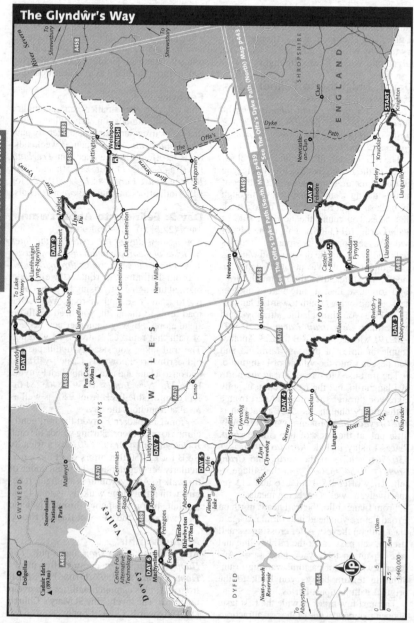

The Glyndŵr's Way

Day 3: Abbeycwmhir to Llanidloes

15.5mi (25km), 6–7 hours

This is a hilly but deeply satisfying day of forests, moorland and grand views. Make sure you carry lunch, as there are no shops on today's route.

The walk leaves Abbeycwmhir opposite The Happy Union and follows a track through forest across a lane before meeting a stream. Here the route climbs the ridge of Upper Esgair Hill – a new section that bypasses the old route along a gloomy forest track. You rejoin the old Way soon enough to descend through open moor to the village of Bwlch-y-sarnau. Another new section, departing north via the path by the phone box, takes you through rather boggy forest. The track improves all the way to Blaentrinant, from where on a clear day you can see the peak of Cadair Idris (893m), in the south of Snowdonia, far to the north-west.

Beyond Blaentrinant the route zigzags rather wildly and you have to keep one eye on your map and the other scanning for waymarks. However, don't allow this to detract from one of the most glorious stretches of the trail. It's fields and stiles for the final 3mi into Llanidloes.

Llanidloes

Beautifully positioned on the River Severn, Llanidloes has a TIC (☎ 01686-412605) and much to offer visitors. The town's most obvious feature is the attractive 16th-century **market hall**, while the 14th-century **church** of St Idloes by the river boasts five magnificent arches brought from Abbeycwmhir in the 1540s.

On a more practical note, Llanidloes has a good range of accommodation and several good pubs, as well as a useful array of services – ideal for a rest day. Places to stay include *Lloyds' Hotel* (☎ 01686-412284), on the edge of town, with B&B from £19.50; the better *Red Lion* (☎ 01686-412270), on Long Bridge St, where B&B starts at £30; and the comfortable *Dyffryn Guest House* (☎ 01686-412129), on a farm just out of town, with B&B from £18.

Many of Llanidloes' pubs offer meals – on Long Bridge St the *Red Lion* and *The Phoenix* both put on a decent spread – and on the main street there's a good *takeaway* serving fish and chips, but get in early as kitchens often close by 8.30pm.

Day 4: Llanidloes to Dylife

16mi (25.5km), 6½–7½ hours

After the familiar stiles and fields, today the trail takes you through pine forest, across moorland and alongside a reservoir. Take advantage of the amenities in Llanidloes as there are no shops until Machynlleth.

Leaving Llanidloes you cross the River Severn to link up with the Severn Way path through an attractive forest. This is a new and welcome section that dispenses with more than a mile of road. Rejoining the road for half a mile, climb steeply and then go left at a cattle grid to pass through Bryntail Farm.

The track now descends into the Clywedog Valley and you suddenly find yourself at the foot of the 65m concrete wall of Llyn Clywedog (Reservoir), where there are the mildly interesting ruins of a 19th-century lead mine. A steep climb takes you back up the other side of the dam to impressive views of the 6.5mi-long reservoir itself. You follow some steep sections of path along the edge of the lake before a new piece of path climbs to the extreme edge of the gigantic Hafren Forest pine plantation.

Rejoining the old path at the western arm of the reservoir, you re-enter the forest and

Abbeycwmhir – The Best-Laid Plans

Little remains of the Cistercian abbey from which the village of Abbeycwmhir gets its name. It was founded in 1143 but never completed, although its plans would have made it one of the largest in Britain after York, Durham and Winchester. Owain Glyndŵr destroyed the abbey in 1401 after finding most of the monks to be English. This halted construction and the damage was never repaired. The abbey was finally closed in 1536 during Henry VIII's Dissolution of the Monasteries.

amble along a flat and wide track and back into farmland. Just past Dolydd, another new section of path heads due north; scan the skies here for red kites cruising the air currents. A gradual climb through attractive moorland takes you to a ridge where you can see Dylife by the road below. You leave the trail here to descend to the pub for the night.

Dylife

This hamlet has one place to stay – the very welcoming *Star Inn* (☎ *01650-521345*) with B&B from £17. The rooms and food are only adequate but the atmosphere in the pub is great. Alternatively, you could press on for 5mi to Aberhosan and have a short day tomorrow.

Day 5: Dylife to Machynlleth

14.5mi (23.5km), 6–7 hours
Today is the finest day of the route, taking in glacial valleys, rugged hills, high mountain lakes, beautiful bird life and cool forest.

Leaving the Star Inn, turn right onto the main road then take the path about 100m to the left and strike uphill to rejoin the trail at the gentle saddle. A new section heads west through lovely moorland, passing close to a dramatic drop into the rugged Afon Clywedog glacial valley. Descending rapidly to cross the Nant Goch tributary, the trail climbs again through more boggy but attractive moorland to the edge of Glaslyn – a lake and waterbird sanctuary, well worth a detour.

Meeting the original path again, you head very steeply downhill, dropping 330m in just under 1.5mi through a picturesque and partially wooded valley. The trail passes half a mile south of Aberhosan, where B&B is available at *Caeheulon* (☎ *01654-703243*) from £19.50.

After a demanding climb up Cefn Modfedd, you leave the old route and head south to begin the largest new section of the trail. It swings expansively south-west, through a short wood and past *Talbont-drain* (☎ *01654-702192*), a beautiful farm charging £19 for B&B and offering superb evening meals.

A steep hill leads into a splendid walk above a valley, before you climb once more

through woodland on Ffridd Rhiwlwyfen and then swing to the far side of Machynlleth to enter town via the so-called Roman Steps.

Machynlleth

Machynlleth is ideal for a rest day. A vibrant little town with a rich history, it's a microcosm of the cultural regeneration being enjoyed by modern Wales. The **Centre for Alternative Technology**, impressive **Celtica exhibition**, an **arts centre**, Internet cafe and organic food cafe all sit comfortably alongside fine old architecture and traditional pubs. For information on accommodation and attractions in the area, drop into the TIC (☎ 01654-702401) on Maengwyn St.

Places to stay in Machynlleth include the *Glyndwr Hotel* (☎ *01654-703989*), the longstanding *Pendre Guesthouse* (☎ *01654-702088*) and *Maenllwyd* (☎ *01654-702928*), all in the centre of town and all with B&B from £20 to £25.

For meals there's a large selection of pubs and restaurants to select from, with *The Quarries* organic cafe (☎ *01654-702339*), on Maengwyn St, a haven of superbly prepared vegetarian meals from £1.95 to £5.50.

Day 6: Machynlleth to Llanbrynmair

14mi (22.5km), 5½–6½ hours
This is a pleasant day's walk through farms and across moorland, before a new section offers fine views high above a valley.

This day's walk used to start with a near-suicidal 3mi stretch of walking along the busy A489, but the new route takes you down the quieter minor road south-east to Forge. From Forge a laneway heads through farmland, back to the main road for 300m and on to Penegoes. Another new section follows a lane due east between hedgerows, before you strike up to the left through some fields and then descend steeply through heavy bracken to the small village of Abercegir.

From Abercegir the route once again climbs onto open moor. Along these hilltops are lovely views of Cadair Idris mountain as you follow a distinct track before descending to Cemmaes Road. At the top of this road is *Cefn Coch Uchaf* (☎ *01650-511552*), a

Pen yr Ole Wen, Snowdonia National Park

Descending Y Garn, with Llyn Ogwen ahead

A well-earned break at the summit of Y Garn, Snowdonia National Park

BRYN THOMAS

Tintern Abbey, Wye Valley, Wales

PATRICK HORTON

Looking for a less strenuous mode of transport?

PATRICK HORTON

Cruising with the narrowboats on the 38m-high Pontcysyllte Aqueduct, Wales

500-year-old farmhouse that offers B&B for £17.50.

The 6mi walk from Cemmaes Road to Llanbrynmair is truly a delight, through rolling hills and pleasant scenic valleys. Although the initial climb out of Cemmaes Road is quite steep, the going is easy. After climbing to a derelict farm, Rhyd-yr-aderyn, the route descends towards Llanbrynmair, before a new section heads north-east up a steepish hill following the fenceline along a very boggy path. A pleasant track takes you half a mile through a pine forest. Once out you descend past a mast and along a minor road to Llanbrynmair.

Llanbrynmair

The little town of Llanbrynmair has a *shop* and a pub, *The Wynnstay Arms* (☎ *01650-521431*), which offers B&B for £17.50 and decent meals.

Day 7: Llanbrynmair to Llanwddyn

17.5mi (28km), 7–8 hours
On the old route this day featured an unpleasant section of bleak moorland but this has been replaced with a delightful jaunt along a range of hills, although boggy ground, innumerable stiles and sheer distance combine to make this a tough day indeed.

Leave Llanbrynmair northwards on a new section of the trail, going under a railway line before heading east through fields to briefly rejoin the old route. It soon strikes north again, following a disused vehicle track up a long, steep hill, but the climb is worth it; you can enjoy terrific views of the valley below as you follow the contour for a mile or so.

Entering a forest the trail becomes a broad, open vehicle track – a very dull section – before you cross several fields and meet yet another vehicle track to rejoin the old Glyndŵr's Way near Dolau-ceimion Farm.

You soon climb to the edge of Pen Coed (360m) and cross a particularly lonely stretch of bracken-covered moor. The waymarking has improved here but still keep an eye on your map and compass. After about a mile cross a stream and follow a path to the left that zigzags a little confusingly through a

host of farms to take you into Llangadfan. This little village has a *shop* at the petrol station, while the *Cann Office Hotel* (☎ *01938-820202*) is a good place for a lunchtime meal and offers B&B for £22. You could stop here but the walk to Llanwddyn is pretty comfortable and the worst is well behind you.

The final 7mi is easy – through the huge plantation of Dyfnant forest. There's a maze of forestry tracks but the waymarking will keep you on course.

Llanwddyn

This little village is a creature of tourism, catering to the steady stream of visitors to **Lake Vyrnwy** and its impressive 33-arched dam. There is plenty to do here if you have a spare day, from exploring one of the many nature trails to spinning round the 11mi circuit of the lake on a hire bicycle. There are also three hides for spotting the many species of local birds (the lake is part of a Royal Society for the Protection of Birds reserve), plus fishing, sailing and canoeing. The helpful TIC (☎ 01691-870346) or visitors centre (☎ 01691-870278) can point you in the right direction.

Places to stay in the area include the *Lake Vyrnwy Hotel* (☎ *01691-870692*), which is expensive (£80/125) but a lovely place if you're cashed up. More affordable is the very welcoming *Fronheulog Caravan Park* (☎ *01691-870662*), about 1.5mi from Llanwddyn (follow the main road east and then south through Abertridwr and then north after a hairpin turn). It offers camping for £2. Or there is *Tynymaes* (☎ *01691-870216*) with B&B for £20, a little farther along the road. Both offer evening meals or you could try the pricey delights of the hotel's restaurant.

Day 8: Llanwddyn to Pontrobert

12mi (19.5km), 4½–5½ hours
This day marks the end of the harder moorland sections. The trail is quite easy from now on, passing through pretty valleys, pleasant riverside walks and gentle farmland.

From Llanwddyn the route follows forest tracks and minor roads, including two sections of new path, to the village of Pont Llogel. Turning left along the path just before the village bridge, follow the River Vyrnwy for half a mile before going left again to higher ground. This section meanders through farmland, down a new path towards Dolwar Fach farm (which cuts a mile off the old route) and eventually into **Dolanog**. There's a small *shop* here but not much else.

The next section is comfortable and attractive, with the route shadowing the Vyrnwy as it undulates through woods before climbing slightly away from the river to follow a lane into Pontrobert.

Pontrobert

The village of Pontrobert is an attractive place with a terrific pub, the *Royal Oak Inn* (☎ *01938-500243*), offering B&B for £19 and good food. If you're lucky, you may spot kingfishers flashing along the river under the old bridge. If you can't get into the pub, Meifod is only another 3mi or so along the trail.

Day 9: Pontrobert to Welshpool

13.5mi (21.5km), 5½–6½ hours
Today is comfortable and quite easy – an enjoyable final day on the trail.

Heading east out of Pontrobert, you wander through gentle farmland before crossing the edge of the wooded Gallt yr Ancr (Hill of the Anchorite) and taking a lane into the rather unimpressive village of Meifod, which nevertheless has a useful *shop*, plus lovely grounds to relax in at the Church of Saints Dysilio & Mary. B&B for £19 is available at *The King's Head* (☎ *01938-500788*), which also has reasonable meals.

Leaving Meifod you encounter a steep but pleasant climb through woods of Broniarth Hill, before looping round Llyn Du ('llyn' means lake in Welsh) and swinging back to the south-west along a minor road. More comfortable farmland walking follows, until you hit the B4392 at Stonehouse Farm. Here you head right along a new section of path that does away with the rather anticlimactic and tiresome 4mi of road into Welshpool that used to conclude this walk. Instead you head south through Figyn Wood, climb to the edge of a golf course and go east through a series of farms to meet the A458, near

Welshpool's Raven Square train station. The main street starts at the nearby roundabout.

A visit to the magnificent **Powis Castle**, a mile south of town, will provide a fitting finale to your walk (see the boxed text 'Powis Castle' for details.)

Welshpool

Known as the 'Gateway to Wales' (although many border towns claim this title), Welshpool is situated in the valley of the River Severn, separated from England by Long Mountain and the Breidden Hills. Architecturally it's Georgian English but culturally it's Welsh through and through. All told, it's an attractive little town and a good spot to finish the walk. The TIC (☎ 01938-552043) is on Church St.

There's a cluster of places to stay near the attractive St Mary's Church on Salop Rd, including *Hafren Guesthouse* (☎ *01938-554112*), *Montgomery House* (☎ *01938-552693*) and the *Westwood Park Hotel* (☎ *01938-553474*), which are all spotless and offer B&B for under £20. If you want a little more luxury to celebrate the end of your walk, *The Royal Oak* (☎ *01938-552217*), in the centre of town, has B&B for £58.50. The TIC (☎ *01938-552043*), near St Mary's, can provide other alternatives.

Evening meals are not Welshpool's strongest point. Many cafes close in the late

Powis Castle

Don't miss visiting Powis Castle, half a mile south-west of Welshpool. Built in the 13th century, it is one of the National Trust's finest properties in Wales, featuring impressive terraced gardens, plus an orangery, aviary and a smattering of niched statues. The castle houses the Clive of India Museum – a collection of artefacts and treasures amassed by the redoubtable Robert Clive during his time on the subcontinent more than 200 years ago. Powis Castle is open Wednesday to Sunday in April, June, September and October, and Tuesday to Sunday in July and August. Hours are 11am to 6pm but last admissions are at 4.30pm.

afternoon and several of the pubs don't offer food at all. However, *The Talbot*, in the main street, is by far and away the best of those that do. Nearby, *The Royal Oak* is reasonably good too, or you could try *The Buttery*, also in the main street. Otherwise, your best option is the very good takeaway, *Andrews Fish Bar*, across from The Buttery. When you're ready to move on, there are several trains and buses each day to Shrewsbury.

The Offa's Dyke Path

Distance	177.5mi (285.5km)
Duration	12 days
Standard	hard
Start	Sedbury Cliffs, near Chepstow
Finish	Prestatyn Beach
Gateways	Newport, Welshpool, Hereford, Chester, Shrewsbury

Summary A popular national trail through varied and historically rich terrain, punctuated by testing gradients. Only for fit, experienced walkers competent with a map and compass. There are also more than 700 stiles to climb, so keep that backpack light.

Offa's Dyke was conceived and executed in the 8th century by the Mercian king, Offa, probably to keep the unruly Welsh within their borders. A grand and ambitious linear earthwork, usually in the form of a bank next to a ditch, it became pivotal in the history of the Welsh Marches (the border of the ancient kingdom of Mercia and Wales). Indeed, even though only 80mi of the Dyke remains, it continues to roughly define the modern-day Wales–England border.

The Offa's Dyke Path National Trail runs from the Severn Estuary at Chepstow in the south through the beautiful Wye Valley and Shropshire Hills to end on the coast at Prestatyn in North Wales. The trail doesn't stick religiously to the Dyke – which is overgrown in some places and built over in others – often detouring along quiet valleys and up sharp ridges, through an astonishing range of scenery and vegetation. You'll walk from river flatland to hill country, through oak forests, heathland and bracken. You'll see dense and dark conifer forest, and a patchwork of green fields bound by hedges, plus high moors and the more exacting mountainous conditions of the Clwydian range in the north. The region's rich and turbulent history is also reflected in the ruined castles and abbeys, its ancient hillforts and remaining sections of Roman road.

The Offas's Dyke Path also continually crosses between England and Wales, meaning villages a mere 10mi apart can be completely different in look, feel and culture, which pretty well sums up the eclectic nature of the route. There's really nothing coherent here at all, but get out and enjoy it – one of its chief delights is that you're never really sure what you'll encounter from day to day.

Direction, Distance & Duration

While the trail can be walked in either direction, it's best done south to north; the sun and wind will be mostly on your back, and most guidebooks describe the walk this way.

The total length of the trail is 177.5mi and we describe it in 12 days, with an average daily walk of 14mi (22.5km) and three particularly long days to start with. This can be pretty hard going in this terrain, and even harder if the weather's poor. It's wise to allow at least two rest days, bringing your venture to an even two weeks. The rest days will also allow you to take in some of the notable sights off the trail, particularly Tintern Abbey and Powis Castle in Welshpool. If you can't avoid carrying a heavy backpack, investigate having it transported between villages (see Baggage Services later) or the going will be tough indeed.

Offa's Dyke is generally well waymarked by the familiar white acorn indicating a national trail, but there are many more public paths and bridleways that crisscross the route, so keep your eyes peeled. Ensure you carry a good set of maps and compass as there are some wild and exposed mountain sections where you don't want to get lost.

For a 12-day walk, the most convenient stages are:

day	from	to	mi/km
1	Sedbury Cliffs	Monmouth	17.5/28
2	Monmouth	Pandy	17/27.5
3	Pandy	Hay-on-Wye	17.5/28
4	Hay-on-Wye	Kington	15/24
5	Kington	Knighton	13.5/21.5
6	Knighton	Brompton Crossroads	15/24
7	Brompton Crossroads	Buttington	12.5/20
8	Buttington	Llanymynech	10.5/17
9	Llanymynech	Chirk Castle	14/22.5
10	Chirk Castle	Llandegla	16/25.5
11	Llandegla	Bodfari	17/27.5
12	Bodfari	Prestatyn	12/19.5

Alternatives If you aren't fond of strenuous walking, you could ease your way in by taking two days to complete Day 1, with a stopover at Brockweir. Otherwise, the days between Knighton and Brompton Crossroads (Day 6) and Llandegla to Bodfari (Day 11) are the most demanding physically. You could divide each of these sections into two days (stopping at Newcastle and Llanferres), taking the duration to 16 or 17 days.

PLANNING
Maps
Take a compass and a good set of maps, as there will be times when you need them. The best maps are the OS Explorer and OS Outdoor Leisure 1:25,000 series. You will need, in order, OS Outdoor Leisure maps No 14 (*Wye Valley and Forest of Dean*) and No 13 (*Brecon Beacons – Eastern Area*), and OS Explorer maps No 201 (*Knighton Presteigne*), No 216 (*Welshpool & Montgomery*), No 240 (*Oswestry*), No 256 (*Wrexham & Llangollen*) and No 265 (*Clwydian Range/Bryniau*).

The route is also covered by OS Landranger 1:50,000 maps No 162 (*Gloucester & Forest of Dean*), No 161 (*Abergavenny & The Black Mountains*), No 148 (*Presteigne & Hay-on-Wye*), No 137 (*Ludlow & Church Stretton, Wenlock Edge*), No 126 (*Shrewsbury & Oswestry*), No 117 (*Chester & Wrexham, Ellesmere Port*) and No 116

(*Denbigh & Colwyn Bay*), but the detail is not as helpful for exploring off the path.

Books
For pure practicality, the official national trail guide *Offa's Dyke Path* is the best on offer, covering the walk in two books – *Chepstow to Knighton* and *Knighton to Prestatyn* – both by Ernie & Kathy Kay & Mark Richards. They feature straightforward route notes, a taste of the history, colour OS 1:25,000 maps and suggested circular walks off the Dyke. However, to get a real sense of the trail's rich heritage, you can't go past *Walking Offa's Dyke Path – A Journey Through the Border Country of England and Wales* by David Hunter. *Langton's Guide to Offa's Dyke Path* by Andrew Durham has a rather regimented approach to the route descriptions but adopts enough background information and good reproductions of maps.

Information Sources
There are TICs at Chepstow, Monmouth, Hay-on-Wye, Knighton, Welshpool and Prestatyn – numbers are given in the route description. The TIC at Knighton (☎ 01547-528753), in the Offa's Dyke Centre on West St, is the best place to contact for route information; this is the base for the Offa's Dyke Association (ODA; ⊜ oda@offasdyke.demon.co.uk, ⓦ www.offa.demon.co.uk/offa.htm) and Offa's Dyke Path Management Service.

Enthusiasts of the ODA publish a number of helpful booklets and pamphlets, including the indispensable *Offa's Dyke Path – Where to Stay, How to Get There & Other Useful Information*, the handy *Backpackers' & Camping List*, *South to North Route Notes*, and a set of strip maps. Some of these are also available at TICs along the route.

Another very useful source of information is the Offa's Dyke Web site (ⓦ www.offas-dyke.co.uk), which has general information on the route, critiques of maps and route guides, and luggage transport and accommodation booking services.

Baggage Sevices
Offa's Dyke Baggage Carriers (☎ 01497-821266) in Hay-on-Wye use local taxis to

collect and transport luggage along the route. The charge varies depending on the length of the day's walk but you're looking at an average of £15. Many B&Bs provide the same service (termed 'luggage' in the ODA booklet), often at substantially cheaper rates. Inquire when booking accommodation.

PLACES TO STAY & EAT

You can cover the entire Offa's Dyke Path using hotels, B&Bs or youth hostels. We provide some recommendations in the route description and there are many more in the ODA *Where to Stay* pamphlet. B&B rates vary throughout the route but you'll need to budget roughly for £20 per night. If you mention that you're walking the trail, the rate can be cheaper.

It's also possible to camp the whole way, as there are several campsites on or near the route, plus many other places on private land where you can pitch a tent; just remember to politely request permission first. We mention some good campsites but see the *Backpackers' & Camping List* for a full selection.

The trail is well served by a range of pubs, cafes, restaurants and shops where you can buy food and drink. Note that many pubs in rural Wales keep traditional hours and will be closed from 3pm to 7pm.

GETTING TO/FROM THE WALK

The Getting Around chapter lists several public transport inquiry lines that provide details of both national and local bus and train services: See the boxed text 'Public Transport Information'.

Bus You can reach Chepstow and Prestatyn by National Express coaches from most parts of Britain. Local bus services to points on or near Offa's Dyke Path are listed in the ODA's *Where to Stay* booklet.

Train You can go by train to Chepstow (usually via Newport) and Prestatyn (on the Chester to Holyhead line), which both have regular services to other parts of the country.

Car Chepstow is reached by leaving the M48 motorway immediately after you've crossed the Severn Bridge coming from England. Parking cars for the duration of the walk is offered, by arrangement, by some of the places to stay (see the ODA's *Where to Stay* handbook for details).

At the end of the walk, Prestatyn is on the A548 between Llandudno and Chester.

THE WALK
Chepstow

Near the confluence of the Rivers Wye and Severn, Chepstow was first developed as a base for the Norman conquest of south-east Wales. It later prospered as a port for the timber and wine trades, but as river-borne commerce declined, so Chepstow's importance diminished to that of a typical market town.

The main attraction is the well-preserved **Chepstow Castle**, on the towering cliffs of the River Wye. Construction began in 1067, making it the first stone castle in Wales, and possibly Britain. Chepstow Castle (☎ 01291-624065) is open daily from 9.30am to 6pm in summer, and until 5pm in winter. The TIC (☎ 01291-623772) is directly across from the castle but, perplexingly, doesn't always stock important ODA pamphlets, so ensure you have these before you arrive.

There is a good range of places to stay in Chepstow. Near the start of the walk there's *Upper Sedbury House* (☎ 01291-627173), on Sedbury Lane, where B&B costs £21.50 (you can also leave your car there). *Langcroft* (☎ 01291-625569, 71 St Kingsmark Ave), a short walk from the centre, charges £20 for rooms in a small house. On Welsh St, the *Coach & Horses* (☎ 01291-622626) charges £20 and has good food all day, while the welcoming *Pendine Guest House* (☎ 01291-623308), on Bridge St, is a comfortable place with B&B from £18.

There are plenty of places to eat along the High St and Bridge St, including *Three Tuns Inn*, *The Castle Inn*, *The White Lion* and the very good *Afon Gwy*.

Day 1: Sedbury Cliffs to Monmouth

17.5mi (28km), 9 hours
This is one of the longest days on the route and is quite demanding, with several testing

climbs, although the sheer beauty of the Wye Valley makes it easier to take.

The official start of Offa's Dyke Path is by a commemorative marker stone by Sedbury Cliffs, about a mile east of Chepstow, with views over the estuary and mudflats of the River Severn. From here the well-marked trail makes its way past a housing estate and along the River Wye to Chepstow Castle, through Chepstow town. It's not particularly picturesque so, if you arrive on the previous afternoon, you could stroll down and get this bit done, then start your walking the next morning from the bridge by Chepstow Castle – an infinitely more pleasing spot.

From the north side of bridge, join the trail and follow it through several small farms and up to Dennel Hill, where you meet with the Dyke proper. Continue through the forest before dropping down into Brockweir, where the **Country Inn** (☎ *01291-689548*) has B&B from £15 and a good lunch menu (from £3.95). Before you head down to Brockweir, there's a path just past the limestone pinnacle, known as the Devil's Pulpit, that takes you down to **Tintern Abbey** (see the boxed text). You can avoid the long slog back up the hill by following the trail by the river to Brockweir.

At Brockweir, the trail divides into upper and lower alternatives. The lower route is an easier and prettier walk along the river but almost a mile longer, while the upper route climbs to follow the line of the Dyke through

The Offa's Dyke Path – Route Highlight

10.5mi (17km), 5½–6½ hours
This is a very attractive – if somewhat demanding – walk that takes you high above the Wye Valley, before crossing the river to Tintern Abbey and following the beautiful Wye Valley Walk back to Chepstow.

From Chepstow Castle follow the Offa's Dyke Path north, taking in the marvellous views of the valley before dropping down to Brockweir. Cross the bridge and look out for the Wye Valley Walk signpost that takes you down the western bank of the river to the turn-off to Tintern Abbey.

Having rested your legs and wandered through the impressive ruins, pick up the Wye Valley Walk again and follow its well-marked route all the way back to Chepstow. It also climbs high above the valley to give you great views to the east and west, providing ample evidence of its designation as an Area of Outstanding Natural Beauty.

Tintern Abbey

The tall walls and empty, arched windows of Tintern Abbey, a 14th-century Cistercian abbey on the banks of the River Wye, have been painted by Turner and lauded by Wordsworth. It's one of the most beautiful ruins in Britain. As a result, the village of Tintern swarms with visitors in summer. The abbey ruins are awe-inspiring, although best visited towards the end of the day after the crowds have dispersed. The abbey (☎ 01291-689251) is open daily from 9.30am to 5pm (4pm in winter) and entry is £2.

enclosed lanes and minor roads. The routes rejoin at Bigsweir Bridge – if you want to call it a day, there are a few B&B options in St Briavels, 1.5mi to the east, including a **YHA Hostel** (☎ *01594-530272*) in a fine 800-year-old castle with dorm beds from £10.15.

The trail climbs steeply again to rise and fall through forest and farmland until a descent into Redbrook, where there's a *shop* and several B&Bs, including *Tresco* (☎ *01600-712325*) for £16. Say goodbye to the Dyke now, as you don't see it again until Kington. From Redbrook you can either trudge up another hill and back down to Monmouth, or follow the more picturesque and infinitely easier Wye Valley Walk (described briefly in the Other Walks in Wales chapter).

Monmouth

This small, attractive town on the Welsh west bank is at the confluence of the Rivers Wye and Monnow. This strategic position resulted in control of the town changing on a regular

The Offa's Dyke Path (South)

basis over the past several hundred years and led the allegiances of war-weary locals to become decidedly local. The town formed its own militia around 1540, a group noted for its propensity to raise arms against both sides whenever caught in the middle of a stoush between powerful neighbours.

Architecturally, Monmouth's main attractions are the beautiful 13th-century stone-gated **bridge** over the River Monnow and the foundations of the **Monmouth Castle** – a building that would be far more impressive had generations of local builders not stripped it down for its stone. The TIC (☎ 01600-713899) is at Shire Hall on Agincourt Square.

Monmouth's Youth Hostel has closed but there's still plenty of accommodation around. You can camp at *Monnow Bridge Caravan & Camping* (☎ *01600-714004*), near the bridge, for £3.50. Most of the 10 or so B&Bs charge between £18 and £25. These include the spotless and welcoming *Verdi Bosco* (☎ *01600-714441*), on Wonastow Rd, and *Burton House* (☎ *01600-714958*), on St James Square. Food at the *Green Dragon* is tasty and well priced but there are other eateries, including *The Gatehouse*, with a great selection of veggie dishes.

Day 2: Monmouth to Pandy
17mi (27.5km), 9 hours
This is another long day but the walking's comfortable through rolling farmland – although you have to cross a lot of stiles.

Route descriptions are pretty superfluous today as the trail is well waymarked. You go through a seemingly endless succession of farms, with hilly and boggy King's Wood, 1mi out of Monmouth, the only significant respite from the fields. The day's highlight is undoubtedly the 12th-century Norman stronghold, **White Castle**, about two-thirds of the way along today's stage. Remarkably intact, it comes complete with moat and instructive displays; open 10am to 5pm daily.

You also pass through a few villages that feature lovely old churches, including the isolated but beautiful **Llanvihangel-Ystern-Llewern**, the austere **St Teilo** at Llantilio Crossenny and castle-like **St Cadoc** at Llangattock Lingoed.

Towards the end of the day's walk, a long, flat mountain comes into view – this is Hatterall Ridge, which you'll cross tomorrow.

Pandy

The *Lancaster Arms* (☎ 01873-890699), on the A465, looks after walkers well and charges from £19 for B&B. Nearby, there's also the more comfortable *Park Hotel* (☎ 01873-890271) for £24 and, on the way into Pandy, the pleasant *Llanerch Farm* (☎ 01873-890432), for £20. If Hatterall Ridge looks too daunting, Pandy is on the bus route between Abergavenny and Hereford.

Day 3: Pandy to Hay-on-Wye
17.5mi (28km), 9½ hours
This is a very long and hard day through the Black Mountains – among the highest and most exposed section of the trail. There are no trees, almost no shelter and limited escape routes. You can get anything from fog and snow to baking hot sunshine up here, and the weather can turn very quickly. In short, be prepared for adverse weather, but on a clear day you'll revel in the wildness and the views are spectacular.

The trail begins with a long, steady climb to the first summit of the Black Mountains at 464m, then continues with an easy, gradual climb to the highest point at 703m. The trail alternates between bracken and peat, and can become very boggy if it's raining. In places the ridge becomes fairly wide and there are a number of confusing paths, so a map and compass are essential. If the visibility is poor or the weather atrocious, strongly consider dropping down west into either Llanthony or Capel-y-ffin. You can either spend the night and hope for better weather tomorrow or follow minor roads and lanes into Hay-on-Wye.

If you opt to stay the night, Llanthony has the small and friendly *Half Moon Hotel* (☎ 01873-890611) where B&B costs £22, while there's a *YHA Hostel* (☎ 01873-890650) at Capel-y-ffin, charging £7.50 for a dorm bed and £3.70 per tent.

From Hay Bluff (Pen-y-Beacon), at the northern end of Hatterall Ridge, there are great views to the east, north and west.

Have a rest here before you negotiate the very steep descent. While Hay might have looked close from the bluff, it's still 4mi away, mostly downhill through farmland.

Hay-on-Wye

If you have time, spend a well-earned rest day here. It's a most attractive little town with an excellent range of places to stay and eat, plus the 30 or so second-hand bookshops for which it's justly famous.

The welcoming *Clifton House* (☎ 01497-821618), on Belmont Rd, is ideal for walkers and charges £25, while the nearby *Rest for the Tired* (☎ 01497-820550), on Broad St, has better rooms for £25 in a 16th-century house. Two good places charging under £25 are *Belmont House* (☎ 01497-820718), on the street of the same name, and *Cwm Dulais House* (☎ 01497-820640), around the corner from the TIC (☎ 01497-820144) on Oxford Rd.

As befits a popular tourist town, most of Hay's many pubs serve good food, with the *Blue Boar*, on Castle St; the *Wheatsheaf Inn*, on Lion St; and the pricier *Black Lion*, round the corner – all worth trying.

Day 4: Hay-on-Wye to Kington
15mi (24km), 7½ hours
This an enjoyable day of contrasts that takes you along the river, through a short forest and up onto a couple of lovely stretches of moor.

Leaving Hay to the west, cross the River Wye and turn right to follow the trail along its pretty banks for several hundred metres, before crossing several fields up to the A438. After a short walk along this busy road, head uphill alongside the Bettws Dingle wood – and briefly through its dark and cool heart – to join a minor road and a succession of fields for the next 3mi into the small village of Newchurch.

Leaving Newchurch, a steep climb takes you up into the undulating moorland of Disgwylfa Hill where the walking is pleasant and the waymarking clear. Turning left at a clear path, follow the dog-leg at Hill House Farm and then negotiate more fields to end up in the village of Gladestry.

From Gladestry you climb again along a bridleway to the open moors of **Hergest Ridge** – an enjoyable 3mi stretch with extensive views in all directions. The descent starts at a disused racecourse and the trail eventually turns into a minor road to take you into Kington.

Kington

Kington is a rather drab little town with no discernible evidence of its Saxon heritage, although the 12th-century St Mary's church is pretty enough.

Accommodation includes the *Royal Oak Inn* (☎ 01544-230484), on Church St, and, across the road, the *Swan Hotel* (☎ 01544-230510), offering B&B for £18 and £20 respectively. There are many private B&Bs in the area, including *Church House* (☎ 01544-230534), on Church Rd (the western extension of the High St), with B&B from £20; and the friendly *Dunfield Cottage* (☎ 01544-230632), on the edge of Kington, with B&B for £18, excellent evening meals and a pick-up service.

Places to eat in the centre of town include the *Royal Oak Inn*, which has a good-value menu, as does the nearby *Talbot* and *The Queens Head*, with meals in the £3.50 to £6.50 range. Other options include Chinese and fish and chip takeaways.

Day 5: Kington to Knighton

13.5mi (21.5km), 7–8 hours

This stretch is relatively short but very attractive as it wanders through rolling hills and features some of the best-preserved examples of the Dyke along the whole route.

Head north out of town and take great care crossing the very busy A44, before embarking on the first of today's many ascents. It takes you up through fields to the highest golf course in England (390m). Continuing through fields to Rushock Hill, you rejoin the Offa's Dyke itself, which will now be your companion most of the way to Knighton.

The rest of the day takes you up and down a succession of green hills with impressive views at almost every turn, punctuated by short stretches of pine forest. Highlights include the historic **Burfa Farm**, a restored

medieval farmhouse at the base of Burfa hillfort, and the well-preserved section of the Dyke at **Ffridd**, the last hill before you descend into Knighton.

Knighton

In Welsh, Knighton is called Tref-y-clawdd – 'Town on the Dyke', and it's the halfway point of the Offa's Dyke Path. For full details on accommodation, food and transport options, see Knighton under Glyndŵr's Way earlier in this chapter.

Day 6: Knighton to Brompton Crossroads

15mi (24km), 9–10 hours

This isn't the longest day on the trail, but it's arguably the toughest. The relentless pattern for today is a steep climb, a relatively level section of ridge and then a steep drop, followed immediately by another brutal climb and so on. It's very tiring and will certainly keep your pace lower than usual. Get an early start to allow for plenty of rest stops.

Heading north out of Knighton, there's a steep climb to Panpunton Hill where you rejoin the Dyke, which the trail follows almost all day. It's at its most impressive from nearby **Llanfair Hill**, the Dyke's highest point at 429m, with fine views to the ruins of Clun castle.

This section passes a mile from the village of Newcastle-on-Clun, where you could split this stage by staying at the *Crown Inn* (☎ 01588-640271) with B&B for £27.50. Alternatively, 3.5mi east of the trail along the B4368 is *Clun Mill Youth Hostel* (☎ 01588-640582) with dorm beds for £9 and camping for £2.80.

Still more demanding hills await you between Newcastle and the Brompton Crossroads, but the Dyke makes navigation redundant.

Brompton Crossroads

The hospitable *Drewin Farm* (☎ 01588-620325), on the path 1.5mi before the Brompton Crossroads, charges £20 for B&B, while a little farther on, friendly *Mellington Hall* (☎ 01588-620456) has rooms from £25 and camping for £2.

WALES LONG-DISTANCE PATHS

Day 7: Brompton Crossroads to Buttington

12.5mi (20km), 6½–7½ hours

The day starts with pleasant, flat walking but includes some stiff ascents as well.

Leaving the crossroads, the trail follows the Dyke straight across the Montgomery plain, passing less than a mile from the historic town of **Montgomery**, worth a visit if you can spare a couple of hours. After crossing a minor road, you start to steadily rise towards Forden, with today's main obstacle, the **Long Mountain**, dominating the skyline ahead and to your right.

After a stretch of road walking, cut through a number of farms before joining a lane which follows the course of a Roman road. It takes you steeply upwards and into Green Wood on the lower slopes of the Long Mountain. From here zigzag up to the summit where the trail swings round the edge of **Beacon Ring**, an Iron Age hillfort.

Keep your eye out for waymarks so you don't stray on the sharp descent that winds through innumerable fields to Buttington.

Buttington & Around

Buttington doesn't offer much except the *Green Dragon* pub. For a place to stay you need to go to *Buttington View* (☎ 01938-552295) in Hope, just south of Buttington, with B&B for £19; or to *Mona Broxton's* (☎ 01938-570225, 1 Plas Cefn) to the north, with B&B for £15. Less than an hour's walk away, Welshpool is a much better prospect, with many facilities, including a good range of places to stay and eat (see Welshpool at the end of the Glyndŵr's Way walk description, earlier in this chapter).

Day 8: Buttington to Llanymynech

10.5mi (17km), 5–6 hours

Today you get a break from your recent exertions with a day of almost completely flat walking. You can make very good time if you stride out, allowing time to squeeze in a visit to Powis Castle if you stayed in Welshpool.

From Buttington the trail joins the serene Shropshire Union Canal and ambles alongside its still waters under shady trees for a couple of miles. After risking life and limb crossing the A483 at Pool Quay, you enter a 4mi stretch of equally flat farmland that meanders along the River Severn, with the Breidden peaks looming above to the right.

Around lunchtime you reach the Four Crosses, which has a couple of pubs – the *Golden Lion Hotel* and the *Four Crosses Inn* – for refreshment. From here the trail follows the Montgomery Canal all the way to Llanymynech. Just before you hit town, the canal crosses the River Vyrnwy via a stone aqueduct – an arresting sight but only a taste of greater things to come.

Llanymynech

In the small, hospitable town of Llanymynech you can stay at *Cae Bryn* (☎ 01691-829055), on North Rd, where B&B costs £22.50 and there's camping for £3. The *Lion Hotel* (☎ 01691-830234) is most welcoming and has B&B for £17.50 in oldish rooms, while the *Bradford Arms*, next door, has a great restaurant.

Day 9: Llanymynech to Chirk Castle

14mi (22.5km), 8 hours

In sharp contrast with the flat terrain of yesterday, today takes you through a Robin Hood's delight of winding tracks, hills with fine vantage points and dense green forests.

A climb up Llanymynech Hill takes you through a wood where you say goodbye to the Dyke for a while. Passing through the villages of Porth-y-waen and Nantmawr, you climb once more to take in the fine views from **Moelydd** (285m), before rejoining the Dyke just before Candy Wood, a lovely section atop a steep ridge.

Clear waymarking makes the route straightforward over the next several miles of hills and farmland. You eventually drop steadily, and then steeply, to the valley floor to cross the River Ceiriog and finish the day at the Castle Mill entrance to **Chirk Castle**. If you've made good time, consider a visit to the elegant state rooms and manicured gardens of this magnificent 14th-century home. It's open Saturday to Wednesday from noon to 5pm during summer.

Castle Mill & Around

Places to stay are fairly scattered around here. Close to Castle Mill is the friendly *Old School* (☎ *01691-772546*), at Bronygarth, with B&B from £15. Otherwise, detour east to Chirk, north to Pentre or Pont-Cysyllte, or west to Llangollen – a popular tourist town and a good place for a rest day. The latter has a *YHA Hostel* (☎ *01978-860330*), at Twndwr Hall, with dorm rooms for £8.25. There's a couple of good places in Pentre – *Cloud Hill* (☎ *01691-773359*), for £18; and *Sun Cottage* (☎ *01691-774542*), for £15.

Day 10: Chirk Castle to Llandegla

16mi (25.5km), 9 hours
Today offers the most varied scenery of the trail, with added architectural attractions.

From Chirk Castle take the optional route through the castle's pretty grounds before making your way on minor roads and through fields to the River Dee and the **Pontcysyllte aqueduct**. Designed and built by engineer Thomas Telford in 1805, the 302m-long arched aqueduct towers 38m over the River Dee and can be crossed on a narrow walkway, for those with a head for heights. Otherwise you can take the official route, which crosses the river to the west.

Next climb through Trevor Wood and along the Panorama Walk where a laneway, then path, takes you up the short ascent to the hilltop fort of **Castell Dinas Bran**, which is well worth the half-hour detour. You end up on a narrow path traversing a scree slope below Eglwyseg Crags – this is a superb section of the route but it can be slippery and dangerous in the wet, so watch your footing.

You next cross a wood, strike across a bracken-covered moor, negotiate a long pine plantation and head into the attractive village of Llandegla.

Llandegla

Llandegla has a good selection of accommodation, including *Hand House* (☎ *01978-790570*) with B&B for £17.50, including an excellent breakfast; and *2 The Village* (☎ *01978-790266*), for £15. The *Willows Restaurant* offers meals from £4.95 to £12.50.

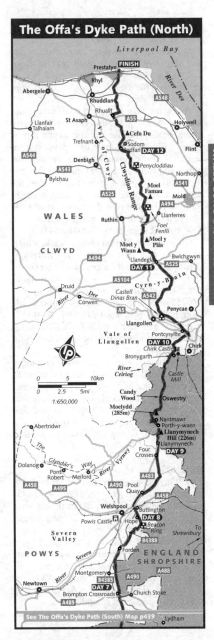

The Offa's Dyke Path (North)

WALES LONG-DISTANCE PATHS

Day 11: Llandegla to Bodfari
17mi (27.5km), 10 hours

This is one of the longest and most strenuous stages of the walk, with several steep ups and downs offset by the wild beauty of the heather-covered moors along the Clwydian Range.

A few miles of farmland takes you to the base of Meol y Waun, from where you climb steadily to the tumulus at the top of Moel y Plâs, a first taste of today's testing terrain. The well-marked path continues to climb and fall past several more peaks, before a brief respite of more farmland walking. You're going up again soon enough, though, this time past the ramparts of Foel Fenlli hillfort to the highest point of the Clwydian Range, **Moel Famau** (544m).

On your way up you cross a track, which will take you east towards Llanferres if you've had enough for one day. The ***Druid Inn*** (☎ 01352-810225) with B&B from £26.50, and ***The White House*** (☎ 01352-810259), for £18, are the best options, although ***Maeshafn Youth Hostel*** (☎ 01352-810320), with dorm beds for £8.20 (book ahead out of season), is only another mile east of town.

Back on the route, you traverse two more peaks to reach an intensely unfair descent to the valley floor and an equally steep ascent past the apex of conical Moel Arthur, before another drop and climb to Penycloddiau hillfort. From here the trail drops 300m in less than 3mi, taking you down to the tiny little village of Bodfari.

Bodfari
You'll arrive very tired in Bodfari and will be delighted with ***Lleweni Hall*** (☎ 01745-812908), a magnificent old farmhouse with cavernous rooms from £19.50 and home-cooked food; or the more modest ***Fron Haul*** (☎ 01745-710301), where B&B costs £23. To reach the latter requires a strenuous walk through the village and up a steep hill (call from the phone box on the A541 for directions). The ***Downing Arms***, on the A541, also puts on a splendid meal.

Day 12: Bodfari to Prestatyn
12mi (19.5km), 7 hours

There are several stiff ascents to tackle on this quite short day, so try to conserve energy in the face of the alluring coastal vistas.

A steep climb out of Bodfari takes you past Sodom villge and along one of the many sections of road today up to Cefn Du peak. More road, punctuated by short sections through fields, brings you to the busy village of Rhuallt, where the somewhat institutional *White House Hotel* (☎ 01745-582155) has B&B for £15 (camping for £2), and the *Smithy Arms* puts on a good lunch.

From Rhuallt, make your way through farmland, along minor roads and over a couple of small peaks to arrive eventually at a hair-raising section of path above a 200m cliff that overlooks Prestatyn. One final steep descent takes you into the main street of Prestatyn, full of tempting pubs, restaurants and shops, but the trail's not officially finished until you reach the TIC on the beach.

Prestatyn
A busy seaside resort, Prestatyn's main street is thronged with tourists during summer. Pubs where you can slake your thirst and raise a glass to your success include ***The Cross Foxes***, at the top of the High St; the gimmicky ***Offa's Tavern***, farther down; and, across the railway line, the more attractive ***Victoria Hotel***. From here you follow the sedate Bastion Rd down to the sea and the TIC (☎ 01745-889092), which marks the official end of the walk. You can walk along the beach and soak up the dubious delights of the seaside with its mini-golf, amusement halls and overpriced cafes. Better food is available at ***Suhail Tandoori***, on Bastion Rd; and ***Primrose Restaurant***, on the High St. Alternatively, there are many takeaways.

There are several B&Bs in Prestatyn, including ***Roughsedge Guest House*** (☎ 01745-887359, *26–28 Marine Rd*); and, closer to the centre, ***35 Bryntirion Drive*** (☎ 01745-853483), both charging under £18. Camping at ***Clwyd View Touring Park*** (☎ 01745-590841), on Marsh Rd, costs £2.50.

Other Walks in Wales

THE WYE VALLEY

The Offa's Dyke Path, described in the Wales Long-Distance Paths chapter, follows, in its early stages, the Wye Valley, which forms the border between England and Wales. This is also an Area of Outstanding Natural Beauty and well worth a visit on foot. A long route called the **Wye Valley Walk** follows the river for much of its distance.

To explore the southern part of the Wye you could base yourself at Monmouth and do day walks up and down each side of the valley. Places to aim for include **Symonds Yat**, the most spectacular section of the River Wye, where it flows through a winding, deep-sided valley edged with woodland. From here you could continue farther along the Wye Valley Walk to **Welsh Bicknor** (on the opposite bank to English Bicknor, naturally), where there's a YHA hostel.

Although Monmouth is in Wales, most of the woodland is in the **Forest of Dean**, which is in England – on the east bank of the Wye. However, the forest has much in common with both countries and is rich in remains from prehistory and the more recent past, when this was a small-scale coal-mining and charcoal-burning centre. There are several waymarked walking routes linking places of interest in the forest and you can get leaflets from local Tourist Information Centres (TICs).

North of the Forest of Dean, the Wye Valley Walk goes through England via Goodrich, Ross-on-Wye and Hereford, and then crosses the border back into Wales at Hay-on-Wye to follow the upper Wye through Mid-Wales to the market town of Rhayader.

The guidebook *Walking Down the Wye* by David Hunter follows the river downstream from source to mouth. For more details on this route you can get maps, leaflets and guidebooks from local TICs.

THE TAFF TRAIL

If your journey through Wales includes Cardiff, the capital, consider taking the Taff Trail, a 77mi (124km) waymarked route between Cardiff and Brecon. Using footpaths, canal towpaths and disused railway lines, the Taff Trail is specifically designed for walkers and cyclists.

The route starts in the Cardiff docklands – originally roughneck Tiger Bay, although recently smartened up and renamed Cardiff Bay – and follows the River Taff north via the fantastical Castell Coch (Red Castle) and the market town of Pontypridd. It then passes through the former heartland of the South Wales coal-mining industry to the rather grim town of Merthyr Tydfil (alternatively Pontypridd to Merthyr can be done by train).

From Merthyr the scenery improves as you go east of the Brecon Beacons, through Pontsticill to Talybont-on-Usk, then along the Monmouthshire & Brecon Canal to Brecon. A handy series of leaflets on the route is available from local TICs.

MID-WALES

Mid-Wales is often overlooked by visitors, appearing as an empty space on the map between the Brecon Beacons and Snowdonia. However, the lack of features (such as main roads and cities) and the presence of several large mountains indicate that this area holds great potential for walkers. In fact, the mountains of Mid-Wales are surprisingly high and wild and no place for novices, but there are also lower walks through valleys, woods and farmland, which are suitable for everyone.

Good bases for exploring mid-Wales include the small market towns of Llandovery (from where you can also reach the Black Mountain section of the Brecon Beacons), Builth Wells and Rhayader, from where you can also saunter along the River Wye – mentioned earlier in this chapter.

Other good bases include Llangurig, Llanidloes and Machynlleth. The **Glyndŵr's Way** (described in the Wales Long-Distance Paths chapter) goes though several of these towns and is an excellent introduction to Mid-Wales. Even if you haven't got time to do it all, following a few stages of the Way would be a great way of seeing the area.

NORTH WALES COAST

If the weather is bad on the high peaks of North Wales (described in the Snowdonia chapter), you could consider some coastal walking.

The north and west of the **Isle of Anglesey** has huge sea cliffs, quaint fishing villages, busy ports and sweeping, sandy beaches. Have a look at the Ordnance Survey (OS) Landranger 1:50,000 map No 114 *(Anglesey)* and you're sure to find some inspiration. You can choose between short day walks (the area around South Stack, an impressive headland and important nature reserve on the western tip of the island, is a good place to start) and a 120mi (193km) circuit of the entire island, or something in between. See *Coastal Walks around Anglesea* by Carl Rogers for more ideas.

On the mainland the **North Wales Path** is a 60mi (96km) route following the coast from Bangor to Prestatyn (also the end of the Offa's Dyke Path). It is possible to complete the path in four to seven days, or you could explore it in single-day circular outings or linear sections using the frequent buses and trains running along the coast. This is a popular holiday area, so B&B options are good. The whole route is described in a handy guidebook *The North Wales Path* by Dave Salter & Dave Worreland, available from local TICs or direct from the publisher Carreg-Gwalch (☎ 01492-642031, ⓔ myrddin@carreg-gwalch.co.uk).

South of Anglesey, the north-western extreme of the Welsh mainland is the **Lleyn Peninsula**. This offers great coastal scenery, particularly between Abersoch and Nefyn, which is quieter than the Bangor to Prestatyn section although less dramatic than Anglesey. The weather here is often good when it's bad on the high ground and other parts of the coast.

TRANS-WALES ROUTES

Long-distance routes that cross Wales include the **Cambrian Way**, winding between Cardiff and Conwy, traversing just about every bit of high, wild landscape on the way. It is described in *The Cambrian Way* by Tony Drake, the Way's instigator. For experienced walkers this is an excellent trip, although the 274mi (441km) make it longer, and much harder, than the Pennine Way. However, help is at hand. An enterprising group of hoteliers along the Cambrian Way has divided the route into five sectors (each of about six days in length) and offer walking holidays along 'their bit'. For more details, contact Nick Bointon at *Llanerchidda Farm* (☎ *01550-750274,* ⓔ *nick@cambrianway.com,* Ⓦ *www.cambrianway.com).*

The other main trans-Wales route is **Snowdonia to the Gower**, which is more direct than the Cambrian Way, although they overlap in the north. Whereas the Cambrian Way goes to/from Cardiff, the other route (as its name suggests) ends on the **Gower Peninsula**, an Area of Outstanding Natural Beauty farther west. *Snowdonia to the Gower* by John Gillham (published by Cordee) is a truly inspirational hardback book with good route descriptions, glossy photos, beautifully drawn aerial views and maps, and fascinating background information. The *Snowdonia to the Gower Companion* is a slim, condensed version of that book, designed to be carried on the route. The same author has another *Snowdonia to the Gower* book (published by Cicerone), still portable but with more than the bare essentials.

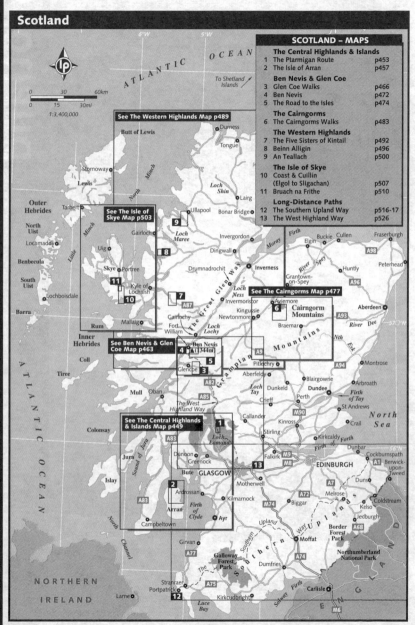

The Central Highlands & Islands

The extensive area south from Crianlarich to the lowland plains and from the islands off the west coast to the edge of Glasgow embraces several groups of mountains. These include the Arrochar mountains on the western side of Loch Lomond, the Trossachs across the water and the higher peaks centred around Ben More to their north. Ben Lomond, the best-known and most popular hill in the area, is featured here, along with the splendid Isle of Arran. Some notes are also provided on the magnificent wilderness of the remote Isle of Jura in the Other Walks section at the end of this chapter.

GETTING THERE & AWAY
For information on travel options between England, Wales and Scotland, see the Getting Around chapter.

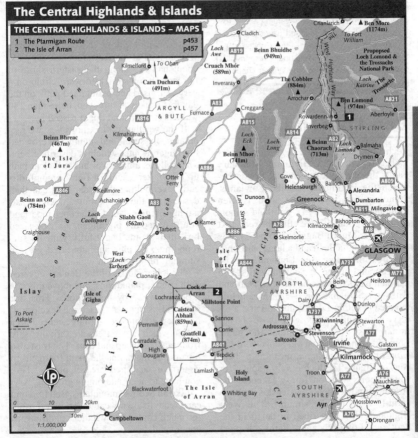

The Central Highlands & Islands

THE CENTRAL HIGHLANDS & ISLANDS – MAPS	
1 The Ptarmigan Route	p453
2 The Isle of Arran	p457

Walking in Scotland

Scotland's northerly location and its more mountainous and less populated terrain have crucial implications for walkers. Quite simply, things are different here to the rest of Britain. You are often in areas classified as remote by British standards, and the weather is likely to be more severe, making walks in the Scottish mountains potentially more serious than those south of the border.

When planning a walking trip in Scotland you should also be aware of the shorter walking season – this is discussed in more detail under When to Walk in the Facts for the Walker chapter. Similarly, it is a good idea to be familiar with the situation regarding access to open countryside in Scotland (see the boxed text 'Access in Scotland & the Concordat'). Rights of way are discussed under Responsible Walking in the Facts for the Walker chapter.

Ben Lomond

Loch Lomond, Britain's largest freshwater loch, straddles the Highland Boundary Fault, the dramatic geological divide between the Highlands and the Lowlands. Standing guard over the loch is Ben Lomond (974m, 3194ft), Scotland's most southerly Munro (see the boxed text 'Munros & Munro Bagging' on p452). It is expected that the loch and a large surrounding area, including Ben Lomond, will be incorporated in one of Scotland's first two national parks (see the boxed text 'National Parks for Scotland' on p478). Meanwhile the area is within Loch Lomond Park, a reserve with similar purposes to those of a national park. It's thought that the name Lomond comes from an old Scots word *llumon*, or the Gaelic *laom*, meaning a 'beacon' or 'light'. The loch is very popular for water sports and, on fine weekends, the droning of power boats and jet skis is all too audible even on the summit. The West Highland Way (described in detail in the Scotland Long-Distance Paths chapter) passes between the loch and Ben Lomond, and many Way walkers take a day off to climb the mountain.

The Ptarmigan Route

Distance	7mi (11.5km)
Duration	4½–5 hours
Standard	medium
Start/Finish	Rowardennan
Gateways	Drymen

Summary A circular route over one of the most popular mountains in Central Scotland, following clear paths with magnificent views of famous Loch Lomond, in the heart of Scotland's first national park.

Most people follow the 'tourist route', which starts at the Rowardennan car park, about halfway along the eastern shore of the loch. It's a straightforward climb on a very well-used and maintained path; on the day this walk was surveyed, more than 130 walkers (and several dogs) passed by.

If the weather is fine, however, we recommend the scenic and slightly less crowded Ptarmigan Route, which is described here. This follows a narrower but still clear path up the western flank of Ben Lomond, directly overlooking the loch. You can then descend via the tourist route, making a satisfying circular walk. On the open moorland you may see the ptarmigan, a chook-sized bird that blends beautifully with its surroundings; its plumage, speckled grey in summer, turns white in winter.

The lower slopes of the Ben are covered with conifer plantations, but above this, the ground, owned by the National Trust for Scotland, is open. At least one 'exclosure' has been established – a large fenced area within which native trees are thriving, safe from grazing sheep and deer. The trust also repairs and maintains the main footpaths in its territory and there are few places where you have to negotiate boggy ground.

Like all Scottish mountains, Ben Lomond can create its own weather, so be prepared for much cooler and windier conditions as you ascend.

Direction, Distance & Duration

The Ptarmigan Route is about 7mi (11.5km) and the ascent 950m. The walking time should be around five hours, for both the circular walk described and the there-and-back route on the tourist path. There are no easy alternative routes; Ben Lomond slopes very steeply down to the loch and tracks through the forest on the eastern side aren't particularly attractive.

PLANNING

Maps & Books

The Harvey Walker's 1:25,000 map *Glasgow Popular Hills* includes Ben Lomond but isn't much help for identifying surrounding features. For this purpose either the Ordnance Survery (OS) Landranger 1:50,000 map No 56 *(Loch Lomond & Inveraray)* or OS Outdoor Leisure 1:25,000 map No 39 *(Loch Lomond)* is preferable.

Walk Loch Lomond & The Trossachs by Gilbert Summers includes several walks around the loch; *Loch Lomond & Trossachs Walks* by John Brooks covers a wider area. For general background information on the region *Loch Lomond & The Trossachs* by Rennie McOwan is recommended.

Information Sources

The nearest Tourist Information Centre (TIC) is at Drymen (☎ 01360-660068) in the public library, Drymen Square. It's open daily from late May to late September. At other times, the library staff can help with information about accommodation, and sales of maps and books. You can check emails at the library; the charge is £1.25 per half-hour. The Loch Lomond Park Centre (☎ 01360-870470) in Balmaha, between Drymen and Rowardennan, has displays about the park's natural and cultural history. By summer 2001 there will be a visitors centre at Rowardennan car park, which will also provide information about the national park.

Guided Walks

Rangers from the National Trust for Scotland (☎ 01360-870224) and from Loch Lomond (☎ 01389-757295) lead walks on Ben Lomond, the latter only during the summer.

Access in Scotland & the Concordat

Traditionally walkers in Scotland have enjoyed 'de facto' freedom of access to private property on the friendly understanding that it is sensible to cooperate with landowners by steering clear of routes that interfere with farming or stalking. However, despite this understanding, 'Keep Out' signs and aggressive, unfriendly owners (not to mention uncooperative walkers) remained a recreational hazard.

During the 1990s the number of people taking to the hills soared as walking became a mass leisure activity, the influence of walker-friendly landowners grew and demand mushroomed for access to lowland areas. In 1996 an Access Forum was initiated, bringing together representatives of land management organisations, 'open-air' recreation groups and appropriate public agencies. The members signed a *Concordat on Access to Scotland's Hills & Mountains*, its principles including:

- Freedom of access exercised responsibly and subject to reasonable constraints for management and conservation
- Acceptance by visitors of the needs of land management and an understanding of how this sustains those who live and work in the hills
- Acceptance by land managers of the public's expectation of having access to the hills
- Acknowledgement of a common interest in Scotland's hills and of the need to work together for their protection and enhancement

It was expected that an early achievement of the Scottish Parliament would be legislation providing greater freedom for people to enjoy the countryside, something already occurring in both England and Wales. In the late 1990s the Access Forum participated in a review of access provisions – the beginning of the long, slow haul towards legislation. In February 2001 the Scottish Executive published a draft Scottish Outdoor Access Code and a draft Land Reform (Scotland) Bill.

PLACES TO STAY & EAT
Loch Lomond

The *SYHA Hostel* (☎ 01360-870259), in the Rowardennan Lodge, is very convenient but also very popular, so it pays to book ahead. The tariff is £9.25 and meals are available. Nearby, the *Rowardennan Hotel* (☎ 01360-870273) has rooms from £35 and reasonably priced bar meals. *Ben Lomond Cottage* B&B (☎ 01360-870411) is right beside the walk and has well-appointed facilities for £25; evening meals are available. The Forestry Commission's *Cashel Camping and Caravan Site* (☎ 01360-870234) is also popular; the average cost per person and tent is £4.40.

The nearest shops of size are in Drymen, to the south, where there are also several pubs, B&Bs, an outdoor gear shop and an ATM.

Across the loch at Inverbeg (see Getting to/from the Walk for ferry details) there's the *Inverbeg Inn* (☎ 01436-860678) for B&B from £38. The nearest hostel is *Loch Lomond* (☎ 01389-850226), about 10mi south of Inverbeg.

GETTING TO/FROM THE WALK

Bus, Train & Ferry Balloch is the terminus of a Scotrail service (☎ 0845-755 0033) from Glasgow. From Balloch, McColl's Coaches (☎ 01389-754321) runs a bus service to Balmaha via Drymen, but there are no buses on to Rowardennan, a distance of 6mi.

Alternatively, in summer use the regular Scottish Citylink (☎ 0870-550 5050) bus service between Glasgow and Fort William as far as Inverbeg, then catch the passenger ferry (☎ 01360-870273) to Rowardennan, leaving at 10.30am, 2.30pm and 6pm, and returning at 10am, 2pm and 5.30pm.

Car The walk starts and finishes at the Rowardennan car park, at the end of the public road from Drymen. Rowardennan can be reached from Glasgow via the A809 or from the east via the A811.

THE WALK
Rowardennan to Ptarmigan

2.5mi (4km), 1½–2 hours

From the car park walk north along the dirt road, past the side road on the left to the youth hostel. Pass a gate and bear left at a fork following the West Highland Way. Beyond the Ardess Lodge National Trust for Scotland Ranger Centre and Ben Lomond Cottage, cross a burn and immediately turn right onto a path through the trees. It climbs beside the burn for a short distance then goes steeply up the bracken-covered mountainside. Straight away you're treated to views of the loch and the mountains on its western

Munros & Munro Bagging

In 1891 Sir Hugh Munro, a member of the recently founded Scottish Mountaineering Club, published a list of more than 500 Scottish summits over 3000ft – the height at which they became 'real' mountains. The metric equivalent, 914m, somehow loses its mystique in translation. Sir Hugh differentiated between 283 'mountains in their own right' (those with a significant drop on all sides or well clear of the next peak) and their satellites, now known as 'tops'.

In 1901 Reverend AE Robertson was the first to climb them all, initiating the pastime of what has become known as Munro bagging. This has grown to a national passion – there are books, CD-ROMs and even a Munro board game. More than 2000 people have completed the full round and the number is growing rapidly. The first person to complete a continuous round was writer Hamish Brown in 1974. Since then at least one continuous round has been completed in winter and the time for the fastest round is lowered regularly. Munro's original list has been revised by the Scottish Mountaineering Club and in late 2000 it totalled 284. List or no list, the great majority of Munros are outstanding walks with superb views.

Once you've bagged the Munros there are other collections of summits to tackle: Corbetts – Scottish mountains over 700m (2500ft) with a drop of at least 150m (500ft) on all sides; and Donalds, Lowland mountains over 610m (2000ft). The extraordinary feat of a complete round of all 728 summits, including 351,000m (1,170,000ft) of ascent, was made in 1998.

side. The path passes a fenced exclosure on the right, climbs steadily across the steep slope and traverses just below a small cliff, with Ptarmigan summit in view. Farther along, above another low cliff, go through a small gate. The path gains more height on an open spur, then zigzags steeply up a grassy bluff to the ridge and on to **Ptarmigan** summit (731m), near a small pond. The fine views include virtually the full length of the loch and its cluster of islands, and the Arrochar mountains to the west.

Ptarmigan to Ben Lomond
1mi (1.5km), 1 hour
The path leads on along the bumpy ridge, through a chain of grassy, rocky knobs to a narrow gap where stepping stones keep you out of the mud. Then the final, steep climb begins through the formidable crags, but natural rock steps and the well-used path make it quite easy. From a grassy shelf there's one more straightforward, rocky

climb to the trig point on the **summit of Ben Lomond** (974m). The all-round view extends to the Isle of Arran in the south-west, the Firth of Clyde, the Arrochar mountains (notably the awl-like profile of the Cobbler), the Campsie Fells and Glasgow to the south.

Ben Lomond to Rowardennan
3.5mi (5.5km), 2 hours
The wide, well-trodden path starts to descend immediately, past the spectacular north-facing cliffs on the left. Soon it swings round to the right and makes a series of wide zigzags down the steep slope to the long ridge stretching ahead, which it follows southwards. Eventually the grade steepens over Sron Aonaich (577m) and the path resumes its zigzag mode through open moorland. Cross a footbridge and continue into the pine forest along an open ridge. The path steepens, becoming rockier and more eroded, down through mixed woodland. Eventually it emerges from the woodland near the toilets and car park at Rowardennan.

The Isle of Arran

Arran is often called 'Scotland in miniature'; the steep mountains and long deep glens in the north of the island are reminiscent of the Highlands, while the rolling moorland and the scattered farms of the south are similar to southern Scotland. There's even a long, straight valley dividing the north from the south, a minor version of the mainland's Great Glen.

The island, in the Firth of Clyde, is only an hour's ferry ride from the mainland and is easily accessible from Glasgow and its hinterland. Consequently it's very popular with families heading for the southern beaches, cyclists, windsurfers, hordes of Glaswegian bikers on bank holidays – and walkers, irresistibly drawn to the rugged mountains. The highest peak, Goatfell (874m), overlooks Brodick, Arran's largest town.

This section covers a circular route up Goatfell and an easy-going outing along the scenic north coast. There are also suggestions for Other Walks at the end of the

The Ptarmigan Route

Ben Lomond (974m)
Coire a' Bhathaich
Ptarmigan (731m)
Glashlet Burn
▲Tom Fithich (499m)
Sron Aonaich (577m)
West Highland Way
Loch Lomond
Rowardennan Lodge
Rowardennan
START/FINISH
To Inverbeg
Ferry Route (summer only)
Hotel
Coille Mhòr Hill (233m)▲
To Balmaha & Drymen
0   500   1000m
0   500   1000yd
1:75,000

THE CENTRAL HIGHLANDS & ISLANDS

chapter, including a challenging traverse of the northern spine of the island.

PLANNING

Wild camping is not allowed anywhere on Arran without permission of the landowner. For camping facilities and other accommodation options, see Places to Stay & Eat.

The planning information in this section is relevant to both walks on the Isle of Arran.

Maps

Arran is covered by two OS maps – Landranger 1:50,000 No 69 *(Isle of Arran)* and Outdoor Leisure 1:25,000 No 37 *(Isle of Arran)*. The Harvey Walker's map *Arran* comprises the whole island at 1:40,000 and the northern half at 1:25,000. It has lots of practical and background information and is highly recommended. It is more versatile than the separate Harvey Superwalker 1:25,000 maps *North Arran* and *South Arran*.

A Geologist's Paradise

The Isle of Arran's geology is amazingly varied. Here you'll find all kinds of rock types, and evidence of many different geological and landscape-forming processes, which have taken place over countless millennia. In fact, a trip to Arran is virtually compulsory for geology students.

The northern rocky peaks, ridges and deep glens consist of granite, sculpted by glaciers during the last ice age. There are several other smaller and more scattered outcrops of granite in the southern half of the island, including Holy Island, opposite Lamlash. In the north the granite mass is almost totally surrounded by much older schist and slate, and some river sediment. Sedimentary rocks – limestone and sandstone – monopolise the north coast.

To demystify the complexities of Arran's geology, two readable publications are available locally. The first is a brochure, *Isle of Arran Trails: Geology*, and the second is the more detailed *Arran & the Clyde Islands: A Landscape Fashioned by Geology*.

Books

Walking in The Isle of Arran by Paddy Dillon describes 41 day walks on the island and is invaluable for an extended visit. Mary Welsh's *Forty-Four Walks on the Isle of Arran* is useful for its flora and fauna notes, but the walk descriptions are vague and practical information is sparse. The brochure *Guide to Forest Walks on the Isle of Arran*, produced by Forest Enterprises, concentrates on southern Arran and is available from the TIC.

For finding out more about local history and heritage, Alastair Gemmell's *Discovering Arran* is the book to have. *Birds of Arran* by John Rhead & Philip Snow is particularly strong on where to see the bird life. Both are available locally.

Information Sources

Brodick's well-organised TIC (☎ 01770-302140, e arran@ayrshire-arran.com) has an array of leaflets, accommodation lists, menus of the several places to eat, maps and guidebooks. The local weather forecast is displayed daily, and the centre also provides a fax and photocopying service.

Guided Walks

The Countryside Rangers at Brodick Country Park (☎ 01770-302462) lead walks during summer, ranging from afternoon wildlife strolls through the low-level forests to days out on Goatfell and other peaks.

PLACES TO STAY & EAT
Brodick

The best base is Brodick, although Lamlash, to the south, is actually the island's principal town. The mainland ferry docks in Brodick and the town is the hub of the island's excellent bus services. Brodick TIC (☎ 01770-302140) is on the pier. There is a post office and two banks, both with ATMs. Arran Active (☎ 01770-302416), next to the Co-op supermarket, is the one place on the island you can purchase the full range of fuel for camping stoves.

A popular walkers campsite is the beautifully situated *Glen Rosa Farm* (☎ 01770-302380), about 2.5mi north-west of Brodick

Pier. It is well placed for Goatfell. Facilities are limited to a basic toilet block and taps; the fee is £2.50. The owner hopes to install showers in 2002. There are more than 20 B&Bs in Brodick – the TIC has a detailed list. In particular, *Tigh na Mara* (☎ *01770-302538*), on Shore Rd, is conveniently located and charges from £18. South of Brodick, at Whiting Bay, is a *SYHA Hostel* (☎ *01770-700339*) where the tariff starts from £7.25.

For places to eat in Brodick, *Stalkers Restaurant* (☎ *01770-302579*) offers good-value meals from a basic menu, with main courses from £6; it's licensed and open daily. Several pubs do bar meals, including the *Douglas Hotel* (☎ *01770-302155*), opposite the pier, which provides a cosmopolitan range of menus, including an Indian set meal for £14. In the Kingsley Hotel at *Duncans Bar* (☎ *01770-302531*) you can sample one of Arran's very own beers (Arran Blonde – light and dark) with a standard bar-menu supper.

For self-catering and picnic lunches, there are two supermarkets (open daily). *Collins Good Food Shop*, on the Auchrannie House access road just north of Brodick, sells health foods and excellent bread and cakes, which you can also sample in their tearoom. *The Arran Brewery* (☎ *01770-302061*), very conveniently located beside the Goatfell path at Cladach, is open daily.

Corrie

Alternatively, you could stay in Corrie, a short distance north up the coast on the A841. At *Blackrock Guest House* (☎ *01770-810282*), with an excellent outlook, tariffs start at £17. The *Corrie Hotel* (☎ *01770-810273*) serves snacks and bar meals.

Lochranza

Perfectly placed for the Cock of Arran walk is the Lochranza *SYHA Hostel* (☎ *01770-830761*); the tariff starts at £8. *Lochranza Golf Caravan & Camp Site* (☎ *01770-830273*) has plenty of grassy pitches; the tariff is £6.

Of Lochranza's two hotels and a guest house, *Lochranza Hotel* (☎ *01770-830223*)

Stalking

Generally walkers are free to roam throughout Arran. However, deer control measures (stalking) are carried out from mid-August to mid-October in the north of the island. Call the Hillphone Answer Service (☎ 01770-302363) for daily updates on where stalking is taking place and which paths should be used or avoided. Note that Access to National Trust for Scotland property is unrestricted at all times.

is the least expensive at £20. There's also a B&B. The hotel is one of the two places to go for a meal; the *Pier Tearoom & Restaurant* (☎ *01770-830217*), looking out across the sea, is the other. There is also a small *shop* in the village.

You can access the Internet at the Pier Tearoom & Restaurant; you'll have to pay £3 for just 15 minutes.

GETTING THERE & AWAY

Bus, Train & Ferry Stagecoach Western (☎ 01294-607007) services run from Edinburgh and Glasgow to Ardrossan, the ferry terminal on the Ayrshire coast.

Several ScotRail (☎ 0845-755 0033) trains reach Ardrossan daily from Glasgow. Make sure you catch one that goes to the harbour, otherwise you'll have to walk or take a taxi from Ardrossan South Beach.

Caledonian MacBrayne (☎ 01294-463470) operates the car ferry between Ardrossan and Brodick, with at least four sailings daily in each direction. The return fare for foot passengers is £7.20. There's also the small summer-only car ferry from Claonaig on the Kintyre peninsula to Lochranza, which has several sailings daily. The return passenger fare is £6.65.

Car Both ferries carry vehicles; the return journey for a standard car costs £43 from Ardrossan and £30 from Claonaig. You can leave your car in a secure place at Ardrossan for £3.40. Ardrossan is about 25mi southwest of Glasgow.

A Goatfell Circuit

Distance	11.25mi (18km)
Duration	6–7½ hours
Standard	medium-hard
Start/Finish	Brodick
Gateway	Brodick

Summary This is quite a demanding circuit walk through scenic Glen Rosa and along steep rocky ridges to outstanding views from the island's highest point.

There are several routes to the summit of Goatfell. The most popular are from the east – from Brodick itself, Cladach (Arran Craft Centre) or Brodick Castle. There's also a good route from the settlement of Corrie up to North Goatfell. A quieter and more pleasing approach is from the west, via Glen Rosa to the Saddle, then up the steep, narrow west ridge to North Goatfell and along Stacach Ridge to the summit. The return to Brodick is via the steep, rocky eastern face, moorland and the grounds of Brodick Castle.

Paths are clear, deeply eroded in places and easy to follow. Maintenance and repair of the main paths is an ongoing task; the path just below the summit to the east was being rerouted and improved in June 2000. There are steep cliffs on both sides of the west ridge and Stacach Ridge, where extra care is needed. It can turn very cold, wet and windy very quickly, so make sure you are well prepared, and don't forget a map and compass.

Brodick Country Park, Goatfell and Glen Rosa are owned by the National Trust for Scotland. Selective culling of red deer by trust staff does not affect public access.

Direction, Distance & Duration

This route can be done in either direction, but clockwise is recommended as the overall ascent is more gentle, although still with some steep bits. The summit comes in the latter part of the route. There are signposts where paths leave the road but not on Goatfell itself. The distance on the map, 11.25mi, includes at least 800m of ascent and some minor scrambling. Allow six to 7½ hours' walking time.

Alternatives Of the alternative approaches to Goatfell, Corrie Burn is preferable to Glen Sannox, which is a boggy sort of a glen with a hair-raising climb to the Saddle at its head. Corrie is a spread-out village on the east coast, 5.5mi north of Brodick and well served by local buses. At the southern end of the village, a sign 'Public Footpath to Goatfell' points along a narrow road. After a few hundred metres leave the road at a sharp bend, just before the settlement of High Corrie, and follow a vehicle track, then a path up Corrie Burn's glen to a saddle below North Goatfell. It's a steep climb most of the way and the ground can be wet in places.

GETTING TO/FROM THE WALK

Bus Stagecoach buses (☎ 01770-302000) circle the island several times daily in both directions. A Rural Day Card (£3) is a good investment, allowing an unlimited number of trips. There are also handy postbus services. All these are detailed in the *Area Transport Guide* available from the TIC.

Car Hendry's (☎ 01770-302274) in Brodick operates a taxi service.

THE WALK
Brodick to the Saddle
5.5mi (9km), 2½–3 hours
From Brodick head generally north along the main road for about 1.5mi to a major junction and turn left along the B880 towards Blackwaterfoot. About 100m along this road turn right down a narrow road, the 'Glen Rosa Cart Track'. Follow this to the campsite, above which the sealed section ends, and continue along a clear vehicle track into the glen itself, with superb views of the precipitous peaks on the western side of the glen, culminating in Cir Mhòr (798m) at its head.

The track becomes a path at the crossing of Garbh Allt, the boundary of the National Trust for Scotland property. Aiming unerringly for the Saddle, the low point between Cir Mhór and the massive, rock-encrusted bulk of Goatfell, the path climbs gently, then quite steeply, to **the Saddle**. From here, among the granite boulders, there's a fine

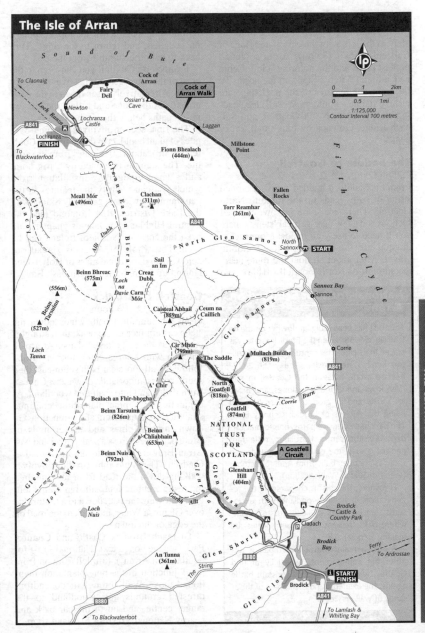

The Isle of Arran

view down Glen Sannox to the sea. Cir Mhòr's alarmingly steep crags rise immediately to the left, with the castellated ridge of Caisteal Abhail (859m), Arran's second highest peak, and the notorious cleft, Ceum na Caillich (Witch's Step), to the north. To the right, the features of the next stage are clearly visible – bouldery West Ridge, leading steeply up to North Goatfell, and Stacach Ridge, crowned by four small, rocky peaks.

The Saddle to Goatfell
1.25mi (2km), 1½–2 hours
From the Saddle, a braided and very eroded string of paths leads up the ridge to North Goatfell. There are some narrow, exposed sections and a few near-vertical 'steps' where you'll need to use your hands. More tricky, though, are the patches of loose granite gravel. After about an hour the route nears the summit of North Goatfell (818m). The

final section is a scramble but, if this is too intimidating, pass below the top, keeping it on your left, and return to the ridge. Turn back to gain **the summit** from the east.

From North Goatfell you can keep to the crest of the ridge, scrambling over the rocky knobs. Alternatively, drop down to the eastern side of the ridge and follow the less exposed paths below the knobs.

The final section involves hopping over piles of giant boulders to the summit of **Goatfell** (874m), about 30 minutes from its satellite. The summit is topped by a trig point and a large topography installation from which you can identify the features in the panoramic view. On a good day Skiddaw in the Lake District, Ben Lomond (see the Central Highlands & Islands chapter) and even the coast of Northern Ireland can be seen. The whole of Arran is spread out below, with the conical mass of Holy Island rearing up from the sea in Lamlash Bay.

National Trust for Scotland on Arran

The trust has been a big landowner on the island since 1958, when the Brodick estate was placed in its care after centuries of the Hamilton family's stewardship. Today the 2833-hectare estate takes in the Goatfell massif, Glen Rosa and its western slopes, and Brodick Castle and its grounds – these last two being the nucleus of Brodick Country Park. The park has extensive paths, fine formal gardens, a visitors centre, trust shop, restaurant and, of course, the castle. The grounds and facilities are open daily from April to October (see also Guided Walks section).

Elsewhere, the trust is encouraging the regeneration of native woodland with exclosures (fenced areas to keep out red deer), where oaks, rowans and other species are making a comeback.

Footpath maintenance and repair is another big commitment, especially around Goatfell, where staff wage a constant battle against the elements and the impact of thousands of walkers' feet.

Goatfell to Brodick
4.5mi (7km), 2–2½ hours
From the summit a path winds down the steep eastern face of the peak, then straightens out as the ridge takes shape. At a path junction with a large cairn, turn right and follow the all-too-clear path south-east then south across moorland, down the Cnocan Burn valley and into scattered woodland. At a junction in a pine plantation, continue straight on and turn right at a T-junction. Go down through pines and the grounds of Brodick Castle, across a sealed road and past Arran Brewery's shop to the main road at Cladach. The route into Brodick involves walking down the road for a few hundred metres to a public footpath sign on the left, then following the path down to a footbridge over Glenrosa Water and back to the road on the edge of the town.

To reach Brodick Castle and Country Park (see the boxed text 'National Trust for Scotland on Arran'), turn left 30m on from the T-junction in the pine plantation mentioned above. Walk through rhododendron-infested grounds and woodland to the ranger centre, and on to the car park and nearby National Trust for Scotland shop.

Cock of Arran

Distance	8mi (13km)
Duration	3½–4 hours
Standard	easy-medium
Start	North Sannox picnic area
Finish	Lochranza
Gateways	Brodick

Summary A fairly easy-going coast walk round Arran's north coast with superb scenery and interesting historical features, mostly following good paths with some rock hopping for variety.

For a change of scene, or if the cloud is too low for a hill walk, the north coast provides fine walking between North Sannox and Lochranza. There are some impressive cliffs, the site of a landslip, isolated cottages, remains of early coal mining and salt harvesting, and the Cock of Arran itself – a prominent block of sandstone, not named after a rooster but probably from the Lowland Scots word meaning 'cap' or 'headwear'. On a good day the views across the Sound of Bute to the mainland, the Isle of Bute and part of the Kintyre peninsula are excellent. There's also a good chance of seeing common seals and a wide variety of birds.

Direction, Distance & Duration

The walk is described from North Sannox to Lochranza but can be done just as well in the opposite direction, depending on the time of day and wind direction. The rise and fall of the tide isn't particularly great, so high tide shouldn't complicate things. The distance of 8mi includes only 60m of ascent, from the coast to North Newton, which should take about four hours. The boulder-hopping sections and some potentially wet stretches of path could easily increase the time taken.

Alternatives Shorter versions of this walk are possible – out and back from either end of the walk described. The distance from North Sannox to Millstone Point and back is 5mi, which should require 2½ to three hours to complete. At the other end, follow the minor road on the north side of Loch Ranza, then the path round Newton Point

and on to the cottage near Fairy Dell, returning to Lochranza by the route described in the main walk. The distance for this walk is 4mi, which should take about two hours.

Yet another possibility is to leave the main walk at Laggan cottage and climb over the ridge rising from the coast, following a path (which could be partly overgrown with bracken in summer) up the mountainside. It reaches a height of 261m on the moorland ridge, then descends across some boggy ground to a minor road at Narachan. Follow this to a junction and turn left to reach Lochranza. The distance is 8mi and you should allow about four hours.

GETTING TO/FROM THE WALK

The walk starts at a picnic area (with toilets) at the end of a minor road that branches off the A841, about 600m north-west of Sannox.

The walk ends in Lochranza. It's possible to park by the road at the north-west corner of the Lochranza golf course or at the end of this road beside Loch Ranza. If you're returning to your car at the start of the walk, you can catch a bus back towards Sannox and get off at the North Sannox turn, from where it's about 300m to the North Sannox picnic area.

THE WALK (see map p457)
North Sannox to Laggan
3.5mi (5.5km), 1½ hours

The forest track leading north from the picnic area gives good views across the Firth of Clyde, a theme sustained for the whole walk. After nearly 2mi the track gives way to a footpath along the shore. At the far end of a shingle beach, the Fallen Rocks, a jumble of massive conglomerate boulders resting at the foot of the steep bracken-covered mountainside, are easily bypassed. The mainly grassy path keeps close to the high tide mark to Millstone Point, where white-painted Laggan cottage comes into view, about 20 minutes farther on.

Laggan to Lochranza
4.5mi (7km), 2 hours

Less than a mile from the cottage the scenery changes with birch and oak woodland on the lower slopes. In summer tall bracken hides the remains of cottages, and the coal pits and salt pans that were excavated here to support local fishing in the 18th century. Ignore paths climbing into the trees and stick to the rocky shore, where you might find scraps of blackish coal. Farther on, although Ossian's Cave is marked on the map, it's invisible from the shore. The pinkish-red sandstone cliffs then start to close in. Around the Cock of Arran, flat red slabs of sandstone line the shore. Below Fairy Dell Cave you have to clamber over and round rough conglomerate boulders, which arrived here in a landslip centuries ago; soon you're back on grass. From the two cottages at Fairy Dell, follow a path from the corner of a dyke visible in the trees, up through bracken to moorland. Then it's down to a gravel road near two cottages, soon with good views of Loch Ranza. Continue down to the minor road along the loch shore and turn left to reach Lochranza.

Other Walks

THE ISLE OF ARRAN
Glen Rosa to Lochranza
The extremely rugged ridge on the western side of Glen Rosa, and its extension from Cir Mhòr via Caisteal Abhail towards the north coast, offers as fine a ridge walk as you'll find anywhere in Britain. Although it looks impossible from below, there are miraculous ways around those crags and peaks that only experienced rock climbers can traverse. The views all along are tremendous, especially westwards. The 11mi (17.5km) walk includes 1360m of climbing, much of which is precipitous and rocky; allow at least seven hours.

Walk up Glen Rosa to the bridge over Garbh Allt. Turn left from the main path and follow clear paths up through two exclosures to the foot of the ridge. The climb to the first summit, Beinn Nuis (792m), is steep and unrelenting. Descending, keep west of large bluffs down to a grassy ridge. On the way up to Beinn Tarsuinn (826m), look out for the striking rock formation

known as the **Old Man of Tarsuinn**. On the next steep descent keep to the left, on grass as much as possible, and continue to Bealach an Fhir-bhogha. Here you leave the ridge to traverse below A' Chir's soaring cliffs on its western side. Return to the ridge about 150m above the gap overlooking Coire Buidhe. **Cir Mhòr** (799m) can easily be bypassed but is worth the effort for an eagle's eye view of Goatfell. Next, Caisteal Abhail (859m) is easy, up grass and small rocks. The more northerly of two summit tors, accessible from the north, is the higher. A path continues north-west from here down a ridge, but soon fades. Where the ridge turns northwards then broadens, head north-north-west and down into Gleann Easan Biorach. The path on the western side of the burn is very boggy between Allt Dubh and the next unnamed stream northwards, but the last stretch is much drier, through a small gorge to the main road on the edge of Lochranza.

THE ISLE OF JURA
Jura is a magnificently wild and lonely island, the wildness of its uplands only matched on the Isle of Rum and on Harris in the Western Isles (see the Other Walks in Scotland chapter). Fewer than 200 people now live here, almost all in the southern corner. The rest of the island, 28mi by about 8mi, is uninhabited and unspoiled.

In the village of Craighouse you'll find a shop and the excellent *Jura Hotel* (☎ 01496-820243), where the tariff starts at £32 and local produce is featured in the restaurant. To reach Jura you catch the Calmac ferry (☎ 01496-302209) from Kennacraig on the Kintyre peninsula to Port Askaig on the Isle of Islay, then the small Western Ferries boat (☎ 01496-840681) to Feolin. From there a local bus regularly goes to Craighouse and occasionally farther north along the east coast.

The OS Landranger 1:50,000 map No 61 (*Jura & Colonsay*) is the one to have. The SMC's guide *The Islands of Scotland including Skye* by DJ Fabian, GE Little & DN Williams covers the mountains with a short section on path walks. Much of the island is managed for deer stalking, so the best time for a visit would be from early May to early July.

The Paps of Jura

These three conical peaks – Beinn a' Chaolais (734m), Beinn an Oir (784m) and Beinn Shiantaich (755m) – dominate the island and are visible from far away. A circuit of their summits provides a fairly energetic and outstandingly scenic day; the distance is 12mi with about 1500m of ascent. Allow at least eight hours – the going is generally rough, the mountains are very steep-sided and paths generally less well beaten than on mainland mountains. A convenient place to start is by the bridge over the Corran River, about 5km north of Craighouse.

The West Coast

Along Jura's west coast, all 40mi of it, you'll find raised beaches, caves, rocky headlands and natural arches. To explore the full length would take a couple of weeks of rugged, self-contained walking, as isolated as any in Britain. Feolin makes a convenient starting point; the track to Glenbatrick from the east coast road (4mi north of Craighouse) is another possibility. If you're a coast walking enthusiast, Jura clearly has enough to offer for several return trips.

THE CENTRAL HIGHLANDS & ISLANDS

Ben Nevis & Glen Coe

Two of Scotland's most famous place names, Ben Nevis and Glen Coe, lie in the Western Highlands, near Fort William. From Glasgow and Loch Lomond, the A82 – also dubbed the 'Road to the Isles' – snakes across remote Rannoch Moor and winds through magnificent Glen Coe, to follow the long finger of Loch Linnhe all the way to Fort William. Ben Nevis, the highest mountain in Britain, is just over 3mi from Fort William and overlooks the town.

The complex geology of this part of Scotland has bequeathed scenery par excellence and there are many great walking opportunities in the area. In this chapter we describe four 'taster' day walks to show you something of the area and inspire you to explore further on your own.

INFORMATION
Maps & Books
OS Landranger 1:50,000 map No 41 *(Ben Nevis)* covers all the walks in this chapter. Details of larger-scale maps are given under Planning for each walk.

The OS Pathfinder guide *Fort William and Glen Coe* details a good range of walks in the area, with several options at the easier end of the scale. *Ben Nevis and Glen Coe* by Chris Townsend also has a good selection of routes. Alternatively for mountain enthusiasts there's *20 Hill Walks: Glen Coe and Lochaber* by Ruaridh Pringle.

Information Sources
The Tourist Information Centre (TIC) at Fort William (☎ 01397-703781) is open all year. Boots and backpacks can be hired at the Glen Nevis Centre, next to the Glen Nevis SYHA Hostel (see the Ben Nevis walk).

Guided Walks
The Glencoe Ranger Service (☎ 01463-232034) takes guided walks from June to August, and the Glencoe Outdoor Centre (☎ 01855-811350) provides activity holidays and courses. Glencoe Mountain Sport

(☎ 01855-811472) offers guides for more serious scrambling and winter routes. Glencoe Ski Centre (☎ 01855-811303), at the top of the valley opposite Kings House Hotel, operates a chair lift, which will take you to 650m for a bird's-eye view of the glen.

In the Ben Nevis area, Highland Countryside Ranger Service offers guided walks from Ionad Nibheis Visitor Centre (☎ 01397-705922). Mountain Craft (☎ 01397-722213) can provide a professional mountain guide.

GATEWAYS
Fort William
Separated from Loch Linnhe by a bypass, Fort William has lost any charm it may once have had to modern development. However, it has good bus and train connections (buses leave from near the train station), and is a good base for walkers wanting to explore the area.

The TIC (☎ 01397-703781) is in the town centre in Cameron Square. There are good outdoor gear shops, including Nevisport near the train station and West Coast Outdoor Leisure at the other end of the High St. Both outlets hire winter climbing, walking and ski equipment. You can get a shower and store luggage at Marco's An Aird Community Centre (☎ 01397-700707), near the train station.

There are numerous accommodation options in Fort William (some streets are almost solidly B&Bs and hotels) and the amount of competition means bargains can be had. Some B&Bs have signs outside advertising rooms for as little as £13. You're best off asking in the TIC or looking around, especially along the A82 approach from Glasgow where there's cut-throat competition. The summer months are very busy, however, so if you want to stay in a specific place (a hostel or a particular hotel), it is advisable to book ahead.

Fort William Backpacker's (☎ 01397-700711), on Alma Rd, is very popular and is a short walk from the train station. A bed costs £11. ***Bank Street Lodge Bunkhouse*** (☎ 01397-700070), on Bank St, charges £10. ***Calluna*** (☎ 01397-700451) offers homely accommodation in a residential area, five minutes from the centre of town, for £9.

The ***Grand Hotel*** (☎ 01397-702928), in the main street, is a large, central hotel with rooms from £27.50. At the top of the scale, the ***Alexandra Hotel*** (☎ 01397-702241, The Parade) is a large, traditional hotel with comfortable doubles for about £45.

For a big meal to celebrate a climb or finishing the West Highland Way, the best place in town is also the best located. ***Crannog Seafood Restaurant*** is on the pier and offers an uninterrupted view over the loch and excellent food. Not in the same culinary league, but with an entertaining touristy floor show, is ***McTavish's Kitchen***, on the High St. The ***Grog & Gruel***, also on the High St, is a traditional ale house with a restaurant. For cheaper meals ***Nevisport***, near the train station, has a cafe-bar with good-value food.

There are also many food outlets offering takeaway and if, you're self-catering, there's a good choice of shops and supermarkets.

If the celebrations are to continue, the Jacobite Bar in the ***Ben Nevis***, on the main street, is a popular music venue and a good place for a drink.

GETTING THERE & AWAY

For information on travel options between England, Wales and Scotland, see the Getting Around chapter.

Bus Scottish Citylink (☎ 0870-550 5050) has a regular run between Glasgow and Fort William via the A82, with around four services a day.

Train The splendid West Highland Railway (WHR; ☎ 0845-748 4950) takes you to Fort William from Glasgow, or even from London on the overnight sleeper (see the boxed text 'The West Highland Railway' on p464).

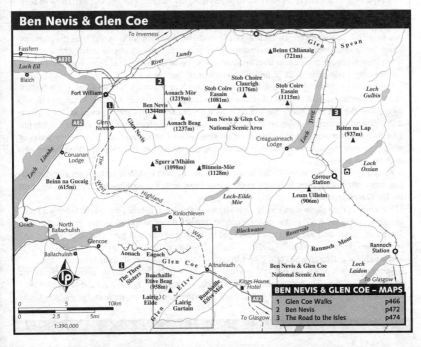

Car The A82 between Glasgow and Fort William runs down Glen Coe.

A Glen Coe & Glen Etive Circuit

Distance	10mi (16km)
Duration	5 hours
Standard	medium
Start/Finish	Altnafeadh
Gateways	Glencoe, Fort William

Summary A rough and quite demanding walk over two high mountain passes. As several streams need crossing, don't attempt this walk during or after heavy rains.

Glen Coe is known as the 'glen of weeping', not because of the rainfall levels (this is one of the wetter areas of Scotland) but because it was the scene of the infamous massacre of the MacDonalds by the Campbells in 1692. Charles Dickens felt it 'bleak and wild and mighty in its loneliness' but these days it is a magnet for tourists, walkers and mountaineers alike.

The impressive glen is the product of not only glacial processes but also its ownership by the National Trust for Scotland and the driving force of one Percy Unna, who intended that 'the land should be maintained in its primitive condition for all time'. Nonetheless, the valley's popularity and accessibility are such that today you are unlikely to be alone unless you strike off the beaten track.

At the head of the glen are the two splendid peaks of Buachaille Etive Mór (see the Buachaille Etive Mór walk description later) and Buachaille Etive Beag. The Glen Coe & Glen Etive Circuit is a rough walk

The West Highland Railway

The West Highland Railway (WHR) runs between Glasgow and Fort William, through some of Scotland's most wild and spectacular mountain scenery, which is also some of Britain's finest walking country. Stations such as Arrochar & Tarbet, Crianlarich, Bridge of Orchy and Spean Bridge allow you to set off on a seemingly endless range of wonderful mountain walks, direct from the platform. There are several opportunities for circular walks, or you can get off at one station, have a good walk, then catch the train again from another station up or down the line. From Fort William Station it's only a few miles' walk to Britain's highest peak, Ben Nevis.

Possibly the most intriguing place to get off the train is at Corrour, which at 408m, is the highest and most remote station in Britain. Corrour Station lies in the middle of Rannoch Moor, so soft and boggy that the line here had to be laid on a platform of earth, ashes and brushwood. It's a tribute to the railway's Victorian engineers that it has remained in place for over a century and nobody has ever managed (or wanted) to build a road up here. From Corrour you can reach lonely peaks or wind your way through remote valleys out of reach to mere motorists. (See the Road to the Isles walk later in this chapter.)

As you go north on the WHR, the magic continues. Beyond Fort William the train runs to Mallaig, from where it's a short ferry ride to the Isle of Skye, with a branch line to Oban, gateway port for the Outer Hebrides.

For a walker this railway is an absolute gift and for any visitor to Britain a ride on the WHR is a must. In summer (May to September) there are four trains per day (three on some Sundays) in each direction. There's also a standard passenger coach attached to the sleeper train that travels between London and Fort William (see the boxed text 'London to Scotland by Rail' in the Getting Around chapter), which is very handy for getting to walks as it comes through Glasgow heading north early in the morning.

For more details phone the national timetable service (☎ 0845-748 4950) or ScotRail reservations (☎ 0345-743 4950). For more ideas on where to go, get a copy of *Walks from the West Highland Railway* by Chris & John Harvey. It covers some 40 walking routes ranging from fairly gentle strolls to the ascents of 18 Munros.

that circumnavigates the base of Buachaille Etive Beag and serves up a flavour of 'primitive' Glen Coe. The appeal of this route is the remote and rugged landscape you pass through. The walk itself is quite a challenge and you might be glad of a walking pole for balance when negotiating stream crossings.

Direction, Distance & Duration

The route is described in an anticlockwise direction because the most difficult stream crossing is encountered at the start. The views down Glen Coe as you walk west are superb too. The 10mi includes more than 600m of ascent. Five hours should see the route completed, but allow longer for stops or if you know you're slow over rough paths. The route follows rights of way.

PLANNING
Maps & Books

OS Landranger 1:50,000 map No 41 *(Ben Nevis)*, OS Outdoor Leisure 1:25,000 map No 38 *(Ben Nevis & Glen Coe)* and Harvey's Superwalker 1:25,000 map *Glen Coe* (which includes a useful little visitor guide) cover the walk.

As well as the books listed under Information at the start of this chapter, there's the National Trust for Scotland's annual guide, *Glencoe*.

Information Sources

There's a seasonal TIC (☎ 01855-811296) at Ballachulish, west of Glencoe village. The National Trust for Scotland Visitor Centre (☎ 01855-811307), on the A82 2mi east of Glencoe near Clachaig Inn, is open from April to October. It has exhibitions and an audiovisual presentation covering the area's history and natural heritage. Glencoe Ski Centre (☎ 01855-811303), at the top of the valley opposite Kings House Hotel, has a museum of Scottish Skiing and Mountaineering. There is also a Folk Museum in Glencoe that is open from May to September.

PLACES TO STAY & EAT
Glencoe

There are many B&Bs and hotels in the village of Glencoe, but a large number of the

traditional walker's haunts can be found spread out along the old Glencoe road that leads east from the village, parallel to the A82. *Glencoe SYHA Hostel* (☎ 01855-811219) is about 1.5mi from the village and charges £9.25. *Leacantium Farm Bunkhouse* (☎ 01855-811256) is next along the road, and charges £6.50 in a large room with triple-tiered alpine sleeping platforms or £7.50 in a farmhouse hostel. *Red Squirrel Campsite*, run by the same people, is a little farther along and is very attractively located between trees and a river. It charges £4. *Clachaig Inn* (☎ 01855-811252) is at the end of the road, 2.5mi from the village. It offers B&B from £23 and has a selection of self-catering mountain lodges available. The inn really comes into its own during the evening, when most outdoor people in the area descend on the climbers bar. The food is hearty, the selection of real ales has won awards and there is regular live music.

If you're into historic ambience then *Kings House Hotel* (☎/fax 01855-851259), at the head of the valley 11mi east of Glencoe on the A82, and arguably the oldest licensed inn in Scotland, is worth considering. (You'll definitely find better service than the Wordsworths did in 1803 when William's sister, Dorothy, wrote in her journal of poor food and damp rooms; the place being 'as dirty as a house after a sale on a rainy day'!). Rooms start at around £24 (above the noisy bar!) with breakfast £7 extra. This hotel is also on the West Highland Way (see the Scotland Long-Distance Paths chapter) and is popular with walkers.

GETTING TO/FROM THE WALK

The route proper starts where it leaves the A82 at a Scottish Rights of Way Society signpost 'to Loch Etiveside', opposite a large 'igloo' cairn just east of 'The Study'. If you are travelling by bus, however, or making this a detour from the West Highland Way, your start will probably be Altnafeadh, 2mi east, where the West Highland Way leaves the A82 to ascend the Devil's Staircase.

Bus & Train Scottish Citylink (☎ 0870-550 5050) buses (which pass through Bridge of

Orchy on the WHR – see Getting There & Away at the start of this chapter) will stop at Altnafeadh, if you arrange it beforehand.

Car Park in a lay-by beside the A82, half a mile west of Altnafeadh, near an Automobile Association (AA) telephone. There's another signpost here pointing towards the 'Public Footpath to Glen Etive'; this is the route you return along.

THE WALK
Altnafeadh to Loch Etiveside Sign
2.25mi (3.5km), 1 hour
From Altnafeadh you have to walk west on the A82, almost to the AA telephone, before escaping right on a path along the old road. This provides some relief from the traffic, but not the noise, as it leads you west below the steep north end of Buachaille Etive Beag. Ahead can be seen the Three Sisters on the south side of Glen Coe, with the high peak

Glen Coe Walks

To Fort William

West Highland Way

0 1 2km
0 0.5 1mi
1:135,000

Stob Mhic/Mhartuin (707m)
Beinn Bheag (616m)

A Glen Coe & Glen Etive Circuit

Glen Coe

Lagangardh

START/FINISH
Altnafeadh

A82

The Study

To Glencoe, Ballachulish & Fort William

Buachaille Etive Mór

Stob Coire Raineach (925m)

Coire na Tulaich

Stob Dearg (1022m)

Allt Lairig Eilde

Buachaille Etive Beag

Coupall River

Stob na Doire (1011m)

Buachaille Etive Mór

Lairig Eilde Pass

Stob Dubh (958m)

Lairig Gartain Pass

Stob na Bròige (956m)

Stob Coire Altruim (941m)

Side Trip

Allt Gartain

Dalness

Etive River

Glen Etive

Alltchaorunn

of Bidean nam Bian (1150m) just peeping over the top. The old road rejoins the A82 about a mile west of the AA telephone, and the traffic must now be endured for another half-mile or so to a sign for Loch Etiveside and the real starting point of this walk.

Loch Etiveside Sign to Lairig Eilde
2.25mi (3.5km), 1 hour
A stony track leads south-west from the 'to Loch Etiveside' signpost. There are excellent views across Glen Coe to the spiky, precipitous ridge of Aonach Eagach. The path leads to the stream of Allt Lairig Eilde, the 'moment of truth'; if it's in spate it is dangerous to cross but even in average conditions it can be difficult so, if in doubt, retreat. If you make it (perhaps with the aid of a stick for balance or with wet feet) you should be able to make all of the remaining burn crossings on this walk.

The well-defined path continues along the north-west side of this burn for about a mile before crossing back more easily. (There is evidence of a faint path on the south-east side of the burn, avoiding the crossings, but the going would be much more difficult.) The way, marked by a few cairns, now leads upwards and bends around to the south. There are views of increasingly wild countryside, including the jagged ridges of Stob Coire Sgreamhach to the west and the rocky gorges below. You may be lucky to see red deer here and, when you eventually reach the top of the **pass** (490m), the views open up across Glen Etive to the impressive peaks beyond.

Lairig Eilde to Lairig Gartain
2.5mi (4km), 1½ hours
Continue down the path on the other side of the pass (*lairig* in Gaelic means 'pass'), crossing a burn. The steep descent continues down to Dalness in Glen Etive. You can avoid about 100m of this descent (and the subsequent 100m ascent) by taking a path that leads to the left when you reach a fenced enclosure on the right, about a mile from the top of the pass. This path traverses round the slope and crosses the burn you

have been following just above a waterfall. Continue the traverse to the next burn, the Allt Gartain, where you join a small path coming up from the right.

Now heading north-east, go up the steep and fairly narrow valley, with the Allt Gartain tumbling down it in a series of small waterfalls. The route up involves some easy scrambling and, on a fine day, there are many opportunities to stop beside the waterfalls and enjoy the views back down to Loch Etive. An alternative but less interesting route keeps to the left, avoiding the trickier section on the lower path. Eventually you reach the **pass**, providing extensive views ahead to the mountains around Loch Treig and a final opportunity to look back at Loch Etive.

Lairig Gartain to Altnafeadh
3mi (5km), 1½ hours
The remainder of the walk back to Altnafeadh can be seen from the pass. This classic, U-shape valley (resulting from glacial erosion) has a more gentle descent than Lairig Eilde but is very marshy. There are some cairns at first; however, the problem is not so much finding the route as avoiding the muddiest places along it. The only useful tip is to keep on the north-west side of the burn, enjoying the fine situation between Buachaille Etive Beag on the left and Buachaille Etive Mór on the right, as you return to the A82, just a few hundred metres west of Altnafeadh.

Buachaille Etive Mór

Distance	6.5mi (10.5km)
Duration	5–6 hours
Standard	medium-hard
Start/Finish	Altnafeadh
Gateways	Glencoe, Fort William

Summary A fine walk on the ridges and summits of one of the most distinctive mountains in Scotland. This is a suitable route for reasonably fit and well-equipped walkers.

Standing sentinel at the head of Glen Coe, Buachaille Etive Mór is one of the most distinctive landmarks in the Scottish landscape

and the appeal of this mountain for walkers is unmistakable. The initial appearance of the mountain, when viewed from the A82 to the east or from the start at Altnafeadh, is one of an impregnable pyramid of buttresses and chasm-like gullies. But looks are often deceiving and a steep, but fairly straightforward, ascent can be made via Coire na Tulaich. The summit, commonly referred to as Buachaille Etive Mór, is actually Stob Dearg (1022m). Behind Stob Dearg the mountain continues to the south-west, with a high-level ridge connecting a further three summits. The sharp cone of Stob na Doire (1011m) provides the other Munro. With such deep valleys on either side, the views and feeling of space from the ridge and summits is exceptional.

In winter the head of Coire na Tulaich becomes a steep snow slope, and should only be climbed by experienced walkers with ice axes and crampons. This snow slope can sometimes persist well into spring. At any other time of the year the high ground is exposed to high winds and can attract thick cloud for days on end. Make sure you check the weather forecast before setting out. The ability to use a map and compass is essential for this walk.

Direction, Distance & Duration
The route is described in a clockwise direction for aesthetic reasons, although it can also be done in the opposite direction. Once the ridge is gained from Coire na Tulaich the walking is quite easy, with only a few short ascents required to reach the various summits. The route described here continues along the ridge and across Stob na Doire, before descending into Lairig Gartain via Coire Altruim. You should allow five to six hours for the route described.

Alternatives As a short option you can simply return down Coire na Tulaich after visiting the summit of Stob Dearg, a walk that will need about three to four hours.

For those who want to maximise distance and effort, Stob na Bròige (956m) can be taken in as a side trip towards the end of the route. Add an hour or more for this option.

PLANNING
Maps & Books
This walk is on OS Landranger 1:50,000 map No 41 *(Ben Nevis)*, OS Outdoor Leisure 1:25,000 map No 38 *(Ben Nevis & Glen Coe)* and Harvey's Superwalker 1:25,000 map *Glen Coe*. Useful books are listed under Maps & Books under Information at the start of this chapter.

PLACES TO STAY & EAT
For information on accommodation and services in Glencoe, see Places to Stay & Eat in the Glen Coe & Glen Etive Circuit earlier in this chapter.

GETTING TO/FROM THE WALK
The walk starts and ends at the lay-by and parking area on the A82 at Altnafeadh. See Getting to/from the Walk for the Glen Coe & Glen Etive Circuit earlier in this chapter.

THE WALK (see map p466)
Altnafeadh to Stob Dearg
2mi (3km), 2 hours
From the parking area follow a wide 4WD track to a large footbridge. Then walk along a good path past Altnafeadh Cottage and gently upwards into Coire na Tulaich. Ignore a path going off to the left (this is used to reach the many scrambles and rock climbs on the buttresses farther east) and follow the path along the right bank of the Allt Coire na Tulaich, which will probably be dry in summer. Higher up the ground becomes steeper and the bed of the stream becomes choked with boulders. The path climbs up to the right, onto easier ground, heading for the scree slopes above. Scree makes for fast descents, but it can make ascents a case of two steps forward and one back. It is easier to stick to the right where, by following the sides of small outcrops, you can find firmer footing. Just below the rim of Coire na Tulaich, you may need to use your hands to scramble over rocky ground before emerging suddenly onto the ridge between Stob Dearg and Stob na Doire (1½ hours from the start).

Turn to the east and climb steadily for around 20 minutes over stony, frost-shattered ground to the summit of **Stob Dearg** (1022m). There are fine views to the east across Rannoch Moor, and to the north and north-west across the shapely summits of the Mamores to the unmistakable, whale-backed profile of Ben Nevis (see the walk description for Ben Nevis later in this chapter). Closer to home, the eye is drawn to the steep north-east face of Stob na Doire, which is next on the agenda.

Stob Dearg to Stob na Doire
1.5mi (2.5km), 1 hour
Descend back to the top of Coire na Tulaich, and head west and then south-west across a lovely, broad ridge with many small lochans filling the depressions between grassy hummocks. Ten or 15 minutes of walking on this ridge should see you at the base of the short, steep haul to Stob na Doire. A well-defined path shows the way to the small **summit** cairn (1011m). The views to the west across Bidean nam Bian now dominate and there are also excellent views south into Glen Etive. To the south-west the ridge of Buachaille Etive Mór continues to Stob na Bròige, while immediately below, in a col, you can make out the red erosion scar of a path heading down into Coire Altruim.

Stob na Doire to Altnafeadh
3mi (5km), 2½ hours
Descend steeply to reach the col and then decide whether you want to continue on to Stob na Bròige, for good views of Loch Etive, or start heading back to Altnafeadh. The return journey to the summit is a little more than 1mi, involves just over 200m of ascent (approximately one hour of extra walking time) and the terrain is quite easy.

From the col, the descent into Coire Altruim is steep but quite straightforward, except for a few wet, rocky steps towards the bottom where a little care is needed. Most walkers take an hour to reach the River Coupall, which may be difficult to ford if in spate. If in doubt simply follow the river back to Altnafeadh and cross it on the footbridge used at the start. If the river is low, cross over and follow the well-defined but boggy path that takes you to the A82, just a few hundred metres west of Altnafeadh (one hour from the col).

Ben Nevis

Distance	9mi (14.5km)
Duration	6–8 hours
Standard	medium-hard
Start/Finish	Ionad Nibheis Visitor Centre, Glen Nevis
Gateway	Fort William

Summary A steep, stony path and a long day to the summit of Britain – an immensely rewarding walk with unsurpassed panoramic views.

There's something irresistible about an attempt on the highest peak in a country, hence many are drawn to Ben Nevis. Despite its popularity, a walk up 'The Ben' should not be undertaken lightly. The mountain measures in at 1344m, the start is virtually at sea level and the ascent is continuous, all the way to the top. You should be well prepared with mountain equipment and adequate food and drink, and be warned that this mountain can be a very dangerous place.

Conditions near the top, in particular, can be extreme. The mean annual summit temperature is below 0°C and snow often remains until early summer. The upper slopes are cloud-covered six days out of seven and navigating off the top is notoriously dangerous – sheer gullies cut into the plateau very near to the line of the path. Ensure that you have the bearings needed to descend from the summit plateau in safety (bearing cards can be purchased in local outdoor gear shops or see the walk description).

All this adds up to a morbid list of superlatives for the Lochaber Mountain Rescue Team, the busiest team in Britain. It is no surprise that 'Nevis' has been traced back to the Gaelic and Irish words meaning 'dread' and 'terrible'.

Despite its dangers, the mountain has a colourful history. The path from Glen Nevis was an old pony track, constructed at the time of the summit observatory (now in ruins), which was opened in 1883. During the previous two summers one Clement

Wragge, soon nicknamed 'the inclement rag', made a daily ascent of the Ben to take weather observations. The observatory closed in 1904 but a small 'hotel' annexe continued to open in summer until about 1918. In 1911 a Model T Ford was 'driven' to the summit as a publicity stunt – a feat that took five days. Nowadays contestants in the Ben Nevis race (first Saturday in September) run up to the top in less than an hour and back down in half an hour!

The old pony track is now known as the 'Mountain Track'. It is absolutely not a jaunt but for properly experienced walkers and, on a good day, the experience of standing on the summit of Britain is unforgettable. If you don't strike it lucky with the weather but still want to explore the lower slopes of the mountain, an alternative route is described.

Direction, Distance & Duration

This route is essentially up and down the same path, but some variation is possible at the start/finish. The Ionad Nibheis Visitor Centre makes a good starting point. Alternatively, the start can be from the SYHA hostel. These two paths meet at a small plantation above the hostel. The route then goes via Halfway Lochan to the summit.

The route is about 4.5mi each way, but the ascent (and descent) of over 1300m and inevitable stops along the way mean that up to eight hours should be allowed for the round trip.

Alternatives If you don't want to go all the way to the summit, or if there is snow, ice or cloud on the upper part of the mountain, a path from just above Halfway Lochan allows splendid views of the intimidating cliffs of the Ben's north-east face. Return by the same route or by the Ben Nevis Low-Level Walk, described at the end of this section.

PLANNING
Maps & Books

The walk is covered by OS Landranger 1:50,000 map No 41 *(Ben Nevis)*, OS Outdoor Leisure 1:25,000 map No 38 *(Ben Nevis & Glen Coe)* and Harvey's Superwalker 1:25,000 map *Glen Coe*.

Many books carry descriptions of the route up Ben Nevis; see Maps & Books under Information earlier in this chapter. Local leaflets also covering this route include *Ben Nevis – Walking the Path from June to September*, produced by the Ranger Service, and *Great Walks No 2* by Fort William and Lochaber Tourism.

Information Sources

Fort William TIC (☎ 01397-703781) is on the High St (open all year). Nevisport, near the train station in Fort William, displays up-to-date mountain weather information, as do the Ionad Nibheis Visitor Centre (☎ 01397-705922) and the SYHA hostel in Glen Nevis. The visitors centre also has interesting

The John Muir Trust

Ownership of Ben Nevis, Britain's highest mountain, changed recently. The Nevis estate, which includes 'The Ben', was put on the market in 1999. The conservation charity, the John Muir Trust, launched an appeal and snapped up the property for approximately half a million pounds.

The area purchased extends eastwards into the Grey Corries and westwards past the upper Glen Nevis gorge. The intention of the trust in buying the land is to safeguard the mountain environment, and manage it in such a way as to preserve and enhance the natural heritage of the area. An integral part of this purchase is to guarantee the right to roam for hill-users, and to improve and manage paths for walkers.

Ben Nevis is the most recent addition to an already impressive portfolio held by the John Muir Trust in Scotland. Six other properties, totalling some 19,000 hectares, have been purchased by the trust since 1987. All of the areas encompass wilderness environments and almost all of them include significant mountain peaks. Over 12,000 hectares are on Skye, and many of the Red Cuillin peaks, as well as one or two of the Black Cuillin summits, are within the trust's ownership. The village of Elgol, Glen Sligachan, and almost all of the terrain covered by the Coast & Cuillin (Elgol to Sligachan) walk (see the Isle of Skye chapter) fall within these boundaries.

The history of the trust is an interesting story in itself. John Muir was born in the fishing port of Dunbar, on the eastern coast of Scotland, in 1838. His family emigrated to Wisconsin, in the USA, when he was 11 years old. He arrived in California at the age of 30, and there he became well known as a pioneer of botanical and geological conservation. Two hundred sites in the USA are named after him, including the John Muir Trail through the High Sierra mountains. Muir's ethos of conservation was formally established in the UK in 1983 with the foundation of the John Muir Trust.

In recent years a number of Scottish estates, incorporating valuable mountain areas, have come up for sale (see the boxed text 'The Black Cuillin for Sale' in the Isle of Skye chapter). This has both ensured the future role of the trust in Scotland and exposed its financial limits as a charitable organisation. The purchase of Ben Nevis (even at a generous discount) stretched the trust considerably and funds to maintain the estate on a year-to-year basis still have to be secured. The trust does not have the financial clout to compete with developers or wealthy individuals who may have less ecologically sensitive plans. Eyes are turning now to the Scottish Executive to examine its responsibility in preserving one of Scotland's most valuable resources – its wild and beautiful mountain landscapes.

For more information about the John Muir Trust, visit the Ionad Nibheis Visitor Centre in Glen Nevis, or contact the John Muir Trust, 41 Commercial St, Edinburgh EH6 6JD (w www.jmt.org).

HUGH D'ANDRADE

displays about the history and geology of Ben Nevis.

PLACES TO STAY & EAT
Glen Nevis

One of the best, most convenient places to stay is *Achintee House* (☎ *01397-702240*). B&B costs from £20 and bunkhouse accommodation is £9, and there is the option of an evening meal or self-catering. Other possibilities are the *SYHA Hostel* (☎ *01397-702336*), where beds costs £12.25 plus £1 extra in July and August. *Glen Nevis Caravan & Camping Park* (☎ *01397-702191*) charges from around £9 for a two-person tent (there are also holiday cottages and caravans for rent). *Glenlochy Guesthouse* (☎ *01397-702909*), quite convenient at Nevis Bridge, charges from £18 for B&B.

Café Beag offers main courses from £6 and *Glen Nevis Restaurant & Bar* has bar meals plus a small shop – all are open during summer months and are between the caravan park and the SYHA Hostel.

GETTING TO/FROM THE WALK

This walk starts 1.5mi up Glen Nevis from Fort William, at the Ionad Nibheis Visitor Centre.

Bus Highland Country Buses (☎ 01397-702373) run 11 buses a day (except Sunday) from Fort William, past the visitors centre and SYHA hostel, and up Glen Nevis as far as the lower falls car park.

Car To reach Glen Nevis take the A82 east out of Fort William (towards Inverness), keeping ahead at the small roundabout on the minor road signed 'Glen Nevis'. Park at the Ionad Nibheis Visitor Centre or just beyond the SYHA hostel.

THE WALK
Achintee to Halfway Lochan
1.5mi (2.5km), 1½–2 hours

From the car park at the Ionad Nibheis Visitor Centre, take the path signposted 'Achintee and Ben Path' across the suspension bridge over the River Nevis. Follow the river bank upstream, below Achintee House, then turn left and climb alongside a stone wall to reach the Ben Nevis path, going up across the slopes of Meall an t-Suidhe ('Hill of Rest' and pronounced mel-an-tee). There's a small plantation where a path comes up steeply from the SYHA hostel. Continue on over a couple of footbridges, to follow a gully, with the Red Burn on your right. As the ground levels off a little, the path turns sharply left. Keep on the path and don't take the short cut. Your route soon turns right again then levels out as Halfway Lochan (its correct name is Lochan Meall an t-Suidhe) comes into view.

Halfway Lochan to Ben Nevis Summit
3mi (5km), 2–3 hours

Just east of Halfway Lochan the path turns right to reach Red Burn Ford. The ruins of 'Halfway House', used in association with the summit observatory, are nearby. (In days gone by walkers were charged one shilling (5p) for walking to the summit, the proceeds being used for path maintenance.) This is the midpoint of the ascent and a good place to take stock. Is the weather fit to continue? Are you? From here to the top and back is a good three to five hours. If in any doubt, enjoy the view and go back down or take the alternative route to the Allt a' Mhuilinn described later.

If you decide to continue start zigzagging steeply up Ben Nevis proper. Keep to the path as short cuts are loose and slippery. The angle of ascent eases at around 1200m and the path forks beside a large, circular stone shelter. The right-hand path is easier, but either will take you across the plateau to the summit cairn and trig point. Take care on this final section as the last bit of the path goes very close to the edge of the cliffs and gullies on the north face of the mountain. Keep especially well clear of any patches of snow. In poor visibility, don't lose sight of the summit cairn until you're ready to descend.

The **summit** is a bit of a wasteland with the remains of the substantial walls of the observatory, several cairns and an emergency shelter, as well as the trig point – all set in a boulder-strewn 'moonscape'. However, the views are exceptional with the islands of Mull, Rum and Skye to the west and, all around, a myriad of mountain peaks as far as the eye can see.

Ben Nevis Summit to Glen Nevis
4.5mi (7km), 3 hours

To return you must retrace your steps. If the cloud is down then, from the trig point, walk for 150m (count your paces – probably about 200) on a grid bearing of 231 degrees, then follow a grid bearing of 281 degrees. This should take you safely off the plateau and on to the path. Remember to allow for magnetic variation. (If you don't know what this means – you shouldn't be up here.) Once on the path, continue to go carefully – most accidents occur during the descent.

Alternative Route: Ben Nevis Low-Level Walk
7.5mi (12km), 4–5 hours

This route offers a pleasant alternative if you don't want to go all the way to the summit or if there is snow, ice or cloud on the upper part of the mountain. Follow the directions for the previous route description as far as Halfway Lochan.

From Halfway Lochan take the path that leads north then east, beneath the intimidating cliffs of the Ben's north-east face. The path continues below Carn Dearg before climbing alongside the Allt a' Mhuilinn (known as the Whisky Burn) to a crossing point about 100m before a private mountain rescue post. From the crossing point take the path heading down on the north-east side of the burn. It gets boggy lower down before meeting a rough, driveable track.

Head left at the first track junction (where the track to the right enters the forest), crossing the Allt a' Mhuilinn at a water intake point. After half a mile or so the track divides. Head downhill on the right-hand fork to a further junction, where again you head downhill. Turn left at a T-junction; you'll shortly pass under some pylon lines

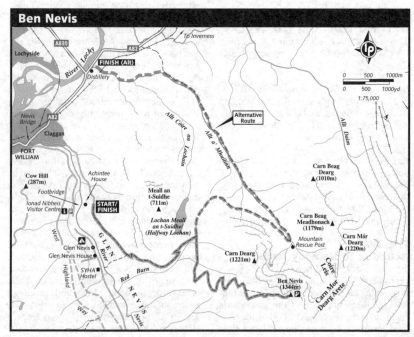

and then cross a small burn. A small sign indicates 'footpath to main road' and you turn right immediately after the bridge to head down alongside the burn, emerging at the whisky distillery, which gives the burn its nickname. The distillery offers tours with a wee dram, after which it is a pleasant walk along the A82 to Fort William.

The Road to the Isles

Distance	14.5mi (23.5km)
Duration	6–9 hours
Standard	medium-hard
Start	Corrour Station
Finish	Glen Nevis roadhead
Gateway	Fort William

Summary A long and remote route with stony, rough and boggy sections, and several river crossings to negotiate. It is best avoided in wet weather. A very satisfying route for experienced walkers.

The Road to (or, indeed, from) the Isles is an ancient route, which traverses the Western Highlands between central Scotland and Skye via Fort William. It was much used by cattle drovers (and cattle thieves) heading for the cattle fairs at Crieff and Falkirk. Armies, their quarries and refugees would march and flee along the route. (The 'Road to the Isles' label is also used by the modern A82, which runs to the south of its original namesake.)

An old Scottish song about the Road to the Isles runs 'By Loch Tummel, and Loch Rannoch and Lochaber I will go'; the walk described in this section goes through the heart of Lochaber. It starts at Corrour Station on the WHR (see the boxed text 'The West Highland Railway' on p464), which at 408m above sea level makes it the highest station on the British Rail network. The station is 11mi from the nearest public road. The Road to the Isles meets up with the railway again at Fort William.

The route follows rights of way, passing between major mountain ranges (Ben Nevis and the Aonachs on one side, the Mamores on the other) before descending through a dramatic rock gorge (mini-Himalayan in character) to the roadhead in Glen Nevis. This walk goes through wild and remote country – although there is a bothy about halfway along the route – and should only be attempted by experienced hill walkers and in suitable weather.

Direction, Distance & Duration

This route is best done from east to west. Following the route in this direction means the majority of your progress will be downhill. It also means your accommodation options will be greater. The total distance from Corrour Station to the Glen Nevis roadhead is 14.5mi. This takes about seven hours of walking, but you should allow at least nine.

Alternatives From the Glen Nevis roadhead it is still some 6mi to Fort William (two to three hours). If you don't want to try and get a lift and prefer to avoid the traffic and tar, there is a track through the forest that starts at Achriabhach, about 250m after the road crosses to the other side of the river. Alternatively, you can leave the road in places to follow the river bank along a series of informal paths.

PLANNING
Maps & Books

The whole route is covered by OS Landranger 1:50,000 map No 41 *(Ben Nevis)*. *Exploring Scottish Hilltracks* by Ralph Storer includes a description of this walk.

Information Sources

The main TIC this area is in Fort William (☎ 01397-703781). So if you're getting the train from Fort William to Corrour Station, call in to check on the weather.

PLACES TO STAY & EAT

The options at Corrour are limited, so don't turn up on spec or you might be unlucky. The simple but popular *SYHA Hostel (☎ 01397-732207)*, at the western end of Loch Ossian, charges £6.75 and is a couple of miles' walk from Corrour Station. Alternatively, the *Corrour Station Bunkhouse (☎ 01397-732236)* offers the unusual experience of staying in a former signal box for £6.50. The station *cafe* offers excellent snacks/meals from 9am to 9pm and also stocks basic provisions, although it is still wise to bring any important items with you.

If you have suitable gear there are bothies at Staoineag and Meanach, about halfway along the walk, which would let you split the walk into two days.

There is plenty of accommodation at the end of the walk in Glen Nevis and Fort William – see the Gateways section and Places to Stay & Eat in the Ben Nevis walk earlier in this chapter for recommendations.

GETTING TO/FROM THE WALK

Train The only way to Corrour Station is by the WHR (☎ 0845-748 4950), either from Glasgow or Fort William, or one of the intermediate stations (see the boxed text 'The West Highland Railway' on p464). There are four services in both directions Monday to Saturday, and two or three services on Sunday. The overnight sleeper service from London will also stop here on request. The platform itself is so small that only one door on the train can be opened to let passengers off; check with the conductor where you should sit to be near the right door.

Car & Bus To reach the Glen Nevis roadhead from Fort William, take the A82 east out of Fort William (towards Inverness) and keep going straight at a small roundabout to join a minor road signed 'Glen Nevis'. Continue up the glen to the end of the road, where there is adequate parking space.

If you haven't left a car at the Glen Nevis roadhead or haven't arranged to be picked up from there at the end of the walk, you might be able to hitch down to Fort William as the glen is a popular day-trip destination. Otherwise it's a 2mi walk from the roadhead to the lower falls car park, at the end of the Glen Nevis bus route (see Getting to/from the Walk in the Ben Nevis walk earlier in this chapter).

THE WALK
Corrour Station to Creaguaineach Lodge
4mi (6.5km), 1½ hours

From Corrour Station, on a clear day, you get a preview of Ben Nevis and nearby mountains. Once you've savoured the view, cross to the west of the railway line and follow the track to the north-west, alongside the line. The track is used by 4WDs, which are better designed for negotiating the bog than your booted feet. Old railway sleepers help to ford wet patches and to cross several small burns.

After about a mile you get to a point where the Allt Lùib Ruairidh runs through an underpass below the railway line. A track from the Loch Ossian SYHA Hostel also comes under here and you join it after crossing the bridge over the stream. Continue ahead on the much better track below the railway line, down to a bridge across the Allt a' Chamabhreac, just before it empties into Loch Treig. There are excellent views of the Mamores and shapely Binnein Beag ahead – you'll pass below this peak about

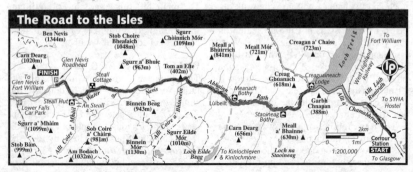

The Road to the Isles

three-quarters of the way along this route and it acts as a marker against which you can measure your progress.

Walking round Loch Treig you may well feel it lives up to its name, which means 'Forsaken', so it's something of a surprise to see **Creaguaineach Lodge** ahead. This is a private lodge that just survived the raising of the water level in the 1930s, when the loch was dammed as part of the hydroelectric scheme for the aluminium works at Fort William.

Creaguaineach Lodge to Lùibeilt
3.5mi (5.5km), 2 hours
Immediately before Creaguaineach Lodge there is a major bridge over the Abhainn Rath (flowing down a small gorge into Loch Treig). At the south end of this is a junction marked by a Scottish Rights of Way Society signpost. Although the original right of way to Glen Nevis, and the path shown on the OS map, follow the north side of the Abhainn Rath, the preferred route (and that indicated by the signpost) keeps to the south side. This is to avoid the river crossing, which is otherwise necessary at Lùibeilt and which can prove a major difficulty after wet weather. The signposted route follows a rough path alongside the river, swinging left to cross two small tributaries and then right where it climbs a narrow section of the valley to a wide level area near Staoineag Bothy.

The path continues along the valley floor, crossing a substantial tributary, to another step in the valley, down which the river tumbles. Above this the valley becomes wide and flat again, and would feel very remote if it were not for the group of conifer trees around Lùibeilt and the nearby Meanach Bothy, now visible ahead. The river meanders here and the optimum route is not always obvious, particularly as another major tributary is reached, but there are stepping stones if you can find them. The marshy ground between here and Lùibeilt is clearly subject to regular flooding but the ground is firm immediately alongside the river.

Lùibeilt itself is a ruin, although much of the roof is still in place, and adjacent to it is

a locked barn. If you need shelter there's Meanach Bothy but to reach this you must cross the river – the very crossing you have avoided by following the south side of the river! A rough, yet driveable, track leads south from Lùibeilt to Kinlochleven, about 7mi away; an escape route if required.

Lùibeilt to Glen Nevis Roadhead
7mi (11.5km), 4 hours
Continuing north-west, follow a track that winds between stony knolls, some quarried for road stone, and then head along a grassy track, back into wild country again. You are now getting near Binnein Beag, which comes into view again on the left. Ahead is the massive Aonach Beag and the outer peak of Sgurr a' Bhuic, which you'll pass to your right.

About a mile after Lùibeilt and shortly before a major confluence in the river, the path ascends a stony slope on the left and then traverses along the side of glacial deposits towards a small metal hut (known as 'The Water Shed') on the far side of the Allt Coire a' Bhinnein. A small dam diverts this burn from its natural course down Glen Nevis towards Loch Treig. Its bed is strewn with boulders and a stick will help you balance when crossing it. The hut is in a poor state and offers limited shelter.

From the hut follow the usually dry river bed to the north for about 200m to join the path on the north side of the infant River Nevis (at this point it's called Water of Nevis), below the hillock of Tom an Eite, then the path turns west.

The ground ahead is often peaty. Where the peat is exposed, the remains of ancient trees are sometimes apparent – relics of the very different vegetation that was once present. As a result there are many boggy stretches making the going slow. Alternative paths do exist but it's tricky finding the best option; the highest is often best.

As you eventually leave Binnein Beag behind, many more fine peaks in the Mamores come into sight and there's a dramatic view of Ben Nevis' north-east profile.

Ahead is what appears to be an enclosed basin and you may begin to wonder how the river finds its way out. On the way down to it there is a substantial bridge over a burn, which drains the corrie between Ben Nevis and Aonach Beag, alongside the ruins of the old Steall cottage. Nearby is a waterfall, An Steall, which cascades down more than 100m of rock slabs. Steall Hut, on the other side of the river, is private and reached by a bridge comprising just three wire ropes – try it if you dare, and imagine negotiating it in high winds with a backpack filled for a week's stay!

The way out of this sanctuary now becomes apparent – the river takes an abrupt turn to the right and tumbles down a steep rocky gorge, the bed of which is filled with massive boulders. Fortunately there is a well-constructed path clinging to the valley side. After a sharp turn back to the left (and an excellent view back up this dramatic gorge to An Steall), you'll soon reach the Glen Nevis roadhead. The last few miles before the roadhead will probably be quite crowded as this is a popular strolling zone.

The Cairngorms

The Cairngorms are the wildest and most extensive area of uplands in Britain and embrace the largest tracts of land over 600m, 900m and 1200m high. The climate is the closest in Britain to an arctic regime; consequently the area is of outstanding ecological importance. Indeed, the Cairngorms will become one of Scotland's first national parks during 2003 (see the boxed text on p478).

The term Cairngorms can refer to the entire area between the River Spey south-east to Braemar on the upper River Dee, but in this chapter the focus is mainly on the vast central Cairn Gorm–Macdui plateau. It's crowned by Ben Macdui (1309m), Britain's second-highest mountain, south of Cairn Gorm (1245m) itself (the peak is spelt as two words). The plateau is separated from neighbouring mountain massifs by the deep gash of the Lairig Ghru pass in the west and the Lairig an Laoigh in the east, and pitted with spectacular, cliff-lined corries on its northern and southern faces.

Originally the Cairngorms were called Am Monadh Ruadh, meaning 'red rounded hills' (referring to the big exposures of pinkish-red granite), but the name of the summit most visible from Strathspey was adopted in the 19th century. Oddly, Cairn Gorm means blue rocky mountain.

Whatever the name, the Cairngorms need to be taken seriously, not the place to go for a casual stroll – the plateau is generally above 1000m. The weather is notoriously fickle with low cloud, mist, strong wind, sleet and snow likely at any time – so always be prepared for the worst. Navigation skills are essential; the paths are well worn

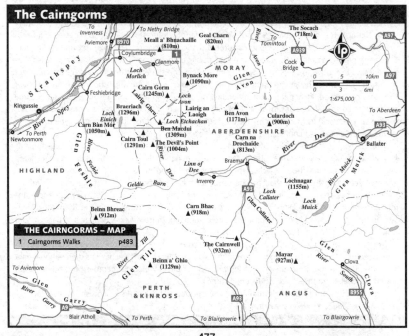

THE CAIRNGORMS – MAP	
1 Cairngorms Walks	p483

but visibility can quickly deteriorate to zero and finding the way can be decidedly tricky in the absence of prominent landmarks. In winter the Cairngorms are one of Scotland's premier mountaineering and ice-climbing destinations and a mecca for downhill and cross-country skiers.

Not only are the Cairngorms outstandingly scenic, they are also exceptionally valuable for wildlife, especially for birds. Golden plovers, ptarmigan and dotterels may be seen on the higher ground; siskins, crested tits and redpolls live in the more sheltered areas and the pine woodlands on the lowermost slopes. Mountain hares also inhabit the

higher ground, red and roe deer are widespread and you may even see reindeer (an introduced species) grazing high up.

Don't be put off if you are not keen on climbing hills. On the northern slopes of the plateau, Rothiemurchus Estate (privately owned by the Grant family, of whisky fame) and Glenmore Forest Park (managed by Forest Enterprise, a government agency) have many low-level walks, suitable for all and ideal for days when the mountains are cloud-shrouded.

In this chapter, two walks – a high-level circular walk over the summit of Cairn Gorm with an optional extension to Ben

National Parks for Scotland

Scotland has had to wait a long time for even one national park – 128 years since the world's first and more than 50 years after they were set up in England and Wales. This is despite having the finest mountain and coastal landscapes in Britain, relatively large areas of undeveloped land and many sites of national and international ecological importance.

Scotland's relative slowness can be attributed to the times: to a strong interest in developing Scotland's, and especially the Highlands', water resources for hydroelectric power; to the opposition by owners of large estates; and to a general lack of public support.

By the late 1990s a host of protective designations had been heaped upon the Scottish countryside – National Nature Reserves, Sites of Special Scientific Interest, National Scenic Areas and several others of EU origin. Most were administered by Scottish Natural Heritage, set up to safeguard Scotland's natural assets, with varying levels of public participation. The creation of a Scottish Parliament and Executive in 1999 provided the inspiration and the opportunity to set up the country's own national parks. The government believed that parks would enhance the long-term future of the areas concerned, local people could become more involved and more resources would become available to solve all kinds of problems. Opponents claimed that national parks would spell disaster for the very landscapes they were meant to protect and that setting up yet another type of reserve would create chaos and confusion.

After much public debate and consultation, the National Parks (Scotland) Act was passed in August 2000, giving the government the means to declare national parks. The first park to be declared will be Loch Lomond & the Trossachs, which should be up and running in 2002, followed by Cairngorms a year later. Although their precise boundaries had not been settled at the time of writing, their core areas are fairly definite. For the Cairngorms, this extends from Nethy Bridge and Tomintoul in the north to the Dee-Tay divide in the south, and from Newtonmore in the west to Ballater in the east. Around Loch Lomond, the core extends south from near Crianlarich to Balloch, and from Arrochar in the west to Callander in the east.

The main aims of park management will be to protect and enhance the area's natural and cultural heritage, alongside social and economic development. Each park will have its own national park authority; its maximum membership of 25 will include directly elected members and others nominated by local authorities and Scottish ministers.

The best source for further information on the evolution of the parks is Scottish Natural Heritage (☎ 01224-642863, **W** www.snh.org.uk).

Macdui, and a medium-level route deep into the range through the Lairig Ghru – give a good introduction to the scale and wildness of the range. In Other Walks at the end of the chapter there are also outlines of the ascent of nearby Braeriach, the third-highest mountain in Britain and a truly magnificent peak; a much shorter climb over Meall a' Bhuachaille, with fine views of the plateau; a long, low-level walk to beautiful Loch Avon; and an introduction to the vast opportunities in the southern Cairngorms.

PLANNING
Maps & Books
Harvey's Superwalker 1:25,000 map *Cairn Gorm* covers both walks very well. The OS Outdoor Leisure 1:25,000 map No 3 *(The Cairngorms – Aviemore & Glen Avon)* is a big, unwieldy double-sided sheet but excellent for detail. The OS Landranger 1:50,000 map No 36 *(Grantown & Aviemore)* would do as an alternative.

The most comprehensive guidebook is *The Cairngorms* by Adam Watson in the Scottish Mountaineering Club's (SMC) District Guide series. Of the several strictly walking guides covering the area, *Walks Speyside* by Richard Hallewell is very compact and describes a good range of walks, while *Cairngorms Walks* by John Brooks has better maps and more generous descriptions. Jim Crumley's *The Heart of the Cairngorms* is a passionate statement of the 'need for wildness' to be recognised in conservation and development proposals. The Cairngorms also feature in the guides to walking in Scotland mentioned under Books in the Facts for the Walker chapter.

Information Sources
The nearest Tourist Information Centre (TIC) is in Aviemore (☎ 01479-810363, e aviemoretic@host.co.uk). It has a good range of maps and guides, local accommodation listings, weather information and an exchange bureau.

Rothiemurchus Visitor Centre (☎ 01479-812345, e rothie@enterprise.net) at Inverdruie is run by the Rothiemurchus Estate and has information about the estate (including guided walks run by the estate's rangers), local maps and guides, and a farm shop.

Forest Enterprise's Glenmore Forest Park Visitor Centre (☎ 01479-861220), beside the Ski Road in Glenmore, concentrates on the surrounding forest park. Its *Guide to Glenmore & Inshriach Forests* includes maps and notes for waymarked walks in the park.

Up at the funicular's base station, the Cairngorms Countryside Ranger Service (☎ 01479-861261) can give expert advice about walks on the plateau. The local weather forecast is posted here daily.

Guided Walks
Guided walks leave from the Rothiemurchus Visitor Centre, or you could join one of the summer guided walks hosted by the Cairngorms Countryside Ranger Service (see Information Sources for details on both).

PLACES TO STAY & EAT
Aviemore
While Aviemore, itself, does not have a great deal to recommend it to visitors, it does provide a range of accommodation options. The TIC (☎ 01479-810363, e aviemoretic @host.co.uk), on Grampian Rd, has details of the numerous B&Bs. The *SYHA Hostel (☎ 01479-810345, 25 Grampian Rd)* has lots of space, is open all year and has an Internet kiosk; the tariff is £13.25. The town has several shops, including a *Tesco* supermarket.

Colyumbridge & Inverdruie
At Coylumbridge, the small *Rothiemurchus Camp & Caravan Park (☎ 01479-812800)*, in pine woodland beside the Lairig Ghru path, charges £3.50. At Inverdruie, *Junipers B&B (☎ 01479-810405)* is welcoming and comfortable; the tariff is £17.

For a meal, between Aviemore and Inverdruie is the *Old Bridge Inn (☎ 01479-811137)*, on Dalfaber Rd, a largely unspoiled traditional pub that specialises in Scottish fare, including venison and salmon – and doesn't ignore vegetarians. Prices represent good value and there's local ale on tap.

For walking gear, the nearest outlet is Cairngorm Mountain Sports at Inverdruie (☎ 01479-810729).

THE CAIRNGORMS

Glenmore

Glenmore (7mi from Aviemore) is the closest settlement to the start of the walks, beside the Ski Road up to Coire Cas. Here Forest Enterprise runs the large and well-maintained *Glenmore Camping & Caravan Site (☎ 01479-861271)*; the tariffs vary according to the season, but you can count on paying up to £9 per pitch.

Opposite is *Loch Morlich SYHA Hostel (☎ 01479-861238)*, a spacious former lodge; the tariff is £9.25 and meals are available – just £4.95 for a three-course evening meal and £3.50 for a cooked breakfast.

A Cairngorms Funicular – Environmental Vandalism?

At the beginning of the 1960s the northern slopes of the Cairngorms were opened up for downhill skiing with the construction of a road from Glenmore into Coire Cas. From here chair lifts ascended to an intermediate station and on to Ptarmigan Centre, the top station and restaurant at 1080m. Other later lifts and tows gave access to the eastern slopes, and a road snaked up from Coire Cas to Ptarmigan.

However, because the plateau is buffeted by winds of stronger than 35mph for more than 50% of the year, the chair lift often had to be closed.

In 1994 the Cairngorm Chairlift Company (CCC) proposed a more reliable and comfortable replacement for the chair lift – a funicular railway similar to those operating in continental European alpine resorts. It was claimed it would attract huge numbers of visitors – up to 200,000 annually was the late 1990s 'guesstimate', compared with a then figure of about 50,000. Consequently, many jobs would be created and the local economy soundly underpinned.

The proposal ignited fierce opposition from walkers, mountaineers and conservation groups, led by the Cairngorms Campaign. They protested that the environmental impact of the development would be disastrous in an area of supreme ecological and scenic importance, that it couldn't possibly be economically viable and would probably drive visitors away rather than draw them in. What's more, snowfalls seem to be on the decline.

The European Regional Development Fund and the Bank of Scotland were eventually persuaded to back the project, anticipated to cost £14.7 million. Scottish Natural Heritage, the statutory environmental agency, sanctioned the proposal (confined to the Cairngorm Ski Area of 598 hectares), subject to mandatory access restrictions to protect adjacent EU-designated conservation areas. The Scottish Executive finally approved the proposal and construction began in August 1999. To minimise the visual impact of the funicular and its support columns, the top 250m of the track to the Ptarmigan Centre will go through a shallow tunnel, blasted out of the hillside.

The funicular will take off in winter 2001, the new base station will open in mid-2001 and the new Ptarmigan visitors centre and restaurant will be operational in spring 2002. The Day Lodge, next to the base station, is being refurbished and the Coire Cas car park is due to be upgraded. The operating company (CCC) will plough the profits back into facilities within the ski area, including footpath repair and construction.

The European money was provided on condition that the funicular operate as a closed system during summer, to ensure the increased number of visitors don't cause severe damage to the fragile mountain environment. According to the official Visitor Management Plan, this means that between 1 May and 30 November funicular riders will not be allowed out onto the mountain – their experience will be confined to displays in the Ptarmigan Centre and what they can (with luck) see from the viewing platform and the funicular carriage. Whereas in the past people have been able to take the chair lift up to Ptarmigan Centre and then walk up to the summit, this is no longer possible. Access on foot is now from Coire Cas only.

For more information about the project, contact the Cairngorm Ski Area (☎ 01479-861261, fax 861207, e info@cairngorm.sol.co.uk).

There's also the friendly Mrs Ferguson's *Cairn Eilrig* B&B (☎ *01479-861223*) at £17; and, farther up the road, **Glenmore Lodge** (☎ *01479-861256*), from £17.50. The *Lochain Bar* at the Lodge specialises in whiskies and serves reasonably priced bar meals, including a vegetarian option, with a marvellous view of the Cairn Gorm plateau and – when you can't see the view – stunning posters of more distant mountains.

The Glenmore *shop*, next to the campsite, has a small range of supplies and liquid fuel and gas; the local forecast is posted outside. The adjacent *cafe* does light meals and snacks and is open during summer evenings.

GETTING THERE & AWAY
For information on travel options between England, Wales and Scotland, see the Getting Around chapter.

Bus Aviemore is easily reached from Inverness, Glasgow and Edinburgh by Scottish Citylink services (☎ 0870-550 5050), which stop at the train station several times a day; the TIC handles bookings and inquiries. From late May to late September, Highland Country Buses (☎ 01463-233371) runs a service from Fort William to Coire Cas via Aviemore train station twice daily, stopping at Inverdruie, Coylumbridge and Glenmore en route. The same company also operates a more frequent (at least three times daily) summer-only service between Aviemore and Coire Cas, with the same intermediate stops as the Fort William to Coire Cas service. In other words there are at least five buses per day between Aviemore and Coire Cas.

Train ScotRail services (☎ 0845-755 0033) linking Inverness with Edinburgh and Glasgow stop at Aviemore, as does the Great North Eastern Railway (GNER) service (☎ 0845-722 5225) from London King's Cross to Inverness via Edinburgh.

Car Leave the A9 12mi north of the Kingussie turnoff or 7mi south of the Carrbridge turnoff to reach Aviemore. From here take the B970 to Coylumbridge, then the Ski Road to Glenmore and Coire Cas.

A Cairn Gorm High Circuit

Distance	7mi (11.5km)
Duration	4–4½ hours
Standard	medium-hard
Start/Finish	Coire Cas car park, Ski Road
Gateways	Aviemore
Summary	An outstanding mountain walk across an exposed plateau, part of the most extensive upland area in Britain, with magnificent wide-ranging views and an optional detour to Ben Macdui.

THE CAIRNGORMS

This is the most popular high walk in the Cairngorms, the highlights being the summit of Cairn Gorm itself, the dramatic peaks of Stob Coire an t-Sneachda and Cairn Lochan, and the awesome corries. It can't be stressed too strongly that this walk is not a doddle. The vast plateau drops precipitously in almost all directions and severe weather is possible at any time; conditions may be fine at Glenmore but up on top it can be completely different. Inexperienced walkers should only tackle this walk in seasoned company.

Direction, Distance & Duration
This walk can be done in either direction; it is described clockwise, going up to Cairn Gorm from the north-east, round the rim of Coire an t-Sneachda, over Cairn Lochan, then down the ridge and back to the start.

The ascent to Cairn Gorm's summit is about 645m and there's an additional climb of about 155m over Cairn Lochan. The walk isn't a particularly long day, allowing plenty of time for enjoying the views.

Alternatives Realistically, the only early escape route on the walk is down Fiacaill a' Choire Chais, the ridge between Coire Cas and Coire an t-Sneachda.

The alternative route to Ben Macdui (described at the end of the walk description) offers even wider views and a greater sensation of remoteness, out of sight of the northern slope developments. The path to Ben Macdui diverges from Cairn Lochan south-west across a gap and up to the undulating plateau studded with crowds of cairns.

The extra distance involved is 8km (with another 200 vertical metres of climbing), for which you should allow at least two hours. Adding Ben Macdui makes for a full day, but one well within the scope of fit walkers.

GETTING TO/FROM THE WALK

Bus For information on the Highland Country Buses service (☎ 01463-233371) to Coire Cas, see Getting There & Away in the introduction to the chapter.

Car From Aviemore take the B970 to Coylumbridge and continue along what is known as the Ski Road to Glenmore and Coire Cas.

THE WALK
Coire Cas to Cairn Gorm
2mi (3km), 1½ hours

Start by walking down the road, away from the car park, to a road junction and take the road to the right for about 90m to a stonework drain on the right. A small cairn in the heather marks the start of a narrow path on the other side of the ditch, parallel to the road. Follow this entrenched old track for about 200m – you'll find that it becomes wider and clearer up the heather-clad slope. After a while cairns mark the route steadily upwards, with views unfolding of the corries and spurs of the Cairn Gorm plateau. The path goes beneath a ski lift, past the top of another, weaving in and out of the picket fences lining the lift routes. Having left the heather behind, the path then crosses gravelly ground. Until the new Ptarmigan Centre opens you need to follow path diversion signs round the construction site. Beyond here a stone-paved path leads fairly steeply up to a boulder field, where cairns and poles clearly mark the route across this minor obstacle course and up to the large cairn on the **summit**, with a weather station nearby.

Among the many features in the panoramic view are the long flat plateau of Ben Wyvis (just west of Inverness) to the north, the sprawling bulk of Ben Macdui nearby, beyond it the sharper profile of Braeriach and, to the south-east, flat-topped Ben Avon, its summit dotted with granite tors.

Cairn Gorm to Cairn Lochan
2mi (3km), 1 hour

Descend sharply westwards over a jumble of big boulders – initially there's no clear path – towards a wide path on clearer ground below. Then, on a broad saddle, diverge a little to the right to a prominent cairn, marking the feature mapped as '1141' at the head of Fiacaill a' Choire Chais (the escape route mentioned under Direction, Distance & Duration earlier), for a great view of the crags on the eastern side of Cairn Lochan.

Follow the broad path round the rim of cliff-lined Coire an t-Sneachda, its flat floor decorated with swampy lochans (small lakes). A cairned route leads up to Stob Coire an t-Sneachda (1176m), peak of the snowy corrie. Drop down westwards to a small gap. The path to Ben Macdui leads south from here (see the Alternative Route later). Otherwise, climb steeply to **Cairn Lochan** (1215m) with its sprawling cairn close to the rim of the plunging cliffs. The beautiful patchwork of broad Strathspey dominates the outlook north-west and west, while Ben Rinnes, a prominent feature along the Speyside Way (described in the Scotland Long-Distance Paths chapter later), stands just to the left of Cairn Gorm's summit.

Cairn Lochan to Coire Cas
3mi (5km), 1½ hours

Continue generally south-west following a cairned route, then descend the steep, mostly rocky slope to the clearly defined path along the north-south ridge rimming the western side of Coire an Lochan. The path loses height fairly quickly down the heathery slope as it bends north-eastwards and crosses a small stream. A well-made path takes over – you can be grateful for the huge stepping stones planted across a very boggy stretch. The excellent path leads on, making it much easier to enjoy the superb views of the northern corries, then across Allt Coire an t-Sneachda and on to the car park.

Alternative Route: Ben Macdui
5mi (8km), 2½ hours

Leaving the gap between Stob Coire an t-Sneachda and Cairn Lochan, follow the clear narrow path leading south then south-west above the shallow valley of Feith Buidhe and down to a wide saddle cradling Lochan Buidhe. Snow can linger on the north-facing slope, just east of the lochan, into late summer. Beyond you can see the dramatic cliffs of Carn Etchachan, while in the opposite direction, across the depths of the Lairig Ghru, Braeriach's magnificent corries look as if some giant hand had scooped them out of the plateau. Follow a cairned route across boulders, then climb the steep slope past a minor peak and on to the **summit of Ben Macdui** (1309m), marked

by a lonely survey pillar. Near this is a low stone shelter and a direction indicator, erected by the Cairngorm Club (Aberdeen) in 1925. It helps to identify the features in the extraordinarily wide view from Ben Nevis and Creag Meagaidh (west-south-west), to Lochnagar (east-south-east) and Ben More Assynt (north-north-west).

To return to the Cairn Gorm High Circuit route, retrace your steps to the saddle of the anonymous lochan. From here keep to the left or westerly path over the broad spur, then it's down – with an awesome view straight into the Lairig Ghru, overlooked by

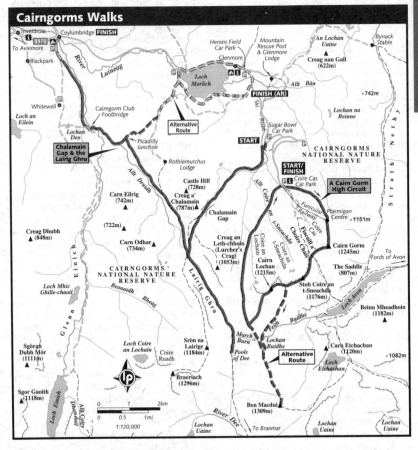

THE CAIRNGORMS

rugged Lurcher's Crag. Follow this path back to Coire Cas as described above.

Chalamain Gap & the Lairig Ghru

Duration	6–6½ hours
Distance	13mi (21km)
Standard	medium-hard
Start	Sugar Bowl car park, Ski Road
Finish	Coylumbridge
Gateways	Aviemore

Summary An energetic walk into the finest mountain pass in Britain, following rocky paths and crossing boulder fields, with a choice of return routes.

The Lairig Ghru is generally regarded as the finest mountain pass in Britain and is accessible only to walkers. It was cut by a massive glacier slicing right through the mountain mass, and provides a natural route from Strathspey to Upper Deeside. Lairig Ghru means pass of Druie – the stream that drains its northern side. It has been in use for centuries for trade and cattle droving and is a public right of way. Traditionally people walked the full distance from Aviemore to Braemar (28mi) but these days many start from Coylumbridge or Glenmore. At the southern end there's nothing for it but to walk right into Braemar. It's possible to do this in a day or you could carry a tent, spreading the journey over two days. There is accommodation in and near Braemar.

The walk described here is a day's outing from Glenmore, through the dramatic Chalamain Gap and up to the top of the Lairig, then back to Coylumbridge through Rothiemurchus pine woodlands.

Direction, Distance & Duration
The best way to do the walk is from Glenmore, starting at a point higher than the finish. Crossing Chalamain Gap involves a climb of 240m and it's another 225m up to the top of the Lairig Ghru. The route is divided into four stages, with the Lairig's summit marking the halfway point in time, although not in distance, but it is downhill all the way back.

Alternatives One possible alternative for the return is to walk back to Herons Field car park on the Ski Road near Glenmore, a distance of 14.8mi; Forest Enterprise charges £1 for the use of this car park.

Alternatively, you can reach the Ski Road near the western end of Loch Morlich via the Rothiemurchus Estate road, although car parking here is less satisfactory. The distance for this version is 12.8mi. An outline of these alternatives follows the main walk description.

GETTING TO/FROM THE WALK
The walk starts at the Sugar Bowl car park, on the north-eastern side of the Ski Road, 1.75mi from Glenmore village. If travelling by public transport, you could take either of the summer Highland Country Buses services (for details, see Getting There & Away in the introduction to this chapter), although the driver will probably stop below the car park for safety's sake. The same services will stop in Glenmore and Colyumbridge on their way down the mountain.

THE WALK (see map p483)
Sugar Bowl car park to Allt Druidh
3mi (5km), 1¾ hours
From the car park cross the road and follow the path down to a footbridge across Allt Mor. Climb up to the right, then, on the rim of the bank, veer left along a paved path and continue past a sign warning that you're entering a wild mountainous area, across moorland. The views here are great, taking in the deep corries and sharp spurs of the northern face of the Cairn Gorm plateau. The path dips to cross a small stream then climbs to the narrow Chalamain Gap. Clamber over the boulders filling its narrow cleft, keeping to the lowest level to avoid the peaty, heathery slopes. It's an eerily quiet place where rock falls seem to happen frequently. On the far side there are magnificent views across the Lairig Ghru to mighty Braeriach and the cairn-topped Sgòran Dubh Mór beyond. The wide rocky, occasionally wet path crosses a shallow valley then descends steeply to the Lairig Ghru path beside Allt Druidh.

Up to the Pools of Dee
2mi (3km), 1¼ hours

The path crosses the stream on enormous boulders and climbs the heathery slope, then emerges onto more open ground, but still with the steep slopes towering above, their cliffs scoured by glaciers eons ago. Elongated mounds of moraine left behind by the retreating glaciers partly block the valley as you climb towards the pass. The path is marked by occasional cairns; follow these carefully, keeping to the left (east) for the final stretch to the crest. Ahead, the rugged peaks of Cairn Toul and the Devil's Point come into view. Continue for another 500m or so to the Pools of Dee – the headwaters of the River Dee – from where you can look far down the southern side of the Lairig.

Pools of Dee to Piccadilly junction
5mi (8km), 2 hours

Retrace your steps to the point where you joined the Lairig Ghru path and continue downstream from here. The rough path crosses steep, rocky slopes, with Allt Druidh far below in a deep trench cut through the moraine. Continue past a path to the right (to Rothiemurchus Lodge), with fine views of the Monadhliath Mountains on the western side of Strathspey and Meall a' Bhuachaille above Loch Morlich. After just over a mile you meet some beautiful Scots pines, the outliers of the Caledonian pine woodland and a precious remnant of the great forests that once covered much of the Highlands. The path junction, known unofficially as Piccadilly, has direction signs to Aviemore (to the left/west) and Loch Morlich (to the right/east).

Piccadilly junction to Coylumbridge
3mi (5km), 1 hour

Follow the track to Aviemore, beside Allt Druidh, past a stream junction and down to the fine footbridge, built in 1912 by the Cairngorm Club over Allt na Beinne Moire (mapped as Am Beanaidh). A short distance farther on, bear right along a path to Coylumbridge. This leads through dense pines,

then through more open pine woodland – where the displays of purple heather in August are magnificent – across small burns and through gates. Pass a path to the left (to Gleann Einich) and continue along the broad track, past the Rothiemurchus campsite, to the road at Coylumbridge. There is a small roadside car park to the left.

Alternative Finish: Glenmore
3mi (5km), 1¼ hours

Here we describe two alternative routes to Glenmore, one via Loch Morlich and the other via Herons Field. For both, turn right off the main route at Piccadilly, along the wide path towards Loch Morlich. This leads through pine woodland to a high deer fence, just beyond which you meet the wide gravel road to Rothiemurchus Lodge. Bear left and continue along the gravel road for nearly a mile to an unsignposted junction.

To reach the Ski Road near the western end of Loch Morlich from here, just continue ahead for 300m. There is some roadside car parking here and there's a Forest Enterprise car park 200m to the right, where the fee is £1. Glenmore village is 1.25mi along the road.

For Herons Field, follow the path from the unsignposted junction to a footbridge across a small burn, then go through a tall gate (where you leave Rothiemurchus Estate and enter Glenmore Forest Park) and left along a wide forest track, skirting the shore of Loch Morlich to the south. Near its eastern end, turn left along a path marked with a red-banded post. Follow the route marked with these posts north and east through cleared land and pines to the car park. Sugar Bowl car park, at the start of the walk, is 1.25mi south along the Ski Road, while Glenmore is 600m to the north.

Other Walks

BRAERIACH
Braeriach (1296m), which means 'brindled upland', is the second-highest peak in the Cairngorms and the third-highest in Britain. It's the culmination of a great undulating

plateau, with the Lairig Ghru on its precipitous eastern side and its western flank rising almost as steeply from lonely Glen Einich. This magnificent massif, with dark mysterious corries scooped out of its northern and eastern slopes, is unspoiled by any alien, damaging developments. For Munro enthusiasts (for an explanation of Munro, see the boxed text 'Munros & Munro Bagging' on p452) it also boasts Sgor an Lochain Uaine (1258m), Cairn Toul (1291m) and Bod an Deamhain (1004m), which means 'the Devil's Point'. All three are perched on the rim above the Lairig Ghru, although the last-named is usually climbed from Corrour Bothy, about 5km south of the Pools of Dee.

The climb to Braeriach starts only after a fairly long walk in, so you'll need a fine midsummer day for this outstanding walk. The distance is 18.75mi and the ascent 1000m; allow about nine hours. The best map is either the Harvey Superwalker 1:25,000 map *Cairn Gorm* or the OS Outdoor Leisure 1:25,000 map No 3 *(The Cairngorms – Aviemore & Glen Avon)*. The SMC's guide *The Cairngorms* is an invaluable reference.

The most popular approach is from the Lairig Ghru path by Allt Druidh to a minor track junction about 150m south of the Chalamain Gap path junction (see the Chalamain Gap & the Lairig Ghru walk earlier). Rather than return the same way, a descent west into and down Gleann Einich makes a much more interesting and varied walk. Extending the walk to Sgor an Lochain Uaine and Cairn Toul would add 4mi (6.5km), 300m ascent and about two hours.

The walk starts and finishes at Whitewell car park at the end of the road between Inverdruie and Blackpark. It is also possible to start from Coylumbridge.

A short path leads to a north-south vehicle track. Follow this to Lochan Deo and head east to reach the Lairig Ghru path near the Cairngorm Club footbridge.

From the Chalamain Gap junction, the first part of the climb, south-west from Allt Druidh, scales the steep heathery slope where the path is deeply eroded in places. Once you gain the ridge, the direction changes to south-east then south up to a broad plateau topped by Sròn na Lairige (1184m). Cross a small saddle then climb to the summit of Braeriach, spectacularly overlooking the Lairig Ghru. Continue along the rim for a few hundred metres then head south-west to cross a burn, the headwaters of the River Dee and the highest spring in Britain at 1190m. Go on to Carn na Criche (1265m).

To reach the other two Munros, keep to the rim all the way, then retrace your steps towards Carn na Criche. About 600m northwest of the saddle, west of Sgor an Lochain Uaine, set a compass course westwards, unless you find a faint path, to the top of the pass into Gleann Einich beside Allt Coire Dhondail

To skip the extra peaks and go directly to Glen Einich from Carn na Criche, head down generally south-westwards on an indeterminate path. The start of the descent is marked with a large cairn beside Allt Coire Dhondail. The path leads to a precarious traverse of a small cliff then descends to the vehicle track near Loch Einich. Follow this back to Whitewell or Coylumbridge.

Keep in mind, for a misty overcast day, that the walk into Loch Einich and back is well worth doing by itself.

MEALL A' BHUACHAILLE

This shapely hill (the name means 'Shepherd's Hill') overlooks Glenmore and Loch Morlich and gives superb views of the whole Cairn Gorm plateau and Braeriach from its summit (810m). A path waymarked with orange banded posts leads north from behind the Glenmore Forest visitors centre and climbs steeply through the pines to open moorland. From here a clear path leads up to a broad saddle between Creagan Gorm (782m) to the west and the Meall, then on up to the summit. To make a circular walk, continue eastwards on the path down the broad spur to Ryvoan Bothy and follow the vehicle track down past beautiful An Lochan Uaine (green lake), Glenmore Lodge and back to Glenmore village. Allow three hours for this 6mi (9.5km) walk, which includes 480m of climbing. It is covered by the Harvey

Superwalker 1:25,000 map *Cairn Gorm* and the OS Landranger 1:50,000 map No 36 *(Grantown & Aviemore)*.

LOCH AVON

Dramatically beautiful Loch Avon is almost surrounded by cliffs – the precipitous slopes of the Cairn Gorm plateau to the north, and Carn Etchachan (1120m) and Beinn Mheadoin (1182m) to the south. It can be seen from the edge of Cairn Gorm's broad summit, glinting in the sun (sometimes!) far below. The loch is the very scenic centrepiece of this long, generally low-level walk, round the eastern side of an outlier of the plateau. The approach to Loch Avon and the lower reaches of Strath Nethy can be very wet, so keep this walk for a dry spell. The distance is 21mi (34km), with 470m of ascent, for which you should allow at least 8½ hours. The walk could be spread over two days, pitching a tent near the tiny Fords of Avon refuge – a windowless stone hut. This would allow time for climbing some of the alluring hills nearby – Bynack More (1090m) and Beinn Mheadoin. Both the Harvey 1:25,000 *Cairn Gorm* and the OS Landranger 1:50,000 map No 36 *(Grantown & Aviemore)* cover the walk.

From Glenmore, walk up the road past Glenmore Lodge and An Lochan Uaine and on to Bynack Stable – a small tin shed. A wide and muddy path continues south-east from here up a broad hillside, over the shoulder of Bynack More, down slightly and on across its eastern slopes to the Fords of Avon. Turn west from the refuge – the path of sorts is faint for several hundred metres until the flanking slopes close in. Keep close to the youthful River Avon up to Loch Avon and continue along its northern shore for just over half a mile to a path diverging uphill. Follow this up to the Saddle (807m), then make your way down Strath Nethy – the path varies from good to invisible – to Bynack Stable and back to Glenmore.

SOUTHERN CAIRNGORMS

Looking south and south-east from the summit of Cairn Gorm, you can see a host of broad-backed hills, many of which are separated by long deep glens. There's enough high- and low-level walking here to occupy several weeks.

The **Lairig Ghru** walk (see earlier) can be extended via Derry Lodge to Braemar on the River Dee; it also links with a right of way southwards through **Glen Tilt** to the village of Blair Atholl (on the A9 and the railway), and another that you can follow west through **Glen Feshie** to finish up at Kingussie in Strathspey.

On the eastern side of the Cairn Gorm plateau there's a long-established route, accessible from Glenmore, via Bynack Stable and the Fords of Avon (as outlined earlier in this section) through **Lairig an Laoigh** to Derry Lodge and the Linn of Dee near Braemar. Thus it's possible to circumnavigate the plateau via Lairig Ghru to Derry Lodge and Lairig an Laoigh.

Farther east in Deeside and south of the town of Ballater are **Lochnagar** (1155m) and **Loch Muick**, both deservedly popular walks. A few miles south of Braemar, **Jocks Road**, a public footpath, crosses high ground not far south of Lochnagar to Glen Doll on the southern fall of the uplands.

Two Harvey Superwalker 1:25,000 maps cover this area – *Cairn Gorm* and *Lochnagar*. You can also use the OS Landranger 1:50,000 maps No 36 *(Grantown & Aviemore)*, No 43 *(Braemar & Blair Atholl)* and No 44 *(Ballater & Glen Clova)*. There are TICs at Braemar (☎ 01339-741600) and Ballater (☎ 01339-755306).

SPEYSIDE WAY

This long-distance path (LDP) links Aviemore and Buckie on the north coast and generally follows the course of the River Spey. An outline of this varied route is given in the Scotland Long-Distance Paths chapter.

THE CAIRNGORMS

The Western Highlands

For serious walkers the Western Highlands is heaven. This is a remote and starkly beautiful highland area, sparsely populated, with lovely glens and lochs, and some of the finest mountains in Britain – some say Europe. The sheer number of peaks and their infinite variety attracts walkers from all over the country, year after year. On these small and crowded islands of Britain, this is as close as it gets to real wilderness. But the emptiness integral to this area's charms can make logistics difficult for walkers on a short visit from abroad, especially if you are relying on public transport. For those who have the time, the effort will be well rewarded. All this is contained in the area between Glen Moriston and Glen Shiel in the south and Ullapool in the north, and bounded in the east by a line running through Garve.

In summer the clear air provides rich colours, and (sometimes) great views from the ridges and summits. In winter the views can be clear but the weather often makes walking a much more serious enterprise. Snow and ice will turn the steep ground on the three walks described into something akin to mountaineering terrain (especially Beinn Alligin and An Teallach). At any time of year the walking can be hard, so this is no place to begin learning mountain techniques. But if you are a fit, competent and well-equipped walker, the Western Highlands will not disappoint.

The routes we describe in this section are nontechnical (ie, no ropes), have relatively easy access (by car or public transport) and

> ### Warning
> One final reminder – all the routes as described in this chapter are for summer. In Scotland this means May to September, although weather conditions can be bad at any time of the year. Scottish mountain walking in winter (October to April) is a different game – more like mountaineering – and not covered in this book.

have good accommodation options nearby. They are but a mere taste of the fine opportunities available, with several other classic walks in each of the Glen Shiel, Torridon and Great Wilderness areas. Farther north, beyond Ullapool, the wild landscapes of Inverpolly and Sutherland offer exciting walks and scrambles on mountains like Stac Polly, Suliven and Quinag (see the Other Walks in Scotland chapter for more details).

INFORMATION
Books
A couple of publications by the Scottish Mountaineering Club (SMC), *The Northwest Highlands* by DJ Bennett & T Strang, and *The Munros Hillwalkers Guide*, edited by Donald Bennett, provide a good introduction to the area.

Information Sources
The main Tourist Information Centres (TICs) for the Western Highlands are in Gairloch (☎ 01445-712130, ℮ gairlochhost.co.uk); Inverness (☎ 01463-234353); Kyle of Lochalsh (☎ 01599-534276, ℮ kyleoflochalsh@host.co.uk); Lochcarron (☎ 01520-722357), which is open Easter to September; and Ullapool (☎ 0184-612135, ℮ ullapool@host.co.uk). All are informative and well staffed, selling maps and guidebooks and providing weather forecasts for the area. The overall Web site for the whole of the Highlands is Ⓦ www.host.co.uk, and the general email address is ℮ info@host.co.uk.

Guided Walks
Mountain guides based in the Western Highlands (at Lochcarron) include well-known and very experienced guide Martin Moran (☎ 01520-722361, ℮ martin.moran@btinternet.com, Ⓦ www.moran-mountain.co.uk), who also has several books to his credit.

As well as localised guided walks, Martin organises a series of courses. Most are for technical rock and ice climbers, but the spring/autumn 'North-West Ridges' course

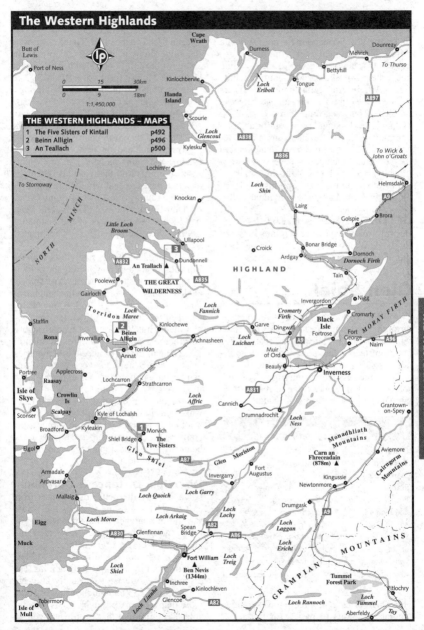

The Western Highlands

THE WESTERN HIGHLANDS – MAPS

1:1,450,000

THE WESTERN HIGHLANDS

is designed for reasonably adventurous walkers to appreciate the hardest mountains of North-West Scotland in the company of a guide. No technical rock climbing is required. Instruction is given in map reading and other 'hill skills'. Mountains include Beinn Alligin, An Teallach, the Five Sisters (all described in this book) and some peaks on Skye. The week-long course costs £320 and includes food and very comfortable accommodation. Martin also runs a 'Winter Munros' course giving a basic foundation in the skills and techniques necessary to approach the Scottish mountains in winter.

For other guided walk options see Planning in the introduction to individual walks.

GETTING THERE & AWAY

For information on travel options between England, Wales and Scotland, see the Getting Around chapter.

Glen Shiel

Travelling west to the Isle of Skye you pass through what appears to be the impenetrable Glen Shiel. The winding road snakes between steep-sided, rock-encrusted mountains, soaring skywards to the north, and rising almost as steeply and ruggedly to the south. The long spiky ridge to the north is known as the Five Sisters of Kintail.

The Five Sisters of Kintail

Distance	7.5mi (12km)
Duration	6¾–8 hours
Standard	hard
Start	car park at Glen Shiel
Finish	Ault a' chruinn
Gateways	Ault a' chruinn, Morvich, Shiel Bridge

Summary One of the finest ridge walks in Scotland – an arduous but immensely scenic walk over rough ground, traversing some narrow ridges along mostly clear, well-used paths.

This chain of elegant, precipitous summits, separated by slits of passes (or bealachs),

falls away vertiginously to Glen Shiel on one side and to the more remote and peaceful Gleann Lichd on the other. To the north-west the ridge drops a little less steeply to the shores of beautiful Loch Duich. Three of the sisters are Munros (peaks over 914m, 3000ft) – Sgùrr Fhuaran, or 'Peak of the Springs' (1067m), Sgùrr na Càrnach, or 'Rocky Peak' (1002m) and Sgùrr na Ciste Duibhe, or 'Peak of the Black Coffin' (1027m). The other two, at the north end of the ridge, are Sgùrr nan Saighead, or 'Peak of the Arrows' (929m) and Sgùrr na Moraich, or 'Mighty Peak' (876m). And that isn't all: There are also two peaks to deal with before you even reach the southernmost sister – Beinn Odhar, or 'Dun-Coloured Peak' (878m), and Sgùrr nan Spainteach, or 'Peak of the Spaniards' (990m). See the boxed text 'The Spanish Connection'.

The ridge commands fine views with the Torridon mountains punctuating the horizon to the north-west, the Isle of Skye spread-eagled across the western skyline and the islands of Canna, Eigg and Rum sailing between the rugged south-western peaks – and much, much more. The whole ridge is within the National Trust for Scotland's West Kintail Estate, so access is at all times.

The Five Sisters are very exposed and can be extremely hazardous in poor visibility, strong wind or rain, so it's worth waiting for the right day for this classic ridge walk. This is also important because there's a lot of loose rock along the ridge, especially on the descents into and climbs out of bealachs, so considerable care is needed for your own and others' safety.

Direction, Distance & Duration

Far and away the better direction is from east to west – walking towards the views, starting at a higher point than where you finish, and with a slightly less steep and knee-jarring descent. The distance given is to Ault a' chruinn. If you're staying at Morvich or Shiel Bridge, add about a mile. The distance of 7.5mi isn't unusually long but the ascent of 1530m, which is nearly 100m more than a romp up Ben Nevis, is remarkable. Keep in mind that even when you've reached the highest point on the walk (Sgùrr Fhuaran) the climbing isn't over – there are still two peaks to go. It should take you about 6¾ to eight hours to complete.

Alternatives Once you're on the ridge, escape routes are few. People do go down to Glen Shiel via the spur from Sgùrr Fhuaran, but this is seriously steep. Routes to and from Gleann Lichd, on the other side, are feasible and, indeed, have much to recommend them. There is a clear path up to the ridge at Bealach an Làpain from Glenlicht House, and the long ridge thrusting eastwards from Sgùrr Fhuaran offers a fairly straightforward climb or descent.

PLANNING
Maps
The Harvey Superwalker 1:25,000 map *Kintail, Glen Shiel* covers the Five Sisters and has some background information and local contacts. The relevant OS Landranger 1:50,000 map is No 33 *(Loch Alsh, Glen Shiel & Loch Hourn)*.

Information Sources
The Glen Shiel TIC (☎ 01599-511264), beside Kintail Lodge Hotel near the end of the walk, is open from Easter to the end of September.

PLACES TO STAY & EAT
Ault a' chruinn
Right at the end of the walk is *Glomach House* (☎ *01599-511382)*, in a superb location, charging from £17.50 for B&B. On the main road nearby, *Port Bhan Restaurant* (☎ *01599-511347)* offers a small menu in pleasant surroundings and also has a takeaway service. There's an off-licence close by. About a mile south is *Kintail Lodge Hotel* (☎ *01599-511275)*, where walkers are particularly welcome at the Trekkers Lodge, which costs £23.50 for B&B; the bar suppers are better than average.

About a mile north of Ault a' chruinn is secluded *Morvich Caravan Club Site* (☎ *01599-511354)*, where camping costs £2.60 per person and £2 per tent on well-grassed pitches.

Shiel Bridge
In Shiel Bridge there's the small *Shiel Bridge Caravan & Campsite* (☎ *01599-511211)*; the tariff is £3 per person plus £1 per tent. Its vintage facilities were due to be flattened and replaced for summer 2001. The nearby *Five Sisters Restaurant* (☎ *01599-511211)* has a rather imaginative menu, including a vegetarian choice, and serves Black Isle and Isle of Skye beers. The adjacent shop has a good range of supplies.

GETTING TO/FROM THE WALK
Bus Scottish Citylink buses (☎ 0870-550 5050) on the Edinburgh and Glasgow to Uig (Isle of Skye) service (via Fort William) stop at Shiel Bridge, as do Scottish Citylink buses on the Inverness to Portree run. Both services are daily. These buses are particularly useful if you need to return to the start of the walk to pick up your car. The nearest bus stop to the start of the walk is at the Cluanie Inn, about 5mi (8km) east of the starting point.

Train Fort William, Inverness and Kyle of Lochalsh (between Glen Shiel and Skye) are served by ScotRail (☎ 0845-755 0033) trains from Glasgow and Edinburgh, but you will, of course, need to connect with buses to reach Glen Shiel.

The Spanish Connection

In the long struggle between government and Jacobite forces, which ended at the Battle of Culloden in 1745, a lesser known battle took place right here in Glen Shiel. In June 1719 Jacobite troops, including a Spanish regiment, landed at Eilean Donan Castle beside Loch Duich. Government troops came from Inverness and the two sides met about a mile west of the starting point for this walk (there is a National Trust for Scotland interpretive sign at the site). The government troops routed the Jacobites and the last to flee were the Spanish, who dashed up the mountainside to the pass now called Bealach nan Spainteach and down into Gleann Lichd.

Car Glen Shiel is on the A87 trunk road, which branches off the A82 (Inverness to Fort William and Glasgow) at Invergarry and extends to Portree (Skye). The walk starts at an informal car park off the A87, identified on the Harvey map (see Maps & Books). The car park is distinguished by a vehicle height barrier and is immediately east of a small open area between pine plantations.

The walk finishes on the minor road to Morvich in the hamlet of Ault a' chruinn, beside Loch Duich.

THE WALK
Glen Shiel Car Park to Sgùrr na Ciste Duibhe
2mi (3km), 2½–3 hours

Follow a narrow path from the western edge of the plantation, next to the car park, and climb the steep bracken and grass-covered hillside. After a few hundred metres of ascent the path angles across to the right (east), to the northern edge of the plantation, which

it parallels for about 200m. Then turn off left (north) along a path leading straight up a subtly defined spur to meet the ridge at Bealach an Làpain. Suddenly you're in a different world – surrounded by mountains and deep glens, for the moment out of earshot of the traffic noise on the road below.

Turn west along the ridge crest and follow the well-worn path up to a breezy arête and on over the twin bumps of Beinn Odhar. Then comes a shallow dip and a rocky climb to Sgùrr nan Spainteach. A scramble down the face of a bluff takes you to the amazingly narrow Bealach nan Spainteach. Make your way up through the boulders to the neat summit cairn on Sgùrr na Ciste Duibhe, the first of the Five Sisters. Here you can look east towards Glen Affric through the gap at the top of Gleann Lichd and, in the opposite direction, contemplate the serrated skyline of the Isle of Skye beyond Loch Duich.

Sgùrr na Ciste Duibhe to Sgùrr Fhuaran
1.5mi (2.5km), 1½–1¾ hours

The ridge changes direction, leading northwest as you continue down to Bealach na Craoibhe ('Pass of the Tree'), keeping to the highest ground in the absence of a clear path. The line of ascent then turns north up to Sgùrr na Càrnach, the second Sister. From here new features in the panorama include Lochs Affric and Benevean to the east. The first bit of the descent is down a narrow cleft to the left, then bear right to regain the line of the ridge and go down to Bealach na Càrnach. A steep, rocky, twisting path takes care of the climb to Sgùrr Fhuaran, the highest point on the ridge and the third Sister. From here the view is just as absorbing as those from her siblings.

Sgùrr Fhuaran to Sgùrr na Moraich
2.5mi (4km), 1¾–2 hours

Leaving the summit cairn take care to head north-west, then north, on this awesome and spectacular descent to Bealach Bhuidhe. The path then traverses above the dramatic sheets of cliffs leading up to Sgùrr nan Saighead, Sister number four. The ridge now changes

The Five Sisters of Kintail

character with more small, rocky knobs to negotiate on the way down and up to Beinn Bhuidhe (yellow hill). A rough path drops down to a narrow gap, with fine views of Gleann Lichd below. Climb straight up and soon the path follows a more even course among rocky outcrops and across grass, for a pleasant change, and finally up to **Sgùrr na Moraich**, Sister number five.

Sgùrr na Moraich to Ault a' chruinn

1.5mi (2.5km), 1–1¼ hours

Having led north-west from the summit, straight towards the Skye Bridge, the path fades into insignificance. Keep well to the left of the broad spur, generally north-west (or about 300 degrees magnetic), as you descend very steeply over grass and heather, steering away from the small cliffs bristling on the crest of the spur. Keep your eye on the crags on the western side of Allt a' chruinn as a guide to the best route down to a narrow path, high above the stream. Follow it down to a stile and continue to a water treatment works. Turn right along a vehicle track, which becomes a bitumen road and meets the Morvich road in Ault a' chruinn, about 200m from its junction with the A87.

Torridon

The celebrated Torridon peaks provide every delectation the rambler could desire: deep corries, imposing buttresses, airy pinnacles and magnificent views. Nowhere in Britain do mountains so proclaim their individuality.

Irvine Butterfield
The High Mountains of Britain & Ireland

The Torridon mountains mark the southern edge of the Flowerdale Forest – a wild and complex area of lochans, moors and peaks. The quote above is just one of many, reflecting the wonder that this area holds for walkers.

Within the Torridon group are three major mountains. Liathach (pronounced lee-attack by English people and lee-agaph by the locals) is a massive wall of a mountain with several peaks along its central ridge, including Mullach an Rathain (1023m) and Spidean a Choire Léith (1054m). Next is Beinn Alligin, again with several peaks, the highest being Sgùrr Mhór (986m). East of Liathach is Beinn Eighe (972m), not quite as high as Liathach but with several outliers, making it bigger 'on the ground'. A fourth mountain in this area is Beinn Dearg (914m), wedged between Alligin and Liathach. At first Beinn Dearg seems insignificant but its full glory becomes apparent when seen from one of the neighbouring peaks.

Beinn Alligin

Distance	6.5mi (10.5km)
Duration	6–8 hours
Standard	medium-hard
Start/Finish	Torridon House Bridge
Gateways	Torridon, Kinlochewe, Gairloch

Summary An immensely rewarding circuit of a horseshoe ridge crossing two major summits. It involves several steep and exposed sections and some scrambling.

Many Torridon routes are serious undertakings, often with technical manoeuvres, and are beyond the scope of this book. However, Beinn Alligin's summit, Sgùrr Mhór (986m) and the peak Tom na Gruagaich (922m) can both be reached without technical difficulties, although this is still a serious mountain walk and not suitable for the unfit or inexperienced. As Scottish peaks go, this mountain is relatively easy to 'do' and is a splendid introduction to the area's walking potential. Sgùrr Mhór and Tom na Gruagaich, both Munros, and three spectacular subsidiary peaks, the Horns of Alligin, are linked by a ridge curving round the huge corrie Toll a Mhadaidh Mor (the fox hole). Even more dramatic is the great gash of Eag Dhubh (the black cleft) in the back wall of the corrie, running from the summit ridge to the base and appearing to split the mountain in two.

According to the commentators, Beinn Alligin means 'Beautiful Mountain' or 'Mountain of Jewels'. Either way, it's definitely a gcm – a mountain that allows walkers to get a feel for the high and wild Scottish peaks without having to be a mountaineer or cover long approach routes. Relatively easy transport and numerous accommodation options are further attractions; you can be on top of the world at lunchtime and safely back down in the glen in time for tea. A further plus is that this mountain is owned by the National Trust for Scotland, so there are no access restrictions.

Like all the Scottish mountain routes described in this book, it should be done in summer only. When covered in snow and ice, many sections of this walk become dangerous. Even in summer patches of snow lurk in shaded corners, the mist can be thick and the winds strong enough to blow you over. There are no signposts and only a few cairns, so map and compass knowledge is essential if the mist comes down (always likely). In places you will find a well-defined path on top, formed by the erosion of many feet, but this should not be followed blindly as side paths can also lead off to dead-end lookouts and other potential difficulties.

Direction, Distance & Duration
This is a circular walk and can be done in either direction. We recommend going anti-clockwise. This way you do the peaks early in the route before fatigue strikes.

On the map the distance is 6.5mi but, on steep and broken ground, this figure is almost meaningless. The route starts near the shore of a sea-loch and you gain almost 1000m on your way to the top, plus another 300m or so between the main peaks, so walking time is likely to be at least six hours. Add extra for lunch and photos, and you'll need at least seven to eight hours.

PLANNING
Maps & Books
The OS Landranger 1:50,000 maps No 19 *(Gairloch & Ullapool)* and No 24 *(Raasay & Applecross)* overlap on Beinn Alligin. OS Outdoor Leisure 1:25,000 map No 8 *(The Cuillin and Torridon Hills)*, neatly covering the area, is much more useful, as is Harvey's Superwalker 1:25,000 map *Torridon*.

Torridon – A Walkers Guide by Peter Barton gives details of low- and high-level routes in the Torridon area.

Information Sources
Torridon Countryside Centre (☎ 01445-791221) is just off the A896, opposite the youth hostel in Torridon. Before heading for the high peaks you can check the weather forecast here. It is open 10am to 5pm Monday to Saturday, and 2pm to 5pm on Sunday, and has displays and information about the landscape and wildlife of the National Trust for Scotland estate. It also sells maps and guidebooks relating to the area. Other TICs in the area are at Gairloch (☎ 01445-712130) and Lochcarron (☎ 01520-722357).

Guided Walks
National Trust for Scotland rangers based at the Torridon Countryside Centre (see Information Sources) organise day walks on Alligin and other peaks in the area. Guided walks are run three times a week during July and August, and cost £5, leaving the visitors centre at 10am. One is a high-level walk but does not climb any mountains, while the other is a Torridon ridge walk. Check with the visitors centre for more information.

The well-known guide, Martin Moran (☎ 01520-722361, e martin.moran@btinternet.com, W www.moran-mountain.co.uk), organises walks in the Torridon mountains starting at £130 per day, which is reasonable if shared between a small group.

Discover Torridon (☎ 01445-791218) also offers guided walks in the area. Island Horizons (☎ 01520-722232) runs a series of week-long holidays in many parts of Scotland, including Skye and the Torridons, starting from £300 all-inclusive. Some weeks are for women only or exclusively for over 60s.

PLACES TO STAY & EAT
Torridon
The small village of Torridon nestles between the steep slopes of Liathach and Upper Loch Torridon. On a good day its situation is inspiring but in bad weather, when mist engulfs the village, the impression can be oppressive.

Torridon Campsite (☎ *01349-868486*), opposite the National Trust for Scotland visitors centre, is run by a friendly local woman who arrives to collect fees (£3 per tent) on a moped, which is sure to wake the heaviest sleeper. It is basic but has water, toilets and a coin-operated shower. The nearby *Torridon SYHA Hostel* (☎ *01349-791284*) is open between February and October and costs £9.25. It has a drying room and posts local weather forecasts daily, but the staff can be pedantic rather than friendly.

There is a small but well-stocked shop and post office, open 9.30am to 6pm Monday to Saturday, and 10am to noon and 4pm to 6pm on Sunday. The nearest bank is 50km away in Gairloch, so bring plenty of cash with you.

Annat

Annat is just across the loch from Torridon and boasts the undoubted top spot of the area. *Loch Torridon Hotel* (☎ *01349-791296*) is elegant and atmospheric, and B&B costs from £50. There is a full dinner menu but prices start from £6 for a pot of tea for two! *Ben Damph Lodge* (☎ *01349-791296*), next door, is affiliated to the hotel but aimed at a more down-to-earth clientele. B&B prices in the lodge range from £46 for a single room to £18 per person in a six-bunk room. There is an excellent bar menu with main courses starting at £5.

There are also several B&Bs in the area. *Annat Lodge* (☎ *01349-791200*), *Mrs MacKay* (☎ *01349-791315*) and *Mrs Wrigglesworth* (☎ *01349-791293*) all offer B&B for £17 to £20 and can all be found within a mile of the Countryside Centre.

There is free Internet access and petrol pumps at Ben Damph Lodge.

GETTING TO/FROM THE WALK
Bus & Train There are good Scottish Citylink (☎ 0870-550 5050) connections from Edinburgh and Glasgow to both Inverness and Kyle of Lochalsh. Inverness also has good rail connections.

Between Inverness and Kyle of Lochalsh there are four trains a day (two on Sunday), in each direction, that stop at Strathcarron. The best trains to connect with the local bus

to Torridon arrive at Strathcarron, from both directions, around 12.35pm.

The local bus runs daily (except Sunday) in summer, and Monday, Wednesday and Friday in winter. Times and services are subject to change so check the latest timetable with the operator, Duncan Maclennan (☎ 01520-755239), or a local TIC.

There's also a postbus service (☎ 01246-546329) leaving Achnasheen (on the railway line between Inverness and Kyle) every day (except Sunday) at 12.10pm, passing through Torridon at 2.55pm and along the shore of Loch Torridon (past the start of this walk, although too late for walkers) to Inveralligin and Diabaig, before returning to Achnasheen.

The start of the walk is a large bridge (Torridon House Bridge) about 2mi west of Torridon. You can start and finish the walk at the village, adding an extra 5mi (two hours) to the overall distance. Of course Beinn Alligin is a popular mountain and you may be offered a lift by other walkers.

Car Torridon lies at the eastern end of Loch Torridon, on the main A890/896 between Kyle of Lochalsh and Kinlochewe, which is on the A832 between Gairloch and Inverness. There is a busy car park beside Torridon House Bridge, the start of the walk, about 2mi west of Torridon on the road to Inveralligin.

THE WALK
Torridon House Bridge to Sgùrr Mhór
3.5mi (5.5km), 3–4 hours
From the bridge a path leads up the east bank of the Coire Mhic Nobuil river, through a small wood and then into moorland. The path leads you into a triangular sloping bowl, between the three main Torridon mountains. Straight ahead is the blunt western wall of Beinn Dearg. To the right (east) is the western end of Liathach and to the left (west) is Beinn Alligin. The path crosses a footbridge and aims roughly north, towards the eastern end of the Alligin horseshoe ridge.

As you get higher the path becomes indistinct but continue up the crest of the broad and very steep ridge, using your hands for balance while negotiating some rocky steps and aim for the three Horns of Alligin. You reach the base of the first horn about 1½ to two hours from the start. You can scramble over this and the next two rocky peaks, or keep your hands in your pockets and take the path that tends left, avoiding the peaks on their southern side.

After the third horn drop to a small col and then go up again, swinging round to the left (north-west) and keeping the steep drop down into the corrie on your left. To your right (north-east) the view really begins to open out – a beautifully jumbled mosaic of lochans, moors and smaller peaks, with Loch Maree beyond and the coast town of Gairloch visible on the bay. Behind, too, the view keeps on getting better – down the corrie and over Loch Torridon, then up again to the mountains around Beinn Damph.

With all this to look at time flies and you soon reach **Sgùrr Mhór** (three to four hours

from the start). With the extra height your view is almost 360 degrees – range upon range of wonderful peaks, too numerous to mention, spread out in all directions. Most notable to the south-west are the Cuillin Hills on the Isle of Skye and to the east the summits of Beinn Eighe, where exposed quartz makes them appear eternally snowcapped.

Sgùrr Mhór to Torridon House Bridge

3mi (5km), 3–4 hours

From the summit head north-west, down a grassy slope and keeping the corrie edge to the left. We've been expounding on the views, but there's more than half a chance of bad weather and limited visibility up here. If this is the case take particular care on this section as the top of **Eag Dhubh**, the giant gash that dominates the view from below, is hereabouts, just waiting to trap the unwary

Beinn Alligin

Beinn Eighe Mountain Trail

If all this high Scottish mountain stuff is just too daunting, but you'd still like to do something on foot in this wonderful area, you might consider the Beinn Eighe Mountain Trail. This waymarked route is only 4mi long and takes in the best low- to mid-level terrain in the Beinn Eighe National Nature Reserve, including beautiful stands of native Scots pine. There is a short, steep section of rocky ground to negotiate to reach the higher section, where the path weaves past secluded lochans and offers a real impression of being in the heart of the mountains. There are also wonderful views of the Beinn Eighe massif and across Loch Maree to Slioch.

The walk starts and finishes on the banks of Loch Maree, a few miles west of Kinlochewe (on the main road to Gairloch), about 18mi from Torridon. You should allow two hours, and take the usual precautions with footwear, waterproofs and food. A booklet produced by Scottish Natural Heritage has a map of the route, and plenty of information about local wildlife and geology. This should be available from the nearby visitors centre or in local TICs.

The ruins of a medieval stronghold overlooking Loch Ranza, on the Isle of Arran

Like a scene from Tolkien, the West Highland Way crosses the ancient peat bogs of Rannoch Moor

The rugged Goatfell massif on the Isle of Arran provides some challenging ridge walks

As the clouds part, a glimpse of sun on the mighty hills of Glen Coe

Rising out of a sea of mist, Buachaille Etive Mór at dawn

walker in mist. If, however, the day is clear, the cliffs on either side of the gully frame the view of the glen far below – one of many classic vistas associated with walking in Scotland. (Don't try to descend this way.)

After Eag Dhubh go steeply up again, over large boulders, to reach **Tom na Gruagaich**, about one to 1½ hours from Sgùrr Mhór. There's a trig point to lean against as you have a last look at the view before starting to descend. It is possible to follow the ridge all the way down but most people take the small corrie between the main western ridge and the one that extends from Tom na Gruagaich. The descent is steep but straightforward. Walk south into Coire nan Laogh, dropping steeply on an eroded path with several small streams gurgling along beside. The steep walls of the corrie funnel you down to a rocky plateau where the descent eases briefly before descending steeply again towards the car park and bridge. The path splits twice on the way down but quickly rejoins, so don't worry when you meet junctions – everything is going to the finish. The last section of path is quite rough and feels difficult after the efforts of the day, passing through an area fenced for native forest regrowth. The descent from Tom na Gruagaich to the finish will take around two hours.

The Great Wilderness

The Great Wilderness is a particularly remote area of the Western Highlands, stretching from Little Loch Broom in the north to Loch Maree in the south, and from the Fannich Hills in the east to the west coast village of Poolewe. In total the area covers about 180 sq mi. For visitors from countries where wilderness areas are a bit larger, this title may seem exaggerated, but within these boundaries there are no roads or houses, and no cafes, pubs or shops selling tartan walking sticks – by British standards, wilderness indeed.

The landscape is mountainous with some fine, austere peaks. There are lochs and

lochans of all shapes and sizes, rivers and waterfalls, peat bogs and grassy valleys, but very few trees. It may seem strange when you see Fisherfield Forest, Letterewe Forest and Dundonnell Forest on the map, but 'forest' here means hunting ground; this is prime deer-stalking country and must be avoided between 15 August and 15 October (see the boxed text 'Stalking' on p499).

An Teallach

Distance	14mi (22.5km)
Duration	7½–9 hours
Standard	hard
Start	Corrie Hallie
Finish	Dundonnell
Gateways	Dundonnell, Gairloch, Ullapool

Summary A long, tough mountain walk in a remote area. Paths are faint, and there is some exposure and scrambling. Bad weather is always a possibility. Aptitude with a map and compass is essential, and the walk is for experienced hill walkers only.

An Teallach is one of Scotland's finest mountains, standing proudly on the edge of the Great Wilderness and a classic in anyone's book. An Teallach (pronounced an chelluck) means 'the forge', a name that bears no relation to its shape ('the castle' might be better) but comes from the mountain's red sandstone, which glows like a smithy's fire when lit by the setting sun. There is no denying the drama of the effect, especially when seen from the coast. The shadows of a summer evening throw into greater relief the fortifications of An Teallach's renowned and rocky ridge, which forms the highlight of the route described.

Like the mountain, the route is a classic – one of Britain's best high-mountain traverses. For Munro baggers Sgùrr Fiona (1060m) and Bidein a' Ghlas Thuill (1062m) can be ticked off, and eight 'tops' are thrown in for good measure. In fine weather the ridge crest is an exciting scramble on good rock, although there are parts that are difficult, with a fair degree of exposure.

These can all be avoided, however, as a path running below the ridge misses the trickiest bits. In bad weather, strong winds, wet rock and slippery ground make the route a much less secure proposition, and in winter the ridge becomes a serious mountaineering expedition.

Whatever the conditions, it is not a route to be undertaken lightly and should be avoided by those who lack the experience or the skills. Once on the mountain there are no paths marked on the map. Escape routes are limited but detailed in the following walk description. There is little water on the ridge so bring plenty, and a short walking rope (and knowledge of how to use it properly) could offer extra security. The weather is also notoriously changeable, so bring clothes in anticipation of all weather conditions.

An Teallach, then, is for connoisseurs and experienced hill walkers who are well prepared, well equipped and adept with map and compass. Its ascent and traverse make for a long and demanding but immensely satisfying mountain walk. From the ridge and summits you have unrivalled views across the Great Wilderness and its less accessible mountain peaks. On clear days you can see to the Torridon mountains in the south, the far-off hills of the distant north, the beautiful coastline of Wester Ross and the islands of the Outer Hebrides. If the cloud is down you will have to imagine it all and buy a nice picture book later.

The Sale of An Teallach

At the time of writing, the ownership of the 2320-hectare Eilean Daroch estate that contains most of An Teallach had just changed hands for a cool £1.7 million. Although the identity of the owner is not known, it is thought that the good access that the public have traditionally enjoyed will not be affected. It was hoped that the John Muir Trust, which recently bought Ben Nevis (see the boxed text in the Ben Nevis & Glen Coe chapter), could have made a bid, but it was already too far stretched by the Ben Nevis purchase.

Direction, Distance & Duration

By following the direction described you start on an easy path leading to the foot of the ridge, which is best traversed south to north. The walk covers a total distance of 14mi but because of the nature of the route, which involves at least 1300m of ascent and some tortuous descents, not to mention tricky navigation, this takes a minimum seven to 8½ hours. Add to this time for rests, lunch, navigation and admiring the view, and you should allow between eight and 10 hours. The nearest accommodation is about 2mi from the start so, if you don't tie in with the bus, allow extra time to walk this.

Alternatives This route can either be circular or almost circular, depending on whether or not you have left transport at the starting point. If you don't have transport it is more convenient to go directly to Dundonnell. Alternative finishes to Corrie Hallie are listed at the end of the walk description.

The second alternative finish offers a continuation of the scrambling encountered on the ridge and provides a more challenging end to the day for those who just can't get enough of a good thing!

As is often the case in Scotland, getting off the mountain is sometimes harder than getting up it. Whichever way you go, navigation is particularly important to avoid dropping into the wrong valley.

PLANNING
Maps

An Teallach and the Great Wilderness are on the OS Landranger 1:50,000 map No 19 (*Gairloch & Ullapool*), which also covers the north Torridons.

Information Sources

The nearest TICs are Ullapool (☎ 01854-612135) and Gairloch (☎ 01445-712130), north and south of Dundonnell respectively. They can advise on local transport and accommodation options.

Guided Walks

Celtic Horizons (☎ 01854-612429), Fraser House, West Shore St, Ullapool IV26 2UR,

Stalking

The estates around An Teallach are privately owned and deer stalking takes place at certain times of the year. There is a tradition of mutual tolerance between walkers and stalkers in Scotland, and if there is stalking in the area walkers are asked to avoid it. The main deer stalking season is between 15 August and 15 October. Before setting out for a walk on An Teallach during these months, check at Eilean Darach Lodge (☎01854-633203).

offers outdoor courses and private guiding in the mountains of Inverpolly (north of Ullapool) and the Great Wilderness.

PLACES TO STAY & EAT
Dundonnell

Accommodation in the area is fairly sparse and is well spread out. In Dundonnell the only option is the smart *Dundonnell Hotel* (☎ *01854-633204*), which charges from £50 for B&B. *Badrallach Bothy and Campsite* (☎ *01854-633281*), 6.2mi along a small road on the other side of Little Loch Broom from Dundonnell, charges £4.50.

The Dundonnell Hotel is the only place for eating out. There is a restaurant and also a bar with good food from £5. There is a petrol station with a small shop (open seven days a week) just opposite the hotel. The larger shop and post office of the Dundonnell Stores are actually 5.6mi west along the A832 in Durnamuck. The Dundonnell Stores is open 8am to 6pm from Monday to Saturday, closed on Sunday.

Camusnagaul

About 1.5mi west of Dundonnell, in Camusnagaul, *Sail Mhor Croft Hostel* (☎ *01854-633224*) has good self-catering facilities and costs £8.50 or £13 B&B. It is family-run, oriented towards walkers and the owners are very knowledgeable about the surrounding mountains. Also in Camusnagaul is *Mrs Ross* (☎ *01854-633237*), who charges £17 for B&B. She also has self-catering chalets and caravans to let.

Northern Lights Campsite, 3mi farther west at Badcaul, is basic and not very flat, and charges £4 per pitch plus £1 per person.

GETTING TO/FROM THE WALK

Bus Dundonnell is one of the stops on the Ullapool to Gairloch and Inverness to Gairloch services operated by Westerbus (☎ 01445-712255). The Ullapool bus service operates on Thursday only, leaving Dundonnell at 10.05am and returning from Ullapool at 1.15pm. The Inverness bus runs on Monday, Wednesday and Saturday, departing from Dundonnell at 9am and returning from Inverness at 5.05pm.

The scheduled stop is outside the Dundonnell Hotel, but the driver will pick you up farther along the road near your accommodation if requested, and can also drop you off at Corrie Hallie, the start of the walk.

Car Dundonnell is at the east end of Little Loch Broom, about 100mi west of Inverness on the A832.

The route starts at Corrie Hallie, 2mi south-east of Dundonnell along the B832. There is a lay-by and car park.

THE WALK
Corrie Hallie to Sail Liath

6mi (9.5km), 2½–3 hours

From Corrie Hallie car park go through a gate onto a well-defined track that runs southwards. Climb gradually through silver birch and bracken (plus bluebells in spring), with a burn on your right that is mostly hidden but refreshingly audible. After crossing some stepping stones the path gets steeper, then reaches a rocky plateau (about 45 minutes from the start), with fine views beginning to open out. To the right (west) is the formidable ridge of An Teallach itself. To the left are the hills around Beinn Dearg and the Fannichs, and ahead the peaks of the Great Wilderness begin to appear.

At this point you leave the track (the junction is marked by two cairns), taking a smaller but well-trodden path on your right, which leads to Shenavall. Continue along this path as it gradually rises towards the broad shoulder of Sail Liath, the first of An

Teallach's tops to be tackled. After about 30 minutes from the junction you leave the path (at about its highest point) and strike right (north-west) up the shoulder of Sail Liath.

From here until almost the end of the walk there is no path marked on the map, although you will pick up occasional paths on the ground. Not here, though, as you make your own route, first up a steep slope of shattered boulders, studded with bilberry, juniper and occasional clumps of wild thyme. There is a bit of a scramble to the top of this first steep rise and then it becomes easier as you pass over a grassy slope to the small, rocky

An Teallach

plateau of **Sail Liath** (954m). There is a cairn, wind shelters and the most wonderful view. You now get a much closer view of the ridge to come – the buttresses of Corrag Bhuidhe leading on to the two summits of Sgùrr Fiona and Bidein a' Ghlas Thuill.

Sail Liath to Bidein a' Ghlas Thuill

3mi (5km), 3–3½ hours

From Sail Liath go westwards, down a slippery drop to a narrow gap, then straight back up a steep, rocky path to a minor top (unnamed on the OS map) above Cadha Gobhlach – the forked pass. Descend again, northwards, to the pass. (If the weather is bad there is a possible escape route leading from here down to the right towards Loch Toll an Lochain.) From the pass take a steep path up to the ridge proper, across a rocky outcrop to the foot of Corrag Bhuidhe and the rocky pinnacles beyond.

The next section, from Corrag Bhuidhe to Sgùrr Fiona, is the steepest and most difficult part of the route, and includes an exposed 10m 'bad step' (hard scramble). These difficulties can be avoided by taking a narrow path running left of the buttress wall, south-west of the ridge crest. Even on this 'easier' option you should take care as sheep and previous walkers have created a confusing selection of tracks. So you don't miss the views, there are several points where you can scramble back to the ridge crest, which should, of course, be approached with care. In order to savour at least some of the ridge's delights, aim to regain its crest before the lofty heights of Lord Berkeley's Seat.

For those who decide the conditions are good enough, and the spirit and flesh are both willing and able, keep to the ridge crest. The rocky pinnacles of Corrag Bhuidhe provide a dramatic challenge and some good scrambling on sound rock. The experience is heightened by the sheer cliff faces dropping down to the loch below. The pinnacles lead up to the narrow top of Corrag Bhuidhe (1036m). Continue to clamber along the line of the ridge to reach the bulky form of Lord Berkeley's Seat (1047m). Ahead is the magnificent pointed peak of Sgùrr Fiona.

Leaving Lord Berkeley's Seat, continue along the ridge. Care must still be taken as the scrambling continues. You know the worst is over when you reach a pleasant sandstone stairway leading up to the sharp and stony summit of **Sgùrr Fiona** (1060m). This is another wonderful lookout and a fine place for lunch. After all the excitement of the ridge, this peak feels like the summit but that honour belongs to Fiona's sister, Bidein a' Ghlas Thuill, which is higher by a massive 2m. Still, stay here awhile to admire the peaks, from Suilven and Coigach to the Fannichs, through the peaks of the Great Wilderness like Ruadh Stac Mhor and Slioch, and on to the Torridons. Perhaps the coast is bathed in sunshine and the Summer Isles are living up to their name.

From Fiona, Bidein seems distant, with a lengthy descent and ascent, but take heart, it's not as far as it looks. It is, however, unpleasantly loose underfoot as you go steeply down to the curved gap between the two summits (in emergencies you can descend very steeply from here to Loch Toll an Lochain) and then up again to the **Bidein a' Ghlas Thuill** (1062m) trig point. Take a break and, yes, once again admire the views. Alternatively, of course, you can sit and curse the clouds, and mutter about the unfair lack of view after all that effort.

Bidein a' Ghlas Thuill to Dundonnell

5mi (8km), 2–2½ hours

From the trig point at Bidein a' Ghlas Thuill the most direct way back to Dundonnell goes northwards, by the minor peak and bealach south-west of Glas Mheall Mór, and then down the ridge to the west and north of Coir a Mhuillinn. About halfway down you meet a path, which eventually takes you down to the main road, only 300m east of the Dundonnell Hotel.

Alternatively, from the bealach you can drop into the Coir a Mhuillinn valley itself and follow the stream in a north-easterly direction, contouring north after 2mi or so to pick up the path mentioned above, which leads to Dundonnell. Other alternative finishes are discussed in the sections following.

Alternative Finish: Corrie Hallie via Glas Mheall Mór

4mi (6.5km), 2–2½ hours

To reach Corrie Hallie from Bidein a' Ghlas Thuill, the most straightforward way (which also bags you another peak) is to head north from the summit and then go east to Glas Mheall Mór. This is gained by a pleasant walk along a gentle, north-easterly ridge to the cairn marking the final top of An Teallach. Then it is a steep scramble down loose scree towards the stream that drains the narrow corrie between Glas Mheall Mór and Glas Mheall Liath. Follow this stream down on its north side, passing a little lochan on your right, and you will meet up with a more distinct path, which is designed to allow less ambitious folk to visit the very pleasant waterfalls, where you might like to loiter a while. Or, with the end so near, you may want to push on, eventually reaching the main road opposite Dundonnell House, about 500m north of Corrie Hallie.

Alternative Finish: Corrie Hallie via Glas Mheall Liath

3.5mi (5.5km), 2–2½ hours

This more challenging way to return to Corrie Hallie from Bidein a' Ghlas Thuill includes the summit of Glas Mheall Liath, and may appeal if you want a bit more scrambling and like the 'completeness' of a mountain horseshoe. This route seems to follow more closely the natural sweep of the mountain, although it involves a rather unpleasant bit of descent at the end.

From Bidein you will see Glas Mheall Liath south-east at the end of a narrow and rocky ridge. A path runs along the southern side of this ridge. On your left are some interesting pinnacles of rock, with scrambling options, and good lookouts. On your right you get good views of the ridge you traversed earlier in the day.

The character of the rock changes as you approach Glas Mheall Liath; the Torridonian sandstone is capped with big boulders of grey Cambrian quartzite, and it takes some concentration as you step across them towards the summit cairn. From here, you continue roughly south-east down these unpleasantly steep boulders to reach a heathery terrace and the great stone slabs of the valley side. Finally you meet the stream that drains Loch Toll an Lochain. Follow this downstream to pick up a rather indistinct path, marked by decidedly erratic cairns. You pass a small lochan, then pick up the good path past the waterfalls mentioned above.

Other Walks

GLEN AFFRIC

Immediately north of Glen Shiel (see The Five Sisters walk), **Glen Affric** is considered the most beautiful glen in the Highlands. Loch Affric is untouched and surrounded by expanding native woodlands.

From the village of Cannich, south-west of Inverness, a road leads to the eastern end of Loch Affric. A public right of way from there traverses the glen to *Glen Affric SYHA hostel* (☎ *0870-870 8808*). It continues to Morvich on Loch Duich, an inlet from the west coast, via Bealach an Sgairne or Fionngleann and Gleann Lichd – an outstanding two-day walk. Along the way several fine mountains can occupy a day or three, notably **Beinn Fhada** (1032m) and **Sgùrr nan Ceathreamhnan** (1151m). From near Morvich there's a good path northwards to the awesome **Falls of Glomach**.

The Harvey Superwalker 1:25,000 map *Kintail* covers most of this area. The relevant OS Landranger 1:50,000 maps are No 25 *(Glen Carron & Glen Affric)* and No 33 *(Loch Alsh, Glen Shiel & Loch Hourn)*. The SMC guide *The Northwest Highlands* is recommended.

GLEN SPEAN

Rising high above Loch Laggan, between the southern reaches of the Great Glen and Strathspey, is a small cluster of peaks dominated by the magnificent Creag Meagaidh (1130m). The peak is the central feature of Creag Meagaidh National Nature Reserve,

owned and managed by Scottish Natural Heritage (SNH). The Creag Meagaidh horseshoe is one of Scotland's classic mountain walks, taking you round the spectacular, cliff-lined Coire Ardair. This 11.8mi (19km) walk involves 1240m ascent and takes seven to 7½ hours. As well as Craig Meagaidh, the route (usually completed anticlockwise) rewards Munro baggers with two extra peaks: Carn Liath (1006m) and Stob Poite Coire Ardair (1053m).

The best times for the walk are mid-May to mid-June and September; access is generally open at all times but check with SNH about stalking activities (☎ 01528-544265).

The OS Landranger (1:50,000) map for the walk is No 34 *(Fort Augustus)*. The Scottish Mountaineering Club's *The Munros*, edited by Donald Bennet, includes this walk.

The walks starts at the car park beside the A86, near SNH's Aberarder office, nearly 20mi (32km) from Spean Bridge and 10mi (16km) from Laggan Bridge. Highland Country Buses' (☎ 01463-222244) summer Munro Bagger service (Fort William to Cairngorm) stops here twice daily between late May and the end of September.

There is excellent accommodation at Laggan Bridge at *The Pottery Bunkhouse* (☎/fax *01528-544231*, ⓔ *lynda@potterybunkhouse.fsnet.co.uk*), on the A889 just east of the village centre. The tariff is £9, plus £1.50 for bedding, or £45 for a room sleeping up to five. There is a small shop in the village. In the other direction (towards Spean Bridge) along the main A86 road is *Station Lodge* (☎/fax *01397-732333*, ⓔ *info@stationlodge.co.uk*), at Tulloch train station on the Fort William to Glasgow railway line. The tariff is £10 for a bed; meals are available and the Lodge is licensed. The nearest TICs for more accommodation information are at Kingussie (☎ 01540-661297) and Spean Bridge (☎ 01397-712576); both offices are open seasonally. You can also check the Web site at ⓦ www.host.co.uk, or email ⓔ infohost.co.uk.

The Isle of Skye

Speed bonny boat, like a bird on the wing,
Over the sea to Skye.
Carry the lad, that's born to be King,
Over the sea to Skye.

The 'Skye Boat Song' is quite possibly the world's best-known song about Scotland, but it's not only the tales of Prince Charlie and his Flora MacDonald that attract visitors to the Isle of Skye. For walkers and climbers there's the allure of some of the most impressive mountains in the British Isles – the spectacular Black and Red Cuillin.

The name 'Cuillin' (pronounced coolin) is derived from the Norse *kjollen*, meaning 'keel-shaped'. Both the Red and the Black Cuillin are igneous formations, but their mineral compositions are very different. The Black Cuillin rocks are mainly gabbro, with sections of smooth basalt on the surface. The gabbro is a coarse crystalline rock, which is rich in iron and magnesium and has a dark colour. The basalt has eroded more readily than the hard gabbro, leaving gullies and chimneys. At the same time glacial action has carved corries out of the rock and the end result is a finely sculpted, jagged ridgeline. A peculiar property of the rocks is their localised magnetic influences – a rather important consideration if you're intending to navigate by compass! The nearby Red Cuillin, by contrast, are a product of late igneous activity and are more rounded in shape. The red granite, which gives them their name, also appears somewhat friendlier than the black gabbro of their more illustrious neighbours to the north-west.

Most visitors to Skye will merely admire the Black Cuillin's jagged ridges, towers and pinnacles from a safe distance. Most of these airy peaks are the domain of fit and adventurous walkers with experience in rock scrambling and a head for heights, and are beyond the scope of this book. However, there are a few places where walkers with some mountain experience can get 'Skye-high' for a closer Cuillin encounter. Should the cloud be down, there are also some rewarding low-level walks along the island's glens and coast.

In this chapter we describe a long low-level walk and a challenging route up Bruach na Frithe onto the Black Cuillin ridge, one of the few peaks on Skye that is accessible to experienced mountain walkers without hands-on scrambling.

INFORMATION
Maps
Both the walks described here are covered by OS Landranger 1:50,000 map No 32 *(South Skye & Cuillin Hills)* and OS Outdoor Leisure 1:25,000 map No 8 *(The Cuillin and Torridon Hills)*.

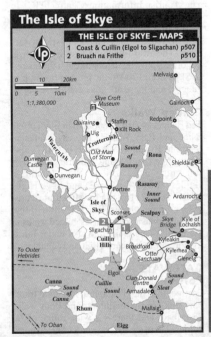

The Isle of Skye

THE ISLE OF SKYE – MAPS
1 Coast & Cuillin (Elgol to Sligachan) p507
2 Bruach na Frithe p510

Books

Skye has inspired many scribes and for the transient visitor there's an excellent little series of guidebooks written and published by Charles Rhodes; *Selected Walks – Southern Skye* covers the area we describe. *Walks on the Isle of Skye* by Mary Welsh describes 35 short walks, while *50 Best Routes on Skye & Raasay* by Ralph Storer has a wide selection of mountain and coastal outings with photos and maps. There's also *Selected Walks – Northern Skye* and *Walks from Glen Brittle* (both locally produced in English and German). Longer 'classics' include *The Magic of Skye* by WA Poucher. The Scottish Mountaineering Club (SMC) *Guide to Skye* is very useful for the serious and experienced walker wanting to spend some time on the island. For those wishing to do some scrambling on the Black Cuillin, *Skye Scrambles*, published by the SMC, is worth a look.

Information Sources

The Tourist Information Centre (TIC) in Portree (☎ 01478-612137) has a fax weather forecasting service. The TIC in Broadtree (☎ 01471-822361) is only open April to October. The award-winning Aros Experience, in Portree, provides a tour through the history of Skye from 1700 to the present (in six languages) and there are adjacent forest walks.

Guided Walks

Ted Badger (☎ 01471-866228) in Elgol offers 'Nice and Easy Walks'. The environmental centre in Broadford (☎ 01471-822487) also runs guided walks and wildlife tours. For something more serious, Skye Mountain Guides (☎ 01478-612682) and Skye Highs (☎ 01471-822116), run by Mike Lates, provide guiding on the Black Cuillin ridge. Martin Moran also organises guided walks in the Cuillin (see Guided Walks under Information in the Western Highlands chapter).

GATEWAYS
Portree

Portree, the island's capital, has good transport links to the mainland and both walks described, and there's a wide range of facilities. There are several outdoor gear shops, various bookshops selling maps and walking guides, banks, and numerous grocery stores and supermarkets. There are also plenty of pubs, restaurants, and fish and chip shops. The TIC (☎ 01478-612137) is just off Somerland Square.

Portree also offers a wealth of accommodation options and it can seem as though every second house is a B&B. Nonetheless, the many visitors in peak season do a good job of filling the spaces and booking ahead is advisable during summer. *Portree Independent Hostel* (☎ *01478-613737*) is centrally located near the TIC, and charges £9.50. *Portree Backpackers* (☎ *01478-613641*) has a homely atmosphere and costs £9, but is a mile away from the town centre up the A87 towards Dunvegan and Uig. There is space for tents only for a charge of £4 per person. *Torvaig Campsite* (☎ *01478-612209*) is a mile up the road to Staffin and charges £3 per person.

Sligachan

Sligachan is a minimalist sort of place, but it is also the main gateway for walkers and climbers venturing into the Cuillin, and thrives throughout the summer. *Sligachan Hotel* (☎ *01478-650204*) is the centre of activity, and charges from £35 for B&B (£40 during July and August). The adjacent *Seamus's Bar* offers bar food until 9pm, including a hearty 'camper's breakfast' served from 7.30am to 10am. *Sligachan Campsite* (☎ *01478-650303*), just opposite the hotel, has laundry facilities and charges £4 per person. There is no shop (save the very basic supplies held at the campsite reception), so bring all the supplies you'll need.

GETTING THERE & AWAY

For information on travel options between England, Wales and Scotland, see the Getting Around chapter.

Ferry, Bus & Train There are two main ways to get to Skye from the mainland. One is to take the ferry from the mainland port of Mallaig to Armadale on Skye. The ferry service is run by Caledonian MacBrayne (CalMac; ☎ 0870-565 0000) and costs £15.25

for cars (excluding passengers) and £2.70 for foot passengers. ScotRail (☎ 0845-755 0033) train services from Glasgow tie in with the Mallaig ferry to Armadale, as does a Scottish Citylink (☎ 0870-550 5050) bus service from Fort William. From Armadale, Highland Country Buses (☎ 01463-222244) have connections to Broadford, Sligachan and Portree several times daily.

There is also a small ferry that plies the narrow Sound of Sleat from Glenelg to Kylerhea (☎ 01599-511302), which runs from April to October.

The other way to get to Skye is via a road bridge from Kyle of Lochalsh on the mainland. There are four trains daily, Monday to Saturday, to Kyle of Lochalsh from Inverness. Two of these trains come through from Edinburgh and Glasgow. There are two trains on Sunday. From Kyle of Lochalsh you can pick up the Highland Country Buses local services to Broadford, Sligachan and Portree. Scottish Citylink buses travel from Glasgow and Inverness to Kyle of Lochalsh, and continue directly on to Broadford, Sligachan and Portree (two buses daily).

Car In 1995 the controversial Skye Bridge between Kyle of Lochalsh and Kyleakin was opened, with a hefty toll of £5.80 each way for cars.

Coast & Cuillin (Elgol to Sligachan)

Distance	13.5mi (21.5km)
Duration	8–9 hours
Standard	medium
Start	Elgol
Finish	Sligachan
Gateways	Portree, Broadford

Summary A spectacular, low-level route that penetrates into the heart of the Black Cuillin to reach the shores of Loch Coruisk. The route also involves the 'Bad Step', a short, exposed rock section some walkers may find problematic.

This low-level route combines coastal paths, mountain views, glen scenery and a short scramble to reach Loch Coruisk in the heart

of the Black Cuillin. The section from Elgol to Loch Coruisk is particularly impressive and has justifiably been described as 'possibly the best coastal walk in Britain'.

Loch Coruisk is the jewel in the crown of the Black Cuillin. The jagged ring of peaks that surround the loch form an impressive fortress and a wild setting for its clear blue waters. Boats can be used to access the loch by sea but, without mountaineering skills, there are only three possible routes in to Loch Coruisk on foot. This walk links two of these routes (the other path is more tenuous and leads in from Glenbrittle campsite, to the west).

If you decide to take two days, the experience of camping at Loch Coruisk is unique, but this is wild terrain and you will need to be entirely self-sufficient. There is also a bothy at Camasunary but tenting at the loch is much more memorable.

Despite its high quality, the route described involves one section of scrambling that may not be to everyone's liking. The 'Bad Step', about 500m before Loch Coruisk is reached, is a 6m-long, 60-degree slab with a narrow ledge for the feet and small handholds for support. It is exposed but is situated about 8m above deep water, so it's not necessarily dangerous if you can swim well! It should be within the capabilities of most fit walkers, but a cool head is required and heavy packs may also increase the difficulty.

If the idea of the Bad Step is too daunting, then it's possible to take a linear route from Elgol to Sligachan straight up Glen Sligachan, avoiding Loch Coruisk altogether. Alternatively you can take a boat in to Loch Coruisk and then walk out. See Alternatives for more details.

Direction, Distance & Duration

There are two reasons for doing this 13.5mi walk from south to north: firstly, transport logistics (see Getting There & Away earlier) are easier; and secondly, the views in this direction are really stunning.

The entire walk takes eight or nine hours to complete and could easily be fitted into a single day. To really appreciate the magnificent surroundings of the Black Cuillin, however, it is preferable to split the walk into two days and camp on the shores of Loch Coruisk, completing the walk to Sligachan on the second day.

Alternatives If you want to adapt the route, Bella Jane Boat Trips (☎ 01471-866244) charges £10 to take you from Elgol across Loch Scavaig to the landing steps near Loch Coruisk. From here you can walk the 7.5mi out to Sligachan, following the walk description from Loch Coruisk to the finish. This option would fit easily into a day and make for a very memorable trip.

Another option is to follow the first part of the route described as far as Camasunary and then continue straight up Glen Sligachan to Sligachan village. There is a sign on the wall of the house at Camasunary that directs you up the valley and the path is very good all the way. This option covers a total distance of 11mi (17.5km) and should take about six hours to complete.

PLANNING
Maps
As well as the OS Landranger 1:50,000 map No 32 *(South Skye & Cuillin Hills)* and OS Outdoor Leisure 1:25,000 map No 8 *(The Cuillin and Torridon Hills)*, the Harvey Superwalker 1:25,000 map *Skye* covers most of this walk.

PLACES TO STAY & EAT
Elgol
Elgol is a small fishing village with an incredible view of the Cuillin. It boasts a small shop, a post office and the friendly *Cuillin View Coffee Shop*, which serves snacks and meals. There are a limited number of places to stay in the village and most of them are closed during winter. There's a B&B at *Rowan Cottage (☎ 01471-866287, e Rowan @rowancott.demon.co.uk)*, charging from £18 with evening meals available. *Coruisk Guesthouse (☎ 01471-866330)* has an excellent tearoom and licensed seafood restaurant, and also does B&B for about £25.

Walkers are welcome at *Strathaird House (☎ 01471-866269, e jkubale@com puserve.com)*, near Kirkibost, 3.5mi out of

Elgol towards Broadford. B&B starts from £25, and lunch and evening meals are available at its *Hayloft* restaurant. One week's self-catering for four people at Strathaird costs £175 to £250.

GETTING TO/FROM THE WALK
To reach Elgol you could take a morning bus (daily except Sunday) from Sligachan (or Portree) to Broadford, connecting with the 10.45am postbus service that leaves from Broadford post office. The service arrives in Elgol at 12.45pm. On weekdays there's also an afternoon postbus from Broadford to Elgol, departing at 3.40pm.

The walk begins about 400m south of Elgol post office and 600m north of the jetty, where a lane leads off to the north from the B8083 (the Elgol–Broadford road). The lane is clearly signposted as a footpath to Camasunary and Sligachan.

The walk finishes at Sligachan, on the main road between Broadford and Portree, which has good transport links.

THE WALK
Elgol to Camasunary
3.5mi (5.5km), 2 hours
Walk up the lane that is signposted to Camasunary and Sligachan. The road soon disappears, leaving a dirt track that ends at two houses. A footpath (signed to Loch Coruisk) continues directly ahead, between the fences of the two houses, and passes through a gate before leading out onto open hillside. The views are immediately impressive; the 'Small Isles' of Eigg, Rum and Canna lie to the south, while the Black Cuillin ridge dominates the skyline to the north-west.

The well-trodden path contours across grassy and heathery slopes all the way to the beach at Camasunary, with views improving along the way. The drop-off to the west is steep in places, passing the lower slopes of Ben Cleat and Beinn Leacach, and care is required over these sections. At Glen Scaladal cross a stile before descending to the pebbly cove, then climb steeply to the broken cliff top from the back of the beach. Duck under the branches of a grove of stunted trees, and watch out for a place where the old path has eroded away and a new track climbs slightly higher up the cliff. Easier ground then leads down to the bridge over the Abhainn nan Leac and a substantial junction of paths, about 3mi from Elgol.

Of the two buildings at Camasunary, the larger house near the bridge is privately owned. The smaller building 500m farther west is the ***Mountain Bothies Association (MBA) bothy*** that offers free accommodation to hill users. At the junction of paths, the 4WD track that descends from the shoulder to the east leads to Kirkibost, about 2mi away. The path that forks right between the bridge and house leads directly up Glen Sligachan to Sligachan, avoiding Loch Coruisk.

Camasunary to Loch Coruisk
2.5mi (4km), 2 hours

To continue to Loch Coruisk, take the path that leads west (left at the fork) along the top of the beach and passes in front of the bothy. Ford the Abhainn Camas Fhionnairigh by following its banks upstream for 100m or so and then crossing on stepping stones. The path on the other side climbs slightly to contour round the craggy lower slopes of Sgurr na Stri. The terrain is rougher than previously, and several rock steps and angled slabs are crossed. As you round the headland another wonderful vista greets the eye; rocky islands nestle at the mouth of the River Scavaig, backed by the looming Cuillin peaks.

The slabs become more frequent as the path veers northward and care must be taken not to lose the main route as it splits in various places. Continue towards the white sand and turquoise water of Loch nan Leachd cove. The notorious **Bad Step** is the very last slab that needs to be negotiated before the beach. A cairn marks the stony path that descends to the difficulties. (It could be a good idea to undo pack straps, just in case of a slip into the water below.) Duck under an overhang and scramble out onto the seaward rock face. Pull yourself up to balance on a ledge that skirts round the slab face, using handholds for support. Shuffle along and at a convergence of fault lines take care to drop diagonally down to the boulders on the beach rather than continuing up the slab.

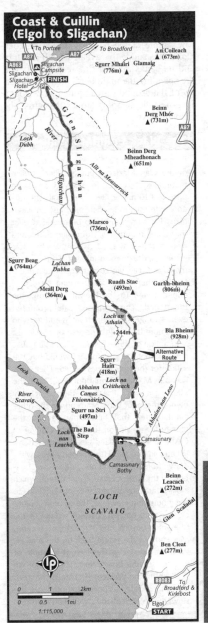

Cross the boulders to the sand of Loch nan Leachd and follow the path inland across the low saddle at the back of the cove. **Loch Coruisk** is suddenly revealed in all its glory and its banks make a fine rest spot. If you are spending the night here, then the majority of flat ground for camping can be found just over the stepping stones that cross the Scavaig River.

The Black Cuillin for Sale

In the early part of 2000 John Macleod (Chief of the Clan Macleod) put the Black Cuillin mountains of Skye up for sale with an asking price of £10 million. Environmental and outdoor interest groups had only just defeated plans for scenic flights to be operated over the same mountains from Sligachan, and were horrified by rumours that wealthy foreigners had expressed interest. Some feared the Black Cuillin would be turned into a mass-tourism theme park or the long history of public access to the mountains would be threatened. The proposed sale prompted even stronger reaction from islanders who were more than a little peeved by Macleod's assumption of title – a suggestion at a public meeting that the government would buy the estate for the people was booed. Their view was that Macleod should not profit from the sale and it was unclear whether he actually owned the mountains. Macleod, on the other hand, stated that he simply needed the money for repairs on the roof of Dunvegan Castle, one of the island's leading attractions.

Later in the year the property was withdrawn from the market pending an investigation by the Crown Estate Commission, which looks after state-owned land, into legal title to the mountains. However, the commission decided not to contest Macleod's claim to the title and, despite the strength of feeling, Macleod put the estate back on the market. With the sale of An Teallach at the time of writing (see the boxed text 'The Sale of An Teallach' in the Western Highlands chapter), a serious debate has been prompted into the stewardship of Scotland's wild mountains.

Loch Coruisk to Sligachan
7.5mi (12km), 4 hours

The path from Loch Coruisk to Sligachan leads round the south-eastern shore of the loch, and then climbs up the right-hand side of a burn that can be seen tumbling down from a smaller loch above. It is a climb of over 300m to the saddle and the terrain is rocky towards the top. A large cairn marks the saddle and there are fine views westwards over the serrated north Cuillin ridge. Veer north-westwards along the ridge to a second cairn 20m away, where a wide, stony path drops down the other side. The path from Camasunary to Sligachan can be seen winding along the valley below. The descent to join it is fairly steep for a section and then evens out, becoming rather wet at the valley floor. Join the main Sligachan path at a large cairn, from where there is a great perspective of Bla Bheinn to the south-east.

From the junction of paths it is about 3.7mi along the valley to Sligachan. The terrain is largely flat and the going easy, although the *Sligachan Hotel* soon comes into view and it can seem like a long time before it moves much closer. The final 500m of the route is along a well-benched path and you exit the mountains at a metal stile. Turn left across the old bridge to arrive at the hotel itself.

Bruach na Frithe

Distance	8.5mi (13.5km)
Duration	6–8 hours
Standard	medium-hard
Start/Finish	Sligachan
Gateways	Portree, Broadford

Summary A fine but strenuous mountain walk with spectacular views of the Black and Red Cuillin. An alternative route on the north-west ridge provides exciting scrambling for those with a head for heights.

The summit of Bruach na Frithe (pronounced bruack na free) is a turning point on the main Cuillin ridge and provides magnificent views along its line in both directions. At 958m (3142ft) this peak is a Munro and has been described as the least difficult of the Black Cuillin peaks to ascend, being the only one not defended by cliffs. The easiest route is up (and down) Fionn Choire, a steep-sided 'bowl', which leads up to Bruach na Frithe. This route follows a steep, zigzagging path up through scree and boulder slopes, and avoids all scrambling.

Direction, Distance & Duration
The approach to Bruach na Frithe follows a right of way from Sligachan to Glenbrittle, over Bealach a' Mhàim (continuing along here would provide another option on a poor day). The total distance covered by the walk is 8.5mi and involves almost 1000m of ascent, so you need between six and eight hours to cover the route.

Alternatives If you're happy to tackle an easy scramble, which is airy in places, an attractive alternative to the summit of Bruach na Frithe is the ascent by the north-west ridge. The impression of exposure is exhilarating. See Alternative Route: via the North-West Ridge in the walk description.

PLANNING
Maps & Books
This walk is covered by OS Landranger 1:50,000 map No 32 *(South Skye & Cuillin Hills)* and OS Outdoor Leisure 1:25,000 map No 8 *(The Cuillin and Torridon Hills)*, as well as the Harvey Superwalker 1:25,000 map *Skye*.

PLACES TO STAY & EAT
For information on accommodation and services in Portree and Sligachan, see Gateways in the introduction to this chapter.

Warning
Due to the magnetic properties of the gabbro rock, compasses give distorted readings on the summit ridge. Also, the route up and down the choire would be far from straightforward in poor visibility. Hence this summit should only be attempted in good weather when the way can be clearly seen.

GETTING TO/FROM THE WALK
The walk starts and finishes in Sligachan. For details of how to reach the town, see Getting There & Away in the introduction to this chapter.

THE WALK
Sligachan to the base of Fionn Choire
2.5mi (4km), 1½–2 hours
From Sligachan Bridge walk west along the A863 towards Dunvegan for a little over 500m. Just after the road passes through a cutting near a lay-by, take the track signed 'Footpath to Glenbrittle' that heads towards Alltdearg House. Just as you approach the house a signed footpath diverts round the grounds to the north, crossing a stretch of boggy ground. The firmest route keeps near to the fence on the left.

You soon pick up a stony path that runs alongside the Allt Dearg Mór, a burn which tumbles down a series of rock ledges. After 2mi the path begins to level out in Coire na Circe and the going becomes soft underfoot. Continue on, fording a sizable tributary, to reach a large cairn. Here the path for Bruach na Frithe forks left across boggy ground and crosses another burn (more easily) about 200m after the cairn. Follow the ascending path for about 20 minutes, keeping Allt an Fionn Choire (a burn with small waterfalls pouring from the corrie above) on your left, until you reach a substantial cairn on top of a rock slab.

This is a good place for a rest while you decide which route to take to the summit.

Base of Fionn Choire to Bruach na Frithe
1.5mi (2.5km), 2–2½ hours
From the large cairn stay on the small cairned path to the right (west) of the burn. After ascending a short way the path reaches the sill at the corrie's edge. You need to cross the burn to reach a large cairn on the other side; this may be easier above a burn junction. From this cairn there is no discernible path but you can pick out a line of small cairns swinging slightly left across the corrie floor towards some rock slabs in the scree ahead.

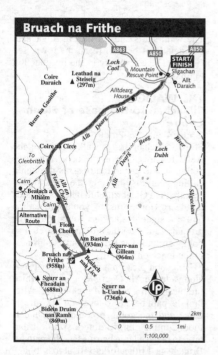

Bruach na Frithe

Fionn Choire to reach Bealach nan Lice, about 400m from (and 60m below) the summit. Turn left down a stony path into Fionn Choire. There is a burn on the left (west) but this disappears in places. In mist the route can be confusing. The standard advice is that by following any of the watercourses leading north, the Allt Dearg Mór flowing down to Sligachan will eventually be reached. However, beware, some of the watercourses are cut into ravines and there are steep sections with small waterfalls. If possible, you're best off sticking to a reverse of the route described earlier. This will lead you back to the path on the north-west side of the Allt Dearg Mór and then down to Sligachan.

Alternative Route: Bruach na Frithe via the North-West Ridge
2mi (3km), 2–2½ hours
From the cairn on top of the rock slab head up the steep slope of grass, boulders and scree on the right. The bearing is south to south-west and there are occasional cairns to guide you. Cross a marshy depression and then, higher again, you'll reach a small pool. Climb the steep up to the left and join a more obvious path (which has come up from Bealach a' Mhàim). This zigzags up steep scree and then grass to a narrowing of the ridge and a brief easing of the angle.

There is a short, steep section before an almost horizontal narrow section about 150m long. This is a superb situation for those with a head for heights. At the end of this is the main ridge scramble. Difficulties encountered near the ridge crest can be avoided by going to the right but don't take the path that traverses round to the right at the start of the rocks. There is plenty of evidence of the routes that have been taken by those who have gone before, and with the occasional use of hands for balance and to help with upward progress you should reach the cylindrical **trig point** with a great feeling of exhilaration and achievement (or perhaps just relief!). Either way, enjoy the superb views and check your compass to see for yourself how the gabbro affects the needle!

After crossing this level stretch a small path ascends to the left of a dry stream bed in a small gorge, where the burn has disappeared below boulders. There are no cairns but a pretty obvious path roughly follows the left-hand side of the burn. Where the angle steepens the route zigzags up the scree and boulders to reach the ridge at Bealach nan Lice, where you turn right on a small path under the rock outcrop of Fionn Choire. This takes you to the east ridge of Bruach na Frithe, which you follow to the distinctive cylindrical trig point on the **summit** and superb views.

Bruach na Frithe to Sligachan
4.5mi (7km), 2½ hours
The descent retraces the main route. From the summit take the east ridge, keeping close to the crest but avoiding obstacles by passing them on their left. Pass below Sgùrr a'

Scotland Long-Distance Paths

This chapter covers Scotland's major long-distance paths (LDPs). The coast-to-coast Southern Upland Way and the famous West Highland Way are described in detail and an outline is provided for the other four: the Great Glen Way, the Speyside Way, the Fife Coastal Path and St Cuthbert's Way (part of which runs through England). They offer excellent introductions to many of the different types of walking in Scotland: from moorland to the coast, from river banks to woodlands, from the Borders to the Highlands.

The Southern Upland Way

Distance	212mi (341km)
Duration	9 days
Standard	medium-hard
Start	Portpatrick
Finish	Cockburnspath
Gateways	Stranraer, Moffat, Dunbar

Summary An extremely challenging, very long route passing through remote country in the west and more settled areas in the east, crossing high ground (up to 700m) and following minor roads, farm and forest tracks, and footpaths.

The Southern Upland Way (SUW), opened in 1984, was Britain's first official coast-to-coast LDP, traversing one of the broadest parts of Scotland through Dumfries & Galloway, and the Borders. The route goes across the grain of the countryside; rollercoasting over hills and moorland, and through conifer plantations, descending to cross rivers and streams, then climbing out the other side. It also passes through deciduous woodlands and agricultural land, mainly on the eastern half of the walk.

You can expect a wide range of weather conditions during a complete crossing; thick mist and strong winds – and warm sunshine – are likely any time between April and September. This is the best, if not the only, time for the SUW. Snow falls on higher ground

are standard during winter when short daylight hours make it impossible to complete the long daily distances before dark.

The going underfoot ranges from sealed roads to muddy forest paths. There are, unfortunately, some long (over 2mi) sealed stretches (although not on busy roads), which some walkers feel should have no place on official routes. There's some comfort in the fact that they do link some very fine paths across the hills and through woodlands.

The route is not very well served with accommodation, so you have to anticipate some long days to get from one roof to the next. Camping or staying in bothies gives more flexibility but all the necessary gear weighs heavily, especially on days of 20mi or more. These factors, combined with the route's length and remoteness, make it a far more serious proposition than the West Highland Way and most, if not all, national trails in England and Wales. Nevertheless, the rewards are considerable; a real sense of moving across the country, becoming attuned to gradual changes in the landscape, meeting fellow walkers and the satisfaction of the first view of the North Sea on the last day. It's essential to be pretty fit before you start, and preferably to have had some experience of long-distance walking. It also helps to get into the right mind frame; taking each day as it comes but still keeping the objective firmly fixed – whatever the weather, track condition or distance to be covered.

Many hosts along the Way provide a vehicle back-up service, picking you up from an agreed spot and returning you next day to continue the walk. Some people will do this gratis, while others may charge, so check first.

Direction, Distance & Duration
Probably the majority of people do the walk from south-west to north-east. It could be said this means the prevailing wind is behind you, but when the Way was walked for this book in this direction, the persistent

north wind was coming either from the side or head-on. There is much to be said, however, for finishing in the east with more open, settled countryside, where shorter days are possible, than in the west with monotonous conifer plantations and some unavoidably big daily distances.

The full walk of 212mi may take as few as nine or 10 days or as many as 14 (although people do spread the journey over a number of years, doing a bit at a time), depending on your best walking speed and the number of rest days. The amount of ascent is also a significant factor when you're planning an itinerary, especially in the central section between Sanquhar and Beattock. It's as well to have some flexibility in your plans as bad weather, likely at any time, may dictate a change of plans, especially in the more remote and exposed western section.

The route is well waymarked with a thistle hexagon logo and signposts but you should still carry maps and a compass in case visibility deteriorates on the exposed stretches. Distances between waymarks vary widely, from line of sight across moorland to miles apart along minor roads. Sections of the route are changed (often for the better) from time to time, so waymarks should always be more reliable than the mapped route.

The nine-day itinerary we suggest is:

day	from	to	mi/km
1	Portpatrick	New Luce	23/37
2	New Luce	Bargrennan	17/27.5
3	Bargrennan	St John's Town of Dalry	24/38.5
4	St John's Town of Dalry	Sanquhar	27/43.5
5	Sanquhar	Beattock	28/45
6	Beattock	St Mary's Loch	21/34
7	St Mary's Loch	Melrose	30/48.5
8	Melrose	Longformacus	25/40 ·
9	Longformacus	Cockburnspath	17/27.5

Alternatives The Way crosses several main roads, along which there are bus services and a railway line with a convenient

train station. These enable you to reach the SUW from many major centres and to walk shorter sections of the trail using public transport for arrival and departure. A brief note on transport connections is included in each day's walk description. Two suggestions for shorter walks are given in the Route Highlight boxed texts in the walk description.

PLANNING
Maps & Books
The Official Guide to the Southern Upland Way by Roger Smith is invaluable. It comes in a pack with four map sheets containing strip maps extracted from seven Ordnance Survey (OS) Landranger 1:50,000 maps covering the full length of the Way. The cost of the pack is less than half that of buying the maps individually. The only catch is that, at the time of writing, in the current 1996 edition some of the route details are outdated. Anthony Burton's guide to the Way has a more up-to-date and livelier description but its 1:25,000 Pathfinder maps are antiquated.

For a really in-depth study of the area, you can't go past the Scottish Mountaineering Club (SMC) guide *The Southern Uplands*. By contrast, Ronald Turnbull's light-hearted *Across Scotland on Foot* includes a humourous chapter on the Way, along with an outline of a truly upland alternative.

Information Sources
Two free leaflets, *Southern Upland Way* and *Accommodation* (updated annually), are useful for preliminary planning. They are available from the Ranger Service at Dumfries (☎ 01387-260000) and Harestanes (☎ 01835-830281), near Jedburgh. The Dumfries service also produces leaflets on the wildlife, history, archaeology and place names of the area, and a booklet describing short circular walks based on the SUW.

Southern Upland Way: Access by Public Transport is available from Technical Services, Scottish Borders Council (☎ 01835-824000), Newtown St, Boswells TD6 0SA. For more general information, the relevant tourist boards are Dumfries & Galloway (☎ 01387-250434) and Scottish Borders (☎ 0175-020555).

TICs based in towns along the route include Galashiels (☎ 01896-755551), Melrose (☎ 01896-822555) and Stranraer (☎ 01776-702595); the Galashiels and Melrose TICs are open seasonally only.

PLACES TO STAY & EAT

Over much of the route (west of Galashiels) opportunities for overnight stops at hotels, B&Bs and hostels are limited. Using bothies or camping can help to compensate for this. Brief details are given in each day's walk description but you'll need the current *Accommodation* guide (see Information Sources earlier) to be sure of what is on offer. You'll also need to anticipate carrying all the food and drink you'll need for the day – there are precious few watering places en route.

GUIDED WALKS

The locally based Scotwalk Ltd (☎ 01896-830515) conducts guided tours of the Way using local experts; it can also organise a self-guided walk along the Way. C-N-Do Scotland (☎ 01786-445703) also has the SUW on its program.

GETTING TO/FROM THE WALK

For information on travel options between England, Wales and Scotland, see the Getting Around chapter.

Bus, Train & Ferry You can reach Stanraer by bus or train from Glasgow or Carlisle, and by ferry from Belfast; there is a bus service from here to Portpatrick about six times per day. Cockburnspath, at the other end of

Laws, Cleuchs & Rigs

As you pore over the maps at home, the names of the hills, rivers and other landscape features of the country you are going to walk through can help give a clearer picture of what it will look like, and can also reveal something of the local history. While Gaelic place names are commonplace in the Highlands and islands to the north, in the Southern Uplands they're largely confined to the south-west, even though Gaelic is now little spoken in these parts. In the Borders, however, the names are mainly from Lallans (Lowland Scots), a distinct language still in use, with origins in the languages of settlers from the east rather than in the Celtic-Gaelic spoken in the west.

Starting at the beginning of the Way, Portpatrick's origin is obvious, given the Irish connection, although it was originally called Portree from the Gaelic *port righ*, meaning 'harbour of the king'. The name Killantringan, the location of the fine lighthouse, includes the Anglicised version of the common Gaelic prefix *cill*, meaning 'church' – in this case of St Ringan or Ninian. Balmurrie, the farm near New Luce, has another widespread Gaelic element – *bal*, meaning 'farm' or 'small township' – in this case of the Murray family.

Laggangairn, the site of the two prehistoric cairns beyond Balmurrie, means 'hollow of the cairns' (*lag* meaning 'hollow'). A bit farther on you climb over Craig Airie Fell – a hybrid of Gaelic and Norse. Craig is derived from *creag*, which is Gaelic for 'cliff' or 'crag'; *àiridh* is Gaelic for 'shieling' (a temporary dwelling); and fell, once a Norse term, is commonly used in the English Lake District to mean 'mountain'. Dalry is from the Gaelic *dail righ*, or 'meadow of the king'. Benbrack, the hill between that town and Sanquhar, is the speckled *breac* (hill), while Fingland comes from the Gaelic *fionn gleann*, meaning 'white glen'.

In the east, the Lammermuir Hills feature prominently in the latter stages; the name comes from the Old English for lamb – still appropriate today.

Among the most common names for geographical features are cleuch, which comes directly from the Lowland Scots for ravine; the similar sounding heugh is a cliff. The name law pops up all over the Borders and is the equivalent of a Gaelic *beinn* (mountain or hill), often isolated and conical in shape. A knowe is also a high sort of place (a small hillock), while a dod is a bare round hill.

Scottish Hill and Mountain Names by Peter Drummond, the Scottish place names guru, should answer almost any query you can come up with.

the walk, has bus services to Edinburgh and Berwick-upon-Tweed, on the main east coast railway line. Basic information about transport services along the route is given in the walk description.

Car Portpatrick is 8mi from Stranraer on the A77; Cockburnspath is just off the A1 between Edinburgh and Berwick-upon-Tweed.

THE WALK
Portpatrick

The peaceful harbour in Portpatrick village was once the port for ferries from Ireland. These days it looks after anglers, sailors and walkers, with a good choice of accommodation, places to eat and a small *shop*.

Carlton Guest House (☎ 01776-810253), on the seafront, is recommended; the tariff is £17. At *Harbour House Hotel* (☎ 01776-810456) nearby you can, with luck, sit outside and enjoy a meal of suitable proportions for the miles ahead, washed down with a pint of real ale.

Stranraer

Eight miles north-east of Portpatrick, Stranraer is a busier town with lots of accommodation. Contact the TIC (☎ 01776-889156), in Harbour St, for full details.

Day 1: Portpatrick to New Luce
23mi (37km), 8–8½ hours
A delightful stretch of about 2mi along the coast from Portpatrick to Killantringan lighthouse at Black Head makes a fine start to the Way. The rest of the stage is mainly along minor roads through farmland, with good views of the area. The total ascent for the day is 370m.

From Portpatrick the Way goes above impressive cliffs (take care, especially in poor visibility) and round scenic coves. It passes a golf course, communications buildings and a little double-hexagonal building at the landfall of a submarine telephone cable connection to Ireland. The route ahead isn't always obvious but trust the thistle waymarks to show the trail from the shore back up to the cliff top. The lighthouse comes dramatically into view and the SUW joins

the minor road leading inland from it. Enjoy the view north across Killantringan Bay, as you'll cover more than 200mi before you reach the sea again.

Minor roads and farm tracks lead to a high point with fine views on a clear day. From here more minor roads, farm tracks and short, sometimes muddy paths take you down past the outskirts of Stranraer to Castle Kennedy. The village has a small *shop* and *Eynhallow Hotel* (☎ 01581-400256) where you can choose between a comfortable room or camping nearby; B&B costs £30 and camping is free if you eat at the hotel.

From Castle Kennedy a sealed drive takes you through the pleasant wooded grounds of the now ruinous castle to a minor road. You soon leave this to follow farm tracks to another minor road, then right round the edge of a cleared conifer plantation. The route descends through trees to a footbridge over a railway line, from where it's down to a suspension bridge over the Water of Luce. New Luce is off the Way, 1mi north along a nearby road. If you feel like putting a few more miles behind you before stopping at New Luce, continue on a muddy track across open moorland, past deserted Kilhern and down to a minor road about 1mi east of New Luce.

New Luce

The fine old *Kenmuir Arms Hotel* (☎ 01581-600218) has rooms for £25 and an adjacent camping and caravan site; there's a small *shop* in the village. A limited bus service run by A&F Irvine (☎ 01581-300345) links the village with Stranraer (one bus each way on Tuesday, Wednesday and Friday).

Day 2: New Luce to Bargrennan
17mi (27.5km), 6¾–7¼ hours
The Way now starts to feel remote as you traverse almost empty upland farming country, pine plantations and moorland. With 340m ascent, it's an easier day than those to come.

Follow very quiet roads to Balmurrie farm, from where the route rises across rough moorland then follows a wide heathery ride (a path specially made for riding on horseback) through a conifer plantation. A short stretch of forest road leads to an open area with old ruins and a timber beehive-shaped *bothy*, which has only sleeping platforms; there is fresh water nearby. Beside the Way are the 4000-year-old **Laggangairn standing stones** with information about their history. Beyond a large cairn the Way follows a different route from that on the official map as it climbs over Craig Airie Fell (320m) for an excellent 360-degree view, including of the Galloway Hills, which lie ahead. The Way then descends past Derry Farm and follows minor roads and tracks east and north-east past Knowe and Glenruther Lodge, over Glenvernoch Fell and down to Bargrennan.

Bargrennan & Glentrool

House O'Hill Hotel (☎ 01671-840243) provides accommodation (£20 for B&B) and serves excellent bar meals. At *Glentrool Holiday Park* (☎ 01671-840280), about half a mile north along the road, it costs around £7 to pitch a tent. There are also B&Bs in Glentrool village, a mile north and off the Way. Stagecoach Western buses (☎ 01387-253496) run several times a day (only twice on Sunday) between Bargrennan and Girvan, on the coast.

Day 3: Bargrennan to St John's Town of Dalry

24mi (38.5km), 9–9½ hours

You now encounter the Galloway Hills, the first significant range of hills along the Way, although the route keeps to lower ground and only reaches an altitude of about 310m. Nevertheless, you'll climb 500m during the day. Most of the time you're in Galloway Forest Park; the going underfoot varies widely.

This stage starts along mossy, partly overgrown paths through conifers. After crossing a minor road (which leads to Glentrool Visitor Centre), the Way passes through pleasant woodlands and follows the Water of Trool to spacious *Caldons Campsite* (☎ 01671-840218), which has a small shop; the fee for pitching a tent is about £6. It then traverses above Loch Trool, with some good views towards Merrick (843m), the highest peak in the Galloway Hills, and drops down to cross

Glenhead Burn. The Way goes up beside the burn briefly, then diverges from the mapped route and heads south-east across country to meet a forest road about a mile west of Loch Dee. *White Laggan Bothy*, a stone-built former lodge, is about 350m off the route to the south.

Past the Loch Dee Angling Club's small hut, the Way crosses the River Dee. From here there's almost no respite from the conifers for about 4mi, apart from a fleeting outlook across Loch Clatteringshaws, until you reach the road to Mid Garrary. There's a scout *bunkhouse* nearby.

The Way leaves the road on a good path through wide clearings between more plantations, rises across moorland and descends to Clenrie Farm. Farther on, and well down into the valley of Coom Burn, the Way cuts east across Waterside Hill and follows the Water of Ken to a fine suspension bridge leading to St John's Town of Dalry (to give it its full name).

St John's Town of Dalry

This large village, often shortened to Dalry, has a couple of hotels, including *Clachan Inn* (☎ 01644-430241), in the main street, where the tariff is £20; and a few B&Bs, of which *Mrs Findlay* (☎ 01644-430420), in Main St, costs £15. There is an excellent licensed *grocer* and another small *shop*.

Bus services here include one to Ayr, on the coast, and another to nearby Dumfries. Buses depart at varying frequencies throughout the week; there is no bus to Dumfries on Sunday. The operator for both services is MacEwan's (☎ 01387-256533).

Day 4: St John's Town of Dalry to Sanquhar

27mi (43.5km), 9¾–10¼ hours

This is a long, challenging day through empty country with some stiff climbs, including one up to Benbrack (580m). The total ascent is 900m.

From Dalry the Way crosses rough grazing land past Ardoch Farm to Butterhole Bridge. Friendly *Kendoon SYHA Hostel* (☎ 01644-460680) is about 1.5mi farther west, off the SUW at Glenhoul (the warden may be able to help with transport from the hostel). The route continues across rough grazing ground to Stroanpatrick, then climbs a wide ride through plantations and skirts the summit of Manquhill Hill (421m). Then it's on past the track (unsignposted) to *Manquhill Bothy* and up to Benbrack for excellent views, including Cairnsmore of Carsphairn (784m) to the west. The Way then takes you down and over a couple of lesser tops into a plantation, past Allan's Cairn and down a forest road past the rather spartan *Polskeoch Bothy* to the scattering of buildings at Polskeoch.

After about 2mi along a minor sealed road, the Way sets off to cross the ridge to the north along tracks which, in places, are badly cut up by cattle. Sanquhar comes into view from the top but there's a long descent into the the River Nith valley (Nithsdale) before you reach the bridge over the river and the path into Sanquhar (pronounced sanker).

Sanquhar

Sanquhar offers a selection of hotels – try *Blackaddie House* (☎ 01659-50270) for a meal – and B&Bs, including the welcoming *Mrs McDowall* (☎ 01659-50751), in Town

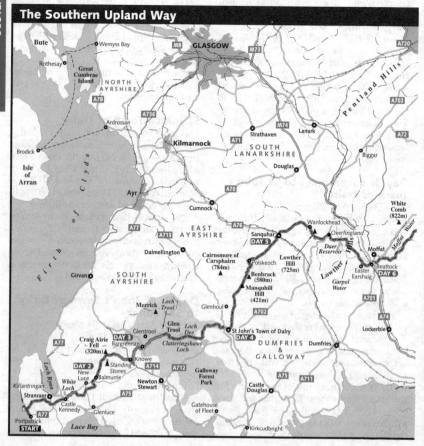

The Southern Upland Way

Head St, where the tariff is £15. *Castle View Caravan/Camping Site* (☎ 01659-50291) is beside the Way at the south end of town and charges £3 to pitch a tent. There are shops and a bank with an ATM in the town centre. ScotRail (☎ 0845-755 0033) trains from Carlisle and Glasgow stop here several times a day, and there's a daily Stagecoach Western bus (☎ 01387-253496) to Dumfries.

Day 5: Sanquhar to Beattock
28mi (45km), 10¼–10¾ hours
This stage includes three highlights: the halfway point of the Way, the highest point on the Way on Lowther Hill (725m), and the highest village in Scotland, Wanlockhead (425m). In spring and from 12 August to 1 November, walkers are requested to follow a deviation from the route between Cogshead and Wanlockhead, firstly to avoid disturbing breeding grouse and very young lambs, and later, shooters and their grouse. This adds about 2mi but saves the climb over Glengaber Hill. Many walkers do manage to complete this section in a day – probably the hardest day you'll ever put in on an LDP in Britain, with 1550m of climbing to contend with.

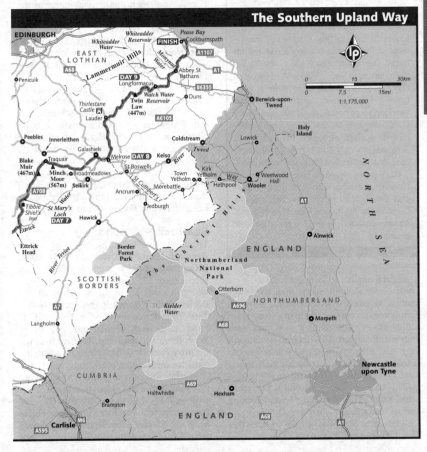

Southern Upland Way – Route Highlight

In the western half of the SUW the most sustained section of the route across open moorland, not blighted with long tedious stretches through pine plantations, is between St John's Town of Dalry (called Dalry) and Overfingland (a large farm) on the A702 south-east of Wanlockhead. The Way crosses several relatively high points, including Benbrack (580m), Glengaber Hill (515m) and the highest point on the entire SUW, Lowther Hill (725m). Wanlockhead, an old mining village, has a museum and extensive remains of the old lead mines.

On this section of the Way you won't spend too much time walking along sealed roads – most of the distance is along forest and hill tracks. The only drawback is the distance between places to stay. It's 27mi (43.5km) from Dalry to Sanquhar, although there is Polskeoch Bothy en route, and the warden at Kendoon youth hostel (about two hours' walk from Dalry) may be able to arrange an intermediate pick-up. However, after a night in Sanquhar, it's only 8mi (13km) to Wanlockhead and another 5mi (8km) to Overfingland.

Dalry is well served by buses from Ayr and Dumfries, Sanquhar is on the Carlisle to Glasgow railway line and you can catch a bus to Dumfries or Edinburgh from Overfingland. Accommodation is covered in the main walk description.

From Sanquhar to Wanlockhead there's a short climb straight away, then two more bumps to cross with Cogshead, a ruined farmhouse, set between them in a steep-sided valley. A steep descent on a good track leads into **Wanlockhead**. This old lead-mining village, with plenty of industrial archaeology, is a striking contrast to the bare, lonely moorland. There's an *SYHA Hostel* (☎ 01659-74252) charging £8.25, several B&Bs and a small *shop*. The **Museum of Lead Mining** and its tearoom are worth a visit.

From here the Way climbs to Lowther Hill, crossing and recrossing the sealed road

to the surreal golf ball domes (containing radar equipment) in an enclosure on the summit. On a good day you can see the Pentland Hills (near Edinburgh) to the north. The Way continues over the highest ground, with valleys falling away steeply on all sides, very steeply up to Cold Moss. It then drops down to the A702 at Overfingland, a large farm in a wide valley. Dumfries and Edinburgh buses, run jointly by MacEwans (☎ 01387-256533) and Stagecoach Western (☎ 01387-253496), stop here three times daily Monday to Saturday (only once on Sunday).

Just beyond the A702, in Watermeetings Forest, you reach the halfway point of the SUW as you climb through a wide clearing in the conifers. Then it's down to a road near the cottages beside the extensive Daer Reservoir. Here a long climb begins over Sweetshaw Brae, Hods Hill and Beld Knowe (507m), overlooking the reservoir. This is inevitably followed by an equally long descent down broad rides through the plantation to Cloffin Burn. The *bothy* at Brattleburn is out of sight, about 400m west of the Way. There's another *bothy*, Rivox, about a mile farther on, and signposted from the Way. The SUW continues its somewhat meandering route generally downhill, still in dense conifers, across a large clearing and Garpol Water, eventually reaching a minor road at Easter Earshaig Follow this to Beattock.

Beattock & Around

There are two hotels in town, of which *Beattock House* (☎ 01683-300403), about 200m south of the Way in the village, with rooms from £35, has an adjacent campsite where it costs £7 to pitch a tent. Of the B&Bs, historic *Barnhill Springs* (☎ 01683-220580) is beside the Way; the tariff is £21.

At Craigielands, about a mile south of the Way, there's a *shop* and the *Craigielands Country Park* (☎ 01683-300591), where the tariff for one camper is £4.

Moffat, just over a mile away, has more accommodation and places to eat (and banks with ATMs), but the A701 road is very busy, so try for a place that provides vehicle back-up. Moffat is well served by buses from Dumfries, Glasgow, Edinburgh and

Carlisle. MacEwan's (☎ 01387-256533) and Stagecoach Western (☎ 01387-253496) are the main operators.

Day 6: Beattock to St Mary's Loch

21mi (34km), 8–8½ hours
Another tough day, when you cross the watershed between streams flowing into the Irish and North Seas at Ettrick Head; the total ascent is 1200m.

From Beattock go under the A74 motorway then across the River Annan, up and over a small hill, then beside Moffat Water through woodland and along field edges. The Way turns uphill and winds through a plantation on a forest road and on to a path up a deep valley. This leads to the **gorge** carved by Selcloth Burn; the path traverses this dramatic cleft, then climbs to Ettrick Head (520m), the boundary between Dumfries & Galloway, and the Borders. Beyond here you soon meet a forest road that leads down to *Over Phawhope Bothy* and a minor road alongside Ettrick Water. Follow this for 6mi down the valley, its natural beauty somewhat compromised by blankets of conifers.

Turn off at Scabcleuch along a signposted footpath, which climbs up a narrow glen then crosses Pikestone Rig and continues down to Riskinhope Hope, where a once-solid stone house now lies in bramble-covered ruins. The route then turns round Earl's Hill and picks up a forest track for the descent to historic *Tibbie Shiel's Inn (☎ 01750-42231)* at St Mary's Loch, scene of the Way's opening in 1984. The inn offers relatively luxurious accommodation (starting at £24) and excellent bar meals (they understand vegetarians!). There's also a *campsite* nearby, run by the inn; the tariff is £2. A limited bus service run by McCall's links the nearby Glen Cafe with Galashiels and Moffat. For timetable details, phone the council transport information service on ☎ 08457-090510.

Day 7: St Mary's Loch to Melrose

30mi (48.5km), 11½–12 hours
Plenty of variety – lakes, hills and open moorland to Traquair, then forest, heather moor, a relatively suburban interlude around Galashiels and a riverside walk into Melrose. This ultra-long day could be split into two, with an overnight stop at Traquair, 12mi (20km) from St Mary's Loch. Of the total climb (1120m), 800m comes between Traquair and Melrose.

From the inn pass in front of the Sailing Clubhouse and follow a path, then a vehicle track, beside the loch, with superb views; farther on, cross Yarrow Water to the A708. The Way crosses the road and returns to open country. Good paths and tracks climb over a spur to Douglas Burn, then it's up again, across heathery Blake Muir and down to the hamlet of Traquair in the Tweed valley, at the junction of the B709 and B7062. Buses link Traquair with Peebles and Selkirk, and there are daily First Edinburgh buses (☎ 01721-720181) from these towns to Edinburgh.

Traquair Mill Bothy (☎ 01896-830515) is a commodious bunkhouse providing vehicle back-up; the tariff is £13. There's more accommodation in Innerleithen, about 1mi north along the B709 (and a bus service to Edinburgh).

Turning your back on Traquair, follow a lane (which can be muddy) climbing steadily into a plantation. Minch Moor (567m) rises on the right and the short detour is well worth the effort for the panoramic view, including the distinctive Eildon Hills near Melrose. The SUW continues along a wide ride through the plantation and rises to Brown Knowe (523m), which also provides good views. The next tops are skirted on the right and left. The turn-off to the *Broadmeadows SYHA Hostel (☎ 01750-76262)*, Scotland's first youth hostel, is signposted and is a mile or so to the south. If you're considering staying here, remember that the nearest shops are in Selkirk, 5mi away. The route continues up to a summit distinguished by three massive cairns known as the **Three Brethren**. Then it's down past conifers and deciduous woodland to Yair and a bridge over the River Tweed.

You then climb over a fairly broad ridge and go down across fields, crossing numerous stiles, to woodland on the outskirts of

Galashiels. The Way follows a rather devious route through parklands and along suburban streets, skirting round Gala Hill. Cross the busy A7 and follow riverside paths and a sealed cycle path along an old railway formation to Melrose.

Galashiels & Melrose

Both Galashiels and Melrose offer a wide choice of accommodation options. The seasonal TICs in Melrose (☎ 01896-822555), Abbey House, Abbey St; and Galashiels (☎ 01896-755551), 3 St John's St, can provide details. At *Gibson Park Caravan and Camp Site* (☎ 01896-822969), on the High St near the centre of Melrose, it costs around £6.20 to pitch a tent. The *Melrose SYHA Hostel* (☎ 01896-822521) is about a mile south of the Way, and has a tariff of £11.25. There are also abundant B&Bs and pubs, and good transport connections to destinations such as Edinburgh, Carlisle and Berwick-upon-Tweed.

The Southern Upland Way – Route Highlight

The eastern half of the SUW comprises the uplands between Beattock and Melrose, and the more settled, agricultural country between there and the coast. The best of the hill country – good views, minimal pine plantations and roads, and plenty of open moorland – is between St Mary's Loch and Galashiels or Melrose. The loch itself, fringed by woodland and overlooked by really high hills, is particularly scenic. Between Traquair and Yair (on the River Tweed) the SUW crosses several tops over 500m with fine wide views.

The walk can be split into two fairly easy days, staying overnight at Traquair or nearby Innerleithen (12mi/20km) on one night and then Galashiels or Melrose (18mi/28km) the next; some details are given in the main walk description.

Buses run to St Mary's from Galashiels, while Galashiels and Melrose are well served by public transport.

Day 8: Melrose to Longformacus
25mi (40km), 9–9½ hours

The first part of today's walk is through mainly agricultural land, along minor roads and farm tracks, and across fields, which can be very muddy in parts. Essentially the route traverses a long ridge between Allan Water and Leader Water, tributaries of the River Tweed. From Lauder there's a very different stretch across extensive grouse moors in the Lammermuir Hills and down to the hamlet of Longformacus. The day involves 750m of climbing.

From Melrose cross the River Tweed, this time by a chain suspension bridge for pedestrians and 'light carriages' only (dating from 1826). The Way goes back up beside the river then heads north, steadily gaining height. There are fine views on a good day from the highest point around flat-topped Kedslie Hill. The walk route passes through several fields occupied by grazing cows – they're very inquisitive but not aggressive. The steep descent into Lauder skirts the local golf course.

Lauder has three pubs and several B&Bs in and near the town, of which *Thirlestane Farm* (☎ 01578-722216) is particularly recommended (the tariff is £23). At *Thirlestane Castle Caravan & Camp Site* (☎ 01578-722254), near splendid Thirlestane Castle, the charge is £4. In the main street you'll find an excellent *baker*, small supermarkets, a *coffee shop* and a bank with an ATM. All of which is just as well – Lauder is the last place where you can stock up on chocolate and other daytime staples before Cockburnspath, at the end of Day 9. Buses from Galashiels and Edinburgh stop here.

From Lauder the Way weaves through the grounds of **Thirlestane Castle** (open to visitors). Cross the A697 and follow a lane up through the curiously named Wanton Walls Farm and steeply up to a small plantation. The trail then wanders up and down across open grassland, where the route may not be altogether clear, then crosses Blythe Water on a substantial bridge. Continue on to Braidshawrig, part of the Burncastle Estate grouse moor. It's essential to keep to the track (although there's no incentive to stray onto the tussocky moor), especially during the grouse shooting season, which always starts on 12 August and ends in early November. The track climbs across the vast empty moors, dotted with shooting butts and old tin sheds providing shelter for stock, to the ridge crest. It then turns right to the high point of **Twin Law** (447m), topped with two giant cylindrical cairns, each with a sheltered seat facing south-east. From here the Tweed valley is spread out before you and the sea apppears at last. The descent towards Watch Water Reservoir is easy – a good track leads to Scarlaw and a sealed road. Continue to Longformacus village (pronounced longformaycus) and the excellent *Eildon Cottage* B&B (☎ *01361-890230*), where you'll undoubtedly appreciate the magnificent four-course evening meal; the tariff starts at £16.

Day 9: Longformacus to Cockburnspath
17mi (27.5km), 6¾–7¼ hours
Paths and tracks through farmland and woodland lead to a fine cliff-top walk, but you have to leave the coast to officially finish in the village of Cockburnspath. The day's ascent amounts to 450m.

After about a mile along a minor road, east of Longformacus, the Way branches off to climb over moorland past some small plantations and down to the B6355. From here the route follows steep-sided Whiteadder Valley through mixed woodland to the hamlet of Abbey St Bathans. Cross Whiteadder Water just below where it joins Monynut Water. In a change from the officially mapped route, the Way follows the Whiteadder for a while then turns north (the *Riverside* restaurant is just across the river here) to follow paths and lanes, crossing some fields in the process. From a minor road at Blackburn you can catch a last glimpse back to the hills. Then it's down to the busy A1; cross with care. Follow an old road between the A1 and the railway to a pleasant green track into Penmanshiel Wood. It seems cruel at this stage but the route climbs through the wood, fortunately

to a very rewarding view of the North Sea and the Firth of Forth. A long flight of steps takes you down to the A1107, beyond which is Pease Dean Wildlife Reserve, where the native woodland is being regenerated.

Skirt the serried ranks of vans in *Pease Bay Caravan & Camp Site* (☎ *01368-830206*), where tent pitches cost around £5, and walk up the road above the bay. The final walk along the cliff top – mirroring the start at Portpatrick – is blessed with impressive coastal scenery, along to colourful Cove Harbour, tucked below. To officially finish the Way turn inland, under the A1 and the railway line, to the mercat cross at Cockburnspath (pronounced coburns-path or just co-path). It takes a while to sink in that you really have walked 212mi from Portpatrick.

Cockburnspath
There are a couple of B&Bs on nearby farms, including *Mrs Hood* (☎ *01368-830499*), who charges around £20; and the excellent *Chesterfield Caravan & Camping Site* (☎ *01368-830459*), where the tariff is £6. Both have a pick-up service. Unfortunately the nearest pub is at Grantshouse, a few miles south along the main A1 road. At least the small *shop* in Cockburnspath is licensed!

The West Highland Way

Distance	95mi (153km)
Duration	7 days
Standard	medium
Start	Milngavie (near Glasgow)
Finish	Fort William
Gateways	Glasgow, Fort William
Summary	Britain's most popular LDP passes through a tremendous variety of landscapes. It is easy to follow but passes over rough or exposed terrain in many places, especially in the northern sections.

The West Highland Way extends for 95mi from the outskirts of Scotland's largest city to the base of its highest mountain. The route is walked by some 50,000 people every year and is officially the most popular path in Britain.

The walk starts from Milngavie (pronounced mullguy), 7mi north of Glasgow's city centre, and passes through some of the most spectacular scenery in Britain. It starts in the lowlands, but the greater part of this walk is among the mountains, lochs and fast-flowing rivers of the Highlands. It runs along the length of Loch Lomond and, in the far north, the route crosses wild Rannoch Moor and passes through magical Glen Nevis to reach Fort William. The route is well signposted and uses a combination of ancient ways, old drove roads along which cattle were herded in the past, the old military road (built by troops to help control the Jacobites in the 18th century) and disused railway lines.

The first section of the walk is fairly easy going as far as Rowardennan. After that, particularly north of Bridge of Orchy, it's quite strenuous and remote. You need to be properly equipped with good boots, maps, a compass, food and drink. There's no shelter on Rannoch Moor if the weather turns bad, which it's quite likely to do. The area has a very high rainfall, and the wind in the narrow mountain valleys and on the more exposed areas can reach gale force.

Direction, Distance & Duration

Since the northern section is more challenging, it is generally advised to start in the south at Milngavie. This also gives the advantage of having the prevailing wind and sun behind you. The walk route is marked with signposts and the Scottish waymark (a thistle within a hexagon), with yellow arrows to show direction.

The official route length is 95mi, although you will need to add extra distance for any diversions off the route, such as an ascent of Ben Lomond. Most people do the walk in six or seven days. The location of accommodation in the north means you will either have some very long days or rather short days in this section.

For a seven-day walk, as described here, the most convenient places to start and end each day are:

day	from	to	mi/km
1	Milngavie	Drymen	12/19.5
2	Drymen	Rowardennan	14/22.5
3	Rowardennan	Inverarnan	14/22.5
4	Inverarnan	Tyndrum	13/21
5	Tyndrum	Kings House Hotel	19/30.5
6	Kings House Hotel	Kinlochleven	9/14.5
7	Kinlochleven	Fort William	14/22.5

Alternatives If your time is limited and you just want to walk a day or two of the West Highland Way, see the boxed text 'The West Highland Way – Some Route Highlights' on p530 for suggestions of the best day walks along the route.

To do the walk in six days, spend the third night in Crianlarich, the fourth night in Bridge of Orchy and reach Kinlochleven on the fifth night, stopping for lunch at Kings House Hotel.

Most people will want to add an extra day in order to go up Ben Nevis (see the Ben Nevis walk description in the Ben Nevis & Glen Coe chapter). Ben Lomond (see the Central Highlands & Islands chapter) and Beinn Dorain are other mountains beside the walk route that are worth attention. Add

When to Walk the Way

The West Highland Way can be walked at any time of the year. May is the most popular month, as many people try to avoid the midges, and spring and autumn can be particularly beautiful. Note that the Conic Hill section is closed for lambing during the last two weeks in April and the first two weeks in May, and the section between the Bridge of Orchy and Fort William is often used for the annual Scottish motorcycle trials around the same time. Diversions are set up, but contact the ranger service (☎ 01389-758216) for further information. The Way itself is unaffected by deer stalking, but detours from the track should generally be avoided between August and October.

another day if you want to walk from Glasgow to Milngavie along the Clyde, Allander or Kelvin walkways.

PLANNING
Maps & Books
Although the route is fully waymarked, a map and compass and the ability to use them is still recommended. The Way is covered by OS Landranger 1:50,000 maps No 64 (*Glasgow*), No 56 (*Loch Lomond & Inveraray*), No 50 (*Glen Orchy & Loch Etive*) and No 41 (*Ben Nevis*), although most people find the best option is to take a purpose-designed all-in-one route map. The excellent Harvey *West Highland Way Map* and the cheap and cheerful Footprint *West Highland Way* are more than adequate, and also include lots of additional practical information for walkers.

The best guidebook is the expensive *West Highland Way* by Bob Aitken & Roger Smith. The guide comes with its own 1:50,000 OS route map. The OS guidebook *West Highland Way* is lavishly illustrated, has good route descriptions and detailed, but dated, mapping at 1:25,000. There's also *A Guide to the West Highland Way* by Tom Hunter and *The West Highland Way* by Terry Marsh.

For details of side trips from the track, or as an alternative challenge for mountain-lovers, *The Highland High Way* by Heather Cannon & Paul Roper details a high-level route from Loch Lomond to Fort William. Walks suggested broadly stick to the traditional West Highland Way route, while taking in 23 Munros along the way (for a definition of Munro, see the boxed text 'Munros & Munro Bagging' on p452 in the Central Highland & Islands chapter).

Information Sources
For a free leaflet listing accommodation on the West Highland Way, contact the Loch Lomond Park Ranger Service (☎ 01389-758216) at Balloch Castle, the Highland Countryside Ranger Service (☎ 01397-705922) at the Ionad Nibheis Visitor Centre in Glen Nevis, or the Scottish Tourist Board (☎ 0131-332 2433).

The West Highland Way Web site (W www.west-highland-way.co.uk) is also very useful, offering practical information, accommodation listings and links to the rangers' email site for further queries. Copies of the free *West Highland Wayfarer* newspaper can be found at Milngavie train station or at TICs in the area.

There are TICs in Glasgow (☎ 0141-204 4400); Drymen (☎ 01360-660068), open from late May to the end of September; Tyndrum (☎ 01838-400246), open between April and October; and at Fort William (☎ 01397-703781).

Guided Walks & Baggage Services
Several companies run walking holidays on the West Highland Way with vehicle support. C-N-Do Scotland (☎ 01786- 445703, e info@cndoscotland.com, W www.cndoscotland.com), Unit 32 Stirling Enterprise Park, Stirling FK7 7RP; and Lomond Walking Holidays (☎ 01786-447752, W www.biggar-net.co.uk/lomond), 34c James St, Riverside, Stirling FK8 1UG, are two of the larger companies.

You can make the going easier by using a pack-carrying service. Travel-Lite (☎ 0141-956 6810) charges £32 to pick up your bag each morning and deliver it to your next B&B or hostel (up to eight collections and deliveries).

PLACES TO STAY AND EAT
Accommodation should not be too difficult to find, although between Bridge of Orchy and Kinlochleven it's quite limited. In May, July and August you must book all accommodation in advance. A company called Easyways (☎ 01324-714132, fax 887766, W www.easyways.com) offers an accommodation booking service.

There are three SYHA hostels on the walk at Rowardennan, Crianlarich and Glen Nevis. There are bunkhouses at Drymen, Inverarnan, Tyndrum, Bridge of Orchy, Kinlochleven and Glen Nevis. Even more basic are the free bothies and camping barns at Rowchoish and Doune, both on Day 3.

Camping is only permitted on the West Highland Way in designated areas. There are several official sites, some hotels allow camping in their grounds in return for evening patronage, and there are also several free, one-night-only backpacker sites without facilities (no fires allowed).

Most B&Bs provide evening meals if requested in advance, and also packed lunches if you ask on arrival. Some B&Bs, particularly those not directly on the route, will send someone to meet yozu and drive you back next morning for a small charge.

GETTING TO/FROM THE WALK

For information on travel options between England, Wales and Scotland, see the Getting Around chapter.

Bus National Express/Scottish Citylink (☎ 0870-550 5050) runs coaches between Glasgow, Fort William and most parts of Britain. There are frequent buses from Glasgow bus station to Milngavie, but they take twice as long as the train.

Train Glasgow has excellent rail links with the rest of Britain – 20 trains a day from London's Euston to Glasgow Central (five hours). It's then a 10-minute walk to Glasgow's Queen St for trains to Milngavie (departures every half-hour). If you only want to do part of the walk, Crianlarich, Upper Tyndrum, Lower Tyndrum and Bridge of Orchy are all served by trains. For timetables and fares contact the National Rail Enquiry Service (☎ 0845-748 4950, W www.nationalrail.co.uk) and for reservations contact ScotRail (☎ 0845-755 0033).

Fort William is on the West Highland Railway and the most scenic way to end your walk is to make the famous train journey back over Rannoch Moor to Glasgow, or onwards to Mallaig (see the boxed text 'The West Highland Railway' on p464). A single from Fort William to Glasgow costs £20, which is more than twice the price of the bus.

Car Milngavie is 7mi north of Glasgow on the A82/A809 (take exit 17 off the M8).

Fort William is 104mi north of Glasgow on the A82.

THE WALK
Glasgow

Glasgow, Scotland's largest city, has excellent transport links, is a good place to get supplies, and offers an array of places to stay and eat. The TIC (☎ 0141-204 4400) is on George Square.

Glasgow's **SYHA Hostel** (☎ 0141-332 3004, 7 Park Terrace) charges £12.75 for a bed, rising to £13.75 during July and August. Nearby, the **Glasgow Backpackers Hostel** (☎ 0141-332 9099, 17 Park Terrace) is only open from July to September. Beds are from £10.50. Just south of here, **Berkeley Globetrotters** (☎ 0141-204 5470, 56–63 Berkeley St) has beds from £10.50. Perhaps the best-value, centrally placed guesthouse accommodation is at **McLay's Guesthouse** (☎ 0141-332 4796, 264 Renfrew St), where B&B costs from £19.

Milngavie

There are several banks and plenty of shops, eating places and B&Bs in Milngavie. For B&B, **Barloch Guest House** (☎ 0141-956 1432), on Strathblane Rd, or **West View Guest House** (☎ 0141-956 5973, 1 Douglaston Gardens) both cost around £20. You can also camp at **Bankell Farm** (☎ 0141-956 1733), about 1mi from the start of the walk, for £2.50. The pick of the places to eat in Milngavie is **Toscana**, Italian-run and good for just a coffee or a tasty pasta meal from £5.

Day 1: Milngavie to Drymen
12mi (19.5km), 4½–5½ hours

The first day offers easy walking through rather unspectacular rolling countryside and farmland. For about 3mi the path runs along a disused railway track that can be muddy if it's wet, then there's a couple of miles along a quiet road. The Beech Tree Inn at Dumgoyne is the only convenient food stop; otherwise you'll need to bring lunch with you.

From the start at Milngavie train station, go through the underpass and up into the pedestrianised town centre. An unmissable granite obelisk commemorates the West Highland Way and is virtually the only point on it where walkers usually get lost! A small sign on a nearby building indicates that you should turn right here. Follow the stream (Allander Water) through the trees to join good paths through Mugdock Wood. At the end of the wood you meet a road; turn left then almost immediately turn right onto a path again. The path soon becomes a vehicle track and there's a good view to your right over Craigallian Loch.

Pass a collection of holiday homes and you will soon arrive at the B821. Turn left along the road and follow it for about 300m until a style leads onto another path to the right. The West Highland Way skirts Dumgoyach Hill (watch out for Bronze Age standing stones to your right just before the hill) and, after Dumgoyach Bridge, joins a disused railway track. After about 800m you pass the path to Glengoyne Distillery, which can be visited from April to October. Another 800m farther on you reach the *Beech Tree Inn* at Dumgoyne, a pub that serves food all day. The village of Killearn is 1.5mi off the route to the right – it has accommodation, shops, pubs and a post office.

The West Highland Way continues along the old railway track to Gartness. Join a minor road, turn left and cross the attractive bridge and weir. The road is then followed all the way to Drymen. A mile after Gartness is *Easter Drumquhassle Farm* (☎ 01360-660893), which has B&B for £18.50. There are also places in wigwams for £7 and camping costs £4. You get your first view of Loch Lomond from here.

Pass an ugly quarry and continue along the road to a sharp left turn. Just before the bend, there's B&B at *Gateside Lodge* (☎ 01360-660215), from £17. Just after the bend, the West Highland Way leaves the road and follows a path to the right. If you're going to Drymen, continue along the road and cross the A811 to enter the village.

Drymen
Mrs Bolzicco (☎ 01360-660566, 8 Old Gartmore Rd) offers B&B for £18. The top place to stay is the *Winnock Hotel* (☎ 01360-660245) with B&B from £43. There's also the only Indian restaurant-takeaway on the route, the *Drymen Tandoori* (☎ 01360-660099), which also offers B&B from £20. The best pub is the *Clachan*, which dates back to 1734, making it Scotland's oldest pub. If you're hungry it has a dozen different steaks on offer, from £12 to £15. There is a grocery *shop* for self-caterers, a *cafe* and several more pubs, as well as a bank. The TIC (☎ 01360-660068) is in the town library.

Day 2: Drymen to Rowardennan
14mi (22.5km), 5–6½ hours
Walking on the second day is still easy going and, apart from the climb up Conic Hill (358m), it is mostly along undulating paths and along the banks of Loch Lomond. The only place for food supplies is Balmaha, around three hours from Drymen.

From where it meets the A811 just outside Drymen, the path turns right and follows alongside the road for a short section. It then veers left onto Forestry Commission tracks and gradually climbs through the dense woods to Garadhban Forest (there is a wild *campsite* here with no facilities). Near the end of the trees, just over an hour from Drymen, a path to the left leads to the road into Milton of Buchanan. This path provides the alternative route when Conic Hill is closed during the lambing season (see the boxed text 'When to Walk the Way' on p522). Milton of Buchanan has two B&Bs, *Dunleen* (☎ 01360-870274) and *Mar Achlais* (☎ 01360-870300), both at around £19, but no pubs or shops. B&B owners offer a pick-up service if you want to go into Balmaha or Drymen.

For most of the year the West Highland Way continues through the trees, over a stile and onto open moorland. Cross a burn and begin the ascent of **Conic Hill**, an altitude gain of 200m. The path contours just north of the summit. It is a short detour to reach the top but the wonderful panorama over Loch Lomond is certainly worth the effort. Conic Hill is a boundary point and a landmark for walkers; from here onwards you're in the Highlands.

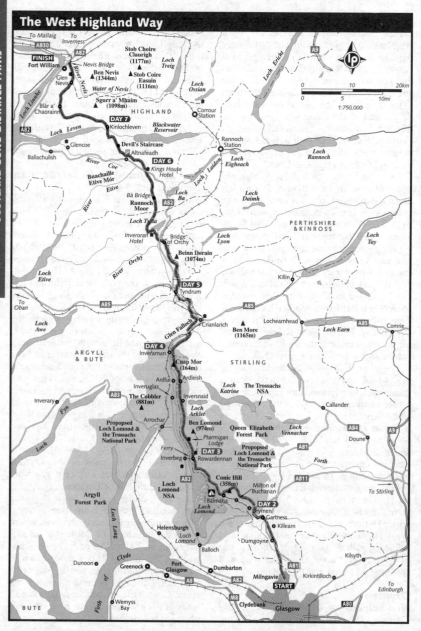

The West Highland Way

The path descends through a pine wood to Balmaha and the loch itself. The *Oak Tree Inn* (☎ *01360-870357*), on the lochside, offers B&B at £20/£27 for singles/doubles, camping for £5 and has food available in the bar. There are several other places offering B&B, including *Bay Cottage* (☎ *01360-870346*), which charges £21. There's a *shop* and *cafe* in the village.

The section between Balmaha and Rowardennan can be busy with day trippers during summer and solitude can be difficult to find. The route begins by hugging the shore, passing a marker commemorating the opening of the West Highland Way in 1980. In less than an hour you reach Milarrochy, where there's a *Camping & Caravan Club campsite* (☎ *01360-870236*), charging £11.80 for a two person tent for nonmembers. There's a shop on site. About 800m beyond, to the left, is *Critreoch* (☎ *01360-870309*) with B&B from £18.

The path now dives into a dark forest, before emerging to follow the road for about a mile. Just after Sallochy House it returns to the trees and climbs through **Ross Wood** to Rowardennan. This oak forest is some of the finest remaining natural woodland in Scotland.

Rowardennan

Rowardennan is really just the *Rowardennan Hotel* (☎ *01360-870273*) with B&B from £35 and bar food served all afternoon. A path leads from the hotel up to the summit of Ben Lomond (974m), a 7mi return trip. (For a description of the route, see the Ben Lomond walk description in the Central Highlands & Islands chapter.)

The *SYHA Hostel* (☎ *01360-870259*) in the Rowardennan Lodge is 20 minutes beyond the hotel. Booking is required from May to August and beds cost £9.25. Two hundred metres to the right of the hostel entrance is a *campsite* without facilities.

Ben Lomond Cottage B&B (☎ *01360-870411*) is right beside the walk and has well-appointed facilities for £25 per person; evening meals are available. The Forestry Commission's *Cashel Camping and Caravan Site* (☎ *01360-870234*) is also very popular; the average tariff per 'unit' (person and tent) is £4.40.

By summer 2001 there will be a visitors centre at Rowardennan car park which will also provide information about the national park. NTS rangers (☎ *01360-870224*) lead guided walks on Ben Lomond

In summer there are ferry services across Loch Lomond between Rowardennan and Inverbeg.

Day 3: Rowardennan to Inverarnan
14mi (22.5km), 6–7½ hours
Today's walk begins with 4mi of Forestry Commission track, followed by a 6mi section down by the lochside. The only place for food along the way is the large Inversnaid Hotel, 7mi beyond Rowardennan.

From Rowardennan follow the unsurfaced road that runs parallel to the loch. After Ptarmigan Lodge an alternative path branches left and takes a low route through the trees, but the path is eroded and heavy going. The official route offers much easier walking and follows the track higher up the hillside. The area around here has seen extensive conservation work in recent years. Large-scale forestry felling is scheduled to take place and the lochside woodlands will be replanted with native broadleaf trees.

From both routes you can reach *Rowchoish Bothy*, a stone shelter with a fireplace, a sleeping platform and a dirt floor. It's free and always open. About 400m after the bothy, the low route meets the high route and soon after the forestry track becomes a path again. The path now dives down to the lochside and there's some occasionally difficult walking along to Inversnaid. Shortly before the village, the path crosses Snaid Burn, just above the impressive Inversnaid Falls. The *Inversnaid Hotel* (☎ *01877-386223*) has 109 rooms at £30. A farther 400m north is the Inversnaid Boathouse, where wild *camping* is permitted. In summer there is a ferry service between Inversnaid and Inveruglas; useful for reaching transport options.

From Inversnaid to the foot of Glen Falloch is one of the most difficult parts of the route, although recent work on the path has improved things greatly. The path goes up and down through wooded slopes (oak and birchwood) and can involve some scrambling. The loch is now much narrower and the valley deeper. The path passes the outlaw Rob Roy's cave, although there's little to see. There's basic accommodation at *Doune Bothy* (with the same facilities as Rowchoish Bothy). Almost a mile beyond the bothy at Ardleish, there's a landing stage used by the ferry crossing to *Ardlui Hotel* (☎ 01301-704243), where B&B costs £30 and camping costs £7 for a two-person tent.

At this point you leave the loch and climb to a col on the hill of **Cnap Mor**. There are good views from here on a clear day, both north towards the highlands and south over Loch Lomond. The path now begins to descend towards Inverarnan. Shortly before arriving at the village, the path crosses the Ben Glas Burn. Just upstream are the spectacular **Beinglas Falls**, a cascade of 300m that forms an impressive sight indeed after heavy rain. Leave the route and cross the river to reach Inverarnan.

Inverarnan

On the way into Inverarnan, on the north side of Gen Glas Burn, is *Beinglas Farm* (☎ 01301-704281), which has wigwam accommodation for £8 and camping for £4.

In the village, the wonderfully atmospheric *Drover's Inn* (☎ 01301-704234) charges £22 for B&B, but service is reported to be very slow in the morning. Opposite is the *Stagger Inn*, where the traditional Scottish food is excellent.

Day 4: Inverarnan to Tyndrum
13mi (21km), 4½–5½ hours
This day is much easier than the previous day and passes through open country next to a river. Unfortunately you're also following the busy road and railway line. Unless you make a detour down to Crianlarich (20 minutes each way), there's nowhere to get food until Tyndrum.

From Inverarnan the route follows the attractive River Falloch most of the way to Crianlarich. At the beginning the valley is

narrow, the river is turbulent and the banks are lined with trees. Soon the valley begins to open out and the river becomes more placid. After 3.5mi the path crosses the river and continues along the west bank. Half a mile farther on it leaves the river and climbs through a small tunnel under the railway line and then crosses under the A82 to join an old military road.

The road climbs out of Glen Falloch towards the trees ahead. At the stile into the forest there's a path leading down to the right towards Crianlarich; this is the approximate halfway point of the West Highland Way. There's no need to go down to Crianlarich, but the village does have a railway station, bank, post office, shops and numerous places to stay and eat. The *SYHA Hostel* (☎ 01838-300260) costs £9.25. There's B&B at *Ben More Lodge Hotel* (☎ 01838-300210) for £31, and at *Craigbank Guest House* (☎ 01838-300279), for £17. The *Rod & Reel* has a good restaurant and is also a great place for a drink.

Returning to the West Highland Way, the route climbs to the left from the stile, offering good views across to Ben More on the right. It then continues on good paths through the trees for about 2mi before crossing under the railway line and over the road again.

The path then crosses the River Fillan via a wooden bridge, where there is a wild *campsite* with no facilities on the west bank. Pass the remains of St Fillan's Priory, turn left and follow the track to reach *Auchtertyre Farm* (☎ 01838-400251) in about 20 minutes. There's wigwam accommodation from £9 and camping for £3.

The route crosses the A82 once more, passes several minor roads and, in less than an hour, reaches Tyndrum, formerly a lead-mining settlement.

Tyndrum
The village is strung out along the A82. The TIC (☎ 01838-400246) is in the car park of the *Invervey Hotel* (☎ 01838-400219). The hotel has a good pub and offers B&B from £25. Other places to stay include *Dalkell* (☎ 01838-400285), where B&B costs from

Only for the adventurous – the remote Black Cuillin range, the Isle of Skye

The imposing peak of Slioch, in the Great Wilderness of the Western Highlands

For Munro baggers, An Teallach (1062m) is a classic among Scottish peaks

The old fishing harbour of Crail, on the Fife Coastal Path, Scotland

£20; and *Pine Trees Leisure Park* (☎ *01838-400243*), alongside the river, charges £8.50 for bunkhouse accommodation and £3.50 for camping. In the village there's also an outdoor gear shop and a self-service restaurant, the *Clifton Coffee Shop*. There's a train station and, if you need it, there's also a taxi and baggage-carrying service available on ☎ 01838-400279.

Day 5: Tyndrum to Kings House Hotel

19mi (30.5km), 6½–8 hours
An early start is necessary for this, the longest day of the walk. Mainly on good surfaces, the walk is not difficult but it does cross Rannoch Moor, the wildest section of the West Highland Way. The only places for food are the pub at Bridge of Orchy and, an hour beyond, the Inveroran Hotel.

From Tyndrum the path runs parallel to the A82 and the railway line for a while, crossing the train tracks twice, before rejoining the old military road. This is easy, clear walking with lovely views. Three miles from Tyndrum you cross a burn at the foot of 1074m Beinn Dorain, the mountain that dominates this section of the path. Just before the bridge there's B&B on the left at *Auch Farm* (☎ *01838-400233*) for £14.

From here it is another 3mi to Bridge of Orchy. The path climbs gradually to pass the entrance to Glen Orchy, crossing the railway again en route. This is the beginning of the really mountainous scenery. Bridge of Orchy is not much more than a train station, a post office and a church. The *Bridge of Orchy Hotel* (☎ *01838-400208*) is the village's dominant feature. B&B costs from £49 and there's bunkhouse accommodation for £9. It has no cooking facilities but the bar serves good food. A new, self-catering bunkhouse, the *West Highland Way Sleeper* (☎ *01855-831381*) is due to open in late 2001 in the old station building and should cost around £8. There is *camping* (no facilities) just over the bridge on the right.

Cross the old bridge (built in 1750) and climb through trees to moorland, from where there are superb views across to Rannoch Moor. The path here has been upgraded

recently and is now very good. The route winds down to the secluded *Inveroran Hotel* (☎ *01838-400220*), where there's B&B for £29. Another *campsite* (no facilities) can be found beside a stone bridge 400m west of the hotel.

The West Highland Way follows the road round a bend before the sealed road turns into a track. It then climbs gently past three tree plantations and out onto the wild moor. There's no shelter for about 7mi and Bà Bridge, about 3mi after the tree plantations, is the only real marker point. It can be very wild and windy up here and there's a real sense of isolation. A cairn marks the summit at 445m and from here there's a wonderful view down into Glen Coe.

As the path descends from the moor to join the road again, you can see the chair lift of the Glen Coe Ski Centre to the left. There's a cafe and skiing museum at the base station, about 500m off the West Highland Way. **Kings House Hotel** is just over a mile ahead across the A82. Dating from the 17th century, the building was used after the Battle of Culloden as barracks for the troops of George III (hence the name).

Kings House Hotel & Around

Kings House Hotel (☎ *01855-851259*) has accommodation from £24 but breakfast costs an extra £7. There's a restaurant and popular climbers bar at the back. Free *camping* (no facilities) is available just behind the hotel.

If you can't get a bed here you may want to consider taking a bus to Glencoe (11mi west), where there's a wider selection of accommodation. See Glencoe under Glen Coe & Glen Etive Circuit in the Ben Nevis & Glen Coe chapter.

Day 6: Kings House Hotel to Kinlochleven

9mi (14.5km), 3–4 hours
The superb mountain scenery continues. This day is not long, but includes the climb up the Devil's Staircase (a 330m gain in altitude) and a long knee-cracking descent to Kinlochleven. There's nowhere to get food en route and no shelter.

From Kings House Hotel the route goes along the old military road, and follows alongside the A82 to a car park on a bend in the road at Altnafeadh. This is a wonderful vantage point from which to appreciate the mountainous scenery of Glen Coe. The conical mountain to your left is Buachaille Etive Mór. The Altnafeadh car park is also the starting point for the ascent of this mountain and for the Glen Coe & Glen Etive Circuit (see the Ben Nevis & Glen Coe chapter).

The West Highland Way – Some Route Highlights

If you want to get a taste of the West Highland Way without attempting the entire path, one of the best sections is between Kings House Hotel and Glen Nevis. It is quite possible to complete these two sections in a single day, although the total distance for the day adds up to a fairly lengthy 19mi (30.5km). Paths are good all the way and the going is fairly quick with just day-packs to carry. Allow about nine hours for the walk.

Start at the Altnafeadh car park on the A82, 3mi north-west of Kings House Hotel. Citylink buses (☎ 0870-550 5050) from Glasgow and Fort William both pass the car park and the driver will stop if you request it in advance. At the end of the day you can either stay at Glen Nevis or catch one of the frequent buses to Fort William, a service run by Highland Country Buses (☎ 01397 702373). See the Ben Nevis route in the Ben Nevis & Glen Coe chapter for details.

One of the other highlights of the route is walking along the wooded shores of Loch Lomond, passing several spectacular waterfalls. The section from Inversnaid to Inverarnan covers 7mi (11km) and can be easily completed as a day walk. A passenger ferry (☎ 01877-386223) from Inveruglas on the western side of the loch will take you across the water to Inversnaid. Both Inveruglas and Inverarnan are request stops on the Glasgow–Fort William bus service run by Scottish Citylink (☎ 0870-550 5050).

From here the West Highland Way turns right and leaves the road to begin a fairly steep, zigzag climb up the **Devil's Staircase**. The cairn at the top is at 548m and marks the highest point of the whole walk. The views are stunning, especially on a clear day, and you should be able to see Ben Nevis to the north.

The path winds slowly down towards Kinlochleven, hidden below in the glen. As you descend you join the Blackwater Reservoir access track and meet the pipes that pump water down to the town's hydroelectric power station. The effect is not particularly pretty but it has been the basis of the town's industrial prosperity for years. Kinlochleven is a factory town that has been built on the smelting of aluminium, and the water pumped in the pipes beside you is what makes it all possible.

Kinlochleven

The town offers a return to 'civilisation', with a bank (open on Thursday only, no ATM), shops, pubs, restaurants and plenty of accommodation. Stay on the west bank of the river as you enter the town and the first accommodation you reach is the new **Blackwater Hostel** (☎ 01855-831253). Beds cost from £10 and camping is £4. **Tailrace Inn** (☎ 01855-831777), on Riverside Rd, offers B&B for £23 and there's good pub grub served all day. Also in the village there's cheap food at the **Harlequin Bakery & Restaurant** and at the **fish and chip shop**.

North of the village, just where the path leaves the road again, is **Macdonald Hotel and Lochside Campsite** (☎ 01855-831539), charging from £24 for B&B and £4 for camping. One of the best places to stay is a 20-minute walk farther along the West Highland Way. Set up on the hillside, **Mamore Lodge Hotel** (☎ 01855-831213) has B&B from £28, with great views over Loch Leven and a pleasant bar.

Day 7: Kinlochleven to Fort William

14mi (22.5km), 5½–7 hours
The final day is one of the hardest but most enjoyable, through varied terrain and with spectacular views that include Ben Nevis.

You need to be prepared for bad weather as there's little shelter. There's nowhere to buy food until Glen Nevis, almost at the end of the West Highland Way, so you need to carry food and drink.

From Kinlochleven follow the road north out of town. The West Highland Way turns off the road to the right, just opposite the school. The path climbs through woodland, crossing over a lane that leads to Mamore Lodge and emerges onto the old military road. At an altitude of about 250m you can see far down the wide glen ahead, which is enclosed on both sides by mountains. The track that you are following runs through the middle of the valley. The highest point is at 335m, which comes shortly before you reach the ruins of several old farm buildings. From here the route continues gently downhill to enter forestry plantations in just under 2mi.

Continue through the woods for 1mi to emerge at Blàr a' Chaorainn, which is nothing more than a bench, but the information panel with Fort William bus and train timetables could be useful.

After Blàr a' Chaorainn the path goes through some more forestry plantations and there are several steep descents to cross streams. Occasionally there are breaks in the trees and fine views of Ben Nevis ahead. At the end of the trees a sign directs you towards **Dun Deardail**, an Iron Age fort with walls that have been partly vitrified (turned to glass) by fires beside them. The fort is just a short detour from the path.

Shortly after the fort, cross another stile and descend into Glen Nevis following the Forestry Commission track. Across the valley the huge bulk of Ben Nevis fills your vision. A side track leads down to the village of Glen Nevis. There are several accommodation options here and this would be a good base if you wanted to polish off your walk with an ascent of 'The Ben'. See the Ben Nevis walk description in the Ben Nevis & Glen Coe chapter for details of both the ascent and accommodation options in Glen Nevis.

Continue along the path if you're pushing on to the bitter end, passing an interesting little graveyard just before you meet the road that runs up the glen. Turn left here and soon after there's a large visitors centre on the right. Continue along the roadside down into Fort William. The West Highland Way ends, like so many other British LDPs, with a bit of an anticlimax; just a sign by the busy but rather anonymous road junction on the edge of town. Thankfully Fort William has enough restaurants and bars for you to go on and celebrate your arrival in your own style.

Fort William

For details on facilities, accommodation options, places to eat and transport links in Fort William, see Gateways in the introduction to the Ben Nevis & Glen Coe chapter.

Other Walks

If you are a long-distance walk fanatic, you may be interested in some of Scotland's other LDPs, especially if the West Highland Way sounds too busy and the Southern Upland Way too long and serious. There are not many LDPs in Scotland, official or otherwise (even the official ones aren't called national trails), reflecting the right to roam in the wilderness tradition of Scottish walking.

THE GREAT GLEN WAY

The Great Glen – the wide, deep trench that almost severs the Highlands from the rest of Scotland – is a natural route for an LDP. The scenery is magnificent, with Ben Nevis and the Nevis Range at the south-western end, and Loch Ness and the Moray Firth at the north-eastern outlet. In between are superb Loch Lochy and Loch Oich and several fine hills. Access by public transport is excellent, towns and villages are conveniently spaced, and there's a good basic chain of paths and tracks. The Great Glen Way (GGW) is set to become Scotland's fourth official LDP and should be opened during 2001. Linking Fort William on the west coast and Inverness on the shores of the Moray Firth in the east, it follows long stretches of the historic Caledonian Canal's towpath, sections of the

Great Glen Cycleway, an old railway formation and quiet roads and tracks.

Direction, Distance & Duration

The GGW could be walked in either direction – both have their strong points. Starting at Fort William you'd be surrounded by mountains, while at Inverness you're near the Moray Firth with the hills in the distance. The prevailing wind is technically from the south-west, but it's almost as likely to be coming from the north or north-east. Fort William is at the northern end of the West Highland Way (see the walk description earlier), so now there's the opportunity for a really long walk of about 170mi (274km), linking Glasgow and Inverness. The GGW is about 70mi (113km) long; spread this over four or five days and you'll have a reasonably comfortable walk. The small amount of climbing involved is mainly at the north-eastern end, between Invermoriston and Bunloit (above Drumnadrochit) and from Drumnadrochit up to the Abriachan plateau.

Planning

There is no official guide or leaflet – yet. An unofficial guide, *The Great Glen Way* by Heather Common & Paul Roper, has basic maps but does not follow the official route in its entirety. Look out for the Rucksack Readers guide, *The Great Glen Way*, with more detailed maps and a handy format. OS Landranger 1:50,000 maps No 26 *(Inverness & Loch Ness)*, No 34 *(Fort Augustus)* and No 41 *(Ben Nevis)* cover the route.

Places to Stay & Eat

There is no shortage of accommodation – hostels, camping grounds and B&Bs – through the Great Glen. The GGW passes through Gairlochy, Laggan, Fort Augustus, Invermoriston and Drumnadrochit. Contact the TICs at Fort William (☎ 01397-703781) or Inverness (☎ 01463-234353) for a Highlands accommodation guide.

Getting to/from the Walk

Bus Scottish Citylink buses (☎ 0870-550 5050) reach Fort William and Inverness from Glasgow and Edinburgh; there are also Citylink and Highland Country Buses (☎ 01463-233371) services through the Great Glen.

Train Fort William and Inverness can also be reached by ScotRail (☎ 0845-755 0033) and Great North Eastern Railway (GNER) trains (☎ 0845-722 5225) from many southern cities and towns.

Car Fort William is on the A82 arterial road from Glasgow. From Edinburgh there are several options, although the route via the M9 to Stirling, then the A84 through Callander and on to Crianlarich on the A82 is recommended. Fort William is 104mi from Glasgow and 146mi from Edinburgh.

The main routes to Inverness from Glasgow are the A82 via Fort William, or the M80 then A roads and motorways via Stirling to the A9, which takes you to Inverness. From Edinburgh take the M90, then the A9 via Perth and Pitlochry. Inverness is 166mi from Glasgow and 155mi from Edinburgh.

THE SPEYSIDE WAY

The River Spey is Scotland's second-longest river and one of its most scenic. Rising in the Monadhliath Mountains west of Kingussie, it flows generally east and north to enter the North Sea at Spey Bay. The Speyside Way, Scotland's third official LDP, has one end at Aviemore in Strathspey, overlooked by the Cairngorm mountains, and the other at Buckie on the North Sea coast, a few miles east of Spey Bay. The Way closely follows the river for many miles and makes use of footpaths, cycle tracks, old railway formations, forest roads and quiet rural roads. It passes through Boat of Garten, Nethy Bridge, Grantown-on-Spey, Cromdale, Aberlour, Craigellachie, Fochabers and Spey Bay. Two spur routes, from Bridge of Avon to Tomintoul (the highest village in the Highlands) and from Craigellachie to Dufftown, provide attractive walks in their own right and are well worthwhile. Speyside is blessed with several whisky distilleries, some close to the Way, and has diverse wildlife habitats ranging from riverine to woodland and moorland.

The Way is well signposted and waymarked with the official thistle hexagon logo.

Direction, Distance & Duration

The Speyside Way can be followed in either direction, depending on whether you prefer to walk down the river or to travel from the sea to the mountains. The Way is 65mi long (105km); the Tomintoul Spur is 14.3mi (23km) one way and the Dufftown Spur 4.3mi (7km) one way. It is possible to do the whole lot in five days, but six or seven allows time for visiting distilleries, the famous Strathspey Steam Railway and the re-opened, scenic Dufftown to Keith railway.

Planning

The Speyside Way Ranger Service (☎ 01340-881266) publishes a free, annually updated *Accommodation and General Information* brochure with a map and details of facilities and places to stay. The service also produces a Public Transport Guide and maintains an informative Web site via the Moray Council Web site (🖳 www.moray.org).

The Harvey Walker's 1:40,000 map *Speyside Way*, the official map for the route, shows facilities and some features of interest. *The Speyside Way* guide, published by Rucksack Readers, has easy to use 1:100,000 strip maps and a load of helpful information. For coverage of the surrounding countryside you'll need OS Landranger 1:50,000 maps No 28 *(Elgin & Dufftown)* and No 36 *(Grantown & Aviemore)*, which also show the route of the Way.

Places to Stay & Eat

The official brochure is invaluable for planning your walk, as it indicates which accommodation hosts will pick up and drop off Way walkers, especially useful where there are long gaps between shelter of any type (particularly between Cromdale and Aberlour). Commercial campsites and those with minimal facilities for Way walkers are spaced so you could camp each night.

Getting to/from the Walk

Aviemore is served by ScotRail (☎ 0845-755 0033) and GNER (☎ 0845-722 5225)

on the Inverness to Edinburgh, Glasgow and London services, and by Scottish Citylink buses (☎ 0870-550 5050) between Inverness and Glasgow and Edinburgh. Buses run between Buckie and Aberdeen and Keith, the latter two on the railway line connecting Inverness and Aberdeen. Several of the intermediate towns have bus services from major centres.

THE FIFE COASTAL PATH

Best known for its dozens of golf courses, and with extensively farmed countryside, Fife isn't a major walking area. However, it does have a scenic and varied coastline, much of it accessible via long-established paths. The Fife Coastal Path (FCP), when completed, will incorporate these paths in a route linking the Firth of Forth in the south with the Firth of Tay in the north, a distance of 78mi (126km). By late 2000 the FCP had reached Crail, more than halfway to the Tay from North Queensferry on the Forth.

More so than almost any other extensive section of Scotland's coastline, Fife's coastal landscape bears the imprints of its industrial and maritime heritage. Mining, quarrying and shipping are still carried on, although generally on a much reduced scale, mainly around Inverkeithing, Kirkcaldy, Buckhaven and Methil. Consequently, a few stretches of the FCP are unlovely (see Direction, Distance & Duration below) and better seen from the window of a bus or car. More pleasingly, the constantly changing vistas are the highlight of the FCP – across the Firth of Forth and along the subtly indented coast. The fishing villages on the east coast – Elie, Pittenweem and Crail – are fascinating, with well-preserved traditional buildings and old harbours. Bird life is quite plentiful, especially along the rocky shores, common seals bask on the rocks in several places and the route passes through many fine woodlands.

Direction, Distance & Duration

With the most walker-friendly section in the north-east, North Queensferry is the place to start – saving the best to last. The distance to Crail, 44.25mi (71km), can be split into three days of quite easy walking, especially if you catch a bus or drive through the black spots. Convenient stages are from Burntisland to Kinghorn (2.5mi beside a busy road) and Buckhaven to Leven Links (with a 4mi walk through industrial towns).

The FCP is easy to follow with blue metal or timber sign posts at road and path junctions, and smaller signs and marked posts displaying the path's logo – a stylised Fife coast shape – elsewhere.

Planning
Contact the TIC in Kirkcaldy (☎ 01592-267775) for an accommodation guide and information about the FCP. They may have some or all of five leaflets, each with a map and outline description, for the sections from North Queensferry to Leven Links. OS Landranger 1:50,000 maps No 59 *(St Andrews)*, No 65 *(Falkirk & Linlithgow)* and No 66 *(Edinburgh)* cover the area concerned.

Places to Stay & Eat
There's no shortage of accommodation but it's almost exclusively B&Bs and hotels. There are no hostels on the coast and many of the caravan parks have limited space for tents. Happily, you'll never be far from a pub or restaurant for a pint and a meal.

Getting to/from the Walk
Fife Council's comprehensive brochure, *Getting Around Fife*, free from TICs, has a map showing all public transport services and gives contacts for inquiries. ScotRail (☎ 0845-755 0033), GNER (☎ 0845-722 5225) and Virgin Trains (☎ 0845-748 4950) from Edinburgh, Aberdeen, Perth and Inverness stop at several stations on the FCP, and buses link almost all the towns through which the walk passes.

ST CUTHBERT'S WAY
St Cuthbert was a 7th-century Celtic saint whose vocation with the church began at Melrose in the Scottish Borders in AD650, where he later became prior of the local monastery. He explored the Borders countryside on foot and was particularly drawn to the coastline. He was eventually appointed Bishop of Lindisfarne (Holy Island), just off the Northumberland coast in England. For Cuthbert, walking was a time for peaceful contemplation when he could feel at one with the natural world.

St Cuthbert's Way links Melrose and Lindisfarne on a route of great variety and interest, passing through places associated with Cuthbert's life and ministry. It crosses the Eildon Hills, and the Cheviot Hills in Northumberland National Park, follows sections of the beautiful Rivers Tweed and Teviot, part of the ancient Roman road Dere Street, and traverses fertile farmland. It follows footpaths, vehicle and forest tracks, and quiet country roads. At low tide you can cross to Lindisfarne by the causeway or by the Pilgrim's Route across the sands.

The route is well waymarked, most prominently with the Way's own Celtic cross logo.

Direction, Distance & Duration
By starting at Melrose you'll follow Cuthbert's lifetime journey and finish with the inspirational experience of crossing the sands to Lindisfarne. The distance of 62.5mi includes 1200m of ascent; this could be walked in four days but you'll probably need to allow five or six to fit in with safe crossing times to Lindisfarne (see Planning following) and to spend time exploring the island. The Way links with the Pennine Way at Kirk Yetholm (see the Northern England Long-Distance Paths chapter) and the Southern Upland Way at Melrose (see earlier in this chapter), thus making possible a grand long-distance walk from Edale in Derbyshire to either Portpatrick or Cockburnspath.

Planning
The relevant OS Landranger 1:50,000 maps are No 73 *(Peebles, Galashiels & Selkirk)*, No 74 *(Kelso & Coldstream)* and No 75 *(Berwick-upon-Tweed)*. The official trail guide, *St Cuthbert's Way* by Roger Smith & Ron Shaw, comprises a detailed guidebook and a 1:40,000 map published by Harvey.

The free, annual *Accommodation & Facilities Guide* is invaluable and can picked up from relevant TICs, including Jedburgh (☎ 01835-863435) and Berwick-upon-Tweed

(☎ 01289-330733). Vital information about safe crossing times to Lindisfarne is available on a fortnightly basis from Wooler TIC (☎ 01668-282123) and is displayed there out of hours. For long-term planning, contact the Berwick-upon-Tweed TIC.

Places to Stay & Eat

There's no shortage of B&Bs and pubs along the Way, many of which will transfer walkers' baggage (usually for a fee) and/or provide transport to/from the Way. There are also hostels and camping grounds, although these are probably too widely spaced to use either type of accommodation exclusively.

Getting to/from the Walk

Melrose is on Scottish Citylink (☎ 0870-550 5050) bus routes from Edinburgh and Berwick-upon-Tweed, which are served by GNER (☎ 0845-722 5225) and Virgin Trains (☎ 0845-748 4950) and by National Express (☎ 0870-580 8080) buses on the Edinburgh to London route.

Local buses call at most towns and villages along the Way; there's a good service between Lindisfarne and Berwick-upon-Tweed from late July to late August but infrequently at other times. For timetables get in touch with the Scottish Borders Council (☎ 01835-823301).

SCOTLAND LONG-DISTANCE PATHS

Other Walks in Scotland

A weighty tome or two is needed to do justice to all the walking areas in Scotland. A selection of the best of the rest follows here. For yet more ideas, look out for Lonely Planet's *Walking in Scotland*.

FAR NORTH-WEST

Scotland's most sparsely populated quarter, north-west Sutherland – between Ullapool and the north coast – contains a good share of the wildest and most rugged mountains and glens in the country.

Several peaks offer an immense variety of walks, magnificent views and a keen sense of remoteness. The most northerly Munro, **Ben Hope** (927m), overlooks the north coast between Durness and Tongue. Its neighbour, shapely **Ben Loyal** (764m), graces the view south from the village of Tongue. Mighty **Ben More Assynt** (998m) and its satellite **Conival** (988m) provide a long, exhilarating day in limestone country. The Star-shaped **Quineag** (808m), above Loch Assynt, comprises three separate summits. The massive tower **Suilven** (731m) is the icon of the north-west. Also worth mentioning are **Canisp** (847m), **Cul Mor** (849m) and serrated, easily accessible **Stac Pollaidh** (612m).

There are few, if any, finer stretches of coast than that between Oldshore More and Cape Wrath, including incomparable **Sandwood Bay**. Start from the cape (via ferry and minibus from near Durness) or walk in to the bay from the road at Blairmore, near Kinlochbervie.

Probably the highest waterfall in Britain, **Eas a' Chual Aluinn**, with a drop of 200m to Loch Beag at the head of Loch Glencoul, is the centrepiece of another first-class walk. The usual approach is from the A894 between Skiag Bridge and Kylesku.

The definitive guide to the region is the Scottish Mountaineering Club (SMC) book *The Northwest Highlands* by DJ Bennett & T Strang. The area is covered by Ordnance Survey (OS) Landranger 1:50,000 maps No 9 *(Cape Wrath)*, No 10 *(Strathnaver)*, No 15 *(Loch Assynt)* and No 16 *(Lairg & Loch Shin)*. Contact the Lochinver Tourist Information Centre (TIC) (☎ 01571-844330) for accommodation information.

THE HEBRIDES

Several of these islands off the west coast provide a wealth of first-class walking, with the unique experience of island walking as an added spice. Here is a selection of what's on offer.

Separated from Morvern in Lochaber by a narrow strait, **Mull** is dominated by **Ben More** (966m), the only island Munro outside Skye, where magnetic rock plays havoc with compasses. East of Ben More, other groups of hills with long ridge walks worth exploring include those centred around **Beinn Talaidh** (761m) and **Dun da Ghaoithe** (766m). The south coast is very fine, indeed, especially the cliffs and arches southwest of the village of Carsaig.

The main ferry service goes from Oban to Tobermory, the principal town on Mull. There's also a ferry that runs across the Sound of Mull from Lochaline to Fishnish. Both are run by Caledonian MacBrayne, known as CalMac (☎ 01631-566688). The TIC on Mull (open year-round) is in Craignure (☎ 01680-812377).

These walks are covered by the OS Landranger 1:50,000 maps No 48 *(Iona & West Mull)* and No 49 *(Oban & East Mull)*. The SMC guide *The Islands of Scotland* is the recommended reference.

The **Isle of Rum**, west of the fishing port of Mallaig, is owned by Scottish Natural Heritage (SNH), whose 30 or so employees are the island's sole inhabitants. The traverse of its **Cuillins**, less formidable than Skye's mountains of the same name, is an absolutely first-class walk. Even the names of the summits are tempting – Hallival (723m), Askival (812m), Trailival (702m) and Ainshval (781m). It's a very long day, making use of an old track from Kinloch, which passes a bothy at Dibidil.

The wild and rugged **north-west coast** is another possibility, and no trip to Rum is complete without an inspection of Kinloch Castle, built by an eccentric former island owner. A CalMac ferry (Mallaig ☎ 01687-462403, central reservations ☎ 0870-565 0000) goes from Mallaig three times weekly. Accommodation is hostel-style or in a tent at Kinloch. There is a small shop where you can buy supplies and even a newspaper. The Rum midges are particularly ferocious, so a springtime visit is recommended.

The OS Landranger 1:50,000 map No 39 *(Rum, Eigg, Muck & Canna)* and the SMC's island guide are essential. For up-to-date information about accommodation and facilities, contact SNH (☎ 01687-462026) .

The Western Isles, stretching 130mi (209km) from the Butt of Lewis in the north to Barra in the south, are a world apart from the rest of Scotland – peaceful, relaxed and a stronghold of Gaelic culture. Of the islands in the group, **Harris** is the most mountainous with a cluster of rugged hills topped by **An Cliseam** (799m), also known as Clisham. On South Uist there are magnificent Atlantic coast beaches and the impressive twin peaks of **Hecla** (606m) and **Beinn Mhòr** (620m), offering challenges greater than many much higher hills on the mainland. Tiny **Barra** has a splendid clutch of hills topping 300m and some fine beaches, one of which is the local airport.

CalMac ferries (☎ 01475-650100) depart the mainland from Ullapool to Stornoway (Lewis), from Uig on the Isle of Skye to Tarbert (South Harris), and from Oban to Lochboisdale (South Uist) and Castlebay (Barra). The main TIC is at Stornoway (☎ 01851-703088). Of six relevant OS Landranger 1:50,000 maps, those most useful are No 14 *(Tarbert & Lock Seaforth)*, No 22 *(Benbecula & South Uist)* and No 31 *(Barra & South Uist)*. Pick up a copy of the SMC guide *The Islands of Scotland including Skye*.

THE SOUTH-WEST & BORDERS

In the far south-west and close to the Southern Upland Way (see the Scotland Long-Distance Paths chapter) are the Galloway Hills, of which **Merrick** (843m) is the highest, offering a fine day out and magnificent views. Farther east, north of Moffat, are **Hart Fell** (808m) and **White Coomb** (822m), as well as the beautiful waterfall, **Grey Mare's Tail**. The big, rolling mountains of the Borders invite longer exploration – try the mainly high 35mi (56km) route linking Moffat and Peebles via St Mary's Loch.

There's much more to walking in the Borders than climbing mountains, however. An excellent series of nine leaflets describes countryside walks near towns such as Jedburgh, Selkirk and Peebles. A booklet, *Walking in the Scottish Borders*, describes 25 low-level routes through woodlands, forests and beside streams. With a historic theme, the **Borders Abbeys Way** links Kelso and Jedburgh, and extensions are planned. For yet more variety, there's a coast path between Burnfoot, Eyemouth and Coldingham.

Several OS 1:50,000 maps cover the area. The SMC guide *Southern Uplands* by Ken Andrew is a mine of information. The Jedburgh TIC (☎ 01835-863 4350) is also a very helpful point of contact.

Glossary

Some English words and phrases commonly used in Britain will be unknown to visitors from abroad, even if they regard English as their first language, so we have translated some of these. We have also focussed on British walking terms, including several Welsh, Scottish and regional English words, mainly to do with landscape, that you are likely to come across during your travels. For those seeking a more in-depth introduction to the British English language, Lonely Planet also publishes a *British phrasebook*.

4WD – four-wheel drive car; all-terrain vehicle

AA – Automobile Association
aber – river mouth (Wales)
abhainn – river or stream (Scotland)
ABTA – Association of British Travel Agents
afon – river (Wales)
allt – stream (Scotland, Wales)
aonach – ridge
ATM – Automatic Teller Machine; machine for extracting cash from a bank; in Britain usually called a *cashpoint* or 'cash machine'
ASL – above sea level
aye – yes or always (Scotland, Northern England)

B&B – bed and breakfast
BABA – book-a-bed-ahead scheme
bach – small (Wales)
bag – reach the top of, as in 'to bag a peak'
bailey – outermost wall of a castle
ban, bhan – white (Scotland)
banger – old, cheap car; sausage
bank holiday – public holiday, ie, when the banks are closed
bap – bread roll (Northern England)
bar – gate (York)
bastle-house – solidly constructed and well-fortified house (Northumberland)
bealach – pass between hills (Scotland)
beck – stream (Northern England)

beinn, ben – mountain (Scotland)
bevvy – any drink (originally Northern England)
bidean – peak (Scotland)
billion – a million million, not a thousand million
bimble – *ramble*
biscuit – cookie
bitter – a type of beer (ale)
black pudding – a type of sausage made from dried blood
bloke – man
bothy – hut or mountain shelter (Scotland)
brae – hill (Scotland)
bramble – berry-cane
bridleway – path that can be used by walkers, horse-riders and cyclists
broad – lake (East Anglia)
broch – defensive tower (Scotland)
bryn – hill (Wales)
BT – British Telecom
BTA – British Tourist Authority
bun – bread roll, usually sweet
burgh – town (Scotland)
burial mound – ancient burial site characterised by a large circular dome of earth and stone covered by grass; see also *long barrow*
burn – stream (Scotland)
bus – local bus; see also *coach*
butty – sandwich, often filled with something hot, eg, bacon or (British speciality) *chips*
bwlch – pass or gap between two hills (Wales)

cadair – chair; stronghold or defended place in the mountains (Wales)
caer – fort (Wales)
cairn – pile of stones to mark path or junction, also (in Scotland) peak
capel – chapel (Wales)
carreg – stone (Wales)
carry-out – takeaway
cashpoint – machine for extracting cash from a bank; *ATM*
CCC – Camping & Caravanning Club
ceilidh – pronounced kaylee, informal evening entertainment and dance (Scotland)

chine – valley-like fissure leading to the sea (south, especially the Isle of Wight)

chips – hot, deep-fried potato pieces; French fries

clach – stone, stony (Scotland)

cleve – steep-sided valley

clint – the bit of rock sticking up between two *grikes*

clough – small valley

clun – meadow (Wales)

coach – long-distance bus

coaching inn – originally an inn along a stage-coach route at which horses were changed

coasteering – working your way round the base of cliffs by scrambling, climbing or swimming

cob – bread roll (Northern England)

coch – red (Wales)

coed – forest or wood (Wales)

coire – *corrie* or high mountain valley (Scotland)

col – hill or mountain pass

common – land that may be private but people have traditional rights of access, formerly for grazing animals, more often now for recreation

coombe – valley (Southern England)

Corbett – hill or mountain between 2500ft and 2999ft high (Scotland)

corrie – semicircular basin at the head of a steep-sided valley, usually formed by glacial erosion; cirque

crack – good conversation, good times (originally Ireland, also Northern England); now also used to mean 'happening', as in 'What's the crack?', ie, 'What's going on?'

craig – exposed rock (Scotland)

crannogh – artificial island settlement

crisps – salty flakes of fried potato, in a packet (what the rest of the world calls chips)

croft – plot of land with adjoining house, worked by the occupiers (Scotland)

cromlech – burial chamber (Wales)

CTC – Cyclists' Touring Club

cut – canal or artificial stretch of water

cwm – *corrie* or valley (Wales)

dale – open valley

DB&B – dinner, bed and breakfast

de – south (Wales)

dead-end road – no through road

dear – expensive

dearg – red (Scotland)

din, dinas – fort (Wales)

dinner – usually evening meal, except in some northern regions where it is the noon meal

Donald – lowland hill between 2000ft and 2499ft high (Scotland)

downs – rolling upland, usually grassy, characterised by a lack of trees

drove road – ancient route, once used for bringing cattle and sheep from the farm to the market

drum, druim – ridge (Scotland)

du – black (Wales)

dubh, duibh – dark or black (Scotland)

duvet – thick padded bed cover

duvet jacket – thick padded coat, usually filled with feathers and down, worn by mountaineers or walkers

dyke – stone wall or embankment; drainage channel (Southern England)

eas – waterfall (Scotland)

East Anglia – Eastern England, usually the counties of Norfolk and Suffolk

eilean – island (Scotland)

eisteddfod – festival in which competitions are held in music, poetry, drama and the fine arts

en suite – a room with an attached private bathroom; also written 'ensuite'

ESA – Environmentally Sensitive Areas

estate – area of landed property, usually large (Scotland)

evensong – daily evening service (Church of England)

exclosure – fenced enclosure to protect trees from grazing stock (Scotland)

fag – cigarette

fagged – exhausted

fanny – female genitals (which is why some people giggle when Fan y Big, a mountain in Wales, is pronounced in the English way, rather than in the correct Welsh way as van er big)

fawr – big (Wales)

fell – large hill or mountain (Northern England); hillside or mountain side

fen – drained or marshy low-lying flat land (south-eastern England)
ffordd – road (Wales)
firth – estuary (Scotland)
fiver – five-pound note
flip-flops – thongs
folly – eccentric, decorative (often useless) building
force – waterfall (Northern England)
fret – to worry; mist from the sea (Northumberland)

garbh – rough (Scotland)
gate – street (York)
geal – white (Scotland)
gill, ghyll – small steep-sided valley (Northern England)
ginnel – alleyway (mostly Northern England)
glan – shore (Wales)
glas – grey, grey-green (Scotland)
glas – blue (Wales)
gleann, glen – valley (Scotland)
glyn – valley (Wales)
gorm – blue (Scotland)
GR – grid reference (on maps)
grand – one thousand
grike – narrow fissure, usually in limestone *pavement* areas
gritstone – hard, course-grained sandstone containing a heavy proportion of silica
grough – *gully*
gully – small steep-sided valley
gwyn – white (Wales)
gwrydd – green (Wales)

haar – fog off the North Sea (Scotland)
hag – bog (Northern England)
hamlet – small settlement
haus – *col* (Northern England)
Hogmanay – New Year's Eve (Scotland)
honeypot – crowded place
horseshoe route – curved or circular route, eg, up one ridge and down another
hotel – accommodation with food and bar, not always open to passing trade
hows – *haus*

inch – island (Scotland)
inver – river mouth (Scotland)
inn – *pub*, usually with a bar, food and accommodation

jam – jelly
jelly – jello
jumper – sweater

ken – know, as in 'Do you ken what I mean?' (Scotland)
kin – head of a peninsula, lake or sea inlet (Scotland)
kipper – smoked herring (fish)
kirk – church (Scotland)
kissing gate – swinging gate, allowing access to people but not animals
knoll – small hill
kyle – narrow strait of water (Scotland)

ladder-stile – two small ladders back to back against a wall or fence, to allow people to pass over
laird – estate owner (Scotland)
lairig – pass (Scotland)
lass – young woman (Northern England)
lay-by – parking space at side of road
LDP – long-distance path
ley – clearing
liath – grey (Scotland)
lift – elevator
linn – waterfall (Scotland)
llan – enclosed place or church (Wales)
llyn – lake (Wales)
loch, lochan – lake, small lake or *tarn* (Scotland)
lock – part of a canal or river that can be closed off and the water levels changed to raise or lower boats
long barrows – Neolithic structure, usually covering stone burial chambers
lorry – truck
lough – Irish word for lake (Northumberland)
lunch – midday meal

mad – insane, not angry
Martello tower – small, circular tower used for coastal defence
mate – a friend of any sex; term of address for males
mawr – big (Wales)
MBA – Mountain Bothies Association
meall – rounded hill (Scotland)
metalled – surfaced (road), usually with tar (bitumen)
mhor, mor – big or great (Scotland)

MOD – Ministry of Defence
moor – high, rolling, open, treeless area
motorway – freeway
motte – mound on which a castle was built
muggy – 'close' or humid weather
mullach – top or summit (Scotland)
Munro – mountain of 3000ft or higher (Scotland)
mynydd – mountain (Wales)

nant – valley or stream (Wales)
navvy – labourer who built canals and railways in the 19th century (abbreviation for navigator)
newydd – new (Wales)
NNR – National Nature Reserve
NSA – National Scenic Area
NTS – National Trust for Scotland

oast house – building containing a kiln for drying hops (Southern England)
off-license, offie – shop selling alcoholic drinks to take away
ogof – cave (Wales)
OS – Ordnance Survey mapping agency

p – pronounced pee, pence (currency)
pasty – hot pastry roll with savoury filling
pavement – sidewalk; any flat area of exposed rock, especially limestone
peat – dark soil, the remains of ancient vegetation, usually wet and glutinous, found in moorland areas
pen – headland or peak (Wales)
pend – arched gateway (Scotland)
pete – fortified houses
PIC – Park Information Centre
Pict – early Celtic inhabitants (from the Latin *pictus*, meaning 'painted', after their painted body decorations)
pike – peak (Northern England)
pint – about 750mL
pissed – drunk (not angry)
pissed off – annoyed
pistyll – waterfall (Wales)
pitch – playing field; tent site
pitched – laid with flat stones, eg, to improve a path
plas – hall or mansion (Wales)
pont – bridge (Wales)
pop – fizzy drink (Northern England, Wales)

porth – bay or harbour
postbus – minibus that follows postal delivery routes and carries passengers
pub – short for public house, a bar usually with food, sometimes with accommodation
pull-in – *lay-by*
punter – customer; somebody placing a bet; somebody punting (ie, poling) a boat
pwll – pool (Wales)

quid – pound (money)

RA – Ramblers' Association
ramble – a relatively short or nonstrenuous walk
reiver – notoriously cruel warrior, bandit (Northern England)
reservoir – artificial lake, usually formed by damming a river
rhiw – slope (Wales)
rhos – moor or marsh (Wales)
ride – path specially made for riding on horseback
round – a natural circuit, mostly along ridges, often in a horseshoe shape
RSPB – Royal Society for the Protection of Birds
rubber – eraser
rubbish bin – garbage can
ruadh – red (Scotland)
RUPP – Road Used as a Public Path

sack – rucksack, pack, backpack
SAE – stamped addressed envelope
Sassenach – an English person or a lowland Scot (Scotland)
scrambling – requiring hands and feet to negotiate a steep, rocky section of path
SDW – South Downs Way
sgorr, sgùrr – pointed hill or mountain
shut – partially covered passage
SMC – Scottish Mountaineering Club
sneachd – snow (Scotland)
SNH – Scottish Natural Heritage (Scotland)
snicket – alleyway (York)
spidean – peak (Scotland)
squeeze stile or **squeeze gate** – narrow gap in wall to let people through, but not animals
sron – nose (Scotland)
SRWS – Scottish Rights of Way Society
SSSI – Site of Special Scientific Interest

staithe – mooring point on a canal
stalking – hunting of deer (Scotland)
stile – steps to allow people to pass over a wall or fence
stob – peak (Scotland)
strath – wide valley (Scotland)
stuc – peak or steep rock (Scotland)
subway – underpass for pedestrians
SUW – Southern Upland Way
sweet – candy
SYHA – Scottish Youth Hostels Association

tarn – small mountain lake (Northern England)
tea – British national drink; light meal eaten late in the afternoon; cooked evening meal in those parts of the country where *dinner* is eaten at noon
teashop – smart cafe, in country areas
thwaite – clearing in a forest
TIC – Tourist Information Centre
tom – hill (Scotland)
top – peak over 3000ft (914m), but without a significant drop on all sides
tor – small and pointed hill (England)
torch – flashlight
torr – small hill (Scotland)
tre – town (Wales)
trig point – pillar, formerly used for the making of Ordnance Survey maps
tube – *underground* railway
tumulus – ancient burial mound
twee – excessively sentimental, sweet, pretty

twitcher – keen birdwatcher
twitten – passage or small lane
twr – tower (Wales)
ty – house (Wales)

underground – subway
Unesco – United Nations Educational, Scientific & Cultural Organisation
uamh – cave (Scotland)
uig – bay (Scotland)
uisge – water (Scotland)
uisge-bha – whisky (Scotland)

VAT – value-added tax, levied on most goods and services
verderer – officer upholding law and order in the royal forests

way – usually a long-distance path or trail, eg, the Pennine Way
wheal – mine (Cornwall)
WHW – West Highland Way
wold – open, rolling country
WTB – Wales Tourist Board
wynd – lane (Scotland)

YHA – Youth Hostels Association
ynys – island (Wales)
yob – hooligan
ystwyth – winding (Wales)

zawn – very steep-sided gully or fissure in a sea cliff (Cornwall)

LONELY PLANET

You already know that Lonely Planet produces more than this one guidebook, but you might not be aware of the other products we have on this region. Here is a selection of titles that you may want to check out as well:

London City Map
ISBN 1 86450 008 5

London Condensed
ISBN 1 86450 043 3

British phrasebook
ISBN 0 86442 484 1

London
ISBN 0 86442 793 X

Britain
ISBN 1 86450 147 2

England
ISBN 1 86450 194 4

Walking in Scotland
ISBN 1 86450 350 5

Walking in Ireland
ISBN 0 86442 602 X

Western Europe
ISBN 1 86450 163 4

Europe on a shoestring
ISBN 1 86450 150 2

Read this First: Europe
ISBN 1 86450 136 7

Cycling Britain
ISBN 1 86450 037 9

Scotland
ISBN 0 86442 592 9

Edinburgh
ISBN 0 86442 580 5

Available wherever books are sold

LONELY PLANET

Guides by Region

onely Planet is known worldwide for publishing practical, reliable and no-nonsense travel information in our guides and on our Web site. The Lonely Planet list covers just about every accessible part of the world. Currently there are 16 series: Travel guides, Shoestring guides, Condensed guides, Phrasebooks, Read This First, Healthy Travel, Walking guides, Cycling guides, Watching Wildlife guides, Pisces Diving & Snorkeling guides, City Maps, Road Atlases, Out to Eat, World Food, Journeys travel literature and Pictorials.

AFRICA Africa on a shoestring • Cairo • Cairo City Map • Cape Town • Cape Town City Map • East Africa • Egypt • Egyptian Arabic phrasebook • Ethiopia, Eritrea & Djibouti • Ethiopian Amharic phrasebook • The Gambia & Senegal • Healthy Travel Africa • Kenya • Malawi • Morocco • Moroccan Arabic phrasebook • Mozambique • Read This First: Africa • South Africa, Lesotho & Swaziland • Southern Africa • Southern Africa Road Atlas • Swahili phrasebook • Tanzania, Zanzibar & Pemba • Trekking in East Africa • Tunisia • Watching Wildlife East Africa • Watching Wildlife Southern Africa • West Africa • World Food Morocco • Zimbabwe, Botswana & Namibia
Travel Literature: Mali Blues: Traveling to an African Beat • The Rainbird: A Central African Journey • Songs to an African Sunset: A Zimbabwean Story

AUSTRALIA & THE PACIFIC Auckland • Australia • Australian phrasebook • Australia Road Atlas • Cycling Australia • Cycling New Zealand • Fiji • Fijian phrasebook • Healthy Travel Australia, NZ & the Pacific • Islands of Australia's Great Barrier Reef • Melbourne • Melbourne City Map • Micronesia • New Caledonia • New South Wales • New Zealand • Northern Territory • Outback Australia • Out to Eat – Melbourne • Out to Eat – Sydney • Papua New Guinea • Pidgin phrasebook • Queensland • Rarotonga & the Cook Islands • Samoa • Solomon Islands • South Australia • South Pacific • South Pacific phrasebook • Sydney • Sydney City Map • Sydney Condensed • Tahiti & French Polynesia • Tasmania • Tonga • Tramping in New Zealand • Vanuatu • Victoria • Walking in Australia • Watching Wildlife Australia • Western Australia
Travel Literature: Islands in the Clouds: Travels in the Highlands of New Guinea • Kiwi Tracks: A New Zealand Journey • Sean & David's Long Drive

CENTRAL AMERICA & THE CARIBBEAN Bahamas, Turks & Caicos • Baja California • Belize, Guatemala & Yucatán • Bermuda • Central America on a shoestring • Costa Rica • Costa Rica Spanish phrasebook • Cuba • Dominican Republic & Haiti • Eastern Caribbean • Guatemala • Havana • Healthy Travel Central & South America • Jamaica • Mexico • Mexico City • Panama • Puerto Rico • Read This First: Central & South America • World Food Mexico • Yucatán
Travel Literature: Green Dreams: Travels in Central America

EUROPE Amsterdam • Amsterdam City Map • Amsterdam Condensed • Andalucía • Austria • Baltic States phrasebook • Barcelona • Barcelona City Map • Belgium & Luxembourg • Berlin • Berlin City Map • Britain • British phrasebook • Brussels, Bruges & Antwerp • Brussels City Map • Budapest • Budapest City Map • Canary Islands • Central Europe • Central Europe phrasebook • Copenhagen • Corfu & the Ionians • Corsica • Crete • Crete Condensed • Croatia • Cycling Britain • Cycling France • Cyprus • Czech & Slovak Republics • Denmark • Dublin • Dublin City Map • Eastern Europe • Eastern Europe phrasebook • Edinburgh • England • Estonia, Latvia & Lithuania • Europe on a shoestring • Europe phrasebook • Finland • Florence • France • Frankfurt Condensed • French phrasebook • Georgia, Armenia & Azerbaijan • Germany • German phrasebook • Greece • Greek Islands • Greek phrasebook • Hungary • Iceland, Greenland & the Faroe Islands • Ireland • Italian phrasebook • Italy • Krakow • Lisbon • The Loire • London • London City Map • London Condensed • Madrid • Malta • Mediterranean Europe • Mediterranean Europe phrasebook • Moscow • Munich • Netherlands • Normandy • Norway • Out to Eat – London • Out to Eat – Paris • Paris • Paris City Map • Paris Condensed • Poland • Polish phrasebook • Portugal • Portuguese phrasebook • Prague • Prague City Map • Provence & the Côte d'Azur • Read This First: Europe • Rhodes & the Dodecanese • Romania & Moldova • Rome • Rome City Map • Russia, Ukraine & Belarus • Russian phrasebook • Scandinavian & Baltic Europe • Scandinavian phrasebook • Scotland • Sicily • Slovenia • South-West France • Spain • Spanish phrasebook • St Petersburg • St Petersburg City Map • Sweden • Switzerland • Tuscany • Ukrainian phrasebook • Venice • Vienna • Walking in Britain • Walking in France • Walking in Ireland • Walking in Italy • Walking in Spain • Walking in Switzerland • Western Europe • World Food France • World Food Ireland • World Food Italy • World Food Spain
Travel Literature: After Yugoslavia • Love and War in the Apennines • The Olive Grove: Travels in Greece • On the Shores of the Mediterranean • Round Ireland in Low Gear • A Small Place in Italy

Index

Text

For a list of walks, see the Table of Walks (pp4–7)

O

P

Bold indicates maps.

Boxed Text

MAP LEGEND

BOUNDARIES

.... International
.... Regional
.... Disputed

HYDROGRAPHY

.... Coastline
.... River, Creek
.... Lake
.... Intermittent Lake
.... Salt Lake
.... Canal
.... Spring
.... Waterfall
.... Swamp

ROUTES & TRANSPORT

M1 .... Motorway
A5 .... Primary Road
A45 .... Main Road
B4530 .... Secondary Road
.... One-Way Road
============ Unsealed Major Road
.... Unsealed Minor Road
.... Track
.... Lane

.... Tunnel
.... Train Route & Stations
.... Disused Railway
.... Chair Lift/Ski Lift
.... Described Walk
.... Alternative Route
.... Side Trip
.... Walking Track
.... Ferry Route

AREA FEATURES

.... Park (Regional Maps)
.... Park (LDP Maps)
.... Park (Walk Maps)
.... Beach
.... Cemetery
.... Urban Area

MAP SYMBOLS

✪ **CAPITAL** ... National Capital	⊠ .... Airport	⛪ .... Museum
◉ **CAPITAL** ... Regional Capital	⊠ .... Battle Site	⊡ .... Park or Reserve
● **CITY** .... City	⊞ .... Castle	P .... Parking
● **Town** .... Town	⊟ ⊡ .... Church	)(............... Pass/Saddle
● Village .... Village	.... Cliff or Escarpment	⊙ .... Picnic Area
	⊡ .... Embassy	⊡ .... Post Office
	❀ .... Gardens	⊡ .... Pub
⬛ .... Camping Area	⋈ .... Gate	⊠ .... Ruin
⬛ .... Hut	❂ .... Golf Course	+100m .... Spot Height
⬛ .... Lookout	⊕ .... Hospital	⛫ .... Stately Home
▼ .... Place to Eat	⚓ .... Lighthouse	.... Stone Row
■ .... Place to Stay	⊠ .... Mine	ⓘ .... Tourist Information
● .... Point of Interest	▲ .... Monument	△ .... Trigonometric Point
⬛ .... Shelter	▲ .... Mountain or Hill	.... Wall

Note: not all symbols displayed above appear in this book

LONELY PLANET OFFICES

Australia
Locked Bag 1, Footscray, Victoria 3011
☎ 03 8379 8000 fax 03 8379 8111
ⓔ talk2us@lonelyplanet.com.au

USA
150 Linden St, Oakland, CA 94607
☎ 510 893 8555 or ☎ 800 275 8555 (toll free)
fax 510 893 8572
ⓔ info@lonelyplanet.com

UK
10a Spring Place, London NW5 3BH
☎ 020 7428 4800 fax 020 7428 4828
ⓔ go@lonelyplanet.co.uk

France
1 rue du Dahomey, 75011 Paris
☎ 01 55 25 33 00 fax 01 55 25 33 01
ⓔ bip@lonelyplanet.fr
ⓦ www.lonelyplanet.fr

World Wide Web: ⓦ www.lonelyplanet.com *or* AOL keyword: lp
Lonely Planet Images: ⓔ lpi@lonelyplanet.com.au